GT
2850
.F666
2011

Food cultures of the
world encyclopedia.

A$D
$380.00

30660000379060

DATE		

FOR REFERENCE

Do Not Take From This Room

MILDRED M KELLEY LIBRARY
THE ART INSTITUTE OF DALLAS
8080 PARK LANE — # 100
DALLAS, TX 75231

GT
2850
.F666

MILDRED M KELLEY LIBRARY

D0714106

BAKER & TAYLOR

Food Cultures of the World
Encyclopedia

Food Cultures of the World Encyclopedia

THE AMERICAS

Volume 2

KEN ALBALA, EDITOR

MILDRED M. KELLEY LIBRARY
THE ART INSTITUTE OF DALLAS
2 NORTHPARK 8080 PARKLANE
DALLAS, TX 75231

 GREENWOOD

AN IMPRINT OF ABC-CLIO, LLC
Santa Barbara, California • Denver, Colorado • Oxford, England

Copyright 2011 by Ken Albala

All rights reserved. No part of this publication may be reproduced,
stored in a retrieval system, or transmitted, in any form or by any means,
electronic, mechanical, photocopying, recording, or otherwise, except for
the inclusion of brief quotations in a review, without prior permission
in writing from the publisher.

Library of Congress Cataloging-in-Publication Data

Food cultures of the world encyclopedia / Ken Albala, editor.
    v. cm.
    Includes bibliographical references and index.
    ISBN 978-0-313-37626-9 (hard copy : alk. paper) — ISBN 978-0-313-37627-6
(ebook) 1. Food habits—Encyclopedias. 2. Food preferences—
Encyclopedias. I. Albala, Ken, 1964–
    GT2850.F666 2011
    394.1'2003—dc22   2010042700

ISBN: 978-0-313-37626-9
EISBN: 978-0-313-37627-6

15 14 13 12 11   1 2 3 4 5

This book is also available on the World Wide Web as an eBook.
Visit www.abc-clio.com for details.

Greenwood
An Imprint of ABC-CLIO, LLC

ABC-CLIO, LLC
130 Cremona Drive, P.O. Box 1911
Santa Barbara, California 93116-1911

This book is printed on acid-free paper (∞)

Manufactured in the United States of America

The publisher has done its best to make sure the instructions and/or recipes in this book
are correct. However, users should apply judgment and experience when preparing
recipes, especially parents and teachers working with young people. The publisher
accepts no responsibility for the outcome of any recipe included in this volume.

Contents

VOLUME 2: THE AMERICAS

List of Abbreviations, vii
Preface, ix

Argentina, 1

Aruba and Bonaire, 7

Barbados, 15

Belize, 31

Bolivia, 37

Brazil, 47

Canada, 55

Chile, 65

Colombia, 75

Costa Rica, 85

Cuba, 91

Curaçao and Sint Maarten, 101

Dominica, 109

Dominican Republic, 119

Ecuador, 129

El Salvador, 135

French Guiana, 141

Grenada, 147

Guatemala, 153

Guyana, 159

Haiti, 165

Hawaii, 175

Honduras, 183

Inuit, 191

Jamaica, 199

Martinique and Guadeloupe, 207

Mexico, 217

Native Americans, 231

Nicaragua, 243

Panama, 249

Paraguay and Uruguay, 253

Peru, 263

Puerto Rico, 273

Suriname, 283

Trinidad and Tobago, 291

United States: The Mid-Atlantic, 303

United States: The Midwest, 313

United States: New England, 325

United States: The Pacific Northwest, 337

United States: The South, 347

United States: The Southwest, 357

Venezuela, 369

About the Editor and Contributors, 375
Index, I-1

List of Abbreviations

c = cup

fl oz = fluid ounce

gal = gallon

in. = inch

lb = pound

mL = milliliter

oz = ounce

pt = pint

qt = quart

tbsp = tablespoon

tsp = teaspoon

Preface

This encyclopedia is the culmination of nearly a decade's work on the *Food Culture around the World* series. As that project expanded to 20 volumes, we realized that many peoples and places, fascinating and important in their own right, had not been covered. Considering that the cultural study of food has become more sophisticated and comprehensive over the past decade, that food has become a legitimate academic topic in curricula at every level of education, and that we seem to become more obsessed with food every day, we recognized that we simply could not leave out much of the planet. The only way to satisfy this growing demand is the set you see before you, which includes material covered in the series plus new articles that span the globe. We have gathered food scholars from around the world—people whose passion and expertise have given them deep insight into the ingredients, cooking methods, and ways of eating and thinking about food in their respective countries.

A number of questions regarding breadth and depth naturally arose in planning this work, particularly about the level of analysis for each article. Could we do justice to the vast array of distinct cuisines on earth? Could we include regional coverage for well-recognized food cultures? That is, rather than the nation-state as the criterion for inclusion, why not add Alsace, Provence, and Burgundy with France, or Sichuan, Hunan, and Canton with China? It became apparent that we would need another 20 volumes or risk very brisk, superficial coverage and that as arbitrary as the construction of nation-states has been historically, in particular the way minority cultures have tended to be obscured, the best way to organize this encyclopedia was by nation. Regional variations and minority groups can, of course, be discussed within the framework of nation-based articles. On the other hand, some groups frankly demanded separate entries—those who stood out as unique and distinct from the majority culture in which they happen politically to be included, or in some cases those people who either transcend national boundaries or even those very small places, whose great diversity demanded separate coverage as truly different from the culture around them. Thus we include the Basques separate from Spain and France, and the Hmong. We have not, however, included every single people merely on the basis of national status. This should not be taken to suggest that these cultures are unimportant but merely that many places share a common culture with those around them, though divided by national borders. In such cases we have provided cross-references. This seemed a preferable solution to suffering repetitiveness or unmanageable size.

The format for each entry also raised many questions. "Eating Out," for example, is simply not relevant in some places on earth. Would forcing each article into a common structure ultimately do injustice to the uniqueness of each culture? In the end it seemed that the ability to conduct cross-cultural analysis proved one of the most valuable assets of this set, so that one could easily compare what's for lunch in Brazil or Brunei. Moreover, tracing the various global currents of influence has been made possible since a shared set of parameters places each article on a common footing. We can trace, for example, the culinary influence of various peoples as they spread around the world. In this respect this work is unique. There are several excellent food encyclopedias on the market, all of which cover individual ingredients, topical themes, cooking methods, and sometimes recipes. None, however, treats individual food cultures as discrete units of analysis, and for students hoping to find an in-depth but succinct description of places, or for those hoping to compare a single food topic across cultures, this is the only source to which they can turn. We anticipate that this work will be invaluable for students, scholars, food writers, as well as that indomitable horde popularly known as foodies.

The other major question in designing this encyclopedia was how to define what exactly constitutes a *food culture*. This term should be distinguished from *cuisine,* which refers only to the cooking, serving, and appreciation of food. Naturally we include this within each entry and in doing so have taken the broadest possible definition of the term *cuisine.* That is, if a people cooks and recognizes a common set of recipes and discusses them with a common vocabulary, then it should be deemed a cuisine. Thus there is no place on earth without a cuisine. A nation, continent, region, and even a small group may share a common cuisine. This encyclopedia, however, covers much more. It explores the social context of consumption, the shared values and symbolic meanings that inform food choices, and the rituals and daily routine—indeed everything that constitutes a food culture. Thus we include religion, health, mealtimes, and special occasions, as well as the way certain foods confer status or have meanings beyond simple sensory gratification. Nor have we neglected the gastronomic angle, as recipes are an essential expression of what people think is good to eat, and their popularity is the outcome of decisions made at every level of society, from the farmer who grows food, and the environment and material resources that make it possible, to the government policy that promotes certain ingredients, to the retailers who market them, to the technologies by which they are transformed, and to the individual preference of family members at the level of the household. To this end we have added food culture snapshots to each entry, which puts a human face on the broader topics under discussion.

As with the series that preceded this encyclopedia, our aim is to present the panoply of human experience through the lens of food in an effort to better understand and appreciate our differences. We will find remarkably common experiences among us, especially as the world increasingly falls under the sway of corporate multinational food industries, but we will also find deep, profound, and persistent distinctions, ones that should and must be preserved because they are essential to who were are and how we define ourselves. These are differences that should not be effaced nor lost as our tastes become increasingly cosmopolitan. I hope that in reading these articles you find, like me, that the world is a marvelously diverse place and what people eat tells us about them in such an immediate and palpable way that in a certain sense you feel you know the people at some level. This, of course, is the first step toward understanding, appreciating, and living with each other peacefully on this small lump of turf we call earth.

Ken Albala
University of the Pacific

Argentina

Overview

The Argentine Republic is located in South America and is the second-largest Latin American country. It is divided into several culinary zones, each distinguished by individual gastronomic characteristics that are difficult to find elsewhere in Argentina. In the central region and las Pampas, dishes with a strong Italian influence, such as pizza, pasta, and polenta, are consumed on a daily basis. Pre-Hispanic dishes and ingredients, such as corn, potatoes, and chilies, are common in the northwestern provinces, while Welsh and Central European immigrants have influenced the gastronomy of the Tierra del Fuego region.

At the same time, the renowned Argentinean barbecue, the *asado,* which always starts with a *picada,* an aperitif, most often Vermouth and cold cuts, cheese, and olives; the preference for drinking red wine and yerba maté instead of other beverages; the passion for eating *dulce de leche* (thick caramelized sweetened milk); and the famous empanadas (small semicircular pies) are culinary examples present in all Argentinean households.

⦿ Food Culture Snapshot

The Russo family manages several hotels in Necochea, a port city on the southern coast of Buenos Aires Province, where they have lived all their lives. Maria del Carmen and Alberto have four grown-up children: two daughters, also in the hotel-management profession, and two sons, the youngest living in Italy. The Russos exemplify a middle-class, Buenos Aires Province

lifestyle, with very conservative culinary practices shown in part by a skeptical view not only of foreign cuisines but also of other regional Argentinean dishes.

Alberto and Maria del Carmen start their days with yerba maté (a hot drink made from the leaves of *Ilex paraguariensis* and drunk from a gourd vessel with a metal straw, or *bombilla*) followed by a light breakfast of *café con leche* (coffee with warm milk) and freshly baked *flautas,* a similar though smaller version of the French baguette, richly covered with butter and marmalade. Lunch is usually eaten around one o'clock and consists of an entrée, often just a steak or oven-baked chicken, with a salad on the side, accompanied by a red wine spritzer. Maria del Carmen's grandchildren are served another light meal called *merienda,* a custom common to countries with Spanish influence, consisting of a glass of milk and sandwiches or something sweet such as cookies or pastries. Adults might join the children with some yerba maté and a small bite of *algo dulce,* "something sweet."

Dinner is the most important meal of the day and is usually eaten at 9:00 P.M. Most often it consists of a single dish with vegetables or a salad on the side. At least twice a week, the Russos have home-delivered empanadas for dinner accompanied by a couple glasses of red wine. Maria del Carmen is enthusiastic about the new time-saving home-delivery services that have become part of their daily lifestyle and finds that the empanadas taste just like homemade. To round off dinner, a light dessert, such as flan (crème caramel), is served along with a cup of coffee or tea. The Russos follow the traditional custom of eating a simple pasta dish on Tuesdays and a homemade, often-filled pasta entrée on Sundays. All generations look forward to the Saturday asado, when family and friends meet for an extended lunch of barbecued beef, spicy pork sausages, blood sausages, salad of lettuce, tomato, and onion, fresh bread, and red wine. A couple of bites of quince fruit paste (*membrillo*) and cheese may round off the meal.

Major Foodstuffs

Argentina is an urban country, with approximately 90 percent of the population living in cities. It is also a mostly self-sufficient nation that has little need to import foodstuffs and exports a surplus of animal products, milk, corn, wheat, sorghum, soybeans, oilseeds, some fruits, and wine.

Beef is the most important staple in Argentina, accounting for the highest consumption rate in the world. Since the arrival of the Spaniards, cattle have thrived on the Pampas, the central flatlands of the country, where the humidity and soil quality result in high-quality grass. Nowadays, Argentinean cattle may be grain or grass fed, but there is an increasing awareness that the meat of grass-fed cattle is healthier. Lamb and young goat's meat are also popular choices for the barbecue, particularly in the Patagonian region. Chicken is often oven-baked or made into the traditional Spanish arroz con pollo (chicken with rice), a favorite in the northwestern parts of Argentina.

Grains such as corn and wheat play an important role in Argentinean cuisine. Corn is a staple of the Andean region and is the base ingredient in *locro,* a pre-Hispanic corn, vegetable, and meat stew, and in polenta, an Italian cornmeal dish sometimes served with tomato sauce and cheese or accompanying beef stews. Wheat is used to produce pasta and as flour for baking bread and a wide variety of pastries and cookies.

Cow milk is inexpensive and the primary ingredient in dulce de leche, a caramelized milk spread similar to toffee and a favorite filling in pastries. Cheese, both fresh and ripened, is an important staple. Argentinean provolone and reggianito, a regional Parmesan cheese, are two of the most popular in the

Argentian barbeque featuring beef asado. (Claus Mikosch | Dreamstime.com)

country. Other dairy staples are *mendicream,* similar to cream cheese, and yogurt, categorized as children's food.

One of the most important beverages in Argentina is maté, a hot infusion made of yerba maté (*Ilex paraguariensis*) leaves grown in the northern part of the country. The leaves are steeped in a small gourd and drunk by sucking the liquid through a bombilla, or strawlike metal rod with a sieve on the bottom, which ensures that the leaves stay in the container. Drinking yerba maté, or *matear,* must follow certain rules: The host fills the gourd with hot water, sucks the liquid, refills the gourd, and passes it clockwise to the next person, who does the same. The gourd is refilled and passed around until the infusion becomes tasteless. This is an important social custom in the country, where friends and family often meet to share a gourd of the infusion. There are several kinds of yerba maté, including ones that are bitter, sweet, or flavored with orange rinds.

The consumption of legumes is not widespread in Argentina, aside from a few dishes such as the *fainá,* an oven-baked chickpea pancake usually eaten with pizza in Buenos Aires. Lentils and beans are used in soups and salads.

Red wine is one of Argentina's largest exports, and grapes are most commonly grown in the regions of Mendoza and San Juan. Climate and geography have played an important role in the cultivation of grapes in these regions. Due to drier weather conditions and higher altitudes, grapes in Argentina do not suffer from as many diseases as their European counterparts. Malbec, Bonarda, Cabernet Sauvignon, Merlot, and Shiraz varieties, among others, thrive in the area. More recently, organic red wine has become very popular.

Cooking

Traditionally, women in Argentina are in charge of feeding their families. However, men may sometimes cook more elaborate pasta dishes and take care of the Saturday barbecue. Families that are able to afford it have a cook. Argentinean cooking methods are simple and straightforward. In cities, kitchens have gas stoves and ovens, and most dishes are prepared by frying, stewing, or baking. Since microwaves are very rare, leftovers are often warmed in ovens. Wood-burning stoves are commonly found in more rural areas of the country.

Barbecuing is an art in Argentina, and two different methods may be used. For smaller cuts of meat, sausages, and vegetables, a regular grill is preferred, but when barbecuing a whole animal (a pig, cow, lamb, or goat), an open pit is used. Seasonings are used sparingly; most often, some salt and nothing else is sprinkled on the meat. However, *chimichurri,* a spicy sauce, accompanies all barbecued meats.

Chimichurri

1 c olive oil

⅓ c white wine vinegar

⅓ c finely chopped onion

3 finely chopped cloves garlic

½ tsp cayenne pepper

1 tsp dried oregano

1 tsp salt

A pinch of black pepper

Put the ingredients in a container with a lid, and blend well. Put in a cool place or in the refrigerator, and let the chimichurri rest for a couple of days so the flavors really blend. Serve as a sauce with barbecued meats and vegetables.

Typical Meals

Even though Argentina is large, the structure of meals, if not the contents, is very similar throughout the country. Usually, Argentineans have three meals a day, breakfast, lunch, and dinner, but children and some adults may also eat a light meal in the middle of the afternoon. Lunch and dinner are the main daily meals, with some kind of meat being the main ingredient.

Breakfast consists of crackers or toast with cream cheese or jam and a cup of coffee or tea. Children may also eat packaged cereals with milk or sometimes have a pastry and drink chocolate milk. Argentinean lunches are eaten around 1 P.M. Since meat is a major staple, most menus are planned according to the type of meat served. A great favorite is beef or veal Wiener schnitzel (flattened breaded cutlets), though sometimes it is made with chicken. It is served with French fries or mashed potatoes, sweet potatoes, or pumpkin. Salads consist of tomatoes and lettuce. Vegetables on the side may include boiled broccoli or cauliflower. Or simple pasta dishes such as boiled spaghetti with melted butter and freshly grated provolone or Parmesan cheese may be served. Red wine spritzers or mineral water are the drinks of choice.

Dinner, eaten at 9 P.M., is the most important meal of the day and a chance for the family to get together after a long day. There are few dishes reserved for dinner menus, and unless it is a special occasion, Argentineans dine on roasted chicken and potatoes. A common starter is *matambre,* literally "hunger killer," made by filling a flank steak with carrots, spinach, and hard-boiled eggs, seasoned with oregano, garlic, and paprika; it is served cold. In the Buenos Aires metropolitan area, gnocchi are a must on the 29th of the month, and many people still maintain this tradition.

Eating Out

Argentineans love eating and will gladly visit restaurants often, if affordable. Recently, Buenos Aires has seen a surge of restaurants driven by young chefs inspired by international cuisines. However,

Argentineans love their meat and are content if they are served a good steak and great bottle of red wine. Regional food restaurants, serving locro, fried empanadas, and other local dishes, are very popular in Buenos Aires. Going out for a pizza with friends is also common, and in this case Argentineans prefer a glass of cold beer instead of wine to accompany their meal. The most popular pizza is a plain mozzarella cheese pizza with a slice of fainá (the flat chickpea bread). Argentinean pizzas are similar to Italian ones, but the crust is thicker and they have a lot more cheese on top. In Buenos Aires all the different regional Italian pizzas are available in the same city. It is thus easy to enjoy a piece of Ligurian fainá (in Italian *farinata*), an Umbrian cheese and onion pizza, and the traditional Neapolitan tomato and mozzarella pizza in the same restaurant.

Empanadas are often served at parties as a starter or main course, or in festivals. Shops specialize in freshly made empanadas, with many flavors and fillings. (Viktorija Kuprijanova | Dreamstime.com)

Eating on the go is considered bad manners in Argentina; therefore, there are few street-food stands. However, the popular *choripán,* a chorizo-filled baguette seasoned with chimichurri, is sold only on the street. Still, this must be eaten by the stand and is not considered take-out food. American-style fast food has become popular during the last few years, and the younger generation often prefers to eat at McDonald's. However, *roticerías,* serving take-out barbecued chicken and vegetable and potato croquettes and empanadas, are still very popular. Other quick meal solutions that have appeared in the last few years are home-delivery services, which range from breakfast served at the home to a wide selection of empanadas. Sushi and Chinese food are recent popular take-out choices in Argentina today.

In Buenos Aires, the tradition of meeting friends for an espresso or cappuccino with grilled ham on toast is still very much alive and has spread to other parts of the country. Going out to ice cream parlors where ice cream from the Italian tradition is served in many varieties is also very popular.

Special Occasions

With a strong Catholic heritage, most Argentinean festivities are related to Christian celebrations. However, some yearly events are celebrated nationally or regionally. Christmas is usually a family affair. Most families attend mass late at night on Christmas Eve and eat dinner around midnight. Christmas menus are flexible, but some dishes are a must on the Argentinean table such as the main course, an oven-baked stuffed turkey or a barbecued piglet. Cider (a carbonated alcoholic drink), Spanish *turrón* (an almond or nut confection that may be either soft or hard), and *pan dulce* (a sweet egg-laden bread similar to the Italian panettone) are irreplaceable elements in Argentinean homes. Cider and pan dulce are also essential on New Year's Eve.

During Easter, Lenten empanadas filled with tuna or sardines are eaten throughout the week. Cod stews are also a part of Easter meals and may be eaten with chickpeas and potatoes. The Ligurian *torta pascualina,* a deep vegetable pie, is often served as a first course. On Easter Sunday hard-boiled colored eggs are used to decorate the table, and children receive candy-filled chocolate eggs. Dessert consists of a *rosca de Pascua,* a sweet Easter bread, which is also eaten on other religious celebrations such as All Saint's Day.

In some parts of Argentina, midsummer, or the Night of Saint John, is celebrated by making huge bonfires in towns and villages. Traditionally, sweet potatoes are cooked in the ashes and then eaten warm. Spring Day, which coincides with Students' Day, is celebrated in all parts of the country on September 21. On this day, high school students converge on parks and have daylong picnics and concerts. They drink maté and eat *sanwiches de pebete con jamón y queso,* sandwiches of ham and cheese on sweet bread.

Diet and Health

Recently, Western health recommendations have become popular in Argentina, though it is difficult for these meat lovers to reduce their intake of meat and add more fish and vegetables to their diet. Those living in urban areas are more health conscious, and many avoid eating too much fat. The younger generations are great fans of American-style fast food, and visiting Starbucks, McDonald's, and Burger King has become a way of life for teenagers and young adults. Still, culinary traditions are very strong, and even though take-out sushi may be the rage at the moment, empanadas and choripán are still a part of the daily life of Argentineans.

Gabriela Villagran Backman

Further Reading

Foster, Dereck, and Tripp, Richard. *Food and Drink in Argentina: A Guide for Tourists and Residents.* Buenos Aires: Aromas y Sabores, 2006.

Lomax Brooks, Shirley. *Argentina Cooks: Treasured Recipes from the Nine Regions of Argentina.* New York: Hippocrene Books, 2003.

Lovera, José Rafael. *Food Culture in South America.* Westport, CT: Greenwood Press, 2005.

Aruba and Bonaire

Overview

Procuring salt, conducting the slave trade, and establishing ports of trade—rather than developing sugar plantations—were the goals of the Dutch explorers who made the six islands of the Netherlands Antilles their colonies. Aruba and Bonaire are part of the ABC islands (Aruba, Bonaire, and Curaçao) that sit 15 miles north of the Venezuelan coast. Saba and Saint Eustatius (and Saint Martin) lie further east, bordered by the British Virgin Islands to the north and the British-held islands of Saint Kitts, Nevis, and Montserrat to the south.

Aruba was discovered and claimed for Spain in 1499, well before the 70-square-mile island was acquired by the Dutch in 1636. This Spanish past influences cuisine on Aruba almost as much as the Dutch ownership. At one time gold and oil dominated the island's economy. Today, tourism supports the population of 100,000.

Bonaire's population is 14,000. Bonaire's present fame comes from its dive sites rather than its sandy white beaches, which are rated the best in the Caribbean and in the world. The jewel of Bonaire's culinary crown lies high up in the hills far inland; the village of Rincon boasts a market of local food.

The Caiquetios, an Arawak tribe, were the original inhabitants of these islands. Before the Africans, the Caiquetios were enslaved by Europeans and forced to cultivate maize (corn) and dyewood (a tree that produces red dye for textiles). The slaves also harvested evaporated salt. The stone hovels in which they lived, less than four feet high and much too short for a man to stand in, are still evident on Bonaire around Rincon and along the saltpans where flamingos are drawn to the brackish water, which harbors their favorite dish, pink shrimp.

Saba, at five square miles, is the smallest island in the Netherlands Antilles; it is a dramatic volcanic island with its highest point, Mount Scenery, dominating the island's profile. Directly south of Saba, Saint Eustatius has a population of 2,900 and is under 12 square miles. Saint Eustatius—often referred to as simply Statia—lies 38 miles south of the jointly held French and Dutch island called Saint Martin or Sint Maarten. In the last decades the Netherlands Antilles have seen a tremendous boom in the tourism industry. This is particularly true for Aruba, Bonaire, and Curaçao, which sit below the hurricane belt.

🍽 Food Culture Snapshot

Mama Lou lives on the hill overlooking Kralendik in a semirural single home with her family—her husband and two daughters, both still in school. She has her own goats—which she raises for meat—and works at Buddy Dive Resort, about a 10-minute drive from her home. If she has breakfast before she drives to work, she may have a sweet bread she has baked herself, plus a fruit such as a banana or mango, and coffee. If there is a special occasion she might shop at Cultimara, the largest traditional grocery store on Bonaire, to pick up a variety of sweet and savory *pasteche* (pies) to share with her coworkers at Buddy Dive Resort. While at Cultimara she might also shop for ingredients for her renowned goat stew: potatoes, tomatoes, green peppers, hot peppers, onions, and *ketjap* (an Indonesian sweet soy sauce) as well as plantains to fry as an accompaniment. She makes this quite spicy with Scotch bonnet peppers and brings it to share with her fellow workers.

On weekends she might prepare a breakfast called *wentelteefjes,* also known as *pain perdu* or French toast, made from day-old bread. However, her husband, Bobby, a dive instructor, prefers to add a Gouda cheese sandwich to his breakfast of fruit and coffee. When lunchtime comes around, the largest meal, they both might be found at a catering truck that stops by just outside the resort and serves ribs and various *stobas,* or stews.

Mama Lou shops three times a week to make dinner for her family. Her favorite is fresh fish. The fish might come from the local fishmonger Doei Diaz next to Richard's Restaurant. Or, if her husband has had time away from diving instruction, he prefers to catch his own fish. This might be snapper, wahoo, or mahi-mahi. She might make a simple fish marinade with lime juice, garlic, peppers, and olive oil.

One of the most looked-forward-to times on Bonaire is the sorghum harvest, or Simadan, in April. A communal feast is prepared that includes *repa*—a pancake made of sorghum meal often served with goat stew, goat soup, or *giambo* (okra soup much like gumbo) and *boontji kunuku,* which is local beans. All these dishes are part of the Bonairean staple diet, although the availability of sorghum meal and boontji kunuku depends on the rainy season. It is held in the village of Rincon, near the Mangasina di Rey (the "Storehouse of the King"), which years and years before had been the main storage place for the island's food stores. Flour is brought, and eggs are collected to prepare the repa for the feast. If the bean harvest is good, the area's kunuku owners bring the beans to Rincon in celebratory processions. After the baskets are blessed at the church, the beans are given to the priest for storage in the Mangasina di Rey.

Major Foodstuffs

Local fruits available on Aruba and Bonaire often include bananas, pineapple, carambola (or star fruit), and *maracudja,* or passion fruit. Vegetables available include pigeon peas or congo peas and *belangere* (eggplant). The vegetable known as the christophene in other parts of the world is called chayote squash on the islands and are frequently included in a mélange or a curry dish. Unique to the locale is an indigenous root called *dashene* or *dachine.* Malanga, another starchy root, can be cooked as we might cook potatoes: boiled and mashed and served as a side dish. *Giraumon* is a local pumpkin or hard-skinned squash. Peppers are available in many varieties and are more often on the superhot scale such as Scotch bonnet peppers.

Beef, pork, and lamb are less available and are quite expensive because they are imported. Poultry is often raised by the locals. *Cabri* refers to goat, which is also a local favorite. Fish is caught fresh and is frequently featured on tables at home and in restaurants. Such varieties found include *chadron* or *oursin,* which is sea urchin; *chatrou,* small octopus; and *balalou,* which can mean any variety of small local fish. *Crevettes* (shrimp) are caught and denoted as *gambas* if quite large. Also appearing are *ecrevisse* or *ouassous,* freshwater crayfish that are rarer than the *z'habitants,* or marine crayfish, a cousin of the lobster. *Lambi* (conch) is harvested as well as *langouste* (lobster). *Morue* (codfish) and *moules* (mussels) find their way onto menus, often with *palourdes,* which signifies clams. If *vivaneau* appears on the menu, this means snapper, that is, the fish rather than a snapping turtle.

Prepared local seafood specialties include *blaff,* a highly seasoned soup of local fish, followed by *chiquetaille,* a shredded, spicy codfish. For shellfish lovers *crabe farci* is a spicy stuffed crab, and if listed as *columbo* this crab is also prepared with curry. *Feroce* is a fiery avocado with chiquetaille. Court bouillon is a steamed fish specialty. Sauce *chien* is a spicy sauce served with fish. Non-fish-oriented dishes might include *calalou,* or callaloo, a stew of herbs and greens, and homemade boudin, a spicy blood sausage. For drinks, there is a *planteur,* which is rum with tropical juices, or *ti-punch,* which is a liberal portion of rum mixed with cane syrup and lime.

Cooking

The Amerindians had a fondness for gathering and therefore often ate such things as turtle and iguana eggs. Sometimes these delicate foods were preserved by smoking, pickling, and salting. If these were not available, then even termites, ants, grubs, and caterpillars appeared on the table. They also developed a cooking method called *brabicot,* which was a wooden framework that held food over hot coals. The Spanish then improved this method, calling it *barbacoa,* and in English this is more familiar as the cooking method called barbecue. The most popular cooking methods include barbecuing (pork is especially prized), followed by stewing for the tougher, more economical meats (goat, lamb, and iguana), coupled with an affection for frying (especially for chicken).

In the past families had to decide on a single source of heat; usually this was wood, and the cooking area was at the rear of the house, for safety and also to allow smoke to leave quickly. Modern conveniences in the form of refrigeration and running water are moderately found outside of the major cities. People do not store much food. Whether this is due to lifestyle or the preference for fresh food is uncertain. Where the temperature is quite warm most of the year, fish is best when at its freshest and cooked immediately. Today, in rural areas it is not uncommon to see a small plot being cultivated for vegetables and herbs.

Keshi Yenaa, traditional delicacy from the Dutch Caribbean involving the shell of a scooped Edam. (Dreamstime)

Keshi Yena

One of the most typical Dutch-influenced and historical dishes is *keshi yena.* Frugality was the keynote of island living in earlier times, when provisions had to last from the visit of one sailing ship to the call of another. In this classic recipe the shell of a scooped Edam (the thin rind remaining after a family had consumed the four pounds of cheese) is filled with spiced meat, then baked in the oven or steamed in the top of a double boiler. For these methods of preparation the red wax must be removed from the empty shell after it has been soaked in hot water. In a more dramatic version the filled Edam, with the red wax intact, is tied in cheesecloth and suspended in boiling water for 20 minutes. The wax melts away in the hot water, leaving a delicate pink blush on the cheese. Use chicken or beef for the filling.

Serves 10–12

1 entire Edam cheese ball, about 2–2½ lb

For the Chicken Filling, Rub with the Juice of Several Limes

1 lb chicken breasts

1 lb chicken thighs

Season the Breasts and Thighs with

Salt and pepper

Poultry seasoning

Minced onion

Let them stand for several hours. Then either arrange the pieces in a shallow baking dish, brown the chicken under the broiler, and then bake it for 1 hour at 350°F, deboning it when cool enough to handle; or choose this more frugal method of preparation: Brown the chicken in 3 tablespoons butter, then place it in a heavy kettle with:

4 qt water

2 tsp salt

12 peppercorns

1–2 onions

1 celery stalk with leaves

Bay leaf, bruised

Bring to a boil, reduce heat, and simmer for 20 minutes, or just until chicken is tender. Strain and reserve the broth, discarding the vegetables. Debone the chicken and set aside.

After the chicken has been prepared by one of the preceding methods, sauté in 2 tablespoons butter:

3 tomatoes, peeled and chopped

4 onions, sliced

1 large green pepper, chopped

1 tbsp parsley, minced, or a few drops Tabasco sauce

Salt and pepper

Add and stir in well:

2 tbsp ketchup

¼ c pimento olives, sliced

1 tbsp capers

¼ c raisins

2 tbsp piccalilli (a sweet, spicy pickle relish that typically includes tomatoes, sweet peppers, onions, cucumber, or other garden vegetables. It gets its bright yellow color from turmeric or sometimes mustard.)

The chicken (or substitute 1 lb ground beef, lightly browned, for the chicken)

Simmer until the tomatoes are reduced, about 20 or 30 minutes. Remove from the fire and permit mixture to cool. If keshi yena is to be baked, preheat oven to 350°F. If it is to be steamed, begin heating water in the bottom of a double boiler.

Beat 3 eggs, reserving about 6 tablespoons for brushing the top, and add the rest to the meat mixture. Generously butter a casserole or the top of a double boiler. Before placing the Edam cheese shell in it, spoon 3 tablespoons of the reserved beaten egg into the bottom of the container. Half fill with the meat mixture and add 1 or 2 hard-cooked eggs.

Fill shell to the top with remaining meat and cover with the original cap of the Edam, from which the wax has been removed, or a few slices of cheese.

Never use soft young cheese for keshi yena; firm cheeses are required for a successful dish.

Drip the remaining 3 tablespoonfuls of beaten egg over the top of the cheese as a sealer. (Place the lid on the double boiler.) Set the casserole in a pan of hot water, or the double boiler top over the simmering water. Cook for 1¼ hours. Invert keshi yena on a heated platter, and keep warm, for the cheese becomes hard and unappetizing if permitted to cool.

In place of the cheese shell, 2 pounds of sliced Edam or Gouda may be used to line the cooking container. The slices should overlap and create the same effect as the shell. Add filling, cover with additional slices of cheese, and set the casserole in the oven at 350°F for 1½ hours. The traditionalist with a great deal of time and patience may scoop out a 4-pound Edam or Gouda, taking care not to pierce the shell.

The open-air market in Rincon on the first Saturday of the month offers at least six stalls of prepared foods such as *kabritu stobá* (a goat stew with vegetables), *kabes ku higra* (a mix of goat brains and liver), and *sòpi di yuana* (iguana soup). Other cooking includes the Dutch-inspired *bokijow*, cod marinated in vinaigrette with hot peppers. *Sopa di banana* is the Dutch term for banana soup, which is often seen on Bonaire and Aruba. *Pika siboyo* is a pepper sauce with onions, vinegar, and two kinds of pepper; one is a hot pepper called Madam Jeanette, and the other is a Scotch bonnet from Venezuela.

Typical Meals

For breakfast, the locals might enjoy fresh tropical fruit and coffee. Sweet pastries are also featured. For lunch the versatile pasteche might appear. This is a plump little pastry filled with spicy meat, shrimp, or fish. It can be found everywhere, around the clock: with coffee, tea, or cocktails; at beach parties; or on the most formal buffet tables. *Bitterbal* are fried meat croquettes served with mustard.

At dinner locals enjoy keshi yena. This dish is sometimes served with *funchi,* a cornmeal pancake, or *pan bati,* a corn pudding formed into pies.

Soppi di pisca, a very popular soup, is actually fish chowder flavored with coconut and also, occasionally, meat. For travelers who enjoy seafood, there are several unique ways of having it prepared. *Keri keri* is a dish of shredded barracuda infused with the South American spice annatto. This is what the Dutch first adopted from their Indonesian colonies, where it is called curry.

Drinks available on Aruba are unique Caribbean soft drinks. Desnoes and Geddes is a company that makes something called *kola champagne* and the more familiar ginger beer. Mixed drinks are also popular, particularly the island's famous rum punch, which is comprised of several types of rum mixed with orange and pineapple juices, sweet and sour mix, and grenadine.

A popular dessert might be *pan bollo,* an Aruban bread pudding that is served with rhum sauce, or a cake called *bolo di tres lechi* made with three forms of milk—condensed milk, evaporated milk, and cream.

Funchi

Serves 6

1¼ c cold water

1½ c cornmeal

1 tsp salt

1½ c boiling water

1 tbsp butter

Funchi is a staple of the Dutch islands. A polenta-like dish made from cornmeal, it is often served with soup.

Mix the cold water, cornmeal, and salt in a heavy saucepan. Stir in boiling water and butter. Bring to a brisk boil over high heat and cook for 3 minutes. Continue cooking an additional 3 minutes, stirring the funchi vigorously with a wooden spoon.

When the mixture is very stiff and pulls away from the sides of the pan, remove from the fire. Turn out into a deep, well-buttered bowl and cover with a plate. Shake the funchi down into the bowl, and then invert it onto a serving platter.

For a special Sunday breakfast, fry sliced funchi in butter and serve with crisp bacon and scrambled eggs.

Eating Out

Meals eaten outside the home by locals differ substantially from those eaten by tourists. It is certainly possible to visit the resorts and never have local food. Cheeseburgers and French fries are widely available, and even the locals are beginning to be more inclined to eat these than take the time to prepare such time-consuming cooked dishes as goat stew. It is even possible, on Aruba, to find such chain restaurants as Hooters and Benihana to please the myriad tourists.

Special Occasions

Monthly market days or even the smaller weekly version (*marshe chikitu*) are celebrations of their own in this arid climate. So are the Simadan (harvest) festival, Día di San Juan, Día di San Pedro, Día di Rincon, and the Bari Festival. Of particular note is the dance known as the Bari, which is still performed during the harvest festival of the same name, as well as during the Simadan festival, and in the period following New Year's (Mascarada). The Bari is led by a solo singer who, very much like a Calypsonian, improvises satirical lyrics based on recent events and local figures.

Typical foods during Simadan include funchi (similar to grits but less coarse) and repa (pancakes made of sorghum meal), served plain or with goat stew, goat soup, giambo (okra soup, similar to gumbo), and boontji kunuku (local beans). All of these dishes are still an integral part of the Bonairean diet, although the availability of sorghum meal and boontji kunuku depends on the rainy season.

In April, Coronation Day and the Queen's Birthday are celebrated. On Antillean Day in October there is a festival commemorating the island's Dutch heritage. In December, holidays are Christmas and Boxing Day, a public holiday exhibiting the island's special flavors of pepper-pot soup with lots of pork, okra, and onions.

A woman selects fruit at one of the many outdoor markets in Aruba. (StockPhotoPro)

Diet and Health

The chief diet and health concerns on Aruba center on obesity and diabetes. For the last 20 years insight and proactive plans have been sought. Focusing on youth, a program called Extreme H Games began. Long-term goals aim to teach children the impact of nutrition and physical activity on health. In 2008 the National Plan for Aruba (2009–2018) for the Government of Aruba for the Fight against Overweight, Obesity, and Other Related Health Issues was launched. The plan was endorsed by the European Public Health Alliance in Brussels, Belgium.

Approximately 6 percent of all deaths are related to diabetes—with poor eating habits being targeted as the main cause. The improvement of these is suggested as the care and cure for 96 percent of cases.

Increased consumption of simple and refined sugars and fried foods paired with a tendency toward little physical activity, or at least not enough to ward off this imbalance, contributes to this problem. With Aruba's inherent Arawak culture and love of dance—calypso, soca, merengue, and a mélange known as *socarengue,* vigorous dancing some might consider risqué, it seems possible that a revitalization of dance for all might hold the key to resolving both diet and health concerns.

Dorette Snover

Further Reading

Aruba Gastronomic Association. http://www.arubadining.com.

Aruba Guide. http://www.aruba-guide.info.

Besson, Jean. "A Paradox in Caribbean Attitudes to Land." In *Land and Development in the Caribbean,* edited by Jean Besson and Janet Momsen, 13–45. London: Macmillan, 1987.

Brathwaite, Kamau. *Roots.* Ann Arbor: University of Michigan Press, 1993.

Brushaber, Susan, and Arnold Greenburg. *Aruba, Bonaire, and Curacao: Alive.* Edison, NJ: Hunter, 2008.

Counihan, Carole, and Penny Van Esterik. *Food and Culture: A Reader.* New York: Routledge, 1997.

Dutch Food. http://www.dutchfood.about.com.

Fiery-Foods: The Fiery Foods and Barbecue Supersite. http://www.fiery-foods.com.

Geddes, Bruce. *Lonely Planet. World Food Caribbean.* Oakland, CA: Lonely Planet, 2001.

Hall, Robert L. "Savoring Africa in the New World." In *Seeds of Change: Five Hundred Years since Columbus,* edited by Herman J. Viola and Carolyn Margolis. Washington, DC: Smithsonian Institution Press, 1991, 161–172.

Houston, Lynn Marie. *Food Culture in the Caribbean.* Westport, CT: Greenwood Press, 2005.

Martindale, Marty. "Curacao: Amazing Island of Diversity." Food Site of the Day. http://www.foodsiteoftheday.com/?p=3841.

McNeill, William H. "American Food Crops in the Old World." In *Seeds of Change: Five Hundred Years since Columbus,* edited by Herman J. Viola and Carolyn Margolis. Washington, DC: Smithsonian Institution Press, 1991, 43–59.

Mintz, Sidney W. "Caribbean Marketplaces and Caribbean History." *Nova Americana* 1, No. 1 (1978): 333–44.

Mintz, Sidney W. "Pleasure, Profit, and Satiation." In *Seeds of Change: Five Hundred Years since Columbus,* edited by Herman J. Viola and Carolyn Margolis. Washington, DC: Smithsonian Institution Press, 1991, 112–129.

Patullo, Polly. *Last Resorts: The Cost of Tourism in the Caribbean.* London: Cassell, 1996.

Scott, David A. "That Event, This Memory: Notes on the Anthropology of Diasporas in the New World." *Diaspora* 1, No. 3 (1991): 261–84.

Wolfe, Linda. *The Cooking of the Caribbean Islands.* New York: Time-Life Books, 1970.

Barbados

Overview

Barbados is situated on the easternmost side of the Lesser Antilles with the west coast of the island on the Caribbean Sea, the east on the Atlantic Ocean. Formed less than a million years ago, the island is believed to have been created by the collision of the Atlantic crust and Caribbean plates during a volcanic eruption. With the formation of coral that accumulated to approximately 300 feet, Barbados is actually two landmasses that merged together over years.

The total landmass of Barbados is 267 square miles (430 square kilometers) and is mostly gently sloping land with some rolling hills and sharp elevations toward the northeastern coastline. Although the island is surrounded by coral reefs, its basic topography consists mainly of coral and limestone with some deposits of clay toward the northeastern side of its coastline. There are many underground caves with streams that create freshwater springs on land. Because of its coral makeup, the island's freshwater is noted to be one of the best on the Caribbean islands. Swept by northeast trade winds, Barbados enjoys a tropical climate and a soil with coralline limestone features that is suited to the growth of sugarcane and most tropical agricultural produce.

A parliamentary democracy, Barbados received its colonial independence in 1966 under the leadership of the prime minister at that time, the Right Honorable Errol Walton Barrow, now a national hero. Up until that time it had been a colony of the British Isles. Approximately 270,000 people live on the island. Quite distinct from others in the Caribbean chain, it follows Jamaica in terms of its uniqueness in expression, culture, and cuisine.

With average temperatures ranging from 75 degrees Fahrenheit (24 degrees Celsius) to 84–86 degrees Fahrenheit (29–30 degrees Celsius), Barbados boasts a climate that is mostly sunny with scattered showers and the occasional hard rainfall. With strong easterly breezes coming off the Atlantic Ocean beating on its east coast, with large rolling waves and a wind that seems interminable, nights are slightly cooler, more so from November to February. Barbados's economy is mostly based on tourism, with sugar and rum being its major exports.

While Barbados is one of the most developed and affluent islands within the Caribbean chain, it has over the years become a society of mixed races. Although traces of Amerindian existence go back thousands of years, there are no documented living descendants of these first inhabitants. With the arrival of the English in 1625 came African slaves, hence Barbados was known as one of the few islands that had both white (English and Irish, with a smattering of Dutch) and black people (Africans). More recently, Barbados became known as the island of opportunity, seeing the arrival of Dutch and Sephardic Jews, Middle Easterners, Indians, and political refugees from Pakistan. Add to this the new arrivals of moneyed North and South Americans, English, Irish, French, Italians, and even Arabs, together with sprinklings of Caribbean people that include mostly Guyanese, Jamaicans, Saint Vincentians, and Trinidadians, and this basically makes up the local society.

An outdoor market in Bridgeport Barbados, 2009. (StockPhotoPro)

🍽️ Food Culture Snapshot

Ena and Norris "Fishmout" Scantlebury live above Consetts Bay in St. John on the east coast of Barbados. Ena was born in Panama to a Barbadian mother and Grenadian father, who sent the child to Barbados to live with her maternal grandmother in the capital parish of St. Michael. Many islanders left their homeland during those days for economic reasons. Ena spent her formative years in Barbados, attending school, then leaving for her father's homeland to teach.

Years later, Ena and Norris would meet in Grenada. Norris's fishing boat, having taken off from Consetts Bay one fine morning toward the south coast, found itself in trouble when the seas began to swell and a harsh easterly high wind rocked the boat from side to side. The ensuing rain blasted the little vessel's only engine as he managed to round the corner of the east coast and the south coast. But by this time the boat was far out to sea, and the raging winds and strong current pushed the boat further and further southeast, until he landed on the shores of Grenada. Fishing can be treacherous work, so if an island boat washes up, help is usually given without a thought. Norris was taken in by villagers while his boat was repaired. Sitting at a local makeshift hut where men gathered after a hard day's work to share in a couple of bottles of white rum, slap a domino or two, and talk of perilous days at sea, Norris spotted Ena taking a walk, and the rest was history. Norris, once home, saved enough money to bring Ena back to Barbados for marriage.

Norris had purchased an acre of land next to the chattel house his parents had bequeathed to him, and with his savings he also got rid of the outdoor latrine and added on a "proper" toilet and bath to greet his new wife. People in the area were proud of Norris; there was a lot of respect for this fisherman who not only had beaten death at sea but also had planned his life carefully when it came to his bride and his home. Now he had even managed to acquire three boats that employed two villagers each.

The village was a serene but cheerful place to live, and Ena spent her days happily there doing remedial work with the odd child who was being kept back at the local school. She loved her acre of land that had turned into a full-time agricultural exhibition, the produce of which went with her every Saturday morning to Cheapside Market in Bridgetown on the other side of the island. It allowed her to mingle with her cultured city folk and reap some extra money to give to the church come Sunday. She grew tomatoes, cabbage, cucumbers, okra, and pigeon peas, as well as yams, cassava, and sweet potatoes. One enormous pumpkin vine never let her down. Nearer to the back of the house where the bathwater flowed easily into the yard, Ena had all the "seasonings" possible—chives, normal thyme and broad-leaf thyme, basil, marjoram, parsley, dill, and, of course, several Scotch bonnet pepper trees. Ena would pick and grind the first six to make "Bajan seasoning," then bottle it. She would keep a bottle or two for herself, save one for the priest at St. John's church, and take the rest for sale in the market. The last six feet to the back of the acre were planted with one breadfruit, two lime, a golden apple, a grapefruit, two guava, three pawpaw, one avocado, one coconut, and approximately 12 to 14 banana trees. Interspersed in the garden were various pigeon pea trees. A trumpet tree stood away from these, a passion fruit vine attached to its trunk. To the side of that in a separate area were the plants required to make bush tea or bush baths, such as cerasee, fever grass, and leaf of life, and those to help in healing, such as aloe vera.

Early every morning Ena prepared a good hot herbal tea for her husband. While Norris sipped his tea, Ena would bring out the fresh salt bread from the brick oven at the back of the house, add a good chunk of cheese or even some sardines to it, and place it before her husband. If the chickens in the yard had left extra eggs, he also got one hard-boiled. Some mornings Norris was treated to porridge made from ground oats, drizzled with Bajan molasses, or two bakes (a kind of bun) made of flour, water, and spice, one of which she would fill with her homemade guava jelly. Ena would pack his *breakfass* in a three-tiered tin canister for the journey. There would be slices of sweet potato and yam, a little rice, and peas; and although he mostly ate fish such as dolphin (not the mammal but mahimahi), marlin, or kingfish, sometimes she would prepare a chicken (if she had killed one) or perhaps a lamb or beef stew. He sometimes got salt fish and *coucou,* and this was Norris's favorite meal. English tea thickened with condensed milk, placed hot in a Thermos, accompanied this feast for the seas.

At six o'clock in the evening they would sit together over a bowl of delicious Bajan soup in which various "provisions" floated, with pumpkin, carrots, and christophene (chayote) for color, a piece of salt pork or beef for taste, and dumplings for the "man-hood." As a drink Ena would always serve juice made from her garden fruits, sweetened with the golden brown sugar received from a nearby sugar plantation just after the crop season had ended. Norris, being a fisherman, would take a bagful of the much-sought-after sea egg (a kind of sea urchin now getting scarcer by the minute) for the nearby plantation owners, and they paid in sugar. Sometimes the exchange of sea egg for sugar produced more, and Norris also returned with a bundle of canes in the back of his truck. These would be squeezed of their juice. There was nothing like an ice-cold glass of cane juice after a hard day's work in the sun.

Every Friday Ena prepared her produce for the market, leaving the herbs, lettuces, and tomatoes for picking at dawn. And every Saturday Norris and she woke up at 2 A.M., packed the back of the truck neatly, and took off for Bridgetown. By 5 A.M. the market was open, and Ena was behind her counter selling her goods, chatting, and getting in touch with the world. Norris would retire upstairs to the food court. Here, Miss Dora ensured that Ena got her share of the delicious Saturday-morning Bajan special—pudding and souse. Norris would prefer to have Miss Harriett's fish broth to start with—later on enjoying one of her dishes of the day: macaroni pie with lamb stew, Creole marlin with peas and rice, flying fish (steamed or fried) and corn coucou, baked pork with green banana, or stewed lamb with sweet potato pie. To wash down these delicious meals, there was always Debbie's *mauby*—a drink made from the bark of a tree. Later he would sit under the trees to the side of the market and slap some dominoes with the men, sharing a flask of rum among them "neat" in plastic cups with a little water on the side.

On Sundays they went to church and invited their grown children for a family meal. Sunday lunch always began with grace. Ena forced Norris to give the prayer every time. She felt he needed to pray more, especially as he was still, in his old age, going out to sea "like eff you is a young gully-boar" she would say. Once that was over, the feast began, and a feast it always was: roast pork with cracklings and thick gravy, roast chicken with stuffing, steamed dolphin or baked snapper, peas and rice, macaroni pie, breadfruit slices, and cornmeal coucou, the yellow butter melting over the golden mound in the dish and the pieces of okra peeking through as if to get a look at the rest of the fare. Sometimes Ena went real traditional, slicing a boiled egg and some cucumbers over the coucou. Coleslaw was also there, as well as salad with fresh lettuce from the garden, sprinkled with chives and herbs. On occasion, if she could save a little from Saturday, Ena would also produce pudding and souse—she knew the children hardly ever ate "the good one," preferring to meet friends at the over-popular Lemon Arbor on a Saturday morning. "It not like ours," Ena would say, even though she had never tasted it. Jugfuls of freshly squeezed lime juice, and passion fruit mixed with a touch of ginger, always sat on the table for anyone to help themselves. Pepper sauce made by Ena from extra peppers always graced the table too. No Bajan worth their life in salt would eat a meal without that good old Bajan pepper sauce, the mustard giving it that traditional yellow color. Dessert depended on Ena, and she loved to surprise everyone, including Norris. Some Sundays it would be bread pudding—a trickle of Red Label sherry giving it that edge—drizzled with Tate & Lyle golden syrup, other times a beautifully decorated rum triffle. Some days the dessert would be two pies baked to perfection, filled with something from the garden like golden apples with cinnamon or mango and bananas. Her favorite, however, was fresh coconut cream pie. She labored with cutting out the flesh from the dried brown coconut, grating it, and squeezing it through a muslin sieve until all the milk was drawn out. She then boiled it, sweetened with condensed milk,

until it was thick, ready to be placed into the pie crust and into the fridge. Later, sprinkles of grated coconut would decorate her specialty. Needless to say, after a lunch like this the family would sit around, sometimes with a cup or two of coffee, talking about the week that had passed. Ena always praised God for her blessings.

Major Foodstuffs

Barbados is one of the most populated islands within the Caribbean. Many years ago, it was covered in organic agricultural land, but this is sadly no longer so. Because of its beauty, as well as its steady economy and governance, Barbados has also become the home that all the rich and famous wish to have. Add to that the average Barbadian, whose interest in owning land and a house continues, and one finds more and more housing developments taking over the rich soil and, therefore, more and more imports happening foodwise. The importation of fertilizers and pesticides to the island in order to push the crops forward has taken its toll as well. Taking into consideration that Barbados is considered one of culinary stops of the Caribbean, with restaurants dotting most of the coastline, one would think that steps would have been put in place a long time ago to allow the island to be self-sufficient in food.

There is, of course, hope. Recently, more and more attention is being paid to culinary tourism and the health of the Barbadians. More and more systems are being put in place to encourage local farming. More and more farmers want to become "organic." The health of the soil is, however, in question now. The Ministry of Agriculture works closely with farmers, and the Inter-American Institute for Co-operation in Agriculture is very much part of this new agricultural drive. Fridays and Saturdays at the various markets across the country see a resurgence in buying local. Although the seas are also showing extreme stress, the fish markets continue to bring in good hauls just about all year round, and fresh fish is very much part of the Barbadian diet. Barbados is still sugarcane country, and the rolling hills of the island are covered with this crop, hiding the few

Tropical coastline and sugar cane plantation in Barbados. (iStockPhoto)

remaining working plantations in-between. Sugar factories have been reduced to two, but during the crop season, from January to June or July, one can see cane cutters—both human and mechanical—working the fields and the canes being taken to the sugar factories. Special tours allow visitors to watch the process.

The island is known for its rum, 99 percent made from molasses, and Barbados was the first in the Caribbean to produce it. Today, Barbados has several brand-name rums, and Barbadians are very loyal in this regard. If a particular brand is favored, they stick with it no matter what. Mount Gay, Cockspur, Alleyne Arthurs, and Old Brigand are but a few of the many available. Falernum, concocted on the island from rum, lime, almonds, ginger, cloves, and vanilla, is a liqueur that is added to many cocktails. Corn & Oil is a traditional drink made with Falernum, rum, Angostura bitters, and a twist of lime. Banks is the Barbadian beer, and Guinness is a drink purported

to give strength and is, therefore, a favorite. Plus is a sweet drink concocted by the Banks Beer Brewery that many locals drink for energy or for "putting it back" after a hard night or day.

The soft drink industry is big in Barbados, with bottling companies creating carbonated drinks in all colors of the rainbow with names like Kola Champagne, Grape, Orange, Banana, and Frutee. Fruit juices of all types, sweetened and unsweetened, are made at the island's well-known and time-honored Pine Hill Dairy, mostly from imported concentrate. The dairy also produces fresh milk, chocolate milk, and vanilla milk—all enjoyed by Barbadians. Evaporated and condensed milk can be found in most homes, the latter used in inordinate proportions. Syrups are also available to be used in the hotel industry or at home; adding water makes a refreshing drink. Mauby is a traditional drink with a slightly bitter taste, made from the bark of a tree and reputed to cleanse the kidneys. Ginger beer and

Brightly painted red "Rum Shop" in Oistins fishing village, Barbados. (StockPhotoPro)

sorrel, the latter usually a Christmas drink, are now served year-round. Mauby, ginger beer, and sorrel can be found in syrup form, to which one just adds water, but these are not as healthy nor as popular as the homemade variety. There are other traditional "strengthening" drinks purported to help men perform their duties better, such as *seamoss* (made by boiling seaweed, then removing the weed and mixing the remaining gel in a blender with condensed milk, water, and spices such as cinnamon and nutmeg). To this all manner of other ingredients such as linseed, oats, eggs, and stout are added for further strength.

In terms of traditional dietary staples, when the English arrived, the Amerindians had actually left for other shores, but there might have been some remnant of their culinary existence, such as cassava, sweet potatoes, corn, and Scotch bonnet peppers. The movement of food began with the island's new settlers, and plantation owners had to feed the slaves who toiled in the canes and those who lived in the great houses. Breadfruit arrived from Tahiti (Captain Bligh's voyage is of note here); yams came from Asia through Africa. This movement created a base of English/African cuisine. Today, Barbados still grows yams, dasheen, and sweet potatoes in abundance, as well as some English potatoes and *eddoes* (a kind of taro root); recent yields of cassava have been excellent. Rice is imported from Guyana, Trinidad, and the United States.

Vegetables and fruit grown on the island are now influenced by the arrival of other Caribbean people, including the Guyanese from the coast of South America, and also by the requirements of the tourism industry (hotels and restaurants). Vegetables include carrots, normal pumpkins and the slightly pear-shaped garden pumpkin, squash, cabbage as well as Chinese cabbage or *pachoy,* okra, christophene (*cho-*

cho), cauliflower, sweet peppers (red, yellow, and green), eggplant, broccoli, tomatoes, cucumbers, onions, various types of green beans, pigeon peas, corn, avocados, and various mixtures of lettuce and microgreens, the most popular for locals being Bajan lettuce. Two types of hot peppers are grown and used widely—the Scotch bonnet is farmed, while the smaller bird pepper grows wild in backyards and sometimes even on the side of the road.

Golden apples (*Spondias cytherea*) are grown as well mangoes, bananas (used ripe and green), plantains, grapefruit, oranges, shaddocks (a large citrus fruit), limes, sour oranges, sweetsops, soursops, and carambola. Growing wild are the famous Bajan cherry, tamarinds, *dunks* (jujubes), sea grapes (not related to grapes but in the genus *Coccoloba*), ackee (not Jamaican ackee but *guinep*—a green oval fruit with a pink interior), hog plums, gooseberries, cashews, and fat pork (*Chrysobalanus icaco*—a plumlike fruit). Barbados has a season for some fruits—mangoes, avocados, golden apples, and nearly all items sold in the markets, supermarkets, and small shops are priced according to the season. At times limes are out of season, meaning mostly that the fruit has been reaped and the next lot will take time to blossom and bear; meanwhile, imported ones with little juice that are more expensive take their place. Most householders know the importance of having a lime tree in their yard. Apart from being used to wash and season meats, lime is a staple juice—lemonade is favored by children and adults above all drinks. Today, a lot of juices are also being made with combinations of greens such as herbs, cucumbers, pumpkin, and carrots, and juice bars are popping up offering all manner of health drinks.

Fish consists of various types. Flying fish is the national darling, with its roe and melts (eggs) being much in demand. Dolphin (mahimahi), kingfish, marlin, yellowfin tuna, billfish, and swordfish are the larger fish brought in by the fishermen. Shark has begun to tickle the taste buds of Barbadians, although in the past it was not considered to be part of the average diet; the odd shark caught was used as dog food. Various types of snapper are offered, and barracuda is also found and revered. "Pot fish" or reef fish such as chub are also enjoyed. Jacks and sprats are caught by net off the shores. Conch and *seacat* (octopus) are eaten with gusto when available and are considered to have aphrodisiac properties. Lobster is enjoyed, but there are very few left on the reefs. Although salt fish is very much an integral part of the Barbadian diet, introduced by the Portuguese traders, sadly not much is salted on the island, and this remains mostly an imported product.

Barbados is known for its pork, which is, after fish and chicken, one of the most consumed meats. Turkey comes next. Several processing plants make ham and ham products including sausages, and fresh pork can be had in all supermarkets, small shops, and fresh from the market. Salt pork, beef, and pig tails are imported in brine and are an integral part of Bajan soup or used in the flavoring of white rice. The chicken industry is by far the largest, with chicken farmers introduced to fast-growing chickens. Although cattle are reared on the island, and the meat is organic, beef imports have harmed the industry. However, enough cattle are still reared for local beef to be sold in the markets. Duck and rabbit are two other traditional meats, usually served stewed. There is a game bird farm that supplies specialized restaurants. There are still a few man-made ponds and private clubs where members spend time during the northern migration of birds for a shoot—these birds are considered a secret delicacy. Blackbelly sheep (a Barbadian breed), although exported for its meat, is also now considered a treat by Barbadians. Although the average Bajan will say this is not so, monkey is eaten "stewed down" as a delicacy in certain parts of the island, particularly on the eastern coast.

Bakeries abound. The small local bakery is fast disappearing with the advent of large modern ones. Barbadians have always enjoyed their breads. The traditional one is the small rounded salt bread baked in ovens, each loaf decorated with a piece of banana leaf (the leaf is also fast disappearing). Salt breads are used for the traditional Bajan *cutter*—a salt bread filled with shop cheese (cheddar), fish, fish cakes (also served alone, these are circular balls of salt fish [salted cod], flour, seasonings, and finely chopped pepper that are fried in hot oil), ham, egg, or pork, doused with yellow pepper sauce (made with mustard). All manner of sweet breads and pastries are consumed such as raisin loaves (called sweetbread), coconut bread, banana bread, currant rolls, Swiss rolls, jam puffs, coconut turnovers, rock cakes, and the well-known lead pipe—the last being a heavy four-inch-long and two-inch-wide rectangle-shaped staple made of pure hard dough—it is said you can give a heavy blow with a lead pipe. Used as a stomach filler when money is not handy, it certainly fulfills its job when downed with a soft drink. Various sponge cakes and cookies are also popular, with supermarkets carrying these made either by the larger bakeries or by small businesses at home. Cassava or cornmeal pone (with the consistency of a hard pudding and made with cassava and coconut) is eaten heartily. Bread pudding, sponge cake, fruit or great cake, rum cake, coconut cream pie, and lemon meringue pie are traditional, although all manner of pastries and cakes can now be found at specialized bakeries and supermarkets. Guava stew and crème caramel are traditional favorites. *Conkies,* made from sweetened cornmeal, pumpkin, coconut, and spices, wrapped in steamed banana leaf, are traditional at Christmas.

A *one in two* is a cutter with two salt fish cakes. Cutters are sold in most rum shops all week long or at specialized spots around the island. There are many savory pastries as well—beef, chicken, and vegetable patties or sausage rolls (a wiener or sausage meat is rolled in a pastry dough and baked). One of the best-known places for these is Beefeaters Ltd. on Swan Street. Roti, which is originally from Trinidad, has become a favorite. The bake made with *dhal* (yellow split peas), it is filled with curried chicken, beef, potatoes, chickpeas, pumpkin, or any combination of these.

Favored snacks range from salted plantain, cassava, or sweet potato chips to corn curls, Chee-Weez, peanuts, and cashews. Local companies and small home businesses do a roaring trade with these, as Barbadians enjoy snacking. Traditional sweets are tamarind balls, sugar cakes (white, brown, and pink, made from sugared grated coconut and colored with vegetable coloring), caramel and chocolate fudge, guava cheese (made from stewing down the fruits with lots of sugar and spices, placing it in baking pans until gelled, then cutting it in squares and rubbing it in white sugar), peanut brittle, mints, and governor plums. Not seen so much but still loved and returning slowly into the area of "exotic" sweets are ginger candy, shaddock rind, and paw-paw candy, just to name a few. Many Indian sweets are finding their way onto the shelves as the population of Indians has increased on the island. Snow cones are a favorite—shaved ice in a cup doused in different colored syrups with flavors of pineapple, strawberry, lime, and so on with an option to have condensed milk poured over that.

Barbados Coucou and Flying Fish

Serves 6

Please note that any fish can be used. Traditionally it is flying fish, but this may not be available readily to others. Salt fish (codfish) can be used instead of fresh fish. Yellow butter is equivalent to the red Irish cooking butter, but if it is not available, normal butter may be used.

Coucou

7 c water

1 small piece of pig tail, salt beef, or salt fish (optional)

2 tsp salt

14 okras, sliced thinly

3 c cornmeal

½ Scotch bonnet pepper, finely chopped, seeds removed

2½ tbsp yellow (red Irish) butter

In a large pot bring water (and pig tail, salt beef, or salt fish if using—this is not traditional but does give taste; if using, reduce salt by ½ teaspoon) and salt to a boil. Add okra, and continue to boil until very soft. Cool 2 cups of this water to room temperature, and stir into a bowl with the cornmeal. Add water if necessary; the cornmeal should be able to be poured. Do not put hot water in with the cornmeal.

Add pepper to the pot of boiling water. Slowly pour the cornmeal into the pot with the boiling water, stirring continuously with a coucou stick or with a large wooden spoon until the mixture is smooth and is turning easily. Add the butter and continue to turn. When mixture begins to stick slightly to the pot it is ready. Grease a glass bowl with butter, and add coucou. Taste for salt. Garnish with more butter, sliced hard-boiled eggs, or finely sliced cucumbers. Serve hot with steamed flying fish (or any other suitable fish).

Steamed Flying Fish

12 filets flying fish, washed in lime and saltwater and patted dry

½ tbsp yellow butter

2 medium onions, sliced in rings

½ red pepper, ½ yellow bell, and ½ green bell pepper, cut in julienne strips

1 whole Scotch bonnet tied in muslin cloth

2 large cloves garlic, finely chopped

1 sprig thyme—whole

1 sprig marjoram—whole

4 large tomatoes, cut in chunks

2 c water

½ tbsp tomato paste

Juice of one lime

Salt and pepper to taste

Seasoning

1 medium onion, finely chopped

2 large cloves garlic, finely chopped

4 sprigs chives, finely chopped

1 tbsp parsley, finely chopped

½ tsp marjoram, finely chopped

1 tsp fresh lime juice

½ Scotch bonnet pepper, finely chopped, seeds removed

¼ tsp each salt and pepper

Make the seasoning by either combining the ingredients in a bowl or using a blender. Spread season-ing over the grooved side of each flying fish fillet, roll like a roll mop, securing it with a toothpick, and set aside. In a large frying pan, melt half the butter and sauté the onions, all the peppers, and the garlic. Add the tomatoes and water. Add salt and pepper to taste. Tie the thyme and marjoram together and place whole into the pan. Add lime and tomato paste. Cover and bring to a boil. Add the rest of the butter. Add the flying fish, allowing it to simmer for approximately 20 minutes, so that the gravy can penetrate it. A teaspoon of rum can be added to the gravy for taste (optional). Place hot in a dish and serve with coucou. When using other fish, use a fillet to make it easier to roll. However, a fish steak can be used; in that case, just place seasoning into grooves made into the fish—this allows the fish to be well seasoned and tasty.

Cooking

Traditional Barbadian cooking cannot be described as labor-intensive; it is, however, particular to the household cook. Everyone has a little secret, a touch of the hand that is seldom disclosed and that makes the food taste just that little bit different. Many Barbadian men pride themselves on their ability to cook and love of cooking—one prime minister, the late Honorable Errol Walton Barrow, even wrote a now-famous cookbook, *Privilege.* Women are, however, traditionally the cooks in the home.

While gas or electric stoves are now the norm, coal pots with their corresponding black buck (iron) pots or huge frying pans are still used in some households, although mostly on the side of the road at night in special areas/streets for frying fish or chicken. In the old days the kitchen was always built on the west side of the house so that smells would not bother the living areas, but this has now changed, the aromas of home cooking being more welcomed these days. Large cooking spoons and pots were and still are a must in the kitchen; a coucou stick had to be, and still is, a part of the cooking utensils. A coucou stick is a flattened spoon used to stir the thick mass of cornmeal and okra that becomes coucou—a dish that originated in Africa and was brought to the island by the slaves. Coucou and steamed fish is a traditional Friday dish.

Barbadians like to season their meats and wash their rice. Seasoning consists of finely chopped chives, onions, garlic, thyme, parsley, marjoram, a touch of Worcestershire sauce, vinegar, cloves, salt, pepper, and hot chili peppers (Scotch bonnet or bird peppers). In the market one can buy bundles of the required fresh ingredients for seasonings. Seasonings are used in most dishes, although primarily it is particular to fish or chicken. Washing consists of placing rice in a sieve and washing it in cold water until the water runs clear; sometimes a little lime juice is used to help this procedure along and to take away the "rawness" of the rice. Rice is usually cooked with some kind of peas—pigeon peas; yellow, green, or brown lentils; red beans (really a pea)—to make a dish that is simply called peas and rice.

Bajans (as Barbadians are called) also love to marinate their meats overnight in the fridge, so that they are ready for frying, baking, or stewing the following morning in time to be served for lunch or dinner. Salt pork, salt beef, pig tail, and salt fish will always be part and parcel of a Bajan kitchen unless one is a vegetarian.

Fish and chicken are both washed with salt, lime, and water before seasoning. Holes are made in both these meats, and these are stuffed with the seasoning. Jars of Bajan seasoning have also become popular as they contain all that is required in the kitchen without the tedious job of all the fine chopping. Flying fish is treated differently; these come already cleaned and boned (mostly) from the fish market, but they are still washed and/or marinated in lime, salt, and water before their grooves are filled with seasoning and they are dipped in egg and a seasoned mixture of breadcrumbs and flour. They are then placed skin down into hot oil and fried until crispy before being turned over and fried on the other side. All fish is served steamed, fried, grilled, or baked. In steamed flying fish the fish is rolled into a sort of roll-mop position, kept in place with a toothpick, and then steamed. Steak fish (filets/steaks of fish, whether boned or not) or flying fish when steamed requires onions, tomatoes,

garlic, chives, and peppers as well as a most important ingredient that is used in a Bajan kitchen to add a taste to just about everything—yellow butter better known as *mello-kreem* or just *shop butter*. It is bright yellow in color, has the consistency of ghee, and is purportedly made from fish oils. Some yellow butters give the ingredients as the same as margarine with coloring added, but the original traditional one was indeed made from fish oil. Fried fish and chicken are usually dusted with seasoned flour before being placed in hot oil to fry on both sides until well cooked. Barbadians do not like their fish undercooked, and of course chicken follows the normal worldwide rules.

Conch and octopus are both treated much the same. Both of them are found on the reefs that surround the island and are revered. The conch animal is removed from its shell, beaten with a wooden mallet, and usually eaten raw with lime and pepper, or it is deep-fried or made into curry, stew, soup, or souse. The shell is then sold to tourists as a decoration. Octopus is cleaned carefully of its ink, chopped into fine pieces, and boiled until soft, deep-fried, or soused. Another seldom-seen item is *wilks,* which are still eaten traditionally on the east side of the island. These are found close to the shores on rocks, plucked from the alabaster shell, and eaten raw, curried, or stewed.

Chicken, as well as other meats such as pork, lamb, beef, rabbit, and duck, is stewed; the first three meats are also baked or roasted. Stewed means the meat is browned first—oil and sugar are caramelized, and the meats are browned in this. Seasonings such as Bajan seasoning and/or onions, garlic, tomatoes, and chives are added, and then later carrots (sometimes potatoes for thickening) and dumplings (made from flour, water, cinnamon, and salt) are added if required.

Chicken is usually cut into quarters for baking, and many times there is a light barbecue sauce that is basted on the meat, basically made up of Bajan seasoning with some ketchup and pepper sauce, or it is roasted whole with stuffing until crispy (usually for a Sunday lunch). Stuffing is made with bread, crackers, the innards of the chicken, and seasonings; some people add nuts and raisins to this. *Steppers,* or chicken feet, are used in soup or in souse (pickled in lime, cucumber, and parsley).

Baked pork is done in chops much in the same way as chicken, seasoned only sometimes or in a barbecue sauce as well. Similarly, lamb is baked in chops, but the seasoning is usually a little different, using rosemary or thyme. Sometimes a little water is added to both pork and lamb just before the baking ends to create a little gravy. Lamb legs or a shoulder or leg of pork are also roasted, usually as a Sunday lunch treat. In the case of the pork leg, crackling is made with the outer skin by rubbing salt and lime over it before scoring it into squares. Nearly all meats except for fish are sometimes curried, but this is not traditionally Bajan.

Ham (the two large processors on the island produce good ham) is always baked, after being marinated with the householder's or cook's special recipe; some use orange marmalade, for instance. If there is a bone it is usually saved for soup. Ham bone soup is made with "peas"—really yellow lentils—boiled down with seasoning until thick.

Breadfruit, yams, sweet potatoes, eddoes, cassava, and English potatoes are usually boiled; for breadfruit, sometimes a piece of pig tail, salt pork, or beef is added for taste. Breadfruit is sometimes roasted in its skin, and the blackened skin is removed once the breadfruit has been cooked. English potatoes and sweet potatoes are also roasted. Breadfruit and yams are also baked. Breadfruit and English potatoes are also fried or deep-fried. Recipes for these will be dealt with in the typical meals section. Rice is boiled, sometimes with pig tail or a piece of salt pork or beef for taste, and sometimes okra is added with seasonings, a dish called *privilege* by the older folk. The latter version is used as a meal. Cornmeal is an integral part of most Barbadian kitchens and is used in savory and sweet dishes.

There are many Barbadians who to this day still pickle or make their own pepper sauces, chutneys, jams, and jellies with much of the available fruit in season, but with the advent of so many good processors of these, this is becoming a dying household art.

Saturday morning is pudding and souse day. Pudding used to be made traditionally with pig's blood, but this has now been discarded and it has been replaced with sweet potato, coloring, and spices. Although some still use the pig's intestine as the casing for the pudding (more like a sausage), this is also a fast-dying art, and it is easier to prepare steamed pudding in a bowl. There is white pudding and black pudding (blood sausage), with the white having no or very little coloring. Souse is traditionally made from pork "features" (nose, ears, cheeks, and tongue), trotters (pig's feet), and bits of the meat itself. Now chicken feet, chicken breast, octopus, and fish souse can be found in specialized places. Today, one can ask for it lean, with fat, or without bone, with the last meaning the trotters. The pork is boiled in seasoning and drained. The pickle is made—finely chopped onions, grated cucumbers, parsley, chives, and hot peppers are placed into lime with some of the water from the boiling of the meat. The pork is placed into the pickle, with some of the latter being reserved for serving. This dish is served with slices of breadfruit, sweet potato, or avocado depending on the season.

Typical Meals

The cuisine of Barbados traditionally is a mixture of colonial and African influences. The Indian influence was the first to peep into the cuisine, and now with Caribbean people integrating a lot more, there is a definite influence of their cooking creeping into what was very much just typically Barbadian. Meals depend on the family's social standing and financial means, and helpers and cooks are the norm for those who can afford it—labor in this area is still fairly inexpensive.

Breakfast or Tea

Barbadians traditionally called breakfast *tea*. And they called lunch *breakfast,* while *dinner* refers to supper. This is now heard only among the older folk or villagers in the countryside. We can safely divide breakfast into *English local* or *local-local,* depending on the family's financial means and/or the social standing, as mentioned earlier. An English breakfast starts with fresh fruit of the season and continues with a cereal such as cornflakes, muesli, or a porridge with milk, honey, or golden syrup, followed typically by eggs to order (scrambled, Creole [with onions and tomatoes], fried, hard-boiled or soft-boiled, poached, or omelet style), bacon, sausage, and toast. Marmalade, guava jam, or any other fruit jam and butter or margarine are served. English tea or coffee is served. Evaporated or condensed milk and brown or white sugar are used.

A local breakfast might include cereal or porridge, eggs, bakes (made of flour, water, and salt, either deep-fried or baked in the oven), and bush tea or English tea sweetened with condensed milk. There might also be salt bread, sweet bread of some kind, or sliced toasted bread with butter and/or fruit jams or jellies. Cutters would be served, as well as various canned fish.

All the preceding choices will be eaten with a juice (homemade or packaged) or a soft drink. Apart from the usual fruit juices, juice is also considered to include mauby, sorrel, or ginger beer.

Midmorning Snacks

Depending on what was had for breakfast, the snack may include a cutter or a sandwich of some sort made with white bread or whole wheat bread; salt fish cakes; or an assortment of fruits; or a combination of these. All are accompanied by a drink. Many do not participate in having a snack at a particular time. Munching on various types of nuts; dried fruits; fresh fruit such as imported apples or local bananas; banana, yam, or potato chips (processed); or bagged salted snacks is normal.

Lunch or Breakfast

Eating in Barbados depends on the financial means of the household. Lunch is usually the heavy meal, although some people still cook early in the morning and then cover the pots, leaving them on the stove to be warmed and eaten in the evening after work. Because of concerns about diet and bacteria, this is a dying art, and light meals are eaten in the evening if a big lunch was had. If not, then food is cooked fresh.

Lunch is eaten at home or in small eateries or restaurants, or it is obtained from van ladies who drive around with a full buffet in the back. For the middle class and more affluent, lunch can consist of a choice of starch and meat. Perhaps it would be easier here to say that Barbadians love a buffet with choices. So defining what a buffet consists of allows the reader to understand the choices that Barbadians might have in their daily feedings. Sunday lunches are usually the big meal of the week and might include several of these dishes.

Soups could be pea, pumpkin, vegetable, beef, or fish. One meat option is pepperpot, originally a Guyanese dish using *cassareep,* a thick black liquid derived from cassava that is used to cure the meats. If reboiled every day, this dish can remain out of the fridge for years. Pepperpot is now embedded in Barbadian buffet culture. Other meats include roast or stewed beef (with potatoes, carrots, and onions); suckling pig with stuffing; roast, stewed, or braised pork or lamb; baked, grilled, fried, or steamed fish (catch of the day); steamed or fried flying fish; and roast, baked, or fried chicken. Accompaniments might be stuffing, the respective gravies, peas and rice, macaroni pie, and boiled and sliced dasheen, yams, and sweet potatoes. Sweet potatoes are often made into a pie with pineapple and baked. Yams can also be found baked, sometimes in their shells, covered with cheese. Breadfruit is either boiled

A typical Caribbean lunch, including fried flying fish, cucumber salad, stewed pork, and macaroni salad. (StockPhotoPro)

or pickled. Breadfruit coucou is also served—it is boiled with salt beef, then mashed with a little milk, and stirred until the smooth and creamy consistency of the cornmeal coucou is reached. Other dishes include cornmeal coucou (just known as coucou), mashed green banana, pumpkin and spinach fritters, baked eggplant, green banana souse (served with pickle), and pork souse (traditionally served only on Saturdays, it is seen on buffet tables during the week). Pickle is a mixture of finely chopped onions, chives, parsley, cucumber, and lime juice. Vegetables such as carrots and christophene are usually served together boiled. Christophene is often seen in a cheese sauce. Mixed salad is always available, as is coleslaw. Beets in their own brine and cucumbers in lime are often served separately. Lunch is usually accompanied by juices as described earlier, or by wine or alcoholic beverages. Desserts can consist of several options as indicated earlier.

Tea

In the traditional great houses of the plantation, a tea similar to an English tea was served, with all the various cookies, cakes, and pies to choose from. Today, very few people drink tea at teatime although the ritual does still exist among the well-to-do. In offices those at work may enjoy a cup of tea or coffee around 3 P.M. High teas are still served around 4 P.M. on Sundays or even later, depending on when lunch was served.

Dinner or Supper

Barbadians have gone from traditionally being at-home eaters to being outside eaters. Dinner is usually picked up at a fast-food outlet, and this may include fried chicken and chips (French fries), fish and chips, or pizza. Chinese food is also very popular. Restaurants are finding more and more locals eating out to avoid having to cook at home. As the pace of life has picked up, the Barbadian diet has suffered. Many villagers still eat in the same way as described in the vignette, but many families very rarely sit and eat together anymore, as television and video games are taking over.

Eating Out

Until the 1970s, Barbados did not really have a huge restaurant culture. Barbadians ate and entertained at home. Businessmen went to a restaurant occasionally for business lunches, and families went on special occasions. Today, although many Barbadian still entertain and eat at home, facilitated by the fact that many middle- to high-class homes have helpers and cooks, the number of restaurant has grown in such proportions that Barbados is being touted as "the Caribbean's culinary island." Tourism, a new influx of residents from other lands, and a growing affluent society of locals have influenced the opening of a bevy of restaurants that are visited by all with gusto, such as Chinese restaurants. Japanese sushi and sashimi bars are becoming popular using local fish. A few restaurants serve Mediterranean fare such as falafel and pita souvlaki. Thai food is also popular. Italian cuisine has always had its place, with lasagna having been incorporated into Bajan fare. One of the first restaurants on the island was Italian. Pizza is much loved, and the New York pizza on the south coast is excellent. Jamaican cuisine has found its place in the hearts of Barbadians, and jerk seasoning has managed to infiltrate Bajan seasoning as the next-best choice. Brazil has made its mark on the island as has India. The many Indians who settled in the Caribbean, having been brought to the islands as indentured slaves to take over when slavery was abolished, particularly in Guyana, Jamaica, and Trinidad, have a vibrant Caribbean Indian cuisine. Caribbean curries are slightly different from real Indian curries but nevertheless infused with wonderful spices. There has been a lot more interest of recent, mostly started by foreign chefs, in using local ingredients to fuse into these gourmet dishes, and this has become what is now known as "Caribbean fusion."

The average Barbadian still prefers good Bajan staples, and to give the fast-food outlets a run for their money, van ladies have cropped up in built-up areas. They have full buffets at the back of the van offering delicious homemade Bajan take-out fare at affordable prices. Small eateries are also dotted around the countryside. With the influence of the

A beach restaurant in Barbados. (Robert Lerich | Dreamstime.com)

Rastafarian movement *ital* (vegetarian) food has become a popular food source for those who consider meat to not be an option, and even raw-food dishes are increasing in popularity.

There are three fast-food chains: TGI Fridays, Kentucky Fried Chicken (KFC), and the local Chefette. The latter serves up pizza, hamburgers, and broasted chicken, with some offering the Bar-BCue Barn with salad bar; grilled steak, fish, or chicken; and baked potatoes. Chefette is locally owned, has 15 outlets around the island, and has managed to stave off other American fast-food businesses by providing colorful, clean, well-organized outlets with drive-through facilities and children's indoor playgrounds.

Special Occasions

Barbados as a small island is definitely on the list of the islands with many festivals. Almost every other weekend there is something going on that denotes food and drink. Clubs and bars abound. Rum shops are plentiful. Jazz, reggae, soca, or gospel on De Hill at Farley Hill brings out all manner of local foods and a bevy of alcohol. New Year's Day (January 1), Errol Barrow Day (January 21), Heroes' Day (April 28), Labor Day (May 1), Emancipation Day (August 1), Kadooment Day (the first Monday of August), Independence Day (November 30), Christmas Day (December 25), and Boxing Day (December 26) are all official holidays in Barbados.

On most days except Christmas Day and Kadooment Day, excursions take place in which families, their baskets filled with all manner of culinary delights, a cooler in hand, board special buses to take them to a particular picnic area—sometimes on a public beach or in special parks allotted for just this purpose. Typically *pelau* is precooked—sugar is burned in oil, seasoned chicken with onions and garlic is added, this is stirred until brown, and then water is added, brought to a boil, and peas and rice are added. Sometimes raisins and nuts are placed into the finished pelau. Fried chicken and fish are also popular picnic foods, served with peas and rice, macaroni pie, coleslaw, and salad. Pig or chicken souse can also be added to the picnic basket. On these days many flock to the beach and then eat at home later, while others take their picnic baskets and coolers with them.

On May Day the celebrations are islandwide, but the biggest one takes place on Bay Street on the beach. The traditional Tukk Bands, Landship, Stilt Walkers, and Junkanoo (dressed in costumes made of bright pieces of cloth sewn up to cover the whole body) perform on stage and in the crowd, while grills sizzle with hot dogs, hamburgers, pork chops, and chicken or fish, and the oil in the buck pots on wood or coal fires bubbles with salt fish cakes or fried chicken parts. Vendors selling cotton candy, snow cones, or peanuts ply their trade. Banks beer and brand-name rums open their tents with cold drinks for sale. Huge speakers begin blasting soca, calypso, and dancehall in between the performances, and there is much festivity and frolicking in the sea for the day.

The yearly Agrofest is attended by people from all over the island. This is a weekend where all local food processors and anyone involved in the agricultural and animal-farming sectors come together at Queen's Park in Bridgetown for a huge fest of food, produce, exhibitions, and sales of flora, as well as competitions for various categories of animals bred on the island. On this day the Inter-American Institute for Co-operation in Agriculture, apart from its general involvement in the fest itself, puts on a Sunday Caribbean breakfast/brunch with various different island dishes; it is usually sold out before the first dish is served.

Another major festival is Crop Over. Based on the days of slavery when the crop had ended and the slaves were allowed a small celebration, it has now become a full-fledged carnival, a celebration of the end of the sugarcane crop season. The festivities that lead to the major costumed frenzy parade on the first Monday in August begin weeks in advance.

Although Christmas Eve and Christmas Day bring special menus offered by hotels and restaurants across the island, they are usually spent at home with family or friends. The fare may consist of any of the following depending on the financial means of the household: split pea and pumpkin soup, roast stuffed turkey, stuffed suckling pig with cracklings (or a roast pork leg or shoulder), baked ham with pineapple rings, roast stuffed chicken and/or duck, and a selection of all the dishes mentioned in the preceding sections. Dessert is usually plum pudding with brandy or rum sauce, rum cake, or black Christmas cake. Eggnog, sorrel, and ginger beer are served. Conkies are eaten throughout the season.

Old Year's Night begins with a dinner at home or at the various restaurants that serve up a special menu, moving on to home parties, clubs, and hotels for the traditional midnight countdown and ensuing fireworks across the island. New Year's Day involves an excursion or picnic or is a quiet day.

Easter Sunday follows the fashion of Christmas except for the Christmas pudding or cake. Hot cross buns are fashionable, and chocolate Easter bunnies fill the supermarkets.

Weddings follow the traditional English wedding but with typical Caribbean flair. They are particularly huge on the island, no matter how affluent the household is. The fruit for the wedding cake (as is done with the Christmas cake) is soaked in rum, brandy, and sherry for months before baking, and then the cake is pricked at intervals for one month prior to the wedding and before the icing is put on. Buffet lunches or dinners are the norm, and most of the dishes already mentioned are found on the tables. Alcoholic beverages and champagne flow like water. Depending on finances the guest list could be from 50 up to 1,000. Some weddings take place in churches, and others at the beach or any particularly specified place—those who can marry a couple will go anywhere on the island including out to sea.

Funerals are huge across the island. People who do not even know the deceased appear from nowhere to attend. Traditionally, the family of the deceased will have a gathering at a home that could be either just a few family members and friends enjoying snacks, full buffet lunches, or a distinctively Caribbean fete (a massive party with music and dancing).

Diet and Health

Barbadians have always been known for their centenarians coming from all walks of life and from all financial sectors of the society. The problem now stands as to whether this reaching of such a ripe old age will continue, for it was attributed to the healthy diet before the influx of imported goods and fast-food outlets. Although Barbadians do lead a fairly healthy lifestyle compared to people who live in big cities, they are subjected to American cable television with its adoration of processed, unnatural, and fast foods. There is also the problem of pollution of the soil through the fertilizers and pesticides imported from the United States (in some cases those banned in that country); through the sudden massive amounts of construction of hotels and homes; and generally through the people's use of everything plastic, including foam containers for fast food, and bad waste and garbage practices.

Today, there is much concern about the diet and, therefore, the health of the average Barbadian. Heart disease, diabetes, and cancer are becoming almost the norm, and health and diet are in such question that government officials and those in the health care sector (doctors, nurses, etc.) have been finally forced into action. Far more information is available on keeping healthy, and an ever-growing number of people are following vegetarian or vegan diets, or simply eating less meat and more fish, fewer carbohydrates and more greens and salads. However, the fight has only just begun.

Organic farmers are popping up, but the soil itself is still in question. Help has also come with the setting up of recycling plants and educational material on problems of pollution. Exercise is now becoming a priority for many, as can be seen on the various boardwalks on the south and west coast, around the Garrison (a race course in Christ Church), or simply in neighborhood streets or in the many gyms across the island. But there is still much work to be done.

Rosemary Parkinson

Further Reading

Elias, Marie Louise, and Josie Elias. *Barbados.* New York: Marshall Cavendish Benchmark, 2010.

Harris, Jessica B. *Sky Juice and Flying Fish: Traditional Caribbean Cooking.* New York: Simon and Schuster, 1991.

Parkinson, Rosemary. *Culinaria: The Caribbean.* Cologne, Germany: Könemann, 1999.

Belize

Overview

Belize is an English-speaking country located in the heart of Central America and measuring 8,866 square miles, slightly smaller than the state of Massachusetts. Its small population numbers about 308,000 people. It is bordered by Mexico to the north and Guatemala to the west and south. The Caribbean Sea demarcates its extensive eastern coastline, which is characterized by over 200 small *cayes* (islands) and has the world's second-largest barrier reef, which runs the length of the country. On land, the country is characterized by diverse ecosystems ranging from open pine forest and seasonally flooded grass wetlands to the low but rugged Maya Mountains, which run parallel to the coast, as well as dense tropical hardwood forest in some portions of the southern and western regions of the country.

Belize was occupied by at least four different Mayan-speaking groups before the arrival of the Spanish in the 1540s. The Spanish never exercised full control, allowing buccaneers and refugees from elsewhere in the Caribbean to settle the coast, exploiting marine resources like manatees and turtles and cutting logwood (used for dyeing clothing in Europe) for export. These early "Baymen" imported African slaves and in the early 1700s began cutting mahogany in the rain forest, which remained the major export until the 20th century. The mercantile export-oriented colonial culture, which centered on natural-resource extraction, led to specific culinary traditions that can be seen in Belize today.

The people of Belize are a varied blend of descendants of immigrants and native groups. The ethnically diverse population encompasses an array of peoples, including three Mayan groups (Yucatec, Mopan, and Kekchi), Afro-European Creole descendants of slaves, the Afro-Carib Garifuna, East Indian, Chinese, Mennonites, and many others. Mestizo or "Spanish" people have replaced the Creole as the majority population during the past 30 years, now making up 48.7 percent of the populace. English is the official language, while Kriol is the lingua franca for much of the population. Spanish, various Mayan languages, Garinagu, and other languages are spoken as well. The population is relatively young, with 37.9 percent under the age of 15. The country is almost evenly divided between rural and urban dwellers, and is now rapidly urbanizing at a rate of 3.1 percent per year. Belize City is the largest settlement, with 25 percent of the nation's population. This rural/urban divide is expressed in many aspects of Belizean culture including food. Full independence from Britain was achieved on September 21, 1981, although the country was given limited self-government in 1964.

Forestry has been succeeded by agriculture and a rapidly growing tourism-based economy. While Belize is better off than its neighbors, its economy was strongly affected by the global recession, and the country has experienced increasing poverty and a broadening income gap in recent years. About 10 percent of the population is involved in agricultural production, with 71 percent in services, including tourism. The tourism sector has been extensively promoted by the government and private sector. Fishing and fish farming as well as the production of sugarcane, bananas, and citrus are complemented by expanding niche markets in organic products such as cacao, spices, and tropical fruits including papaya and *pitahaya* (sold in the United States as dragon fruit).

 ## Food Culture Snapshot

Linda Flowers is an urban Creole, a full-time single maternal grandmother and legal guardian of two teenagers, Janelle and Lewis. She is also raising a neighbor's son, James, whose parents migrated to New York and are planning to fetch James once they have good jobs. Such arrangements are common because so many Belizeans move back and forth to the United States. Janelle and Lewis's parents, Natalie and Don, are separated but live in Los Angeles, where Natalie works in a hospital as a nurse's aide and Don is unemployed. Natalie sends money home on a semiregular basis to help raise the children. James is not in school and often eats outside the house, but Janelle and Lewis are students, so they can come home every day to have their grandmother's rice and beans for lunch. The entire family appreciates her early-morning johnnycakes with jam, butter, and honey. On Sundays and special occasions such as Easter and Christmas, Linda cooks large meals and makes special desserts to celebrate the season.

Far to the south in the rural district of Toledo, Emilia Choc, a Kekchi Maya mother of seven children, three girls and four boys, lives with her husband, Eduardo, in Blue Creek, a small agricultural village with a mixed Maya population. All but her eldest son, Lorenzo, are in school; Lorenzo works in the tourism industry at the beach town of Placencia in the north and regularly sends money home to help pay for his siblings' schooling and other expenses. Eduardo farms rice and organic cacao for sale, and corn and beans for subsistence, while Emilia tends a garden near the house to provide vegetables and root crops for the kitchen. Every morning she gets up early with her eldest daughter, Teresa, to prepare corn tortillas for the entire family. Often for the evening meal she cooks stew beans and tamales accompanied by the ubiquitous corn tortillas and hot pepper. The youngest children come home from grammar school for lunch, but the older ones have to travel to reach the nearest high school, and so they buy food there or bring a few corn tortillas along instead of returning home.

Major Foodstuffs

Urban Belizeans in places like Belmopan and Belize City may buy groceries at supermarkets, but most Belizeans purchase their foodstuffs at open-air markets and dry goods stores, and some farmers grow a significant portion of their own food. Because of the broad diversity of Belize's people, there is a lot of variety in foodstuffs and recipes across the country. However, certain dishes are omnipresent. Rice and beans and stew beans and rice (dishes distinguished on the basis of predominance of one ingredient or the other) are two popular staple foods that can be found in every corner of the country. The beans are almost always red kidney beans, initially imported into Belize from New Orleans but adopted as the nation's favorite bean, over the native black beans.

Rice, another introduction from the Old World, was quick to replace corn among urban Belizeans, although rural farmers and Maya groups still depend on corn, in the form of corn tortillas, as a staple. Mestizos and other urban folk consume factory-made corn tortillas and other corn-based street foods, such as tamales, *garnaches* (a fried tortilla topped with refried beans, cheese, cabbage, and other garnishes), and *panades* (fried corn dumplings stuffed with shredded shark or catfish). Imported wheat flour is also used, especially in towns, to make flour tortillas. Wheat flour is also used to make fry jacks and johnnycakes, which are both eaten as breakfast breads; yeast breads such as coconut-based Creole bread; and holiday treats such as black fruit cake.

The Garifuna people make a staple bread from cassava, which is grated, washed, and processed to remove poisons, then cooked on a griddle into durable large round wafers. Declining in popularity, it is still sold in places such as gas stations and eaten as a snack. Cassava is also eaten extensively in soups and stews, along with other root crops like cocoyam, soup yams, sweet potatoes, and potatoes. Green plantains and bananas are grated or cooked, mashed, and made into dumplings called *maltilda foot* or *bundiga* by the Garifuna. They and other cooking bananas are fried when ripe and commonly served alongside rice and beans, stew beans and rice, and other entrées as a side dish.

Belizeans enjoy a wide range of meat and fish. Especially along the coast, fish, lobster, conch, and shrimp have long been a part of local cuisine. Along the rivers freshwater fish are commonly consumed. Chicken, pork (including imported salted pork such as pig tail, which is used to flavor beans), and some beef are the most common meats. All three are often prepared stewed and served with rice and beans or stew beans and rice. Cow-foot soup and chicken *escabeche* (a vinegar and onion soup) are other common and popular meat dishes. Various large wild birds, deer, large rodents such as *gibnut* and agouti, armadillos, iguanas, and peccaries (similar to a wild pig) are eaten in the countryside and valued by all at holidays. Imported canned meats such as corned beef, Spam, and Vienna sausages are also eaten, though they have become relatively expensive as the price of chicken has gone down.

Almost all Belizeans love spicy food and enthusiastically apply hot sauce or hot peppers to every dish. The most famous Belizean hot sauce is Marie Sharps, made from fiery habaneros. Pepper plants are often grown around doorways or in yards to provide spice on demand. People make their own hot sauce with vinegar, onions, and hot peppers; it is kept in a jar on the table.

Until recently, all dairy products were imported, with canned milk a regular feature of the diet and an ingredient in most desserts. In recent decades the Mennonite farmers have established a local dairy industry, and fresh milk, yogurt, and some cheese are now available, while imports have also rapidly increased. Coconut milk and oil have traditionally been used instead of butter and milk. Lard, and now vegetable shortening, is another staple fat. Coconut oil is used in rice and beans and to flavor meat and fish dishes, while coconut milk is used to flavor breads and in many Garifuna soups and stews. Coconut is also used to flavor desserts and candies. Lethal yellow disease has been killing most coconut trees since the mid-1990s, so imported dried or canned coconut milk has become popular.

Belizeans eat a variety of vegetables including Old World introductions such as cabbage, carrots, onions and garlic, and okra, as well as tomatoes, peppers, and others from the Americas. Other popular vegetables include callaloo (amaranth) leaves, chayote, cucumbers, tomatoes, onions, carrots, and, in the countryside, a variety of wild leaves, mushrooms, and vegetables. Coleslaw made from cabbage is associated with Creoles and is served in most Belizean restaurants, and various salads are increasing in popularity as they are promoted as healthy foods and demanded by tourists.

Belizeans love and regularly eat a wide variety of fruits including pineapple, bananas, mangoes, watermelon, citrus fruits, and lesser-known tropical fruits such as golden plums, soursops (*guanábana*—a prickly green fruit), mameys (a kind of sapote that is round and light brown with a creamy interior), custard apples, cashew fruit, tamarind, and *craboos* (a small round yellow fruit). Children especially relish green fruits dipped in salt and chili powder.

Many of these fruits are used to make beverages; lime juice is especially common and often served with meals. Tamarind drink is also quite popular. Many fruits are fermented to make homemade wines. Cashew wine is particularly famous and is also commercially produced. A strong corn beer called *chicha* is also made at home, especially by the Maya groups. A thick beverage made with seaweed is often sold in markets or on the street as sexual fortifier. Sodas of various flavors, called soft drinks, are very popular, as are imported beers, especially Jamaican Red Stripe and Guinness. Locally produced Belikin Beer is the brew of choice for most, and rum is the traditional hard liquor, locally produced from sugarcane. Black tea, a colonial legacy, is popular, as is instant coffee, both served with imported sweetened condensed milk. Herbal teas, especially lemongrass (*fevergrass*), are also popular as both medicine and drink.

Rice and Beans

1 lb dried red kidney beans

½ lb salted pig tail, salt pork, or cured pork hock

8 c water

2 cloves garlic

1 large onion, chopped

12 oz coconut milk (fresh or 1 can)

1 tsp black pepper

1 tsp salt

½ tsp thyme or ground allspice

2 lb long-grain white rice

Soak beans overnight or for a minimum of 4 hours. Boil the pig tail or salt pork once for about 5 minutes to remove salt, and discard the water. Repeat if necessary. Cook the beans in a covered pot in the 8 cups of water, with garlic, chopped onion, and pork, until tender. Add the coconut milk, black pepper and salt, and thyme or ground allspice, then cook for about 10 more minutes. Add the dry rice, and stir thoroughly. Cover well, and cook over a low flame until all the water has been absorbed and the rice is tender (about 25 minutes). Add a small quantity of extra water if needed, but don't worry if a crust forms on the bottom.

This is typically served with some type of stewed meat, fried plantain (*bluggo*) or another type of cooking banana called *flaggo,* and coleslaw made with carrot and cabbage and dressed with imported "salad cream."

Typical Meals

Most Belizeans eat three meals a day: breakfast, lunch, and supper, which is often called tea. Breakfast can vary from a few fresh corn tortillas and leftover beans to more elaborate fry jacks (puffed fried dough), refried beans, eggs, cheese, and fried bacon or canned meat. Biscuits like johnnycakes and powder buns are often hawked on the street or sold door to door by children. Breakfast is usually eaten quite early, especially in rural areas.

Lunch is normally eaten at noon, particularly in urban areas, when school lets out and government offices close. The meal is traditionally the heaviest of the day, with rice and beans providing the bulk of the calories, usually accompanied by fried bananas, potato salad, and fried or stewed fish or meat. This is often followed by a brief siesta. While traditionally students and workers go home for lunch, nowadays it is often more convenient for some of them to buy food from street vendors. In agricultural areas men may return home for lunch or, if they are working far from the house, may pack a lunch of corn or flour tortillas and cheese or meat. Convenience foods like canned soup and soda crackers have been used for many years, and now ramen noodles have also become common.

Supper is eaten relatively early, usually between 6 and 8 P.M., although in the cities this dinner may be later. This meal is usually much lighter than lunch and may consist of leftovers or even just a couple pieces of bun and cheese, often served with tea, either imported black tea or local herbal infusions, often mixed with milk and heavily sweetened.

Eating Out

Urban Belizeans often purchase street food during the day, especially if they live too far from home to return for lunch or if there is no one at home to cook. Small "cool spots" serve cold drinks and plates of rice and beans, barbecued chicken, fish, and stewed meat, or "Spanish" foods such as garnaches; while vendors in the street hawk tamales, panades (small crescent-shaped pies), conch fritters, *dukunu* (a green corn tamale), and various breads and buns. These same vendors cater to rural Belizean families on market days and to men drinking together in town bars (which often serve conch fritters, ceviche, or other snacks). In Belize City a wide range of different restaurants, including many Lebanese and Chinese, as well as Mexican, Indian, pizza, and Japanese restaurants, may be found. The influence of East Indians means that many Belizean restaurants serve curried chicken along with rice and beans. Chinese fast-food shops, known for their fried chicken, are a fixture of Belize City street corners. Especially on Saturdays the smell of barbecued chicken fills the air in many towns as grills are set up along roads and beaches.

The Shak, one of many beach restaurants in Placencia, Belize. (StockPhotoPro)

Special Occasions

Most Belizeans are Christian, with 49.6 percent Catholic and 27 percent Protestant. Fourteen percent espouse other religions, including Islam and the Baha'i faith, while 9.4 percent do not claim any religion. Christianity has blended with Maya and Garifuna religions to create hybrid practices and beliefs. An offering of food and drink to the ancestors is a common practice in Garifuna ritual.

Christmas is an especially important holiday for most Belizeans and is typically celebrated with imported goods and food. This tradition dates back to the logging days, when the holiday was marked by mahogany crews streaming back to town from distant camps to spend their earnings. Special drinks such as *rum popo,* a very strong eggnog, and foods like turkey, ham, and black fruit cake, are essential parts of the festivities. Imported grapes, apples, and pears are sold at extravagant prices and are purchased for stockings and treats for children. The old custom of the "Christmas Bram" involved a crowd of merrymakers wending their way from house to house, eating and drinking at each one. The custom has been adapted into a two-week-long celebration where most work in the country comes to a halt.

Easter, which falls during the beautiful weather of the dry season, is associated with trips to the islands for those living near the coast, and fishing or barbecuing for those inland. A special dish made with river turtle (*hicatee*) and parboiled rice is a customary Easter dish in the Belize River valley.

Secular holidays such as the September Celebrations commemorating independence and the Battle of Saint George's Caye Day are occasions with high levels of alcohol consumption, in addition to street celebrations and parades. Many vendors congregate to sell food, drink, and snacks to the celebrants.

Diet and Health

Lifestyle diseases are common in Belize, especially heart disease, stroke, and diabetes. Today, many Belizeans, especially those of middle age, try to eat healthier although the most popular foods still contain too much sugar and saturated fat. The sudden death of the Belizean world music star Andy Palacio from a heart attack in 2008 shocked the entire nation and dramatized the problem of a sedentary lifestyle and unhealthy diet. The influence of American relatives and mass media such as television on Belizean attitudes toward food and bodily health and appearance is also apparent, especially in more cosmopolitan places such as the capital Belmopan and Belize City, where even diet television dinners can be purchased at American-style supermarkets.

Lyra Spang and Richard Wilk

Further Reading

Jermyn, Leslie. *Belize.* New York: Marshall Cavendish, 2001.

Mallan, Chicki, and Patti Lange. *Belize Handbook.* Chico, CA: Moon, 1998.

Wilk, Richard R. *Home Cooking in the Global Village: Caribbean Food from Buccaneers to Ecotourists.* New York: Berg, 2006.

Bolivia

Overview

Bolivia, one of the poorest and least developed countries in South America, is one of the hemisphere's highest, most isolated, and most rugged landlocked nations. Bolivia is bordered by Brazil to the north and east, Paraguay and Argentina to the south, and Chile and Peru to the west.

Bolivia's topography and climate are varied, from the peaks of the Andes in the west to the eastern lowlands, situated within the Amazon basin. Its topography includes some of the earth's coldest, warmest, windiest, and steamiest locations: the dry, salty, and swampy natural landscapes of the dry salt flats of Uyuni; the steaming jungles of the Amazon; and the wildlife-rich grasslands of the southeast.

Bolivia is a democratic republic, divided into nine regions, and it is home to more than seven million people. Bolivia has a concentrated indigenous population (60%) with heritage including Aymará, Quechua, Guaraní, and over 30 other ethnic groups. Famous since Spanish colonial days for its mineral wealth, modern Bolivia was once a part of the ancient Inca Empire. After the Spaniards defeated the Incas in the 16th century, Bolivia's predominantly Indian population was reduced to slavery. The remoteness of the Andes helped protect the Bolivian Indians from the European diseases that decimated other South American Indians. But the existence of a large indigenous group forced to live under the thumb of their colonizers created a stratified society that continues to this day. Wealthy urban elites, who are mostly of Spanish ancestry, have traditionally dominated political and economic life, whereas most Bolivians are low-income subsistence farmers, miners, small traders, or artisans.

Bolivia is a country rich in natural resources, with key exports including gas and zinc. The country's agricultural exports include soybeans, coffee, sugar, cotton, corn, and timber, as well as coca, sunflower seed (for oil), and organic chocolate. Despite these rich resources, Bolivia continues to be one of the poorest countries in Latin America, with almost two-thirds of its people, many of whom are subsistence farmers, living in poverty. Population density ranges from less than 1 person per square mile in the southeastern plains to about 25 per square mile (10 per square kilometer) in the central highlands. The annual population growth rate is about 1.45 percent (2006).

Bolivia's estimated 2006 gross domestic product (GDP) totaled $10.3 billion. Economic growth was estimated at about 4.5 percent, and inflation was estimated at about 4.3 percent. The average annual earnings are around US$900, and GDP per capita is around US$2,900 (2005 estimate).

The economy of Bolivia has had a historical pattern of a single-commodity focus. From silver to tin to coca, Bolivia has enjoyed only occasional periods of economic diversification. Political instability and difficult topography have constrained efforts to modernize the agricultural sector. Similarly, relatively low population growth coupled with a low life expectancy and high incidence of disease has kept the labor supply in flux and prevented industries from flourishing. Rampant inflation and corruption have also thwarted development. The mining industry, especially the extraction of natural gas and zinc, currently dominates Bolivia's export economy.

There is widespread underemployment; a large percentage of the underemployed supplement their income by participating in coca production, mainly in the Yungas, and in the informal street-market economy. The government remains heavily dependent on foreign aid. A large part of agricultural revenue comes from the illegal growing and processing of coca leaves. The Bolivian government has tried to have coca replaced by other crops, but this has given rise to a number of problems, and the coca leaf remains one of the major sources of national revenue.

🍽 Food Culture Snapshot

Acarapi and Claudia live in La Paz, one of the more affluent areas of Bolivia. Acarapi works in the local mines, while Claudia is the primary domestic provider, looking after their four children and managing the household and all other household duties including the cooking. Their lifestyle is common among the more affluent neighborhoods of La Paz, and their diet is made up of a combination of meat and potato dishes.

For Claudia, shopping for food to prepare meals is a daily ritual. Bread is purchased daily fresh from a street vendor or bakery. Breakfast is taken in the local market or in the home and is a simple preparation of coffee, tea, or a hot maize beverage (api) served with bread.

For Acarapi and Claudia, following Bolivian tradition, lunch is the main meal of the day. According to Acarapi, because of the altitude and work ethic in Bolivia, most people don't eat dinner until very late, and they don't like to go to bed on a full stomach. Acarapi returns home every day to eat lunch with his family. Lunch typically consists of soup, up to three "main" dishes, and sometimes dessert. Most lunches would include some potatoes—fried, boiled, or whipped together with other foods.

Meat, normally beef, chicken, or sausage, accompanies most dishes, and vegetables usually include red onions, tomatoes, shredded lettuce or cabbage, carrots, peas, and broccoli. All meals are usually accompanied by llajhua, a hot spicy salsa made from tomatoes and hot peppers ground on a large stone.

Claudia begins making lunch around 10:30 and continues preparation for several hours. Meals in Bolivia are a big challenge, with no premade ingredients available, so lunch takes considerable time to prepare. Around 5 P.M. the family may have a snack of tea and rolls with jam or dulce de leche (caramel sauce). A light dinner is usually served around 9 P.M.

Major Foodstuffs

Though Bolivia is currently self-sufficient in sugar, rice, and beef, it still has to import certain foodstuffs. The chief Bolivian crops are potatoes, cassava, sugarcane, coffee, maize, rice, and soybeans with a major share of farm income derived from the illicit growing and processing of coca leaves, the source of cocaine. The relationship between access to land, poverty, and food security appears to be a kind of vicious cycle, particularly for the rural altiplano population in Bolivia. In the context of widespread poverty and limited access to institutional social security, access to land is a crucial factor in creating favorable conditions for subsistence agriculture and hence food security.

The typical diet is abundant in carbohydrates but deficient in other food categories. In the highlands, the primary staple is the potato (dozens of varieties of this Andean domesticate are grown), followed

Two women harvesting in their potato field in Bolivia. (iStockPhoto)

by other Andean and European-introduced tubers and grains (e.g., *oca,* quinoa, barley, and, increasingly, rice), maize, and legumes, especially the broad bean. Freeze-dried potatoes (*chuño*) and air-dried jerky (*ch'arki*) from cattle or Andean camelids (llama, alpaca, and vicuña) are common, although beef forms an insignificant part of the daily diet.

Bolivia is self-sufficient in almost all food staples with the exception of wheat. Highland crops include tubers, maize, and legumes. Other crops (e.g., peanuts, citrus fruits, bananas, plantains, and rice) are grown in the Oriente, while large cattle ranches are prominent in the departments of Beni and Pando. In eastern Santa Cruz, large agricultural enterprises supply most of the country's rice, sugar, eating and cooking oils, and export crops such as soybeans. Enormous forests provide the raw materials for the lumber and wood-products industry (deforestation is an increasing problem). The coca leaf, which is fundamental in Andean ritual, social organization, and health, has always been cultivated in the eastern regions, but the international drug trade has made Bolivia the third-largest coca-leaf producer and exporter in the world.

The simultaneous processes of demographic transition and urbanization currently underway in Bolivia are having a significant impact on cooking traditions and the use of traditional recipes and ingredients in the family home. Food preparation is an important daily ritual for Bolivian families, with family meals playing a critical role in family relationships and socialization. Until the mid-1970s, the average Bolivian family consisted of close to seven children per woman, and the average family as of 2008 is estimated at four children. Food preparation and cleanliness are closely associated with national folklore and taboo; the family kitchen is a space where food is the focus, and the rituals associated with making the raw cooked and the dirty clean are primarily the responsibility of female family members.

Bolivia is in a situation of chronic food insecurity, which seems to be particularly acute in the traditional rural settlements of the altiplano and the valleys. Heavy-handed state intervention has resulted in some improvement in the food supply in recent years, with families being able to enjoy fixed prices for staples such as flour, bread, and oil. Purchasing groceries is increasingly occurring at specialized shops set up by the government where rice, flour, red meat, poultry, and oil are sold at lower prices. The availability of produce significantly influences the family meal and its preparation, as do the strong social and cultural mores of the Bolivian people.

Cooking

Bolivia is home to numerous culinary styles, each with its own personality representative of the nation's diverse climatic and geographic conditions. Bolivian dishes consist mainly of meat, fish, and poultry blended with herbs and spices. The diet also consists of fresh fruit and vegetables. When using meat, every part of the animal (particularly cows) is consumed. Tongue, kidney, stomach, and all cuts of meat are used during cooking.

Bolivians typically prepare and eat *salteñas* in the morning and empanadas in the afternoon (both of these are meat or vegetables pies) and can have up to five small meals a day. Meals generally consist of potatoes, meat, a large assortment of breads made from corn or quinoa, and pastries. Fresh fruit juices are also abundant and can include blackberry, peach, and lemonade. In the more traditional rural areas, coca leaf is often chewed in the evening after a meal. Bolivian food preparation is dominated by meat dishes, accompanied by potatoes, rice, and shredded lettuce, and food is often accompanied by traditional hot sauces made from tomatoes and pepper pods.

Some typical Bolivian dishes include *ají de lengua,* spicy cow's tongue; *lechón al horno,* roast pig, served on New Year's Day; *fritanga,* spicy pork and egg stew; *majao,* a rice-and-meat dish served with fried egg, fried plantain, and fried yucca (tapioca); *cuñapes,* a bread made of cheese and yucca starch; *pan dulce,* a sweet bread served at Christmas; *chuño phuti,* freeze-dried potatoes; *escabeche,* pickled vegetables; *cicadas,* coconut candies; *leche asada,* roasted milk (a dessert); and *helado de canela,* cinnamon sorbet.

Some traditional dishes include majao, *silpancho* (meat served with rice and potatoes), *pacumutu* (a rice dish with grilled beef, fried yucca, and cheese), salteñas and empanadas, *locro* (a soup made with rice, chicken, and banana), and *chicharrón de pacu* (made with the local Pacu fish, rice, and yucca).

Some potatoes are freeze-dried after they are harvested. Bolivians cover raw potatoes with a cloth and leave them outside during the cold nights and dry days of early winter. The potatoes freeze at night, and the next day the people stomp on them to press out the water the vegetables retained. After a few days, the potatoes have been freeze-dried and are called chuño (CHEW-nyo). They last for months, even years, and can be cooked after being soaked overnight in a pot of water.

Corn is also used to make the fermented maize drink called chicha (CHEE-chah). It is a sacred alcoholic drink for the Incas. They drink it from bowls made from hollowed gourds. Before and after drinking it, Bolivians spill a few drops onto the ground. This gesture is meant as an offering to the Inca earth goddess Pachamama, to ensure a good harvest.

Traditional cooking methods revolved around use of a fire for the majority of dishes. Meals were prepared by placing food directly on the heat or grilling it on wooden sticks in order to smoke it. Food is sometimes placed over the embers or on flat pottery or covered with leaves and buried to cook over stones heated from the fire. The subsequent influences of numerous global cuisines have seen these traditional cooking methods replaced or adapted in some areas, particularly the more urban centers.

Picante de Pollo (Chicken in Spicy Sauce)

Picante de pollo is chicken in a special spicy sauce, and there are many variations of this traditional Bolivian dish.

Ingredients

3 lb chicken, cut into medium-size pieces

2 c white onion, cut into small strips

1¼ c carrots, julienned

1 c turnip, diced

1 tbsp salt

3 c chicken stock

¼ c fresh *locoto* or chili pepper, finely chopped

1 tsp ground cumin

1 tsp ground coriander

1 tsp ground black pepper

2 garlic cloves, peeled, chopped

In a large casserole dish combine the chicken pieces with the onion, carrot, turnip, and salt. Pour the chicken stock over this, until all ingredients are covered. Cook over high heat until the dish is bubbling. Turn heat to low and simmer for 90 minutes until the chicken is soft. Stir occasionally and continue to check on the level of chicken stock. If it seems low, add more stock, as you need some liquid to serve the dish. Add the fresh locoto or chili pepper, cumin, coriander, ground black pepper, and garlic, and stir and cook for 30 minutes. Serve with steamed rice.

Typical Meals

Like the people of the other nations of the Andean highlands such as Peru, Colombia, and Ecuador, Bolivians prefer to eat a good breakfast, a substantial lunch, and a small dinner. As the main meal of the day, lunch is eaten with family whenever possible and often consists of soup, a main dish, and perhaps dessert. Bolivian meals are heavy on the pork and potatoes, with chicken, rice, and vegetables also being popular choices. The potato is the main staple, served at most meals, sometimes with rice or noodles. Potatoes, originally cultivated by the Incas in this region, are often served with meat. They are the country's number one crop, and more than 200 different varieties are grown. The most popular meat is beef. No part of the cow is wasted, not even the tongue, which is used to make a popular spicy cow-tongue dish. Bolivians also enjoy chicken and llama—they even eat llama jerky. In rural areas, rabbits and guinea pigs are also eaten.

Bolivian food is not often spicy, with the majority of heat and spice found in condiments such as a sauce la llajhua which is made with tomato and locoto (hot chilies). Maize beer (chicha) is a traditional and ritually important beverage in the highlands.

In the Oriente, rice, cassava, peanuts, bananas, legumes, and maize constitute the cornerstone of the daily diet, supplemented by fish, poultry, and beef. Favorite national delicacies include guinea pig (also consumed during important ceremonial occasions) and deep-fried pork (chicharrón). Meals are served with hot pepper sauces.

The people of Bolivia start their day with a light breakfast. Many people eat empanadas—cheese- and meat-filled turnovers. People often wash them down with api, which is a sweet breakfast tea made from corn, lemons, cloves, and cinnamon. This is common in the cities and towns, with the api often served with bread. Breakfast is followed by a mid-morning snack of salteñas (sawl-TAY-nyahs). Similar to empanadas, salteñas are sweet meat pastries filled with a wide variety of ingredients such as diced meat or chicken, vegetables, potatoes, raisins, and

hot sauce. Along with empanadas, salteñas can be purchased from many street vendors, and in marketplaces hot meals and stews are also consumed. In the countryside, breakfast sometimes consists of toasted ground cereals with cheese and tea, followed by a thick soup (lawa) at 9 or 10 A.M.

The most important meal of the day is lunch (almuerzo), which in upper-class urban households and restaurants typically is a four-course meal. It usually includes soup and a main dish. The soup typically contains beef, vegetables, potatoes, and quinoa. Peanut soup is also popular. The main dish that follows the soup usually includes meat, potatoes, rice, and vegetables. Favorites include *pique macho* (PEE-kay MA-cho)—grilled chunks of meat, tomatoes, onions, and hot peppers. The spicy chicken dish picante de pollo is also popular. Silpancho, beef that is pounded thin and served on a bed of rice or

Street vendors sell bananas, melons, and a variety of potatoes, including chuno (preserved potatoes), at an open air market in the mining town of Oruro, Bolivia. (Anders Ryman | Corbis)

potatoes with a fried egg on top, is another favorite. Lunch for those living near Lake Titicaca may include fresh lake trout. Bolivians in this region tend to enjoy fish grilled, fried, stuffed, steamed, or served covered in a spicy sauce. Frogs' legs from the lake's frogs are also eaten and are considered a delicacy. Peasants and lower-income urban dwellers have a lunch of boiled potatoes, homemade cheese, a hard-boiled egg, and hot sauce (llajhua) or a thick stew with rice or potatoes.

Corn, a major crop in Bolivia, is the main ingredient in *humitas* (ooMEE-tahs), which are a popular side dish. Corn kernels cut off the cob are combined with spices and wrapped in a small package made from corn husks. The package is tied with string and steamed in a pot of simmering water. Another popular meal choice is quinoa. Quinoa grows well in Bolivia's cold and arid climate. For meals the outer coating is removed to reveal seeds, which are ground or boiled in water and used for baking breads or as an ingredient in soups and stews.

A much lighter meal is eaten at around seven in the evening. Bolivians also snack on locally grown fruits including oranges, grapes, apples, peaches, cherries, papayas, pears, and avocados. Sweeter options include sweet pastries, ice cream, sorbets, and coconut candies called cicadas.

Eating Out

Eating out is not a common occurrence in Bolivia, with most families eating in the home. Bolivians tend to eat out when celebrating major occasions, or if they have traveled, there is a tendency to eat out more often or entertain friends at home. Typically the restaurants in La Paz and other affluent

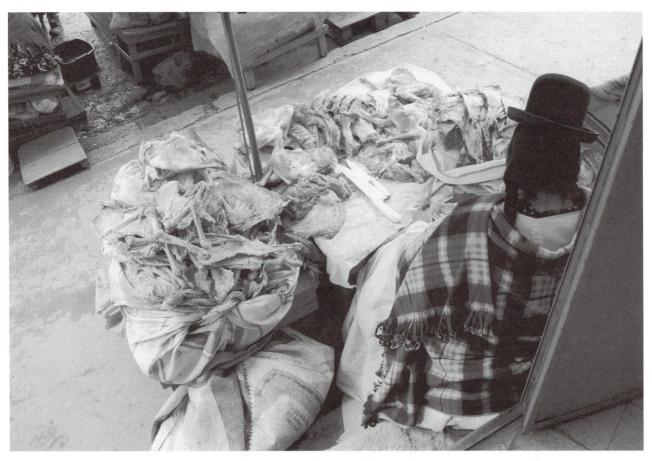

A meat vendor at an outdoor market in La Paz, Bolivia. (Shargaljut | Dreamstime.com)

areas in Bolivia, such as the tourist resort areas, are not restricted to traditional Bolivian dishes. Increasingly, cuisine from all over the world can be found in Bolivia including Asian, Indian, Middle Eastern, and other international tastes. Fast-food chains are also increasing due to their convenience and family-oriented style. The cost point also makes the eating-out experience more accessible for the less-affluent Bolivians.

Special Occasions

There are many holidays and festivals held throughout Bolivia. Many holidays celebrated in Bolivia are of religious or political origin, usually celebrating a Catholic or Indian saint or god, or an event such as a historic battle. Festivals or carnivals typically feature local music, bands, costumes, parades, dancing, fireworks, alcohol, and food.

The most elaborate and hearty meals, with abundant fresh vegetables and beef, chicken, or pork, are eaten at ceremonial occasions, such as the life-cycle events of baptism, marriage, and death. Public displays of generosity and reciprocity, offering abundant food and drink not often available at other times of the year (e.g., bottled beer, cane alcohol [*trago*], and beef), are an important cultural imperative. On All Souls' Day, meals are prepared for the recently deceased and those who are ill. Many important meals mimic those of upper-class restaurants in the major cities, including dishes such as *ají de pollo* (chicken smothered in hot chili sauce and served with rice and/or potatoes).

Social life is punctuated by many rituals that coincide with major agricultural seasons and/or are linked to the celebration of Christian deities, with specific foods associated with many of these rituals. For example, Epiphany or the Twelfth Night on January 6 is a celebration where gifts are given to children to celebrate the Day of the Kings. Children place their shoes outside the door, and the Three Kings (usually the family) fill them with candy and pastries at night. These can include sweet fritters, or *tawa-tawas*. The Bolivian version is unique in the use of cane syrup in the final product.

In Bolivia, Christmas (Navidad) continues to be deeply religious, maintaining the original meaning and purpose of the holiday. Most families set up a *pesebre* (nativity scene) in their homes, and families gather to feast together at midnight after mass, others on Christmas Day. As these holidays take place during the hottest time of year (summer in the Southern Hemisphere) meals usually feature *picana,* a soup made of chicken, beef, corn, and spices that is eaten traditionally on Christmas. The table is also set with salads, roast pork or roast beef, and an abundance of tropical fruit. For the same reasons, the table is usually adorned with fresh flowers. At midnight the families toast with champagne or wine and eat taffy-filled wafer cookies called *turrón*.

The *canastón* is another important holiday tradition. A large gift basket, it is given by employers to their employees on the day prior to taking their vacation. The canastón is a simple but usually large basket (sometimes a plastic washtub is used) filled with the basic food staples such as ketchup and mustard, bread, jam, crackers and cookies, sugar, rice, flour, and sometimes chocolates or candy. These canastónes are almost never decorated, except for a clear plastic covering closed off with a large red bow. A *panetón* (a delicious traditional holiday sweet bread with raisins and nuts) and a bottle of *cidra* (sparkling nonalcoholic cider) are included.

On New Year's Eve the family gathers again, feasts at midnight, and toasts with champagne. Each family member must also eat 12 grapes at midnight.

Bolivians celebrate All Saints' Day on November 1 to honor the Catholic saints. This has been combined with Día de Todos Santos, also known as the Día de los Muertos, or the Day of the Dead. Like many other Catholic celebrations, this melds existing indigenous festivities with the "new" Catholicism and "old" pagan beliefs. The dead are honored by visits to their grave sites, often with food, flowers, and all family members. In Bolivia, the dead are expected to return to their homes and villages. During this time, families and guests, who enter with clean hands, share in traditional dishes, particularly the favorites of the deceased. Tables are laden with bread figurines called *t'antawawas,* sugarcane, chicha, candies, and decorated pastries. At

Cocoa leaves are often used in Bolivia for their medicinal properties. (StockPhotoPro)

the cemeteries, the souls are greeted with more food, music, and prayers. Rather than a sad occasion, the Día de Todos Santos is a joyous event.

Death, marriage, and almost any other social or religious ritual in Bolivia will include an offering of coca. "Guard its leaves with love," warns the "Legend of Coca," an 800-year-old oral poem. "And when you feel pain in your heart, hunger in your flesh and darkness in your mind, lift it to your mouth. You will find love for your pain, nourishment for your body and light for your mind."

Diet and Health

Most Bolivians, particularly in the rural areas and low-income neighborhoods surrounding the large cities, lack access to basic medical care, with most sick people cared for by family members. While Bolivia has improving trends in terms of food supplies, these have not been sufficient to overcome widespread poverty, particularly in rural areas, and there is still a high incidence of hunger and malnutrition.

Many only partially understand and accept Western biomedical ideology and health care, as Bolivian health beliefs and practices typically revolve around rituals and ritual practitioners such as diagnostic specialists, curers, herbalists, and diviners. Divination, rituals, and ritual sacrifices are important in treating illness, as is the use of coca leaves, alcoholic beverages, and guinea pigs. Traditional medicine attaches importance to the social and supernatural etiology of illness and death, which often are attributed to strained social relations, witchcraft, or the influence of malevolent spirits. Dozens of illness categories, many psychosomatic, are recognized. Many curing rituals emphasize balanced, reciprocal relations with deities, who are "fed" and offered drink to dissipate illnesses.

The coca leaf is used extensively for traditional medicines for a supply of nutrients and natural energy. For high-altitude dwellers of the Andes, the leaf, when chewed or brewed into tea, acts as a palliative and stimulant, and a certain amount of cultivation is allowed for local use. Chewing of coca leaf is a common practice among peasant farmers, miners, laborers, and night workers. Soothsayers and indigenous priests use it in rituals passed down by their ancestors. And in many hotels in La Paz, foreign guests are welcomed with a cup of coca-leaf tea, which helps to relieve altitude sickness. Ancestral beliefs, confirmed by scientific research, credit coca-leaf chewing with alleviating hunger, fatigue, and sleepiness.

Bolivia has one of the highest infant mortality rates in South America—between 68 and 75 per 1,000 live births. Major causes of infant and child mortality include respiratory infections, diarrhea, and malnutrition; almost 30 percent of infants under age three suffer from chronic malnutrition. In Bolivia, more than one-quarter of infants are stunted. But between 1994 and 1998 the number of overweight women increased 9 percent, with the greatest increases seen among women with less education. The infant death rate is between 68 and 75 per 1,000 births, higher than anywhere else in Latin America. Life expectancy is 62 years, compared to the Latin American average of 69. Indigenous women prefer to deliver at home because they do not feel confident in hospitals, mainly because their customs are ignored or denied in such health services.

In Bolivia, a culture of rural midwifery known as *partera* is adopted, where midwives speak the local language. Some of them understand the importance of evaluating risks, and for that purpose they use a sort of oracle, based in coca leaves. In traditional deliveries, women can choose the position. Most of them choose to squat, with their family around, and drink infusions of medicinal plants. Soon after the childbirth, women must keep warm and avoid contact with cold water.

Many projects supported by international organizations have been implemented over the past decades with very low success in terms of decreases in maternal mortality. Currently, the Bolivian government is developing a new strategy based on an intercultural reproductive health care approach, which incorporates the religious and traditional medicinal approach of the Bolivians with Western technologies and practices, uses the indigenous languages, takes advantage of the regional resources, and respects the habits and traditions of the people.

The annual expenditure for health care in Bolivia is $125 per capita. Health care providers are scarce, with only 3.2 physicians per 10,000 people and even fewer nurses. It has been estimated that 80 percent of the curable diseases in Bolivia are caused by polluted water. Although the country has abundant supplies of water, very little drinkable water is available to the people. Privatization of water delivery has resulted in price increases and "water wars" among providers.

Katrina Meynink

Further Reading

De Franco, M., and R. Godoy. "The Economic Consequences of Cocaine Production in Bolivia: Historical, Local and Macroeconomic Perspectives." *Journal of Latin American Studies* 42. 3 (1992): 375–406.

Goldstein, D. "Performing National Culture in a Bolivian Migrant Community." *Ethnology* 37 (1998): 117–32.

Gonzalez, Gerado. "Population Ageing, Sustainable Development and Food Security in Rural Areas of Bolivia and Chile." Paper prepared for Population and Development Service, Sustainable Development Department, Food and Agriculture Organization of the United Nations. Rome, Italy: Food and Agriculture Organization Rome, 2005. http://www.fao.org/sd/dim_pe1/docs/pe1_050906d1.pdf.

Hugo, R., A. Zubieta, B. McNelly, and C. Dunford. "Household Food Insecurity and Food Expenditure in Bolivia, Burkina Faso, and the Philippines." *Journal of Nutrition* 135, No. 5 (May 2006): 1431–37.

Johnson, Louise. "Hybrid and Global Kitchens—First and Third World Intersections (Part 2)." *Gender, Place, and Culture* 13, No. 6 (2006): 647–52.

Johnsson, Mick. *Food and Culture among Bolivian Aymara: Symbolic Expressions of Social Relations.* Stockholm, Sweden: Almqvist & Wiksell International, 1986.

Larson, Brooke. "Unresolved Tensions: Bolivia Past and Present." *The Americas: A Quarterly Review of Inter-American Cultural History* 66, No. 1 (July 2009): 136–38.

Lovera, José Rafael. *Food Culture in South America.* Westport, CT: Greenwood Press, 2005.

Orlove, B., and E. Schmidt. "Swallowing Their Pride: Indigenous and Industrial Beer in Peru and Bolivia." *Journal of Theory and Society* 24, No. 2 (April 1995): 271–98.

Perez-Cueto, F.J.A., A. Baya Botti, and W. Verbeke. "Prevalence of Overweight in Bolivia: Data on Women and Adolescents." *Obesity Reviews* 10, No. 4 (July 2009): 373–75.

Poole, N. "Leaves on the Line." *The Guardian,* August 2000.

Williams, Sean, ed. *The Ethnomusicologists' Cookbook: Complete Meals from around the World.* New York: Routledge, 2006.

Brazil

Overview

In a letter written in 1500, the first document describing the land and the native people of what later became Brazil, scribe Pero Vaz de Caminha reported to the king of Portugal, D. Manuel I, that apparently the new land had so many riches and the nature was so exuberant and well favored that "rightly cultivated it would yield everything." The Portuguese explorers landed on the Brazilian seacoast in April 1500. At the time, it was inhabited by roughly five million native people, with different cultures and languages, in a territory spanning from the equator to well below the Tropic of Capricorn.

The new arrivals settled down with the objective of extracting the riches and exploiting the land; to this end, they slashed down forests, at first for brazilwood, used as a red dye during the Renaissance, and later for huge sugarcane, cotton, and tobacco plantations. Coffee, for which seeds were smuggled in from French Guiana, and cocoa beans, a native species from the Amazon rain forest, became export products only in the 18th century. Because of its climate the country was a major haven for many new plant and animal species, and nowadays almost nobody is aware, for example, that bananas and coconuts were transplanted from India and Sri Lanka and are not native trees. The new settlers brought a variety of Mediterranean fruits and vegetables, such as oranges and sugarcane, which had been brought to the Iberian Peninsula by the Arabs. Today, Brazil and the United States are the world's biggest producers of concentrated orange juice.

The new colonial inhabitants were, in turn, introduced to corn, prepared in many different ways, by the natives. Some roots, such as manioc, were ground into flour; the capsicums pepper, either wild or cultivated in small quantities, was used for medicinal purposes. Peanuts, sweet potatoes, pumpkins, and beans of different colors and sizes, all native species that had migrated from different regions of the Americas, soon became staple foods for the newcomers. The beaches, devoid of coconut trees, were thickly populated with huge cashew trees, a source of vitamin C. In the 16th century, the Portuguese settlers introduced rice.

The Portuguese learned how to hunt and tame wild animals that did not exist in Europe, such as *capivaras* (capybaras—a rodent the size of a small pig), *pacas* (spotted cavies—a kind of guinea pig), *tatus* (armadillos), *cotias* (agoutis—a relative of the guinea pig), deer, and *antas* (Brazilian tapir). The newcomers brought chickens and dairy cows, as well as horses and mules for transportation. The native population did not use salt systematically for seasoning or for food conservation. Brazil's extensive seacoast became the location of salt works that are still producing salt.

The Portuguese colonizers came to Brazil to develop a large colonial business. To this end, they brought slaves from Africa, who introduced to their new country their foods and eating habits. The slave trade between the two continents, especially between the state of Bahia and Angola, was very active from the 16th until the early 19th century, when the transport of slaves was banned.

Rice, beans, and manioc flour, the key foods of Brazilian cuisine, originally the nourishment of the native population, became staples in the course of the first two centuries after the arrival of the Portuguese settlers. The Brazilian diet is still based on these three ingredients. Ever since then, the combination of native, Iberian, and African foods has been enriched by the influence of Spanish, German, Polish, Turkish, Greek, Lebanese, Palestinian, Syrian, Hungarian, Bolivian, Argentinean, Japanese, Chinese, Korean, and Russian immigrants.

🍽 Food Culture Snapshot

Nowadays, since the majority of the population lives in cities, Brazilians buy their dried goods and the very basic items of their local kitchen in large multinational supermarket chains. A typical shopping list will include coffee and milk (for breakfast), either dark brown or black beans, rice, manioc flour and its different starches, corn flour (which can be found in many grinds, some very soft, known as *fubá mimoso,* "delicate flour," used in a very traditional cake), wheat flour, sugar, onions, garlic, bay leaves, red pepper (*capsicums*), and a typical cheese from Minas Gerais, in the central region, to be served with guava paste as dessert. Fresh food is bought at the supermarkets, too, although local street markets still have a very good reputation as providers of better produce. Bread is bought in huge bakeries.

A typical visit to a street market begins with a stop at a pastel stall. The *pastel* is a dumpling made of a thin dough with a filling; these are fried right in front of the customers in huge oil woks. The most popular flavors are hearts of palm (*palmitos*), chicken with olives, cheese, cheese and banana spiced with cinnamon, and pizza (cheese, tomatoes, and oregano). These open-air markets, with their exuberant colors and smells, attest to the variety of nature in the tropics. The stalls sell all sorts of very fresh fruit in large amounts, such as mangoes, papayas, bananas, apples, pears, persimmons, grapes, and different kinds of citrus fruits. Shoppers can buy vegetables, legumes, roots, fish, chicken, dried and cured meats, and beautiful flowers; because of the mild climate, seasons are extended, and most produce is available all year long.

Everyday meals, both lunch and dinner, in the large cities consist of a mix of rice and beans, one vegetable, and either red meat or chicken, prepared either grilled or stewed. The use of seasonings and herbs varies according to regional preferences. Fish is eaten along the extensive Brazilian coast, which measures 5,592 miles (9,198 kilometers), while the Amazon River basin offers many delicious freshwater fish like the *pintado* (*Pseudoplathystoma corruscans*), the *pirarucu* (*Arapaima gigas*), and piranhas (*Serrasalmus* spp.), the ferocious meat eaters. The South Atlantic has a wide variety of cold-water fish (sardines, flounder, and sole), shrimp, crab, and squid, which are regularly consumed. However, because of the price difference, a typical family would generally eat shrimp for dinner or serve it at a special occasion and have fried fish for lunch.

The cooking may seem labor-intensive, but the food has acquired a specific preparation methodology throughout the years that still makes it possible to eat a full traditional meal at home. Beans are cooked in a pressure cooker and frozen, rice takes no more than 20 minutes to be ready, and the meat of choice is grilled as the family members sit down to eat.

Major Foodstuffs

The structure of each meal, regardless of social class, is supported by only five ingredients: rice, beans, manioc flour, coffee, and sugar. Meals are planned around them. Rice and beans is the staple dish for daily meals at home and at popular restaurants. Cooked beans mixed with only manioc flour are an important part of the menu in the surrounding countryside. The type of beans and the ingredients added during cooking vary from one region to another. Coffee has been a traditional drink in Brazil since the 19th century. In some regions, it is mixed with manioc flour to make a kind of porridge. Corn, especially in the central and southern regions, is used to make sweets and snacks.

Manioc, or cassava, is a native root that was readily adopted by Brazil's European and African populations. In colonial times, the roots would be washed to remove the hydrocyanic acid they contain, then toasted over live embers and eaten with salted butter, as a substitute for bread. The natives ate peanuts and cultivated manioc roots and corn, which had migrated from Central America. They used each of these plants to make different products such as flour, tapioca, alcoholic beverages, or lightly fermented beverages for rituals.

Brazil has many kinds of native beans. Since precolonial times, fresh or dried beans have been cooked to soften them. Excellent hunters and fishermen, the natives cooked fish and game over small fires. As the natives were always roaming around the countryside, they taught the foreign conquerors who explored the hinterlands how to feed themselves and prepare the food they would have to take on their reconnaissance expeditions into the wild country, where they went first to search for gold and later to occupy land for farming. The natives showed the newcomers how to preserve different kinds of meals for traveling or for daily consumption, like the *paçoca*—a combination of salt-seasoned jerked beef and manioc flour. Paçoca was the main staple food for those long trips. Brazilians ate it frequently well into the 20th century. Today, every child will eat a small sweet with the same name that is a mix of ground peanuts with sugar.

Cattle became part of the national diet later on. In the beginning, the Spaniards established huge cattle ranches in the south of Brazil, a region that is now Uruguay. Soon thereafter, cattle ranches began to migrate northward and provided beef for Brazil's other regions. In the northeast, which had been settled much earlier, cattle were raised in the semi-arid climate of its hinterlands, and the meat was processed as jerked beef to be sold in large cities. As in many other countries, milk and cheese are part of the diet. Cheeses are often country-specific, and many typical specialties are the result of the need to preserve them for longer periods of time. One very popular cheese is *requeijão,* or twice-coagulated cheese, a version of cream cheese. The coagulated curds are broken and stirred until a creamy consistency is obtained. It is found in all supermarkets, and Brazilians spread it on bread at breakfast or eat it with fruit compotes for dessert.

Brazil has been one of the leading sugar producers of the world since the 16th century, and the availability of sugar in large amounts has led to an excessive love for sweetness in confectionary, cakes, fruit pastes, and compotes. Although one shouldn't generalize—given that taste is something very individual—there is a common consensus among Brazilians that sweets must contain a high amount of sugar, much higher than is accepted in European countries, for instance. The excessive availability triggered the creation of typical desserts such as guava or banana paste and syrupy desserts with eggs and all sorts of fruits.

Because Brazil is one of the world's largest soybean producers, many soy by-products are readily available in supermarkets. Food is usually cooked with soybean oil or margarine, and the beans are sold for cooking or salted as appetizers. However, the oriental soy sauce and tofu, although easily found in chain stores, especially in the southeast of the country, are not part of the everyday diet. There are many

A Campesihno pressing sugar as his son looks on. (Corel)

other uses such as for heavy oils for machinery or polymers for making plastic objects, and so on.

The traditional Portuguese cuisine includes a wide variety of pastries, prepared with a high content of eggs and sugar. Most of these recipes can also be prepared with additions of coconut milk and grated coconut. *Cocadas* (coconut wafers), pies, *bolos de aipim com coco* (manioc cake with coconut), tapioca puddings, luxurious creams made with egg yolks cooked in coconut milk and sugar and served with almond cakes, *beijus* (fine tapioca pancakes), and fruit preserves are some of the best-loved sweets in Brazil, which has a delicious and rich tradition.

Typical Meals

Each region in Brazil has its own specialty, and in some cases these regional specialties are served in other parts of the country as well, such as the *churrasco* (meat barbecue), which is typical of the very large plains on the frontier with Uruguay and Argentina. The cuisine of many regions has an African influence, especially in recipes that call for *azeite de dendê* (palm oil), used mainly in Bahia in the northeast. A large number of cakes and desserts mix native ingredients and Portuguese cooking techniques, like the recipes for egg-based desserts. Many Portuguese desserts took on a Brazilian nature through the addition of coconut milk to the list of ingredients, as is the case for *ovos moles,* a traditional egg-cream recipe from Portugal's Aveiro region, the Brazilian version of which is called *baba-de-moça* (ladies' dribble—there are quite a few sweet dishes with ribald names like this one, and they are part of the Catholic tradition not only in Brazil). Many of the dishes served in Brazil on special occasions stem from the ritual foods of the Candomblé, an Afro-Brazilian religion that has many followers. The following list of dishes shows the richness of Brazilian cuisine and its regional variations.

From Pará in the north, there is *pato no tucupi,* a delicious duck stew cooked in a scalded cassava broth called *tucupi,* a liquid extracted from cassava. Tucupi contains hydrocyanic acid, but when cooked for several hours, the liquid becomes harmless.

Jambu leaves are added to the dish when the duck is ready to be served. Jambu (*Spilanthes oleracea*) is a low-growing plant whose leaves cause numbness of the lips when they are eaten.

Caruru, originally a Candomblé ritual dish, was brought to Bahia in the northeast together with slaves from Africa. To avoid being punished for religious practices that differed from Catholicism, the official religion, the Africans created deities that corresponded to the Catholic saints. For example, the martyr saints Cosmos and Damian are honored in the month of September. But when the children of the local community are served caruru, as tradition dictates, the people are actually honoring the *Erês,* free and innocent spirits that exist in each one of us. Caruru is a stew made with okra, smoked shrimp, peanuts, cashew nuts, and palm tree oil.

Moqueca is a savory stew prepared with fish, shrimp, and herbs such as parsley, basil, onions, garlic, and cilantro; it comes from Espírito Santo in the southeast.

Grouper Moqueca

Serves 4

4 or 5 lb grouper or any fish that will not break up as it cooks

Juice of 1 lime

2 onions

1 red pepper

1 yellow pepper

1 jalapeño pepper

8 tomatoes, seeded

1 big garlic bulb

3 or 4 large basil leaves

8 sprigs fresh cilantro (optional)

1 bundle each parsley and chives

2 bay leaves

Salt to taste

Black pepper to taste

Ask the fishmonger to gut the fish and cut it crosswise into four or five large pieces, the head included.

At home, wash the grouper in running water, and rub it with the lime juice and a bit of salt. Place the pieces of fish side by side in a clay or iron pot big enough to fit all the pieces in one layer.

Shred and mix the peeled onions, the peppers (seeds and ribs removed), and the tomatoes in the food processor. Cover the fish with this mixture. Spread the herbs on the top, side, and bottom. Add the whole peeled garlic cloves. Place a lid on the pan and cook the stew at low temperature for roughly 15 minutes. The pieces of fish must remain covered with the sauce. Taste the sauce and add salt if necessary. Cook for 5 more minutes. Serve with white rice and pepper sauce.

The story goes that slaves on coffee plantations created the black-bean stew *feijoada,* cooked with pork parts that are usually rejected, such as ears and tails, plus different kinds of sausages. Allegedly, the prime cuts were reserved for the landowners. These stories are somewhat exaggerated, as each culture has its own bean-stew dish cooked with different kinds of meats and sausages made from the leftover meat of local animals. The French have cassoulet, made with goose legs, whereas foie gras and goose *magret* are sold in luxury food markets. The Portuguese have their own baked bean casserole, made with white beans and sometimes with seafood and small fish left over from the day's catch, or with regional sausages. Feijoada has become a national favorite despite its regional origin in Rio de Janeiro in the southeastern part of the country.

Eating Out

For centuries, ships would stop at Brazilian ports to replenish their supplies before sailing for Africa and India or when traveling south to cross to the Pacific Ocean. From the 20th century on, a cosmopolitan way of life spread throughout the coastal cities, always ready to welcome their visitors. Associations, clubs, theaters, cabarets, hospitals, and restaurants serving a variety of cuisines opened. Nowadays, places like São Paulo, with its 18 million inhabitants, offer a wide range of options to cater to all kinds of tastes.

There is a wide array of different kinds of restaurants in Brazil. The food ranges from traditional cuisine, with a strong Portuguese influence, to French and Italian cuisine, to the *churrascarias,* the barbecue palaces that serve tons of meat nonstop. The churrasco is the typical dish of the pampas, the frontier region on the borders of Brazil, Uruguay, Argentina, and Paraguay. New restaurants and young chefs have added a new twist to the traditionally heavy food from Brazil's rural regions, and they look for forgotten—albeit important for local culture—ingredients from Brazil's history. Leaves of native palm trees are used to add a finishing touch to sauces; fruits from the Amazon region, such as the *açaí* (*Euterpe oleracea Mart*), are used to make soups and ice cream.

In addition to traditional restaurants, bistros, and restaurants where one can eat "today's specials," there are two kinds of restaurants that are specific to Brazil, the so-called *por quilo* and *rodízio* restaurants. At the first kind, people help themselves to a buffet lunch, weigh their full plates on a special scale, and sit at tables while waiters bring drinks and desserts. These restaurants are normally open only for lunch. Patrons can select what they want from a wide variety of dishes, which include different kinds of salads, rice, beans, meat stews, steamed

Feijoada, the national dish of Brazil, is a typical Brazilian dish made with black beans and several kinds of meat, mainly pork. (iStockPhoto)

vegetables, and even Japanese food. The equally creative rodízio is somewhat different: Patrons choose the side dishes when they are already seated at the table, while waiters offer slices of different kinds of meat, fish, or pasta nonstop.

Pizza parlors are one of the most popular spots for eating out in São Paulo, in the country's southeastern region. The enormous influence of the Italian immigrants ensures excellent restaurants, but the pizzeria is the restaurant of choice to celebrate birthdays, to get a bite to eat after a soccer game, or to take the kids out for Sunday dinner. Some Brazilians proudly insist that Brazilian pizza is the best in the world.

For a romantic dinner, restaurant goers can choose from a wide selection of French, Spanish, or Japanese restaurants. The city of São Paulo is home to more than 300,000 Japanese descendants, many of whom live in a typically Japanese neighborhood and celebrate many traditional Japanese feasts. The Japanese influence on daily meals is attested to by the many sushi and *temaki* fast-food restaurants in the city.

One of the most popular activities all over Brazil is to go to a bar and eat delicious *salgadinhos,* which are small savory snacks. They come in a huge variety, each one tastier than the next—*bolinhos de bacalhau* (small, round codfish cakes), delicate chicken croquettes shaped like a chicken leg, and *empadinhas* (small, delicate pies filled with palm heart, shrimp, or meat), among many other tasty delicacies, which taste wonderful with ice-cold beer. Ice cream made from regional fruits is also a popular delicacy, because of Brazil's warm weather during most of the year.

Fresh fruit juice bars are found everywhere. There is a huge variety of fruits all year round—oranges, passion fruit, guavas, watermelons, mangoes, strawberries, açai, *mangabas, sapotis,* coconuts, cacao, and tamarinds, among other varieties. *Erva-mate* (known in the United States as yerba maté or *Ilex paraguariensis*) and *cachaça*—fermented sugarcane juice—are the original beverages. In the south, erva-mate is prepared as a hot infusion and people drink it like tea; in Rio de Janeiro, people drink ice-cold mate. Cachaça, a distilled beverage made from fermented sugarcane juice, differs from rum, which is made from molasses. Cachaça can be consumed pure and young, usually a white-colored beverage, or it can be aged and golden-colored. Today, the cachaças on the market vary from very plain ones to others aged in oak barrels in order to add a certain depth to their bouquet. They sometimes also have flavors added. But the favorite way of drinking them is as a summer drink with ice and fruit juices—they are called *batidas.* The combination of cachaça and fruit juice results in a typical cocktail called *caipirinha,* prepared with lime in its conventional flavor.

Caipirinha

1 small glass of the kind used for whiskey on the rocks

1 average-size lime

1 tsp sugar

Ice to fill the glass

40 mL (1.3 oz) cachaça

Cut the top and bottom of the lime off and then slice it into four equal wedges; remove the seeds and the rind; cut each one in half. Place them in the chosen glass with the pulp facing upward; sprinkle the sugar over them, and mash the two ingredients with a muddler to release the juice. Fill the glass with crushed ice, and pour the cachaça on top.

Special Occasions

Such a rich regional culinary tradition means that delicious and decoratively arranged food is served all over the country on special occasions. There are many religious feasts in Brazil, and very frequently saints' days and different religions' meaningful dates are celebrated by everyone. In the northeast and in the state of Minas Gerais, the São João (Saint John's Day) festivities last throughout the month of June, and special dishes made from fresh and young corn are served during these celebrations, since it is also its harvest time. Before the corn is dried, the kernels are baked in cakes; churned with cream for ice cream; cooked into different porridges, called *curau,* some with hard batter and other softer and mixed with coconut; and fermented with water and sugar to be served as a beverage with a low alcohol content.

In Bahia, caruru, a stew made with okra, dried shrimp, peanuts, and pepper, is served in September to honor Cosmos and Damian; actually, these are a Roman Catholic representation of a spirit of the Afro-Brazilian religion, the Erês or Ibejis. In Bahia, where the African culinary influence is stronger, there is a series of stews with shrimp and fresh fish, called moquecas, which are traditionally served on Sunday lunch for family gatherings.

In the former capital of Rio de Janeiro, New Year's Eve is one of the biggest celebrations. A lentil salad, grapes, and pomegranates are served for good luck. It is also the occasion when the population near the sea honors Iemanjá, the Brazilian goddess of the sea, with gifts and songs at the beaches. Family festivities, celebratory dinners, birthday parties, and Sunday lunches follow the same ritual, when an array of sweet and salty dishes is served.

The most beloved sweet is usually served at children's parties, and adults and kids love it. It is a very small chocolate sweet, similar to a truffle, called the *brigadeiro,* meaning "air marshal." The name honors a former military officer who was a presidential candidate during the 1940s. This sweet is made with a mixture of chocolate and sweet condensed milk cooked until caramelized and then rolled into small balls.

Diet and Health

The Brazilian diet and consequently the population's health are guided by regional cultures and the different levels of economic development, which demonstrates a tremendous variation, although the country is one of the 10 most industrialized in the world. As Brazil's territory lies within several climate zones, there is not one single common diet, and there are also different food consumption levels, which depend on the highly heterogeneous availability of foods. People in the south plant extensive apple tree groves and will eat fruits and vegetables of European origin, such as spinach, red beets, lettuce, and carrots, to name a few. In the northeast, where the climate is drier, fruit consumption tends to be low, with the exception of the local tropical fruits, such as the wonderfully scented *seriguelas, pitombas, graviolas* (soursop fruit), and cashews.

It is important to notice that fruits play a very significant role in the local diets due to the variety of the species, whether native or introduced in the last 500 years. The same cannot be said of vegetables. Large areas do not consume them as part of their everyday lives. There is instead a preference for starches: potatoes, cassava, sweet potatoes, and yams as a side dish. A significant part of the northeast lies in a semiarid zone, where the climate resembles that of a desert. The Amazon rain forest is the northernmost region, and the Amazon territory also includes part of the Pantanal, the vast area of wetlands with seasonal inundations. Each region has its own specific plants and animals, both native and immigrant populations. Eating habits were influenced by the farm production of the colonial period and evolved according to the migration of people within Brazil, a constant event in Brazil's history. For instance, maté tea, which is a beverage in the pampas, the region that lies on the border with Uruguay and Argentina, is also widely consumed in Roraima, which lies on the border of Venezuela. This is due to the migration of people from the south to the far north as they followed the expansion of soybean plantations.

The preference for a specific type of bean might vary according to the region, but beans, which are full of iron, vitamin B, and amino acids, are a staple food all over Brazil, even though they are prepared in many different ways. Manioc flour is also produced and consumed from north to south, on the seacoast and in the countryside. Manioc flour is used in different ways, in both sweet and savory dishes, much like rice.

The fact that core nourishment is based on cooked beans, either accompanied by meat or, in very hard times, served with cassava flour, made it possible to avoid huge famines from historical times. Unfortunately, today their consumption is diminishing, and a new dietary parameter is establishing itself, more

Tropical fruit being sold in the market. (Corel)

as a consequence of the country's urbanization and industrialization: high consumption of saturated fats and industrialized sugars, as well as a more sedentary life, resulting in a lower consumption of fresh vegetables and fruits, which are replaced by small industrialized snacks that are leading to obesity. The local dishes are losing importance in everyday life and more and more are turning into restaurant fare, as in most places in the Western world.

Marcia Zoladz

Further Reading

Câmara Cascudo, Luís da. *História da Alimenta-ção no Brasil.* 3rd ed. São Paulo, Brazil: Global Editora, 2004.

Embrapa Arroz e Feijão (National Rice and Beans Research Center Site). http://www.cnpaf. embrapa.br/english/index.htm.

Hamilton, Cherie Y. *Brazil: A Culinary Journey.* New York: Hippocrene Books, 2005.

Idone, Cristopher. *Brazil: A Cook's Tour.* New York: Random House, 1995.

Zoladz, Marcia. "About Eggs, Two Countries and a Cake." In *Eggs in Cookery, Proceedings of the Oxford Symposium on Food and Cookery 2006,* edited by Richard Hosking, 322–32. Blackawton, UK: Prospect Books, 2007.

Zoladz, Marcia. "Cacao in Brazil or the History of a Crime." In *Food and Morality, Proceedings of the Oxford Symposium on Food and Cookery 2007,* Susan Friedland, ed., 309–20. Blackawton, UK: Prospect Books, 2008.

Canada

Overview

Covering about 5.6 million square miles (almost 10 million square kilometers), Canada has the second-largest landmass of any country in the world. Its climatic and geographic variety is as vast as the land itself—mountainous terrain, great plains, three seacoasts (Atlantic, Pacific, and Arctic), fruitful valleys, and northern tundra. The food culture is likewise diverse.

The 2006 agricultural census indicates that only 1 percent of the nearly 33 million Canadians are involved in agriculture, working on approximately 230,000 farms. Over the course of the country's relatively short history, Canadians have slowly but steadily moved from the countryside to the city, a move that has impacted both what Canadians eat and how they produce it. The majority of the Canadian population can be found in the urban centers of southern Ontario, British Columbia, and western Quebec. As more people leave the bounty of the countryside for the bustle of the city, not only have eating patterns changed but farms have continued to grow in size to meet increasing demand.

Despite the changes that have occurred since Canada was founded in 1867, the Canada of today is strongly influenced by its colonial history: The French and British competed for eastern and central Canada—what is now Ontario through to the Atlantic provinces—beginning in the 1400s. The Treaty of Paris established British rule over what became New France (now Quebec) in 1763. British and French culinary traditions still strongly influence these areas and were adapted to the available foodstuffs of the regions. They were sometimes fused with the culinary traditions of Canada's three indigenous peoples—the First Nations (as Native Americans are called in Canada), Inuit (formerly referred to as Eskimos), and Métis (those of mixed heritage now accorded aboriginal status, with a distinct culture).

Following colonization, years of immigration from the world over have led to an unusually diversified food culture. When the Germans arrived in Ontario, the Scottish in Nova Scotia, the French in Quebec, the Chinese in British Columbia, and the Ukrainians in Alberta, the bounty of the Canadian soil meant that their cultural and culinary traditions were adapted to the available ingredients, creating a unique nutritional and cultural milieu.

¶◎¶ Food Culture Snapshot

Joan and Ken Craig live comfortably in Guelph, a bedroom community of 130,000 people west of Toronto, Canada's biggest city. Housing is expensive in Toronto; the average price in November 2009 for a home in Toronto was CDN$420,000, compared to around CDN$280,000 for Guelph, turning people such as Ken into commuters. Mass transit leading into Toronto from Guelph is underdeveloped, so Ken drives about an hour a day, depending on traffic. Financially, Joan and Ken are comfortable—he's a national marketing manager for an imported-auto manufacturer, earning CDN$190,000 annually along with a company car. Joan works as an administrative assistant at the local university, earning CDN$40,000 a year. They have two children, Lilly, age five, and Watson, age three.

Ken is usually harried, so his morning diet is often poor and built on fast food. Typically, he hits the main highway into Toronto at 5:45 A.M., to avoid as much rush hour traffic as he can. Just before the on-ramp, he stops at a drive-through coffee shop called Tim Horton's—started by a famous Canadian hockey player—for a "double-double" (two spoonfuls of sugar, two portions of milk) American-style coffee and a blueberry or bran muffin, or a chocolate doughnut on Fridays as an end-of-the-week treat. That might be all he eats until noon, at which time he will have a ham or peanut butter sandwich he slapped together on wholegrain bread at home that morning. Or he will run across the street to a fast-food shop for a submarine sandwich or perhaps a lettuce salad with raspberry vinaigrette. Another coffee follows in the afternoon, around 2:30 P.M., likely from the office dispenser, and possibly a snack, such as a granola bar. Then at about 5:30–6 P.M. Ken fights traffic for at least another hour on the way home.

Joan, a lacto-ovo vegetarian, has the main food-preparation responsibilities. She can get an excellent selection of fruits and vegetables whether in or out of season (citrus, root vegetables, etc.) at any of the five major grocery stores in the city. She may go to the local health-food store for her whole grains, such as oatmeal and brown rice. But she may also run to discount stores, which have the fastest-rising market share. Joan will try to buy as much as a week's worth of food at a time, especially in the winter. It is not unusual for a city such as Guelph to get hit with a major snowstorm that shuts down the city for one to three days, and householders need to stock up.

Joan works five days a week, but she does not start until 8:30 A.M. and she is done at 4:30 P.M. sharp. So she often has time to get the kids from the daycare and still get home to cook something for supper, which they will eat around 6:30 P.M. One of the family's favorite dishes is Elora Road butternut squash soup, adapted from Anita Stewart's *Flavours of Canada.*

Elora Road Butternut Squash and Buttermilk Soup

Makes 6 to 8 Generous Servings

Butternut squash has deep orange-colored flesh. Buttercup or Hubbard squash may also be used. This is such an intensely flavored autumn soup that it can be garnished with yogurt. The name comes from a road near where butternut squash are grown.

2 tbsp canola oil

1 large onion

2 cloves garlic, peeled and minced

1 tbsp minced fresh ginger

½ tsp black mustard seeds

1 tsp cumin seeds

1 tbsp garam masala

4 c diced butternut squash

4 c chicken stock

Salt and freshly ground pepper to taste

2 small cobs of corn, husked *or* 1 c frozen corn

1 sweet red pepper, seeded and minced

1 c buttermilk or half and half cream (10%)

Plain yogurt, as needed for garnish

Heat oil in a large soup pot over medium heat. Add onions, garlic, and ginger; cook and stir for 3–5 minutes or until beginning to turn golden. Add mustard seeds and cumin. Stir and cook for 30–60 seconds until the mustard seeds begin to pop. Add garam masala, and stir the entire mixture thoroughly for another 30 seconds. Stir in squash, tossing to coat with the spice mixture. Add chicken stock, cover, and bring to a boil. Reduce heat to low, simmering till squash is tender. Season to taste and remove from the heat. Let cool for 10 minutes before pureeing either with a hand blender or in a food processor. Return to medium heat. While soup is reheating, carefully cut kernels from the corn. Add to simmering soup with red pepper. Cook, covered, for 3–4 minutes. Stir in buttermilk or cream, and reheat till steaming.

Serve in heated soup bowls, topping with a spoonful of yogurt.

In some countries, vegetarians such as Joan would insist on organic produce. Canadians are less fussy. Canada was one of the first countries in the world to embrace genetically modified food. Here, organic food's market share is growing, but it still accounts for just 2 percent of the total production.

On days when Joan is too busy to cook, she might pop a frozen pizza in the oven. In Canada, the demand for frozen pizza has skyrocketed since just before the new millennium, jumping more than 400 percent. That makes it the leading frozen food in Canada, in terms of growth. If the Craigs do have pizza, however, vegetarian Joan might have to pick hers apart: Pork-based ingredients take the top three positions as the most-menued sources of protein on pizzas. At the top of the list is bacon, which appears on 18 percent of offerings.

Major Foodstuffs

Food production is not important solely for meeting the demands of the domestic market; agricultural products are one of Canada's main exports, and food has always been vital to the economy. In 2006, the agricultural and agrifood system contributed almost CDN$90 billion to the country's gross domestic product, or 8 percent of the Canadian economy. Its relevance is increasing. The agricultural and agrifood system has been growing at an average rate of 2.4 percent per year over the past decade. The sector employs more than two million individuals, representing almost 13 percent of Canadian active human resources and directly providing one in eight jobs.

The predominance of agriculture and food in the economy is all the more remarkable given that little more than 7 percent of the nation's landmass is used for agriculture. That is almost microscopic compared to a nation such as Britain, where nearly 70 percent of land is dedicated to agricultural production. The relatively low land-use percentage is, to a large extent, due to the Canadian climate, which varies considerably across the nation's large landmass, limiting the amount of arable land.

Canada's history also explains why very few truly local foods exist—in fact, most foods came from abroad and were planted in Canada's fertile soil. About a millennium ago, aboriginal peoples brought corn, beans, and squash from the south along the well-established, intricate trading routes that spanned North America. In turn, Canada's foodstuffs have

Saint John City Market (built in 1876), New Brunswick, Canada. (Jamie Roach | Dreamstime.com)

influenced international cuisine; Basque sailors harvested the Grand Banks off Newfoundland and took shore-salted cod home to France and Spain in the 1500s, offering the basis for regional specialties that can still be tasted in those nations today. In the 1800s, Canadian cheddar cheeses and Westphalian-style hams went back to Great Britain, and today, ingredients such as mustard, flour, and oils all head to Europe and Southeast Asia.

Canada is also the number-one producer of mixed grains, linseed, and oats and the second in blueberries, mustard seed, canola, and cranberries. That means fine Italian pastas are made with Canadian durum wheat (semolina). In fact, Ireland's Guinness beer is founded on Canadian malt barley.

Canada's agrifood system is best understood by breaking the country into five regions, moving from west to east: the province of British Columbia; the prairies (the provinces of Alberta, Saskatchewan, and Manitoba); Ontario and Quebec; the Atlantic provinces (Prince Edward Island, Nova Scotia, New Brunswick, Newfoundland); and the northern territories (Yukon, Nunavut, and the Northwest Territories).

British Columbia

Situated on the beautiful Pacific shore, the food production of British Columbia reflects both its bountiful coast and fruitful interior. Foods originating from the coast include Pacific salmon, which has become a staple food in British Columbia since it was first harvested by the indigenous peoples of the region and, eventually, its settlers. Currently, farmed Atlantic salmon is relied on to meet the demand for British Columbian salmon, both domestically and internationally. Clams, oysters, and kelp are also farmed in the coastal waters of British Columbia.

Just west of the Rocky Mountain range, the Okanagan Valley provides an excellent climate for fruit production, including grapes. The Okanagan is at the heart of British Columbia's expanding viticulture industry. The Fraser Valley is also an important agricultural-production area, providing an ideal location for growing vegetables and berries and supporting the production of fresh milk, eggs, chickens, turkeys, and pork. Cow/calf operations are also common in the interior of British Columbia.

The Prairies

The provinces of Alberta, Saskatchewan, and Manitoba make up Canada's prairie region, the nation's breadbasket. The west was initially opened in Canada when the trans-Canada railway was constructed in the second half of the 19th century. The fertile grasslands of the southern prairies are contrasted with the fish-filled lakes of the north, which eventually give way to northern tundra. Despite the diversity of the prairie climate, it is the grasslands of the prairies that often characterize the region, supporting grain, oilseed, and wheat production, as well as cattle ranches. The cattle of today have replaced the great plains bison of yesteryear that sustained the indigenous populations for thousands of years before large-scale bison drives eventually collapsed the population.

Canadian prairie farmers are one of the world's main producers of canola, a staple high-oil-yielding and nutritionally improved variant of rapeseed, developed in Canada, with reduced erucic acid. Canola production has become a cornerstone of Canadian agriculture and is used to produce oil low in saturated fat.

Canada is also one of the world's largest producers and exporters of pulses, the edible seeds of legumes, including dry peas, dry beans, lentils, chickpeas, and fava beans. The Canadian pulse and specialty-crop industry produces and exports more than CDN$1 billion worth of products to thousands of customers in over 150 countries each year. About 75 percent of the Canadian pulse production is exported. Most of this production comes from Saskatchewan.

Ontario and Quebec

Like many Canadian provinces, Ontario is best analyzed with a north/south view, for nearly anything. For example, in Ontario's north, game hunting (deer, moose, ducks, and geese) is a way of life and sustenance, as the growing season is shorter. In contrast, the fertile soils of southern Ontario have been supporting agricultural production for more than a millennium. The Iroquois people had grown corn in what is now southwestern Ontario since 500 A.D. They expanded their agricultural production to include beans and squash in the centuries after their first crops were planted. Crops grown now in Ontario are varied and include soybeans (the biggest cash crop, with two million acres), corn, wheat, and a variety of legumes. Vegetable production is also strong, with asparagus opening the growing season. The fall harvest begins in September and includes root vegetables, squash, and corn, to name a few cultivars.

Within the province of Ontario is another of the nation's main fruit-producing regions—the Niagara Peninsula. Similar to the Okanagan, the Niagara Peninsula is a prime area for tree-fruit production and is known for its plums, pears, peaches, apples, and grapes. Like the Okanagan, Niagara is one of the few areas in Canada that can support a substantial wine industry. Ice wine is a Canadian delicacy, and although it was first vinified in British Columbia, it has become one of Ontario's most widely recognized alcoholic beverages. To make it, grapes are allowed to ripen fully, then freeze on the vine. They are then pressed, and the juices are vinified, producing a sweet signature product for the Niagara Peninsula.

Another great Canadian signature food is maple syrup, which is made from the sap of the maple tree (the leaf of which is found on the Canadian flag). The sap is collected throughout the maple forests of eastern Canada but primarily in Quebec, where the food traditions are notably different and strongly influenced by the French settlers who came to Canada. Settlement occurred along the majestic Saint Lawrence River, with agricultural plots extending on either side of the river. Today, Quebec is home to a strong culinary tradition that has merged French cuisine with the available foodstuffs of the region. Situated on the Canadian Shield, the harsher climate and less-hospitable soil mean some of the staple crops grown in Ontario cannot be found

Held from April 2 to 6 in the Beauceron region of Quebec, the Beauceron Maple Festival celebrates the area's traditional production of maple syrup and includes stands that sell stacks of syrup-laden pancakes. (Corel)

throughout Quebec. Instead, Quebec is known for its unique ingredients and artisanal foods. Maple syrup production is still a strong cultural heritage, drawing many Quebecers to *les cabanes au sucre,* or sugar shacks, in the early spring. Dairy production is also important, and Quebec is well known for its yogurt production and artisan cheese makers. The eastern coast of Quebec, the Gaspé region, ushers in the Atlantic Ocean and is well known for its seafood, including lobster.

The Atlantic Provinces

Lobster is really the possession of the Atlantic provinces, but it is not as readily available as might be expected. The fisheries of the Atlantic provinces are strictly regulated to ensure fish stock sustainability. Conservation efforts have been only marginally successful. Fish, such as cod, have been mercilessly hauled out of the Atlantic, and the stock is significantly depleted.

Atlantic Canadians are great foragers and rely on the natural bounty of the earth, which includes berries, other wild fruits, and mushrooms. Fiddleheads are a special spring treat. Young ferns that have not unraveled and exposed their leaves are eagerly sought in May and June.

Northern Canada

Traditional farming is a challenge for much of the Canadian north as the growing season is short, or sometimes absent altogether. However, the long daylight hours in the summer months (the average is 20 hours, but some regions enjoy 24 hours of sun in the peak of the summer season) and sufficient frost-free days mean that the climate is favorable for growing short-season crops. That is especially true in the western regions of the northern territories, which are more hospitable to agriculture. But despite the ability to grow some grains, berries, and vegetables (often in greenhouses), agriculture in the Canadian north is mostly seen as an act of import substitution, as most of the food for the region's inhabitants is imported from the rest of Canada and internationally. Local agriculture is a means by which to reduce the dependency on imports.

Other forms of agriculture, including wild game herding (such as caribou and musk ox), are also practiced. Food production is new to the north, which has been historically populated by small groups of aboriginal peoples, particularly the Inuit, who have their own food culture that includes hunting seal, whale, and game animals. Canada's governor general Michaelle Jean caused an international stir when she obligingly ate raw seal heart, an Inuit tradition, on a visit to Nunavut in 2009.

Cooking

The Canadian culinary tradition of fusing international influence with local flare began with the first French in L'Acadie, in what is now known as Nova Scotia, and lives on today. The Acadians began harvesting *dulce* (seaweed), samphire (sea asparagus), and goose-tongue greens, as they once had done in France. Soon the dishes of old France began to appear on the maritime tables but with a twist: The flour was the maritimers', the vegetables were grown on small farms, and the meat was slaughtered communally.

Despite the proliferation of regional cuisine and all its intricacies, there is only one cooking method that is indigenous to Canada—that is, the bentwood box on the north coast of British Columbia. Planks of cedar are notched, soaked, and bent before being lashed to form a tight cooking vessel. Four to five hours before cooking, a fire is lit, and rocks are placed into it. The hot rocks are then picked up with a split alder branch and placed into the water-filled box; seafood is added—prawns, scallops, clams, chunks of halibut or salmon—and a woven mat is placed over it to hold in the steam.

Otherwise, Canadians roast, boil, bake, stir-fry, microwave, pickle, freeze, preserve, pit cook, and barbecue ad infinitum. During the Canadian growing season (between April and September, depending on the region) a great plethora of grains, fruits, and vegetables are produced. The Canadian winter demands that the bounty of the growing season be saved for survival over the long winter months.

Before the increased globalization of food trade, Canadians stayed fed all year round by tapping into prepared preserves. Canning is a great Canadian tradition in which the summer's fruits and vegetables are preserved for storage over winter. Pickled beets, beans, and cucumbers, as well as canned peaches, pears, apples, apricots, and tomatoes, meant that the Canadian pioneer would have a supply of fruits and vegetables over the long winter months.

While the plight of Canadian settlers is long past, remnants of their food culture persist today. Typical Canadian kitchens are set up for food storage and cooking that reflects the tendency to horde food for survival. Canadians typically buy groceries to last for several days, meaning most kitchens are equipped to handle long-term food storage, including a large refrigerator, freezer, and cupboard space for dried goods. Most food is cooked either

Two women preparing fruit to can in New Brunswick, Canada. (Alanpoulson | Dreamstime.com)

on an electric or gas stovetop or in the oven, or it is warmed up in the microwave. With constant food availability, fewer Canadians use fruit cellars (a cool, dry room, usually in the basement) where preserves and vegetables were typically stored in the winter months. Canadians now expect a great variety of fresh fruits and vegetables to be available all year. Imported fruits and vegetables come from progressively further away as the winter wears on: tomatoes from California, then Mexico, and apples from Canada, then the southern United States, and, finally, New Zealand. In 2005 the Food and Agriculture Organization ranked Canada 12th among importing nations, bringing in more than CDN$15.5 billion of food into the country that year. But the bounty of Canada was shipped internationally as well. In the same report, the Food and Agriculture Organization ranked Canada 9th among exporting nations, sending CDN$21 billion outside its borders.

The increased globalization of food has had far-reaching consequences in Canada. Some Canadians argue that it has resulted in a homogenization of food, as processing increases and taste decreases. Environmental concerns regarding the distance food needs to travel to make it to people's plates, and the resulting mental separation between the individual and the origin of the food, have contributed to a growing grassroots movement to reassess existing food systems. A manifestation of this reassessment is the burgeoning eat-local movement, sometimes called the 100-mile diet.

Typical Meals

Canadians mostly eat three meals a day: breakfast, lunch, and dinner ("supper"). While the meal structure is reasonably consistent, there is little uniformity regarding what is actually found on any given Canadian's plate. The Canadian Food Guide recommends that available foods be broken down into four categories: vegetables and fruit, grain products, milk and alternatives, and meat and alternatives. Canadians are encouraged to eat a balanced diet with a focus on fresh fruit and vegetables as well as whole grains and low-fat, low-sugar options.

However, there is a growing disparity between what is recommended, and Canadians' eating habits. For example, there is a strong emphasis on fresh fruits and vegetables, but many Canadians eat a high percentage of processed foods. The Canadian food- and beverage-processing industry had sales of approximately CDN$78 billion in 2006, with CDN$68 billion accounting for food purchases alone.

Breakfast is typically eaten in the early morning before the beginning of the workday. It usually involves a cereal or grain of some kind—either processed or cooked—as well as fruit, yogurt, or eggs. A hot drink, such as coffee or tea, usually accompanies the meal. On weekends, brunch (a late breakfast combined with lunch) is popular. Hearty meals are always in vogue such as a combination of fried eggs, sausage or bacon, toast, pancakes, and/or fruit.

The changing socioeconomic terrain means that many Canadians are working longer hours in offices than ever before. This often results in a quick lunch that is eaten out or packed to take to work. For most Canadians, lunch is a light meal, and the emphasis is placed on dinner. Dinner is usually eaten at the end of the workday, between 6 and 7 P.M.

Vegetarianism is on the rise in Canada, with approximately 4 percent of the population following a vegetarian lifestyle. While the cultural diversity of Canada guarantees that some of the vegetarian choices are based on religious reasons, much of the vegetarian population has made changes based on lifestyle and moral concerns.

Eating Out

The history of Canadian restaurant culture reflects the country's history and liberal immigration policy, which has long encouraged and invited newcomers. The variety of cuisine available reflects the nation's diversity—Italian, Chinese, Greek, East Indian, Thai, Vietnamese, and more can all be found. British Columbians eat out the most. The province has 27.3 food-service locations per 10,000 inhabitants, compared to the national average of 25.2. At the other end of the scale is Manitoba, with 18.2 units per 10,000 people, the lowest in Canada.

The local-food movement is sparking some dining activity. One of the best examples in Canada is the Borealis Grille in Guelph, with its commitment to local foods and beverages. Chefs try to source more than 95 percent of the food from Ontario. Steaks, flatbreads, fish, pasta, and barbecue items make up the main menu. Olive oil has been replaced by cold-pressed soy, canola, and sunflower oils from the province. The beverage selection is almost exclusively local. The wines are predominantly Ontario VQA with some Okanagan wines and a few brands from the United States and South America to round out the list. All the draft beers are microbrewed within a 100-kilometer (62.1-mile) radius.

Despite the growing market for locally sourced restaurants, some ingredient providers are at loggerheads with buyers. For example, the Canadian Restaurant and Food Services Association, a lobby group, is pushing hard against a long-standing and highly political Canadian tradition called supply management, which it says distorts food prices, especially dairy, and exaggerates the price of restaurant meals. Under supply management, the amount of milk, poultry, and eggs that can be produced and their price are tightly controlled by legislation, as are imports of these commodities. Farmers say border protection is necessary; otherwise, they will get swamped by imports. They argue that cheap food is not necessarily safe food. For their part, Canadians do not seem to mind paying more for peace of mind and supporting Canadian farmers.

A man and woman preparing ribs as part of the World's Longest Barbecue in Guelph, Ontario, Canada, 2008. (Dreamstime)

Special Occasions

Canadian diversity means that nationally celebrated feasts are few and far between; however, there are a couple notable celebrations that attract the participation of a large number of Canadians. Thanksgiving (the second Monday in October) and Christmas (December 25) are the main culinary-related holidays in Canada, usually recognized from a culinary perspective with a feast centered on roast turkey. For birthdays, people normally get a birthday cake. The same goes for weddings. Owing to Canada's multicultural nature, many other religious, secular, and ethnic holidays are also recognized, many with their own food traditions.

A food-related event called the World's Longest Barbecue, which is expanding into Food Day Canada, dubbed "a coast to coast to coast celebration of great regional foods," is informally recognized on the first weekend in August, traditionally a national holiday in Canada (Civic Holiday). The barbecue started in 2003 to help beef farmers rebound after an animal with bovine spongiform encephalopathy was found among the Canadian herd, prompting the United States, Canada's biggest trading partner, to close the border. Now, tens of thousands of Canadians light their grills on that weekend in support of farmers and Canadian food.

Diet and Health

Canadians have a culture of eating "pioneer" food—high protein, high fat, high carbohydrates—and lots of it. This pattern dates back to the relatively recent settling of the land, and the hard-working rural and farm population. Now, only a fraction—less than 1 percent—of the population lives on farms. But some Canadians eat as if they still routinely drove a horse-drawn plow (which they do not).

Health Canada, a branch of the Canadian government, is entrusted with Canadians' good food and nutrition. The Canadian government calls maintaining the safety of the country's food supply a "shared responsibility" among government, industry, and consumers, based on what it calls evidence-based nutrition policies and standards. These policies and standards are reflected in Canada's Food Guide. The guide makes recommendations by suggesting food options rather than daily allowances of nutrients. Offering choices from four basic food groups is intended to supply Canadians with the proper intake of nutrients, but it does not account for the specific needs of all individuals, such as women who need more iron.

Furthermore, Health Canada recommends to Canadian consumers that they eat at least one dark green and one orange vegetable each day; have vegetables and fruit more often than juice; make at least half of grain products whole grain each day; drink skim, 1 percent, or 2 percent milk each day; have meat alternatives such as beans, lentils, and tofu often; eat at least two Food Guide servings of fish each week; include a small amount of unsaturated fat each day; and, lastly, satisfy their thirst with water. These messages do not seem to be getting through to the public, though.

Despite—or perhaps because of—Canadians' limited adherence to health precepts, new crops aimed at better health are constantly being monitored, trialed, and introduced into the food system. Value-added crops continue to be an area of exciting development, particularly those with health benefits. For example, Canadian-grown oilseeds such as canola, sunflower, and flax are known today for their health benefits, and the industry has successfully developed a strong market based on these qualities. Canola was developed in Canada and is often the nation's most valuable crop, with annual exports of canola seed, oil, and meal valued at more than CDN$3 billion. Canola is an achievement of Canada's research community and is a testament to how responding to consumer demands for quality and nutrition pays big dividends over time. Canadian wheat is renowned the world over for its quality as well. Looking into the future, an organization called the Advanced Foods and Materials Network is Canada's front line of research and development in the area of advanced foods and biomaterials, including improved frozen-food quality and reduced salt intake.

Owen Roberts, Rebecca
Moore, and Anita Stewart

Further Reading

"Canada: Recipes and Cuisine." Whats4Eats: International Recipes and Cooking around the World. http://www.whats4eats.com/north-america/canada-cuisine.

Duncan, Dorothy. *Canadians at Table: Food, Fellowship, and Folklore. A Culinary History of Canada.* Toronto, ON: Dundurn, 2006.

Food Network Canada. http://www.food network.ca/.

Hamilton, Janice. *Canada.* Minneapolis, MN: Lerner, 2008.

Munro, Derek B. *Vegetables of Canada.* Ottawa, ON: NRC Research Press, 1997.

Chile

Overview

The Republic of Chile has 15 provinces; it stretches 2,640 miles in length but is little more than 100 miles wide, and it is bordered by the Pacific Ocean and the Andes range. Its geographic extremes range from the Atacama Desert, the Earth's driest place, to the fertile Central Valley, from where produce and wines are shipped around the world, to the south, where volcanoes and virgin forests give way to Patagonia's glaciers and Antarctica. Stories vary as to the origin of the country's name. *Chile* may refer to an Inca word, to a Peruvian valley, or to indigenous Mapuche Indians' word *chilli,* possibly translated "where the land ends."

About 85 percent of Chile's 16 million people live in its Central Valley, and almost a third of those live in Santiago, the capital. About two-thirds of Chileans claim mixed indigenous and European descent. The indigenous Mapuche make up about 10 percent of the country's population and are among the poorest of Chileans.

Allowing for some regional specialties, the same foods are enjoyed and the same eating habits are practiced throughout the country. There's an abundance of seafood from the country's endless coastline, and beef, pork, and chicken are popular. The produce is excellent and plentiful. Chile's thriving wine industry continues to expand to new areas.

Chile's oldest cooking traditions come from the Incas, whose agriculture and irrigation methods in turn influenced the Mapuche. The Spanish intermarried freely with the indigenous cultures from their arrival in the 1500s and contributed their eating habits and some foods to the cuisine. In the following centuries, French cooking techniques were embraced, as was the food influence of those who came from Britain, Germany, Italy, and other countries.

The vineyards in the Elqui Valley, Chile often contrast beautifully with the dry valley walls and the clear, blue sky above. (iStockPhoto)

🍽 Food Culture Snapshot

Juan and Cynthia live in Santiago's upscale suburb of Barrio Los Condes. Juan works in his family's fruit export business. Cynthia is a housewife. They have two children, ages 8 and 12. Juan's family history has British roots that date back to the early 1800s, mixed with both Indian and Spanish ancestry from the 1500s and before. Cynthia is from the south of Chile, where her family's German ancestors settled in the late 19th century.

Cynthia shops several times a week in both the nearby supermarket and the *feria,* the open-air markets. Daily meals are planned around fish (shrimp, mussels, and conger eel, as well as farm-raised salmon), beef, or chicken, served alone and in soups and stews, often with rice or mashed potatoes and fresh vegetables, especially salads with lettuces, avocados, tomatoes, carrots, green beans, and others. Cynthia serves such fresh fruit as apricots, peaches, cherries, plums, *lúcuma* (a fist-sized green or yellowish fruit with a big brown pit), pears, grapes, strawberries, and cherimoyas, which grow in abundance in Chile's Central Valley. Fruit is served at every meal except breakfast, alone or with pudding or cake for dessert.

During the week, the family eats breakfast together. Juan eats the midday meal out with business associates, and the children eat lunch at school. Cynthia has a sandwich or salad at home. When the children return from school, Cynthia sits down with them for *onces,* a light teatime snack. Cynthia and Juan have a maid who comes in daily to help prepare meals and do household work. The family eats together in the early evening. Occasionally, Cynthia and Juan go out for dinner out about 9:30 in the evening.

On weekends, *almuerzo,* the midday meal, is a relaxed dinner, sometimes consisting of several courses. Often, they invite their siblings and their families or friends, or they join them as guests. Guests may be invited for weekend onces, a heartier version of the weekday snack, including a selection of pastries, as well as bread and cheese, desserts, and tea and coffee.

Major Foodstuffs

Chilean cooking draws on thousands of years of food traditions. The rugged *altiplano* in Chile's north is still home to the Aymara and Atacama Indians, who herd llamas, alpaca, and sheep in the high desert adjacent to Bolivia and Peru and grow potatoes, quinoa, and barley. Today, quality olive oil and Chile's famous *pisco* (distilled alcohol) come from this region.

In the south, the Mapuche cook from the ancient food trilogy of potatoes, corn, and beans. The Mapuche also raise livestock and gather the piñon, the pine-cone seed of the araucaria, or monkey puzzle tree. These ingredients, as well as squash, the grain quinoa, and chilies, are found in many of Chile's most popular modern dishes; the style is called *Chile Criolla.* Chilean Creole cuisine grew out of the melding of Spanish and indigenous foods and cooking methods.

The Spanish introduced grapes, citrus and other fruits, olives, nuts, rice, sugar, and garlic to Chile, as well as chicken, cattle, sheep, pigs, and rabbits. Milk, cheese, and chorizo were all Spanish contributions. Spanish food had already been influenced by medieval Moorish cuisine when the Spanish arrived in Chile in the 1500s. The fried bread sopaipilla, made with pumpkin and lard, has Arab pastries as its ancestor, for example.

Fruits and vegetables in Chile, largely grown in the Central Valley, are of the best quality and widely available throughout the country. Grapes, plums, apples, cherries, peaches, nectarines, berries, and avocados are diet staples. Native Andean fruits include cherimoya, the custard apple; lúcuma, a fruit with orange flesh, a sweet aroma, and a slightly bittersweet flavor that is pureed for creamy fillings and ice cream; and the *pepino dulce,* related to the tomato but with a mild melon flavor. The modern strawberry has a berry ancestor native to Chile.

The country's unusual geography means that fresh fish and seafood are never more than 100 miles away from most of the population. However, it's bread that the Chileans eat most often, about 200 pounds per person per year, second only to the Germans worldwide. About 80 percent of the bread is purchased fresh daily from bakeries, often carried warm from the shop. Fresh bread is the basis of breakfast and of the late-afternoon onces. Pasta is a diet staple in Chile. Rice is eaten less often.

Fish and seafood choices abound in Chile. Paleontologists have found and studied piles of shells from ancient meals of clams, abalones, and mussels, dating back 12,000 to 14,000 years. The diversity of Chilean fish and seafood is owed to the Humboldt Current, which carries frigid water from Antarctica northward along the west coast of South America. Chileans enjoy *centolla* (the king crab), *albacora* (albacore tuna), *pejerreyes* (whiting), *bacalao* (cod), *róbalo* (haddock), *merluza* (hake), *almejas* (clams), *choritos* (sea barnacles), *erizo* (sea urchin), and *jurel* (mackerel). Among the species distinct to Chile are *machas* (clams), *congrio* (conger eel), *cholgas* (mussels), and *locos* (Chilean abalones).

Fish is an important export, both as whole fish and as processed fishmeal. Salmon and trout are farmed intensively in southern Chile, raising concerns about disease and pollution, even while Chile has become the second-largest exporter of salmon worldwide after Norway. *Corvina* (Chilean sea bass) has been overfished to the point of concern about extinction.

Seaweed has been eaten in Chile for as long as seafood has. Seaweed varieties are nutritional powerhouses, being excellent sources of iodine, iron, protein, and such trace elements as cobalt copper, and manganese. Traditionally, seaweed was an inexpensive meat substitute. The variety *chochayuyo* grows up to 50 feet long among the coastal rocks and is a substitute for meat in the stew *charquicán,* which is renamed *charquicán de chochayuyo* when made with seaweed.

Grass-fed Chilean beef is leaner and less tender than the beef raised across the border in Argentina. Beef, pork, and chicken often are grilled or used as the basis for soups and stews. In southern Chile, there are excellent hams and sausages, a result of the area's German food traditions. Patagonian lamb is prized for its flavor due to the grass varieties on which the sheep graze. Chile's most popular cheese is the semihard, ripened *chanco,* known for its soursalty flavor and tiny holes. It accounts for half of all the cheese sold in the country.

The traditional indigenous tea, maté, is served in a special cup with a filtered straw designed especially for the drink. The cup's shape is based on the gourds that people used for the drink hundreds of years ago. Yerba maté's dried green leaves are high in vitamin C and antioxidants. The drink is enjoyed throughout South America, in Brazil, Argentina, Paraguay, and Uruguay, as well as in Chile.

Chilean cuisine has several ingredients, spices, and seasonings distinct to the country. Caramelized sweetened condensed milk, *manjar,* is spread on bread and poured over fruit. The Mapuche spice *merquén* (*merken*) is enjoying a resurgence in contemporary dishes as chefs and home cooks find new ways to use this mixture of dried, smoked chilies, cumin, coriander, and salt. Chili peppers are used in Chilean cooking but only lightly. The cuisine is not spicy hot, though the ground, hot Andean chili pepper, *ají,* is a common ingredient but in small amounts. *Ají de color* is Chile's paprika and a necessary ingredient in the traditional dishes. Chileans serve the salsa *pebre* in restaurants and at home with empanadas, sopaipillas, scrambled eggs, and grilled chorizo. In short, pebre's combination of finely chopped garlic, chilies, onions, cilantro, salt, oregano, vinegar or lemon juice, and tomatoes goes with everything.

Wines

Long before the Spanish arrived, the Mapuche and other indigenous people made fermented beverages from fruit, potatoes, and the grains corn and quinoa. The Mapuche called it *chichi.* Today, it's made from lightly fermented grapes or apples and widely drunk in rural areas and for Chilean Independence Day.

A Spanish priest planted the first vineyard in Chile in 1548 to fulfill the sacramental need for wine. Wine production grew far beyond the needs of the Catholic Church, and wine was even exported to Peru and Mexico during colonization. Chile's ideal combination of hot, sunny summers, frost-free winters, good soils, and optimum humidity proved to be splendid; it is now considered one of the best wine-growing regions in the world.

Spanish grapes gave way to French vines in 1851, with more sophisticated wines resulting from the Old World Cabernet Sauvignon, Cot (Malbec),

Foods typically found in Chile including cazuela, bread, fruit, and pebre. (Ene | Dreamstime.com)

Merlot, Pinot Noir, Sauvignon Blanc, Sémillion, and Riesling varieties. By the late 1800s, Chilean wines won acclaim in Europe as the vineyards thrived. When the tiny phylloxera aphid infested and destroyed the original plants in France, Chile's geographic isolation proved an advantage, leaving its vineyards untouched. The industry was further aided when French, Italian, and Spanish winemakers brought their expertise to Chile as immigrants in the late 1800s. Chilean winemaking stagnated under political constraints in the mid-20th century.

In 1979 a Spanish winery introduced state-of-the-art winemaking technology. When democracy returned to Chile in 1990, the wine industry was poised for innovation and success. There are at least dozen wine-growing valleys in Chile, the newest just a few miles from the Pacific Ocean. In the 1990s DNA testing proved that one grape variety considered to be Merlot was actually Carmenére, a grape believed lost in the aphid devastation a century earlier. A further distinction for Chilean wines is research that has shown that its Cabernet Sauvignon has the highest levels in the world of antioxidant flavonols, which have a protective effect against heart disease.

Another Chilean signature, also claimed by Peru, is pisco, the basis for the cocktail *pisco sour.* Named for a pre-Incan bird, pisco has been produced since the 1500s, at first from the inferior grapes not used for wine. Peru's pisco, generally, has a more refined flavor. Chile's robust, clear, brandy-like liquor is produced from Muscat, Torontel, and Pedro Jiménez varieties in the microclimate valleys of the Atacama Desert and Coquimbo. Chileans and Peruvians both claim, as well, the cocktail pisco sour, made by blending pisco, lemon juice, powdered sugar, and ice. Finally, Chile has a wealth of *bajativos,* liqueurs made from the whole range of Chilean fruits: raspberries, strawberries, blackberries, peaches, plums, and even celery. These after-dinner drinks are meant to be sipped and aid digestion.

Cooking

Chileans have modern kitchens separate from the dining area. Middle- and upper-class families hire household help, who may do the cooking with or without added help from the woman of the house. Kitchens have gas or electric ranges with ovens; only upscale homes have dishwashers. Kitchens are stocked with the pots and pans that are familiar to North Americans.

Common cooking techniques are roasting, baking, stewing, and frying. Knives are kept sharp for chopping fresh vegetables for the variety of Chilean salads. Small kitchen appliances such as food processors are uncommon. However, green beans have their own tool, a tiny hand-held gadget that shreds a single bean at a time.

An *asado* (roast) is a relaxed outdoor meal in Chile. The open gas or charcoal grills are the man's domain. Chilean asado calls for large, boneless cuts of meat and long cooking times. *Choripán,* literally *chorizo en pan,* or sausages in bread, are grilled alongside the meat and served while the main-dish meat cooks.

Typical Meals

Chileans' daily eating habits are much more alike than the dramatically diverse geography of the country would suggest. Chileans eat three to four meals a day, starting with *desayuno* (breakfast), followed by the day's large midday meal, almuerzo (lunch), onces (afternoon tea), and *la cena* (supper) in the evening. Evening restaurant dining is always late, about 9:30 P.M.

Desayuno is built around bread, either rolls or toast, often warm from the bakery and eaten with cheese, butter, and thick fruit jams. The most popular bread in Chile is *marraqueta,* also known as *pan batido,* a French-style roll with a fold in the middle. It has a soft center and medium crust. Dimpled rolls called *hallalas* are a richer version of the same white-flour bread but made with lard. When bread is made at home, *pan amasado* is the classic recipe. Even one of Chile's national dishes is bread based. The meat-filled empanada uses tender yeast dough as the wrapping. Fruit is not universal at breakfast. Across a range of backgrounds, fruit is considered detrimental to digestion in the morning if eaten with milk products.

Chileans drink coffee or tea with breakfast and for afternoon tea, as well as after meals. Chileans' coffee of choice is instant Nescafé, usually prepared with hot milk and served as *café con leche.* When Nescafé was introduced in Chile in the 1970s, it became an instant hit as a large number of people chose it over brewed coffee, now called *café-café.* Brewed coffee is available in the growing number of coffee shops, including international chains, as well as upon request in restaurants.

Traditionally, the midday meal has been the centerpiece of an afternoon break from school and work between 1 and 4 P.M., allowing time for a leisurely lunch and a nap. Urban dwellers in Santiago and increasingly in Valparaiso have adopted a schedule that omits the afternoon break. Children eat lunch at school, and working Chileans eat almuerzo away from home. The tradition continues in smaller cities and in rural areas during the week. In urban centers on weekends, almuerzo remains a relaxed break in the day.

Families sit together at the table for the meal. Meals can be relaxed or served in several courses, including an *entrada* (appetizer), perhaps *sopa* (soup) or pasta before the *plato de fondo,* a hearty main course with meat or fish, followed by a *postre* (dessert) and coffee or tea. Wine may be served with the meal and a bajativo (liqueur) afterward.

Main dishes are as simple as grilled fish or meat or a casserole or stew. *Chile Criolla* dishes are popular for family meals. *Pastel de choclo* is a classic with its layer of *pino* (seasoned beef filling laced with raisins, olives, and quartered hard-boiled eggs) and whole pieces of chicken topped with sugar-crusted corn pudding. Chile's empanadas may be baked or fried and filled with pino, seafood, or cheese. The chicken soup called *cazuela de gallina* is filled with chicken, potatoes, and pumpkin. Chile's tamale is called *humita.* The bean dish *porotos granados* is made with dried beans, pumpkin, corn, garlic, and onions.

Pastel de Choclo

Serves 8–10

6–8 medium ears corn on the cob, or 3½ c fresh or frozen, defrosted corn kernels

4 tbsp butter

¼ c milk

2 eggs

8 basil leaves, thinly sliced

4 tbsp vegetable oil, divided

1 lb boneless chicken breasts, cut in 3-in. pieces

Salt and pepper to taste

1 lb very lean ground beef

2 medium onions, chopped

2–3 cloves garlic, minced

2 tsp paprika

1–2 tsp ground cumin

1 tsp salt

½ tsp ground black pepper

¼ c raisins, soaked in hot water for 20 minutes and drained

12 black olives

2 hard-boiled eggs, quartered

¼ c confectioners' sugar

If using corn on the cob, grate corn into a bowl. Or process corn kernels in batches in a food processor. In a medium saucepan, heat butter and milk, add corn, and cook over medium heat until mixture boils and thickens, about 5 minutes. Remove from heat. Whisk the eggs in a bowl. Spoon a few tablespoons of the warm liquid into the eggs and whisk again. Then stir into the corn mixture, all at once, along with the basil leaves. Stir until thickened and bubbly, about 7 minutes. Set aside.

In a large skillet, heat 1 to 2 tablespoons oil, add chicken, seasoned with salt and pepper to taste, and sauté over medium heat until browned on all sides and cooked through, about 15 minutes. Remove and keep warm.

In the same skillet, heat 1 to 2 tablespoons of the remaining oil. Add ground beef and cook until lightly browned. Drain if necessary. Stir in onions and cook until translucent. Stir in garlic, paprika, cumin, salt, pepper, raisins, and olives, and let cook about 5 minutes to blend flavors.

To assemble: Place beef filling in a 3-quart casserole and press chicken into filling. Distribute hard-boiled eggs over the surface. Top with the corn pudding to seal the edges. Sift confectioners' sugar over the top. Place in a 350°F oven and bake for 30 to 40 minutes or until golden brown and bubbly.

Chile's seafood inspired the Nobel Laureate Pablo Neruda to write "Ode to Conger Chowder" in honor of *caldillo congrio,* with its oniony-tomato broth. *Chupe de mariscos* is a rich casserole of shellfish baked with bread and cheese. Chilean clams are enjoyed baked as *machas de la Parmesana.* The seafood platter *mariscal* joins a selection of fresh seafood with an irresistible chopped green sauce of green onion, cilantro, parsley, chilies, and salt.

Chile's fresh vegetables are as ubiquitous as its fruits and often served as salads. Chile's signature salad, *ensalada Chilena,* is simply fresh tomatoes and slices of onion dressed with oil and vinegar and a sprinkle of cilantro or parsley and salt and pepper.

Desserts often feature Chile's wonderful fruits. One of the simple favorites is sliced bananas, apples, or peaches with either sweetened condensed milk or the caramelized version called manjar. Other fruit desserts include ice cream, compotes, baked flan (custard) mixed with fruits, and crisp meringues topped with fruit and whipped cream.

The late-afternoon onces ranges from a quick snack after school to a more substantial meal including bread, cheese, meats, butter, and jam, along with hot chocolate, maté, café con leche, or tea. A hearty onces may be the day's final meal. For a home evening meal, Chileans have vegetable salads, pizza, pasta, empanadas, or lighter fish, meat, or chicken dishes. Fruit, again, is dessert.

In the Andean highlands, the regional specialty is *charqui,* dried meat, from llamas, goats, or cattle. The English name *jerky* for dried, seasoned meat comes from *charqui,* coined by the Spanish. The stew of vegetables and jerky called charquicán is considered a Chilean original.

Residents of Chiloé, an island in the south of Chile, keep alive an outdoor seafood bake tradition called *curanto,* similar to a New England clambake and many Native American earth oven traditions. The process starts with stones, spread in a hole in the ground and covered with a blazing wood fire. Once the stones are hot, the cook assembles layers of *nalca* (Chilean rhubarb) or cabbage leaves,

Typical chilean dish named curanto, based on shellfish. (Francisco Javier Espuny | Dreamstime.com)

chorizo, mussels, clams or other seafood, pork chops, chicken legs, potatoes, other vegetables, and the dense potato-wheat bread called *chapaleles,* finishing with a layer of leaves before covering it with earth to seal in the heat while the food cooks. Cooks steam smaller proportions in a pot on the rangetop.

Eating Out

In the mid-19th century wealthy Chileans brought French chefs to cook for their families. Later the chefs opened restaurants. Santiago's elegant Restaurant del Hotel Crillon embodied the ideal led by Chef Carlos Aranda, who published a cookbook in 1951. The introduction promises foods from the "heroic land" of the Three Musketeers including cassoulet, coq au vin, and *tripes a la mode.*

French and Continental European influence dominated Chilean restaurants until recently. While those traditions continue in high-end places, Chile's economic prosperity has fueled a wider restaurant bonanza especially in Santiago and Valparaiso. To the benefit of both adventurous chefs and appreciative diners, creative cuisine is thriving in Chile alongside the quality of its wines.

Many Peruvians have immigrated to Chile during the economic expansion and have opened restaurants featuring a cuisine that is one of the world's oldest and most diverse. The restaurants are among Santiago's most popular, ranging from inexpensive to highly sophisticated. Chilean Peruvian food tends to be less spicy than in Peru. Celebrated *cebiche,* citrus-marinated fish laced with onions and seasonings, comes in many forms. The potato holds a place of honor in Peruvian cooking in such dishes as *causa rellena,* yellow potatoes mashed with lime and hot pepper and stuffed with chicken or fish. Diners love *lomo saltado:* sautéed beef with onions, tomatoes, and chilies over French fries. *Suspiro limeño* is a meringue-topped vanilla custard.

Chilean *parrilladas* are grill restaurants offering meats, sweetbreads, and sausages cooked over an open fire. They are another restaurant category that ranges from the cheap to the most expensive ones, which feature seared meats or fish over foie gras. In the middle range, Italian and Middle Eastern restaurants are abundant, as are Cantonese Chinese places. There are a growing number of Japanese, Southeast Asian, Indian, and Korean restaurants as well.

Renewed interest in indigenous foods and the *Chile Criolla* tradition is influencing the country's chefs. Chefs from a selection of the country's restaurants are promoting Chilean food products abroad, and their energy, in turn, is bringing fresh interpretations back to familiar dishes. The *picadas* (small joints) are the places to find such home cooking as *arrolloado* (pork roll) and delicious *cazuelas* (stews). Then there's the famous pork sandwich, *lomito:* slow-cooked, marinated pork with avocado, tomato, and mayo, and even cheese and sauerkraut, piled high on a six-inch-wide bun.

Locals still eat at the picadas in Santiago's Central Market, operated continuously since 1872 in a classic art nouveau structure. The market has seafood restaurants and stalls selling fresh fish, fruits, vegetables, free-range poultry, goat cheese, local olives, and Chilean wine. Markets with good food for diners and shoppers are found elsewhere in Santiago and the length of Chile in the larger cities. Valparaiso has the Cardonal and Bombay Port, La Serena's market is called Revoca, and Angelmo is near Puerto Montt. Temuco, the heart of Mapuche culture, has the Municipal Market. Markets are also found in Coquimbo, Chillan, Concepción, and other cities of size.

In general, restaurant diners find salt but not pepper on restaurant tables. Usually, there's a cruet of vegetable oil to drizzle on potatoes and other side dishes. Salads are dressed simply with vegetable oil and vinegar or lemon juice. Many restaurants provide two napkins: one for the lap, the other for daubing the mouth during dining.

Special Occasions

The highlights of the national Chilean calendar are Christmas, New Year's, and September 18, Chilean Independence Day. Fiesta Patrias commemorates Chile's 1810 independence from Spain. The official date is September 18, but in reality, the celebrations go on for a week or more in homes and in fairs set up across the width and length of the country. The holiday centers around the asado, the outdoor barbecue, and the foods highlight the indigenous-Spanish Chile Criolla traditions. Menus feature empanadas, the meat pies filled with meats, seafood, or cheese; choripán, grilled sausage on a French roll; *anticuchos,* skewers of grilled beef, pork, chicken, and onions; bowls of pastel de choclo; and even whole roasted pig and lamb. For dessert there's *mote con huesillo,* a drink made of wheat berries and dried peaches. Chileans wash it all down with wine, beer, the lightly alcoholic *chicha,* soft drinks, coffee, and tea.

Chile remains largely a Catholic country, if a less strictly observant one than during much of its 450-year history. Christmas is a warm-weather holiday with beach vacations. The cultural symbols have been adapted from the Northern Hemisphere including nativity scenes of the Holy Family, Christmas trees, and snow suggested by puffs of cotton. Children anticipate the arrival of the *Viejito Pascuero* (Old Man Christmas) in full costume by reindeer-drawn sleigh. The bearer of gifts enters homes through the window instead of the chimney.

On December 24, families gather for midnight mass. Then, the holiday feasting begins, which may include roast turkey, beef, or chicken, or salmon or shrimp, accompanied by fresh vegetable salads, potatoes, tomatoes, avocados, peas, carrots, celery, green beans, and, of course, fresh bread. Chile's Christmas bread is *pan de Pascua,* packed with nuts, raisins, candied fruit, and spices. It resembles Italian panettone. In the south of Chile, there's always the German Christmas bread, stollen. While children open presents, the adults share glasses of *cola de mono* ("monkey's tail"), a rum- and milk-soaked coffee drink, served cold with a cinnamon stick. Holiday desserts range from *buche de noel* (Yule log cake) and Black Forest cake to layered meringue cakes filled with creamy cherimoya, raspberry, or lúcuma fillings. Strawberries, blueberries, and raspberries are stirred into mousse and layered into trifles.

A week later, families celebrate *Feliz Año Nuevo.* Traditionally, serving lentil stew with chorizo or lentil soup brings good luck for the coming year. Besides wine, Chileans toast with wine-and-fruit mixtures such as *borgoña* (red wine with strawberries) or white wine with peaches, ending with bajativos, the after-dinner liqueurs made from Chile's endless selection of fruits.

In addition to birthdays, saint's days have traditionally been celebrated in Chile. A saint's day notes the birth date of a saint in the Catholic Church. For example, Saint Francis was born on October 3, and that is the saint's day for those named Francisco or Francesca. When families gather in honor of a birthday or saint's day, the centerpiece is *torta de mil hojas.* The cake starts with either wafer-thin cookie slices, thin layers of baked cake, or pancakes that are layered with a creamy *dulce de leche* (cooked-down caramelized milk), often homemade, frosted with meringue, and finished with fresh fruit or flowers.

Diet and Health

Chile's traditional diet—the blend of indigenous foods and those introduced by the Spanish—forms the basis of a diet with plenty of fruits and vegetables, legumes, grains, dairy foods, abundant seafood, and some meat. Until the late 20th century, many Chileans practiced this variation of the nutrient-dense, lower-fat Mediterranean diet coupled with a lifestyle that brought families together at the table for meals. During the midday meal break from 1 to 4 P.M., offices and schools closed, giving a relaxing break from school and work. At the same time, among Chile's poorest citizens, malnutrition and infant mortality were high.

Chile's growing economic prosperity from the 1990s on fueled a radical change in eating habits across the entire population. Malnutrition practically disappeared, infectious diseases decreased, and life expectancy increased to one of the highest in South America. The Chilean story is similar to the one in many countries where the abandonment of traditional foods and lifestyle choices and the choice of more highly processed foods and faster-paced urban lives have been followed by an increase in childhood obesity (at 20.8% for primary-school students in 2008) and risk for cardiovascular disease.

A vendor at the fish market in the Pacific port of Puerto Montt, Chile. (StockPhotoPro)

Heart disease is the cause of 28 percent of deaths, topping all other causes.

Chronic illness, including high blood pressure and obesity related to cardiovascular disease, increased significantly. Researchers are limited by the fact that Chile doesn't collect nationwide nutrition data. They rely on targeted studies, including a 2003 *National Health Survey* reporting that 38 percent of adult Chileans were overweight and 23 percent were obese, with higher rates among women and in lower socioeconomic groups. A third of Chileans had high blood pressure.

Chileans are selecting more energy-dense foods and meat for an average 25 percent increase in both calorie and fat consumption between 1988 and 1998. Per-capita consumption of soft drinks and tea is among the highest in the world. More people in Chile have moved to the cities, and rates of alcohol and drug abuse have increased. Add to that the high incidence of smoking (42% of adults) and

the serious air pollution in Santiago, one of Latin America's most polluted cities. Chileans are also not keen to exercise: 90 percent of adult Chileans report a sedentary lifestyle.

One unusual finding in Chile's nutrition transition has been among the indigenous rural populations, who continue a traditional diet along with plenty of physical activity growing crops and tending animals. Despite being among the poorest of Chileans, the Mapuche in southern Chile and the Aymara in the north have each been found to have a very low incidence of diabetes. However, when the Mapuche move to an urban setting (about 60% of Mapuche are urbanites), the numbers of diabetics doubles from 4.1 to 9.8 percent, as does obesity. Among the rural Aymara, the incidence of diabetes was 1 percent. Researchers are intrigued because, unlike the rural Aymara and Mapuche, North American Indians, rural as well as urban, have epidemic rates of diabetes. Preliminary data point to the preventive effect of the traditional diet and the activity it takes to produce it.

Chile does have a well-established national public health system with a succession of rural posts, public health centers, and hospitals. Since the mid-1990s, those involved in nutrition programs and academia have been actively advocating to better link that system with a stronger nutrition policy. Through that system, health-promotion messages have increased across the country, and programs have begun in schools to promote exercise and better eating habits. Advocates are pushing for laws to restrict advertising for cigarettes and alcohol and to limit advertising for energy-dense, nutrient-poor foods on television, especially during children's prime viewing times.

Mary Gunderson

Further Reading

Caskey, Liz. "Chilean Food and Wine Experiences." *Eat Wine.* http://eatwineblog.com/.

Del Pilar Roa Baker, Gloria. "Chilean Home Cooking." *Canela Kitchen.* http://canelakitchen.blogspot.com.

"Flavors of Chile for the World." Pro Chile. http://www.chileinfo.com/publicaciones.php.

Freire, Wilma. *Nutrition and an Active Life: From Knowledge to Action.* Washington, DC: Pan American Health Organization, Regional Office of the World Health Organization, 2005.

Lovera, José Rafael. *Food Culture in South America.* Westport, CT: Greenwood Press, 2005.

Reyes, Carlos. "Chilean Food and Restaurant Guide." *Unocome.* http://unocome.blogspot.com/.

Stuart, James. "Chilean Food, History, and Culture from Santiago." *Eating Chile.* http://eatingchile.blogspot.com/.

Umaña-Murray, Mirtha. *Three Generations of Chilean Cuisine.* Los Angeles: Lowell House, 1996.

Van Waerebeek-Gonzalez, Ruth. *The Chilean Kitchen.* New York: HP Books, 1999.

Colombia

Overview

Among the cuisines of South America, Colombia is second only to Peru in combining the culinary traditions of the native populations with those of the Europeans who arrived in the 1500s. The country's long coastline and historical trade routes have also fostered a strong Afro-Caribbean influence. That hybridization, along with the varied produce of a country with several distinct climatic regions, makes Colombian cuisine particularly interesting to study.

The volcanic Andes Mountains divide into three roughly parallel ranges as they enter Colombia, so that broad plateaus and valleys of high fertility occupy the center of the country. Those valleys, called the *tierra templada,* comprise only 6 percent of the land area but support over a quarter of the country's population. Along the Pacific coast are the world's rainiest tropical jungles, a sparsely populated area broken up by slow-moving rivers. The Caribbean coast is more dry and hospitable and includes relatively temperate zones, vast marshy lowlands, and a desert peninsula. The Andean foothills extend to this area, and the majority of the country's population is in this region where the central highlands slope to the Caribbean. Colombia also has sovereignty over a Caribbean archipelago that has an Anglo-African culture with no Spanish roots.

The natural flora of most of the country is thick jungle, which provided abundant fruit and game to hunter-gatherers, and there are still tribes that live in the same way as their Neolithic ancestors. The principal preconquest tribes of Colombia were the Tairona (or Tayrona) along the Caribbean coast and the Muisca in the highlands to the south. Both the Muisca and Tairona developed urban centers, and a Spanish chronicler of 1538 noted extensive plantings of potatoes, maize, and cassava in the highlands. The natives also raised beans, chili peppers, *arracacha* and malanga roots, and squashes. The coastal Tairona ate seafood, tortoises, manatees, tapirs, and iguanas and raised cassava. Their diet included fruits such as the tamarillo, papaya, guava, *guanábana* (soursop), and passion fruit, but whether these were actively cultivated before the arrival of Europeans is open to question. Lake and river fish were caught; insects, including snails and ant queens, were eaten; and they may have raised animals to supplement the birds and game that they hunted. There was some commercial activity in food and spices; coastal Taironas developed a salt trade with the interior tribes, though not with the Muisca, who had their own mines in the highlands.

About the only cooked item in modern Colombian cuisine that we can be certain is the same as a Mesoamerican dish is the arepa. This corn pancake probably gets its name from a word for corn in the Chibcha language, which was spoken by the Muisca and other tribes. (It is hard to tell because speaking Chibcha was illegal from 1770 until 1991.) In its most basic form an arepa is a thick fried cake made of ground corn, water, and salt, but modern arepas are often stuffed with cheese or topped with salad. A relative of the arepa, called the *casabe* and made from cassava root, is native to the area around the border between Colombia and Venezuela. Though it is now associated with Venezuela, it was probably eaten all along the southern Caribbean seaboard.

Arepa, breads made of corn flour popular in Colombia and Venezuela, usually filled with egg or cheese. (Raphael Chay | Dreamstime.com)

The natives also brewed a kind of corn beer and, in the highlands, made both alcoholic and nonalcoholic versions of *chicha,* a beverage incorporating corn and fruit. The latter caught on with the Spanish, who added citrus; in 1627, when Fray Pedro Simon first recorded it, he noted that the Spanish had "made it cleaner, more curious and gifted."

The colonial era brought Spanish techniques and ingredients that became integral to Colombian cuisine. The tierra templada of Colombia was the only part of northern South America suited to large-scale cattle ranching, and the importance of this industry led to the establishment of the Viceroyalty of New Granada, centered at Santa Fe de Bogotá, in 1739. The administrators in Bogotá were primarily from the Spanish regions of Andalusia, Aragon, and Valencia, and they brought a taste for paella and blood pudding that survives to this day. Though they initially tried to keep their culture and cuisine as Spanish as possible, in time native foods became part of their diet and a cuisine called *criolla* was born. This used Spanish foods such as pork, beef, chicken, and cheese along with imports from other parts of the empire such as plantains, rice, carrots, and sweet potatoes.

Bogotá's rival for cultural precedence was Cartagena, the gateway to the Caribbean, which had the advantage of being the port of call for the Spanish galleons and the disadvantage of frequent raids by pirates and enemy forces. Cartagena developed a distinctive seafood-heavy cuisine that uses the locally popular *sabalo* fish as well as shrimp, sea bream, carp, and the tiny local oysters. Among the signatures of Cartagena-style food is abundant use of coconut milk and rice. Plantains, originally imported by Portuguese missionaries from Southeast Asia, are eaten in many ways, including the delightfully named "kitten's head," in which they are baked and mashed with fried pork and pork skin.

The exceptional example of Afro-Caribbean cuisine in Colombia is the Raizal cuisine of the San Andrés and Providencia islands, which are owned by Colombia even though they are far closer to Nicaragua. The typical dish here is *rondón,* consisting of fish, sea snails, breadfruit, yucca root, and plantain boiled in coconut milk.

🍽 Food Culture Snapshot

Santiago and Carolina live in a high-rise building on the edge of Bogotá and wake up every workday at 6 A.M. when the radio plays the national anthem. Like most of the inhabitants (who refer to themselves as *Santafereñas*), they enjoy a breakfast of *changua,* soup made from eggs poached in milk with scallions, cilantro, and bread. This they wash down with locally grown coffee, strong and black. They feed their children—Alvaro, Ernesto, and Maria—the same breakfast before sending them to school, though instead of coffee, the children drink fruit juice. It isn't necessary to pack a lunch for them, because, as in many schools, a lunchroom serves healthy meals. The children would rather run to a nearby stand that sells *perro caliente Colombiano*—the Colombian hot dogs that are topped with coleslaw, pineapple, ketchup, mustard, mayonnaise, and potato chips—but Carolina does not approve of junk food.

Santiago drives to his job in the accounting department for a coffee broker, while Carolina takes a bus to the hospital where she is an administrator. Her mother is old-fashioned and would prefer that she stay at home, but like almost half the women in the country, Carolina prefers to work. She doesn't expect to rise to executive level nor to join the men who are at that level for social occasions, but she takes her morning snack, known as a *medias nueves,* with co-workers at a similar level in the hierarchy. The medias nueves is likely to be a roll with coffee or a glass of *aguapanela,* a drink made from sugarcane and water.

Santiago and Carolina have their main meal of the day around one in the afternoon, both dining with their coworkers. Since Carolina works for a hospital, her place of business does not close, but like most of Colombia, Santiago's department closes for lunch. She eats at the hospital's canteen, while he dines at a fine restaurant, but both have similar meals; they start with a bowl of *sancocho,* meat or fish stewed with yucca, plantain, and vegetables. The second course, called *el seco,* or the "dry dish," is usually a grilled fish or meat, and it is followed by a glass of juice and coffee. After lunch, anyone who can fit it into their schedule takes a brief nap, the siesta, awakening refreshed by 3 P.M. to go back to work.

Both Santiago and Carolina are home by 7 P.M. and help the children with their homework while drinking glasses of passion fruit or mango juice. Carolina doesn't start to make dinner until after 8—they won't be eating until 10 P.M. When they do, it is a light meal: arepas or empanadas, savory little corn-flour turnovers; fried green plantains called *patacones;* and a small portion of the soup called *ajiaco,* made with chicken, several kinds of potatoes, and the aromatic herb called *guasca.* Santiago prefers his patacones with a spoonful of *ají picante,* the vinegary hot sauce made with habanero peppers, but the rest of the family likes them plain or with a dusting of cheese. The adults have coffee, the children hot chocolate, and after dinner Santiago enjoys a glass of rum mixed with water, lime, sugar, and cinnamon.

On weekends the family invites friends over for an afternoon meal of empanadas, followed by *parrillada,* the traditional barbecued mixed grill. This is served with grilled or boiled corn on the cob, yucca or potatoes, and spicy green garlic sauce. Afterward, while the children play, the adults enjoy glasses of fermented chicha, the corn-based fruit punch that turns mildly alcoholic after a night in the refrigerator. They have to drink it all that day, since it turns sour quickly, but the sweet, fruity taste is so enjoyable that there is rarely any left. When Santiago and Carolina can get an aunt to watch their children, they enjoy going out to dine, usually at restaurants featuring food from Colombia rather than from other parts of the world. They enjoy the food of their own country and don't see a reason to go beyond its culinary borders.

Major Foodstuffs

Though the climate and altitude variations in Colombia are extreme, an extensive road system means that produce from all areas of the country is available in the cities. This has been true even during period of insurgency and civil unrest; it was dangerous for the drivers and transport workers, but fresh ocean fish was available in the highlands, and beef went from the plateaus to the lowlands.

This is especially impressive because Colombia's largest crops, bananas and coffee, are both grown more for export than local consumption. Colombians prefer green plantains to the yellow bananas that are popular overseas, and though they are voracious coffee drinkers, the greater part of the crop is grown with overseas sale in mind. In fact, though the coffee business employs fully one-fourth of the country's agricultural labor and coffee is the country's largest cash crop, the coffee served in cafés in Colombia is often not very good, since the best beans are exported. Lower-value beans stay at home and are often overroasted.

Colombia's lowlands produce sugarcane for both export and local consumption, but the sugar that stays in the country is not mixed into coffee—most Colombians drink theirs black and bitter. The sugar is refined into *panela,* a solid mass of fructose and sucrose sugars that is used in drinks and desserts, and the leftover molasses is made into local rum and *aguardiente,* a distilled clear spirit.

Other major lowland crops are rice, plantains, cassava, cocoa beans, tobacco, and fruit for both export and local consumption. The most popular fruits in Colombia are the coconut, passion fruit, orange, guanábana (soursop), mamey, mango, and varieties of guava, though star fruit, tamarillos, limes, cherimoyas, and others are eaten widely or made into juice drinks. Avocados are widely grown and used in soups and beverages, and tomatoes are a minor crop.

Colombian coffee farmer harvesting their coffee, 2006. (Hsahjd 2010 | Dreamstime.com)

in almost every restaurant. The tuna fishery on the west coast has long been important, but concerns about sustainability have led to restrictions and decline. Freshwater fish from the tributaries of the Amazon is also widely available. There are over 800 known species of freshwater fish in Colombia, but the most popular is catfish, which sometimes reaches colossal size. The *bocachico* fish used to be eaten widely, but the construction of a dam almost wiped out the species, causing concern about how ongoing water projects affect the sustainability of freshwater fisheries.

Pigs and chickens are raised and eaten everywhere, and in the mountains barbecued *cuy,* a breed of guinea pig, is regarded as a delicacy. Wild tapirs are eaten by natives of the Amazon but are not raised commercially, and their numbers have been falling due to overhunting.

Colombian cuisine is not highly spiced as a rule, though chili peppers and garlic are used in moderation in many dishes. The most distinctive native Colombian herb is guasca, which is slightly similar to basil. Other commonly used spices are cilantro, chives, cumin, onion, and achiote (annatto seed).

As the land rises from the Caribbean coast into the foothills of the Andes, cattle ranches and family farms growing corn, beans, yucca, and squash take over. Colombia exports beef and some cheese, but the country makes few aged cheeses; instead, there are soft farmer cheeses, cottage cheese, and the crumbly, slightly acidic *queso fresco* (fresh cheese). Milk is drunk by both adults and children, usually mixed with juices or cinnamon and other spices.

In the highlands, the staple is the potato—or rather, many different varieties of potatoes, each suited to different climates, altitudes, and purposes. Potatoes in Colombia come in colors from almost pure white and yellow to red and deep purple, and they vary in size from tiny spheres to large and irregular.

Fish, mussels, shrimp, and lobster from both the Caribbean and Pacific coasts are popular throughout the country, and the *mojarra* (tilapia) is offered

Cooking

Colombian cuisine is simple, and Colombian kitchens are comparatively free of the special gadgetry that is popular in many countries. Daily meals are rich in soups, and most kitchens will have many well-used large pots. In rural areas and in old-fashioned families, or among gourmets who have embraced traditional ideas, cooks will use "Tolima" clay pots of the type made by the Chamba people of the Magdalena River basin. This pearl-gray cookware has become a prestige item and is often displayed where guests may see it. Like all well-made clay cookware, it is naturally nonstick, holds heat, and heats food evenly. Since Chamba cookware has been discovered by outsiders and praised by modern cooking gurus such as Paula Wolfert in her book *Clay Pot Cooking,* the price of the best clay pots has risen to the point that many Colombians can't afford them.

Many Colombians believe that even soups and other items that never touch a fire will taste better when cooked over wood, so woodstoves are popular even where gas and electricity are available. Until the early 1990s, when tax laws designed to keep out imported items changed, electric kitchen appliances were very expensive. Their popularity has grown slowly but steadily, and one particular item has taken off—the electric arepa maker. Traditionalists scoff at these contraptions, which are similar to waffle irons, and claim superior flavor for old-fashioned arepas made in a cast iron skillet or using a special perforated grill that is set on a wood fire.

There will be a variety of skillets in any household, including a very large one that is used for *fritanga,* fried assorted meats. Most homes will also have an outdoor grill for making parrillada, or grilled meats. Large households may have a fire pit with a spit or a vertical roasting rack for this purpose.

Typical Meals

Though there are regional differences between the Afro-Caribbean–influenced northeast and the Andean-influenced southwest, some things about any Colombian meal are universal: There will be soup, there will be corn or rice, and fruit or fruit juice will make an appearance somewhere. This is not a society with a profound difference between the meals of the rich and the poor; the wealthy will have better-quality ingredients, eaten from nicer dishes and in more formal circumstances, but except among the very poorest or the tribes who are subsistence farmers or hunter-gatherers, the general pattern will be the same.

Poor people live like their remote ancestors on a diet of beans and rice supplemented with vegetables, small amounts of meat, and the fruit that grows wild and abundant in the jungles. The national bean of Colombia is the *cargamanto,* a large red bean with white flecks that is nutritious and high in protein. Black beans are fried and served with rice in a style similar to the Cuban dish "Christians and Moors," and white canary beans are boiled with onions and served as a side dish or used in soups.

Sopa de Frijoles Canarios (Canary Bean Soup)

This is a traditional Colombian dish. *Sazón preparado* is a popular seasoning mix throughout the Caribbean. The Goya brand is most popular in Colombia, but it contains more monosodium glutamate than many other versions.

Serves 6–8

Ingredients

1 garlic clove

¼ c onion, chopped

¼ c red bell pepper, chopped

¼ c green pepper, chopped

1 scallion, chopped

1 lb canary beans (or kidney, pinto, or cranberry beans), soaked overnight

2 lb pork ribs, cut into pieces

14 c water

2 c grated carrots

1 cube chicken bouillon

½ tbsp ground cumin

½ tbsp sazón preparado with saffron

½ c chopped cilantro

1 large potato, peeled and diced

Salt and pepper

1. In a food processor, combine garlic, onion, red bell pepper, green pepper, and scallion and process until finely chopped.

2. In a large pot over medium heat, combine the processed vegetables, beans, pork ribs, water, carrots, and chicken bouillon. Slightly cover and simmer for 1½ hours.

3. Add the ground cumin, sazón preparado, cilantro, and potato. Simmer for 30 to 40 minutes more, or until the beans are tender.

4. Season with salt and pepper. Serve with white rice and hot sauce on the side.

Even simple meals may begin with empanadas as an appetizer. Though savory turnovers called empanadas are found from Mexico all the way to Argentina, Colombian empanadas are different. First, they are usually fried rather than baked, and, second, they are made with a mixture of corn and wheat flour. Colombian empanadas are usually filled with a mixture of minced chicken and onion but may also be filled with beef or cheese. In the Caribbean region you might also have *carimañolas,* yucca fritters stuffed with meat or cheese and served with garlicky hot sauce. Plantains feature throughout Colombian meals and may be served as an appetizer, either cut into pieces and fried; sliced lengthwise and baked with cinnamon; or mashed, salted, and fried (called patacones).

The first main course is almost always soup, of which there are many varieties. The most popular nationwide is sancocho, originally from the Tolima region. The iconic version is made with a whole cut-up hen, sliced green plantains, yucca, corn, and potatoes. It is seasoned with salt, black pepper, cilantro, and a seasoning paste called *aliños* that is made from green and red bell pepper, onion, scallions, cumin, garlic, and saffron. Aliños is used as a soup base throughout Colombia, and every family has its own recipe.

There are other bases as well, such as *mazamorra,* ground corn soaked in fern ash or lye (similar to American hominy grits, and also known as *peto*). This features in *mazamorra chiquita,* a soup made of beef ribs, tripe, onions, green peas, lima beans, carrots, several types of potatoes, garlic, pepper, and cumin.

The Caribbean coast is home to the spiciest food in Colombia, which in practice often means the soups contain a larger amount of aliños. On both the long Caribbean coastline and the shorter and sparsely populated Pacific coast, soups with coconut milk, rice, and fish are popular. The most exceptional example of this type of soup is from the San Andrés and Providencia islands, which are owned by Colombia but are actually far closer to Nicaragua. The people and cuisine here are called Raizal, and their signature dish is rondón, made from fish, sea snails, breadfruit, yucca, and plantain simmered in coconut milk.

In a Colombian meal, following the soup is the seco, the dry dish. In coastal regions this will usually be fried or grilled seafood with coconut fried rice on the side. Inland, roasted chicken or beef is extremely popular. As with coffee, much of the best Colombian beef is exported, but the cuisine is rich in techniques for making the most of tougher cuts. A specialty of Bogotá is *sobrebarriga,* flank steak simmered in beer until it is extremely tender, then rolled in breadcrumbs and broiled. It is then served half-submerged in the beer broth, thus a steak served in soup.

Sobrebarriga Bogotá (Flank Steak)

Ingredients

2 lb flank steak

2 medium tomatoes, chopped

1 white onion, chopped

1 carrot, chopped

2 cloves garlic, chopped

1 tbsp Worcestershire sauce

1 tbsp prepared mustard

1 tbsp lime juice

1 bottle dark beer

Beef stock or water

2 tbsp melted butter

1 c breadcrumbs

Preparing the Roll (*Prep Time: 15 Minutes; Marinating Time: 24 Hours*)

1. Lay out flank steak on a cutting board and trim off excess fat.

2. In a bowl mix together tomatoes, onion, carrot, garlic, Worcestershire sauce, mustard, and lime juice.

3. Spread the mixture on the steak, and roll along the grain so that when you slice it, you will be cutting across the grain.

4. Secure the steak with butcher's twine. The easiest way is to tie a slip knot once every couple of inches.

5. Place the steak in a large freezer bag, pour over any filling that has leaked out, and allow to sit in the refrigerator for at least a day.

Cooking the Steak (*Cooking time: 2 Hours, 15 Minutes*)

1. Place steak in a large saucepan, and add the beer. Fill the pot with enough beef stock or water to fully submerge the steak.

2. Bring to a boil, and then reduce heat to low and allow to simmer for 2 hours.

3. Preheat broiler 15 minutes before the steak is ready.

4. Remove steak from the cooking liquid, and increase the heat to reduce the liquid to a sauce while you broil the steak.

5. Place the steak on a baking sheet and drizzle melted butter over the top of the steak, then sprinkle with breadcrumbs. Place under the broiler until the breadcrumbs have browned, about 10 minutes.

6. Remove from the broiler, remove twine, allow to sit for 10 minutes, and slice across the grain.

7. Skim any particles from the top of the cooking liquid, and then pour it into a gravy bowl.

Among the nontraditional but popular methods of cooking beef are marinades using Coca-Cola; the citric acid helps tenderize meat and also adds a touch of sweetness. Beef in Colombia is usually sliced very thin and served medium-well—a Colombian steak covers a plate but is still a modest portion compared with an English or American portion of roast beef or prime rib.

The quintessential celebratory dinner is par-rillada, a mixed grill that might be composed of beef, pork, tripe, *morcilla* (a blood sausage similar to boudin), sweet pork *longaniza* sausage, chorizo sausage heavily flavored with coriander, and other meats, served with corn and potatoes. If this same assemblage of meat is served fried instead of barbecued, it is called fritanga. By any name, it is an imposing spread that makes a siesta afterward seem like a wonderful idea.

Another dish with an impressive variety of meats is *bandeja paisa,* a combination of meats and vegetables from the region around Medellín in the northwest. This is a mixed grill distinguished by its accompaniments—the thinly sliced steak, pork skin with attached meat, and sausage are always accompanied by rice, beans, avocado, sweet fried plantains, arepas, and a fried egg.

To finish, Colombians enjoy simple desserts that are often based on milk, coconut milk, or fruits. Among the baked sweets is flan (custard), either plain or mixed with guava, pear, or other fruits. Fruit desserts include preserved *uchuva* (a type of gooseberry), tree-tomato juice, chopped fruit mixed in soda or orange juice, and fruit-stuffed crepes. Finally, there are simple sweet breads topped with *arequipe* caramel (the local version of *dulce de leche*) or ice cream. An unusual after-dinner sweet is candied *hormigas,* the queens of the world's largest species of ant. While the Guane Indians eat these ants fried as a savory, city dwellers prefer them enrobed in caramel or chocolate.

Bandeja paisa, a mixed grill distinguished by its accompaniments—the thinly sliced steak, pork skin with attached meat, and sausage are always accompanied by rice, beans, avocado, sweet fried plantains, arepas, and a fried egg. (StockPhotoPro)

Colombians of all ages enjoy fruit juices, either straight or mixed with milk, or aguapanela, sugarcane juice mixed with water. The other homemade soft drink is *chicha morada,* the traditional Andean fruit punch with corn and cinnamon. Chicha is usually homemade, but despite problems with a short shelf life, bottled versions have entered the market in the last decade. Colombians also enjoy sweet carbonated sodas, the most popular of which, Cola-Champaña, has been made by the Postobón company since 1904. Other popular bottled soft drinks are Pony Malta, a sweet nonalcoholic beer, and Kola Roman, a very sweet fruity drink popular in the Caribbean region. Colombiana, a tart soda made with tamarind, is also popular along the coast. In the mornings or on cool evenings, Colombians enjoy hot chocolate. In Bogotá this frequently has cheese melted into it and is called *santafereño.*

Among alcoholic drinks, the alcoholic version of chicha is popular, but there are no commercial producers due to its very short shelf life. Alcoholic chicha is drinkable for only about a week after it has finished fermenting—after that it turns very sharp and sour. Multiple attempts have been made to stabilize and commercialize chicha, but as of this writing none has been successful.

As might be expected in a hot country, beer is popular, with light lagers dominating the market. Rum drinks are popular, especially those that use local fruits, but it is also drunk with Coca-Cola or on the rocks. The other popular strong drink is aguardiente, a strongly flavored variant of rum that often contains anise. There is some regional market segmentation, with aguardiente most popular inland and rum drunk mainly along the coast.

Finally, there is coffee, the country's national beverage, which is drunk from morning to night by almost every adult. As might be expected, alcoholic coffee drinks involving rum or aguardiente and milk or cream are very popular as a nightcap.

Eating Out

While Colombians enjoy dining out, they are not generally adventurous, and the overwhelming majority of restaurants serve regional Colombian cuisine. The exception is at the high end, where the most expensive places boast their fidelity to traditional Spanish cuisine. In the last decade other European cuisines have achieved a foothold in major cities, but they are still struggling to find a market beyond business dinners and the most sophisticated younger people.

Restaurants are patronized at all times of day, with cafés specializing in breakfast, called *desayunerías,* opening very early. The slang word for restaurants serving home-style food is *corrientazo,* literally meaning "a place to get energy." Whether a simple corrientazo or a top-notch restaurant, the evening pattern is similar—they open for dinner at about 7 P.M., but the rush begins around 9, and people will still be dining until almost midnight. Tourists are often amazed that they can be seated in the best places at 7 or 8 and don't realize that by local standards that is ridiculously early. Tourists also stand out because they are excessively casual; at all but the most modest restaurants, people are expected to dress up for dinner. In most restaurants, as at Colombian homes, the oldest person will always be served first, and it is expected that even finger-friendly items like empanadas will be eaten with a knife and fork.

Special Occasions

As is the case throughout Central America, special versions of tamales appear at Christmas and Easter. One is the tamale Tolimense style, made with beef, pork, chicken, and vegetables with ground corn, boiled or steamed in corn-husk casings. Fruit and dessert tamales are also made. Colombian tamales are usually milder than Mexican versions but are otherwise similar and are almost always accompanied by hot chocolate.

Many Christmas pastry treats are deep-fried instead of baked. These include cheese fritters called *buñuelos* and *bolillas,* fried round doughnuts that are served with chocolate or coffee. *Hojuelas,* flat fried cookies topped with powdered sugar, are almost identical to the Polish Christmas cookie called *kruschicki,* though it is hard to establish a connection between the two seasonal treats. Other seasonal treats are *natilla,* a coconut-milk custard that is sometimes fortified with rum or aguardiente, and *champus,* a drink similar to chicha but with chunks of fruit, extra spices, and orange leaves added.

Diet and Health

The most famous living Colombian artist, Fernando Botero, famously portrays his countrymen as pudgy sensualists who are obsessed with food. His sometimes cruel, sometimes sympathetic portraits are an exaggeration of a fact; a 1999 study showed that over 40 percent of the country's citizens are obese, and that figure may be rising. It is ironic that a government that has historically focused on getting its rural and native citizens enough to eat now must change its focus to convincing them to switch to healthier foods. The popularity of sugary sodas and a diet heavy in meat, coconut milk, and cream, plus the increasing use of motor vehicles instead of walking for everyday tasks, are probably to blame. Colombians who can afford it often get weight-loss surgery rather than change their diets, and more of these operations are performed there than anywhere else in South America.

When Colombians do fall ill, traditional practices that are based on a diet of scarcity are actually counterproductive. Traditional ideas of health prescribe aguapanela, the mix of sugarcane juice and water, for almost any illness, and especially in diabetic people this can make things much worse. Colombians also ascribe characteristics of hot and cold to many foods and give beef broth the kind of reverence accorded to chicken soup in eastern European cultures.

There is a specific regimen called the *dieta* that mothers are supposed to observe for 40 days after giving birth. Besides never being exposed to direct sun, a new mother is supposed to eat sancocho and hot chocolate; at the end of this period, she takes a bath in herbs before going outside and resuming normal life. If the baby becomes sick at any time, putting slices of cucumber on its head is supposed to help protect it from sinus infection.

The influence of Colombian traditional healers has been growing, and the commercialization of their remedies based on Amazonian plants has been a boon for people who want to preserve jungle regions. Colombian culture is very macho, and there are many recipes for aphrodisiacs. Some of these involve eating insects such as leafcutter ant queens, a logical choice for someone obsessed with fertility, since ant queens are literally egg machines. Since leafcutter ant queens are high in protein and have low levels of saturated fat, this at least does no harm, unlike more toxic alternatives.

Richard Foss

Further Reading

Karpf, Helln. *The Cuisine of Cartagena de Indias: Legacy of Spanish Cooking in Colombia.* Santa Fe de Bogotá, Colombia: Ediciones Gamma, 2001.

Montaña, Antonio. *A Taste of Colombia.* Bogotá, Colombia: Villegas, 2001.

My Colombian Recipes & International Flavors. http://www.mycolombianrecipes.com.

Costa Rica

Overview

Costa Rica is located at the crossroads of three distinct geographic regions: Mexico and Central America, South America, and the Caribbean. Costa Rican foodways have transformed over time as different cultural groups (Europeans, former Caribbean slaves, and Americans) have arrived and intermingled, creating new tastes. Costa Rica is often separated into three cultural sections: the Mesoamerican-influenced Guanacaste to the north, the Hispanic-based Central Valley, and the Afro-Caribbean Atlantic coast. Socioeconomic status also plays an important role, both contemporaneously and historically, in the development of Costa Rican taste. Today, international fast-food chains and cooking products compete with local ones, often garnering a place in the new eating habits of the middle class and wealthy and in the minds of those without the economic capital to partake.

🍽 Food Culture Snapshot

Midmorning on Saturdays, Hilary typically bursts into the family home, arms laden with plastic grocery bags, with a taxi filled with more bags waiting outside beyond the gate. At 35, Hilary is the oldest daughter still living with her parents in their lower-middle-class home in Puntarenas, the southern province of Costa Rica. Another grown sister, Sandra, and brother, Mau, also live in the home of their parents, Don Mauricio and Doña Pilar, as well as two grandchildren, Jonathan and Gabriel, who are the sons of another daughter who does not live in the home. The daughters support the family through their work, one as an environmental educator and the other as a social security associate. Though nuclear families exist in Costa Rica, this household, comprised of multiple generations who at times contribute to the economic and social reproduction of the household, is equally common.

Outdoor markets are rare in Costa Rica, although a few farmers often bring some goods to town plazas once a week to sell. Instead, Costa Ricans purchase the bulk of their goods from chain supermarkets, with last-minute supplements from neighborhood *pulperías* (corner stores). Hilary's weekly purchases are dominated by large bags of white rice and red beans (though most Costa Ricans favor black beans). Knotted white bags contain cuts of pork, beef, and chicken, which poorer families rarely eat and middle-class families serve at least once a day. Two cartons of eggs are bought, though neighborhood families with roaming chickens often sell or share their eggs. Coffee, palm oil (used for frying), boxes of milk, bunches of green and ripe plantains, a carton of strawberry yogurt, flour or corn tortillas, boxes of gelatin, bologna, and packets of tomato paste, dehydrated soups, and spices are purchased weekly. Yellow onions and sweet red peppers are ubiquitous, and red cabbage, lettuce, carrots, papayas, apples, pineapples, potatoes, chayotes (vegetable pears), yucca (a starchy tuber), and *limones* (lemon-lime hybrid) will occasionally appear. Most Costa Ricans who live in the countryside grow their own fruit (limones; *mamones chinos,* which have mild-tasting, fleshy fruit; and mangoes) and spices (cilantro and oregano). Those who have enough space grow corn, beans, and other vegetables. Snack foods and sweets are purchased in small portions from pulperías.

Major Foodstuffs

As has been the case for centuries, maize remains the staple food and gastronomic marker of identity for many of Costa Rica's northern Mesoamerican neighbors: Guatemala, El Salvador, and Honduras. Archaeological data in Costa Rica point to a similar history of maize-based foodways, although an influx of foods from other populations over time has downplayed corn in current usage. Outsiders often assume that Costa Rican foodways align closely with those of the country's northern neighbors. Tourists are often overwhelmed by the national culinary emphasis on rice and beans and the comparably scant attention paid to maize-based foods. Costa Rican foods also tend toward the use of savory aromatics (onion, garlic, sweet red pepper, cilantro, oregano) as opposed to the spicy or stronger tastes of Mesoamerica.

The Spanish influence on Costa Rican and other Latin American cuisines is indisputable. Perhaps no single food has been more influential on Costa Rican foodways than rice. Unlike beans, rice is not a domesticated, native food in the Americas. In Costa Rica, the cultivation of rice, albeit in small quantities, dates to the late 1700s among the Spanish. Today, the dish of mixed rice and beans is one of the principal meals of the culturally diverse region. The meal likely originated among emancipated slaves who migrated in the late 1800s to Costa Rica's Atlantic coast to work on railroads, banana plantations, and the Panama Canal. Bread and sugarcane are other important European contributions.

Central Valley cuisine has become the mainstay in Costa Rican food. *Gallo pinto* is the national dish. On the Atlantic coast, *gallo pinto* is called "rice and beans" in English; there, the rice is prepared with coconut milk instead of water, and red beans (although black can be used as well) and a special *pimienta roja* (locally grown spicy red pepper) that gives the dish a kick are used. Notably, the rice-to-bean ratio greatly favors the rice, which is different from other versions in Costa Rica, which have a roughly even mixture. In Guanacaste, *pinto* is often toasted to a crisp and called the full name, *gallopinto*. In the Central Highlands, locals say only *pinto* and include plenty of oil to make the mixture moister. Some families cook with red beans, but most Costa Ricans prefer black beans.

Gallo Pinto (Beans and Rice)

Remove any small stones from the dry beans, and wash them. Cover the beans with a lot of water (later to be eaten as a soup), and add cilantro, sweet red pepper, onion, and garlic, all finely diced. Also add salt. Cook until tender.

Rinse the rice several times. Cover it with water, and add cooking oil, salt, and sweet red pepper, onion, and garlic. Bring to a boil, then simmer about 20 minutes until done.

Prepare the frying pan to mix the rice and beans together. Dice onion, sweet red pepper, and garlic, and fry them in cooking oil. Add the cooked beans, a small bit of their broth, and salt, mixing them with the aromatics. If desired, mash the beans a bit. When the beans have dried to your satisfaction, add the cooked rice and chopped cilantro. Stir the rice and beans together and heat thoroughly. If desired add Salsa Lizano (which tastes like Worcestershire sauce).

Serve for breakfast with coffee, sour cream, eggs, fresh cheese, fruits, bread, tortillas, or meats.

While most Costa Ricans currently do not base their diets on maize-based foods, such foods remain integral to their conceptions of themselves as members of a Central American culture. In learning about Costa Rican foodways, or those of any culture, one must pay attention to the difference between typical and popular foods. Typical foods are those eaten daily, perhaps with little thought as to why such foods are consumed, whereas popular foods are often invested with considerable outwardly symbolic meaning. Corn is such a food in Costa Rica. In Guanacaste, however, maize more closely approaches ubiquity. Costa Ricans differentiate the northern province of Guanacaste as culturally separate from the rest of the country, perhaps owing to its recent acquisition in 1828 from Nicaragua. Many present-day residents are of Nicaraguan descent or are Nicaraguan immigrants, further casting the territory as a borderland between the two nations. In addition to daily tortillas (flatbread), other maize-based foods include empanadas (turnovers) made with masa (corn flour) and fresh cheese, *atoll* (a purple, gelatinous drink), *chorreadas* and arepas (hotcakes made with masa), and various tamales (masa filled with meat such as pork and steamed in plantain leaves, as opposed to the Mesoamerican tradition of corn husks).

Contemporary alimentary strategies of indigenous peoples in Costa Rica stem from and make use of ancient practices. In southern Costa Rica, the Chibchan practice slash-and-burn agriculture and plant polyculture fields, referred to as "homegardens." The most commonly cultivated crops include plantains, cacao, oranges, peach palms, *manzanas de agua* (watery apples), mangoes, and *Inga* species (pod fruit). Bananas and plantains are grown as monoculture crops. Of the foods cultivated by the Chibchan, oranges, bananas, and plantains are the principal nonnative crops. On the Caribbean coast among the Bribri and Cabecar nations, plantains have recently overtaken cacao as the most common crop. Maize nearly ties plantains in its popularity among the Bribri and Cabecar peoples, followed by rice. Beans figure less prominently in the diet when compared to other Costa Rican populations because of the region's high humidity. *El ñame, el yuca,* and *el tiquisque* are other commonly eaten tubers. Meats include pacas (large rodents known

Ripe cacao pods ready for harvest. (Pindiyath100 | Dreamstime.com)

locally as *el tepezcuintle*), deer, freshwater shrimp, and iguanas.

Cooking

Cooking is a domestic task primarily undertaken by the grown women in a family. In a household comprised of a mother and grown daughters, the daughters take on an equal share of the responsibility for preparing foods. Family members cherish the traditional foods made by mothers and grandmothers, such as handmade corn tortillas. In contrast, daughters often include more modern foods, such as spaghetti and cakes, in their repertoire.

Cooking revolves around the preparation of rice and beans. Women prepare rice fresh each day, often using an electric rice maker. Beans are frequently cooked on the stove or range once every few days using a pressure cooker. Poorer families in the countryside continue to cook with open fires outdoors, and Costa Ricans agree that food cooked this way always tastes better. Rice and beans are rarely refrigerated but are reheated as needed. The large pot of beans is brought to a boiling temperature daily to kill bacteria.

Costa Ricans love fried foods. For economic reasons, few people own ovens. Those who do tend to use the ovens to store already-cooked foods. Meats are always fried. Traditionally, pork lard was used for frying, but increasingly palm or vegetable oil is preferred. Frozen or prefabricated foods are uncommon, particularly among working- and middle-class families. Aside from the occasional use of dehydrated broths or packages of spices, foods are prepared from scratch, and Costa Ricans often disparage American culture for its reliance on fast foods.

Typical Meals

At breakfast, gallo pinto comes accompanied by some combination of fried or scrambled eggs, fried sausage or bologna, fried or plain salty cheese, store-bought corn tortillas, toast or bread with sour cream, fried green or ripe plantains, fresh fruit (pineapple, mango, papaya, or watermelon), avocados bathed in salt, and coffee with plenty of sugar

Central valley coffee region in Costa Rica. (Corel)

and perhaps milk. Occasionally, fresh corn tortillas, arepas, or empanadas will appear. Despite its popularity in cultural discourse, gallo pinto does not appear on the breakfast table in the homes of all Costa Ricans, and when it does, economic resources dictate which foods sit beside it on the plate. Wealthier Costa Ricans or the children of middle-class Costa Ricans often prefer cereal with milk. Poorer Costa Ricans subsist on bread or tortillas and coffee.

Lunches in Costa Rica are large and follow a standard prescription. Lunches cooked at home revolve around a large plate of rice that has been prepared fresh that morning with finely diced sweet red pepper, yellow onion, garlic, and cilantro. If beans have been cooked that day, a favorite food is *sopa negra,* or a bowl of the broth with some beans and a hard-boiled egg. Another popular soup, one that stems from the colonial era and can be traced to Spain, is known as *olla de carne.* This dish contains large pieces of stewed beef on the bone and several large pieces of vegetable, including corn on the cob,

carrots, green plantains, yucca, potatoes, and chayote. Other popular entrées include *picadillos,* comprised of cooked vegetables (potatoes, green beans, or chayote) and finely chopped meats stewed together in a hash; rice with chicken; and spaghetti. A small portion of beans and a light salad often accompany the meal. To drink, Costa Ricans prefer freshly made fruit juices, often from fruits gathered from their own trees. Flavors include *cas* (guava), blackberry, pineapple, mango, strawberry, lemon, carambola (star fruit), and tamarind (pod fruit). Drinks made from oatmeal and rice are also popular.

Dinners vary by family custom, though the foods are the same as those served at lunch and often are whatever was served for lunch that day reheated. Sometimes Costa Ricans add a freshly prepared side dish, such as *patacones* (fried green plantains). Between lunch and dinner, many Costa Ricans enjoy a quiet time called *cafecito,* in which they sit alone or gather with family or friends to share a fresh coffee and possibly sweet or salty breads, crackers, tamales, or cookies. Desserts rarely follow meals directly, but they are served with cafecito or as snacks. Rice pudding, *tres leches* (three-milk cake), flan (custard), and *pudín* (gelatinous cake) are all popular.

Eating Out

Restaurants in Costa Rica primarily feature the same foods that are cooked at home. Working Costa Ricans eat out most often for the midday meal. When bought on the street from small restaurants, called *sodas,* these meals are called *casados.* Separate rice and beans are accompanied by a picadillo, salad (often cabbage and grated carrot), and a choice of meat, whether pork, chicken, or fish. A soft drink or a fresh juice accompanies the meal.

In the past decade young professional couples have begun to dine out together after work, most frequently in American chain restaurants. As has been occurring in other countries, the McDonaldization of foodways in Costa Rica is a current trend. Pizza Hut, Taco Bell, Papa Johns, KFC, and McDonalds dominate the urban restaurant-scape, with their bright, multicolored buildings and multistory plastic playgrounds. In the 21st century, Costa Rican allegiance to American fast food is mixed, as resistant discourses argue that such food is unhealthy and does not speak to Costa Rican culture, even though McDonalds does serve gallo pinto. Furthermore, not all of Costa Rica's residents have access to these food choices (because of geographic or economic disparity), pointing again to the elusive difference between daily alimentary practices and desirable imagined foods. Rural and poor Costa Ricans may claim to love pizza and hamburgers, without consuming them at regular intervals.

In the urban areas of Costa Rica's Central Valley, a variety of upscale, ethnic restaurants exist. Chinese eateries are perhaps the cheapest, most commonly frequented, and most likely to be accessible in less urban areas. Costa Rican Chinese food involves plentiful portions of fried rice or lo mein with a few vegetables and mixed meats.

One final type of desirable restaurant cuisine can be found in Costa Rican bars. Ceviche (in coastal towns), patacones with refried black beans, nachos, fried yucca, and fatty fried pork cuts called *chicharrones*

are the most popular. Beer is the near-ubiquitous alcoholic beverage, although men and women will occasionally order whiskey, wine, or *cacique* (a sugarcane-based liquor) with ginger ale and *limón.*

Special Occasions

Holy Week and Christmas Eve are the two Costa Rican special occasions with the most well-known foods. The female members of an extended family often plan get-togethers during Holy Week to prepare various corn-based snacks. Palm-sized baked rings called *rosquillas* are popular, as well as empanadas filled with sweetened *chiverre,* a large gourd. Families gather together for large dinners on Christmas Eve, where pork tamales take center stage. Eggnog is a common drink at this time of year. While many Costa Ricans grew up preparing these foods at home, today many people prefer to purchase ready-made holiday treats at the supermarket.

Diet and Health

The Costa Rican diet, grounded in a protein-laden rice-and-bean mix and supplemented by proteins from meats, eggs, and cheeses, as well as fruits and vegetables, seems quite healthy, aside from a tendency to prefer frying over other cooking methods. Additionally, Costa Ricans favor generous portions at lunch and breakfast, and light dinners. A simple diet combined with a national health care system fosters a relatively healthy population. Costa Rica even boasts one of the longest-living communities in the world, in the country's northern province, Guanacaste.

Nonetheless, changes in lifestyles and increases in unhealthy globalized foodways have spurred health concerns. Costa Ricans complain of constant gastritis and constipation. Better infrastructure and access to cars and public transportation mean that many Costa Ricans do not benefit from daily exercise. Recently, gyms and workout classes have come into fashion, but not all socioeconomic classes can afford such luxuries. Instead, rates of dieting, eating disorders, and self-medication with expensive medicines and health products are growing. A discourse of healthy eating and favoring natural foods and medicine has grown in the media and on the ground, though practices are slower to follow.

Theresa Preston-Werner

Further Reading

Chang, V. Giselle. "Comidas Regionales." In *Nuestras Comidas.* San Jose, Costa Rica: Coordinación educación cultural centroamericana (CECC) Libro 4. Serie Cultural Populares Centroamericanas. 2001.

Preston-Werner, Theresa. "*Gallo Pinto:* Tradition, Memory, and Identity in Costa Rican Foodways." *Journal of American Folklore* 122, No. 483 (2009): 11–27.

Preston-Werner, Theresa. "In the Kitchen: Negotiating Changing Family Roles in Costa Rica." *Journal of Folklore Research* 45, No. 3 (2008): 329–59.

Ross González, Marjorie. *Entre el comal y la olla: Fundamentos de gastronomía costarricense.* San José, Costa Rica: Editorial Universidad Estatal a Distancia, 2006.

Vega Jiménez, Patricia. "Alimentos e identidades (trabajadores de las bananeras costarricenses 1934)." *Ciencias Sociales* 98 (2002): 99–110.

Whiteford, Michael B. "From *Gallo Pinto* to *Jack's Snacks:* Observations on Dietary Change in a Rural Costa Rican Village." *Ecology of Food and Nutrition* 27, No. 3–4 (1992): 207–18.

Cuba

Overview

Cuba is the largest country in the Caribbean. Cuba has almost as much land area as the rest of the Caribbean islands combined. It is north of Jamaica, west of Haiti, and southwest of the Bahamas. The northernmost point of Cuba is located just 90 miles south of Key West, Florida. The island contains three mountain ranges: the Sierra de los Organos, the Sierra del Escambray, and the Sierra Maestra in the southeast. However, the majority of the country is flat plain. Cuba has a tropical climate, but trade winds keep the temperatures relatively cool, with averages between 70 and 78 degrees Fahrenheit. The dry season is from December to April, and the rainy season is from May to November. Cuba is often hit by tropical storms and hurricanes from July to October.

Since 1962 Cuba under Communist rule has had a national food-rationing system. Under this system the Cuban national government centrally collects food and redistributes it in an equal manner, so that every Cuban family has the same basic foods that they need to survive and no one goes hungry. All Cuban citizens are eligible for a ration card, and with this card they can get their monthly allotment of food items. They do still have to pay for this food, but the prices are very heavily subsidized so it is only about 25 Cuban pesos, or one dollar. The food provided in the monthly ration varies; they try to provide people with the scarcest food items and do not include items that are readily available, such as bananas, mangoes, and other tropical fruits. A typical month's food ration would include 5 eggs, 5 pounds of refined sugar, 5 pounds of raw sugar, 5 pounds of white rice, 5 pounds of beans (black beans, red beans, or split peas), 0.4 pints cooking oil, and 200–500 grams (7–17 ounces) of pork or ground beef mixed with soy. Additionally, everyone gets one roll of bread per day, which is delivered to the house each evening. Children under the age of 7 get a liter (about a quart) of milk per day, and children from ages 7 to 14 get a liter of yogurt. The food ration is essential for basic nutrition in most Cuban households, but many people need to supplement their monthly food rations by buying food in other places as well. Cubans supplement their monthly food rations through state-run stores that sell in the Cuban national peso, and state-run stores that sell in Cuba's second currency, known as the CUC, which is worth about 25 times what the national peso is worth. They also get food at farmers' markets, through workplace cafeterias, and through the black market.

Cuban food on the island has some similarities to Cuban cuisine in the diaspora, including in American cities such as Miami and New York, but there are also many differences. The major differences between Cuban food on and off the island are due to the fact that Cuban food is rationed on the island, so many ingredients that were once a part of Cuban cuisine either are very difficult to access or are simply not available. For example, many Cuban dishes call for beef, but since beef is usually available to Cubans only as ground beef and rarely in other forms, Cuban beef dishes are rarely served in Cuban homes.

Typical state run grocery store in Havana, Cuba, with almost empty shelves. (Ulita | Dreamstime.com)

🍽 Food Culture Snapshot

Pati lives in the heart of downtown Santiago, Cuba. She lives in a three-bedroom house with her five-year-old son, Gorgi; her mother, Susi; and her father and brother. They have lived in this house for many years. Pati's grandfather first moved into the house in the 1920s. Pati works as a secretary for the state legal services, her father works in construction, and her brother is in school studying to be a dentist. Her mother stays at home with Pati's son and does most of the household food preparation. Their lifestyle is typical for a relatively well-off urban household in Cuba.

For breakfast, the family starts off the day with strong Cuban coffee made with lots of sugar and served without milk. Gorgi drinks milk instead of coffee for breakfast. The family also eats half of a loaf of bread, which they either dip in the coffee or eat with homemade jam made with seasonal fruits. An assortment of seasonal fruits will also be served, including fresh mangoes, bananas, papayas (*fruta bomba*), grapefruit, cherimoya, passion fruit, and pineapple.

After breakfast Pati and her father head off to work, her brother goes to school, and Susi will take Gorgi out to pick up the ingredients for the day's food. First, they will stop at the ration station to pick up any dry goods, such as beans, and eggs. Then they will go to the *carnicería,* or butcher, where they pick up the ration of meat products. Susi picks up pork, because it is what is available, and she can use it for both the day's lunch and dinner. At both of the ration pickups, they may have to wait in line for up to an hour before it is their turn. Then Susi will head to the state market to pick up onions, garlic, and any other fresh herbs, vegetables, and fruit that they may need. Susi will buy whichever products are inexpensive, and she will have to buy whatever is in stock, since there is often not much variety.

Lunch is a big meal in Cuba, although not as big as it used to be. Some Cuban workers are able to go home for lunch, and many Cuban children will come home from school or someone will drop off a hot meal for them. Lunch breaks are not as long as they are in other Latin American countries, and most Cubans do not take a siesta after lunch as people do in many other Latin American countries. Susi prepares white rice and pork for lunch for herself, her husband, and Gorgi. The rice is prepared in a rice cooker that was provided to each Cuban family by the government; these cookers help save electricity. Pati and her brother do not come home for lunch because they eat a free meal at their workplace cafeterias.

For dinner Susi will prepare a stew. To flavor the stew she will use the leftover pork pieces and the drippings from lunch and add chopped onions and garlic to prepare a roux. Adding water, she puts the roux ingredients into the pressure cooker, also provided by the government to help conserve electricity. She adds the beans from the ration, and if she has some potatoes or taro, she will cut them up and add them. This will simmer in the pressure cooker until later in the evening when everyone is home from work. The stew is served over rice. Susi prepares enough rice for both lunch and dinner at the same time.

Moros y Cristianos (Cuban Black Beans and Rice)

1½ c dry black beans

2½ c chopped green peppers

3 c chopped yellow onions or shallots

¼ c olive oil

4 cloves garlic, crushed

1 8-oz can tomato paste

2 tsp oregano

3 tsp ground cumin

1 bay leaf

3 tbsp white vinegar

Salt and pepper to taste

3 c white rice, cleaned and washed

4½ c chicken stock

Place beans in a saucepan, cover with water, and bring to a boil for about 5 minutes. Remove from heat and let stand for 1 hour. Drain and rinse the beans, place back in the saucepan, and add enough water to cover them again; bring to a boil, reduce heat to low, and cook for about 45 minutes or until tender. Once the beans are tender, drain them, and run cold water over them until they are clean.

In a large pot with a lid, sauté the onions or shallots with the green peppers and olive oil until tender. Add black beans, garlic, tomato paste, oregano, cumin, bay leaf, and vinegar. Cook about 7 minutes, stirring continuously.

Add the cleaned rice, and stir in the chicken stock. Bring to a boil, and then reduce to a simmer, cover, and cook for about 30 minutes or until rice is done. Add salt and pepper to taste. Place in a serving dish, and drizzle some olive oil over the dish before serving.

Major Foodstuffs

Cuba's tropical climate and rich soil allow a wide variety of crops to grow on the island. Since colonization by the Spanish, sugar has been one of the most important crops for the Cuban economy. Sugar, tobacco, coffee, citrus fruits, and fish are among the top commodities exported from Cuba. Despite these rich resources agriculture makes up less than 5 percent of the Cuban gross domestic product. Currently, many of the foods eaten in Cuba are imported from countries such as Venezuela, China, and Spain.

Rice is a very important part of Cuban cuisine. Cubans eat rice with lunch and dinner nearly every day. Rice is provided in the ration. Currently, Cuba imports most of its rice from Vietnam. Beans are also a very important dietary staple in Cuba. Different kinds of beans are provided in the food ration, including black beans, red beans, chickpeas, and mung beans. Beans are almost always served with rice. In eastern Cuba, also known as Oriente, the most popular way of preparing beans and rice is called *congri*. To prepare congri, first a *sofrito* is prepared. A sofrito is a sauce made with finely chopped onions, garlic, tomato, and sometimes bell peppers. These ingredients are slowly sautéed in olive oil and added to the rice and beans, which are cooked together. In western Cuba, a very similar dish, referred to as Moros y Cristianos or *Arroz Morro,* is the preferred way to prepare rice and beans.

In addition to rice and beans, root crops known as *viandas* are an essential part of Cuban cuisine. The category viandas includes yucca, sweet potatoes, yams, potatoes, pumpkin, some squash, and plantains. Viandas are almost always served with lunch and dinner. Viandas can be prepared in many different ways. Although they are often boiled, many families prefer to slice them up and fry them. Others prefer to have mashed viandas with cream and sugar added, or they might take little balls of the mashed viandas and deep-fry them to make *tostones.* Viandas are rich in many different important nutrients and amino acids, including potassium, magnesium, manganese, and vitamins A and C.

Pork is the most commonly eaten meat in Cuba and a very important source of protein. Pork is prepared in many different ways, but it is rarely cured or prepared into forms such as bacon, pepperoni, or sausages. Pork is often bought and served on the bone. It is sometimes prepared with a sauce called a *mojo* sauce or *mojito* (not to be confused with the drink). The mojo sauce is thought to have been brought to Cuba by slaves and slave traders, who learned to make it in the Canary Islands. A mojito sauce is made of oil, garlic, paprika, and cumin. These ingredients are all sautéed together, and sometimes vinegar or the juice of a lemon, lime, or orange is added for additional flavoring. Stuffed pork is also a popular Cuban dish; in this case the bone is removed and the pork is tenderized, marinated, flattened out, and then wrapped around the stuffing. The stuffing might include ham and cheese or some other savory combination.

Chicken dishes are also popular in Cuba, although chicken is somewhat less available than pork in Cuban cities because pork is provided in the ration more often than chicken is. Chicken is often prepared in the same manner as pork by marinating and cooking the meat in a mojo sauce. Beef is rarely eaten in Cuban homes. Although beef dishes were once an important part of Cuban cuisine, currently beef is very difficult to find in Cuba. Cattle farming

A traditional Cuban feast of roast suckling pig (*lechón asado*), complete with signature Cuban rice and beans (congri), *yuca con mojo, malanga,* and a variety of side items. (Ted Henken)

uses a lot of resources, so beef is difficult to produce in Cuba. Cubans get beef in their diet through the ground beef provided in the food rations; this ground beef is often mixed with soy to help stretch the limited supply on the island. Cubans in the diaspora are more likely to eat beef dishes, such as *ropa vieja,* a shredded beef dish.

Fish is another important part of the Cuban diet and is also a great source of protein. Mackerel, or *jurel,* is a type of fish often available in the food rations. Canned fish such as sardines are available for purchase at the state food stores. Recreational fishing is relatively uncommon in Cuba, compared to other island nations. Furthermore, many of the fish from commercial fishing are exported; therefore, fresh fish is a less common source of protein in Cuba compared to other island nations.

Cuban food is often prepared using the same basic ingredients to flavor the dishes. Cuban food is not usually very spicy, but the flavors are rich and savory. Onion, garlic, salt, and oil or pork fat provide the basic flavoring for many Cuban dishes. Sugar is added to many dishes as a flavoring and is a very important part of Cuban cooking. Sugar has been a central part of the Cuban economy and everyday Cuban life since colonization.

Tropical fruits grow very well in Cuba. Cubans have access to fruit throughout the year, eating different fruits as they are in season. Many urban and rural families have fruit trees in their patios and yards from which they get fruit for much of the year. Families will often have more fruit than they can eat on their own, and they will share or trade fruit with extended family and friends. Mangoes are a very common fruit in Cuba; there are many different varieties of mangoes on the island. Other common fruits include bananas, papayas, grapefruit, cherimoyas, passion fruit, and pineapple. Fruit is eaten as a snack, as breakfast, or as a dessert after meals. These tropical fruits are also used to make fresh fruit juices.

Water is usually served with meals in Cuba. Sodas and packaged juices are served only on special occasions or in more affluent households. Malta is a Cuban favorite. It is a nonalcoholic carbonated malt beverage made from barley, hops, and water. Malta is often served mixed with condensed milk for an ultrasweet drink. Cubans often make smoothies as a snack or special drink. The smoothies will often use the milk or yogurt provided in the children's ration, mixed with whichever fruits are in season. Cubans drink small cups of coffee made with a lot of sugar, served without milk, a few times a day. Coffee is a very important beverage in Cuba.

Cooking

Cooking in Cuba can take several hours and is usually done by an older woman in the household. Younger women will often help with various cooking-related tasks. Some families have cooks or paid workers who help with food preparation. In recent years, Cuban kitchens have changed drastically. Whereas before most people cooked on kerosene gas stoves with one burner or with charcoal over an open fire, today most Cuban households use many different kitchen appliances to cook their food. In an effort to save on fuel and electricity the Cuban government distributed many of these appliances to Cuban households. The rice cooker is one of the most important appliances. Soups, stews, and meat dishes are often prepared in the "multipurpose cooker," which is an energy-conserving electric pressure cooker. Blenders are also very important

kitchen appliances for making smoothies and fresh juices.

In addition to these electric kitchen appliances, many Cuban dishes are prepared on the stovetop. Most Cuban households have old gas stoves from the 1950s or earlier, although some have newer imported gas stoves. Sautéing and deep-frying are used to prepare many Cuban dishes. Pans are often made of aluminum or stainless steel. Because it requires a lot of gas and gas is expensive and difficult to access, baking is rarely done at home; usually baked goods are purchased from a neighbor who makes baked goods for extra cash or from small local bake shops. Bread is provided in the rations and delivered to each Cuban household daily.

In some households charcoal fires are the predominant cooking method. Charcoal is often cheaper than gas and will sometimes be used in situations where there is no electricity. Some families prefer the taste of foods cooked over charcoal over that of foods cooked over gas, so they choose to make a charcoal fire. To cook with a charcoal fire, a big cast iron pot is used. Usually soups and stews are slow-cooked over charcoal in a large outdoor area.

Typical Meals

Although there is a great deal of diversity in what Cubans eat in different regions of the island and in the diaspora, many elements of Cuban cuisine are found in most, if not all, varieties of Cuban food. Most Cubans eat three meals a day—breakfast, lunch, and dinner—as well as a small snack in the afternoon. Cuban meals do not usually arrive in courses; everything is placed on the table and usually mixed together on each individual's plate and eaten together. The exception to this is dessert, which is served after the meal. Very few Cubans are vegetarian, since meat is a mainstay in the Cuban diet.

For most Cubans, breakfast is a relatively light meal, consisting of bread and coffee. Sometimes jam will be spread on the bread, or the bread will be lightly toasted on the stovetop. Many enjoy dipping the pieces of bread into coffee. Coffee in Cuba is made with a lot of sugar, but milk is added only when it is available. Sometimes fruit or eggs will be eaten at breakfast as well. In the country-side breakfasts tend to be heartier than in Cuban cities; rural families are more likely to enjoy eggs or meat with their breakfast as well as some rice for carbohydrates.

Some Cubans eat lunch at work, at school, or on the go during their workday. In these cases, they will stop at their workplace cafeteria or a government cafeteria for a subsidized meal. These meals might consist of a sandwich with ham or ham spread and mayonnaise on a bun, along with some fruit and a coffee. Other cafeterias will service rice and beans with a small piece of pork and plantains. Some Cubans are able to eat lunch at home. Lunch at home will often be a heartier meal, and it is eaten more slowly since it is eaten in the company of friends and family. Home lunches will include rice and a bean-based soup with some fruit or vegetables on the side.

Cuban dinners consist of pork, chicken, or fish dishes with sauces, served with rice, beans, and viandas. Dinners often include the popular Cuban salads. Two of the most common salads are the tomato salad, which consists of sliced tomatoes and sliced raw onions doused in olive oil, and the avocado salad, made of sliced avocados and sliced raw onions doused in olive oil. Sometimes salt is sprinkled over the salads for extra flavoring. Cubans rarely eat leafy lettuce salads, but during the late summer months when lettuce is in season, lettuce salads may appear on the Cuban dinner table. *Picadillo,* or ground beef cooked in a sofrito sauce, served over white rice, is another common Cuban dinner.

Between meals, Cuban snacks are popular ways to ward off hunger. *Bocaditos* are small bite-sized sandwiches with ham spread. *Pastelitos* are small pastries filled with meat, cheese, guava, or guava and cheese. While street vendors sell bocaditos and pastelitos, many people also sell them out of the window or front door of their houses. Little personal pizzas are also a common snack food, sold in government cafeterias and out of neighborhood houses. Croquettes, made of deep-fried minced pork, are very popular Cuban snacks, but they are more likely to be eaten at a street fair or festival than for everyday snacking.

Although most Cuban households are able to eat three meals a day along with a snack, some households may not have adequate resources to do so. Hunger and malnutrition are rare in Cuba, but some evidence shows that due to the lack of iron-rich foods in the Cuban diet, rates of anemia in eastern Cuba can be as high as 56 percent among children under two years old and 20 percent among children between two and five years old.

Although historically the cuisines in different regions of Cuba varied a lot, today with the nationalized food-rationing system, much of the food eaten in Cuba is the same across the island. There are a few exceptions to this, however. People are eating the same thing, but the items may have different names in different parts of the island. For example, in western Cuba a banana is called a *plátano,* but in eastern Cuba it's called a *guineo.* In central Cuba, it is common to have flatbread made out of cassava served with meals, but this is very rare in other parts of the island.

Picadillo

Ingredients

1 lb ground beef

1 tsp oregano

1 tsp cumin

Salt and pepper

2 yellow onions

1 green pepper

7 cloves garlic

1 c tomato sauce

½ c water

1 tbsp olive oil

Combine ground beef, oregano, and cumin, and add salt and pepper as desired. Chop onions and green pepper, and mince the garlic. In a saucepan on the stove, heat the olive oil, and sauté the onions, green pepper, and garlic. Cook until soft. Add tomato sauce and water, stirring continuously, then simmer for 10–15 minutes. After the beef is cooked, remove the cover, and cook for an additional 5 minutes or until the liquid has evaporated. Serve over warm white rice.

Eating Out

In Cuba, there are many ways to eat outside of the home. In addition to foods and snacks from street vendors, Cubans also eat at government-owned restaurants or at privately owned restaurants called *paladares,* and on rare occasions Cubans may eat at hotels where many foreigners and tourists are likely to eat. In some cities, such as Havana, there is a vibrant Chinatown area where Cubans can eat excellent foreign dishes, but for the most part Cuban restaurants serve only Cuban food.

There are many privately owned restaurants, or paladares, all over Cuba. The Cuban government started allowing private restaurant ownership in 1997. The paladares are essentially a way for Cuban families to open up their homes and sell food to foreign or Cuban guests. Paladar owners must purchase and apply for a permit, and they must pay a monthly fee to keep their business going. Paladar menus often consist of a wide range of traditional Cuban dishes, but most of the time only a few of the menu options are available. Some patrons find this frustrating about paladares, while others have simply grown accustomed to always asking which menu items are available that day. Many paladares are known for having very slow service, but a few stand out because of their polite waitstaff and relatively quick service. Paladar prices vary widely: Some are quite affordable for most Cubans, while others have set prices

A Cuban man drinks at Bilbao, a bar in Havana. (StockPhotoPro)

that only foreign clientele can afford. Many paladares will have two different menus, one with affordable prices for Cubans and another with the same menu items set at high prices for foreigners.

Cuban Chinese food is a popular type of cuisine that many Cubans eat in restaurants. Many Cuban cities have Chinese restaurants, and Havana has the largest Chinatown of any country in Latin America. Over 100,000 Chinese people immigrated to Cuba in the 1800s as migrant workers, and many of their ancestors remain in Cuba. Chinese Cuban food is somewhat different from other Chinese foods since the ingredients are quite different due to Cuba's food-rationing system and the types of foods that the Cuban government is able to import. Nonetheless, many Cubans feel this is the best food to experience when eating outside the home since the dishes are not easy to make and are not common in Cuban home cooking. The prices at Chinese restaurants in Cuba tend to be very reasonable, making this an affordable option for the occasional dining-out experience in Cuba.

There are some government-owned fast-food restaurants in Cuba; El Rapido and Burgui are two of the most common chains. El Rapido sells hamburgers, hot dogs, pizza, and sandwiches along with Cuban-made soft drinks. Most Cubans rarely eat fast food both because they do not find it to be a filling or satisfying meal and because the prices are somewhat high.

Special Occasions

Cubans celebrate many different occasions throughout the year. Many Cubans follow the Christian calendar as well as celebrating some of the saints of Santeria or other Afro-Cuban religions. In every Cuban city, Carnival and the anniversary of the 1959 Revolution are celebrated, as well as weddings, births, and deaths. Fasting is uncommon in Cuba; most celebrations involve feasting.

During Carnival many Cubans will celebrate by attending and eating at the local festivals. During this time street vendors set up along the streets with whole roasted pigs from which they sell sandwiches. Croquettes and bocaditos are also for sale during this time. Others vendors sell sweets and desserts such as sugar-roasted peanuts, candies, or cotton candy. During this time state-subsidized beer is also sold from very large kegs placed along the streets. The beer is very cheap, but all must bring their own cups because these are not provided. Some Cubans celebrate Carnival with a special dinner at home. It is common to share a roasted pork leg served with a tomato salad and boiled or fried viandas. After dinner, family members and guests might also have a few glasses of rum as they share stories and listen to Cuban music.

During Christmas and New Year's, Cubans will also celebrate with a special meal. This meal might include croquettes or tostones as appetizers along with marinated olives. The main meal consists of black beans and rice, viandas, Cuban salad, and roasted pork. Desserts for these holidays are often much more elaborate than everyday desserts. Many families serve rice pudding (*arroz con leche*), Cuban flan, *tres leches* cake, or homemade jams and jellies with cheese. Rum is usually shared following special-occasion meals, and smokers will enjoy a good Cuban cigar. For New Year's Eve, some Cubans will eat 12 grapes at the stroke of midnight to celebrate the 12 months of the year.

Birthdays and wedding celebrations are also very important in Cuba. Usually, these occasions are celebrated at home with a special meal rather than by going out to celebrate. At a typical birthday or wedding celebration the host will serve a macaroni or potato salad with lots of mayonnaise, chunks of cheese, and ham. Smoothies or fruit juice will be served along with a cake bought from a local cake maker. At weddings and adult birthday parties, guests will drink Cuban beer or rum together throughout the celebration.

Diet and Health

Recently, in Cuba, the government has tried to encourage people to eat more vegetables and less fatty foods. Many Cubans claim that this is very hard for them, as they have grown accustomed to eating fried foods and a lot of pork, which can be a very fatty meat. For a long time fresh vegetables were hard to find in Cuba, so many Cubans are not used to eating vegetables daily. However, fresh fruits have always been an important part of a healthy Cuban diet, and most Cubans eat several servings of fruit everyday. Nearly all of the grains Cubans eat—mostly rice—are refined grains. The white rice that is eaten daily has far less nutrients in it than brown rice would; however, brown rice is nearly impossible to find in Cuba and, even if it were, Cubans are not accustomed to eating it.

In addition to encouraging healthier eating, the Cuban government encourages Cubans to get plenty of exercise and take part in healthy physical activity. Eating more fresh vegetables and exercising daily is thought to help reduce the chances of getting heart disease or acquiring other related health problems.

Hanna Garth

Further Reading

Benjamin, Medea, Joseph Collins, and Michael Scott. *No Free Lunch: Food and Revolution in Cuba Today.* Princeton, NJ: Princeton University Press, 1984.

"Cuba Food." Havana-Guide. http://www.havana-guide.com/cuba-food.html.

Cuba Recipes. http://www.cubanfood.org/.

Funes, Fernando, Luis Garcia, Martin Bourque, and Nilda Perez. *Sustainable Agriculture and Resistance: Transforming Food Production in Cuba.* Oakland, CA: Food First Books, 2001.

"Old Havana Foods." *Havana Journal,* January 29, 2009. http://havanajournal.com/culture/entry/old-havana-foods-offers-a-variety-of-cuban-food-favorites/.

Curaçao and Sint Maarten

Overview

The five islands of the Netherlands Antilles are divided geographically into the Leeward Islands (northern) group (Saba, Saint Eustatius, and Sint Maarten, which is the Dutch half of the island shared with France, known as Saint Martin) and the Windward Islands (southern) group (Bonaire and Curaçao). In October 2010 the Netherlands Antilles was broken up. Curaçao and Sint Maarten became autonomous territories of the Netherlands, and the remaining smaller islands were given the status of cities.

Curaçao was first settled 6,000 years ago when the Arawak Indians journeyed to an island 35 miles to their north, Curaçao, the middle island in what is known as the ABC islands (Aruba, Bonaire, and Curaçao). The group of Arawaks that settled on Curaçao were the Caiquetios, who some historians believe gave the island its name. Others trace the name to the island's reputation as a place to cure scurvy-stricken sailors. The indigenous population was followed by large numbers of Spanish who settled on the island. However, by the early 16th century the Spaniards abandoned the island because of the lack of a freshwater supply and valuable minerals.

In 1634, long after the Spanish had abandoned Curaçao, the Dutch West Indies Company claimed the island. The natural harbor of the capital, Willemstad, was ideal for trade. Commerce and shipping became the center of Curaçao's most important economic activities. Curaçao played a pivotal role in the Atlantic slave trade. During this period, the local language, Papiamentu, a mixture of Portuguese, Spanish, Dutch, and African dialects, began to develop, and it became the primary means of communication between slaves and their owners.

The capital city of Willemstad became a UNESCO World Heritage Site in 1997, putting it on the list of some the world's most famous landmarks. Willemstad's Saint Anna Bay became one of the busiest ports in the Caribbean. Raw materials from South America were traded for finished goods from Europe and North America.

The end of slavery in 1862 led to an economic downturn that lasted until Shell built an oil refinery on the island in 1915. Curaçao became the seat of government for the newly autonomous Netherlands Antilles in 1954. However, the 1970s oil crisis ended the long economic boom and reduced international investment, leading to further economic decline. Shell closed the refinery in 1985. Curaçao's government took over the refinery in the 1990s and leased it to a Venezuelan company. Other industries like tourism, offshore banking, shipping, and ship repair all make a considerable contribution to the economy.

Curaçao's population of 192,000 spreads out over 182 square miles. The official language is Dutch, but English, Papiamento, Spanish and Portuguese are also spoken. With respect to religious affiliation, 85 percent are Catholic, while the remainder are Methodists, Seventh-Day Adventists, Pentecostals, and other Protestant denominations. The Jewish congregation on Curaçao dates back to 1651 and is the oldest in the Americas.

Curaçao is the largest island of the Netherlands Antilles, whereas the island of Saint Martin is the smallest landmass in the world to have been harmoniously shared for 350 years by two independent countries; the French owned Saint Martin and the Dutch the territory of Sint Maarten. The border between north and south is all but invisible, and in most ways Saint Martin/Sint Maarten is simply a strikingly beautiful neighborhood with two distinct cultures.

The French side (Saint Martin) has first-class beaches and exclusive restaurants. Marigot is their "Mediterranean resort," with yachts in the harbor and open-air markets lining the waterfront. On the north side, Grand Case is known for the island's best restaurants. The Dutch side (Sint Maarten) also boasts white sand beaches and offers casinos, historical sites, shopping venues, and lots of nightlife. Philipsburg, a duty-free port, is the main entry point for cruise ship passengers.

🍽 Food Culture Snapshot

For breakfast a Curaçaon might rise early and search out the "schooner" market along the Ruyterkade in Willemstad, the capital. Here, Curaçaons may shop for melons, pineapples, plantains, chilies, limes, oranges, papayas, mangoes, potatoes, tomatoes, peppers, okra, fresh nutmeg, and cinnamon sticks for the next few days' menus filled with *stobas* (stews) More so than 50 years ago, the tourist trade has increased the choices at open-air markets, grocery stores, and the docks.

While shopping Curaçaons may opt for a stand-up breakfast of *pastechi,* fried pastries filled with savory cheeses, tuna, ham, chicken, or, more rarely, beef. In addition to shopping for supplies, a small percentage of islanders raise a few chickens or iguanas and/or enjoy fishing for their own supper.

At the modern grocery store they would purchase other staples such as coarse-ground cornmeal and peas for such dishes as *tutu,* which is cornmeal with black-eyed peas, or *funchi,* a cornmeal porridge much like *fufu* or the African *ugali.* Because of the humidity, cornmeal and any flour or sugar items are stored in refrigerators, but the dried beans are shelved in kitchen pantries. At times these pantries are still called closets, like in Europe.

Caribbean people are descendants of Europeans and Africans, among other groups. Those of European descent have typically been the ruling classes. Though European customs prevail in terms of shopping a little each day, the spirit is decidedly Caribbean. Wealthy families dine late in the evening, sipping on wine and scotch as well as the ubiquitous rum and, of course, Curaçao liqueur, which is a sweet lurid blue drink flavored with the peel of the Lahara citrus fruit, a descendant of the Valencia orange. The name of Curaçao may have originated in part due to the "cure" part of the drink's reputation. No actual Curaçao liqueur made in Curaçao is imported into the United States.

Later in the day after work, Curaçaons may stop at a fishmongers as the fresh catch is brought in, to prepare a *guiambo,* a seafood and okra stew. If it is Christmas time they may purchase salt cod to make *pekele,* a dish similar to the *bacala* eaten elsewhere in the Caribbean—a dish of cooked salt cod and potatoes. Another very specialized holiday ritual dish is *hallaca,* which are cornmeal cakes stuffed with beef, pork, chicken, olives, capers, and raisins, then wrapped in plantain leaves, tied with string, and boiled or steamed. Recipes and ingredients appear in the local papers in early December to give ample time to gather the long list. The true hallaca are made during a matriarchal family fest that produces hundreds to last the entire season.

It is favorable for Curaçao, as well as Bonaire and Aruba, that the island is located below the hurricane zone, but it can still be challenging to receive any fresh produce and meats from Venezuela if a hurricane is rolling through the Caribbean.

Major Foodstuffs

Market women ("hucksters") offer tubers, including yams, potatoes, dasheen, *tannia* and *eddoes* (both small starchy root vegetables), and cassava (the flour of which is used to make farina), as well as citrus, bananas and plantains, and breadfruit, in the floating local markets. An 18th-century soldier's diary mentions "syrup beer and a country drink called mawbey," a bittersweet drink made from the bark of a tropical tree. *Mauby*'s taste is perfect with the salty sea urchins called sea eggs. Slave markets offered a significantly broader range of items than the historical record has suggested. Staples such as rice, wheat flour, beans, corn, and salted meats were imported, both from Europe and the United States, except during interruptions caused by war.

Various herbs are sold and used for both culinary and medicinal purposes; in Obeah, Voudun, and other Afro-Caribbean religious ceremonies; and in the past as a poison against slave masters and in rebellions. Tropical and semitropical fruits include bananas, mangoes, citrus fruits, papayas, guavas, and pineapples. Dietary staples like potatoes, tomatoes, and green peppers were brought by the Dutch. Families who live on Curaçao often raise goats, iguanas, chickens, rabbits, and pigs. Fresh fish found in the waters and used extensively include kingfish (*mala*), sea bass (*mero*), king dolphin (*dradu*), and some very fine shrimp and warm-water (i.e., tropical) lobster. Dairy products are all imported. Salt is an important part of Sint Maarten's history, as it is for Bonaire.

Cooking

On Curaçao, cooking is a bit more Spanish than on Sint Maarten but still filled with common key local foods. Oil is involved in making the all-time favorite breakfast, *mangú,* a green plantain puree with fried eggs, fried cheese, or sausage. Variations include other tubers and vegetables as well as potatoes and bread. Strong coffee with milk is part of the daily morning ritual.

The roots and tubers used in the local cuisine are preferably cooked, and that is more the focus rather than presenting fresh vegetables, even tomatoes and

The famous floating market market at Willemstad in Curacao. (Dreamstime)

peppers, raw in salads. Noon is considered lunch-time. Lunch is the largest meal of the day. Again, the preferred cooking technique is stewing with generous use of fresh ingredients and spices. The mainstay is rice, either cooked with beans or served with any type of bean on the side. Beans are stewed in a flavorful liquid to a creamy state and served over the rice. Meat, perhaps served only twice a week (from leftovers), is either chicken, beef, pork, or goat, generally stewed in Creole fashion with pimentos and tomatoes.

Dinner is at 7 to 8 P.M. and is similar in proportion to breakfast. Plantains are served mainly, but variations do include boiled roots and bread, accompanied again by bread or sausage, eggs, or leftovers from lunch. Because of the weather, meal patterns remain similar, except for holidays, throughout much of the year. Spicy braised pork and hot peppery stews of seafood as well as barbecuing are popular.

Guavaberry is the legendary folk liqueur of Sint Maarten. It was first made here hundreds of years ago in private homes. People made as much as they needed to serve family and friends. Guavaberry became and still is an integral part of the local island culture. The word itself conjures up memories of the olden days, folk songs, and stories. The guavaberry itself is a wild local berry that is found in the warm hills at the center of the island. Guavaberry fruits are rare and seasonal, making the liqueur even more unique.

There are Curaçao cucumbers, which are small spiny vegetables with a long stem, not to be confused with cucumbers used in salads, which are used in the classic stew *stoba di komkomber*. Prickly pears grow wild, as do *melon di seru,* or mountain melons.

Iguana Stew

Fresh tuna or chicken can be substituted for the iguana. This is a rough approximation of the dish. This stew is quite hot.

Serves 4–6

2 lb iguana meat (if unavailable, substitute tuna or chicken, in large chunks)

Juice of 1 lime

3 c water

1 c coconut milk

10 small potatoes, diced

3 tomatoes, chopped

3 bell peppers, cut into 1-in. pieces

1 c noodles, such as macaroni

2 bay leaves

½ tsp oregano

1 sprig parsley

1 sprig thyme

3 stalks celery, cut into ½-in. pieces

2 habanero chilies, seeds and stems removed, chopped

3 cloves garlic, chopped

Salt and pepper to taste

1 oz whiskey of choice

In a bowl, toss the meat with the lime juice. Cover; while the meat is marinating, combine all the remaining ingredients, except the whiskey, in a large pot or stockpot, and bring to a boil. Reduce the heat, cover, and cook over low heat for 45 minutes.

Add the marinated meat, adjust the consistency if necessary with coconut milk, cover, and cook over low heat for the following times: iguana, 1 hour; tuna, 20 minutes; chicken, 40 minutes.

Just before serving, add the shot of whiskey and stir well.

Other dishes may include local green papaya, a special kind of cucumber, or cabbage, this being stewed with corned beef. Okra and cactus soup is also part of the local cooking as well as a sweet soup made from plantains and vegetables seasoned with peppers and cinnamon. *Ayaca* are savory meat tamales wrapped in banana leaves. *Keshi yena* is a Dutch holdover and is a whole Edam cheese stuffed with stewed meat, raisins, olives, and capers and baked until the cheese melts. Then come the Dutch favorites of pickled fish, salted herring, salmon, and mackerel marinated with onions, hot peppers, and spices. Pickled pig's ears and feet are cut into thin strips, soaked in brine, and flavored with onion and spicy peppers. *Bolo pretu,* the black cake, is reputed by the islanders to be the world's best fruitcake. Another dessert is *sunchi,* or meringue "kisses" made from sugar, egg whites, and food coloring. *Panseiku* is a praline of toasted peanuts and almond essence cooked in a brown-sugar brittle. *Djente kacho* ("dog's tooth") is coconut cooked in sugar syrup. *Kokada* are patties of freshly grated coconut. *Tentalaria* is ground peanuts or cashews cooked till tender in a sugar cream, and *zjozjoli* are chewy sesame seed bars.

Curaçao is known and recognized the world over for its Curaçao liqueur, which was discovered by accident. The liqueur is made from the peels of the bitter Lahara orange. The Spaniards had brought juicy sweet Valencia oranges to the island, but the fruit was unable to flourish because of the very different climate, which changed the flavor, transforming the sweet Valencia orange into the sour Lahara orange. Decades later, it was discovered that the peel of Lahara oranges contains sweet-smelling oils that could be used to make the Curaçao liqueur. These oils were combined with exotic spices, which results in the familiar liqueur millions recognize and enjoy. Amstel Brewery makes its home on Curaçao too.

Typical Meals

Breakfast embraces the breads that are an important part of Sint Maarten's culture. *Pan dushi* (often made for New Year's) or *pan serra* (a dense loaf of bread with a Holland heritage) are common, as are pastechi.

A typical roadside resturant in Sint Maarten specializing in krioyo. (Dreamstime)

For lunch there is the wide variety of local cuisine, called *krioyo*. Roadside stands, called *truki pan*, on Sint Maarten are quite sought after. Dishes offered include *morro*, which is rice and beans, often served with fried plantains or banana *hasa* (*gebakken banaan*, baked banana). *Sopa pika* is fish stew; if made with shellfish, it is called *zarzuela*. *Kadushi* is a hearty soup made of the kadushi cactus with fish, more vegetables, and herbs. Ayaca is chopped beef wrapped in banana leaves. *Cachapas* is a cornmeal and beef tamale with a huge reputation for being delicious. Stoba are stews. They can be made of goat or lamb and include such ingredients as capers, cumin, celery, garlic, ginger, olives, limes, sweet peppers, hot peppers, cucumbers, and shallots. *Berehein na forno au aubegine* (eggplant) in coconut milk is also popular on Sint Maarten. Often by 1 P.M. the roadside stands have shuttered their windows as they are completely sold out.

At dinner time *sopito* may be featured; this is a seafood chowder made with coconut milk, salt pork or corned beef, onions, tomatoes, garlic, peppers, fresh cream, and a variety of spices as well as whatever seafood the boats have brought to shore that day. Though a Curaçao meal often centers around fish or meat, many a Curaçao meal ends with sweets, a custom stemming from the colonial era that aided the northern Europeans by giving the body sugar to help in tolerating the extreme heat.

Eating Out

Restaurant culture began after the Dutch arrived. Foreign travelers to Curaçao and Saint Martin are likely to come in contact with a broad range of dishes professed to be authentic in character. Most food produced for tourists reflects the particular tradition of transatlantic shipping from which not only the foodstuffs but also the contemporary populations emerged. Perhaps the most contentious debate among contemporary scholars of the Caribbean concerns the origins of the region's cultural influences. Many argue that African cultural influences define the region.

Resort restaurants feature dishes as worldly as the tourists who arrive into Curaçao, but the Dutch influence can be seen in such dishes as Dutch pea soup. A few restaurants even boast authentic windmills that were dismantled and shipped from Holland and reconstructed on the premises. *Callaloo*—which means "herb porridge"—is served often, even at lunchtime roadside stands or shacks. Another favorite dish on Sint Maarten is *christophene farci*, which is stuffed chayote squash. Chinese restaurants serve the traditional *rijstaafel*, a 21-course meal created by Dutch colonial rulers in Indonesia, since there are few Indonesians here. French fries are served with an African-influenced peanut sauce.

Special Occasions

For special occasions, two culinary traditions may still be found in well-to-do households. The birthday reception is basically an open house held from sunup to sundown on the day in question. It should be well attended by everyone who even slightly knows the person having a birthday. Another social time well anointed with cultural significance and food is teatime. When in the past circles of friends and acquaintances were more manageable, this was a very important time. The servants of these households often whispered that this was the gossip hour, and in Papiamento this would be called *awa di redu*, or gossip water. Such a traditional teatime menu would include pastechi, cachapas, and also another chopped beef delicacy stuffed inside banana leaves.

Curaçao's fine restaurants provide for vacationing tourists, and as such the locals struggle to preserve traditions. They are often so busy working that they cannot celebrate, at least not with the vigor they used to have.

For weddings they make a cake called bolo pretu, which includes nuts, figs, citron, almonds, raisins, currants, dates, prunes, Angostura bitters, brandy (both regular and apricot), vermouth, cherry cordial, Curaçao liqueur, rum, and spices. It is important to bake the cake a day or two before the wedding. It is baked in round pans and iced with fondant. The decorated cakes are cut into squares, wrapped in wax paper, and placed in a small tin for guests to take home.

Diet and Health

Pork- and fat-laden "resort" food is consumed on Curaçao and Sint Maarten. It is recommended that locals return to their original foods and seafood and avoid the trap of fast foods, which, while quicker to consume, also pose greater health and long-term risks as well as leading to a loss of food culture. When eaten, chicken, goat, and iguana are high in protein and, depending on the cooking method, may contain less fat. As on many of the Dutch Antilles, iguanas are now protected and are now often raised on farms instead of depleting the already-challenged wild population.

Irish moss is a beverage consumed for health and aphrodisiac purposes. It is made with Malta, a nonalcoholic beverage and a seaweed. It is thought to aid in the cure of bronchitis, tuberculosis, and intestinal dilemmas. Ginger beer is often offered as a tonic for digestion and menstrual cramps and as an alternative to aspirin.

Dorette Snover

Further Reading

Besson, Jean. "A Paradox in Caribbean Attitudes to Land." In *Land and Development in the Caribbean,* edited by Jean Besson and Janet Momsen. London: Macmillan, 1987, 13–45.

Brathwaite, Kamau. *Roots.* Ann Arbor: University of Michigan Press, 1993.

Brushaber, Susan, and Arnold Greenburg. *Aruba, Bonaire, and Curaçao: Alive.* Edison, NJ: Hunter, 2002.

Counihan, Carole, and Penny Van Esterik, eds. *Food and Culture: A Reader.* New York: Routledge, 1997.

Geddes, Bruce. *Lonely Planet. World Food Caribbean.* Oakland, CA: Lonely Planet, 2001.

Hall, Robert L. "Savoring Africa in the New World." In *Seeds of Change: Five Hundred Years since Columbus,* edited by Herman J. Viola and Carolyn Margolis. Washington, DC: Smithsonian Institution Press, 1991, 161–172.

Herskovits, Melville J. *Myth of the Negro Past.* Boston: Beacon Press, 1990. (Originally published in 1958.)

Houston, Lynn Marie. *Food Culture in the Caribbean.* Westport, CT: Greenwood Press, 2005.

Karin's Dutch Food Blog. http://www.dutchfood.about.com.

Martindale, Marty. "Curacao: Amazing Island of Diversity." Food Site of the Day. http://www.foodsiteoftheday.com/?p=3841.

McNeill, William H. "American Food Crops in the Old World." In *Seeds of Change: Five Hundred Years since Columbus,* edited by Herman J. Viola and Carolyn Margolis. Washington, DC: Smithsonian Institution Press, 1991, 43–59.

Mintz, Sidney W. "Caribbean Marketplaces and Caribbean History." *Nova Americana* 1, No. 1 (1978): 333–44.

Mintz, Sidney W. "Pleasure, Profit, and Satiation." In *Seeds of Change: Five Hundred Years since Columbus,* edited by Herman J. Viola and Carolyn Margolis. Washington, DC: Smithsonian Institution Press, 1991.

Mintz, Sidney W. *Sweetness and Power: The Place of Sugar in Modern History.* New York: Viking, 1985.

Patullo, Polly. *Last Resorts: The Cost of Tourism in the Caribbean.* London: Cassell, 1996.

Scott, David A. 1991. "That Event, This Memory: Notes on the Anthropology of Diasporas in the New World." *Diaspora* 1, No. 3 (1991): 261–84.

Dominica

Overview

Officially the Commonwealth of Dominica, Dominica is nestled between two of the last vestiges of French Caribbean colonialism, Guadeloupe to the north and Martinique to the south. The most northerly of the Windward Islands, at 15° north and 61° west, Dominica is 291 square miles (750 square kilometers) in area, 29 miles (47 kilometers) long and 18 miles (29 kilometers) wide.

The island was formed by volcanic action, evident in the verdant majestic mountains as well as numerous volcanic fumaroles and hot water springs. With two-thirds of the island covered in a lush rain forest canopy hiding towering waterfalls and rivers flowing through valleys, as well as boasting an array of colorful and interesting flora and fauna, Dominica is paradise for nature lovers and a top scuba-diving destination. Warm but sometimes very wet, the temperature in this tropical climate ranges from 80 degrees Fahrenheit (26 degrees Celsius) in January to 90 degrees Fahrenheit (32 degrees Celsius) in June. The heaviest rainfall occurs between July and November, and the interior has the highest average annual rainfall at around 275 inches (700 centimeters).

Dominica was first claimed by France in 1635 and, after a period as a neutral island, was ceded to the British in 1760. Now a republic within the British Commonwealth, Dominica became an independent island nation on November 3, 1978. With a small population, challenging topography, historical dependence on agriculture, and devastating hurricanes, Dominica's economy has suffered many setbacks. Agriculture, especially banana exports, was the dominant sector, but recent decisions by the World Trade Organization heralded an end to the preferential treatment given by the United Kingdom. This has led to a sharp decline in the sector. The island is now trying to diversify its economy and is expanding tourism, focusing on ecotourism and attempting to vary its agricultural exports.

The population, estimated at around 72,000, is an ethnic mix, the majority of whom are descendants of West African slaves brought to work the plantations. The remainder consists of Amerindian descendants and a small percentage of Europeans, Lebanese, Syrians, and Asians. Dominica is one of the few places in the Caribbean that still has a population of pre-Columbian indigenous people, the Kalinago (Caribs). Numbering around 3,000, the Kalinago mainly live in the east, in an area secured for them in 1903. This dedicated Kalinago Territory, unique in the Caribbean, is communally owned. The remainder of the population mainly resides in the coastal villages, with the capital Roseau on the southwestern coast being the most densely populated, and Portsmouth on the northwestern coast being the second-largest town. This vibrant synthesis of French, African, Amerindian, and British influences has created a unique but distinctly Creole culture that is evident in the language (French Creole or patois), traditional dress, customs, music, dance, and cuisine.

🍽 Food Culture Snapshot

John and Sylvia Charles live in the Roseau Valley village of Trafalgar with their children, Robert (age 13),

Zoe (age 8), and Joshua (age 4). Sylvia's mother, Petula, also lives with them. It is 6:30 A.M. on Friday, and Sylvia, who works as a bank clerk in Roseau, has already returned from her morning walk, has eaten her perfunctory two oranges under the tree in the yard (a knife is kept tucked away in the branches for this purpose), and is now preparing breakfast. At the same time she is getting the lunch ingredients ready for when the helper arrives later in the morning.

Lunch will be tuna in Creole sauce, which she already seasoned last night. Yesterday John picked some lettuce and tomatoes from their little backyard garden, and his brother David, who lives nearby, brought over carrots and string beans from his garden earlier in the week. Sylvia puts a bag of white rice on the kitchen counter, checks the pot of lentils left soaking on the cooker overnight, and gets the last of the figs (as green bananas are called here) from the pantry.

She then writes her shopping list. They don't need much, as it's nowhere near payday and things are already tight. Some garlic, onions, butter, ultrapasteurized and evaporated milk, and macaroni, perhaps. She will, however, have to pick up some whole wheat bread from the depot even though she knows the children will complain. Making a start on breakfast, the thought crosses her mind how this meal has become a trial. The children no longer want to eat her usual offerings of porridge oats—Joshua in particular refuses to eat anything but the very expensive chocolate-flavored cereal he saw on TV. She and John will have fried plantains and boiled eggs and share the leftover bread with the children.

Sylvia begins to prepare cocoa tea for the kids, grating the rolled chocolate her husband's brother brought in fresh the week before, boiling the water, and adding the chocolate to "melt" before pouring it into hot milk and placing a couple of teaspoons of brown sugar into the mixture. Milk would have to do today for the cocoa tea although dried coconuts sat on the counter ready for the inner hard flesh to be removed, which would then be grated; the far more nutritious milk would then be forced out by repeatedly pouring hot water over the grated coconut. Sylvia herself has already downed her ginger tea, made fresh from the grated ginger that she had grown in the garden.

Suddenly, the morning peace is shattered by the sound of the boys running down the wooden stairs. Zoe is good girl and has always given Joshua his breakfast before getting him ready for school. Robert, however, is a typical teenager, as sullen as his grandmother, so he arrives fretting as usual. John, a forestry officer at the nearby Trafalgar waterfall, walks in and tells the children to be quiet—peace is required before his daily routine of ensuring the forests and its wild animals are kept safe. Hunters out of season are penalized severely for catching *manicou* (opossum) and agouti (wild meat revered by Dominicans) on this island—even the now-almost-extinct "mountain chicken" (an edible frog)—but although these laws have worked well as a deterrent, one still has to keep a sharp eye out for the odd criminal.

During breakfast Sylvia plans out the weekend in her head. The family will probably go to the local barbecue stall in the village after grocery shopping tonight. She can almost taste the deliciousness of that well-seasoned chicken. Tomorrow, Saturday, John will go to the Roseau market, make his social rounds, and pick up some hot stone-oven bread, blood sausage, and souse for their breakfast. He will also buy what vegetables, fruit, provisions, and herbs they need for the week and whatever fish is available from the nearby fisheries complex. On Sunday they might visit John's parents in Castle Bruce village and take a tour of the Kalinago model village on the way. Sylvia has always wanted to go there and hopes they have fresh cassava bread. Or maybe if the weather is fine they will join friends for a picnic on Mero beach after mass. She makes a mental note to add some Irish potatoes and mayonnaise for potato salad and chicken for frying to her shopping list, just in case. Sylvia has always insisted that weekends become a special treat for her family.

Major Foodstuffs

Dominica has small-scale farming including traditional subsistence horticulture or backyard gardens; the fertile volcanic soil lends itself to growing a large variety of crops. The most common include bananas, plantains, "provisions" (these include root crops such as yams, dasheen, *tannia,* cassava, and sweet potatoes, as well as other starchy foods such as breadfruit and green bananas, known locally as figs), chayotes, seasoning peppers, hot peppers, avocados (known locally as pears), lettuce, carrots, tomatoes, pumpkins, ginger, coconuts, and a variety of pulses. A selection of seasoning herbs are also grown, like chives, thyme, parsley, celery, and bay leaf as well as an assortment of herbs for bush or herbal tea, like vervain and sacred basil (basilic).

In an effort to diversify the agricultural sector, cacao is one of the crops being targeted for increased production, and coffee cultivation is likely to grow with talk of a Venezuelan-funded coffee plant. The local Café Dominique, a pure ground coffee made from the roasted arabica bean, is produced by PW Bellot & Co. Limited.

Fruit trees are all over, and local fruit juices are drunk on a regular basis. Fruits include citrus, such as oranges, limes, grapefruit, and tangerines, and exotic fruits, like passion fruit, West Indian cherry,

carambola, soursops and sweetsops, sapodillas, guavas, tamarinds, pawpaws (papaya), and a variety of mangoes. Pineapples and watermelons are mainly grown on the drier west coast.

Native rums are produced by Belfast and Shillingford Estates. The Shillingford *macoucherie* rums are distilled from pure sugarcane juice using sugarcane that is still cultivated on the old estate lands. These rums form the basis of a wide variety of punches, bush rums, and cocktails. Bush rums are overproof rums infused with spices or herbs—these are usually found in every home or bar.

Cattle and poultry are reared for local consumption, including beef, chicken, pork, lamb, mutton, goat, and, more recently, rabbit. Across the island the sound of the queen conch shell being blown signifies that fishermen have returned or that a truck with fish is nearby. The catch can include tuna, marlin, or dorado (also known as mahimahi, and locally

A small backyard farm on the island of Dominica. (StockPhotoPro)

as *dolphin* or *dowad*) and flying fish. Jacks, snapper, and *balao* (a thin fish with a long pointy beak) are caught inshore, and during hunting season there is fresh river crayfish. Spear fishermen hunt for reef fish, lobster, and octopus. Imported codfish (salt fish) is also used in a variety of dishes. The tiny *titiri* is revered. Caught three to four days after the quarter moon using huge nets at the mouth of the rivers (particularly the Layou River), it is washed of sand, seasoned well, and made into *titiri accra* (spoonfuls of a seasoned fish/flour mixture are fried in buck pots of hot oil).

Crab Backs

Ingredients

¼ c oil

½ tbsp soy sauce

2 cloves fresh garlic, grated

1 large onion, finely chopped

2 mild chili peppers, finely chopped

1 stalk fresh celery, finely chopped

1 sprig parsley, finely chopped

5 sprigs chives, finely chopped

2 sprigs thyme, finely chopped

1 tbsp lime juice

¾ lb crabmeat, fresh or canned

2 tbsp tomato paste

1 hot Scotch bonnet pepper, seeded and finely chopped

3 tbsp breadcrumbs

Salt and black pepper to taste

6 crab back shells, cleaned and scrubbed

Heat oil in a deep frying pan. Add soy sauce, garlic, onion, chili peppers, celery, parsley, chives, and thyme. Stir and let steam for just a few seconds. Add lime juice. Let steam for another 5 minutes. Add enough water to cover ingredients. Add all the crabmeat. Stir. Add tomato paste and hot pepper, and sprinkle breadcrumbs over the mixture, stirring constantly until a good thick consistency is reached.

More crabmeat than breadcrumbs is preferred. Add salt and pepper to taste. Reduce heat. Let steam for another 2 minutes just to get rid of excess water. Place mixture into crab backs, sprinkle with more breadcrumbs, and brown under a grill just before serving. Crab backs can also be prepared and frozen; when ready for use, remove from freezer, defrost, and use same way as described. Serve with a sprig of parsley as garnish. Two crab backs are usually served per person.

Bread is a major staple, and there are several family-owned bakeries with satellite bread depots in most of the populated areas. A few still bake using the traditional stone oven. The bread types include *mastiff* (a long, dense bread), *jackery* (a small square bread with small holes on the surface), and *butterflap* (a roll that is folded and filled with salted butter). Rolls and sandwich loaves, including whole wheat, are also available.

Most bakeries also bake meat pies, pasties, and a selection of sweet breads, cakes, and pastries such as raisin bread or buns, coconut cake or turnovers, sponge cakes, and bread pudding. Cassava bread and *kanki* (a sweet made with cassava/manioc roots, sugar, and spices and steamed in banana leaves) can be found in the Kalinago territory.

There is currently no local dairy, and all dairy products are imported. Milk is predominantly evaporated, ultrapasteurized, or powdered. Items such as rice, sugar, flour, pasta, garlic, onions, and Irish potatoes are additional major imported foodstuffs.

Cooking

The native Carib Kalinago influence can still be seen in some culinary styles and dishes such as smoked meat and fish or even in the traditional cooking method of the island, in which large black iron pots sit above a wood fire or coal-fired coal pots (iron or earthenware pots). The word *barbecue* is in fact derived from *barbacoa,* the indigenous method of cooking meat or fish over a fire. The use of *roucou* (annatto) as a natural food coloring and of cassava flour (known locally as *farine*) to make bread also stems from Kalinago culture.

One of the most important steps in Creole-style cooking, influenced by the French, is the use of seasoning and the marinating of meat and fish prior to cooking. Seasonings, including seasoning peppers (these are slightly different in shape from hot peppers and have flavor and no heat), garlic, ginger, thyme, parsley, celery, salt, and sometimes onion and chives, are chopped and used in meat preparation and to flavor a variety of dishes. Meat and fish are washed with salt, lime, and water and marinated in seasonings overnight.

Chili peppers are widely used, both in dish preparation and sprinkled over cooked food. The main varieties grown are the West Indian red and Scotch bonnet, and households and eating establishments will have a bottle of one of the locally produced hot pepper sauces. Curry is also used to season, and although not a traditional Dominican dish, curried goat is common.

Caribbean jerk chicken served with red beans, rice, and plantains. (Eddie Lepp | Dreamstime.com)

The main dishes usually consist of meat or fish, a mixture of fresh seasonal vegetables, salads or coleslaw, rice or pasta, and pulses and are cooked in the following manner: Seasoned and marinated meat, largely chicken, pork, lamb, mutton, and beef, can be stewed in a light curry or Creole sauce or roasted. Chicken and pork can also be baked plain or in a barbecue sauce, and chicken can additionally be served fried. Fish is served steamed, fried, grilled, or baked and often in a Creole sauce.

Pulses including kidney beans, black-eyed peas, and lentils are bought dry, soaked overnight, and boiled with seasonings or heated from cans. Rice, normally white rice, is washed to remove excess starch, seasoned, and boiled, and sometimes pulses are added. Vegetables are served boiled, and provisions are served as boiled chunks or sometimes in the form of a deep-fried seasoned "puff" or *accra* (fritter).

Light stews such as goat, fish, or *shatou* (octopus) water and soups made of vegetables, cow heel, or pumpkin are eaten in the early evening. These are also considered to be aphrodisiacs—soups to "put it all back in." *Callaloo* soup is made from young dasheen (taro) leaves or spinach and is sometimes cooked with land crab. Flour-and-water dumplings can be added to soups. The ears, nose, tail, and trotters of the pig are boiled in seasoned brine for a traditional dish called souse. It is served with a mixture of cucumbers with lime juice.

Putting all the ingredients into one pot is a common cooking style. The one-pot *braf* (a broth made from a variety of provisions, dumplings, and seasonings, flavored with smoked meat or fish and cooked in a large iron pot over an open fire) and stewed chicken *pelau* (a seasoned rice dish) are examples.

Wild meat such as manicou (opossum), agouti, and wild pig is revered but available only during hunting season. Land crab also comes under this heading. The mountain chicken (*Leptodactylus fallax*) has almost become extinct because of a viral infection affecting these frogs, and efforts are underway to study not only the problem but also the solution, as this meat (frog legs) was a staple in most Dominican households.

Manicou or Agouti (Dominican Game)

Any smoked or unsmoked meat or wild meat can be used for this recipe.

Serves 4

1 whole smoked manicou or agouti

2 tbsp vinegar

¼ tsp crushed fresh garlic

¼ lb onions, peeled and chopped

1 tbsp soy sauce

1 tsp thyme

1 tsp celery powder

½ tsp fresh grated ginger or ground ginger

3 mild chili peppers

1 slice hot pepper or ½ tsp cayenne

1 sweet pepper

1 tbsp butter

2 bay leaves

¼ c red wine

1 tbsp tomato paste

1 c water

1 c cornstarch

Cut the manicou or agouti into small pieces with a sharp Chinese chopper and wash with vinegar. Season with garlic, onion, soy sauce, thyme, celery powder, ginger, and chili peppers. Melt butter in a heated iron pot on the stove. Add the meat, bay leaves, and red wine, and stir vigorously. Stir in tomato paste and water. Cover the pot and let boil over moderate heat for 15 minutes or until meat is tender. In a separate bowl make a paste of the cornstarch and a little water. Add the paste to the pot and boil for another 30 seconds. Serve with plain boiled rice or slices of boiled dasheen. Boil a plantain in its skin, peel and slice, and serve with the meal.

Rastafarians who are Italists (eating a vegan diet that also excludes canned and dried food and often alcohol) and other vegans and vegetarians in the community prepare similar dishes, but the meat is replaced with vegetables, pulses, nuts, tofu, soy chunks, or mushrooms.

Baking is another traditional form of cooking, and baked or roasted dishes (in addition to meat, bread, cakes, and other desserts) are macaroni and cheese, yam and sweet potato pies, vegetables au gratin, casseroles, and roasted breadfruit. These days, although coal pots and open fires are still used, most households cook on propane gas or electric stoves and use microwaves.

Typical Meals

The average person would start their day with one or more of the following: Cereal or porridge made from oats, figs (green bananas), farine, or arrowroot; bread filled with local fruit jam, boiled egg, smoked herring, codfish, tuna, or cheese; plain *bakes* (deep-fried dough made of flour, water, and salt) or bakes stuffed with smoked herring, codfish, tuna, corned beef, or cheese; farine and pear (cassava/manioc flour mixed with avocado); fresh fruit; and cocoa tea (made with grated cocoa sticks, nutmeg, cinnamon, water, and milk or coconut milk), herbal bush tea, or coffee. If a more substantial breakfast is required, then boiled provisions, fried breadfruit, or plantain may be included.

Coconut water fresh from a jelly coconut, blood sausage, pork souse, and deep-fried accras (made with codfish, tannia, or *titiwi*) are Saturday favorites. On Sundays, smoked herring, codfish, or tuna may be cooked Creole style with onions, garlic, and tomato and eaten with boiled eggs and salad. Codfish *sancoche,* made with coconut milk, or ground and boiled codfish, seasoned and fried with onions and sweet pepper (codfish *bulljaw*), are also eaten on a Sunday morning or for lunch.

Daytime snacks include local plantain or breadfruit chips; plain or stuffed bakes; accras, meat or fish pies and patties; barbecued or roast chicken, corn, or plantains; or imported crisps, chocolate bars, and biscuits. Roadside stands sell children's favorite sweets: tamarind balls, coconut cheese/tablet (a kind of sweet coconut fudge), guava cheese, gooseberry sticks, shaddock rind, and peanut brittle as well as fruits like *kenips* (genips or *mamoncillo,* a little, oval green fruit) and governor plums. On hot days, snow cones (flavored syrup poured over shaved ice in a cup), frozen joys (sweet, fruit-flavored frozen ice pops sold in small plastic bags), and locally made ice cream are welcome treats.

Lunch is normally the heaviest meal of the day, and many families get up early to prepare the meal so it is ready when they come home between 1 and 2 P.M. It typically consists of meat or fish, provisions, fresh vegetables, salads, rice or baked macaroni and cheese, and some sort of pulse. Lighter lunches include pelau, soup, sandwiches, or roti (a flatbread stuffed with curried chicken, fish, or vegetables). As Dominica is a primarily Catholic country, many Dominicans eat only fish on a Friday. Beverages such as carbonated drinks, imported and local fruit juices, natural spring water, coconut water, sugarcane juice, sorrel, sea moss (made from seaweed, milk, and spices), and ginger beer complete the meal. Sunday lunch is traditionally a sit-down meal with roast meat or fish and a selection of the mentioned accompanying dishes. The last meal of

the day, supper, is usually very light. It could consist of soup, bread or toast, and English or herbal bush tea.

Eating Out

Dominicans rarely eat out in the evening, but over the last few years this has been changing. There is a good selection of dining establishments to suit all budgets, commonly serving traditional cuisine. The majority are located in or near the capital Roseau and in the second-largest town, Portsmouth.

Snackettes are the most prevalent eating establishment, very casual and inexpensive, serving everything from snacks to full lunches. The larger hotels and restaurants offer both local and international dishes. Ross University, a U.S. offshore medical school located in Picard, Portsmouth, has meant that eating establishments in that area normally offer a more varied international menu. There are also

Restaurants line the water on the port of Roseau in Dominica. (Richard Goldberg | Dreamstime.com)

several Chinese restaurants and a few French restaurants, extending the variety of what's on offer.

Fast-foods outlets, although not as prevalent as on other Caribbean islands, are slowly making their way to Dominica, and Kentucky Fried Chicken, pizza franchises, coffee shop franchises, and Subway ready-made sandwiches are available. Friday night is barbecue night, and in most of the towns and larger villages, vibrant roadside barbecue stalls will offer barbecued chicken, fish, and pork ribs, accompanied by various side dishes like chips, green salad or chow mien, and potato salad.

Special Occasions

Throughout the year Dominicans celebrate a range of religious, community, and national events, most of which involve a strong emphasis on food. Village feast days are associated with a patron saint; after a church service and procession through the village, the music, drinking, and eating begin. Weddings, christenings, first communions, and confirmations, as well as funerals, normally offer buffet-style fare. At Carnival and during Independence time, Dominica's culinary heritage is really in the spotlight. Traditional Creole favorites include crab callaloo, crab back (flesh of a land crab is mixed with a secret blend of spices and served in its shell), breadfruit and codfish, *fachine* (cattle skin boiled in seasoned brine), and the stewed or smoked bush-meat delicacies of agouti and manicou. The island's national dish, "mountain chicken," Dominica's largest frog or *crapaud,* would normally be a delicacy at this time, but due to the decimation of the population by the chytrid fungus, it is strictly forbidden to eat or hunt the mountain chicken.

Recent additions to the calendar of celebrations include the community-based Titiwi Festival held in Layou village and Cochrane's Rabbit Festival. At these events, against a backdrop of music and other entertainment, residents and visitors get to sample titiwi (a tiny translucent fish) or rabbit cooked in a variety of different ways. Most bank holidays and some weekends often involve a family outing or beach picnic. On these occasions lunch is prepared and packed, or goat water, fish braf, or

breadfruit is cooked in the open air, over a fire made with branches and twigs.

Christmas is another special time for food. Blood sausage, pork souse, and braf are served after midnight mass together with *chaudo* (eggnog), ginger beer, and sorrel. The main course on Christmas Day would be similar to meals during the rest of the year, with the addition of smoked pork, baked ham, and roast turkey or chicken. For dessert, there would be a slice of rich, dark fruitcake made with currents and sultanas soaked in cherry wine or other liqueur for several months.

Alcoholic beverages such as spirits, ginger wine, and Guinness are found at most social occasions or celebrations. Rum punch is also common and normally made with a lime or passion fruit base. Beer selections are the local Kubuli or imported Heineken, Carib, and sometimes Corona.

Diet and Health

The nutritious local food, the use of herbal remedies and bush teas, the more traditional methods of cooking, and Dominica's clean natural environment, which is more conducive to a healthy lifestyle, all contribute to the island's fast-growing reputation as a center for mental and physical well-being. The high ratio of healthy centenarians per capita is testimony to this.

But there is doubt whether this phenomenon will last very much longer, as the lifestyle of younger Dominicans is changing and many do not lead the same active lifestyle as their parents and grandparents or follow the same healthy diet. Tobacco smoking is on the increase, as is drug and alcohol abuse. Food imports are also on the rise, as local food production has begun to decline. The largely unregulated diversion of former agricultural land into real estate development raises concerns about the nation's long-term ability to feed itself.

The prevalence of noncommunicable diseases is rising. Stroke, heart disease, diabetes, and cancer account for a high percentage of deaths. Initiatives such as healthy eating campaigns, screenings, and government proposals to combat noncommunicable diseases, as well as organizations like the recently established Dominica Organic Agriculture Movement, will likely help reduce some of the underlying causes of ill health.

Celia Sorhaindo and
Rosemary Parkinson

Further Reading

Crask, Paul. *Dominica—Bradt Travel Guide.* Chalfont St. Peter, UK: Bradt Travel Guides, 2008.

Dominica Food and Drink Guide. 2nd annual ed. June 2009. ISSUU: You Publish. http://issuu.com/caribbean_homes_lifestyle/docs/food_and_drink_guide_dominica_2009.

Elwin, Hyacinth I. R. *A Taste of Nature Island Cooking—The Cuisine of Dominica.* Oxford, UK: Macmillan Caribbean, 1998.

Parkinson, Rosemary. *Culinaria: The Caribbean.* Cologne, Germany: Könemann, 1999.

Dominican Republic

Overview

Christopher Columbus arrived on an island in the Greater Antilles during his first voyage in 1492. He named the island Hispaniola, and it figured prominently in the Spanish conquest of the Caribbean and the Americas. However, the French gained control over the western third of the island, and this portion was named Haiti in 1804 when the African slaves revolted and successfully achieved independence. The remainder of the island, then known as Santo Domingo, tried to gain independence in 1821. They were not successful and were conquered by the Haitians, who ruled them for 22 years. By 1844, the Spanish on the eastern portion of Hispaniola gained independence and named it the Dominican Republic.

The original inhabitants of Hispaniola were the Arawak/Taino Indians, a group believed to have arrived from as far away as South America, island-hopping until they found themselves on the island of Hispaniola. The Taino built canoes, some large enough to carry 100 people, used for deep-sea fishing as well as for trade among the islands. Long-distance travel by canoe was done from March to August, guided by the North Star and the constellations of the Milky Way.

Subsequent Spaniards who arrived brought no women. The children they had with Taino women resulted in a mix called mestizo. The Carib Indians had been fierce enemies of the Taino, forcing them northeastward in gradual retreat. In time the Taino were devastated by diseases, which gradually forced their assimilation into the Spanish culture.

The Dominican Republic, the second-largest country in the Caribbean, is equal in size to Vermont and New Hampshire combined. The country has over 1,000 miles of shoreline, bordering the Caribbean to its south and the Atlantic Ocean to its north. Possessing a variety of highland and lowland areas, the Dominican Republic has a favorable amount of land suitable for agriculture. The country, a representative democracy, has a population of nearly 10 million. The capital city, Santo Domingo, is also the largest city in the country, with nearly three million people, and it is also the oldest European city in the New World.

The Dominican Republic itself has four rugged mountain ranges bisecting it from the northwest to the southeast. The highest is the Cordillera Central; its Pico Duarte is the highest point in the Caribbean, at over 10,000 feet. Three large, agriculturally friendly valleys lie between the ranges. One, in the southwest, contains Lake Enriquillo, a saltwater lake with crocodiles.

Annual temperatures in the Dominican Republic average 77 degrees Fahrenheit. Any change in seasons is determined by amounts of rainfall. The summer months, May to October, are the hottest, reaching around 87 degrees during the day with nighttime temperatures around 72. The high humidity makes it feel hotter than it is. Annual rainfall is close to 58 inches per year, and the western part receives the most rain. The heaviest tourist season is from December through April.

The Dominicans have relied on agriculture as a base for their economy, and sugarcane is their most important crop. Other major crops are coffee, cotton, cacao, tobacco, and rice. The mining of minerals is growing in importance. The country has deposits of nickel, bauxite, gold, silver, and limited amounts of other minerals. There has been an increase in light manufacturing of textiles and clothing thanks to free-trade zones. Tourism is also important for the economy. Outward migration from the Dominican Republic has been large due to globalization. The United States, only 600 miles away, is already home to a million Dominicans. There is also a large population of former Dominican citizens in Puerto Rico, Canada, the Netherlands, Spain, and Venezuela.

🍽 Food Culture Snapshot

Christy Garcia lives with her husband and two children. She cooks a Dominican diet for her husband

A Haitian migrant worker cuts sugarcane in Barahona in July 2003. The Dominican Republic's economy is agrarian-based; the main crop is sugarcane. (AP | Wide World Photos)

every day in their home in Santo Domingo. "The mornings start with breakfast at 7:00, and we usually have a cup of hot chocolate with a piece of bread called water bread in English (*pan de agua*). The typical chocolate milk is made with a hard chocolate bar called Embajador. To make it we have to boil it in water to dissolve it, then we add sugar, a stick of cinnamon for flavor, and a very small amount of salt. We buy the fresh bread from the store. Sometimes we add butter and cheese, but not usually because the typical way was just wetting the bread with the chocolate. Some people add milk to the chocolate, but again, the typical way was just dark chocolate with water.

"Then lunch is about noon, and the typical white rice is made with boiled water with some oil and salt. We just add the rice, simmer it for a few minutes, turn it off, and wait till it is dry. We have it with red beans. The beans are boiled for a few hours because they are dried, not canned, and then we add a seasoning called *recaito,* which is made from lots of condiments and vegetables. If we don't use the recaito from the store, we fry a big onion till it burns a little (is caramelized), then add tomato paste, tomatoes, peppers, garlic, other vegetables, and salt.

"For the evening meal, at about 7:00, we mostly have chicken with the same seasonings as for the beans. In a hot pan we put oil and sugar till it burns a little. Once it is really hot, we put the chicken into the pan and watch it, adding water when needed. Once it has a nice color and taste, the chicken is ready. We also have yellow sweet plantain. We peel each of them, cut them into six pieces, and then we fry them. Sometimes we will make sweet white rice (*arroz con leche*), made by boiling water with lemon and salt in it, adding the clean, white rice, and then, once it is soft, adding sugar, a stick of cinnamon, and canned Carnation milk. After it is on the plate, we sprinkle it with powdered cinnamon. This was also used as dessert once in while."

Major Foodstuffs

Before Columbus, the Tainos arrived in the Dominican Republic with *barbacoa* (barbecue), yucca or cassava, and cassava bread. Other cultures contributed foods as well. African slaves brought plantains and bananas, as well as the custom of eating the organs of animals; the ears, feet, and heads of pigs;

and cows' intestines. People from the British West Indies brought johnnycakes, the Middle Easterners brought kibbe (ground lamb and bulgur) and tabbouleh (bulgur, parsley, and vegetables), and the Chinese a chicken and seafood stew.

As the early Tainos settled in, they were fortunate to have their skills as canoe makers, fishermen, and sailors and navigators. Thanks to their seamanship skills, they hunted ducks and turtles and fished with homemade nets made from cotton they grew. On land, there was a scarcity of wild animals, so they relied on birds, snakes, rodents, and any other small animals.

The Taino's early system of agriculture was far from labor-intensive. Crops were raised in *conucos,* large farming mounds they protected from erosion with a system of stacked leaves. They also planted a wide variety of foods to ensure an adequate harvest, no matter the type of growing season they experienced. Crops planted were a lot of cassava (also known as yucca or manioc), a staple in their diet; this is a root crop that contains a poisonous juice that needs to be extracted. It is then baked in a slab, resulting in flat bread. It was used as a wrap for fish, meat, and vegetables. They also planted garlic, potatoes, *yautías* (a root vegetable), mameys (or sapotes, a fruit), and guavas. The early Dominicans also grew corn (maize), squash, beans, chili peppers, sweet potatoes, yams, and peanuts, and they cultivated fruits such as guavas, papayas, and pineapple. Besides cotton, their other nonfood crop was tobacco, used in religious ceremonies.

Today, rice is the country's most important crop, while sugar is the Dominicans' largest crop, and as many as 30 percent of the population work in it. Additionally, many thousands of cane cutters, frequently Haitian immigrants, are necessary for harvesting. Other major food crops included starchy staples such as plantains and an assortment of tubers such as cassava, taro, sweet potatoes, and yams, which are easy to grow. Plantains are usually fried and are popular due to their sweet taste. Grains planted were usually corn, sorghum, and wheat, which they exported. Much of the corn is used for animal feed. Fresh ingredients raised by Dominicans are fruits, vegetables, and spices. These include bananas, peanuts, guavas, tamarinds, passion fruit,

soursops, coconuts, tomatoes, carrots, lettuce, cabbage, scallions, cilantro, onions, and garlic.

The Dominicans take much pride in their coffee production. They drink coffee in small cups, very strong and with lots of sugar. In fact, most brew their coffee together with sugar. It is usually served alone at any hour. Their arabica coffee is grown in the southwestern and northern sections of the country. Regardless of social class, Dominicans are eager to share it with guests. They also export their coffee, and the demand for it is increasing. The coffee bushes need the shade of trees, which is discouraging deforestation in the region. A local brand, Santo Domingo, is affordable, in demand, and considered smooth and rich.

Cooking

The cuisines of the Dominican Republic, Cuba, and Puerto Rico are similar because they are all based on available foods and Iberian influences. Because their foods are mostly fresh, cooks do not rely heavily on spicing. Popular pantry items include achiote oil, an oil that has been flavored with achiote (annatto) seeds. This makes the oil bright yellow. It is used in yellow rice and as a coloring for other dishes. *Achiotina* is lard flavored and colored with achiote seeds.

Adobo is a mixture of garlic, herbs, and spices used dry as a rub for meats or used wet with a little oil as a marinade. *Sazón* is blend of seasonings available in small foil packets. It is used with annatto for yellow rice. *Sofrito* is a sauce that is added to many dishes. It can be purchased, but it tastes better if made at home from crushed canned tomatoes, Anaheim-type peppers, yellow onions, garlic, olive oil, sweet paprika, and cilantro or parsley. These are sautéed and then simmered for about 10 minutes. Recaito is basically the same as sofrito but without the tomatoes. Dominicans' favorite spices include anise, *bija* (annatto), cinnamon, *clavo* (cloves), *malagueta* (allspice—not be confused with the chili pepper or *melegueta* pepper from West Africa), *nuez moscada* (nutmeg), oregano, *sal en grano* (sea salt), and *tomillo* (thyme).

Dominicans also eat a lot of beans. Beans are high in protein and low in fat, calories, and salt, as well as being cholesterol free. The most commonly used beans are black beans, chickpeas, pink beans, kidney beans, navy beans, and pigeon peas. The popular Dominican beans and rice dish is also called *LaBandera* for their national flag. The rice used is long-grain white rice. Frequently, instant rice is used. Shorter-grain rice is used for paella and rice desserts. Most fresh fruits, vegetables, and herbs have a short shelf life in the tropics and are purchased close to the time of use.

Dominicans also use a wide variety of utensils. A *caldero* is a cast iron cooking pot, similar to a Dutch oven, with a tight-fitting lid. A flan mold is used to make flan, an extremely popular caramelized custard dessert; various molds exist to make it into interesting shapes. Fryers are electric pots that hold deep fat heated to a controlled temperature. Seasoned cooks use their calderos and adjust the heat based on the food's appearance. Rice cookers are often used. These are a small electric pot that cooks rice automatically until the rice is soft and the liquid has been absorbed by the rice. Experienced cooks accomplish this in their basic caldero.

The *pilón* (mortar and pestle) is also essential. In Latin Caribbean cooking, it is used to crush, grind, and mash ingredients, herbs, and seasoning. Mortars and pestles can be made of ceramic, metal, stone, or wood. Some use a coffee grinder for dry items or a food processor for wet ones. A plantain press, or *tostnera*, can be made from wood, plastic, or metal. One type is used to flatten sliced plantains for frying. The other is used to stuff plantains. It has a ball on one end and a hole on the other. Many cooks improvise and don't have one. *Loco con los platanos* is a three-piece unit that comes with a plantain peeler, a smasher, and a cookbook.

Some sandwiches are pressed, like Italian panini sandwiches, in a special gadget. One can invest in a panini press or a handheld grill press. As a substitute, one can use a cast iron skillet to press down the sandwich or place a heavy foil-wrapped brick on top.

Typical Meals

Most Dominicans, who are not rich, get their calories from rice and fried plantains, as well as fruits like papayas, pineapples, bananas, and avocados. They get very little of their protein from beef, most of which is exported, and some pork when they can afford it. More plentiful sources of protein are chicken and fish, usually shrimp, marlin, mahimahi (dorado), or lobster. Dominicans' diet is less spicy hot than food in most other Latin American countries. They depend on onions, garlic, cilantro, oregano, and sweet *cubanelle* peppers for flavoring. Their one exception to this is *chivo picante,* a goat stew. They also avoid cold gazpachos based on the theory that hot soups eaten in hot weather cause perspiration, which is more cooling to the body.

Typical breakfasts consist of eggs or meat, and maybe some cheese; a strong favorite is mashed plantains (*mangu*).

Mangu

4 large plantains, peeled

2 tbsp oil

2 large onions

2 tsp salt

1 tbsp vinegar

4 tbsp butter

1 c cold water

Boil plantains in salted water until very tender. Meanwhile, put oil in a skillet, and sauté the onions, then add salt and vinegar. Reserve. Drain plantains and mash with butter and cold water until smooth. Garnish with onion, and serve with eggs or meat.

Another popular way to serve plantains is called *monfongo*. Here, green plantains are fried, seasoned with garlic, olive oil, and pork cracklings, and mashed with a little liquid. Still another favorite plantain recipe is fried plantains or plantain chips. Unripe ones are peeled, cut into pieces, and fried in deep fat. They are then flattened with the base of a bottle and quickly fried once more.

Lunch is usually a mix-all dish they term *LaBandera Dominica,* the Dominican flag. When possible, workers return home for this meal. This dish is usually composed of white rice with beef, pork, chicken, or goat, accompanied by beans, sometimes white, red, or black. The following dish has three variables—the meat, the beans, and the vegetable—and it can be the base for almost all lunches.

LaBandera Dominica (Basic Beans, Meat, and Rice)

4 tbsp oil

2 c boiled or canned beans

2 c squash, cut into small cubes

½ lb pieces of meat

3 bay leaves (optional)

I tsp thyme leaves

2 tsp cilantro, finely diced

I chicken stock cube (optional)

I large green pepper, diced

3 tsp crushed garlic

2 tbsp tomato paste

4 c water

Salt

4 c rice

Heat half the oil in an iron pot, and add beans, squash, meat, seasonings, stock cube, green pepper, and garlic. Sauté until well combined. Add tomato paste and water. Bring to a boil, adjust salt, add rice, and stir regularly to prevent sticking. When water has been absorbed, add remaining oil, cover, and place over low heat for 15 minutes. Remove from heat, cover, and wait 5 minutes. Rice should taste done. Remove any bones and bay leaves. Serve hot.

The following fish dish is a favorite and very popular during Lent. It is made with potatoes; however, it is also served with rice. The salted codfish must be soaked in many changes of fresh water overnight.

Bacalao a La Criolla (Codfish a La Dominicana)

2 lb salted dried codfish

I lb potatoes

2 tbsp oil

I small red onion, sliced

¼ c pitted olives, sliced

2 green bell peppers, diced

4 plum tomatoes, each cut into 4 quarters

½ tsp mashed garlic

2 tsp Tabasco sauce (optional)

2 tbsp tomato paste

Salt

2 lemon wedges (optional)

Boil the codfish and potatoes in 2 quarts of water until tender. Flatten the codfish, and peel and dice the potatoes. Set aside. In a skillet, heat oil, and sauté onion, olives, pepper, tomatoes, and garlic. Add I cup water and simmer for 3 minutes. Stir in codfish, Tabasco sauce, and tomato paste. Add another cup of water and the potatoes. Let simmer until potatoes are cooked, and there is a thin sauce. Season to taste. Serve with rice and garnish with lemon wedges.

A suitable luncheon dish utilizing eggplant and eggs can be made simply on the stovetop. To sautéed onions, peppers, tomatoes, garlic, and vinegar, add roasted, skinned, and mashed eggplant and simmer until the liquid is absorbed. Next, add four eggs and simmer until they harden.

Camarones Guisados (Shrimp Stew)

2 tbsp oil

I small onion, cut into strips

4 plum tomatoes, cut into strips

2 bell peppers

8 chopped, pitted green olives

½ tbsp crushed garlic

2 lb shrimp, peeled and cleaned

I tbsp tomato paste

I c water

Tabasco to taste

Salt

Heat oil, and sauté onion, tomato strips, peppers, olives, and garlic. Add shrimp, tomato paste, and water. Simmer for 3 minutes. Add Tabasco and salt to taste. Serve with fried plantains or rice.

A conch stew can also be made using the preceding recipe: Just omit the olives and cook the conch about six minutes until tender.

The heartiest meal is at lunchtime, and evening meals are light and simple, often variations of breakfasts. Usually there are also leftovers available. Fresh fruits and fruit beverages are also evening favorites.

Holiday foods are elaborate in the Dominican Republic. Besides personal family days of joy and celebration, every February is Carnival time and the celebration of Dominican independence. The end of August is the annual Merengue Festival, and on June 24 they celebrate the feast of St. John the Baptist. These are in addition to the Christian holidays of Easter and Christmas Eve, which is celebrated on January 5. At these times everyone eats and drinks heavily.

A favorite is banana-leaf bundles (*pasteles en hoja,* similar to tamales). Sautéed chopped vegetables, spices, and minced beef is simmered with tomato paste and water until the liquid is reduced. In a separate bowl they combine. A mixture of cooked, mashed yautía root, *name* root, plantains, and bouillon powder is spread onto a banana leaf, and then it is topped with some of the meat mixture. The leaf is then folded, tied, and placed in boiling water for 35 minutes. They are served with hot sauce and ketchup.

Another popular dish at Easter is *habichjuhelas con dulce,* described later, but no holiday season is complete without pork roast:

Puerco Asado (Pork Roast)

1 5-lb shoulder roast of pork

½ c sliced pitted olives

½ c capers

1 large onion, diced

4 tbsp mashed garlic

1 tsp parsley, finely diced

4 tbsp ground oregano

2 tbsp ground black pepper

1 c green peppers, diced

2 tbsp vinegar

2 tbsp oil

¼ c salt

Mix all the ingredients for the seasoning. With a sharp paring knife carve deep holes in the meat, each a few inches apart. Using a teaspoon, stuff the holes with the seasoning mixture, and spread the remaining seasoning on the surface of the meat. Marinate for at least 5 hours before cooking. Put in a 350°F oven. Baste every 30 minutes. A meat thermometer should register at 170°F when it is done. Serve with pigeon peas with rice and coconut, as well as a green salad.

The most celebrated holiday dish is a seven-meat stew called *sancocho.* This dish is expensive due to the amount of meat required, as it calls for lemon-rubbed beef bones, goat meat, *longaniza* sausage, pork, chicken, pork ribs, and smoked ham bones. These are browned and simmered with root vegetables, plantains, lemon, vinegar, and many spices. Near the end cheese-filled fritters are added. Sancocho is served with white rice.

An almost-universal holiday and family-occasion favorite is Dominican cake (*bizcocho Dominicano*). Its status is also heightened because the cake is difficult to make. There are three parts to it. First, there is the very rich cake, and then comes the equally rich pineapple filling. The cake is then topped with a caramel-infused meringue.

Beverages are important in a hot climate. Most milk is reconstituted from powdered milk. Smoothies (*batidas*) are popular and are made from fresh fruits and condensed milk. Particularly favored is ginger and lemongrass tea, as well as thick hot chocolate drinks. Their coffee is strong and served in three-ounce cups. The local beer is Presidente, and local rums are Barcelo and Brugal.

Empanadas, johnny cakes, and fritters. (Dreamstime)

Eating Out

The culture of the cuisine of the Dominican Republic is referred to as *Comida Criolla,* a blend of Spanish, African, and Taino heritage adapted to the availability of local ingredients, cooked with ancient methods. Besides formal restaurants, there are three distinct venues to in which to eat out: (1) Comedors, popular with locals, can be a room in a private home where plain Dominican foods are served. (2) Basic cafeterias are found on almost every street, some of them in chain supermarkets. These specialize in the locals' favorites of red beans and rice, and also meat stews. These are also very popular with locals. (3) Food stands serve street food, both snacks and small meals. Some sell barbecued pork, while others specialize in local-style hamburgers, pork skins, fried meats, and homemade sausages. Sandwiches are popular from store fronts. Barbecue stands serve chicken with yucca or ba-

nana. Other establishments serve *chimichurri* (*chimmi*), which are Dominican-style hamburgers, hot dogs, and pork sandwiches.

Ice cream (*helados*) is very popular in the Dominican Republic and is made with tropical fruit. It is sold in a cone or in a cup with a plastic spoon. Candy is called *dulces* and may have the consistency of fudge but be flavored with pineapple, coconut, or guava. Their peanut brittle is very popular as well.

The Dominican diet rests heavily on healthful fresh fish, seafood, and locally grown vegetables and exotic fruits. Beef is expensive, which makes pork and goat more popular. Locally made rum and beer are cheaper than hard liquor, which must be imported. Some favorite foods are red beans and rice, pork rinds, fried chicken, and soup with meat and vegetables.

Local restaurants fall into the categories of barbecue, seafood, Dominican, international, Mexican, Italian, Middle Eastern, Chinese, and Caribbean. Most resort menus reflect what management believes will cater to U.S. and Continental tastes. However, a few local influences may be evident.

Special Occasions

Music is a way of life in the Dominican Republic. Births, weddings, deaths, comings-of-age, all victories, falling in love, planting, harvest—these are all gala excuses for music, singing, and dancing. Merengue, salsa, and *bachata* ring forth in many public spaces, either live with homemade instruments, over the radio, or from professional musicians.

Every February is Carnival time with even more dancing, singing, and music. It is also a celebration of Dominican independence. The annual Merengue Festival is at the end of August and in early September. Every Easter each town's patron saint is celebrated widely, and June 24 is a very special day celebrating the feast of St. John the Baptist.

Dominican national holidays include January 1, New Year's Day; January 6, Three Kings Day (Dominican children receive their gifts on this day, not on December 25); January 21, Feast of Our Lady of Altagracia (Dominican patroness); January 26, Duarte's Birthday (first of the three founding fathers);

and February 27, Independence Day. Dates vary for Good Friday, Easter Sunday, the National Carnival Celebration at Malecon, Labor Day, Corpus Christi Day, Independence Restoration Day, Lady of Mercedes Day, and Constitution Day. Note that Christmas Day is casual for most Dominicans. The real Dominican nativity celebration takes place on January 5, when families get together to share a heavy late-night dinner and have a lot to drink.

The following are some celebratory dishes served on holidays:

Pasteles en Hoja (Banana-Leaf Bundles)

Combine chopped green pepper, onion, oregano, salt, and pepper with minced beef. Cook evenly in oil. Add a small amount of water and tomato paste, and simmer until the meat is cooked and liquid is reduced. In a separate bowl, combine yautía root, name root, plantain, chicken bouillon powder, and salt. Place 2 tablespoonfuls of this mixture in the center of a banana leaf, add 1 teaspoon of the meat mixture, and cover with 2 more tablespoons of grated root mix. Fold shut and fasten all sides with string. Place in boiling water and boil over medium heat for 35 minutes. Cool, unwrap, and serve with hot sauce and ketchup.

Habichuelas con Dulce (A Popular Easter Dish)

Puree red kidney beans in a food processor until smooth. Combine beans, coconut milk, and some milk in a pot and boil. Add more milk, sugar, cinnamon sticks, raisins, and sweet potatoes, and cook over low heat for 20 minutes. Add coconut milk and cloves, and simmer until smooth. Serve chilled over browned cassava bread.

Sancocho (Holiday Stew)

This is a special, hearty, seven-meat stew served throughout the holiday season. Brown and combine goat meat, pork sausage, pork meat, beefsteak, chicken, pork ribs, and smoked ham. Season with lime, garlic, oil, bell peppers, thyme, yam, celery, cassava root, potatoes, plantain, oregano, coriander, cilantro, and hot sauce. Stew all until tender. Serve with avocado slices and rice.

Pudín o Bizocho (Special Dominican Holiday Cake)

This dish is probably the one way to declare a totally festive occasion. It is made in four parts: the cake itself, its filling, caramel icing, and a stiff meringue.

The cake is composed of butter, margarine, lime peel, orange juice, flour, sugar, vanilla, baking powder, and eggs. The caramel icing is made of sugar and water. The filling is cubed fresh pineapple, water, sugar, and vanilla extract. The meringue is made with five egg whites, fine granulated sugar, salt, and cream of tartar. Beat until peaks are formed, then very slowly add in the caramel icing.

Popular beverages are eggnog (*poncho de huevo*) with or without rum. As an after-dinner drink, monkey anise (*anis del mono*) is enjoyed. A gingerroot beverage (*jengibre*) is made of boiled gingerroot, cinnamon, and lots of sugar.

Diet and Health

Type 2 diabetes is prevalent in the population of the Dominican Republic. This is no doubt aggravated by diets high in rice, sugar, starchy roots, fatty meats, and sugars from many fresh fruits. Additionally, dietary problems in the Dominican Republic tended to be concentrated in the areas of deficiencies in iodine, vitamin A, and iron, and approximately 5 percent of school-age children have goiter problems. The severity varies regionally, and the World Health Organization has enforced use of iodized salt in cooking since 1920.

Marty Martindale

Further Reading

"Dominican Republic, Spanish Foods". Colonial Zone, October 2009. http://www.

colonialzone-dr.com/food-spanish_food_words.html.

"Dominican Republic." Librarians' Internet Index. October 2009. http://lcweb2.loc.gov/frd/cs/dotoc.html.

Drago, Lorena. *Beyond Rice and Beans: The Caribbean Latino Guide to Eating Healthy with Diabetes.* Alexandria, VA: American Diabetes Association, 2006.

Gonzalez, Clara. Aunt Clara's Dominican Kitchen. October 2009. http://www.dominicancooking.com.

Gonzalez, Clara, and Ilana Benady. *Traditional Dominican Cookery.* Santo Domingo, Dominican Republic: Lunch Club Press, 2005.

Rouse, Irving. *The Tainos: Rise and Decline of the People Who Greeted Columbus.* New Haven, CT: Yale University Press, 1992.

Ecuador

Overview

Ecuador lies on the equator in western South America, bordered by Colombia to the north, Peru to the south, and the Pacific Ocean on the west. The Galapagos Islands also belong to Ecuador. It measures 283,561 square miles and has a population of about 14.5 million people. This region enjoys an incredibly rich biodiversity with a remarkable number of unique species, especially on the Galapagos. The country is divided into three distinct regions: the coast, which is tropical and very humid; the Sierra, or highlands, which is cooler and drier and spans a section of the Andes Mountains; and, lastly, the Oriente, a part of the Amazon basin that is rain forest. The altitude is also a crucial factor in determining which crops can be grown, with tubers more common in higher areas and rice in the lowlands. More than half the population lives in cities, the largest of which is Guayaquil on the coast, but the capital is Quito, which sits at 8,464 feet and has a beautifully preserved historic center.

People of mixed heritage (Spanish and Native American), or mestizos, make up 65 percent of Ecuador's population, with indigenous Amerindians making up 25 percent. The latter come from a variety of groups, the majority of which in the highlands are Quichua, but there are also Caranqui, Otavaleños, Cayambi, Pichincha, and others. There are also many indigenous peoples of the Amazon. A small number of white, mostly Spanish, inhabitants comprise 7 percent, and there is a smaller number of people of African and mixed African descent, at 3 percent. Most people speak Spanish, but there is a large number of people who also speak Quichua (as it is called there). About 95 percent of Ecuadorians worship officially as Roman Catholics, though historically in practice this religion has incorporated many elements of indigenous religious beliefs and festivals. There is also a great disparity of wealth in Ecuador, with marked social inequality. Many people, especially the indigenous population, live well below the poverty line.

The cuisine of Ecuador, like its people, is a mix of indigenous and European components, with many native New World species forming the basic staples and many Old World plants and animals combined with these. Likewise, the culinary techniques span a broad range of styles, some of which are clearly descended from medieval Spanish cuisine, while others are still completely indigenous, in addition to many completely unique combinations of the two. It is also important to remember that what is today Ecuador entailed many indigenous cultures through history, only the last of which, centered in Quito, was engulfed by the Inca Empire in 1463. Not long after this, the Incas in turn were conquered by the Spanish under Francisco Pizarro in 1533. In 1809 Ecuador was also the first Latin American country to declare independence from Spain, but it did not become an independent republic until 1830.

🍽 Food Culture Snapshot

Hector González Vargas and his wife, Concepción, live in the city of Guayaquil. They have a two-year-old daughter named Manuela. Hector has a university education and works as a petroleum engineer for a large multinational company. His wife works in the home, does all the cooking, and takes care of the baby. Her mother still lives in the northern highlands, in a small village called Atuntaqui, which is known for its textiles. Concepción learned to cook from her mother, so she knows many traditional dishes, but Hector prefers modern international cooking and sometimes eats fast food in the city for lunch with his colleagues. As an educated urbanite, Hector is anxious to buy modern appliances for his household, though his wife prefers cooking at a leisurely pace, taking time to make traditional dishes. She fears that expensive imported foods not only will drain the household budget but will also make Hector fat. Concepción is often found making *humitas*, a kind of tamale from Ecuador that she folds delicately in corn husks and ties with a torn strip of husk, then steams in a special pot that her mother gave them as a wedding present. Sometimes she fills them with onions and cheese, or sometimes she makes them sweet, studded with raisins and a pinch of cinnamon. She hopes some day to pass on her love of cooking to her own young daughter.

A vendor cooks potatoes at a market in Otavalo, Equador. (iStockPhoto)

Major Foodstuffs

The starchy staples of Ecuador, sometimes grains and sometimes tubers, depend primarily on the region, though most are enjoyed to some extent throughout the nation. The most important indigenous plants are potatoes, corn, quinoa, and yucca (or cassava). Potatoes were domesticated in the Andes and represent this area's greatest contribution to the world food supply. One of the unique Ecuadorian dishes, which derives from the highlands, bears the delightful name *llapingachos.* They consist of boiled potatoes, mashed and rolled into balls that are filled with cheese. These are flattened and cooked on a griddle. They are usually colored yellow with achiote (annatto) and can be served with a peanut sauce (*salsa di maní*) or with sausages on the side. They are now enjoyed throughout the country practically as a national dish.

Maize, or corn, was domesticated to the north but may have been introduced to this area and cultivated here as early as 10,000 years ago, making its cultivation roughly contemporaneous with the development of agriculture in the Middle East. Corn features in many dishes, often simply roasted on the cob or sliced into rounds on the cob and cooked in soups. This is not the sweet corn with which North Americans are familiar but instead *choclo,* a huge-grained, chewy, and very flavorsome variety that is used extensively in soups and stews. Preparations familiar elsewhere in Latin America are common too, though. Freshly ground corn is steamed in corn husks to make humitas, which are something like tamales from Mexico and can be either savory or sweet. Field corn that has been nixtamalized—soaked in lye or calcium hydroxide so that the kernel swells and the outer pericarp comes off—is ground into dough and cooked in various ways. The whole kernels, called *mote,* similar to hominy in the United States, are also cooked into various dishes, like *mote pillo,* in which they are mixed with eggs, chives, and cilantro. An even more unique corn dish is *cancha,* which is a fried corn kernel that puffs up a little and becomes crunchy, familiar in the United States as corn nuts. Popcorn is also a familiar food, served interestingly with the raw fish dish of ceviche.

Quinoa was in precolonial times one of the most important grains, though its connection to fertility rites and indigenous religion meant that the Spanish did everything they could to eradicate it. This is a shame since it has one of the highest protein contents of any grain on earth; it has recently enjoyed a resurgence outside of South America among health-food enthusiasts.

Yucca, also known as cassava, is a starchy root, used primarily in the rain forest. It is familiar in the United States only as tapioca, which is made from the starch. There are both bitter (poisonous) and sweet varieties of the plant, and it is remarkable that indigenous peoples learned to process it thousands of years ago as a staple food.

Bananas, introduced ultimately from Southeast Asia, apart from being one of the principal agricultural products of Ecuador and one of its main exports, are also used in cooked dishes, especially green plantains, which are starchier than the types eaten out of hand. These may be simply fried, squashed, and refried as a snack called *patacones,* known throughout Latin America under various names. Plantain chips are also known as *chifles,* eaten as a snack. The more interesting plantain variants include the *bolon de verde,* a fried plantain dumpling that is also featured in soups, as discussed later on.

Surprisingly, rice, another Asian plant, is today one of the most popular side dishes in Ecuador. It is often served as *arroz amarillo,* meaning yellow rice, with achiote (annatto seeds) taking the place of saffron, which would have been used in Europe.

Squash in the Cucurbitaceae family were almost certainly the earliest domesticated plants in this region, though archaeologists debate exactly how their cultivation developed and what connection it might have to permanent dwellings and the use of ceramics. Today, squash is added to many soups and stews or even made into fritters called *pristinos.* The pumpkin (*calabaza*) is first cooked, then combined with flour, baking powder, and cheese to make a dough that is then rolled out, cut into circles, and fried. They are sometimes served with cinnamon syrup as well. This is a perfect example of a native plant being used in a thoroughly European recipe. Squashes like zucchini are American and are used throughout Ecuador.

Beans are one of the most important sources of protein historically, and the lima bean is native to western South America. Beans are used in countless soups and stews, as are other members of the *Phaseolus* genus, as well as chickpeas and lentils. The latter are used in the popular soup referred to simply as *menestra.* There is even a kind of bean called *nuñas* that is used specially for popping like corn. Peanuts, in the same large family of legumes, are another very important South American native and are used extensively in Ecuador in sauces (salsa di maní) as well as in a soup made with potatoes, onion, and ground peanuts. For flavorings there are all the familiar herbs and spices, but everywhere one finds chili peppers used in *aji,* a hot sauce, though in general Ecuadorean cooking is not very spicy.

Although the *cuy,* or guinea pig, is probably the domesticated animal most readily associated with Andean cuisine since ancient times, Ecuadoreans enjoy a broad range of proteins including beef, pork, goat, and to a lesser extent chicken and turkey, though the latter is an American native. Beef can be sliced thinly and served with onions and tomatoes as a *lomo salteado,* but more often it appears in stews; likewise, pork is used in stews like *seco de chanco* and chicken in a *seco de pollo.* These usually also include a variety of vegetables, perhaps beans or grains, and are filling, especially when served with rice, avocado, and perhaps a slice of lime.

On the coast, seafood is the favorite, with various fishes such as tuna, sea bass, shark, and snapper finding their way into soups and stews, as well as a

Guinea pigs (*conejillos de indias*) or cuy as they are called in Ecuador, are cooked over an outdoor grill. (David L Amsler)

wide array of shellfish such as shrimp (which form one of Ecuador's major industries), clams, mussels, squid, octopus, and scallops. Perhaps the dish most readily associated with the South American coast is ceviche, and justly so. Ceviche is a kind of fish salad marinated in lime juice, which "cooks" it by firming up the proteins and killing the bacteria. Its history is a matter of speculation, and it has been suggested that before the introduction of citrus fruits by the Spanish it was soured with *chicha,* a fermented corn drink. The dish also bears some relation to a medieval Spanish dish called *escabeche,* which was cooked, but cold, fish marinated in vinegar. The fish is soaked in lime anywhere from 30 minutes to a couple of hours, along with chili peppers, cilantro, often tomatoes in Ecuador or some tomato sauce, and pickled onions (*cebollas encurtidas*). It is light and refreshing and in the heat of summer can form a meal unto itself.

There are dozens upon dozens of fruits native to Ecaudor. Apart from those familiar in the United States, there is the *naranjilla,* a small fruit in the Solanaceae family related to tomatoes, which is eaten fresh or juiced. There are several kinds of passion fruit: the standard *maracuya,* as well as the *taxo,* or banana passion fruit, so called because it is longish and yellow, as well as the smaller round, yellow *granadillo.* The tamarillo, or tree tomato (*tamat de árbol*), is used for juice as well as in a spicy salsa. Cherimoyas are also popular.

Cooking

Most familiar cooking methods are used in Ecuador, with some having a longer pre-Columbian history and some having been introduced in the past five centuries. Roasted foods (*horneado*) are especially appreciated, in particular, pork with potatoes. Grilled foods (*a la brasa*) and steamed food (*al vapor*) are also common and of ancient use. The most popular dishes, however, are stews like *seco,* while deep-fried foods (*brosterizado*) and breaded fried foods (*apanado*) are more recent introductions. The following is a simple recipe that can be made with practically any fish and variety of vegetables on hand:

Chupe de Pescado (Fish Soup)

Serves 4

2 stalks celery

1 green bell pepper, chopped

1 onion, chopped

2 large tomatoes, finely chopped

¼ tsp annatto

2 carrots, peeled and cut into slices

2 parsnips, peeled and cut into slices

2 small waxy potatoes

8 oz hominy (or 1 can)

1 bay leaf

Pinch of oregano

1 8-oz container fresh lump crabmeat

½ lb shrimp, raw in shell

1 egg per person

Sauté the first three ingredients in olive oil until lightly browned. Add the tomatoes and stir vigorously. Then add the annatto. Add 4 cups of water or more as desired, and bring to a boil. Add all the other vegetables and herbs, and lower to a simmer for about 15 minutes. Before serving, add the crabmeat and shrimp and just cook through. Serve hot with a little of each vegetable in each serving and a few shrimp on top. Just before serving crack in the egg raw. It will cook in the soup. You can use any fresh fish with this recipe as well. You can also sprinkle crumbled fresh white cheese on top if you like.

Typical Meals

Ecuadorean meals usually comprise three parts: a soup, main dish, and dessert. Breakfast is usually small, consisting of a basic starch or bread, pastry, fruit, and coffee, though laborers may often sit down to a bowl of chicken stew with rice or a hearty seafood stew to fortify them for the day. Lunch and dinner are usually larger meals, with lunch (*almuerzo*) usually the larger of the two. Dinner may even be as light as bread and coffee, or steamed humitas.

Soups are perhaps the most important range of dishes in the Ecuadorean repertoire. There is a very popular potato soup with cheese and avocado called *locro,* as well as a potato soup sprinkled with lamb's blood called *yaguarlocro.* There are fish soups with vegetables like chupe de pescado, and one particular soup, noted for its ability to promote virility, is made with boiled cow's hooves and called *caldo de pata.* On the coast there are various menestra made with lentils or chickpeas simmered in a *refrito,* or sauce of tomato, peppers, and onion. Soups can even be extremely elaborate like the *caldo de bollas* from Guayaquil, which includes plantain dumplings stuffed with meat served in a beef broth with corn segments and other vegetables. Likewise, there is *encebollado* with onions, tuna, yucca, and tomatoes with a dash of lime for acidity. The most popular soup is eaten on Easter, a vegetable soup called *fanseca.* Stews are equally important and can be made of virtually any combination of meats, vegetables, and grains or tubers.

Drinks that accompany meals include the familiar soft drinks, imported wine, and beer, but there are unique indigenous drinks as well. The most important of these is chicha*,* made with corn that traditionally had been chewed and mixed with saliva to start the fermentation. Today, the corn is ground, and bacterial cultures are added. Chicha can also be made with rice or yucca, and it is essentially a kind of thick creamy beer that is light in alcohol.

Ecuador also produces distilled *aguardiente,* which is a legacy of Spanish influence. It is normally made of sugarcane or the by-products of sugar manufacture (i.e., molasses) and thus can be similar to rum, but it tastes quite different and is normally unflavored. It literally means "burning water" and can be drunk straight but is more often found in mixed drinks like *canelazo,* which is made from boiling water, lemon, sugar, cinnamon, and aguardiente. This spirit can also be distilled from virtually any grain or fruit, but the best is from sugar. Fruit juices are also very popular and can be made of virtually anything, though the most familiar kinds are pineapple and passion fruit.

Coffee is one of Ecuador's principal cash crops as well as one of the most significant causes of environmental degradation and loss of rain forest. Some regions have turned to coffee as their sole monoculture industry, leaving them particularly vulnerable to fluctuations in price on the international market.

Eating Out

Street foods are very popular in Ecuador, and one find a variety of fritters and fried doughs like *buñuelos*—a kind of donut—and other pastries. Much simpler is choclo, the large chewy Andean corn barbecued, though this corn also features in empanadas (small pies), which include meat or other vegetables.

There are many restaurants in Ecuador, whose height of business is the lunch hours since many people eat out at midday. In rural areas restaurants may even be closed at night. Some serve local food or cater to tourists in larger cities. In recent decades many fast-food restaurants have also appeared, including all those common in the United States as well as McDonalds, which is very popular. One can also find various ethnic restaurants, most notably Chinese. In fact, there is still a Chinese community that originated in the 19th century, and most Ecuadoreans would be familiar with dishes like fried rice with chicken, which goes by the name *chaulafan de pollo.*

Special Occasions

Since the majority of Ecuadoreans are Roman Catholic, they follow traditional fasting restrictions during Lent and on other fast days, when meat and meat products are prohibited, as well as celebrating Christian festivals such as Christmas and Easter. Celebrations are nonetheless often syncretically mixed with indigenous religious practices so that holidays like All Saints' Day may bear little resemblance to the holiday elsewhere. Certain foods are associated with holidays, especially fanseca for Easter. *Guaguas de pan*—stuffed breads shaped like children—are eaten on November 2, the Día de los Fieles Difuntos (Day of the Dead), and *colada morada* is drunk, a sweet purple drink made from blackberries, a kind of blue berries called *mortiños,* pineapple, and spices and thickened with corn flour. On this day families dress up and visit cemeteries, where they make offerings of flowers, crosses, and paper crowns as well as fruits, cooked eggs, and bowls of cooked food.

Diet and Health

Ecuador is a country of great disparities in income and food security. While a privileged minority enjoys general good nutrition and health, a significant proportion of the indigenous rural population as well as the urban poor is undernourished. This has partly been the result of failed government policies to implement equitable food distribution, but it means that iron-deficiency anemia is a serious problem and as many as 15 percent of children's growth is stunted. There is also an extremely high infant mortality rate. Water-borne illnesses are a serious problem, and many people have no access to clean water. Parasites are also a problem, as are malaria, hepatitis, and typhoid.

Ken Albala

Further Reading

Archetti, Eduardo P., and Valentina Napolitano. *Guinea Pigs: Food, Symbol and Conflict of Knowledge in Ecuador.* New York: Berg, 2001.

"Ecuadorean Food and Recipes." Ecuador Explorer. http://www.ecuadorexplorer.com/html/ecuador_food.html.

Minster, Christopher. "Traditional Ecuadorean Food." Suite 101. http://south-american-food.suite101.com/article.cfm/ecuadorian_food_main_dishes.

Weismantel, Mary J. *Food, Gender and Poverty in the Ecuadorian Andes.* Philadelphia: University of Pennsylvania Press, 1988.

El Salvador

Overview

El Salvador is the smallest country in Central America, sandwiched between Guatemala and Honduras, and the only one without an Atlantic coastline. The country was originally inhabited by Native Americans, specifically the Pipil tribes. The Spanish controlled the area from the 1500s until the 1821 revolt for independence.

Nearly 97 percent of the 7,185,218 inhabitants of El Salvador are mestizos, or a blend of Native American and Spanish descent. The remainder of the population is comprised of indigenous Americans, Africans, and Creoles, or people of unmixed European descent. There is a large income gap between the country's wealthiest and poorest citizens, with nearly 50 percent of the population subsisting below the national poverty line. The country survived a 12-year civil war that ended in 1992, which had a definite impact on Salvadoran cuisine with respect to availability and the division of cooking labor within the home.

🍽 Food Culture Snapshot

Julia Garcia is a single Salvadoran mother raising her three children, Jesus, Juanita, and Pedro, in a rural town north of San Salvador, the capital, near the foothills of Mount Guazapa. The town is a new *comunidade* (community) given to the leftist Farabundo Marti National Liberation Front (FMLN) guerrilla organization and their land-poor families as part of the peace agreement signed to end the civil war in 1992. Julia was a guerrilla with the FMLN during the war and was rewarded with a small bit of land, materials, and money to restart her life. Although it is rural and surrounded by dirt roads, Julia has enough space in her 30 by 10 foot cement dwelling for beds for herself, her children, and her mother and father, who also live with her and help run her *milpa*, or farm.

The Garcias grow corn, rice, and beans and raise the occasional chicken or cow. Not only does this provide income for the family but also their daily food. The morning starts early for Julia, who wakes up at 6 A.M. to start grinding the maize (corn) for the day's tortillas. Most meals in the Garcia household revolve around tortillas and beans. For breakfast, Julia fries up leftover beans and rice from the previous night's dinner into a dish called *casamiento*, which she serves to her family with tortillas that are still warm from the griddle and coffee.

Lunch is made of freshly cooked black beans with more warm tortillas and slices of banana from her neighbor's milpa. Dinner is more beans and tortillas accompanied by *sopa de pata*, or a soup made with tripe, cow feet, and corn, flavored with lemon and chili. The family recently butchered their cow, and the extra pieces that are not sold in the market are saved for family dinners. On the weekends, Julia's mother treats the family by making a *semita*, a coffee cake filled with papaya jam.

Major Foodstuffs

Indigenous American populations in El Salvador were mainly vegetarian prior to European settlement, cooking with little fat and eating meat only on special occasions. When the Spanish took control of the country in the 1500s, they brought along with them a variety of new cooking methods like frying and sautéing and ingredients like animal fat and rice that influenced the native cuisine.

The climate in El Salvador is tropical, with a rainy season between May and October and a dry season between November and April. Mountains encompass most of the terrain, along with a central plateau region, as well as slender coastlines. The focus of food production in El Salvador revolves around coffee, rice, beans, and corn, as well as shrimp and grass-fed beef. All of these ingredients figure into the average daily diet of a Salvadoran depending on their social class. For example, beef is highly prized and part of at least one meal a day for middle- and upper-class families, but it remains a rare indulgence

A girl picks coffee beans on the San Salvador Volcano in San Salvador in October 1997. El Salvador's economy, heavily dependent on agriculture, has been weakened during the 1990s and into the 2000s because of civil war and weather phenomena. (AP | Wide World Photos)

for the poor. Seafood and pork are also eaten, and rural diets can be enhanced with *cusuco,* a breed of armadillo. Corn is used daily to make tortillas, *pupusas* (stuffed tortillas), tamales, drinks, and desserts.

Volcanoes are found all across Central America, and they have made the soil incredibly rich in nutrients and ideal for growing many kinds of produce. These include but are not limited to mangoes, watermelons, papayas, guavas, lettuce, coconuts, tamarinds, cabbage, bananas, squash, yucca, peppers, and tomatoes. The plantain is a staple starch in El Salvador, even more so than potatoes, and can be used unripe (green) in savory applications or ripe (black) in sweet applications.

An important ingredient in Salvadoran and Central American cooking is annatto seeds, which come from an indigenous tree known as achiote and were used by the indigenous population for special rituals, body and pottery painting, and even currency. Today, the seeds are ground into a paste with salt, pepper, lime or sour orange juice, and vinegar to be used as a marinade for meats. Before refrigeration, achiote paste prevented the meat from spoiling, and although flavorless raw, the flavors are emphasized through the application of heat.

Salvadorans value fresh, seasonal produce and prefer making food from scratch, so shopping at an open-air market is often a daily occurrence. Community marketplaces are considered to be social venues where one can catch up with family and friends. Most Salvadoran culinary traditions are passed down orally, and the marketplace is where families share and trade cooking tips. In middle- and upper-class families, which tend to have a family chef, one member of the family is assigned to help the chef cook the family's style of cooking, so the home kitchen is another place where Salvadoran oral culinary history and traditions are passed along.

Purified drinking water is not available to the entire population, and tropical, sugary fruit juice drinks called *aguas frescas* are popular. Kolachampan is a sugarcane-flavored soda, and *ensaladas* (literally, "salad") are blended mixed-fruit juices. Corn is used to make several different drinks, including a warm glass of *atole,* a filling drink served salty or sweet, and *chicha,* an indigenous alcoholic beverage. Pilsner is the beer of choice in El Salvador.

Cooking

Corn is a popular Salvadoran ingredient, but it takes a great deal of work to make it usable. Dried corn is soaked in a lime-water solution until soft, then ground (with an appliance or by hand) into masa, a soft corn dough that is used as the base for tortillas, tamales, empanadas, and more. To make tortillas, a small bit of dough is rolled or pressed out into a circle of the desired size, then quickly cooked on a hot griddle. The same dough can be made into tamale dough with a slight adjustment of ingredients, filled with meat or cheese, then wrapped in banana leaves before being steamed or boiled.

Another well-liked Salvadoran dish that uses masa is the pupusa. Said to be created by the Pipil tribe that used to inhabit El Salvador, a pupusa is a stuffed tortilla, a common street food. The method is similar to that for making tortillas, except that the dough is wrapped around a range of fillings including cheese, *chicharrones* (pork rinds), beans, squash, and so on before being griddled. It is served with *curtido,* a spicy pickled mix of cabbage, carrots, and chili peppers that is said to enhance the pupusa's subtle flavors.

Cheese-Stuffed *Pupusas*

Serves 4 people (1 pupusa each)

Ingredients

Dough

2 c masa harina

1 c water

1 tbsp olive oil

Salt and pepper to taste

Filling

½ c crumbled *queso fresco* (fresh cheese)

½ c white melting cheese, like Chihuahua

Method

Mix the masa harina, water, and olive oil in a bowl until combined into a soft dough. Taste for flavor, and then adjust seasonings with salt and pepper to your preference.

Split the dough into 8 evenly sized balls, roughly 2 inches in diameter. Roll out each ball into a 6-inch circle. Sprinkle cheese evenly over the middle of the tortilla, then top with another rolled-out tortilla, pinching the edges to seal the filling inside. Place the stuffed tortilla on a preheated ungreased griddle, and cook on both sides until the tortilla is crispy and the cheese is melted and warm, a few minutes. Serve with spicy, room-temperature curtido (recipe follows).

Curtido

Ingredients

¼ head red cabbage, thinly sliced

¼ head green cabbage, thinly sliced

1 carrot, peeled and grated

2 scallions, thinly sliced

1 c water

1 jalapeño pepper, minced

1½ c apple cider vinegar

½ tbsp salt

1 tsp brown sugar

½ tsp Mexican oregano

Place the cabbage, carrots, and scallions in a large bowl. Bring the water, hot pepper, vinegar, salt, sugar, and oregano to a boil in a small pot. Pour the hot pickling liquid over the bowl of vegetables, and stir. Cover and let sit for at least 24 hours, then pack into a container and store in the refrigerator for 2 to 3 weeks. Let the curtido come to room temperature before serving with pupusas.

Rice is another important staple ingredient in Salvadoran cooking, and it is said that cooks are judged by the fluffiness of their rice. After the rice has been rinsed, the grains are browned in oil with some onion, which allows the rice to remain fluffy after it is cooked and flavors it as well. Most meat is marinated in citrus juices, which help to flavor and tenderize the meat, especially in dishes like *carne asada* (roast meat).

Cooking was traditionally handled by the woman of the house, especially if the man of the house (if there was one) worked outside of the home. It wasn't until after the civil war ended in 1992 that women's rights became an important cause in Central America. Women gained a right to education and began working outside the home. Another positive result of the war was that men started helping out more at home, especially in the kitchen. Fathers, husbands, and sons are pitching in to assist with grinding the daily corn, helping to cook a family meal, and even cleaning up, as the civil war emphasized the importance of all people, men and women, rich and poor, being considered equal.

Typical Meals

For breakfast, beans and tortillas are the most common and affordable dish in El Salvador. Tropical fruits are also served, such as bananas, papayas, and mangoes. *El huevos picados* (scrambled eggs with vegetables) is a popular dish, along with cheese. *Plátanos fritos* is another popular breakfast dish,

Traditional tamales, a mix of meat and vegetables with rice or corn folded in a banana leaf and then steamed. (Raphael Chay | Dreamstime.com)

made from deep-fried plantains, which can be served savory (unripe plantains) or sweet (ripe plantains).

For lunch and dinner, a variety of popular Salvadoran dishes can be made or purchased, depending on the situation. Pupusas are stuffed tortillas, a popular street food that is quick and cheap. Other popular street foods include empanadas (flour pastries stuffed with meats or vegetables) and tamales, which are stuffed with meat or sweet corn and wrapped in banana leaves before being steamed.

Sopa de pollo (Salvadoran chicken soup) is another common dish, made from chicken, chickpeas, potatoes, yucca, cilantro, onions, and lime. Beef is a standard meat for those who can afford it, and Salvadorans grill it in carne asada (grilled skirt steak) and cook it in *bistec encebollado* (beef simmered with onions). Since El Salvador is a coastal country, seafood and fish are commonly eaten, typically in stew or soup form. Snacks are often fried, like chicharron (pork rind), *yucca frita* (fried yucca), and *pacalla* (cornmeal-breaded palm flowers fried and served with tomato sauce).

Hot chocolate and coffee are the most popular drinks in the country, along with *refrescos,* or fruit drinks. Common Salvadoran desserts include *tres leches* cake (cake made with three kinds of milk), *arroz con leche* (rice pudding), and semita (coffee cake–type pastry filled with different jams or preserves). The Salvadoran quesadilla is another famous dessert, essentially a sweet cheese pound cake flavored with sour cream, sesame seeds, and queso fresco or Parmesan cheese.

Eating Out

In major cities throughout El Salvador, fast-food restaurants and more expensive, sit-down restaurants thrive. Subway, Pizza Hut, Burger King, and several other American fast-food chain restaurants have made their way down to major Salvadoran cities. Outside of the cities, the most common style of restaurant is the *comedores,* which function like cafeterias with either a menu to order from or a buffet to choose from, and a waitress that brings the food to the table. Also, street-food vendors are popular all over El Salvador; they sell items like pupusas with curtido for busy workers with no time to cook. Pupusas are also sold in *pupuserías,* or restaurants that specialize in making pupusas.

Special Occasions

Much of El Salvador is Roman Catholic, so Christmas and Semana Santa, or Holy Week (the week before Easter), are especially important occasions in the average Salvadoran life. Tamales are one traditional food made for such celebrations, as are pupusas with curtido and *panes con chumpe,* which are Salvadoran turkey sandwiches typically made on Christmas Eve or New Year's Eve.

Diet and Health

The general diet of El Salvador, which consists of corn and beans supplemented with meat, dairy, and fresh produce, is healthy. Tortillas and beans provide more than enough complex protein for the body; beans provide fiber, magnesium, and vitamin B, among other nutrients, and tortillas gain zinc and iron from being ground on a grinding stone. Tropical fruits that are native to El Salvador, such as mangoes, bananas, sour oranges, and papayas, offer plenty of carotenoids and vitamin C.

With almost half of the population living below the national poverty level, financial distress often prevents families from getting a well-balanced, healthy diet in El Salvador. Fresh fruits and meats like beef and chicken are not affordable to all income levels, and the little meat purchased by the poor tends to be high in fat and low in nutrition, like sausages. Food security in El Salvador has been threatened by natural disasters (including an earthquake and a mudslide), rising food prices, little education, lack of food production, and financial hardship. Sixteen percent of rural families do not make enough money to buy food. A civil war in the 1980s displaced rural communities that had been relied on to produce cereals for the country, which has led to reduced food supplies. Malnutrition in children under the age of five has led to an increase in stunted growth among Salvadoran children.

Leena Trivedi-Grenier

Further Reading

Balladares-Castellon, Enrique. "Central America." *Encyclopedia of Food and Culture,* edited by Solomon H. Katz, 1:340–46. New York: Gale Cengage, 2003.

"El Salvador." The CIA World Factbook Web Site. https://www.cia.gov/library/publications/the-world-factbook/geos/es.html

Gorkin, Michael, Gloria Leal, and Marta Pineda. *From Grandmother to Granddaughter: Salvadoran Women's Stories.* Berkeley: University of California Press, 2000.

Hubbard, Kirsten. "El Salvador Food and Drink." About.com. http://gocentralamerica.about.com/od/elsalvadorguide/p/ElSalvador_Food.htm.

McDonald, Michael R. *Food Culture in Central America.* Westport, CT: Greenwood Press, 2009.

"Salvadoran Food." Salv Aide Web Site. http://www.salvaide.ca/salvadoranfood.html.

Sanjur, Diva. *Hispanic Foodways, Nutrition, and Health.* Boston: Allyn and Bacon, 1995.

French Guiana

Overview

French Guiana, called La Guyane in French, has a complex and intriguing history that has had a direct effect on the country's food culture. It is an overseas department of France (*département d'outre-mer,* or DOM). Located on the northeastern Atlantic coast of South America, between Suriname and Brazil, it is a small country in terms of area and has a population of approximately 220,000. The capital and largest city is Cayenne, with a population of a little over 60,000. The country has a tropical climate, with coastal access, low plains, mountains, and dense rain forest that covers the majority of the land.

Historically and culturally, French Guiana is more akin to the Caribbean rather than other countries in South America. The area was originally inhabited by Amerindians (predominantly Carib, Arawak, and Kali'na tribes), long before European colonization. The Amerindians gave the area an appropriate name based on the ocean and many rivers, as *Guiana* means "land of many waters."

Christopher Columbus explored the coastal area near French Guiana on his third voyage in 1498, but it was the French who began to settle the region during the first half of the 17th century, albeit with pushback from the Portuguese. They managed to establish Cayenne in 1643 as a trading port, along with setting up some small plantations in the region. Facing more attacks, the French made Cayenne a permanent settlement in 1664. Throughout the latter half of the 17th century, the area switched hands a number of times between the Dutch, French, British, and Portuguese. The regular fighting over the land hindered the area that is now French Guiana from developing as substantially as in the rest of the Guianas, where the Dutch had more control. Sugarcane, though, was the main product here as well, which saw slaves from West Africa being brought over to work the plantations.

The territory was seized by the combined British-Portuguese forces based in Brazil in 1809, and it was under Portugal's control until 1814, when the French regained the land after the signing of the Treaty of Paris. The plantations almost collapsed after the abolition of slavery in 1848, but, as in the rest of the Guianas, laborers were brought in from India and China to fill the void.

Devil's Island, off the coast of French Guiana, became home to a penal colony from 1852 until the mid-20th century, with convicts from mainland France being sent there to carry out their prison terms. The infamy of the prison was captured in the book and movie *Papillon,* based on the life of an inmate there. French Guiana became an overseas department of France in 1946.

Demographically, the country is very diverse. Today, the population of French Guiana consists of Creoles (those with African ancestry), Europeans (not surprisingly, mostly French), Chinese, East Indians, and Amerindians, as well as immigrants from Haiti, Suriname, and Brazil. The majority of the population lives in the coastal towns. There are also Hmong refugees from Laos, who arrived in the 1970s and settled in smaller rural farming communities, such as Javouhey and Cacao. Most are market farmers, growing fruits and vegetables that they sell in the cities, and actually supply the country with the majority of its produce. Maroons (escaped slaves) established themselves deep in the interior rain forests, preserving a lifestyle and culture closely tied to their African roots. These communities, descendants of the original Maroons, still exist today.

French Guiana's economy is dependent on France, relying on subsidies, which makes the standard of living one of the highest in South America, at least in the cities. The rural villages are poorer, and the Amerindians and Maroons live a subsistence lifestyle inland. Unemployment is high.

Even though the soils are fertile, a small percentage of the land is cultivated; a good amount of the food in French Guiana is imported. Fishing is one of the main industries, particularly for shrimp. Rice, manioc (cassava), sugar, rum, livestock, gold, and timber are among other important industries. The space center, Centre Spatial Guyanais, was established in 1964 near Kourou and accounts for about 25 percent of the gross domestic product (GDP).

 Food Culture Snapshot

Jean-Claude, Marie, and their children live in Cayenne, the largest city in French Guiana. They start the day with a stop at the local bakery to buy croissants for breakfast. Today is market day, so they go to the open-air market, as do most residents in Cayenne. There, they purchase fresh fruits and vegetables for their meals from a Hmong family who grew the items themselves and brought them in from Cacao. While at the market, Jean-Claude and Marie also look for fresh seafood and chicken to round out their upcoming meals. Rice and other staples are purchased at the supermarkets.

Major Foodstuffs

Starches, such as cassava (also called manioc or yucca), sweet potatoes, yams, taro root (dasheen), and plantains, are staples in the French Guianese diet. Rice is also an important staple, eaten with

A shrimp trawler in the early morning in French Guiana. (StockPhotoPro)

most meals. With the majority of the population living near the coast and the many rivers, the incredibly wide variety of seafood is a major part of the diet. Shrimp is one of the main industries in French Guiana and as such is widely eaten. Snapper, tuna, shark, and anchovies are among the fish found in the country, as well as many native South American species, such as *acoupa, atipa, jamais goûté, machoiran, pirai,* and *pacu*. Chicken and other meats, such as duck, beef, pork, lamb, and local wild game, are also consumed as protein sources but do not hold the same place as seafood does in the French Guianese diet.

Vegetables in the diet include tomatoes, zucchini, cucumbers, bitter melons, Chinese long beans, red (kidney) beans, eggplant, and pumpkin. Tropical fruits are plentiful, including mangoes, papayas, coconuts, bananas, and citrus fruits, such as oranges and lemons. Fruits not common in other areas of the world grow in French Guiana, too, such as the sugar apple, the Cayenne cherry, and the acerola cherry.

Cooking

French Guianese cuisine is a reflection of the various ethnic and cultural groups that have, over the history of the country, contributed and adapted their dishes and techniques with local ingredients, merging them into a unique food culture. A strong theme in French Guianese cooking is using French technique with local ingredients. An example is the many soups and stews that feature the country's variety of fish and meat. Aromatics, such as onion and garlic, are often used in them. Soups and stews often simmer on the stove for most of the day. These stews also have their roots in African foodways. A carbohydrate-rich starch is inevitably a part of the meal, served along with the protein. Vegetables can be either included in the dish or served on the side. Root vegetables are also prepared as gratins, another nod to combining local ingredients with French technique.

When prepared other than in soups or stews, seafood or meats are sautéed, grilled, broiled, poached, or fried. Herbs and spices, such as cinnamon, cloves, nutmeg, ginger, and hot peppers, flavor many dishes. A popular way to serve fish and meats, such as

chicken, is to wood-smoke it (*boucané*). This technique is believed to date back to the Amerindians in the region, as a way of preserving their protein sources.

Typical Meals

Breakfast is similar to the Continental French breakfast, usually coffee and a baguette, croissant, or pastry, either eaten at home or found at the cafés and bakeries in the towns and villages. Lunch may be anything from a sandwich or crepe to Asian noodles. For dinner, cod fritters (*accras*) and blood sausages (boudin) are often served as appetizers, as well as marinated fish or shrimp. Smoked chicken or fish boucané is often served cold, on salads. The main dishes, including the soups and stews, are almost always served with rice. *Couac,* toasted cassava flour, is an alternative staple served with meals. Red (kidney) beans often accompany the main dish. *Blaff* is a court bouillon (broth) made with celery, onion, garlic, herbs, and spices in which fish or shrimp is poached. *Pimentade* is similar but contains tomatoes. *Colombo* is a well-liked stew with vegetables and chicken or pork in a spicy curry sauce. Fricassees, meat stews in a rich sauce, are considered specialties here. Wild game from the forests is especially popular prepared this way.

Bouillon d'awara (also spelled *aouara* or *awarra*) is considered French Guiana's national dish, served only on Easter and Pentecost. It is a dish of vegetables, cured meats, smoked fish, crab, prawns, and chicken, made with the fruit of the awara (*Astrocaryum vulgare*) palm tree that grows in the savannas in French Guiana and nearby regions. According to legend, anyone who tries this will be certain to come back one day to French Guiana.

Bouillon d'Awara

Serves 10

Cooking time: 7 hours plus overnight soaking

Ingredients

1 lb corned beef, diced

1 lb salt-cured ham

1 lb pig tails

3 lb *awara* (*aouara*) paste

1 lb smoked bacon, diced

1 lb roast chicken

1 lb roast pork

2 lb green or white cabbage, chopped

2 lb green beans

1 lb cucumbers, chopped

1 lb eggplant, cubed

1 lb shrimp

1 lb crabmeat

1 lb smoked fish

2 lb spinach

Salt, pepper, and assorted spices, to taste

Instructions

1. Soak the corned beef, ham, and pig tails in water overnight. Change the water in the morning, and leave them in the clear water for another 2 hours.

2. Fill a very large soup pot about halfway with hot water. Mix in the awara paste until dissolved.

3. Put the cured meats, including the bacon, in the awara liquid, and cook over low heat for 2 hours.

4. Add the chicken, pork, cabbage, green beans, cucumbers, and eggplant to the bouillon.

5. Stir, and cook over low heat for 6 or 7 hours. The bouillon will be very thick and reduced.

6. Add the shrimp, crab, smoked fish, and spinach, and season with salt, pepper, and spices. Cook for 5 minutes more, or until the shrimp are cooked through and the spinach is wilted.

Considering the history of sugar production in French Guiana, rum is popular and is made into various drinks and cocktails. A local favorite is *ti'punch,* a mixture of rum, sugar syrup, and lime juice. It is usually served as an aperitif, without ice, and drunk in one shot. *Punch planteur* is another rum drink, made with fruit juice.

Eating Out

Restaurants are found mainly in larger cities in French Guiana, such as Cayenne and Kourou. The range of cuisines reflects the population, so one can find Creole, French, Brazilian, Laotian, and Chinese restaurants, to name a few. French cafés and restaurants serve typical Continental French dishes, along with wine imported from France. Inexpensive food stalls are found in and around the city markets. Asian noodles and fried rice are sold, as well as foods such as French crepes and sandwiches.

Special Occasions

Many of the holidays and special occasions in French Guiana center on religious and national festivities. As the majority of the population is Roman Catholic, holidays such as Christmas and Easter are an important part of the culture. Bouillon d'awara is made only during Easter and Pentecost. Carnival in French Guiana is considered one of the liveliest, including costumes, music, parades, and dancing, stretching from Epiphany to Ash Wednesday. *Galette des rois* (king cake) represents the Three Kings and Epiphany and kicks off Carnival. Blaff is commonly eaten during Carnival, seen as a means of sustenance during the celebrating.

Bastille Day (the national French holiday, July 14) is cause for a big celebration each year in French Guiana, with plenty of food and wine. The capital city holds its own yearly celebration, Cayenne Festival, every October 15. Abolition Day is celebrated countrywide on June 10, to commemorate the end of slavery. In the areas with Asian communities, holidays such as the Chinese New Year are celebrated.

Diet and Health

The French Guianese diet is rich in fresh fruits and vegetables and seafood, yet with a poor economy, some may not have access to a healthy, balanced diet. Relying too heavily on inexpensive starches, such as rice, could deprive one of important nutrients and lead to malnutrition, especially among children. With the country's geography, access to a safe water supply is also an issue. The country's status as a French overseas department means that the population has access to health care that otherwise would not be available, including implementation of public health services and health education.

The Hmong, in the smaller villages, have been able to maintain some of their traditional ways of life and culture, including religious beliefs such as shamanism, even if they have converted to Christianity. Appeals to shamans for improving health often involve animal sacrifices. The Hmong are also fairly healthy, growing and eating their own fruits and vegetables and keeping fit through the physical demands of farming.

Erin Laverty

Further Reading

Burton, Richard D. E., and Fred Reno, eds. *French and West Indian: Martinique, Guadeloupe and French Guiana Today.* New World Studies. Charlottesville: University of Virginia Press, 1995.

Clarkin, Patrick F. "Hmong Resettlement in French Guiana." *Hmong Studies Journal* 6 (2005): 1–27. http://www.hmongstudies.org/ClarkinHSJ6.pdf.

Consiel national des arts culinaires (CNAC). *Guyane: L'inventaire du patrimoine culinaire de la France, Produits du terroir et reccettes traditionnelles.* Paris: Albin Michel, 1999.

Crosby, Alfred W. Jr. *The Columbian Exchange: Biological and Cultural Consequences of 1492.* Westport, CT: Praeger, 2003.

La Cuisine Guyanaise. http://www.destination.fr/guyane/lacuisineguyanai.html.

Horth, Régine. *La Guyane gastronomique et traditionnelle.* Paris: Éditions Caribéennes, 1988.

MacKie, Cristine. *Life and Food in the Caribbean.* New York: New Amsterdam, 1992.

"Maroon Foodways." Creativity and Resistance: Maroon Cultures in the Americas.http://www.folklife.si.edu/resources/maroon/foodways/marfood.htm.

Mintz, Sidney W. *Sweetness and Power: The Place of Sugar in Modern History.* New York: Penguin, 1986.

Skelton, Tracey, ed. *Introduction to the Pan-Caribbean.* New York: Oxford University Press, 2004.

Grenada

Overview

Grenada is located in the eastern Caribbean at the southernmost tip of the Windward Islands between Saint Vincent and the Grenadines to the north and Trinidad and Tobago to the south. The nation of Grenada comprises three main inhabited islands plus around 30 islets and rocky pinnacles.

Grenada is the principal island of the three; the capital of the entire country is Saint George's, which is located on the southwestern coast. Grenada is about 21 miles (34 kilometers) long and around 11 miles (18 kilometers) wide. It has a mountainous, forest-covered interior, and its coastline has an abundance of attractive beaches and bays. Known as the "Isle of Spice," Grenada became world famous for its nutmeg and mace, though these spice crops were severely impacted by two devastating hurricanes in 2004 and 2005, leaving the industry in disarray. Today, the island is still in the process of recovering and successfully combines its traditional spice and agricultural industry with a thriving tourism sector.

Carriacou and Petite Martinique are Grenada's other two main islands. Carriacou is located some 23 miles (37 kilometers) to the north of Grenada. It is approximately 7 miles (11 kilometers) long and 3 miles (5 kilometers) wide. Largely dry, this pretty island has undulating hills, a number of idyllic beaches and bays, and a national park. Carriacou is famous for its tradition of boat building, sailing, and its Big Drum Dance festivals. Petite Martinique is a tiny island located 3 miles (5 kilometers) to the northeast of Carriacou. Just 1.2 square miles

(2 square kilometers) in size, it also has a tradition of boat building and fishing.

Grenada was granted full independence from Britain in 1974. In 1979 the incumbent prime minister, Eric Gairy, was overthrown in a bloodless coup by the People's Revolutionary Government, led by the enigmatic Maurice Bishop. In October 1983, Bishop himself was overthrown and, together with a number of his supporters, executed on the orders of his former comrade, Bernard Coard. In a move to rid Grenada of its Cuban-backed regime, the United States initiated Operation Urgent Fury just a few days later. This military action lasted just a week. Free elections were held a year later, in 1984, and Grenada has been a peaceful place since then.

The majority of Grenadians are the descendants of slaves that were brought to the islands by the British and French from the 1700s to work plantation estates that grew sugar, coffee, cacao, and later nutmeg. Like most of the Caribbean, the islands were originally inhabited by Amerindian people, collectively referred to by the Europeans as Caribs. These indigenous people migrated from the Amazon River delta and were proficient canoe builders, hunters, and fishermen. With the arrival of Europeans, most Caribs were enslaved, murdered, or absorbed into the new society. Many died of diseases against which their bodies had no immunity. Following emancipation, many plantation estates were abandoned, and in their place villages were formed and a new nation built. Today, the islands of Grenada are English-speaking, and the government, judicial, and education systems are still based on the old British model. Grenadian culture is shaped by a combination of African and European heritage, as indeed is its cuisine.

🍽 Food Culture Snapshot

Louisa decided to cook a traditional *oil-down* (pronounced *oil-dong*) for her four guests. Right now they were off hiking to the island's pride and joy—the very pretty Concord Falls—and she planned to meet them on their return for a cook-up on the beach close by. Though her guesthouse was quite small and unassuming, she had developed a good reputation for attention to detail and for taking care of "her people." Today would be no exception.

Michael, a local gardener, had brought yams, coconuts, plantains, green bananas, and sweet potatoes early this morning just as Louisa was seasoning the chicken wings with garlic, thyme, onions, and seasoning peppers that grew in her kitchen garden. She had the salt fish (cod) plumping overnight in water, and that sat on the counter, waiting to be drained and later added to the pot. During the early hours of the morning, Louisa had peeled and chopped the ground provisions (starchy staples), cut open the coconuts, and squeezed the pulp in a muslin cloth to extract the delicious milk. She now packed all these things into a cooler, together with a dozen bottles of Carib beer and three bottles of rum punch—she was revered for this traditional West Indian drink that followed the recipe one of sour (lime), two of sweet (sugar syrup), three of strong (rum), and four of weak (water), although she tended to cheat a little, adding only three of weak and relying on ice to make up the four. Nutmeg and Angostura bitters had to come along as well.

By the time her guide, Gerry, arrived with her four guests, a fire was burning and the ingredients were all cooking in a large pot. The waterfall hike had been great fun, and now all her guests were ready for something to drink. Knowing her rum punch well, they chose this readily. Louisa poured the punch into plastic cups filled with ice, added a dash of Angostura bitters, and, with her little portable grater, grated the fresh nutmeg straight into the same. Traditions are not to be messed with. Two drinks each, and it was time to take a bath in the sea—this allowed her guests and herself to freshen themselves up. The waters of the Caribbean were warm and gentle, but Louisa had her pot that needed attention now. Leaving her guests, she clambered to her duty, tasting her oil-dong every now and then to ensure perfection. Once all the ingredients had boiled down, the turmeric giving the dish just that slight nutty flavor and a touch of yellow color, the coconut oil and the shop butter now coating the fish, chicken, provisions, and dumplings, all cooked to perfection, Louisa called out to her guests and opened a beer for each one as they gathered around the pot, their bowls being filled with the goodness of this Grenadian dish, its sweet aroma of pepper and spice filling the air. She remembered the first time this lot had tasted her oil-dong and how they had never heard of plantain before and couldn't imagine eating cooked unripe bananas. With full stomachs, weary limbs, and a liqueur in hand—Louisa had not forgotten the bottle of De La Grenade nutmeg liqueur they so loved after this heavy meal—they all sat in comfortable silence on the beach, watching the sun now setting, the skies slowly bursting into flames of yellow and red.

Major Foodstuffs

Grenada's volcanic soil is very fertile, and a variety of crops are grown on the hillsides of the island's mountainous interior. Though no longer a significant export, grown largely for domestic consumption, bananas are cultivated all around the island. In addition to the banana we all recognize, several other varieties are farmed, including plantains and *bluggo,* which are usually cooked before eating. Ground provisions such as yams and dasheen are also very traditional and commonly grown foodstuffs.

It is for its spices that Grenada has become famous, and despite recent hurricanes, nutmeg, cacao, cinnamon, allspice, cloves, star anise, and black pepper are still farmed in the island's lush green interior. Nutmegs thrive in a cooler, more elevated habitat, which unfortunately makes them vulnerable to severe weather. It is said that nutmegs were first planted as an experiment in the mid-1800s and were so successful that, just 100 years later, Grenada was the second-largest exporter in the world behind Indonesia, where the crop originated. When ripening, the roundish, thick yellow pods that cover this evergreen tree begin to split open, revealing a tough kernel. Within this kernel is the nutmeg itself, and around the nutmeg is a reddish, lacy coating called mace. After harvesting, the mace is removed from the nutmeg and dried. It is used in cooking and also as a natural meat preservative. Nutmegs are usually ground into a powder and used for flavorings, often in desserts. They also contain an essential oil that is used in the cosmetic and pharmaceutical industries. Bay leaf is native to the Windward Islands, and although also used in cooking, it is primarily used in bay rum. Not to be imbibed, bay rum is an essential in every home's medicine cabinet, used as an after-shave lotion. Turmeric and ginger are also grown. Cacao is grown both on smallholdings and on large estates. The Belmont Estate on the east of the island grows organic cacao that is used to make Grenada's very own chocolate.

Carriacou and Petite Martinique are both dry, and water is usually in scarce supply. This means that the variety of crops is quite limited. Traditional staples are pigeon peas and maize, which are often seen growing together in smallholdings and back gardens. These gardens also tend to house a small chicken shed and may also be home to a goat or two.

Interior of a nutmeg factory in Grenada. (PhotoDisc)

Grenadian Oil-Down

3 dry coconuts or 6 cans coconut milk

1-in. x 2-in. piece fresh turmeric, peeled and grated

½ c vegetable oil

2 lb chicken wings

1 lb salt fish, soaked in water overnight

1 salted pig tail, whole

6 green bananas, peeled and cut in half

1 whole breadfruit, peeled and cut into chunks

12 medium-sized leaves of callaloo bush

1 leaf *chadon bennie* (also known as *shadow-bennie*), finely chopped (or a handful of cilantro can be used instead)

4 onions, peeled and finely chopped

6 cloves garlic, finely chopped

3 sprigs parsley, finely chopped

6 stalks fresh chives, finely chopped

3 leaves broad-leaf thyme, finely chopped

4 fresh mint leaves, finely chopped

6 leaves fresh basil, finely chopped

1 red hot pepper or Scotch bonnet, seeded and finely chopped

2 red hot peppers or Scotch bonnets, whole

2 seasoning peppers, finely chopped

1–2 tbsp butter

Salt and pepper to taste

Dumplings

2 c flour

½ c butter

1 tsp salt

1 tsp ground cinnamon

Break the coconuts, and remove and grate the hard interior white flesh. Add the turmeric to the grated flesh. Pour hot water over this mixture and squeeze through a muslin bag until all the coconut milk has been extracted. When substituting this method with 6 cans of coconut milk (unsweetened), add the turmeric, bring to a boil, and still put the liquid through a sieve in order to remove the grated turmeric, just keeping the coloring, which should be a bright yellow in both cases.

Place a large iron pot on the fire. Add vegetable oil. When hot, add chicken wings and brown slightly. Add the turmeric coconut milk. Add all other ingredients except the whole peppers. If there is not enough coconut milk to cover these, add a little water or normal milk. Add the whole peppers, tied in muslin cloth in case they break. Cover until mixture begins to boil.

Meanwhile, in a bowl, begin the dumplings by mixing the flour and butter. Crumble the mixture. Add the salt and cinnamon and mix well. Add enough water to make a sticky but firm dough, form the dough into small balls, roll into 4-inch lengths, and set aside.

Allow the oil-down to slowly boil for approximately 45 minutes, adding the dumplings 20 minutes before it is finished, while there is still liquid. Cover for 5 minutes. Remove cover, stirring now to ensure that the bottom of the oil-down does not begin to burn. When finished and all ingredients are cooked but not mushy, serve in calabash bowls (or ceramic bowls) and eat with a spoon. The pepper can now be removed from the muslin cloth and mashed, and a little can be placed on the oil-down for those who can tolerate the pepper. Salt and pepper can be added to taste.

In addition to pigeon peas and maize, vegetable plots will also usually include carrots, cabbages, potatoes, peas, and beans. Fruit trees grow in the wild and in orchards. Common fruits include several varieties of mango, grapefruit, lime, pawpaw (papaya), guava, passion fruit, pineapple, watermelon, and breadfruit.

The sea provides Grenadians on all three islands with a variety of fish and crustaceans. Tuna, mahimahi (dorado), marlin, and kingfish are regular catches. Queen conch, known as *lambie,* and lobster are caught to supply Grenada's restaurants and hotel resorts. Both are also revered by locals.

A Rastafarian man cooks oil-down, a traditional dish in Grenada. (Dreamstime)

Cooking

Caribbean Creole is the predominant culinary style in Grenada and is a combination of African and European influences. Traditional dishes are usually quite simple and are a good reflection of seasonal fruits, vegetables, and fish catches. Staples are rice and ground provisions. Grenada also has an Indo-Caribbean community, particularly on the east coast, and some spiced curry dishes, such as roti (a circular Indian-type bread wrapped around fillings), reflect the diversity of the island's heritage. The preparation and cooking of meals usually take place in an indoor kitchen over a gas stove, though many still enjoy an outdoor "cook-up" on a beach, especially as a weekend treat.

Meats are usually seasoned in advance, either with prepared, dried seasonings or with a combination of seasoning peppers, garlic, thyme, salt, and pepper. Fish and chicken are often washed with lime before cooking. Marinating meats is a common practice and may often be done the day before. Vegetables and ground provisions are either bought from local markets or roadside stalls or harvested from gardens. Queen conch (or lambie) is extracted from its shell and beaten with a wooden *cosh* to tenderize before it is cooked, often in a curry or hot Creole sauce.

The national dish of Grenada is pronounced oil-dong but written as oil-down. Its traditional ingredients include a selection of spices, turmeric, ground provisions, breadfruit, green (unripe) bananas, and plantains combined with pig trotters (feet) and salt fish, with callaloo (young dasheen leaves—taro) placed on top to retain steam and add flavor. Today, the recipe has changed little except for the meats, which could be one or a combination of beef, pork, the more inexpensive chicken wings, salt pork (pig tail), or salt beef. Everything is cooked in one large pot together with coconut milk and spices until the liquid reduces down to leave an oily residue at the bottom of the pot that coats the meat and provisions. Often cooked outdoors over a fire, oil-dong is typically eaten on special occasions or as a weekend picnic.

Another very traditional dish that also employs coconut as an ingredient is *cou-cou*. Again cooked in a single pot and usually outdoors over an open fire, cou-cou is made from cornmeal, flour, a selection of seasonings, and coconut milk. Everything is cooked together and continually "turned" until the mixture thickens. In Carriacou, cou-cou is often eaten with fresh fish and pigeon peas.

Typical Meals

Lunch has traditionally been the main meal of the day in the Caribbean, though with modern lifestyles and the introduction of fast food, the increasing variety of restaurants, and prepacked sandwiches in plastic lunch boxes from well-stocked supermarkets, things are steadily changing. Whether it is lunch or dinner, the typical main meal in Grenada will consist of meat or fish accompanied by a selection of vegetables, rice cooked with peas, and ground provisions. Perhaps one of the most popular

accompaniments is callaloo, the stewed young green leaves of the dasheen plant.

Because of Grenada's appeal to overseas visitors, investors, and returnees, not to mention the impressive St. George's University medical school, traditional cooking is now far more entwined with international culinary influences. This is particularly true along Grenada's southwestern peninsula where luxury resorts, boutique hotels, yachting marinas, supermarkets, bars, and haute cuisine restaurants line the powder-white sand beaches and sublime natural anchorages. Elsewhere in Grenada, particularly in the more remote villages of the north, a traditional breakfast of locally baked bread, local jams, and fresh fruits may be followed by a lunch of meat or fish, rice and peas, provisions, and vegetables. Dinner or supper is often a lighter affair, perhaps consisting of leftovers or a freshly stewed callaloo soup.

Eating Out

Grenada's southwestern peninsula offers an excellent choice of high-class and local restaurants. Finding somewhere to eat in the rest of the island can, however, prove to be a little more challenging, though there are some hidden gems. In Carriacou there are some very nice restaurants in and around Hillsborough and along the waterfront at Tyrell Bay.

Some of Grenada's restaurants are truly world class, serving a sumptuous selection of international and traditional Creole dishes. Many profess to use local ingredients and locally caught fish and shellfish. The renowned British chef Gary Rhodes has a restaurant on the L'Anse Aux Épines peninsula, and several others have been the recipients of international culinary awards. On Carriacou, dining options reflect the island's love affair with the sea, and queen conch, or lambie, is a particular favorite.

For those looking for something a little more casual or inexpensive, Grenada's southwestern peninsula offers plenty of variety, from bar meals to local snackettes. A fabulous option for anyone traveling on a budget is roti, a dish with East Indian influence that is comprised of a flatbread that is stuffed with either curried vegetables, chicken, or fish. Roti and a range of local snacks such as fried chicken, fish, and *titiwi* cakes (a seasoned, fried fritter containing small fish) can be found at eateries all over Grenada.

Fish Friday takes place every week from around 7 P.M. in the village of Gouyave on Grenada's west coast. A vibrant atmosphere fuses with a wonderful selection of seafood dishes, including freshly caught and barbecued lobster. It is a lovely way to pass an evening, eating delicious food, sampling local rum, and enjoying the sounds of a steel pan band.

Special Occasions

Village maroon festivals on Carriacou are cultural occasions where communities come together for an outdoors cook-up, some drinks, and a traditional Big Drum Dance. Commonly referred to as a *saraca,* a village maroon (cook-up) usually consists of smoked meats, cou-cou, ground provisions, rice, and pigeon peas. Traditionally, it is held to give thanks for a bountiful harvest or to pray for one, along with rain, ahead of planting.

A rather haunting occasion, and also very traditional on Carriacou, is the tombstone feast. On the first anniversary of a burial, the deceased's headstone is carried to the grave site and put in place. Rum and water are sprinkled around the tomb, and sometimes an egg is broken to symbolize a new beginning for the surviving family. The ceremony is followed by a traditional saraca, drumming, and dancing. A parent's plate is a food offering to ancestral spirits. At a village maroon and a tombstone feast, a plate of food rests on a white tablecloth along with a candle. After midnight, when the spirits have had their fill, the plate is removed and people eat from it.

Diet and Health

Despite the arrival of fast-food franchises in Grenada, the typical diet is a healthy one. Fresh fruits, vegetables, and ground provisions have not yet become foods that are scorned by the young in favor of hamburgers and southern fried chicken. With fishing villages along the coastlines of all three islands, fresh seafood is also a healthy staple of the Grenadian diet. Combine this fresh food with sunshine and the great outdoors and there is no reason why anyone should put on too many extra pounds—though some of those wonderful restaurant desserts may indeed prove too much to resist.

Paul Crask and Rosemary Parkinson

Further Reading

Parkinson, Rosemary. *Culinaria: The Caribbean.* Cologne, Germany: Könemann, 1999.

Wilkinson, Wendy, and Lee Wilkinson. *Morgan Freeman and Friends: Caribbean Cooking for a Cause.* Emmaus, PA: Rodale Books, 2006.

Guatemala

Overview

With a land area of about 42,000 square miles and a population of 14 million, Guatemala is one of the largest of the small countries on the isthmus of Central America. Guatemala borders on and shares many features of its culture, climate, and topography with Mexico, Belize, Honduras, and El Salvador. At the same time, the natural and social landscape within Guatemala is varied enough that highland Mayan farming communities and Caribbean fishing villages can exist at the same latitude, and door-to-door tortilla vendors and trendy baristas can be residents of the same city.

Guatemalan legal documents officially recognize the country as "multiethnic, pluricultural and multilingual," and not only does Guatemala have the largest Maya community in the Americas but indigenous Maya make up anywhere from 40 to 60 percent of the population. (Some surveys classify only those who speak a Mayan language and wear traditional Mayan dress, or *traje,* as indigenous, while others include all Guatemalans who chose to identify themselves as such.) Guatemala's population encompasses more than 20 distinct Mayan ethnic groups (the most populous among them are the K'iche, Mam, and Kaqchikel) and as many as 50 distinct languages and dialects. By many accounts from both within and outside Guatemala, mixed-race, mixed-culture *ladinos* (or mestizos) make up the majority of the population. Some Guatemalans of European descent choose to identify themselves as white or *criollo.* Other ethnic groups in Guatemala include the non-Maya indigenous Xinca, the Afro-Caribbean Garifuna, and recent immigrants from Asia, the Middle East, and elsewhere, though all of these groups together make up only about 1 percent of the population. The majority of Guatemalans identify themselves as Catholic, but up to 20 percent of the population has joined an evangelical Protestant movement that began in the late 20th century.

Guatemala's history has been one of voluntary and often-involuntary cultural and economic exchange. In pre-Columbian eras, cacao (or chocolate) traveled complex routes from lowland Mayan villages to the highland Maya and Aztec kingdoms in the region. Spanish colonists established an international trade in Guatemalan cacao and also replanted indigenous squash, tomatoes, chilies, and maize in Europe. Over several centuries, European conquistadors, entrepreneurs, scholars, and missionaries introduced crops from colonies in Africa and Asia to Central America; rice (most often combined with beans) has become a definitively Guatemalan food, and once-foreign crops such as bananas and coffee have shaped Guatemalan trade, particularly with the United States, from the 19th through the 21st centuries.

⅋ Food Culture Snapshot

Sandra lives on a busy street in Antigua, a small, volcano-surrounded town at an elevation of 5,000 feet that has the dual distinction of being Guatemala's colonial capital and—with its cobblestoned streets and striking Spanish churches partially demolished by an 18th-century earthquake—the contemporary tourist capital of the Central American country. Of her immediate family, only Sandra's 25-year-old daughter lives with her, but the house is always buzzing with students from the United States, Germany, Holland, and elsewhere in the world who attend a nearby Spanish-language school and who board with Sandra for several weeks or even a few months at a time.

On a typical day, Sandra is up well before 6 A.M., slicing fruit for breakfast. From the abundantly available local produce, she often selects papayas and bananas though she avoids berries, which are more expensive and more likely to be contaminated by food-borne illnesses. She lights the gas on the stove and begins to cook the beans that have been soaking overnight. A woman selling corn tortillas comes to the house around this time, and Sandra buys at least a dozen, transferring them from their large straw basket to a smaller one of her own and wrapping them in a kitchen towel to prevent them from drying out. Before noon, Sandra will walk five blocks to Antigua's traditional market (where dozens of individual produce, meat, and dry goods vendors set up their stalls under a heavy tarp) to buy a particular variety of squash indigenous to the region. She will also buy a few avocados (the vendor will ask if they are for today or tomorrow and help her select ones with the appropriate ripeness), a few other vegetables, and small bunches of the herbs cilantro and *hierba buena*. Since she's not cooking meat today, Sandra doesn't visit her regular butcher in the market. Next, she buys *pan francés,* a basic white bread, at a bakery nearby but not inside the market; she buys just enough bread for tonight—it will be stale tomorrow, good only for making breadcrumbs or dunking in tea or coffee. Antigua has two supermarkets, both within walking distance of Sandra's house, but she shops there only for staple processed foods like ultrapasteurized milk and chicken bouillon powder. In rural areas—where about 60 percent of the population lives—supermarkets are not available at all, while the capital, Guatemala City, is home to several branches of an upscale supermarket chain now owned by the American giant Walmart.

At lunch, Sandra reheats last night's *caldo* (a general word for stew), choosing to serve the tender chicken and potatoes without the broth today, accompanied by rice (fried lightly with carrots, tomatoes, onions, and garlic) and the black beans that she cooked this morning and pureed in the blender immediately before the meal. Along with lunch, she serves the fresh tortillas and a Guatemalan-style *guacamol,* which differs from Mexican guacamole in that it contains no ingredients other than avocado, lime juice, and salt. For dinner, Sandra follows a recipe she clipped from a magazine for *soufflé de güicoyitos,* a crustless quiche made with the squash she bought this morning. She places a salad of thinly sliced tomatoes and cucumbers on the table, along with the pan francés. Much of Guatemalan cuisine, like tonight's dinner, is not spicy, though it is common to pass around a small dish of pickled chilies.

Major Foodstuffs

The religious book the *Popol Vuh,* often called the bible of Guatemala's K'iche Maya, presents a creation story is which the ancestors of all human beings were molded by the gods from maize dough. Such a dough—made by soaking corn in lime (calcium oxide) to remove the tough outer coating of the kernels and then grinding it either by hand or by machine—is still the basis for Guatemala's essential tortillas (flat cakes cooked on a griddle, smaller and denser than North American supermarket varieties) and tamales (dense packets stuffed with sweet or savory fillings, wrapped in corn husks or banana leaves, and steamed). Today, Guatemala produces over a million metric tons of corn annually. A study carried out in the rural region of Tecpán found that 98 percent of households in that particular area grew corn and beans on subsistence plots known as *milpas.*

Major cash crops grown in Guatemala's fertile volcanic soil, such as coffee, bananas, and cardamom, are produced almost exclusively for export. Cacao (an indigenous crop) and sugar, both grown in Guatemala's balmy lowland Pacific coastal region, were historically strong export crops but are now primarily consumed locally (the production of sugar also allows for the distillation of a wide variety of rums). Animal husbandry practices, along with meat and cheese production, bear the influence of European settlers, including not only the

Spanish colonists but also German and Swiss coffee farmers who arrived in the late 19th and early 20th centuries. Nontraditional crops like broccoli, snap peas, and French beans are increasingly a part of Guatemala's export economy but have yet to make a significant impact on local cuisine, while cabbage (a cousin of broccoli) came to Guatemala with the Spaniards and is now an important part of the pickled slaw called *encurdito* used as a topping for many snacks. Guatemala's extremely varied terrain is responsible for some striking variations in cuisine; fish and seafood stews made with coconut milk are common on the Caribbean coast near the Belizean border, while the sparsely populated jungle in Guatemala's northern Petén region borrows culinary traditions from Mexico's Yucatán Peninsula.

Cooking

The ancient Mayan technique of grinding ingredients into a powder or paste by using a slightly concave stone slab, called a *metate,* together with a matching piece that resembles a rolling pin, called a *mano,* is still an essential part of Guatemalan cooking. Tortillas and tamales are made from treated and ground maize. Cacao is ground together with sugar and cinnamon (European introductions) and then whisked into water or milk to make chocolate drinks. Peanuts, sesame seeds, and squash seeds are often ground up and used in recipes for beverages called *atoles* and *pinoles* and in a variety of stews. Households in very remote areas without a lot of income may rely on metates and manos as the only

A vegetable market in Chichicastenango, Guatemala. (Shutterstock)

technology for preparing ingredients in this way. In more central and financially stable villages, commercial grinding services (by machine instead of by hand) are available. Affluent homes have easy access to food processors, though they may keep a metate or a mortar and pestle for special recipes.

Purchasing purified water is routine in Guatemala, except in impoverished homes that cannot afford to do so, because municipal water supplies are not reliably potable. Running water is not universal, and many houses have only a single tap in a central courtyard rather than a sink in the kitchen. The Guatemalan culinary tradition is one in which fresh produce is readily available and refrigeration is limited and unreliable, so menus tend to emphasize cooking from scratch instead of reheating leftovers. Several appliances are standard in Guatemalan kitchens, including blenders and pressure cookers. Even modest homes may hire a worker (almost always a woman) to help with cooking and cleaning, and affluent families normally employ a household staff, something that is no longer either the social norm or an economic possibility in most European and North American homes.

Typical Meals

Guatemalan food can best be described as a constellation of traditional ingredients: maize, beans, and squash. Several rich stews combine indigenous and European ingredients and flavors to create singular dishes that are distinctly Guatemalan. *Pepián* is slow-cooked beef in a smoky and flavorful combination of spices. *Jocón* is a chicken stew in a tangy green sauce made with *mil tomates* (usually called tomatillos in Mexico and the United States). *Kakik* is a restorative soup traditionally made with a wild turkey.

Pepián

Serves 8, with rice and tortillas

1 whole small onion, peeled

4 whole garlic cloves, peeled

½ c whole tomatillos

1 whole small ripe tomato

2 dried chilies, such as *guajillos*

2 corn tortillas

2 lb beef chuck, cut into 2-in. cubes

5 c water

1 tsp salt

2 oz sesame seeds

2 oz squash or pumpkin seeds (*pepitas*)

10 peppercorns

1 1-in. cinnamon stick, broken up

1 leafy stalk of cilantro, chopped

1 *güisquil,* chayote, or zucchini, cut into ½-in. cubes

1 small potato, peeled and cut into ½-in. cubes

Char the onion, garlic, tomatillos, tomatoes, and chilies either by holding them directly over the flame of a gas burner (turning them regularly) or by heating them in a dry skillet.

Quickly char the tortillas by holding them over the flame of a gas burner with tongs (turning them over a few times), or toast them in the oven or toaster oven until they are crispy.

Bring the water and salt to a boil, add the beef, and simmer for about 1 hour, until tender.

While the beef cooks, add the tortillas to the boiling water for 5 minutes, then remove the tortillas, tear them into pieces, and set them aside.

Toast the sesame and squash seeds in a dry skillet until they are dark but not burned. Grind the seeds into a fine powder in a coffee grinder or food processor. Add the peppercorns and cinnamon, and process the mixture until everything is finely ground.

Combine the ground seed mixture, the moistened tortillas, the chopped cilantro, and the charred onion, garlic, tomatillos, tomatoes, and chilies with 1 cup of the cooking liquid from the beef in a food processor or blender until smooth.

When the beef is almost tender, add the cubed potato and güisquil or other squash, and continue simmering until the vegetables are cooked through, about 10 minutes.

Add the sauce to the beef and vegetables, and simmer for an additional 10 minutes, or until the sauce is thick and chocolate brown.

Small items such as green beans (*ejotes*) or hot peppers stuffed with ground beef (*chiles rellenos*) dredged in egg batter and fried make popular snacks and side dishes. In addition to the *atol* drinks made from ground seeds and nuts, there are several common soft drinks or *refrescos,* including limeade, steeped hibiscus flower, and a tamarind-infused drink. Eating *camotes* (sweet potatoes) in honey or syrup as an after-dinner treat is probably a millennia-old tradition, and the candy makers of Antigua have been selling molded marzipan and condensed milk sweets at least since 1613, when they formed a confectioners' guild.

What constitutes an everyday meal varies from household to household, region to region, and income level to income level. By some estimates, 80 percent of Guatemalans live below the poverty line, and for many Guatemalans eating is more a matter of survival than pleasure.

Eating Out

The elegant restaurants run by charismatic chefs and the convenient restaurant chains in Guatemala City, Antigua, and a few other pockets of the country take their cues from global rather than local culinary culture. European travelers and speculators who arrived with the coffee trade in the mid-19th century were surprised to find that Guatemala had so few cafés or salons where people could meet, and visitors to Guatemala today may have a similar reaction. In the 21st century, social gatherings are still less likely to be in restaurants than in someone's home, a custom influenced both by the cultural importance of hospitality and by a persistent occurrence of violent crime in public places in the wake of a heavily armed 36-year civil war that ended only in 1996. Most towns and urban neighborhoods have at least one *comedor* serving simple meals to workers who cannot return home for lunch and other passersby. While Guatemalans have access to several American chains, by far the most popular fast-food restaurant is the nationally owned Pollo Campero, which specializes in fried chicken; in recent years, several branches of Pollo Campero have opened in the United States. Some of the tastiest and most traditional foods consumed outside the home are served at informal stalls or stands on busy streets. Common street foods include roasted corn, sliced mangoes coated in powdered chili and salt, the same *pupusas* that are popular in El Salvador (thick tortillas stuffed with cheese or another filling before they are cooked), and *enchiladas,* which bear no resemblance to the food of the same name in Mexico (here, they are a crisp tortilla topped with cabbage-and-beet encurdito, tomato sauce, and salty cheese).

Special Occasions

The ancient Mesoamerican tradition of preparing specific kinds of tamales for special occasions continues into the present day at Mayan festivals and during Catholic holidays like Christmas and Easter. Meat grilled over a charcoal fire or roasted on a spit, accompanied by guacamol or a condensed tomato sauce called *chirmol* along with grilled scallions, fresh bread or tortillas, and cold beer is a popular celebratory meal for a large crowd. Without a doubt, the most distinctive Guatemalan holiday meal is *fiambre,* a vibrant and pungent salad whose seemingly endless list of ingredients includes the local stalky vegetable *pacaya,* just-caught shrimp, imported capers, and Spanish-style chorizo, all mixed together with several different broths and pickling agents that take days to prepare; fiambre is served during the consecutive Catholic holidays of All Saints' Day and All Souls' Day in November, and the meal is sometimes eaten as a picnic at the local cemetery to commemorate the lives of parents, grandparents, and past generations of ancestors.

Diet and Health

Healthy communities in Guatemala are tied both physically and metaphorically to healthy maize harvests. For thousands of years, Maya households have blessed a single ear of corn, which is neither planted nor eaten for the entire season, at the beginning of the harvest. To this day, corn is a symbol of life and health, and many families continue to practice the ancient birthing ritual of cutting the umbilical cord above an ear of corn. Contemporary Maya shamans make use of carefully guarded herbal recipes employed for both religious and medicinal purposes.

Today, lack of access to clean water severely compromises good health for many Guatemalans. While Guatemala's traditional staple foods are the core of a healthy diet (beans combined with maize to make up a complete protein, a diversity of vitamin-rich vegetables, little meat, and many dishes prepared without animal fat of any kind), struggles related to diet in Guatemala and throughout Central American include diabetes provoked and agitated by increased consumption of processed foods and rampant malnutrition as a consequence of extreme poverty.

Emily Stone

Further Reading

Coe, Sophie D. *America's First Cuisines.* Austin: University of Texas Press, 1994.

Coe, Sophie D., and Michael D. Coe. *The True History of Chocolate.* 2nd ed. New York: Thames and Hudson, 2007.

Fischer, Edward F., and Peter Benson. *Broccoli and Desire: Global Connections and Maya Struggles in Postwar Guatemala.* Stanford, CA: Stanford University Press, 2006.

Hearst, Cinnamon, ed. *Guatemala.* Emeryville, CA: Avalon Travel Publishing (Moon Handbooks), 2007.

Marks, Copeland. *False Tongues and Sunday Bread: A Guatemalan and Mayan Cookbook.* New York: Primus, 1985.

McDonald, Michael R. *Food Culture in Central America.* Westport, CT: Greenwood Press, 2009.

Pendergrast, Mark. *Uncommon Grounds: The History of Coffee and How It Transformed Our World.* New York: Basic Books, 1999.

Schlesinger, Stephen, and Stephen Kinzer. *Bitter Fruit: The Story of the American Coup in Guatemala.* Exp. ed. Cambridge, MA: Harvard University Press, 1999.

Tedlock, Dennis. *Popol Vuh: The Definitive Version of the Mayan Book of the Dawn of Life and the Glories of Gods and Kings.* New York: Touchstone, 1996.

Guyana

Overview

Guyana is a land of diversity geographically, ecologically, and culturally. Situated on the northeastern coast of South America, Guyana has a history and culture that are distinct from the rest of the continent. The country is surrounded by Venezuela, Suriname, Brazil, and the Atlantic Ocean. It is the only English-speaking country in South America. With a tropical climate, Guyana's geography is a combination of the coastal region and nearby low plains, mineral-rich hills inland, and dense rain forests still further in.

The history of Guyana has shaped its food culture, influenced by the diverse ethnic groups that have come to the country. Guyana is considered to be part of the Caribbean, based on a common culture and history, despite it being in South America. Guyana was originally inhabited by Amerindians (Arawak and Carib tribes), long before Europe entered the picture. The original name for the area, *Guiana,* is said to come from an Amerindian word meaning "land of many waters"—fitting, based on the number of rivers that run through it.

Although the area that is now Guyana saw various European explorations over the 16th century, including the Spanish and the British (Sir Walter Raleigh went in search of the fabled El Dorado), it was first colonized by the Dutch toward the end of the 16th century. In 1616, they set up a permanent trading post in Essequibo that became part of the Dutch West India Company. The Dutch expanded their settlements in the area, including Berbice and Demarara, throughout the 17th century, with agriculture, mainly sugarcane, the focus. As

the production grew, the Dutch began bringing in slaves from West Africa in the mid-16th century to fill the void in labor. Slavery on the sugarcane plantations and the resulting sugar, molasses, and rum production remained the backbone of the economy in Guyana and of Dutch rule throughout the 18th century. The area was fought over and changed hands several times between the Dutch, British, and French in the late 1700s, with the British taking control in 1796. After it returned to the Dutch for a short period of time, the British took over once again, with the colonies being ceded to them in 1814. The colonies were united as British Guiana in 1831 and remained so for over 130 years.

Although the slave trade was abolished in 1807, full emancipation was not reached until 1838. With the freeing of the slaves, the plantation owners began desperately looking elsewhere for a workforce, first in Madeira, Portugal, then for indentured laborers from India and China. The country gained independence from Britain on May 26, 1966, with its new name, Guyana, and on February 23, 1970, Guyana became a republic.

Today, Guyana's population is approximately 770,000, with people of East Indian heritage at 43.5 percent of the population, followed by people of African heritage at 30.2 percent, people of mixed heritage at 16.7 percent, Amerindians at 9.2 percent, and others, including Portuguese, Chinese, and whites, making up the rest of the population. The coastal towns are home to the majority of the population. Georgetown, the capital, is the secretariat headquarters of the Caribbean Community (CARICOM). With a per-capita gross domestic product

(GDP) of about $4,000 per person, Guyana ranks as one of the poorer countries in the world. Guyana's main economy centers on agricultural exports, in particular, sugar and rice. Shrimp and livestock are significant industries, along with gold, bauxite, and timber. Production of molasses and rum, derivatives of the sugar industry, also plays an important role in Guyana's export economy. The different ethnic backgrounds and cultures that have shared in the history of Guyana have contributed to and influenced the food culture of Guyana today. Guyanese cuisine is similar in some ways to that in other parts of the Caribbean, based on a shared history and foods grown in the area.

Chandana Jagunandan cooks vegetable pakoras in her Queenstown home in Guyana. (AFP | Getty Images)

Food Culture Snapshot

Sam, Betty, and their two children live in Georgetown. They start the day with a trip to Bourda Market, a large open-air market in town. There, they purchase fresh fruits and vegetables for their meals, as do most people. Another stop for buying food and other household items in downtown Georgetown is Stabroek Market. They also look for meat, especially chicken, and fresh seafood at the open-air markets. These markets also allow people to purchase food at better prices than in the supermarkets. They do stop by the supermarket, though, for food staples, such as rice, seasonings, and hot sauces. When visiting relatives in a smaller village on the coast, the family is able to buy fresh seafood directly from the fishermen.

Major Foodstuffs

Ground provisions (a term used to describe root vegetables and fruits) are staples in the Guyanese diet and are part of or served with most meals. These include cassava (also called manioc or yucca), sweet potatoes, *eddoes* (also called taro root or dasheen), and plantains. Rice is also an important staple and is eaten with most meals. Corn plays a dominant role in the diet, as do beans, peas, and other legumes (such as pigeon peas).

Chicken is eaten often as a protein source and is found in many Guyanese dishes. Seafood is plentiful, given the coastal access and many rivers. Shrimp, tilapia, snapper, and trout are among the fish found in Guyana. Salt cod is also consumed. Other meats, such as beef, pork, and goat, are eaten but in smaller amounts than chicken and fish.

Vegetables in the Guyanese diet include okra (often called *ochroes*), tomatoes, cucumbers, pumpkins, squash, *bora* beans (also known as Chinese long beans), eggplant (called *boulanger*), and breadfruit. Tropical fruits abound, such as guavas, pineapples, mangoes, papayas, bananas, soursops, and citrus fruits. Coconut is used extensively in Guyanese cooking, including the meat, water, and coconut milk as a flavoring in some soups and rice dishes.

Cooking

The foodways in Guyana have become a true melting pot. The different ethnic and cultural groups that came to the country, many by force, contributed their own familiar ingredients, dishes, and techniques that have melded into the Guyanese cuisine that is now consumed by everyone, regardless of their origins. So, dishes that originated in India, for example, are now prepared and enjoyed by those other than just the Indo-Guyanese.

Food and cooking in Guyana typically revolve around the family, especially on the weekends. Hearty one-pot dishes, stews, and soups are often cooked, simmering on the stove for most of the day.

A thick split pea soup is an example, made with chicken, beef, or pig tail as well as ground provisions, such as potatoes, yams, cassava, or plantains made into dumplings. A carbohydrate-rich ground root vegetable or starch, like rice, is almost always a part of the meal, many times incorporated into or used as the basis for a dish. A smaller amount of protein, such as chicken, fish, salt pork, or beans, and vegetables and seasonings are cooked with the carbohydrate. Alternatively, chicken and fish are often fried and served over rice.

Herbs and spices, such as thyme, cinnamon, cloves, ginger, and fresh hot peppers, flavor many dishes. Aromatics, such as onion and garlic, are often used in one-pot dishes. Bottled hot pepper sauces are always on the table and used as a condiment.

Guyanese do use certain methods in cooking that are particular to their dishes. When preparing bitter cassava, for example, it must be grated, the juice squeezed out of it, and allowed to dry in order to make it edible. A *matapee,* which is a long, cylindrical basket that originated with the Amerindians and is used to squeeze out the juice, is still used today. When making roti flatbreads, Guyanese use a *tawah* (also called *tawa* or *tava*), a round, cast iron flat plate, which is East Indian in origin.

Typical Meals

Guyanese typically eat three meals a day. Breakfast is usually fairly hearty—a hot cereal or porridge made from a starch such as cornmeal, cassava, plantains, or rice, made with milk or water and brown sugar, and served with tea or coffee and bread. Eggs are also commonly eaten at breakfast. One of the most popular Guyanese breakfasts is salt fish and bake (bakes are bread dough that is fried, not baked). Dried, salted codfish has been eaten in Guyana since colonial times. It was imported from North America, and slaves on the plantations were given an allowance of it to last throughout the week. While some start their day with hearty stews and one-pot meals, these mainly make their appearance at lunch and dinner. *Pepperpot,* a stewed meat dish that originated with the Amerindians, is considered the national dish of Guyana. *Cassareep,* a sauce made from the liquid of the bitter cassava, which is poisonous until cooked, is a key ingredient. (It is also sold in stores.) Cassareep is used as a preservative for the stew. It is said that through the addition of more cassareep and meat to them, pepperpots can last indefinitely. There are rumors of the stews lasting 25 years or more. Pepperpot is always served at Christmas.

Pepperpot

Serves 8

Ingredients

1 cow heel, quartered, or 2 pig trotters

2 lb beef stew meat

2 lb oxtail

1 c cassareep (recipe follows, or use bottled)

1 large onion, chopped

3 cloves garlic, chopped

2 red hot peppers

1 cinnamon stick

3 cloves

2 tbsp brown sugar

1 bunch fresh thyme, or 1 tsp dried thyme

Salt to taste

Instructions

1. Clean meat. Place the cow heel or trotters in a large, covered soup pot. Cover with water, and bring to a boil. Cover with lid, reduce heat to a simmer, and cook for about 1 hour. Skim any accumulated fat off top.

2. Add beef and oxtail. Add more water to cover. Cover with lid and cook for about 1 hour.

3. Add remaining ingredients, and simmer until meat is tender. Serve hot.

Cassareep

Makes about 1 cup

Ingredients

4 lb bitter cassava

1 c water

1 tbsp brown sugar

1 cinnamon stick

1 tbsp cloves

Instructions

1. Peel and grate the cassava.

2. Place grated cassava in a dishtowel or cheesecloth. Twist and squeeze to extract liquid into saucepan. Discard the solids, or reserve for another use. (The liquid at this stage is poisonous until cooked.)

3. Add water, brown sugar, cinnamon, and cloves. Bring to a boil, reduce heat, and simmer, stirring occasionally, until the mixture becomes thick and syrupy.

Other one-pot dishes include *cookup rice*—the Guyanese version of rice and peas, made with coconut and salt pork—and *metemgee,* a stew made with plantains, yam, okra, coconut, meat, and salt fish.

Curry with roti, East Indian in heritage, is a very popular meal for lunch or dinner. The curry may be meat, fish, or vegetarian, such as *dhaal* (peas). Roti is a flatbread made of flour and a little fat. The curry is often stuffed inside and eaten as a wrap. The Chinese introduced their noodle dishes, lo mein and chow mein, into Guyanese cuisine. Made as an entire dish, they contain vegetables and sometimes meat. Chinese fried rice is another popular complete dish, often served with fried chicken.

Pastries, found in all shapes and sizes and made with a variety of ingredients, are no doubt a British influence. Examples of popular Guyanese pastries are *pine* (pineapple) tarts, cheese rolls, cassava pones, *salara* (coconut roll), meat patties, and tennis rolls (which are sweet rolls flavored with lemon).

Black cake is made around Christmastime. It is similar to fruitcake in the United States and western Europe, although it is closer to, and stems from, British plum pudding. Fruits such as raisins, prunes, and cherries, considered luxuries compared to the local tropical fruits, are soaked in rum for several weeks to several months, even up to a year. The fruit is then ground and, along with brown sugar and spices, made into a dense cake.

Most Guyanese prefer homemade beverages, with soft drinks made out of local fruits and spices. Ginger beer, sorrel drink, and *fly* (made with sweet potatoes or mangoes) are popular, especially during Christmastime. *Mauby,* made from the bark of a local tree, is a favorite. Homemade wine is made out of anything from potatoes and rice to mangoes and corn. Rum is ubiquitous in Guyana, considering the history and prevalence of the sugar plantations and rum factories.

Eating Out

Many Guyanese can rarely afford to eat out; it is much more common to visit family and friends for entertainment, rather than going to restaurants. Restaurants in Guyana usually serve foods similar to what people make in their homes. Nonetheless, there are street snacks, like fried plantains and *channa* (roasted chickpeas) and casual takeout-type places, often for lunch, serving things like curry and roti, macaroni pie, and Chinese fried rice and chicken.

Special Occasions

Religious and national holidays and festivals mark times to celebrate in Guyana. Christmas is one of the biggest celebratory times of the year, and food plays a major role. Pepperpot is always made; ham is a special treat, along with black cake. Ginger beer, mauby, and sorrel drink are especially popular this time of year. There are always huge parties on Christmas Eve, Christmas Day, and Boxing Day (the day after Christmas), influenced by British culture.

The season's parties continue into the New Year, with celebrations happening on New Year's Eve, New Year's Day, and the day after New Year's. As the holiday party season comes to a close, Guyanese tend to rev up the intensity of their parties, in a sort of competition, putting everything into a party before the end of the holiday season.

For entertainment year-round, people usually have parties at home and invite family and friends over, rather than going out. Social occasions revolve around food and music. Guyanese parties include day-to-day foods, but the mark of a successful party is the quantity and variety.

Religious customs around food are observed by the various groups in Guyana. For example, fasting is observed during Lent by Christians, and Hindus and Muslims in Guyana observe various religious holidays and festivities. Hindus celebrate Phagwah, or Holi, the Festival of Colors, in the spring. Another Hindu celebration, Diwali, the Festival of Lights, takes place in October. The sharing of sweets is a significant part of this celebration. With the melting-pot culture of Guyana, non-Hindus also participate in these celebrations. Guyana has a notable number of Muslims, and Eid al-Fitr is a celebration marking the end of Ramadan, the holy month of fasting.

Republic Day, also called Mashramani (or "Mash" for short), is celebrated on February 23. Established in 1970, the day commemorates Guyana becoming a republic. It is a colorful, festive day, with parades, costumes, music, and dancing. Food is, of course, a big part of the celebration. Guyana also celebrates Independence Day and Emancipation Day.

Diet and Health

The Guyanese diet is full of a variety of foods, but the goal is to maintain a healthy, balanced diet, which can be difficult, particularly in rural areas. With a poor economy, relying too heavily on inexpensive and plentiful ground provisions may mean missing out on important nutrients, which could lead to malnutrition, especially among children.

The Food and Nutrition Unit of Guyana's Ministry of Health is working hard toward making sure the country's citizens have access to and maintain a healthy diet.

Erin Laverty

Further Reading

Carnegie School of Home Economics. *What's Cooking in Guyana.* 2nd ed. Oxford: Macmillan Education, 2004.

Crosby, Alfred W., Jr. *The Columbian Exchange: Biological and Cultural Consequences of 1492.* Westport, CT: Praeger, 2003.

Harris, Dunstan A. *Island Cooking: Recipes from the Caribbean.* Berkeley, CA: Ten Speed Press, 2003.

Houston, Lynn Marie. *Food Culture in the Caribbean.* Westport, CT: Greenwood Press, 2005.

MacKie, Cristine. *Life and Food in the Caribbean.* New York: New Amsterdam, 1992.

Mintz, Sidney W. *Sweetness and Power: The Place of Sugar in Modern History.* New York: Penguin, 1986.

Narine, Nirmala. *In Nirmala's Kitchen: Everyday World Cuisine.* New York: Lake Isle Press, 2006.

Narine, Nirmala. *Nirmala's Edible Diary: A Hungry Traveler's Cookbook with Recipes from 14 Countries.* San Francisco: Chronicle Books, 2009.

"Recipes from Guyana and the Caribbean: A Part of Guyana Outpost Web Site." Guyana Outpost. http://guyanaoutpost.com/recipes/recipes.shtml.

Smock, Kirk. *Guyana: The Bradt Travel Guide.* Guilford, CT: Globe Pequot Press, 2008.

Haiti

Overview

Covering a total of 10,700 square miles, only 28 percent of which is arable land, the republic of Haiti comprises 10 departments (*departements*) and lies adjacent to the Dominican Republic on its eastern border. Both countries cohabit the island of Hispaniola in the Caribbean Sea. Formerly a French colony called Sainte Dominique, in 1804 Haiti became the only nation in the world to have undergone a successful slave rebellion. Haiti is the poorest country in the Western Hemisphere: Over 80 percent of Haiti's 8,400,000 inhabitants live in poverty. Most Haitians live in rural areas, with a large proportion of the population centered in the capital of Port-au-Prince, though this is less the case since the devastating earthquake in January 2010. Many wealthy Haitians and foreigners live in Petionville, a French-like suburb located north of Port-au-Prince high in the mountains surrounding the city. Exports traditionally have been based on the major agriculture and industries in Haiti: baseballs and clothing manufacturing, coffee, sisal, sugar, bananas, cacao, cotton, textiles, rice, rum, and fish. Deforestation contributes to soil loss and subsequent problems with cropping, agriculture, and food supplies.

With respect to religious affiliation, the population includes 80 percent Roman Catholics and 16 percent Protestants; the remainder follows other practices. Over half the population practices vodun (voodoo), regardless of their primary religious beliefs.

The average caloric intake in Haiti runs around 1,730 per day, in contrast to the 3,330 average in the United States. Most Haitians eat a vegetarian diet, not because they choose to, but because they cannot afford meat. The percentage of calories from meat comes to about 0.8 percent of total intake. Grains provide approximately 43.8 percent, while roots chip in 10.6 percent, milk and eggs 1.8 percent, and beans 9.6 percent.

Haitian cooking results in a true melting pot— French, West African, native Indian, and Spanish, sprinkled with a bit of Syrian and Lebanese tastes from waves of immigration in the 19th century. Some regionalism is apparent, as in the use of nuts like cashews in the north around Cap Haïtien and fish and seafood in the south near Jacmel and on down to Jeremie. Geographic isolation and seasonal factors have affected the diet of Haitians over the centuries, and still do. In 2010 a catastrophic magnitude-7 earthquake struck near Port-au-Prince, killing thousands and leaving perhaps a million people homeless.

🍽 Food Culture Snapshot

Claude and Marie-Louise Latortue live off John Brown, a major thoroughfare in Port-au-Prince, Haiti. Claude works for one of the many nongovernmental organizations offering humanitarian assistance to Haiti, and Marie-Louise teaches at a local high school. Their four children range in age from 2 to 15 years. Living with the Latortues is Claude's mother, Celeste, who does most of the food shopping and the cooking, although three times a week a young woman named Ritha comes to help with house cleaning and the laundry.

Celeste still likes to shop at the huge Marché en Fer (Iron Market), also called Marché Vallières, in the center of Port-au-Prince, built from iron girders originally destined for India but delivered instead to Port-au-Prince, another twist in the turbulent history of Haiti. If she doesn't have time to shop at the Marché en Fer, Celeste goes to the street next to the cathedral in Petionville, where the "Madame Saras" (female street vendors) set up their wares on the ground. Following local custom, Celeste always buys from the same vendor and, therefore, in return for her loyalty, receives excellent quality for less money. Bargaining often helps Celeste to bring the prices down considerably. Celeste also shops occasionally at a French butcher shop on Delmas, another busy street leading down from Petionville to central Port-au-Prince. When she needs certain special foods, she goes to the only large Western-style supermarket, the "Caribbean," also located in Petionville.

A wide range of foods—both local and imported—are available to the Latortues, many of which they buy only for holidays and feast days. Celeste usually fills a typical weekly market bag—a large basket-like bag modeled on those of French country housewives—with the following foods: salted fish, beef, pork, chicken, evaporated milk, red beans, white rice, cornmeal, smoked herrings, spaghetti, hot dogs, yams, cassava, Scotch bonnet peppers, seasonal fruits, plantains, avocados, peanut butter, a pumpkin-like squash called *joumou*, okra, onions, shallots, garlic, thyme, parsley, Maggi bouillon cubes, sweetish Haitian bread, and oatmeal.

The Iron Market gate's cupolas rise above a sea of stalls and vendors, Port-au-Prince, Haiti. (National Geographic | Getty Images)

Major Foodstuffs

Because Haiti is so mountainous and arable land is so scarce, Haitians use ingenious methods of terracing to increase the land available for planting. The most important Haitian food is *diri,* rice. The old saying goes that without rice in the meal, "Nou poko manje" (we haven't eaten). Other grains of importance include corn, wheat, and millet, although only the extremely poor eat millet (*piti mi*). The majority of the calories available to the average Haitian come from grains and other carbohydrates, eaten as porridges, noodles, and mush. One interesting item illustrating the fusion of foodstuffs in Haiti is the bulgur wheat brought to the islands by Syrian and Lebanese immigrants in the 19th century. Although in the larger cities, and particularly in the capital Port-au-Prince, bakeries provide French-style baguettes, the bread of choice for most Haitians regardless of class is bread baked in a square shape, with a slight sweet taste and a fluffier texture than the French bread.

Beans, or legumes, play a vital role in the Haitian diet. A daily favorite of Haitians from all economic levels, rice and beans together form the bulk of the diet for many Haitians. The flavor of the beans, and the different colors (red, pinto, black, petite, pigeon, Congo), cause people to feel they're not eating the same thing again and again. In addition to beans,

Men and women winnowing rice in Haiti. (StockPhotoPro)

½ tsp freshly ground black pepper

½ small Scotch bonnet pepper

In a large, wide, heavy stainless steel pot, heat the oil over medium heat until almost smoking. Add pork cubes and turn them frequently with a wooden spoon to brown them on all sides. Stir in the onions, shallots, orange and lime juices, water, thyme, salt, black pepper, and hot pepper. Bring mixture to a boil over high heat, cover, and reduce heat to low. Simmer for about 30 minutes. Uncover the pot, turn heat up to high once more, and stir often to keep meat from sticking. Cook for about 10 minutes, or until the sauce thickens to a syrupy glaze.

peanuts add protein and flavor to the Haitian diet, chiefly as spiced peanut butter and in the form of peanut brittle.

Pork and other meats form only a small part of the diet for most Haitians. In 1978, because of fear of African swine fever, the United States and the U.S. Agency for International Development eradicated the native Haitian black pigs, the *cochons noirs* sacred to the *loas,* or vodun gods. The newly introduced pink American pigs never really took the place of the beloved black pigs, because they ate everything with no discrimination. Other meat—in the form of beef, goat, and lamb or mutton—appears on Haitian tables, regularly for the wealthy and only occasionally for the poorer citizens.

Griyo (Glazed Pork)

Serves 4

¼ c peanut oil

2 lb boneless pork, cut into 2-in. cubes

1 c finely chopped onions

¼ c finely chopped shallots

1 c fresh orange juice

¼ c fresh lime juice

¼ c water

½ tsp crumbled dried thyme

1 tsp salt

Poultry plays an important role in Haitian cooking; chiefly chicken is used, but turkey, duck, and guinea fowl end up in pots and frying pans, too. Eggs tend to be sold in the markets rather than eaten by people in the rural areas.

Because Haiti enjoys a long 1,100-mile coastline, seafood figures prominently in the diet of some of the population. Most coastal dwellers include some fresh fish in their diets: shrimp, conch, and *tri-tri,* a small, almost-invisible fish that some say resembles plankton, only larger, used to flavor rice. Lobster, prized for its succulent white flesh, often ends up sold to tour companies for beach parties, grilled on racks set right on the sand over flaming wood fires. Dried, smoked, and salted fish also augment the Haitian diet, much as they did during the days of slavery and early years of freedom, and they remain one of the very West African–influenced components of the Haitian diet.

As a country situated on a tropical island, Haiti enjoys a rich variety of fruit. Mangoes, oranges, loquats, mandarins, *quenepa* or *mamoncillo* (a small, tart, oval green fruit), pineapples, bananas, papayas, coconuts, passion fruit, limes, lemons, cantaloupes, soursops, star apples (a purplish fruit with a star-shaped seed pattern inside), watermelons, and even strawberries from the mountains of Kenscoff high above Port-au-Prince—all contribute to the astonishing variety of the Haitian diet and form the basis for many delicious drinks.

Many types of vegetables grow in Haiti, most brought from elsewhere, joining some of the native varieties. Root vegetables like malanga, yams, sweet potatoes, and cassava provide another source of carbohydrates other than bread in the Haitian diet. Other vegetables include beets, corn, cabbage, pumpkin-like squash (joumou), eggplant (aubergine, bélangère), hearts of palm (chou palmiste), okra (gombo), green beans, carrots, tomatoes, green peas, watercress, sweet bell peppers, christophene (mirliton, chayote), and breadfruit.

Flavorings run the gamut from the usual black pepper and salt to onions, shallots, garlic, parsley, thyme, cilantro, Scotch bonnet peppers, cashew nuts, cloves, and tiny black mushrooms called djondjon, usually added to rice to turn it black. Picklises, vegetables cut up and pickled in vinegar with hot peppers, turn up in a multitude of dishes, but diners also add spoonfuls of picklises (or pikliz) to their food at the table. Fats used in Haitian food preparation include lard, shortening, peanut oil, and vegetable oil. Butter appears in some European pastries and in upscale restaurants catering to the wealthy and to foreigners.

Sugarcane served as the mainstay of the slavery-driven economy of the French colony of Sainte Dominique. Nowadays, most of the sugarcane on the island grows in the Dominican Republic, but Haitians still chew sugarcane stalks and suck out the juice from the fibers. Haitian sugarcane forms the basis for some of the best rum in the world. Another product that comes from sugarcane is clairin, a clear, raw alcohol produced only in Haiti and drunk by many rural people and poor people in the cities. Haitians also use raw clairin and drinks called trempés, steeped with medicinal herbs, in vodun ceremonies and practices. Tafia is another strong drink made from sugarcane.

Cooking

Haitians say of a woman who is a good cook, "Li gen dis dwet li," or "she has her 10 fingers." History has influenced modern Haitian cooking considerably. A veritable cauldron of culinary stew, Haiti's cuisine hints of Africa, France, Spain and the Middle East, and native Taino and Arawak Indians.

The Black Code of 1685 of Louis XIV decreed the following for food per week for the slaves over age 10: 2.5 pots of manioc, 3 cassavas, and 2 pounds salted beef or 3 pounds salted fish. Salted fish was one of the ways in which slaves were paid for, other than rum and Spanish coins. Slave dishes still part of the Haitian diet include diri ak djon-djon (rice with djon-djon), diri ak pwa kole (rice with beans in their own sauce), lambi (conch), griyo (griots, or fried pork cubes), and akra de mori (salt cod fritters) mixed with malanga (yautia). Pen patat (pain patate), a popular pudding-like dish, is made with sweet potatoes. Cooks make thiaka, a stew of corn and beans, which is also called mange-mete and thought to be a favorite of Azzaca, the vodun god of agriculture. Akassan, a beverage made with corn, resembles the horchatas of Mexico and Spain. Slave names stuck with these despised foods, particularly names for animal parts. Food-gathering traditions common to all slaveholding areas—gardening, fishing, salting, and smoking—persist in Haiti.

Wealthy families employ cooks. They may also have a few restaveks (from the French rester avec, "to stay with"), a modern version of child slavery. Poor families hand over their children to a wealthier family in return for small fee and the added relief of not having another mouth to feed. In families with restaveks, the restaveks cook their own food, generally cornmeal with the heads of dried herring. The restaveks assist the other servants in their chores, including cooking.

Aside from the wealthier families, who possess Western-style kitchens but don't always use them for cooking typical food, most Haitians cook over small one-burner grills called rechos, fueled with small gas or propane tanks or charcoal (charbon). The need for this traditional cooking fuel is the chief reason for the devastating deforestation all over Haiti.

Because of the simplicity of most Haitian kitchens, the most used cooking techniques are boiling, sautéing, frying, and grilling. Pots generally are aluminum, and except in very remote areas, plastic tubes, bottles, and other equipment help cooks in meal preparation. Measuring utensils include dis-

Typical cooking equipment in a makeshift kitchen in Haiti. (iStockPhoto)

carded cans. Large wooden mortars and pestles, similar to those still used in Africa, provide a mechanism for pulverizing corn, millet, and other foods. Long wooden spoons carved from tree branches serve as stirrers for corn porridge.

A number of flavoring methods assist in making blander foods like cornmeal more palatable. As is the case with many cuisines, Haitians prepare a sort of mirepoix, or aromatic base that flavors many dishes, called *zepis* (derived from the French word *épices,* or spices), consisting of garlic, bell peppers, onion, scallions, cilantro, parsley, and oil. Pikliz (picklises, pickles) provide another flavoring agent with a bite. Essentially pickled Scotch bonnet peppers, the mixture also includes shredded vegetables—cabbage, carrots, onions—as well as other vegetables like green peas or green beans, garlic, black peppercorns, cloves, and vinegar. Cooks use Maggi cubes of differing flavors, including one manufactured with the flavor of djon-djon, the beloved Haitian black mushrooms.

Typical Meals

In Haiti, people tend to follow a pattern of three meals a day. In rural areas, people tend to share utensils, and not everyone can eat together at the same time because of the lack of utensils for each person. Because tables and chairs are also in short supply, the oldest people sit (or the father sits),

while others squat down and eat off of a plate or from a dish made out of a calabash. The poor eat a mixture of red beans, corn, and yams with their fingers and might utilize old cans as drinking glasses. Manioc bread takes the place of the more expensive wheat bread usually found in the larger towns and cities.

Sos Pwa Rouj (Red Beans in Sauce)

Serves 8

2 c small red beans, cleaned and picked over

½ small white onion

3 tbsp peanut oil

2 cloves garlic, peeled and finely chopped

¾ c fresh flat-leaf Italian parsley, finely chopped

Salt

Freshly ground black pepper to taste

Put beans and half onion in a large pot with enough water to cover the beans by 2 inches. Bring to a boil. Cover pot, reduce heat to low, and simmer about 1½ to 2 hours, or until beans are very tender. Drain, retaining the cooking liquid. There should be about 3 cups of liquid. If there is too much liquid, boil it down. If too little, add water to reach 3 cups of liquid. Take 1½ cups of cooked beans, and put into a blender or food processor along with 1 cup of bean liquid. Puree. Stir the puree into the remaining liquid and remaining whole beans.

Heat the oil in a heavy frying pan. Add the garlic and ½ cup of the parsley and cook briefly, making sure to avoid burning the garlic. Stir in the bean mixture, and season with salt and about ½ teaspoon of ground black pepper. Heat the sauce gently, until the raw garlic taste is no longer apparent and the sauce is the consistency of thick buttermilk. Stir in the remaining parsley and check for seasoning. Serve over white rice with griyo and hot sauce.

Breakfast usually occurs between 6:30 and 7:30 A.M., before people rush off to school or work.

The meal generally always includes sweetened coffee (café au lait) and could consist of bread with spiced peanut butter called *mamba;* cornmeal mush with sliced avocado and smoked herring; oatmeal; breakfast spaghetti with a light tomato sauce and sliced hot dogs; rice pudding; small boiled breakfast plantains with hard-boiled eggs and smoked herring with onions and tomato sauce; or yams or cassava served with hot dogs in a tomato sauce. Cold, dried breakfast cereals are perceived as food for the wealthy.

The big meal of the day, lunch, takes place when people come home from work or school during the midday break, which usually lasts several hours. The menu is generally rice and beans cooked with ham hocks if the family is wealthy enough, peas, and meat in a sauce (chicken, goat, pork, turkey). Occasionally there is fish or some wild game. Dumplings made with wheat flour are also added to stews at times. Families might place a Scotch bonnet pepper on the table so people can cut off a bit to put on their own plates to eat with the meal. Otherwise, jars of pikliz or bowls of *sauce ti-malice* —a hot pepper sauce made with peppers, tomato paste, garlic, and onions—provide the fire that many Haitians love so much.

The evening meal is small and consists of simple foods, such as sweetened oatmeal or a fried rice–like dish, plantain puree (a sweetened porridge-like dish), or boiled sweet potatoes with rice and beans. Generally cornmeal is not eaten at night.

Eating Out

Haitians living in rural areas eat at home. Occasionally, they might eat something on the street made by the numerous women cooking fried dough like *marinades* or *patties* and other street snacks. Eating street food most often is a trend in cities and larger towns. The cries of the vendors—*Akasan cho* (hot corn drink) and *Mayi bouyi* (cornmeal mush with red beans)—ring through the air, adding to the chaotic cacophony of sound. Another popular dish eaten on the street is griyo (griots), fried pork cubes drenched in a lime sauce.

One long-standing Haitian custom, the weekly Saturday parties or get-togethers called *bamboches,* allows people the opportunity to eat outside the home. Friends and families gather to drink, eat, and tell stories. *Legim* (*legumes,* or vegetables) is eaten on Saturdays, rich with beef stewing in it. Eaten with rice, cornmeal, or boiled root vegetables, eggplant, and/or cabbage, legim is a dish influenced very much by African cooking traditions.

In Port-au-Prince and Cap Haïtien, restaurant-going plays a larger role in the daily food experience, especially among the wealthier classes. A number of high-class French restaurants always remain open and serve menus that anyone could find on the Boulevard St. Germain in Paris. One of the most famous of these restaurants was located in the arty gingerbread-facaded Hotel Oloffson, made famous in English novelist Graham Greene's *The Comedians* (1966). Lebanese restaurants also serve a wealthier clientele, and the food appears to be the same as that served in Beirut or elsewhere in the Middle East—lamb kebabs, kibbe, and hummus, accompanied by pita bread. Pizza places like Domino's Pizza in Petionville provide Italy's most famous dish as well.

Other opportunities exist for eating out at the various beach resorts dotted across the country but mostly located in Jacmel and south of Gonaive. Like the restaurants in Port-au-Prince, the fare leans toward French cuisine with a Caribbean twist, including lambi (conch) creole or breadfruit beignets.

Special Occasions

Haiti, because of its Roman Catholic heritage, follows the feast-day calendar of the Roman Catholic Church and celebrates a large number of holy days. Several other major holidays occur throughout the year, including many associated with vodun. In addition to the official church or national holidays, birthdays, weddings, christenings, and funerals provide people with special festive food.

On January 1, New Year's Day (also Haitian Independence Day), *soup joumou* appears on menus across the country and wherever Haitians live around the world. Made with a pumpkin-like squash and beef, this thick minestrone-like soup is usually served with homemade grenadine sherry. The following day, January 2, is Ancestors' Day, when Haitians pay tribute to those who fought for Haiti's independence from the French in 1804. Families serve turkey as they prepare the largest meal of the year in a feast not unlike the American Thanksgiving feast but cooked very differently from the U.S. manner—piquant pikliz vinegar seasons the turkey.

Carnival-like festivities take place on January 6, the day of Epiphany in the Roman Catholic Church, and again in May. Just before Lent, on Mardi Gras, *benye* (beignets) or fried fritters satiate appetites. Roving *rara* bands dance and sing in the streets, asking listeners for food and money during Carnival and Lent and on Good Friday. People give them whatever they have. On Good Friday, cooks prepare meals featuring the white beans usually cooked on Sundays. For breakfast, people might eat herrings, boiled eggs, and bread, while the dinner menu includes fish, root vegetables, salad, white rice, and more white beans.

A summer pilgrimage celebration of the Virgin Mary takes place on July 16—also the day of Our Lady of Mount Carmel—in Saut d'Eau, a site where an apparition of the Virgin Mary appeared in the 1800s. This celebration also commemorates Erzulie, the vodun goddess of love. A number of cows and goats are sacrificed, and people drink a lot of clairin, dance, and throw themselves into the water.

The Day of the Dead, November 2, is the Roman Catholic All Souls' Day, as well as a vodun feast day, Fete Gede, which honors the family of *loa* or spirits associated with death and fertility. In Fete Gede celebrations, people rub themselves with hot pepper juice for "possession" and drink coffee and peppered alcohol. Fete Gede is like a New Year's Day for the dead; the practice originated with slaves brought from Dahomey, Yorubaland, Congo, and Angola. A typical menu, subject to variation, features greens, yams, macaroni and cheese, cornbread, red beans and rice, cabbage, baked chicken, fried red snapper, and sweet potato pudding. People also eat thiaka (also called mange-mete) or cornmeal mush with red beans. The day serves as a way for Haitians to get in touch symbolically with their familial roots.

As in the Mexican Day of the Dead practices, Haitians celebrating Fete Gede build altars for remembering their dead and all the good things they liked while alive. A typical altar in honor of Gede might include cigarettes; clarin spiced with Scotch bonnet peppers; a picture of a small white skull; white, black, and purple candles and satin cloth; numerous crosses; a miniature coffin; sequined bottles; and a portrait of St. Gerard, the Catholic saint associated with Baron Samedi, the vodun god of death, along with the mandatory top hat and cane, symbols of the baron. In November, along with the Day of the Dead celebrations, Manje-Yam, a harvest festival celebrating the yam, takes place.

Christmas Eve celebrations tend to follow the French pattern of *reveillon,* or "reawakening," with a large meal after midnight mass. Children are allowed to drink anisette. On the following day, Christmas, families offer guests *kremas,* a type of eggnog often made with pineapple; fried pork (griyo); pickles (pikliz); fried plantains; and sweet potato pudding (pain patate).

Other special occasions include all the family-related events like Sunday dinners and get-togethers, when white beans, macaroni and cheese, and chicken or Haitian turkey load down the tables in wealthier families. Weddings, first communions, funerals, and wakes see such traditional foods as *akra* (fried patties) made with malanga, patties, and roasted or fried goat being served. Traditionally, goats were slaughtered for family reunions, first communions, and confirmations.

Birthdays bring out the best in cooks. A typical menu in a wealthier household might include fried plantains, *tassot* (beef), chicken, green salad, *macaroni au gratin,* potato salad, *gratin pomme de terre* (potatoes au gratin), and diri ak djon-djon (rice with djon-djon mushrooms) with shrimp and green peas.

Another special occasion for Haitian villagers is the *coumbites,* or common work parties, when people work together on a community project. Either

Flowers are sold to observers of Day of the Dead celebrations at the National Cemetery in Port-au-Prince, Haiti. (Getty Images)

yams with milk or cornmeal covered with red bean sauce are served at the end of days spent working on coumbites.

Diet and Health

Aside from some of the foods associated with vodun, Haitians profess beliefs about food as it relates to health. In Haiti, bread soup is said to have properties similar to those of chicken soup in U.S. culture. Pineapple-skin juice is thought to be a blood and body cleanser, while people believe that drinking beet juice will rejuvenate and invigorate people, by putting more red in their blood, and give them strength for difficult and trying times.

Humoral medical theories, based on ancient Greek ideas passed down through the centuries by groups throughout the Mediterranean, still hold sway in Haiti, particularly in rural areas. Many people in rural Haiti suffer from varying degrees of malnutrition. Hot–cold beliefs impact greatly on nutritional status, particularly that of pregnant and lactating women. One practice illustrating the poverty of Haiti is the eating of clay by pregnant women, which may increase their calcium intake, a practice also common in parts of Africa.

Clay eating is not limited to pregnant women. Mudcakes, called *teh,* are eaten in conditions of extreme hunger. People take what vegetables they can find and mix these with mud that has been strained to get out the stones and other debris. They form the mud and vegetables into flat cakes and then dry them in the sun. People eat them like that, without further cooking or preparation. In contrast, obesity is becoming a problem among those Haitians with more money to spend on food.

Cynthia D. Bertelsen

Further Reading

Dash, J. Michael. *Culture and Customs of Haiti.* Westport, CT: Greenwood Press, 2001.

Deren, Maya. *Divine Horsemen: The Living Gods of Haiti.* New Paltz, NY: McPherson, 1983.

"Haitian Cuisine." Everything Haitian. http://www.everythinghaitian.com/HaitianCuisine/Default.aspx.

The Haitian Institute. *The Art and Soul of Haitian Cooking.* Kearney, NE: Morris Press, 2001.

"Haiti: Cuisine and Recipes." Whats4Eats.com. http://www.whats4eats.com/caribbean/haiti-cuisine.

Houston, Lynn Marie. *Food Culture in the Caribbean.* Westport, CT: Greenwood Press, 2005.

Menager, Mona Cassion. *Fine Haitian Cuisine.* Coconut Creek, FL: Educa Vision, 2006.

Wolkstein, Diane. *The Magic Orange Tree and Other Haitian Folktales.* New York: Schocken Books, 1997.

Yurnet-Thomas, Mirta. *A Taste of Haiti.* Exp. ed. New York: Hippocrene Books, 2007.

Hawaii

Overview

Hawaii is an isolated archipelago in the Pacific Ocean located thousands of miles from the nearest continent. Of the hundreds of islands comprising the chain, only seven are occupied by humans: Niʻihau, Kauaʻi, Oʻahu, Molokaʻi, Lanaʻi, Maui, and Hawaii. Polynesians originally settled the Hawaiian Islands more than 1,000 years ago, bringing with them many of their principal foodstuffs. Western contact began in 1778, when Captain Cook encountered Hawaii for the first time. The independent Kingdom of Hawaii was eventually annexed by the United States and, in 1959, became America's 50th state.

Since contact, subsequent settlers have added foods from their homelands to Hawaiian cuisine. Hawaii has a diverse population, with no single ethnicity constituting a majority. Many Hawaii residents have mixed ethnic backgrounds and claim numerous modern ethnicities as their own. The population is roughly 56 percent Asian, which includes a mixture of Japanese (39%), Filipino (36%), Chinese (10%), and Korean (5%). Caucasians make up 34 percent of the population. Only 11 percent of Hawaii's population now claims Pacific Islander descent. Hawaii's mixed heritage is reflected in the eclectic local foodways common throughout the islands.

🍽 Food Culture Snapshot

The Baker family live in Mililani, on the island of Oʻahu. Katie Baker is an attorney who commutes to downtown Honolulu for work. Her husband, Nic Baker, is a chemist and works for a local diagnostic laboratory. Their young daughter, Eleanor, attends preschool. Like most middle-class Hawaiian residents, the Bakers' foodways are diverse and, despite personal preferences, fairly representative of contemporary Hawaiian foodways.

The Bakers do most of their grocery shopping at one of the large supermarkets. Dry goods, produce, meats, and dairy are all readily available from any one of the chains located near their house. Nic takes Eleanor to a farmers' market every Sunday morning to shop for additional veggies and fresh bread. The Bakers also make occasional trips to specialty shops, such as a fish store, wine shop, bakery, or chocolatier.

Much of what the Bakers buy are foods that they prepare at home themselves. This includes basic ingredients such as meats, vegetables, and staples like flour, sugar, and eggs, as well as commercial products like dried pasta, bottled sauces, and canned or frozen goods. They also buy some prepared foods, like bread. Additionally, child-friendly foods are purchased for Eleanor, such as animal-shaped crackers or fruit juice. These foods are only supplementary; Eleanor usually eats the same foods as her parents. The Bakers, who are environmentally conscious, buy many items in bulk with reduced packaging and employ reusable containers for portioning these foods and beverages.

Breakfast is made and eaten at home, early in the day, after which point Katie and Nic pack lunches for themselves, often including leftovers from the preceding night's dinner that they will reheat at work. Both Katie and Nic occasionally eat out for lunch, frequently with colleagues or clients. A hot lunch consisting of typical local food is provided for Eleanor at preschool. Dinner, which Nic usually cooks, is eaten together as a family in the evening. Meals are somewhat health conscious, to encourage Eleanor to develop healthy eating habits. The Bakers also eat dinner out at least once a week. The Bakers' routine is relaxed on weekends, when mealtimes change, foods may be more elaborate and/or luxurious, and snacking is more common.

Major Foodstuffs

Hawaii produces very little of its own foodstuffs. Once the host of pineapple and sugar plantations, Hawaii now produces very little of these products. High land values and the cost of labor have made Hawaii unattractive for agricultural use. Specialty goods, which fetch higher prices, have managed to remain successful in Hawaii. There is some commercial coffee production and a large grass-fed beef industry on Hawaii Island. Most of these products, however, are exported. Small-scale production of fruit and vegetables is becoming more common and provides farmers' markets and fruit stands with their goods. Beyond this, almost all of the food residents of Hawaii consume is imported.

One exception is fish. Hawaii has a multi-million-dollar fishing industry that is one of the largest in the United States. Hawaii residents fish recreationally, as well as commercially, with more than a quarter of the population participating in some form of fishing annually. While fish is one of the chief exports, it is also one of the most popular local foods. Hawaiians, on average, consume more than twice as much fish per person per year as other Americans. Although most of the seafood consumed is locally caught, some cold-water varieties, such as salmon and mussels, are imported to Hawaii.

Salmon Poke

1 lb raw salmon, cut into bite-sized cubes

½ c soy sauce

¼ c green onion, diced

½ tsp Hawaiian salt

1 tsp honey

1 tsp sesame oil

2 tbsp orange juice

¼ tsp orange zest

½ tsp fresh ginger, grated

½ tsp minced garlic

3 tbsp *yasai fumi furikake* (Japanese rice seasoning)

Mix ingredients in a bowl. Cover and refrigerate at least 3 hours. Stir and serve chilled.

Tropical fruit is also consumed in large quantities in Hawaii. Some of these fruits were introduced from tropical Asia, while others are South American in origin. Many fruits, such as bananas and papayas, are grown on a small scale for year-round consumption. Locals favor petite apple-bananas, which have a firmer, sweeter, but also slightly tangier flesh than the common Cavendish bananas, known in Hawaii as "mainland bananas." Papayas are often cultivated but are also known as an invasive weed species. Several types of guavas are available, including common guavas, lemon guavas, and strawberry guavas, the last of which are also considered a weed fruit. Tart yellow passion fruit, called *lilikoi* in Hawaii, is a more seasonal fruit that is popular for its strong flavor but is also an invasive vine in the wild. Mangoes are one of the most popular seasonal fruits in Hawaii, ripening in the late summer and early fall. Hadens are, by far, the most common variety of mangoes, although dozens of others can be found as well. Mangoes are not exported from Hawaii due to the prevalence of mango seed weevils in the state. Coconuts, both green and ripe, can also be found, but derived coconut products are more common than the actual fruit. A firm pudding made of coconut milk, called *haupia,* is a popular dessert often served at luau or as part of a traditional Hawaiian meal.

Wheat and rice are the most important grains in Hawaii. Wheat flour is used for bread as well as for noodles. Bread is eaten on its own, as an accompaniment for meals, or as the basis for sandwiches, much like in the continental United States. White bread made from refined flour is predominant, but healthier whole wheat and multigrain breads are gaining popularity as Hawaii residents become more health conscious. Wheat noodles, such as the thin ramen-like *saimin* noodles, are a regular part of the Hawaiian diet and reflect Japanese and Chinese influences. A strong Asian influence is also witnessed in the preference for short-grain white rice, which has become a staple in Hawaii, accompanying many, if not most, meals.

Many native Hawaiian foods are still eaten. The most important of these foods is taro, known as *kalo* in Hawaiian. The kalo plant has several edible parts, including the leaves, the stems, and the corm, which is the starchy bulbous portion of the stalk found underground. All parts of kalo must be cooked well to break down the calcium oxalate crystals, which can cause an itching or burning sensation in the mouth and throat if not treated properly. Kalo is distinguished by the color of the corm (white, pink, yellow, purple) and whether it was grown in a marshlike wetland field system or a dryland field system. Kalo is prepared in a number of different ways, but *poi,* a paste of cooked and mashed corm, was the cornerstone of the Hawaiian diet and is still eaten by locals. Poi can be eaten

when it is freshly prepared, but it may also be left to ferment for several days so that it requires a stronger sour flavor and a more favorable texture.

The other principal native Hawaiian food still eaten today is the sweet potato (*'uala*), which was introduced to Hawaii from Polynesian contact with South America hundreds of years before Western contact. Other native Hawaiian foods, such as *'ulu* (breadfruit), a starchy arbor crop; bananas (*mai'a*); coconuts (*niu*); and mountain apples (*'ohi'a 'ai*), are all still part of the modern Hawaiian foodscape. The native Hawaiians also cultivated *ko,* a grassy plant originally domesticated in Southeast Asia and Papua New Guinea. Eventually ko was commoditized and became an important part of the emerging global economy. Although ko production has all but vanished from Hawaii, it is still, at least in the United States, strongly associated with the Hawaiian Islands. Ko, more widely known by its English name, sugar, is still a large part of the modern Hawaiian diet but in an increasingly less healthy way.

Cooking

The cooking techniques of Hawaii are the same as those found in most westernized kitchens in developed countries. Electric rice cookers are commonly employed to make the steamed white rice that is one of the islands' staples, as already discussed. Baking, roasting, and broiling are done in modern ovens, and boiling, steaming, sautéing, and frying are done on modern gas or electric ranges. Quick cooking techniques, such as sautéing and broiling, are favored due to Hawaii's largely tropical climate, which makes the heat from slow cooking methods unpleasant, especially in summer months.

The warm weather also results in the relishing of cold and raw foods. Frozen and iced desserts are especially popular, and fresh fruit is a readily available room-temperature treat. Hawaii has indigenous raw-fish traditions, as does Japan, whose culture has so heavily influenced the Hawaiian Islands. *Poke* consists of chopped, usually raw, seafood, which is marinated and eaten, similar to ceviche. Poke is featured at most local picnics and cookouts, and it can be purchased at any supermarket or fish shop.

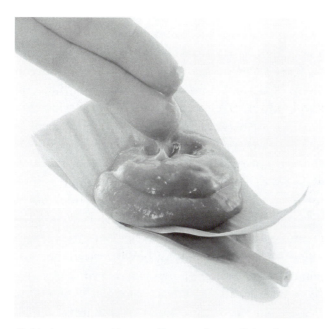

Poi being scooped by two fingers, the traditional way to eat it, on a tea leaf. (808isgreat | Dreamstime.com)

The climate also favors outdoor cooking. Outdoor grilling and roasting are common practices in the evening on weekdays or for lunch or dinner during weekends. Self-contained grills, either gas or charcoal, are used for this purpose. Portable grills are also popular and are set up at beaches or in parks so hot meals can be prepared away from home, often as part of a social gathering or celebration. Occasionally food is roasted over a small open fire or a beach bonfire, usually whole fresh-caught fish, but this practice is becoming rare as restrictions on fires become more stringent.

Another outdoor cooking method is the use of an *imu,* or underground earthen oven. Imu, one of Hawaii's most traditional ways to cook, were common in precontact times. Imu are now reserved for special occasions because their use requires more labor and time than do other cooking methods. To construct an imu a large hole is dug in the ground, into which parcels of food are placed with hot stones from a fire and then buried, allowing the food to steam-roast for hours. Many of the native Hawaiian foods favored for celebrations were cooked using this method, which is still occasionally used today.

Prior to Western contact, cooking was the provenance of native Hawaiian men. Many foods were considered *kapu,* or sacred, and were, therefore, not thought suitable for consumption by women. Women were not allowed to handle kapu foods because it was believed that contact with kapu items might endanger those women. There was also a fear that women might contaminate kapu foods they had contact with and the men who consumed them. To safeguard consumers from supernatural peril, men prepared not only their own food but also the women's food as well, keeping men's foods and women's foods separate. Today, after decades of American and Asian influence, women do the majority of domestic food preparation. Men, however, still dominate professional cooking.

Typical Meals

Hawaiian food habits result from the combination of cultures that make up the islands' mixed population. Forks and knives, along with spoons, are the most common eating implements, although chopsticks are also ubiquitous. Most locals learn to use chopsticks as children and will use them for Asian, or predominantly Asian, foods.

Meals are typically eaten socially. Until relatively recently eating took place at a table surrounded by chairs or at a *chabudai,* a low table where diners sit on mats or cushions on the floor. Tables and chairs were set in designated eating areas in kitchens, in dining rooms, on *lāna'i* (outdoor porch areas), or in a living room. Gathering around a table for a social meal is becoming increasingly less common, mirroring the trends found on the mainland and elsewhere. Many meals are now taken individually, on the go, and/or in front of the television. The meal pattern in Hawaii is also very similar to that of the American mainland. Breakfast is eaten in the morning, followed by lunch at midday and dinner in the evening. Snacking has become increasingly common and can take place at any time before, after, or between meals.

Breakfast ranges from simple to elaborate and can be either sweet or savory. The most common breakfast is cold cereal, eaten with milk. It is a fast meal, popular with both children and adults, and is often eaten with quick accompaniments such as toasted bread and fruit juice. Many of these cereals are high in sugars, although healthier options are also available. Other sweet breakfast items include assorted pastries, French toast, or pancakes. Tropical ingredients, such as bananas and macadamia nuts, are frequently incorporated into such dishes, which are served with tropical fruit sauces, such as coconut or guava syrup. Many sweet dishes are accompanied by savory side dishes of meat products, such as Spam or Portuguese sausage. Eggs are the basis for many savory breakfasts, alongside meat-based dishes such as corned beef hash. Savory breakfasts combine American and Asian elements. Rice is usually served in lieu of potatoes. White rice is the most common, but fried rice or kimchi fried rice is also sometimes available. *Loco moco,* a dish made of rice, hamburger patties, and fried eggs, topped with brown gravy, not only is eaten for breakfast but is popular for lunch and dinner as well.

Lunch is a variable meal that is eaten outside of the home more often than not. Workday lunches are brought from home or are purchased from restaurants, cafés, or cafeterias. Brownbag lunches often feature a sandwich or leftovers from a previous dinner. Pre-prepared items offered by stores, such as sushi sets, are frequently purchased items. Restaurant offerings are almost innumerable. Fast-food chains are also numerous, which offer their standard fare as well as some local adaptations, such as Hawaiian burgers, which include teriyaki sauce and pineapple. Most schools offer catered lunch options, which, like fast food, are criticized for the less-than-ideal nutrition they offer. Many parents opt to pack lunch for their children in order to provide a healthier meal. Weekend lunches vary greatly. Lunch may be eaten in the home, at a restaurant, at the beach, on the go, or not at all.

Dinner is typically the most substantial meal of the day and is arguably the most variable. It is eaten in the evening and often provides leftovers for future meals. Dinner is most commonly eaten in the home or at one of the thousands of restaurants in Hawaii. Local foods are eaten as well as a wide variety of ethnic food from all over the world. Many people in Hawaii finish dinner with a sweet dessert, which can be anything from simple desserts like fresh fruit or ice cream to elaborate cakes and pies.

Periodic snacking has become increasingly common in Hawaii, and there are a number of snack items frequently offered there that are not common to the rest of the United States. Favored Asian snack items include the small Japanese rice crackers called *arare,* wasabi-coated peanuts, dried shredded cuttlefish, and a variety of candies coated in salty-tart Chinese *li hing mui* powder. Li hing mui–coated fruit, both fresh and dried, is also popular, as well as a variety of pickled fruits. *Mochi,* made from sweetened rice dough, are flavored or stuffed with a variety of fillings and sold fresh or packaged. These items are found alongside typical American snack foods in grocery, drug, and convenience stores, as well as in specialty snack shops, known locally as "crack seed stores."

Many people in Hawaii are coffee drinkers, and although coffee may be drunk throughout the day, coffee is most typically an accompaniment of breakfast, regardless of what breakfast may be. Iced coffee beverages are popular in Hawaii due to its tropical climate. Tea is also consumed with meals or on its own, and like coffee, tea may be served hot or cold. Green and oolong teas are the most common. Soda is very popular, as well as sweetened juice drinks that feature local flavors such as guava, lilikoi, and lychee. Meals are typically served with a beverage, even if that beverage is plain tap water. The tap water in Hawaii is potable.

Eating Out

Eating out has become common practice in Hawaii, and there are restaurants that cater to almost every taste and budget. Inexpensive and midrange restaurants make up the majority of dining establishments, although fine dining options are available as well. Local tastes are largely represented, but restaurants catering to tourists are also prevalent, especially in the major hotel zones.

Restaurants representing Asian cuisines are numerous in Hawaii, as are many American-style restaurants. These range from cheap take-out counters to expensive restaurants that serve as special-occasion destinations. European and Latin American foods are rare and relatively expensive, while offerings from elsewhere, such as Africa, are nonexistent. Native Hawaiian food can be purchased from a number of specialty restaurants, although some of the more common Hawaiian foods, such as *lau lau,* a ti-leaf-wrapped package of fish, pork, and kalo leaves, can be purchased at many local-style restaurants. (The ti plant was introduced from Polynesia and has broad, sturdy leaves, also used to make hula skirts.)

Hawaii has many local-style restaurants that enjoy great popularity. Diner-like restaurants, sometimes called drive-ins, serve Hawaiian plate lunches. They typically include two scoops of white rice, a scoop of macaroni salad made with a mayonnaise base, and a choice of meat, such as chicken *katsu* (a fried dish based on the Japanese *tonkatsu*), fried fish, or *kalbi* (Korean-style grilled spareribs). Chili is usually also on offer at plate-lunch establishments, where it is eaten with rice or as a sauce for a plate lunch. These meals tend to be heavy, with large amounts of starch and protein. Many plate-lunch establishments have responded to health-conscious trends by offering smaller portions, grilled options, and brown rice. Despite the name, plate lunches are not eaten only at lunch. Many plate-lunch restaurants offer breakfast and dinner as well. Saimin shops are common, and ramen shops serving Japanese-style noodle soups are an inexpensive favorite with locals and tourists alike.

Street food is uncommon in Hawaii, but occasionally vendors offering marinated grilled or smoked meats, like *huli huli* chicken, can be found. O'ahu's north shore is also known for the shrimp vendors near the towns of Haleiwa and Kahuku, who sometimes sell live prawns from the local farms in addition to shrimp sautéed in garlic sauce. Sweets are often purchased as well. Baked goods, such as guava cream pies and haupia cakes, are sold both whole and by the slice. Shave ice, known elsewhere as snow cones and consisting of fluffy snowlike ice topped with flavored syrups, is especially popular in hot weather and is often eaten with azuki beans, ice cream, and a drizzle of sweetened condensed milk called a "snow cap."

Hawaiian-Style *Kalbi*

4 lb beef short ribs, sliced thin

2 c shoyu (soy sauce)

2 c sugar

3 cloves garlic, minced

I tbsp fresh ginger, grated

I tsp sesame oil

¾ c green onion, diced

I tsp toasted sesame seeds

Mix beef, shoyu, sugar, garlic, ginger, sesame oil, and ½ cup green onions in a bowl. Cover and refrigerate overnight. Remove short ribs from marinade, and grill over high heat until well cooked. Remove from heat, and sprinkle with sesame seeds and remaining green onion. Serve hot.

Fine-dining restaurants are most commonly found in the larger cities or luxury resorts. These restaurants tend to be more informal than their mainland counterparts but just as expensive. Most Hawaiian diners prefer a relaxed atmosphere and dress code. Hawaii boasts several internationally acclaimed chefs who have helped develop the Pacific Rim fusion offered in most of these high-end restaurants. American, Asian, Hawaiian, and European elements are blended to create Hawaii's fancier food, much in the same way everyday Hawaiian cuisine has been formed. These restaurants rely heavily on tourism as Hawaii residents tend to reserve such dining for special occasions.

Special Occasions

Special occasions are celebrated in a number of ways. As on the mainland, dining out at nice restaurants is popular for small or intimate celebrations. When a larger celebration is desired, a party is held, either at a home, at the beach, or in a park. These are Hawaii's most famous form of celebration: the luau. A luau is a festive gathering with native Hawaiian roots that includes feasting. Similar to an American cookout, a luau is normally held outside, sometimes under a party tent. Family and friends gather to eat and drink and, more often than not, sing and dance. Local-style food is served in copious amounts. It is common for guests to bring a dish or beverage to share, although the hosts typically provide a full meal. Luau dishes often include chicken long rice (a noodle dish similar to Korean *japchae*), poke, rice, *lomi lomi* salmon (made from minced salt-cured salmon massaged with diced tomatoes and onions), roasted sweet potatoes, adobo (a savory Filipino stew), spareribs, squid *lu'au* (made from squid and taro leaves cooked in coconut cream), sweet bread (like the Portuguese *pau doce*), macaroni salad, lau lau, poi, and haupia. Luau are held for birthdays, graduations, anniversaries, and even weddings. Some of the largest luau are held to celebrate a child's first birthday, which is given special significance in Hawaii.

Commercial luau offered by hotels and tourism outfits are an entirely different affair. These luau

Traditional food that would likely be served at a luau in Hawaii. (StockPhotoPro)

are Polynesian dance showcases performed by professionals for tourists. Such events may or may not include dinner, depending on the package. When dinner is served it usually includes a variety of native Hawaiian, local, and American dishes.

Many major religious and secular holidays are celebrated in the same manner in Hawaii as they are on the U.S. mainland or elsewhere. The food served at such events often demonstrates some local variation but is in keeping with the parent tradition. Thanksgiving turkeys, for example, may be basted with soy sauce, called by its Japanese name shoyu, and dressed with rice stuffing. The day prior to Ash Wednesday, known elsewhere as Fat Tuesday, is known in Hawaii as Malasada Day. Warm *malasadas,* a fried doughnut of Portuguese origin, are eaten in revelry on this day in preparation for Lent, at which time luxuries, such as sweets, are given up by members of some Christian orders. Bon season, or Obon, is also celebrated in Hawaii. Many Hawaii residents enjoy attending Bon dances, a

Japanese Buddhist custom that honors one's ancestors. Many temples host food festivals to showcase Japanese food during Bon. Watermelon and other summer foods are offered to both ancestors and festival participants alike.

Makahiki, however, is a festive period unique to Hawaii. Sometimes called Hawaiian New Year's, Makahiki celebrates the return of Lono, the god of agriculture, rain, and prosperity. Makahiki, which lasts approximately four months, was a time of peace for native Hawaiians. Offerings were made to the chiefs, religious ceremonies were conducted, family was visited, and feasts were held. Makahiki is still celebrated by native Hawaiian practitioners today, although on a much smaller scale. Traditional native Hawaiian foods are served, and food offerings may be given to Lono. Makahiki is related to other traditions in Polynesia, such as the Matariki celebration in Maori culture.

Diet and Health

Prior to Western contact native Hawaiians enjoyed relatively good health. The combination of regular light manual labor and a diet high in nutrients and low in fat was beneficial to the majority of the population. Kalo and 'uala are good sources of vitamins, minerals, and dietary fiber. Native Hawaiians supplemented these starchy foods with fruit, vegetables, and fish. Necessary fats were provided by regular consumption of food such as coconuts and the occasional consumption of pork, dog, and chicken.

Western contact had catastrophic effects on the native Hawaiian population, who had no resistance to the illnesses common to Europe and Asia. Many died in a short period of time, and much was lost. The introduction of new foodways has also been detrimental to native Hawaiians' health. Many new foods, such as white rice, are high in calories and low in nutrients. Eaten in moderation they pose no threat, but these foods have been incorporated into daily life, and Hawaiian portion sizes remain large despite an increasingly sedentary lifestyle. This new diet has led to a number of health problems that continue to plague the native Hawaiian community.

Native Hawaiians are significantly more likely to suffer from obesity, heart disease, and diabetes than members of the other major ethnic groups in Hawaii. These conditions have been directly linked to diet. Native Hawaiians are also more likely to suffer from many forms of cancer, including breast, lung, colon, rectal, and prostate cancer. Native Hawaiians are among the poorest Hawaii residents and some of the most underserviced in terms of health care. They are less likely to receive preventative care, diagnostic care, or treatment than other ethnic groups.

Overall, Hawaii's population is relatively healthy when compared to the rest of the United States. Hawaii has one of the lowest overall rates of adult and childhood obesity. This reflects the active, healthy lifestyle associated with the local culture. Eating patterns in Hawaii are moderate, and dietary excess is offset, in part, by outdoors activities, such as hiking, swimming, and surfing. The obesity rate, however, is following the national trend and increasing. Hawaii's population needs to embrace a healthier diet, but it doesn't necessarily need to give up tradition to do so.

Kelila Jaffe

Further Reading

Corum, Ann Kondo *Ethnic Foods of Hawaii.* Honolulu, HI: Bess Press, 2000.

Laudan, Rachel. *The Food of Paradise: Exploring Hawaii's Culinary Heritage.* Honolulu: University of Hawaii Press, 1996.

Titcomb, Margaret. *Native Use of Fish in Hawaii.* Honolulu: University of Hawaii Press, 1982.

Trubeck, Amy B. *The Taste of Place: A Cultural Journey into Terroir.* Berkeley: University of California Press, 2009.

Yim, Susan. *We Go Eat: A Mixed Plate from Hawaii's Food Culture.* Honolulu: Hawaii Council for the Humanities, 2008.

Honduras

Overview

Honduras, or *Guaymura* as it was originally called, covers approximately 43,000 square miles, with 510 miles of coastline, in Central America. Bordered by the Gulf of Fonseca on the south coast and the Caribbean Sea on the north coast, Honduras abuts El Salvador in the west, Guatemala in the north, and Nicaragua in the south. Honduras resembles the U.S. state of Tennessee in size, with a total population of almost eight million, 48 percent of whom live in urban areas. Only 9.53 percent of Honduras's land is arable, due to the mountain ranges cutting through the center of the country.

History, as well as geography and tropical climate, also affected the cuisine of Honduras. Christopher Columbus landed in the Bay Islands on his fourth and last visit to the New World. The Spanish brought numerous Old World foods to the area. English pirates settled the Bay Islands, and people there still speak an archaic form of English. Later, U.S.-based multinationals—United Fruit Company and Standard Fruit Company—moved in to grow and export bananas, tying Honduras to U.S. culture. Another cultural infusion came from the Lebanese and Palestinians who settled in Honduras in the early 20th century.

In spite of its Mayan heritage, amply illustrated by the classic Mayan ruins at Copán, where a stone for grinding corn for *nacatamales* (large square tamales nowadays wrapped and steamed in banana leaves) dates to 1300 B.C., Honduras today is 90 percent mestizo, or mixed Spanish and Native American. Modern-day Native American groups make up only 7 percent of the total population. Some of the cultural groups include Pech or Payas, Lenca, Xicaques, Miskitos, Chortí, and Tawahka. Another group, the Garifuna, or Black Caribs, live mostly along the north coast and contribute unique flavors to the cuisine in that region.

Religious beliefs influence some culinary practices, most centering around the 97 percent of the Honduran population professing Roman Catholicism, with the other 3 percent Protestant. The Black Caribs, or Garifuna, who live along the north coast, retain certain deities resembling those of Africa, including Liwa Mairin, a sea goddess and protector of lobster fishermen.

Caloric intake varies with social class. Over 50 percent of Hondurans live in poverty. An average of 2,400 calories per day is available to the wealthy class, in contrast to 1,972 calories per day for the poorer strata of society. Grains supply 50 percent of total calories in the Honduran diet, with fats providing 11 percent and dairy 7.4 percent.

❏ Food Culture Snapshot

Juan and Elvira Sanchez live in a *colonia,* or neighborhood, in Tegucigalpa, the capital and Honduras's largest city. Juan works for a bank as a loan officer, and Elvira enjoys her secretarial position with another bank. Their three children attend a Catholic parochial school not far from their house. Elvira counts on her maid, Clara, to keep the household running by cooking, shopping, and cleaning.

Clara shops in the traditional open-air San Isidro market most of the time, but she will go to the modern Paiz supermarket as well, if she needs an ingredient not readily available at the open-air market. Clara buys a number of local foods for the Sanchez pantry, including small red beans, oil, white rice, *mantequilla crema* (a slightly soured cream with a consistency between sour cream and heavy cream), wheat flour for making bread and wheat tortillas, beef, pork, chicken, cilantro, limes, tomatoes, cabbage, salty white cheese like farmer cheese, chicken- and beef-flavored Maggi bouillon cubes, ground corn masa for making tortillas, oranges, papayas, eggs, sugar, and coffee. She prefers the big cones of sugar, called *rapadura de dulce,* which she grates for the corn-based drink *atol,* unless she makes it using the instant *Maizena El Bebe* or *pinol* mixture made with ground toasted corn kernels and cacao beans. She sometimes buys beef to make *salpicón,* a shredded beef filling for tortillas; ground beef for *picadillo,* a filling reminiscent of many Arab meat fillings; or *chuletas,* pork chops. Occasionally she buys fish or shellfish, because she likes to cook some of the dishes she learned growing up as a child in La Ceiba on Honduras's north coast. If she's in a rush and pressed for time, Clara buys the thin, ready-made tortillas at the *tortillería* around the corner from the Sanchez house.

Major Foodstuffs

Honduras's geography and history influence what foods appear on Honduran tables. Its rich bounty has changed little since pre-Hispanic times. Grains play a vital role in Honduran cuisine. Corn, native to the Americas, forms the hub around which the Honduran diet revolves. In the form of corn on the cob, it is a snack, and, in ground form, it provides tortillas and other similar breadlike foods. Ground corn thickens stews and, when toasted, adds even more flavor. Rice and wheat also contribute tremendously to the cuisine, with rice being almost as important as corn in some areas and among certain social strata of the country. Wheat-flour tortillas and bread are major staples, as are noodles made from wheat flour.

Beans, along with corn, are central to the Honduran diet, serving as a source of protein for those without the means to eat animal protein on a daily basis. Most people choose the red bean for their meals, but black beans grace their tables at times. Beans can be eaten boiled or refried (that is, mashed and then cooked briefly in oil, generally lard).

Meat is a highly desired food item in Honduran culture, a major source of animal protein. Cattle, their importance stemming from the Spanish emphasis on herds and horses, provide beef. Pork and chicken appear frequently in recipes on tables, chiefly those of the wealthier classes. *Carne asada* (grilled meat) is one of the most popular Honduran dishes. Chorizo sausage is another highly desired food. Iguanas also are eaten, but Honduran law prohibits this; in fact, conservation projects attempt to protect iguanas. Game animals provide protein in some areas but do not form a regular supply of food.

Carne Asada

Serves 4–6

2–3 lb flank or skirt steak

1–2 medium onions, thinly sliced

Juice of 2–3 oranges

Juice of 1 large lime

Salt and freshly ground black pepper, to taste

¼ c extra-virgin olive oil

In a large stainless steel or glass mixing bowl, coat the meat with the onions, orange and lime juice,

Carne asada grilling at a Latin American food festival in Honduras. (Andrea Skjold | Dreamstime.com)

salt, pepper, and oil. Cover and marinate at least 1 hour or overnight.

Heat the grill, using mesquite charcoal if possible. Remove the meat from the marinade. With paper towels, pat dry. Grill over a hot flame until well browned on one side, about 5 to 7 minutes. Flip the meat over, and grill on the other side until cooked to desired doneness. Place on a clean platter, and let sit for about 5 minutes. Serve with rice, beans, *chilmol* (salsa), and *tajadas* (plantain chips).

Apart from the coastal areas, seafood doesn't play a big role in Honduran cooking. Fish, shrimp, spiny lobster (caught in traps baited with cow hides preserved in salt), conch, dried salted fish, turtle, and sometimes clams add protein and flavor to the cooking of many Honduran households.

Honduras's geographic location assures the growth of a vast choice of tropical fruit. Coconuts, papayas, mangoes, *guayaba* (guavas), limes, lemons, sour oranges, pineapples, *zapotes,* passion fruit, avocados, cherimoyas (custard apple), plantains, and bananas all provide much-needed vitamins, calories, and sweetness in the diets of many Hondurans. People turn these fruits into a wide variety of juices and other drinks.

Baked Sweet Plantains with Cheese

Serves 4–6

2 ripe plantains (*plátano maduro;* the skin should be almost black)

1/3 c butter

1 c mantequilla crema or crème fraîche

2 tbsp brown sugar

¼ tsp cinnamon

¼ c *queso fresco* or farmer cheese, crumbled

Preheat oven to 350°F.

Peel plantains and slice in half lengthwise; cut each slice in half. There will be 8 slices.

Heat 2 tablespoons of the butter in a heavy skillet until just foaming. Add the plantains and fry lightly until just golden brown. Remove from heat. Drain on paper towels.

Place the 8 slices of plantain in a greased baking dish just large enough to hold them. Cut the remaining butter into small pieces and distribute it on top of the plantains. Cover the plantains with the mantequilla crema, sugar, and cinnamon. Sprinkle the cheese on top. Cover with foil and bake at 350°F for 25 minutes, remove foil, return to oven, and bake another 5 minutes or until bubbly and golden brown.

Vegetables grow well in Honduras, and markets abound with cabbage, carrots, squashes of various types, green peppers, hot peppers, greens, onions, garlic, tomatoes, and chayote. Cassava, white potatoes, malanga (taro), yams, and sweet potatoes all add calories and substance to the Honduran diet.

Milk products in Honduras tend to be somewhat limited. Mantequilla crema, a sour cream–like condiment, is used on refried beans and in numerous other dishes, including baked ripe plantains. *Queso blanco* (salty, crumbly white cheese), *quesillo* (white cheese similar to jack cheese), and *dulce de leche* (formed from thick, caramel-flavored, boiled-down whole milk) round out the roster of common Honduran dairy products. Ice cream, especially a homemade type called *paletas,* is very popular.

Flavorings commonly used in Honduran cooking include ground cumin, cilantro, *culantro,* chilies, salt, black pepper, achiote, cinnamon, cloves, vanilla, citrus juices, vinegar, and lard. Other fats used include palm oil, mostly on the north coast; shortening; and vegetable oil. Sugar flavors food as well and ranges from the raspadora type to fine sugar for cakes and frostings.

As in many areas close to the Caribbean, Honduras has many alcoholic beverages and products. With respect to rum, there's Flor de Caña and Bacardi, made from molasses or sugarcane juice. *Aguardiente* derives from sugarcane as well but is a rawer, less expensive product than rum. *Guaro* is another strong drink, clear and slightly sweet, made from sugarcane. When United Fruit Company owned half the north coast of Honduras, every male employee at a certain level received a bottle of Johnny

Walker Black Label scotch for Christmas. *Chicha,* made from fermented pineapple slices, is a household product, accessible to anyone with pineapples. The Garifuna make *giffity,* a liquor made with herbs and spices.

Cooking

Cooking typically takes place on a small burner over a charcoal- or propane-fueled fire, sometimes in an outdoor kitchen or fire pit, unless a family possesses a modern Western-style kitchen. And even in those cases, the taste of the food is thought to be better if cooked in the traditional way with its smoky aura. Eye and lung damage from cooking smoke caused the government to start a program among indigenous groups like the Pech to ensure that people installed chimneys called *lorenas* in their houses. Among groups like the Pech, cooking equipment consists of wooden bowls and spoons, plastic and metal utensils, and terra-cotta and metal pots.

Boiling, baking, frying, stewing, roasting, and grilling—all cooking methods commonly used around the world—are techniques called on by cooks every day in every sort of Honduran kitchen. The principal foods of the country, tortillas and beans, both begin the cooking process by boiling. The corn is treated with *cal,* a form of lime (not the fruit but an alkali called calcium hydroxide), and ground to make masa, a process called nixtamalization. With the freshly ground masa, women traditionally spent hours patting out tortillas by hands. Thicker than the commercially produced tortillas, the hand-patted ones are becoming a thing of the past. To cook beans, cooks add water to beans and cook them until tender, a process that requires a lot of fuel.

Honduran cooks prepare foods with several different flavoring agents. One such agent is a simple *recado,* similar to the Caribbean *sofrito.* Consisting of garlic, onions, bell peppers, garlic, and perhaps achiote (annatto), this mixture goes into hot oil first. Some cooks add *aiguaste,* or toasted ground squash seeds, which thickens the liquid in a dish, an ancient practice found in many cuisines. Then cooks add the recado to meat, soups, stews, rice, or beans. On the coast, palm oil is used, as is just plain vegetable oil.

Another flavor generator is chilmol, a fresh salsa very similar to Mexico's *pico de gallo,* made with tomatoes, onions, peppers, and salt. Cilantro, ground cumin seeds, and oregano flavor a number of dishes. Thick fuzzy culantro leaves are used for meat. Cinnamon, sugar, chocolate, and vanilla flavor sweet dishes. Coconut, and coconut milk, imparts its unique flavor into numerous dishes, including soups and stews, as well as desserts. Turmeric adds yellow coloring instead of the more expensive saffron. Some local, native plants—unknown to cooks outside Central America—provide flavor. *Juniapa (Piper auritum),* with its heart-shaped leaves, flavors fish dishes on the north coast of Honduras.

Cooking techniques also add flavor. In Honduras, cooks fry dry rice first in recado, or just with onion. Then they add water and salt and cook the rice until tender. The prefrying adds a layer of taste absent from just plain white rice. Leaves add flavor as well. The ubiquitous tamales come wrapped in plantain leaves, which add a nutty and fresh flavor to the corn dough surrounding the various fillings used for tamales. Grilling is popular, as in the case of carne asada, or roasted meat. *Pinchos,* or grilled kebabs, are also popular and easy to prepare.

Cooks take discarded pineapple skins and make pineapple vinegar or an alcoholic beverage called chicha. Another preservation method is found in *encurtidos,* or pickled vegetables, using pineapple vinegar.

Typical Meals

Meals in Honduras tend to follow fairly strict patterns on a daily basis, reflecting what's in the market and what culinary skills the cooks possess. Rice, beans, and tortillas form the core of meals. Breakfast begins early, around 6:30 A.M., and generally consists of the *plato típico:* fried eggs, refried beans, fried plantains, mantequilla crema, sausage, tortillas or bread, and thick sweet coffee. Some people eat milk soup for breakfast, which is boiled milk flavored with cinnamon, sugar, and lime wedges to which small cubes of bread are added.

At noon, people make their way home, if they can, and eat lunch, another version of the plato típico: meat (beef, pork chops, chicken), beans, rice, salad, tortillas or bread, and juice. Or they may just eat *sopa de olla,* a stewlike soup made with whatever meat and vegetables might be in the pantry. A jar of encurtidos (vegetable pickles) usually sits on the table to be enjoyed in small bites with the meal.

The evening meal, or *cena,* starts very late in the evening because people generally do not get home from work until around 6 or 7 P.M. The meal can be similar to lunch, but meat dishes may be *encebolleada* (smothered in onions) or *entomatada* (smothered in tomatoes) instead of grilled or roasted. Or they might just eat a simpler meal of *enchiladas* (more like Mexican tostadas, with the fillings on top), quesadillas (cheese-filled tortillas), or tortillas with beans, mantequilla crema, and a small salad of shredded cabbage. Soups like *mondongo* (tripe soup) or chicken soup with tortillas often suffice. Rice is always served, along with bread or tortillas.

Another common dish is rice and whole beans, called *Moros y Cristianos,* a linguistic tribute to Spanish history and Spain's fight to drive out the Arabs, or Moors, around the time Columbus discovered the New World. *Casamiento* (marriage) is yet another name for rice and beans, not used as much now as in the past. Stews and soups also appear often on Honduran tables. In the north, along the coast, fried fish with lime and garlic joins *bando,* a fish stew, and *sopa de hombre,* a fish soup thought to be excellent for curing hangovers. *Sopa de caracol* (conch soup) is another favorite and practically a national dish. Picadillo (ground meat scented with ground cumin and sometimes enriched with chopped zucchini-like squash) adds zest to plates of beans and rice, as well as serving as a filling for tortillas.

Like people in many countries bordering on the Caribbean, Hondurans utilize tropical fruits and tubers in unique and flavorful ways. Shredded coconut or coconut milk appears in many dishes, including rice and stews, but especially in desserts like coconut flan or coconut bread, a specialty of the Garifuna (Black Caribs) on the north coast. Another bread baked by the Garifuna is *casabe,* made with cassava. Guavas, made into a thick paste and

Moros y Cristianos, the Honduran version of black beans and rice. (StockPhotoPro)

served with salty white farmer cheese, form a simple dessert with Spanish roots that is well loved by many Hondurans. Plantains, both green and mature, augment many meals. Tajadas (fried plantain chips; also called *caras de gata*), salted lightly, make a tasty snack with drinks, both those made with alcohol and fresh fruit juices.

Snacks such as *fritas,* cornmeal mixed with milk and sugar and fried on a griddle, are popular, as are the various drinks called *pozols* or *horchatas,* similar to those made in Mexico, made with ground rice, corn, or seeds for thickening. Tamales, filled with various ingredients, provide a hearty snack, a simple meal, or a ritualistic dish for special occasions. Another snack, often prepared for men going off to work all day in the fields, is the *burra* or *pupusa,* thick tortillas with beans and a little meat, if available, and a little piece of rapadura or cone sugar used traditionally in *torrejas* (a sweet dessert made with roasted fresh corn kernels). Placed in a square of clean cloth tied at all four ends, the burra can ride on a person's belt, leaving the hands free. Another popular tortilla-based snack is the *baleada,* a tortilla filled with beans, cheese, and many other things. On the north coast, ceviche made from fresh seafood appears on many tables. And *pastelitos,* fried corn-crust turnovers, crackle with their rice and meat fillings. For dessert, there might be a simple *arroz con leche* (rice with milk) or *tres leches,* a yellow cake made with three different types of milk.

Eating Out

With modernization, eating outside the home has become more common in Honduras, where most people still eat at home for the main meal of the day. In the past, and still, small eateries called *comedores* served the plato típico to travelers and tourists. Now, in the larger cities of Tegucigalpa and San Pedro Sula, U.S.-based fast-food chains provide quick food.

In Tegucigalpa, a number of upscale restaurants serve a wide range of foods, including sushi, Chinese fare, French haute cuisine, Middle Eastern kebabs, and Italian dishes, as well as Honduran specialties like carne asada and *anafres,* little braziers filled with refried beans and topped with mantequilla crema. Open-air restaurants along the north coast feature fried fish and fish stews made with coconut milk.

Street food is especially popular. Vendors selling *licuados* (smoothies), *jugos* (juices), and small plastic bags filled with chunks of fresh fruit set up shop on street corners. Other sell pinchos (grilled meat kebabs), baleadas (bean- or meat-filled tortillas), grilled corn on the cob, *chicharrones* (fried pork rind), tajadas (plantain chips), pupusas (bean- or cheese-stuffed tortillas), *semitas* (sweet bread), and *rosquetes* (corn dough rings, also called *rosquillas*). Shops sell *sambuseks,* a Middle Eastern meat-filled pastry, as well.

An old tradition still exists of meeting at friends' houses at 3 P.M. for a *cafecito* (little coffee) and sweet breads. Bar-going, particularly for men, offers another opportunity for eating and socializing outside the home. Beers commonly drunk include Salva Vida, Port Royal, Barena, and Imperial.

A vendor grills corn on the streets in Tegucigalpa, Honduras. (Owen Franken | Corbis)

Special Occasions

The predominance of Roman Catholicism in Honduran culture ensures that most holidays revolve around the major religious holidays of Easter and Christmas. Other holidays include baptisms and christenings, wakes and funerals, weddings, and birthdays. Nowadays, often no special food is prepared since most meals are Americanized buffets catered by companies hired by families, particularly wealthier families. Nacatamales, or tamales, are one of the major special-occasion foods, served for many events, including weddings, Sunday family get-togethers, and Christmas. Elaborately decorated cakes are another food item commonly served on many special occasions.

Birthdays merit very special preparations, with piñatas (candy- and toy-filled papier mâche in the shape of animals and other objects) and fancy decorated cakes for young children. The traditional girls' party, the *Quinceañera,* celebrates young women's arriving at womanhood at the age of 15. Caterers generally provide the food, and the parties tend to be held by wealthier people.

In the villages, people celebrate the Day of the Dead (November 2) in a manner similar to that of Mexico, visiting cemeteries and cleaning ancestral graves. In the larger cities, particularly among the wealthier classes, U.S. Halloween customs hold sway. Nine days after funerals, families get together for coffee and *panes dulces* (sweet breads).

Christmas is one of the biggest holidays of the year. Like Mexicans, Hondurans also follow the idea of *posadas* (similar to caroling), but this practice tends to be limited. Some smaller villages have posadas and serve *ponche infernal,* which is served hot and contains pineapple and aguardiente, or *rompopo* (an eggnog-like drink imbued with rum) to the singers. On Christmas Eve, families prepare punch and other foods, including tamales to hand out to people who come by singing. Feasting after midnight mass generally includes banana or plantain leaf–wrapped nacatamales filled with chicken or pork and some combination of rice, potatoes, garbanzos, peas, and green olives. People drink rompopo and eat grapes and apples. A typical Christmas dinner can include roasted pork leg. A special dessert associated with Honduran culture is dough called *torrejas,* fried and soaked in syrup flavored with cinnamon and brown sugar. Or the family may serve rosquetes (corn dough rings) with the same syrup. Stuffed ham with a beef/pork meat filling is popular. Some families serve dried-fish soup, yucca appetizers, stuffed turkey, chicken, meringue sweets, and *horchata de arroz,* a drink made with sweetened rice. Other foods commonly served on Christmas might be carne asada (grilled meat) and *plátanos fritos* (fried plantains). The day after Christmas, most Hondurans take the opportunity to visit relatives and friends. Food is secondary; people eat leftovers or go to restaurants.

At Easter time, artists create elaborate sawdust carpets in Comayagua during Holy Week. Cooks, especially in the north, prepare *sopa de pescado* (fish soup) with fish and egg patties cooked in a broth made with fish heads and garlic, *pan de yema* (egg-yolk bread), and *torrejas de piñol* (fried dough), glazed with boiled honey. Some families spend time at the beach on the north coast, where both men and women of the Garifuna (Black Caribs) make casabe, a flat cassava bread eaten spread with butter.

For folkloric, and national, festivals called Fiestas Catrachas, celebrating the Honduran nation, menus consist of carne asada, beans, tamales, baleadas, cassava with chicharrones (fried pork skins), and tortillas. Different ethnic groups within Honduras celebrate their own special days. The Miskitos, for example, celebrate July 23 as their Day of the Dead, called the Parayapti, similar to the Garifuna's Novenario. To feed all the people, at least three cows are slaughtered.

In western Honduras, particularly in the towns of Gracias, Lempira; Ilama, Santa Barbara; and Texiguat, El Paraiso, a corn-based drink called *chilate* is made for use in a ceremony called the *guacaleo,* or "ceremony of peace," dating to Mayan times. Starting with atol, people add cacao and perhaps a little chili pepper to this slightly fermented drink.

Diet and Health

As is the case in many cultures, Hondurans associate various foods and dishes with good health and with cures for sick people. Some of these beliefs include the idea that meat tenderizers like papaya cause stomach ulcers. Sick people, including those with ulcers, should eat *leche dormida* ("sleeping milk"), made with part of a rennet tablet and sweetened to taste, resulting in a dish very similar to yogurt. Many old beliefs—such as the old hot-cold theory—no longer hold, but some people still drink sour orange juice when they don't feel well to balance out their systems. Drinking lemongrass tea for nerve problems is still common in some areas. Folk belief has it that drinking a tea made from *kalaica,* a plant that grows wild in Honduras, will help anemia, as will drinking an infusion made with beets. Many beliefs surround the states of pregnancy and lactation, including the exclusion of certain foods from the diets of pregnant and lactating mothers.

In Honduras, people still experience severe malnutrition, particularly children. One out of four Honduran children under the age of five still suffers from life-threatening bouts of malnutrition, exacerbated by diseases like chickenpox and measles.

Cynthia D. Bertelsen

Further Reading

Gold, Janet N. *Culture and Customs of Honduras.* Santa Barbara, CA: Greenwood Press, 2009.

Griffin, Wendy. "Coca-Cola's Competition: Honduras' Traditional Grain Beverages." *Honduras This Week,* October 13, 1997 (Online Edition 75). http://www.marrder.com/htw/oct97/cultural.htm.

"Honduran Food." Sidewalk Mystic. http://sidewalkmystic.com/Honduras_Recipes_Food.htm.

Marks, Copeland. *False Tongues and Sunday Bread: A Guatemalan and Mayan Cookbook.* New York: M. Evans, 1985.

McDonald, Michael R. *Food Culture in Central America.* Westport, CT: Greenwood Press, 2009.

Theroux, Paul. *The Mosquito Coast.* Boston: Mariner Books, 2006.

White, Christine. *Reconstructing Ancient Maya Diet.* Salt Lake City: University of Utah Press, 1999.

Inuit

Overview

Inuit is a general term for a group of culturally similar indigenous peoples inhabiting the land above the Arctic Circle in Canada and Greenland. In 1977 the term *Inuit* replaced the term *Eskimo* in Canada and Greenland based on the erroneous belief that the term *Eskimo* has pejorative associations. In English the word *Eskimo* is of uncertain origin. It is believed by some to have come from the French word *Esquimau*. Others believe that the term *Eskimo* comes from an Ojibwa word that is translated as "eater of raw meat," hence the pejorative connotations. However, linguists now believe that the term *Eskimo* was actually derived from a Montagnais name, *ayassime'w,* a name that refers, in the upper western North Shore dialect, to the Micmac and, in the central and lower North Shore dialect, to the Eskimo. Regardless of the origins of the term, *Eskimo* is no longer used in Canada and Greenland but is still used in Alaska to refer to the Arctic peoples of that state. While the indigenous peoples of Alaska prefer to be called by their autonyms, for example, the Yup'ik, they do not mind being collectively referred to as Eskimo. They do, however, object to being referred to as Inuit. The term *inuit,* in the native languages of Greenland and Arctic Canada, is the plural of *inuk,* meaning "real, genuine person."

Three-quarters of Canada's Inuit population lives in Nunavut, a territorial subdivision of the former Northwest Territories. Nunavut comprises the part of the Canadian mainland and Arctic Islands that lies north and northeast of the tree line as it runs from the west end of the Dolphin Strait to 37 miles (60 kilometers) south of the point where the Tha-anne River flows into Hudson Bay. The Inuit of Greenland are descendants of the Dorset and Thule cultures who moved into Greenland from Canada between 900 and 1500 A.D. The population of Greenland is 55,000, the majority of whom are Inuit.

The Inuit are subsistence hunters and gatherers and are therefore seasonally nomadic. In preparation for the seal-hunting season, during which the Inuit move out onto the ice to hunt, the Inuit start building large dome-shaped snow houses in early winter. The snow houses feature a central workspace; radiating from the sides of the central workspace are tunnels. At the end of each tunnel are family living quarters. In the spring season, nuclear family groups spend the summer hunting and gathering on the tundra. Housing in the spring and summer is traditionally caribou-skin tents; however, in the modern era tents are typically made of canvas. In addition, small, semipermanent huts of plywood are built on the tundra for use during the inland hunting season. During the spring and summer the Inuit also travel great distances to trade and to obtain the raw materials needed for carving. When fall comes the Inuit begin the trek to the wintering grounds where they congregate in larger groups to prepare their winter clothing and hunting equipment. Despite the availability of modern winter clothing, most outer winter clothing continues to be homemade. Traditional Inuit clothing is made from seal pelts, seal intestines, caribou skins, animal fur (including polar bear), and canvas. The traditional materials are warmer and more adaptable to the environment in which the

Inuit are working. Clothing is layered, with an inner jacket of fur facing inward and an outer jacket of fur facing outward. Outer fur jackets may also be layered with jackets made of down or duffle cloth.

Inuit religion is based on the relationship between humans and the spirits of the animals on which the Inuit depend for their food and livelihood. It is therefore important to the Inuit that they observe proper rituals and taboos when hunting. An animal spirit who is offended through the violation of a taboo, through the omission of a ritual, or through a lack of proper respect might take revenge on the group. Illness, starvation, and death can occur. Conversely, an animal that is treated properly by a hunter will share the good news with other animals, bringing good fortune to the hunter.

Today, the Inuit live in a modernized world. They regularly use snowmobiles and all-terrain vehicles to get to their hunting and fishing grounds. Many Inuit live in settlements in housing provided by the Canadian and Greenland governments. In the towns, amenities, such as running water, are provided, as are social services and education. While the traditional subsistence hunting, fishing, and gathering lifestyle is still highly valued among the Inuit, more and more young people are choosing to enter the wage economy. The options for employment in the towns are limited; therefore, young Inuit may choose to cater to the tourist industry by becoming hunting and fishing guides. Other Inuit turn to arts and crafts as a living and carve soapstone statues and create other art forms for sale in the southern cities. There is also an increasing demand for designer clothing made from sustainably harvested seal pelts. Students at the Nunavut Arctic College are learning to be furriers, and the fur design industry in Nunavut is seen as an example of the melding of traditional cultural heritage with a modern economic strategy. Regardless of the choice of occupation and place of residence, traditional Inuit food remains a central focus of Inuit identity and culture.

🍽 Food Culture Snapshot

Jimmy Nirlungayak and his wife, Elisapee, live in the Arctic near a small town in Nunavut. They are among the respected elder members of the community and pride themselves in being traditional Inuit. The Nirlungayaks eat what some call "Inuit style" and most others call "country food." This means that they continue to eat a traditional Inuit diet and depend primarily on subsistence hunting and gathering for their food supplies. Their annual income does not provide enough ready cash to purchase all their food from the Northern or from the Co-Op Store, especially given that the cost of buying groceries in the north can be two or three times higher than the cost in the south. Therefore, the Nirlungayaks' store purchases are limited to flour, baking powder, sugar, and tea. To get the money needed to purchase these staple supplies, the Nirlungayaks used to process and sell sealskins and carve small soapstone carvings. However, the Nirlungayaks are among those Inuit impacted by the antisealing campaigns that started in 1983. While these campaigns were primarily targeting commercial sealers around Newfoundland and the Gulf of Saint Lawrence, the banning of imports of seal products into the United States has impacted the Inuit economy. In 2009 the European Union also moved to ban the import of seal products, an action that caused the market to experience a further decline. As a result, the Nirlungayaks now rely more and more on their carvings as a source of income, and they have joined the many Inuit who depend on welfare.

Major Foodstuffs

The environment of the Inuit peoples dictates that the majority of their foods will consist of meat and fish; however, the local environment, which varies greatly for the different Inuit groups, as well as resource availability, ultimately dictates what the Inuit will be able to eat in any given season. During the winter season the Inuit depend primarily on seals. A seasonal shift from seal hunting in the winter to fishing in the spring and summer to caribou hunting in the fall is common. The Inuit will also hunt, either seasonally or year-round, a variety of land and sea mammals as well as ptarmigan and waterfowl. In addition, and only during the summer months, they will gather roots, greens, and berries. The discussion of foods here gives a representative sampling of the kinds and varieties of food that the Inuit eat.

Seal is the primary, and most important, food of the Inuit, and they make use of the many seal varieties that live in the Arctic. Seal hunting is conducted with the help of snowmobiles, and seals are hunted along the edges of the ice floes and at their breathing holes. The bearded seal (*Erignathus barbatus*), the harp seal (*Phoca groenlandica*), and the ringed seal (*Phoca hispida*) are all hunted by the Inuit. And, as with all animals hunted by the Inuit, all parts of the seals are either eaten or used. The blubber and meat of the seals are eaten raw, while the intestines are either boiled or eaten raw. At times the Inuit will also boil the meat and blubber of the seals; however, the liver of the bearded seal is never eaten because the high levels of vitamin A found in the liver are toxic to humans and can cause acute hypervitaminosis A. Ringed seal blubber may also be liquefied and aged, and the meat may also be aged. The ringed seal's liver, heart, brain, eyes, and blood are eaten raw. The pups of the ringed seal are also taken, and the meat is eaten either raw or boiled.

The beluga whale (*Delphinapterus leucas*) and the narwhal (*Monodon monoceros*) are both toothed whales living in the Arctic and are hunted by the Inuit. The blubber of the beluga is eaten either raw or boiled, and the meat is often eaten raw or dried for later use. The *maktaaq,* or skin and underlying blubber, of the beluga is eaten raw or boiled. Beluga whale oil is kept and aged for later use. Narwhal blubber and maktaaq are eaten raw, boiled, or aged, and the maktaaq of the flippers is aged. The blubber may also be aged. The meat of the narwhal is dried for later use.

The walrus (*Odobenus rosmarus*) is another of the sea mammals eaten by the Inuit. Walrus blubber is either aged, boiled, or eaten raw. The liver is eaten raw, and the meat is eaten raw, boiled, or aged. The maktaaq of the walrus is eaten raw or aged. More and more often, however, walrus meat is being cooked before it is eaten because of the presence of *Trichinella,* a tiny parasitic roundworm, in the meat. *Trichinella* can cause trichinosis, a gastrointestinal illness with flulike symptoms that, in severe cases,

Subsistence hunting for narwhal whales remains an integral part of the Inuit culture in Alaska. (Corel)

can cause death. Alternatively, walrus meat is being stored until it can be tested by laboratories in Kuujjuaq, Quebec, for the presence of *Trichinella*. Walrus meat is digested slowly, and an individual may eat large quantities of walrus meat without getting sick. This ability is adaptive and allows the Inuit, who may go a long time without any food, to remain out on the ice hunting.

Among the land mammals eaten by the Inuit, the polar bear (*Ursus maritimus*) is certainly the most dangerous animal hunted. Polar bears are hunted primarily for their fur. However, when a bear is taken, it is eaten so as not to waste the food. The fat is boiled or eaten raw. Polar bear meat would traditionally be eaten raw; however, as with walrus, there is concern about the parasite *Trichinella* in the meat, so polar bear meat is most often boiled. The liver of the polar bear, like the liver of the bearded seal, is never eaten because the concentration of vitamin A in the liver is toxic to humans and can cause acute hypervitaminosis A.

Another large mammal that the Inuit depend on for food is the caribou (*Rangifer tarandus*). As with all animals hunted by the Inuit all parts of the caribou are used. Caribou meat is prepared in a variety of ways. It may be eaten raw, or it may also be aged, dried, boiled, or roasted. The liver and tongue of the caribou are also eaten raw or baked. The stomach, brains, heart, lungs, and kidneys may be eaten raw, and the brain, heart, and kidneys may also be boiled or roasted. The bone marrow is collected and eaten raw or aged. The fat is eaten raw.

Other large mammals that are hunted by the Inuit are the moose (*Alces alces*), the musk ox (*Ovibos moschatus*), and the black bear (*Ursus americanus*). Moose meat is eaten raw, cooked, smoked, or dried. The fat and bone marrow may be eaten raw or cooked, and the fat may also be dried. Moose kidneys, livers, lungs, and blood are eaten raw. Musk ox meat, blood, and fat are eaten raw. Bear meat is eaten raw or smoked.

Many small mammals are also hunted and eaten. The Inuit will eat muskrat (*Ondatra zibethicus*), rabbit (*Lepus* sp.), and beaver (*Castor canadensis*). The meat of all these animals is eaten raw or baked. Beaver meat may also be dried.

Among the birds eaten are the black scoter (*Melanitta nigra*), the Canada goose (*Branta canadensis*), duck (*Anas platyrhynchos*), ptarmigan (*Lagopus mutus*), and grouse (*Dendragapus canadensis*). The meat of these birds is all eaten raw or either oven- or fire-roasted. The innards of the Canada goose may also be boiled, and the lungs of the goose are roasted. In addition, the eggs of the fowl are eaten.

Traditionally, fishing grounds would have been accessed by foot. Today, however, all-terrain vehicles are common, and a network of trails now exists in the tundra. Among the fish that Inuit eat are arctic char (*Salvelinus naresi*), cod (*Boreogadus saida*), inconnu (*Stenodus leucichthys*), burbot (*Lota lota*), salmon (*Oncorhynchus*), sculpin (*Myoxocephalus* ssp.), whitefish (*Coregonus clupeaformis*), lake trout (*Salvelinus namaycush*), and grayling (*Thymallus arcticus*). Fish are eaten either raw, dried, salted, smoked, boiled, or baked. The Inuit also gather shellfish, and the meat is eaten raw or boiled. Among the shellfish gathered are mussels (*Mytilus edulis*) and clams (*Mya* sp.).

During the long summer days the Inuit take full advantage of all the plants and fruits that grow in the northern environment to supplement their diet. Among the favorite foods gathered are the many berries that grow in the tundra and northern woodlands. These include blackcap berries (*Rubus leucodermis*), black hawthorn berries (*Crataegus douglasii*), blueberries (*Vaccinium uliginosum*), bog blueberries (*Vaccinium uliginosum*), gray blueberries (*Vaccinium ovalifolium*), watery blueberries (*Vaccinium alaskaense*), mountain bilberries (*Vaccinium membranaceum*), red huckleberries (*Vaccinium parvifolium*), cranberries (*Vaccinium vitis-idaea*), rosehips (*Rosa nutkana*), bunchberries (*Cornus canadensis*), crowberries (*Empetrum nigrum*), high bush cranberries (*Viburnum edule*), kinnikinnick berries (*Arctostaphylos uva-ursi*), red elderberries (*Sambucus racemosa*), salmonberries (*Rubus spectabilis*), wild raspberries (*Rubus idaeus*), saskatoonberries (*Amelanchier alnifolia*), soapberries (*Shepherdia canadensis*), stink currant berries (*Ribes bracteosum*), swamp gooseberries (*Ribes lacustre*), green gooseberries (*Ribes oxyancanthoides*), purple gooseberries (*Ribes oxyancanthoides*), wild currants (*Ribes laxiflorum*), thimbleberries (*Ribes parviflorus*), wild strawberries (*Fragaria vesca*), and cloudberries (*Rubus chamaemorus*). Of these berries, only the elderberry and wild "green gooseberries" are usually cooked; all the others are eaten raw. Some berries may also be used in bannock (flatbread). And, although not a berry, the fruit of the wild crab apple tree (*Pyrus fusca*) is also eaten.

The greens most commonly gathered and eaten are mountain sorrel leaves and stems (*Oxyria digyna*), cow parsnip (*Heracleum lanatum*), fireweed shoots (*Epilobium angustifolium*), lamb's-quarter (*Chenopodium album*), salmonberry shoots (*Rubus spectabilis*), thimbleberry shoots (*Ribes parviflorus*), wild "green gooseberry" leaves (*Ribes divaricatum*), sheep sorrel (*Rumex acetosella*), stinging nettle (*Urtica dioica*), seaweed (*Porphyra perforata*), and kelp (*Rhodymenia* and *Laminaria* sp.). All the greens, including kelp, are eaten raw with the exception of the seaweed, which is dried.

In addition to greens and berries, the Inuit also eat a variety of roots. Among the roots eaten are those of cinquefoil (*Potentilla pacifica*), clover (*Trifolium wormskioldii*), wood fern (*Dryopteris expansa*), licorice fern (*Polypodium glycyrrhiza*), lupine (*Lupinus nootkatensis*), and riceroot bulbs (*Fritillaria camschatcensis*). The ferns are either eaten raw or steamed. The cinquefoil and clover are steamed, and the lupine, licorice fern, and riceroot are eaten raw. The Inuit also eat the inner bark of cottonwood trees

(*Populus trichocarpa*), the dried leaves of Labrador tea (*Ledum decumbent*), and parts of the arctic willow (*Salix arctica*) and the netted willow (*Salix reticulata*).

Cooking

The Inuit eat only two main meals a day, although they do snack between meals. Traditionally, much of Inuit meat and fish is eaten raw or frozen. After a hunt the hunters are served first, eating their prey raw where it has been caught. Their first choices of foods to eat are liver and blood. Another delicacy is brain mixed with seal fat. The women and children eat after the hunters. Their food of choice is the intestines and any remaining liver. No fish or meat can be cooked where it is caught.

Food that is to be cooked must be transported far away from where it was caught, and when it is cooked the Inuit have taboos that prohibit cooking products of the land and sea in the same pot. This taboo extends to the storage of products of the land and sea as well. Thus, seal meat may not be placed next to caribou meat when stored. Traditional Inuit cooking was done over the central fire of the igloo or tent, and the cooking vessels were made of carved soapstone. Currently cooking pots are available in the stores, and cooking is done over camp stoves when out in the bush or in modern kitchens in their homes in the towns. When cooked, meat is often stewed in a large pot, with very few spices or other seasonings. In the winter the pot would be packed with snow and meat and left over the fire or on the stove until the snow melts and the meat is thawed and warmed.

Arne Lange, a 39-year-old Inuit fisherman and his family have a family seal meat barbeque. (Getty Images)

Typical Meals

Country food, or Inuit-style meals, consists mostly of meat or fish with bread, jam, and fruit on the side. When fresh meat or fish is eaten, slices of raw meat or fish are simply sliced off the whole animal or fish by each individual and eaten. When dried fish is eaten it is commonly dipped in a dish of aged seal blubber to moisten it. With the easy availability of soup seasonings and cooking pots, fish heads can now be stewed as an additional way of using as much of the fish as possible.

Other Inuit meals consist of bearded seal flippers soaked in blubber for two weeks, after which the flesh is stripped from the flippers and eaten. Maktaaq, the outer covering of the whale including the skin and blubber, which is one to two inches thick, is cut in blocks from the whale. The maktaaq is left hanging to dry for two days and then cut into smaller pieces. The maktaaq is then boiled until tender and stored in a cool place in oil in a 45-gallon drum.

Bannock, a typical home-prepared bread product consumed by the Inuit, as well as other First Nations peoples of Canada, is one of the staples of the Inuit diet and can be fried in a small amount of fat or baked in an oven, over a campfire, or on a camp stove in a covered pot. However, Inuit bannock is typically prepared in large rounds that will fit in a cast iron frying pan, and these are cut into wedges or squares for individual servings. While many different recipes for bannock exist, it is typically prepared from two cups of white flour, a half teaspoon of salt, a quarter cup of sugar, two teaspoons of baking powder, a quarter cup of fat (oil, lard, vegetable oil, or shortening), and a half cup of milk, reconstituted powdered milk, or water. Other recipes for bannock include one egg, berries, dried fruit, and nuts. When baked in a conventional oven the temperature is set at 350 degrees, and the bread is baked for 15 to 20 minutes.

During the summer months, when berries can be found, *akutuq,* sometimes called "Eskimo ice cream," is a favorite treat for many. This delicacy is a dessert made with whipped fat and berries. To make this dessert one recipe calls for grated reindeer tallow, seal oil, and water. All the ingredients are whipped until white and fluffy, and then the fresh berries are added.

During an Inuit meal the chunks of food will be presented on sheets of cardboard, metal, or plastic, and guests are invited to use their own knives or to borrow a knife to slice off a portion of the raw meat or fish. The meal is typically eaten sitting on the ground or on the kitchen floor with the food in the middle of the circle.

Eating Out

Given the isolated nature of their traditional hunting and gathering territories, Inuit people do not have a history or culture of eating out that is comparable to that of their white neighbors. Acculturated Inuit living in northern Arctic towns will visit the various fast-food restaurants that have proliferated in places such as Whitehorse and Yellowknife. In addition, there are a variety of small cafés and family restaurants, not to mention the ubiquitous Chinese restaurants, which Inuit families will frequent when visiting or living in town. Also present in many northern towns are more expensive restaurants catering to the tourist clientele; these restaurants focus on northern game meats and country food such as musk ox, caribou, arctic char, pickerel, whitefish, whale meat, clams, turbot, shrimp, and waterfowl.

Special Occasions

Winter is the season for festivities. Traditionally, ceremonial snow houses, called *qagli* among the Copper Inuit, were built for the festivities. Because of the winter storms and blizzards that frequently sweep across the Arctic tundra, many days are spent indoors. Playing games, drum dancing, and observing shamanic performances therefore passed the time.

Traditionally, food is shared among the Inuit, and distribution occurs with both kin and non-kin and follows a preestablished pattern. For example, among the Copper Inuit, each seal that is caught is divided into 12 to 14 parts, and each part is given to a predetermined exchange partner who would then reciprocate in the future with the same body part. A hunter's parents determined the hunter's *piqatigiit,* or seal-sharing partners, at the time of the hunter's first kill. The partners are all members of the same generation as the hunter, which helps forge a bond among age-mates. Other forms of food distribution, which function on a volunteer or ad hoc basis, also occur. Some food-distribution forms involve giving meat to a hunter who did not make a successful catch during a hunt or giving food to a member of the kin group who has no food because of age or illness, while other forms involve communal eating after a hunt. Today, food distribution appears much more idiosyncratic than in the past; however, it has been found that modern sharing continues to take forms that range from highly formalized gift giving to the informal sharing of prepared meals.

Faced with rapid social change the Inuit see food as the connector to everything that surrounds Inuit culture. The hunting and gathering, preparation, and eating of country food are an especially key aspect of Inuit identity. The sharing of food reminds the Inuit of their cultural heritage and serves as a connector to their past. In addition, food sharing highlights the interconnectedness between Inuit families and households. Hunting is seen as being more than simply providing food for families; hunting is also about sustaining the Inuit language and culture. The teaching of hunting skills from one generation to another is a way to build solidarity between generations and within families and remains an important part of a young person's maturation process.

Diet and Health

Increased modernization and the availability of *qallunaat,* or white people's food, has had an impact on the health of the Inuit. The shift from the traditional diet of meat and fish to a diet of processed foods high in sugar and carbohydrates has caused an increase in obesity, cardiovascular disease, acne, anemia, dental cavities, and type 2 diabetes. To try and understand the paradox of the Inuit diet—the fact that eating a diet of seal meat, which is high in fat, prevents the very diseases that are common throughout much of the Western world—researchers at McGill University's Centre for Indigenous

Peoples' Nutrition and Environment have carefully documented the traditional foods eaten by Inuit peoples, complete with a nutritional and caloric analysis of each of the different Inuit foods.

What has been discovered is that is that there are no essential foods, only essential nutrients. And the Inuit get these nutrients in their traditional diet. Vitamin A, for example, which is usually found in fruits and vegetables, is available to the Inuit in the oils of cold-water fish and sea mammals, as well as in the animals' livers, where fat is processed. These dietary staples also provide vitamin D, another oil-soluble vitamin needed for bones. Vitamin C is found in raw caribou liver, seal brains, and maktaaq, and in even higher levels in kelp. The traditional Inuit practices of freezing meat and fish and eating them raw conserve the vitamins, which are easily cooked off and lost in food processing.

The Inuit are genetically well adapted to process a diet that is high in protein. However, protein can't be the sole source of energy for humans; anyone eating a high-protein diet that is low in carbohydrates must also have fat. While fats are considered to be detrimental to Western health, it is the kind of fat that is eaten that is important. Processed and farm-animal fat is high in trans fats, whereas wild animal fat is healthier because it is less saturated and more of it is in a monounsaturated form. In addition, the traditional Inuit diet consists of cold-water fish and sea mammals that are high in omega-3 fats, while a Western diet is high in omega-6 fats. Omega-3 fats help raise high-density lipoprotein (HDL) cholesterol, lower triglycerides, and are known for anticlotting effects. These fatty acids are believed to protect the heart from life-threatening arrhythmias that can lead to sudden cardiac death. In addition, omega-3 polyunsaturated fats help prevent inflammatory processes, which play a part in atherosclerosis, arthritis, diabetes, and other diseases commonly associated with a Western diet.

While the positive aspects of eating traditional Inuit food have been accepted, data also show that there is an increase in the levels of cadmium, lead, and mercury in the traditional meat and fish eaten by the Inuit. Increased levels of PCBs (polychlorinated biphenyls) and DDT (dichlorodiphenyltrichloroethane) have also been found in traditional Inuit foods. The ingestion of metals and chemicals has been found to affect the neurological development of fetuses and children and can affect the immune systems of children. The primary foods that account for a higher level of intake of metals and chemicals are ringed seal meat and liver, caribou meat, narwhal maktaaq, beluga meat, and beluga maktaaq.

Despite the potential dangers of eating country food, the Inuit remain strongly tied to their traditional diet. For the Inuit the connection between eating seal and Inuit beliefs about health, physiology, and identity is stronger than the fears associated with the contaminants found in Arctic foods, and thus country food remains the main diet choice for Inuit today. The traditional Inuit diet is more nutritious and less expensive than commercial food, and it is believed to have healing properties. If an Inuit is feeling well, then he can eat store-bought food with no ill effects, but if he is ill or depressed, he needs country food to make him well. The Inuit believe strongly that their diet of seal meat is life giving. Inuit blood is believed to be thick and dark like seal blood, so when one eats seal blood and seal meat, one is rejuvenating one's blood supply. Eating seal meat, they believe, warms them in the cold Arctic weather, and when the body is warmed by seal blood, then the Inuit's soul is protected from illness and harm.

Laura P. Appell-Warren

Further Reading

Borré, Kristen. "Seal Blood, Inuit Blood, and Diet: A Biocultural Model of Physiology and Cultural Identity." *Medical Anthropology Quarterly* 5, No. 1 (1991): 48–62.

Collings, Peter, George Wenzel, and Richard G. Condon. "Modern Food Sharing Networks and Community Integration in the Central Canadian Arctic." *Arctic* 51, No. 4 (1998): 301–14.

Condon, Richard G. *The Northern Copper Inuit: A History.* Toronto: University of Toronto Press, 1996.

Gadsby, Patricia. "The Inuit Paradox: How Can People Who Gorge on Fat and Rarely See a Vegetable Be Healthier Than We Are?" *Discover Magazine,* October 2004. http://discovermagazine.com/2004/oct/inuit-paradox.

"John Tyman's Inuit." http://www.johntyman.com/arctic/inuit104.html.

Kuhnlein, Harriet, Oliver Receveur, and Amy Ing. "Energy, Fat and Calcium in Bannock Consumed by Canadian Inuit." *Journal of the American Dietetic Association* 101, No. 5 (2001): 580–81.

Scott Polar Research Institute. "Museum Catalogue: Arctic Material Culture Collection." http://www.spri.cam.ac.uk/museum/catalogue/armc/categories/cooking+vessels/.

Simon, Mary. "Inuit on Sealing: We Want Your Mind, Not Your Money." *The Globe and Mail,* March 11, 2009. http://www.theglobeandmail.com/news/opinions/article13031.ece.

Jamaica

Overview

Jamaica is a Caribbean island located about 90 miles south of Cuba. It is the third-largest island in the Caribbean and exhibits beautiful natural features such as world-famous coastal lowlands, a limestone plateau, and the Blue Mountains, which are famous for producing high-quality coffee. Jamaica's diverse terrain has contributed to producing a wide variety of crops.

Jamaica is an English-speaking country, although it has a Creole dialect called Patois, which is influenced mostly by West African languages. Approximately 95 percent of the country's population is of African descent, and nearly the whole population is native-born Jamaican.

Jamaicans enjoy the country's tropical maritime climate. The mean daily temperature ranges from a seasonal low of 79 degrees Fahrenheit in February to a high of 86 degrees Fahrenheit in August, averaging around 80 degrees Fahrenheit. Jamaica's tropical climate and its miles of beautiful white beaches have attracted many tourists from all over the world. The island is also constantly exposed to hurricanes and recently suffered more than $210 million in damage when Hurricane Gustav hit in 2008.

As for religions, Christianity is the dominant religion in Jamaica. The main denominations in Jamaica include the Church of God, Seventh-Day Adventist, Baptist, Pentecostal, and Anglican. The Rastafari movement, a religious movement that originated in Jamaica, contends that Haile Selassie I, the former emperor of Ethiopia, is the incarnation of God. The lifestyle the Rastafarians follow has created a unique food culture. Some adherents follow the dietary laws of the Old Testament; others are strict vegetarians, eat only natural foods, and abstain from alcohol.

Jamaica is proud of its unique culinary history. Enid Donaldson, author of *The Real Taste of Jamaica,* argues that Jamaica's culinary evolution, described as "out of many one pot," reflects the history of the island. The Taino, a group of the Arawak Indians who had inhabited the Greater Antilles in the Caribbean Sea before Columbus's arrival, came from South America about 2,500 years ago. The Tainos named the island *Xaymaca,* which meant "land of wood and water." They grew various crops such as cassava, sweet potatoes, maize, fruits, vegetables, callaloo (a green, leafy, spinach-like vegetable), beans, cotton, and tobacco. Fish and shellfish, along with wild animals such as iguana, were also a major part of their diet. The *barbacoa,* which is a wooden grate standing on four forked sticks placed over a slow fire, was a special technique Tainos used. Jamaicans nowadays call it *jerk*. In addition, Tainos created a habit of making a soup pot with meat, vegetables, and seasonings. Saturday beef soup is still served in most Jamaican households.

The arrival of the Spanish in Jamaica in 1494 greatly influenced the further creation of a modern Jamaican cuisine. The Spaniards brought cattle, goats, pigs, horses, and lard to the island. Not only animals but also plant products, such as citrus fruits, ginger, date palms, coconuts, plantains, grapes, sugar, and bananas, were brought by the Spaniards. Some popular dishes such as *escoveitched fish* (a variation of Latin American ceviche) originated in Spain.

After the Spanish, the English started controlling Jamaica in 1655. The English settlers started growing crops that could easily be sold in England, such as tobacco, indigo, cacao, and sugar, which became the main crop for the island. Sugar, rum, and molasses were taken back to England and were also traded for flour, pork, and salt fish, a present staple food of Jamaica. The English, who also had colonies in different parts of the world, brought important food items such as breadfruit, ackee, mangoes, spices, and coffee to Jamaica.

Africans who were brought to Jamaica as slaves also contributed greatly to the creation of today's Jamaican cuisine. The Spanish turned to trading slaves from Africa's west coast for labor. The slaves brought with them okra, peanuts, and a variety of peas and beans, all of which are considered staples in today's Jamaican cuisine. Africans blended their traditional foods with foods that were already available locally in Jamaica. Some signature dishes of Jamaica, such as ackee and salt fish or Jamaican *rundown,* were invented by African peasants.

Many slaves, unhappy with their harsh conditions, escaped from the plantations and joined the Maroons in the remote mountains of Jamaica. Later, trading in African slaves was declared to be unlawful. The British made into law the Emancipation Act in 1834, and full freedom was granted to the slaves in 1838. After the abolition of slavery, Indians and Chinese were brought to the country by the British as cheap laborers. Just like Africans, these two ethnic groups blended their culinary traditions with food products available in Jamaica and created popular dishes such as curry goat.

In 1962, Jamaica was finally granted its independence from England. The constitution provides for freedom, equality, and justice for all who dwell in the country. Just like the country itself, Jamaican culinary art continues to evolve with its rich history and diversity that Jamaicans are proud of.

🍽 Food Culture Snapshot

Natalie and Michael Campbell live in a suburb of Kingston. Natalie is a secretary for a food company, and Michael works as a sales representative for the same company. Natalie is originally from Port Antonio, a beautiful town located 62 miles (100 kilometers) northeast of Kingston. Michael is a native of Kingston.

They get up early to avoid Kingston's notorious heavy morning traffic. At 6:30 A.M., they eat chicken patties and drink instant coffee with condensed milk. They occasionally eat ackee (an indigenous fruit with a texture and color like scrambled eggs) and salt fish, a typical Jamaican breakfast, with *bammy* (cassava bread). They leave home around 7 A.M. and arrive at their offices around 7:30 A.M. They get fresh coconut juice from a street vendor in front of their office building in New Kingston. Sipping fresh coconut juice is a great way to start their work.

They have a quick lunch at a local cafeteria near their company around noon. Although there are numerous fast-food chains in New Kingston, they prefer to eat traditional Jamaican foods rather than hamburgers and fries. Natalie's favorite is curry goat. Michael likes to have callaloo and salt fish. When they are on the go, they get light meals to go from roadside vendors. For a dessert, they enjoy chewing fresh sugarcane, which is cut into smaller pieces by the street vendor with his sharp machete.

After getting back home, Natalie goes to a local market to buy various food items. At the local market, she buys popular fruits and vegetables including callaloo, *chocho* (chayote), ackee, breadfruit, green bananas, and mangoes. She also realizes that she is almost out of kidney beans, the important ingredient for "rice and peas." There is a new supermarket three bus stops away from their house. Although the supermarket sells some imported foods Natalie has seen in television commercials, Natalie prefers to go to the local market where she can chat with the vendors she knows.

Michael's friend Damian is a Rastafarian from Port Antonio, and he has invited the couple for dinner. Damian doesn't use salt in his *ital* cooking due to his Rastafarian beliefs, which demand that nothing impure or processed be put in his body. Out of his thick clay pot, Damian serves a small fish dish flavored with a large amount of coconut milk and various herbs and spices such as pimento (allspice) and thyme that he grows in his backyard. Callaloo and boiled green banana are also served with the dish. Damian also serves a sweet herb tea in the beautifully carved calabash bowls his Rastafarian friend made for him. In rural areas such as Port Antonio, people still enjoy cooking foods from scratch.

Major Foodstuffs

Starches

Jamaican dishes almost always consist of some roots, tubers, or starchy fruits such as breadfruit, yams, cassava, plantains, and green bananas. Breadfruit, native to the Pacific Islands, was brought to Jamaica in 1793 by Captain Bligh and was an inexpensive food for slaves. Breadfruits can be roasted or baked. They are often made into puddings. Yams are also popular in Jamaica. There are different types of yams, such as the yellow yam, renta yam, St. Vincent yam, sweet yam, and Tau yam. Cassava is another tuber that was once the Arawaks' staple food. A round, flat bread called bammy is made from grated cassava and can be served with escoveitched fish and other dishes. Bananas are eaten ripe or green. Ripe bananas can be eaten raw or grilled. Jamaicans enjoy baked ripe bananas with coconut milk for dessert. Boiled green bananas are often served with meat and fish.

Animal Protein

Chicken is a popular meat in Jamaica. Both locals and tourists enjoy highly seasoned chicken barbecued on a sweltering pimento wood grill over a small pit: jerk chicken! Boston Beach, located in Port Antonio, is considered the birthplace of the spicy jerk seasoning and is known for authentic jerk pork and chicken. Other meats commonly consumed in Jamaica include beef and goat. Curry goat was introduced by the East Indians.

Fish and Shellfish

Fish is also commonly consumed in Jamaica. Codfish, kingfish, blue marlin, and mackerel are popular. Popular fish dishes include ackee and salt fish (salted codfish), mackerel rundown (fish simmered

Proper readying of Jamaican pepper shrimp. (Corel)

in coconut milk with tomatoes, onions, scallion, and pepper), jerk fish, and escoveitched fish, which is a variation of Latin American ceviche, except that the fish is seasoned and fried. Kingfish or snapper is often used for escoveitched fish. Shrimp, lobster, crab, and conch (sea snails) are popular shellfish in Jamaica. They are boiled, frittered, or grilled and are often part of delicious soup dishes.

Plant Sources

Just as in other Caribbean countries, coconut is central to Jamaican food culture, used for many types of dishes. Jamaicans seem to know how to take advantage of every part of the coconut. They enjoy refreshing coconut water that is sold on the street. Coconut milk is used for numerous dishes such as rice and peas, curried goat, and mackerel rundown. Coconut oil is a popular oil that gives foods a nice authentic flavor. Jamaicans make soup out of *copra* (a by-product of coconut). Jamaicans enjoy cooking kidney beans together with rice in coconut milk. The dish is called rice and peas and is often served as a side dish.

Callaloo may mean different things in different countries of the Caribbean. For example, callaloo is a green leafy vegetable stew made with okra in Trinidad and Tobago. Callaloo is quite important in Jamaica, where it refers to a green, leafy, spinach-like vegetable served as a side dish or in dishes. It is also used as a popular filling in patties. Besides its use for dishes, callaloo is also well known for its ritual and spiritual use. Chocho, also called chayote in some Latin American countries, is a pear-shaped, light green, light-flavored squash and is a nice accompaniment for famous Jamaican dishes such as escoveitched fish.

Jamaicans enjoy many tropical fruits grown on the island. There are fruits unique to Jamaica. Ackee, native to West Africa, is the national fruit of Jamaica and is used to make ackee and salt fish, the Jamaican national dish. Ackee must be harvested, prepared, and cooked properly since raw ackee contains toxins that can be fatal. Because it is illegal to export raw ackee to the United States, canned ackee has become a major export product in Jamaica. Ugli fruit is another fruit unique to Jamaica. It appears to be a cross between a Seville orange, a tangerine, and grapefruit. It is mainly grown in Jamaica and is exported to the United States and Europe. Ugli fruit has a rough, lumpy, greenish-yellow skin and is sweeter than grapefruit.

Group of spices and other condiments commonly found in Jamacian cooking, including allspice. (Dreamstime)

Spices

Jamaica is a spice island. The culinary history of Jamaica shows that people from different parts of the world, such as Africans, Indians, Chinese, and others, brought their culinary traditions accompanied by their unique use of various spices. Jamaicans enjoy using many kinds of spices including pimento (allspice). Jamaica grows the majority of the world's supply of allspice. Allspice is used for a numerous dishes including jerk dishes. Jerk flavor comes from meat seasoned with pimento placed on top of a grill made of pimento leaves and wood and slowly cooked.

East Indians brought their traditional habits of using many spices for cooking to Jamaica. Curry powder, often a mixture of turmeric, fenugreek, coriander, cumin, anise, and pepper, is used for various curried dishes, such as curried chicken, goat, and shrimp. Ginger, often used in Chinese dishes, is also used for making ginger beer. *Escallion* (a Jamaican culinary herb similar to scallions) and thyme, which grow well in Jamaica, are used together for Jamaican meat dishes. The essence of Jamaican cuisine is the use of herbs such as thyme, according to Norma

Shirley, who is often referred to as the Julia Child of the Caribbean. Finally, the Scotch bonnet pepper is one of the hottest varieties in the world and is used for many dishes including jerk dishes.

Coffee

In 1728, Sir Nicholas Lawes, then governor of Jamaica, imported coffee into Jamaica from Martinique, and it was discovered that the island was suitable for growing coffee. Today, blue mountain coffee, cultivated in the area of the Blue Mountains located in the northeastern part of the country, is considered one of the highest-quality coffee crops in the world. Blue mountain coffee is exported to other countries. Many locals drink instant coffee with condensed milk.

Rum

Jamaica produces a great variety of types and flavors of rum, and Jamaican rum is famous for its high quality. The history of rum in Jamaica is closely associated with the nonsweet history of British colonization. In the 17th and 18th centuries, sugar was at the center of the triangle trade: Molasses was produced by African slaves on the Caribbean sugar plantations. Molasses was transported to New England for distillation into rum, which was shipped to Africa in exchange for the slaves. Today, rum is the spirit of Jamaica. Jamaicans enjoy a shot of rum on different occasions, and no Jamaican Christmas is complete without sorrel made from rum. Sorrel is a punch made with hibiscus and ginger.

Cooking

One of the unique cooking methods native to Jamaica is called jerk. To make jerk, meats are rubbed or marinated with spices such as allspice and Scotch bonnet peppers. The history of jerk has been well documented. Taino, who had inhabited the Greater Antilles in the Caribbean Sea before Columbus's arrival, would build a platform of sticks above a shallow pit of ashes of pimento (allspice) wood and place the meat on the grid and cover it with pimento leaves and seeds to enhance the flavor of allspice.

Jamaicans also use preparation methods commonly found in other parts of the world, such as boiling, roasting, seasoning, drying, baking, and frying. Many stews are specialties in Jamaica. The use of spices and coconut is a unique cooking style in Jamaican cuisine.

The cooking style among Rastafarians is quite different from that of non-Rastafarians in Jamaica. Because of their beliefs that follow the laws of nature, many Rastas avoid foods that contain food additives such as artificial colorants, flavorings, and preservatives, as well as salt. Devout Rastas avoid canned or dried foods and even prohibit the use of metal cooking utensils; instead, clay and wood cooking pots, crockery, and cutlery are used. Ital food, which reflects a natural and healthy way of life, is served as a one-pot stew made without meat, salt, or other preservatives. The stew is often served in carved calabashes accompanied by calabash spoons.

Typical Meals

Breakfast

Jamaicans enjoy a hearty breakfast that consists of a main dish accompanied by delicious side dishes. Ackee and salt fish is a popular breakfast menu. Salt fish is also served with callaloo or okra. Mackerel rundown and escoveitched fish are other breakfast

A round flat bread called bammy is made from grated cassava. Here, it is topped with breaded grouper. (Rui Dias Aidos | Dreamstime.com)

dishes. Codfish fritters can be served for breakfast or as an appetizer. *Bully beef* (a corned beef dish) is also a typical Jamaican breakfast dish.

Dumplings, breadfruit, bananas, potatoes, and yams go well with Jamaican breakfast dishes. Bammy (cassava bread) is a wonderful accompaniment to fish dishes, and rice and peas goes well with any main course.

Among the poorer families, the morning meal frequently consists of just a cup of bush tea prepared by steeping the leaves in hot water. A small portion of carbohydrate-rich foods such as a piece of bread or a little cornmeal porridge may be served along with the tea.

Lunch

The dishes for breakfast can also be served for lunch. However, the most popular Jamaican lunch item would be *patties and coco bread.* Patties, delicious crescent-shaped flaky pies, are Jamaicans' favorite choice for lunch. There are a number of patty shops across the island where patties are made into a sandwich with coco bread, which despite the name is just a sweet soft bread roll that does not contain coconut. In Kingston, one sees a line of people at a patty shop during lunchtime when people want something quick and delicious. There are spicy beef patties, curried chicken patties, and vegetable patties that contain callaloo and other vegetables. Meat dishes accompanied by rice and peas are other popular lunch items in Jamaica.

Dinner

A variety of dishes are served for dinner. Rice and peas with either chicken or beef are served with some side dishes. Curried chicken, curried shrimp, escoveitched fish, steamed fish, oxtails, stew peas, stew pork, tripe and beans, and cow feet are all popular. Curry goat may be served, but it is mostly reserved for special occasions.

Chicken, rice and peas, raw and cooked vegetables, and a fruit drink are typical Sunday dinner menu items among most Jamaicans. More vegetables are consumed on Sundays than on weekdays. In addition, desserts are consumed on Sundays, mainly potato and cornmeal puddings or ice cream.

Eating Out

Jerk dishes (chicken, pork, fish) are popular, and jerk-dish stands are everywhere. Locals enjoy stands and casual restaurants that serve traditional Jamaican foods. For snacks, patties are one of the most popular food items.

Today, there are numerous fast-food restaurants in Kingston and popular resort areas such as Montego Bay. There are also restaurants that serve international cuisines including Italian, Japanese, and Thai. In addition, there are elegant and innovative Jamaican cuisine restaurants such as those run by Norma Shirley, which are famous for their use of fresh and local ingredients.

Special Occasions

Jamaicans enjoy celebrating various special occasions; curried goat is often served for celebrating a special occasion. *Mannish water* is a spicy goat-head soup that also contains a goat's intestines, green bananas, and a variety of root vegetables like yams or potatoes. Believed to be a tonic, mannish water is often served at wedding receptions.

Christmas Day is a special occasion for many Jamaicans who follow Christian faiths. On Christmas Day common dishes served include chicken, oxtail, curry goat, roast ham, roast beef, and rice and *gungo* peas, which are in season in December. One or two weeks prior to Christmas Day, Jamaicans begin soaking fruits in rum to prepare Jamaican-style Christmas cake, another special food for Christmas. The cake is eaten with sorrel, a popular drink for Jamaicans during the Christmas season. It is made from sorrel sepals (hibiscus), cinnamon, cloves, ginger, sugar, orange peel, and rum. As a favorite Easter dish, *bun* is a spicy bread that is eaten with cheese. Popular fish recipes for Easter include Jamaican escoveitched, fried, and stewed fish.

Nine nights, influenced by African religious and cultural traditions, is an extended wake to give comfort and support to the relatives of the deceased. Fried fish and bammy are served along with 100-proof Jamaican white rum.

Easter Spice Bun

2 c brown sugar

1 beaten egg

1 tbsp butter

¾ c whole milk

3 tsp baking powder

1 tsp grated nutmeg

1 tsp cinnamon

Pinch of salt

1 tbsp vanilla

1 c raisins

½ tsp lime juice

Grease a loaf tin and line it with greased paper.

Preheat oven to 350°F for about 15 minutes.

Add sugar to beaten egg, and then add melted butter and milk

Add all dry ingredients, and beat until smooth.

Add vanilla and the fresh raisins to the mix, plus lime juice, and then pour into the lined and greased tin.

Bake for approximately 1 hour.

Glaze

½ c brown sugar

½ c water

Boil water and sugar until thick.

Spread the glaze on the Easter bun, and return to the oven for an additional 5–8 minutes.

If desired, press a few whole cherries into the top of the bun.

Diet and Health

Various medical and belief systems from the indigenous Arawak Indians, African slaves, and Europeans, primarily Spanish and British, have influenced the contemporary Jamaican folk medical system. Indigenous people developed knowledge of medicinal herbs that were available on the island. The Europeans brought the Hippocratic humoral system, based on the idea that the body is regulated by four fluids, blood, phlegm, black bile, and yellow bile, each of which is described as being hot or cold and wet or dry.

During the slavery era, slaves adapted and utilized the concept of obeah, a morally neutral spiritual power, folk magic, or sorcery, which was derived from Central and West African origins. Later, obeah practitioners, yard healers, and bush doctors or herbalists, who normally combine their spiritual and herbal knowledge, became primary healers during the postemancipation era.

Today, most Jamaicans employ both Western biomedical and folk medical systems. Jamaicans attempt to treat an illness first at home using their herbal knowledge or with help from herbalists or bush doctors. Some herbs are linked to the supernatural roles they play in healing. A number of herbs that have been recognized as medicinal are available in Jamaica. "Duppy" (spirit) coconut, "duppy cherry," and "duppy cotton" are some examples of herbs that are related to spirits. If the home remedy is not effective, Jamaicans go to the biomedical doctor that practices Western medicine. If this does not work, some of them ask spiritual practitioners for help or use both biomedical and folk medicine concurrently. Physicians and patients often have different concepts about causes of illness, symptoms, treatment, and lifestyle factors such as diet, which often creates miscommunication.

Besides the use of plants to prevent or treat illnesses, Jamaicans perceive that diet is associated with their health. The Rastafarians are a group of people who generally follow strict guidelines regarding diet. Eating pork and crustaceans is universally prohibited among Rastas. They also tend to be vegetarians and avoid eating other meats such as beef, chicken, and goat. Many Rastas also avoid consuming fish with no scales or large fish, which are perceived to have more developed souls. Most Rastas believe in not killing other creatures and, therefore, prefer a vegan lifestyle, which is referred to as ital, meaning a natural and healthy way of life. Because of their adherence to nature and their belief that their bodies are the temple of the living God, most Rastas also avoid processed foods, which are not ital and pollute their bodies. The use of any added salt is discouraged among Rastafarians.

Because Rastafarians believe in nature's magical healing properties, they rely on herbs and trees instead of pharmaceuticals. Religious healers called Rasta doctors practice in their "balm" yard, an herbal healing garden where the doctors practice their magic, utilizing different herbs as nature (herbs) provides remedy to any illness.

Obesity has become a major public health issue in many developed and developing countries including Jamaica. Diet has been identified as a major factor associated with onset of obesity in those countries. Recent studies have demonstrated that increased fiber intakes in women, as well as increased vegetable consumption in both genders, were associated with a lower body mass index, indicating that promoting a traditional food culture that emphasizes the consumption of fiber-rich vegetables, fruits, and grains may be important to prevent obesity and noncommunicable diseases in Jamaica. At the same time, child undernutrition, especially stunting, is still a public health issue in Jamaica. Researchers in Jamaica recently revealed that stunting was associated with poor psychological functioning in late adolescence. Just like other middle-income countries, Jamaica is experiencing the coexistence of under- and overnutrition, and globalization and lifestyle changes appear to play an important role in Jamaica's nutrition transition.

Keiko Goto

Further Reading

Asprey, G. F., and Phyllis Thornton. *Medicinal Plants of Jamaica. Parts I and II.* http://www.herbaltherapeutics.net/Medicinal_Plants_of_Jamaica.pdf.

Burrell, Bernard. "Nine Nights: Death and Dying in Jamaica." *American Visions,* October–November 1996.

David, Erin. "Nature in the Rastafarian Consciousness." The Dread Library. http://www.uvm.edu/~debate/dreadlibrary/david.html.

Donaldson, Enid. *The Real Taste of Jamaica.* Toronto, ON: Warwick, 2000.

Higman, B. W. *Jamaican Food: History, Biology, Culture.* Kingston, Jamaica: University of West Indies Press, 2008.

Higman, B. W. "Jamaican Versions of Callaloo." *Callaloo* 30, No. 1 (2007): 351–68.

Houston, Lynn Marie. *Food Culture in the Caribbean.* Westport, CT: Greenwood Press, 2005.

Jackson, M., S. Walker, T. Forrester, J. K. Cruickshank, and R. Wilks. "Social and Dietary Determinants of Body Mass Index of Adult Jamaicans of African Origin." *European Journal of Clinical Nutrition* 57 (2003): 621–27.

Payne-Jackson, Arvilla. "Biomedical and Folk Medical Concepts of Adult Onset Diabetes in Jamaica: Implications for Treatment." *Health* 3, No. 1 (1999): 5–46.

Payne-Jackson, Arvilla, and Mervyn C. Alleyne. *Jamaica Folk Medicine: A Source of Healing.* Kingston, Jamaica: University of the West Indies Press, 2004.

Samuda, P. M., R. A. Cook, C. M. Cook, and F. Henry. "Identifying Foods Commonly Consumed by the Jamaican Population: The Focus Group Approach." *International Journal of Food Sciences and Nutrition* 49, No. 1 (1998): 79–86.

Martinique and Guadeloupe

Overview

Martinique and Guadeloupe are two of France's four overseas departments (the other two are French Guiana, on the mainland of South America, and Réunion, an island in the Indian Ocean). Martinique and Guadeloupe are thus fully French territories that fly the French flag, and their inhabitants are French citizens who speak French and Creole. Both are islands in the Caribbean Sea, part of the Lesser Antilles island chain located to the east of Puerto Rico, Hispaniola (Haiti and the Dominican Republic), Jamaica, and Cuba. Martinique is a single island with an area of 417 square miles and a population of 399,000. Guadeloupe is considered an archipelago. The two main islands, Grande-Terre and Basse-Terre, resemble a single butterfly-shaped island whose sections are divided by a narrow sea channel called la Rivière Salée. The other smaller islands of the Guadeloupe archipelago are Désirade, the Saintes, Marie-Galante, Saint Martin, and Saint Barthélemy. All together, the Guadeloupe archipelago has an area of 687 square miles and a population of 458,000. Martinique and the main islands of Guadeloupe are separated from each other in the Lesser Antilles chain by the island of Dominica.

The two islands were home to Arawak and Carib populations who were largely killed or chased off the islands by the French, who first settled there in the 17th century. The islands supported tobacco and then sugar and indigo plantations through the period of slavery (1635–1848) and later. Export agriculture based on crops and products such as bananas, sugar, and rum is still a major sector of the economy of both islands. The current inhabitants (Martiniquais and Guadeloupians) are the mixed descendants of native Caribs and Arawaks, small numbers of original French settlers, much larger numbers of African slaves brought by the French to work the plantations, Indian and Chinese indentured laborers who were brought in the 19th century for the same reason, and other European, Carib, and African mixed peoples of neighboring Caribbean islands and the American mainlands. The culinary practices of Martinique and Guadeloupe's inhabitants thus reflect the tropical Caribbean geography of the islands themselves and this colonial global history that resulted in the transplantation of both people and foodstuffs. For instance, French supermarkets selling metropolitan French dietary staples are common on the islands, where open-air market vendors also sell a mix of local foodstuffs, *local* in this case meaning both native crops and those imported across oceans long ago to feed both captive and free populations. Through this mix, the culinary cultures of Martinique and Guadeloupe contribute in clearly identifiable ways to the vast panoply of cuisines of the African diaspora.

🍽 Food Culture Snapshot

Odile and Maximilien Chivallon live in central Fort-de-France, the capital of Martinique since 1902 when Mount Pélée erupted, destroying the historical capital of Saint Pierre. Odile, who grew up in Gosier, a small town close to Point-à-Pitre, Guadeloupe, is an account advisor at the local branch of BNP Paribas, a major French bank, and Maximilien, who was raised in a Martiniquais family in Seine-Saint Denis, a suburb of Paris, is an archivist with the Archives départementales de la Martinique, located in Schœlcher, a short distance from Fort-de-France. Both start the day with typically small breakfasts: Maximilien has the remainder of a coconut cake that Odile prepared the week before, accompanied by strong black espresso coffee with sugar, and Odile has the same coffee at home before she leaves and then picks up a *pain au chocolat* (chocolate-filled pastry), croissant, or other pastry (*viennoiserie*) at a bakery close to her workplace.

When working, both Odile and Maximilien often buy lunch from nearby bakeries: sandwiches such as baguettes filled with flaked dried cod, grated carrot, and sliced tomatoes, dressed with a mustard-based vinaigrette, or perhaps two or more *petits pâtés salés*, small, savory wheat-flour pastries stuffed with spicy pork, chicken, or crab fillings, or with guava or other fruit fillings for dessert. Both finish their lunches with more espresso coffee. More substantial evening meals at home, featuring dishes such as lentils with marinated salt cod, or octopus fricassee, both served with plantain or pumpkin or both, are eaten at 8:30 P.M. or later.

When buying food to prepare at home, Odile and Maximilien shop at open-air markets, large supermarkets, and neighborhood grocery stores. Open-air markets such as the Lafcadio Hearn market in Fort-de-France are ideal and inexpensive sources for coconuts, fruit, many varieties of bananas and plantains, ginger and other spices, peppers, and a large range of locally grown tubers. In large supermarkets, Odile and Maximilien can find many products imported from France: canned vegetables (beans, peas, carrots, soups), cheeses, yogurt, butter, other dairy items, biscuits and cookies, dried sausages, canned fish, lentils, rice, and pasta. Supermarkets also have fresh meat sections selling a variety of both imported and local meat. As well as selling convenience food such as canned goods, smaller neighborhood grocery stores often carry a range of local manufactured products such as coffee, dried cod and other fish, fruit juices, and sugar syrups.

Major Foodstuffs

The dietary staples of Martinique and Guadeloupe, like those of many of the other Caribbean islands, are the extensive range of local tubers and roots that have supported populations since before the arrival of Europeans in the 15th century; although the two islands share similar histories and tropical climates and ecosystems, the names of some crops differ. These crops provide the essential carbohydrate base for the dietary regimes that developed historically and that have adapted to the significant transformations brought about by French colonization and settlement over the last five centuries. The historically dominant tuber is manioc, of which there are two main types: The larger bitter manioc is intensively processed to produce a range of edible goods: a thick starch used for baby food and as a thickener for soups and stews, a coarse meal that can be cooked like rice, a finer meal that can be sprinkled on top of other dishes, and the flour that is the base of cassava bread, one of the region's best-known specialties. The smaller sweet manioc (*kanmanioc* in Guadeloupe), which needs no processing other than peeling, is simply chopped and boiled in salted water and then eaten as an accompaniment to main dishes.

Other important tubers include the many varieties of yam (*igname*; both native American varieties such as *couscouche* and the African varieties that had served as provisions for slave ships during the Middle Passage); sweet potatoes (*patate* or *patate douce*); taro, originally from Asia (*madère* in Guadeloupe from its transatlantic associations with the island of Madeira, and *dachine* in Martinique, literally meaning "from China"); malanga (*chou caraïbe*), whose leaves are eaten as well as its roots; and Jerusalem artichokes (*topinambours*).

Legumes such as beans and peas also play a vital role in the carbohydrate complex of Martinique and Guadeloupe, much as they do in other African diasporic cuisines. Again there is a vibrant mix of local varieties such as *pois-savon* (a kind of butter bean), lima beans, red kidney beans (*haricots rouges*), and peanuts (*cacahuète*, from the Aztec *cocohuat*), in addition to African varieties such as pigeon peas (*pois d'Angole*) and black-eyed peas (*pois de canne* in Guadeloupe and *pois-chique* in Martinique). In addition, this carbohydrate base includes foodstuffs technically classified as fruits, such as the many types of banana (starchy green and sweeter yellow ones) and plantains, as well as breadfruit (*fruit à pain*) with its edible seeds, *chataigne-pays,* or "local chestnuts." Although cultivated and eaten, rice and maize are less significant on the islands than on the mainlands of the Americas.

Other vegetables eaten widely on the islands are okra (*gombo*), onions and garlic, a wide range of peppers (*piments*), squashes such as *christophine* (chayote) and *giraumon,* and a plethora of leafy green vegetables, often derived from the tubers already described and other local plants, as well as those imported from Europe during the first generations of colonial settlement, such as lettuce and sorrel (*oseille*). These leaves are often cooked together in a kind of stew known as *calalou,* a name that also refers to a specific plant whose leaves are typically used in its preparation. Herbs and spices such as thyme, cinnamon, allspice (both leaves and berries), and vanilla are grown locally and used widely. The best-known French Caribbean spice mix is Colombo powder, also associated with Réunion, the French overseas department in the Indian Ocean, and it contains *curcuma* (turmeric), cumin, coriander, fenugreek, pepper, cloves, mustard, and ginger; cardamom, saffron, fennel seed, and anise are other spices that can be added. This spice mix is directly related to the Indian populations of the islands, particularly on Guadeloupe, and it is used in the preparation of several classic dishes such as *colombo au poulet* (stewed chicken with Colombo powder) or *riz jaune* (yellow rice).

Like other Caribbean islands, Martinique and Guadeloupe are home to a vast number of fruit trees and plants. Here again are local or mainland American fruits such as pineapples, several types of guavas, papayas, apricots, avocados, passion fruit (*maracuja*), star apples (*caïmite*) and sugar apples (*pomme cannelle*), the purple *mombin* (*prune-chili*), sea grapes (*raisins bord-de-mer*), and sapodillas (*sapotille*) growing today next to nonnative varieties. Fruits imported across the Atlantic or Pacific oceans from the colonial period on include the bananas, plantains, and breadfruit already mentioned, as well as mangoes, figs, jackfruit, and, importantly, the many varieties of citrus fruits now growing there,

including grapefruit, lemons, limes, pomelos, and sour oranges, first introduced to the Caribbean by Columbus in 1493.

The native Arawak and Carib diets of Martinique and Guadeloupe traditionally supplemented this array of tubers, other vegetables, and fruit with the mollusks, crustaceans, fish, and other seafood that are abundant in the Caribbean Sea, and this is still the case today. Widely consumed shellfish include sea urchins (*oursin*) with their eggs (*chadron*), conch (*lambi*), clams (*palourdes*), shrimp of various sizes (*z'habitant* and *ouassou*), langoustine, and small octopus called *chatou.* A wide range of fresh fish also makes its way into common dishes: Well-known types include red snapper (*vivaneau* or *poisson rouge*), sea bream (*daurade*), shark (*requin*), and,

Vendor at the fruit market in Fort-de-France, Martinique. (Corel)

especially in Martinique, the flying fish (*poisson volant*) and king mackerel (*thazard*). Lesser-known fresh fish such as *coffre* and *balaou* are caught by artisanal or small-scale fishermen and are difficult to find in large markets. In the realm of seafood, colonial history also lives in the present day, here in the form of dried cod, which is a ubiquitous filling for sandwiches and other savory baked goods and can appear as a main dish as well. This cod originated in the North Atlantic fishery off of Newfoundland and in the Gulf of the Saint Lawrence, first developed by the British and the French in the 17th century, largely to feed their slave populations in the West Indies.

Although large quantities of meat and poultry are imported, there are also local sources that provide the basis of several Martiniquais and Guadeloupian specialties, beef cattle, goats, and pigs all having been introduced to the islands by the Spanish. Goats, in particular, are raised on a small scale, and goat meat (*cabri*) is found in many stews and fricassees and is eaten in dried form (*cabri salé*). Pigs are also raised on a relatively small scale, making local pork available today, *cochon créole* being particularly prized in Guadeloupe. Pig tails, trotters, blood (in boudin), and offal such as tripe make up a substantial portion of pork consumption, and there is a well-established tradition of sausage and ham production (charcuterie). Although the great majority of beef consumed on the islands is imported, beef cattle are raised on Guadeloupe (*bovin créole*) and are used in stews and roasts; the Martiniquais specialty *peau saignée* is made from frying or slowly simmering a dice of the flesh and skin of the cow's head.

Cooking

There is a range of typical ways of preparing dishes on Martinique and Guadeloupe. Both islands have long traditions of baking, beginning with cassava bread, which depended on the processing of bitter manioc in order to rid the tuber of its poisons. The traditional labor-intensive process that the French and Africans learned from the Arawaks and Caribs involves peeling, soaking, and grating the tuber, after which the grated mass is pressed, then dried and sifted. Liquid and other products including starch and flavorings are added to the meal, which is then formed into cakes and roasted in metal vessels placed over a fire. The process of drying grated pulp to produce flours that then serve as the base of baked goods is common to other tubers, roots, and fruit as well; examples include sweet potatoes, yams, coconuts, and bananas. These manufactured flours are available in local grocery stores. The ubiquity of refined and unrefined sugar, sugar syrups, and rum and the deeply rooted French baking traditions—evident in the many *boulangeries* and patisseries (bakeries selling bread and pastry)—have also contributed to the large assortment of sweet and savory baked goods available on the two islands. As well as the baguettes and *flûtes* familiar to all Frenchmen and Frenchwomen, local specialties such as *zacharie, pain au beurre, galette moussache,* and *jalousies* abound. Also, because of the easy availability of local fruits and their involvement in sugar production, the islands have a long history of candy and jam making (*confiserie*).

One-pot cooking is very common on Martinique and Guadeloupe: Main dishes are often rich stews or fricassees in which onions, garlic, aromatics, and seasonings such as peppers are added to the pieces of meat and often vegetables, which are then cooked together for a long time in stock or water, producing a gravy. Sometimes the meat has been marinated beforehand to tenderize it: In Martinique and Guadeloupe these marinades almost always include lime or lemon juice, peppers (piments), and thyme. This stew or fricassee is commonly accompanied by what can be a surprising amount of quite bland carbohydrates: Small quantities of plain boiled yam, plantain, banana, breadfruit, and taro can be found on the same plate as a small portion of pasta and cheese and/or rice and peas.

Another important method of cooking is deep-frying, which is used in preparing the wide array of fritters and croquettes available on the islands. The most well known are *accras de morue,* small deep-fried battered salt cod fritters, often spiced with Scotch bonnet peppers, but *accras* in general can be based on any other seafood or vegetable such

Accras de morue, small deep-fried battered salt cod, spiced with Scotch bonnet peppers. (StockPhotoPro)

as giraumon or taro. Unlike the rice-based accra found elsewhere in African diasporic and French New World cuisines, such as those traditionally prepared in New Orleans, on Martinique and Guadeloupe, the batter is made from wheat flour.

Soups also play a vital role in the cuisines of Martinique and Guadeloupe: There are a number of widely known bean soups—*soupe z'habitants* and *soupe à congo*—in which local beans are cooked in combination with a large quantity of other vegetables (giraumon—a kind of squash, sweet potatoes, yams), seasonings, and sometimes meat. Calalou, another dish common throughout the African diaspora, is made of a large quantity of different leafy green vegetables, four or five or more varieties. These greens are often the tops of tubers and roots eaten separately; the greens are cooked in water, often in combination with a small quantity of lard or smoked ham, garlic, piments and other seasonings, and okra.

Typical Meals

The structure and frequency of meals in contemporary Martinique and Guadeloupe resemble those in metropolitan France, particularly for middle-class and urban residents. Most people begin the day with a light breakfast, often of baked goods such as coconut or banana cake, if not packaged cereal,

followed by strong coffee. Indeed, breakfast often takes the form of a pastry bought at a local bakery. However, much heartier breakfasts based on local foodstuffs were traditionally consumed in the past by agricultural workers: One classic example is *ti-nain morue,* a dish in which small, starchy green bananas are stewed with soaked salt cod and seasonings such as garlic, lemons, and cloves; toasted manioc meal is often sprinkled on top. A traditional breakfast beverage would be coconut water (*dlo coco* in Creole), considered to have a very high vitamin and mineral content; or a tea called *té péyi* ("country tea" in Creole) made from infusing the bark and leaves of a local tree (*Capraria biflora*) in hot water.

Lunch and dinner meals are often based on a one-pot stewed or fricasseed dish accompanied by a selection of boiled tubers such as yams, breadfruit, plantain, and rice and peas. In recent generations pasta such as macaroni cooked in a cheese sauce and then cut into squares formed another common accompaniment to main dishes.

Blaff de Poisson Blancs (Fish Blaff)

Blaff de poisson blancs, a dish common to both islands, is cooked in another style: It is fish poached in a classic French court bouillon although the dish itself is associated with early Dutch settlers to the Caribbean. The word *blaff* derives from the sound that the fish apparently makes as it is lowered into the poaching liquid. This dish is traditionally accompanied by a selection of boiled yam, breadfruit, sweet potatoes, taro, and so on.

2 to 3 lb firm-fleshed white fish (such as swordfish, sea bream, or king mackerel), scaled, gutted, and cleaned; they may be left whole if small or cut into thick slices if large

4 limes

4 garlic cloves

1 allspice leaf (or bay leaf)

1 Scotch bonnet pepper, chopped finely after removing the seeds and inner veins (use latex or other kitchen gloves and pay special attention to not touch your face or eyes after preparing)

1 French yellow onion (regular cooking onion), diced

3 local onions (these resemble American shallots; use French shallots—échalotes—if not available), chopped

1 bouquet garni (a sprig of thyme, an allspice or bay leaf, and 3 sprigs of flat-leaf parsley tied in cheesecloth)

1 tbsp neutral vegetable oil such as grape seed

3 sprigs flat-leaf parsley, finely chopped

Salt and pepper to taste

Limes and Scotch bonnet peppers, for garnish and/or consumption

1. Rub the fish, or slices of fish, with the cut halves of one of the limes, paying special attention to the insides of the fish if left whole. If the whole fish are thick, make small slices at regular intervals so that the seasoning penetrates. Place fish in a shallow dish with the juice of 3 limes (including the one you have already sliced), one minced garlic clove, the allspice or bay leaf (roughly crushed), the diced Scotch bonnet pepper, and salt and pepper. Add a little water until just covered, and let marinate in the refrigerator for 1–2 hours.

2. Ten minutes before the end of the marinating time, prepare the court bouillon by bringing all of the onion (both types if available), 2 crushed garlic cloves, the bouquet garni, salt (in Guadeloupe the blaff is always very salty), and pepper to a boil in a large stew pot or Dutch oven in 1½ quarts of water. Simmer for 10 minutes on a medium flame.

3. Remove the fish from their marinade, drain them, and immerse them in the court bouillon, putting in the largest whole fish or fish slices first. Bring the court bouillon back to a boil, and let simmer for 5 to 15 minutes, depending on the type and size of the fish. Remove the fish or fish slices as soon as they are cooked through, and keep warm.

4. Place all of the poached fish on a large shallow plate. Discard the bouquet garni from the court bouillon. Mash the remaining garlic clove with the tablespoon of oil, the juice of the last lime, and the chopped parsley. Add this mixture to the court bouillon, and when all is well blended, pour the court bouillon over the poached fish so as to present it bathed in its cooking liquid. On a separate plate, arrange quartered limes and peppers for presentation (and consumption for those who wish).

The evening meal in contemporary Martinique and Guadeloupe often begins with an aperitif (before-dinner drink), in the French style, served with a selection of small appetizers such as spicy fritters, croquettes, small crepes, or puffs made from a variety of vegetables such as sweet potatoes or from seafood such as salt cod or crab. The most common aperitif on the islands is *ti'punch* ("small punch"), a cocktail made of sugar syrup, sections of lime, and rum, with the proportion of syrup to rum ranging from 1:3 to 1:8. Purists prefer the cocktail without ice cubes, but it is often served with them as well. A large variety of sugar syrups are available, ranging from dark ones that can resemble molasses in taste and appearance (*sirop de batterie*) to syrups that are clearer in color and lighter in taste (*sirops de canne à sucre*). There is an even larger range in the varieties of rum available: Rum is one of the most important exports of both islands, and there are many *rhummeries* producing rums of differing tastes, ages, and qualities. The two main categories of rum are *rhum agricole,* a more artisanal product distilled directly from the fermented liquid of the crushed sugarcane; and *rhum industriel,* a larger-scale product distilled from the fermented molasses, a by-product of the refining of sugar. As well as these two categories, rum is also distinguished by the number of years it has been aged, ranging from 3 to 15 years, or even older, and the French system of *appellation d'origine contrôllée* is in place for rum from Martinique and Guadeloupe, restricting the use of names, geographic identifiers, and manufacturing terms according to strictly regulated criteria.

Féroce D'avocat

Féroce d'avocat, a spicy avocado and salt cod dish, is a common appetizer served with the aperitif.

Serves 4

Step 1: *Morue en Chiquetaille* (Shredded Codfish)

1 lb dried salt cod (choose a piece that is as thick as possible and preferably from the tail)

1 French yellow onion (regular cooking onion), finely diced

3 local onions (these resemble American shallots; use French shallots—échalotes—if not available), finely diced

2 cloves garlic, finely diced

2 sprigs flat-leaf parsley, finely chopped

2 sprigs thyme, leaves removed and stems discarded

1 Scotch bonnet pepper, chopped finely after removing the seeds and inner veins (use latex or other kitchen gloves and pay special attention to not touch your face or eyes after preparing)

Juice of 2 limes

5 tbsp neutral vegetable oil

1. Scrape the cod before soaking in order to remove as much surface salt as possible. Cut into strips and grill directly over a gas flame, browning the strips lightly. Then place cod strips in a bowl, cover generously with cold water, and soak for 1 hour. Drain them carefully and shred the strips as finely as possible, making sure to remove all the skin and fine bones you find.

2. Place the shredded cod in a salad bowl with the aromatics (onions, garlic, parsley, thyme, pepper). Mix carefully to fully combine all ingredients, sprinkle with the lime juice, and then slowly add the vegetable oil. Let marinate for at least 2 hours

Step 2: *Féroce D'avocat*

2 large ripe avocados

1 Scotch bonnet pepper, prepared as in Step 1 (optional: this will make the dish extremely spicy)

¾ c cassava (manioc) meal

Salt and pepper

1. Slice avocados lengthways, remove the pit, and scoop out the flesh, keeping the skins intact and putting aside. Mash the avocado flesh, and add the *morue en chiquetaille* and the second Scotch bonnet pepper, if desired, combining until you obtain a smooth texture.

2. Add the cassava meal and combine again. Taste for salt and pepper, and mound the mixture into the avocado skins for presentation. Another common method of presentation is to shape the mixture into small balls and place on a plate.

Eating Out

There are many options for eating outside of the home on Martinique and Guadeloupe. Traditionally, there has been a wide selection of casual eating establishments in the marketplaces of towns and urban centers; these serve stews, fricassees, boiled roots, rice and peas, fresh fruit juices, and baked goods, alone or in combination, particularly at lunchtime. These eateries are often partially or wholly out of doors. In addition, there are many indoor cafés and casual restaurants that serve similar dishes away from marketplaces during the daytime; some combine them with extensive baking facilities. Full bakeries are a well-established institution on the islands. In addition to selling French breads, cakes, pies, and pastries, they prepare sandwiches for lunchtime crowds. All of these places typically close in the evening.

Tourism is an extremely important sector in the economies of Martinique and Guadeloupe, with many metropolitan French visitors owning second homes on the islands and spending their annual vacations there. Their presence and that of other international tourists have encouraged the development of a range of mid- and upscale restaurants that cater to them in towns, cities, and resorts and on beachfronts throughout the day, but especially for evening meals. The growing number of middle-class Martiniquais and Guadeloupians are also clients for these businesses. Many of these restaurants, and the network of formally trained chefs who invest and work in them, consciously offer dishes with

A bakery van filled with bread on the streets of Le Diamant, Martinique. (Philip Gould | Corbis)

traditional touches reflecting the islands' creolized history and in this way support the blossoming of a *cuisine antillaise* that is continuing to gain in popularity and recognition.

The large fast-food chains such as McDonalds, Kentucky Fried Chicken, Pizza Hut, and Quick (a French hamburger restaurant) have not implanted themselves on Martinique and Guadeloupe as they have in metropolitan France, although there is a Hippopotamus (a French fast-food chain) on each island. Nevertheless, there are local versions of fast-food restaurants in most urban centers on both islands that are open in the evening. These establishments sell a combination of Western fast food that has both Caribbean and French touches: French fries (*frites*), grilled brochettes of conch and other seafood, pizza, hamburgers and other hot sandwiches, and couscous.

Special Occasions

Festivals and other special occasions, often linked to harvests or the Catholic calendar, are celebrated on Martinique and Guadeloupe with special foods or food rituals. One of the most important is Christmas, which is celebrated with a *réveillon* (Christmas Eve party) before going to midnight mass on December 24. Three traditional foods commonly eaten as appetizers at this party are small, spicy blood sausages (boudin), savory stuffed pastries (petits pâtés salés), and Christmas ham (*jambon de Noël*). All three make extensive use of pork: Boudin is prepared from pork blood, seasonings, manioc, sweet potato meal or breadcrumbs, and lime juice, which are stuffed into casings after being cooked together and the casings are tied off with string at four-inch intervals. The strings of boudin are then boiled until cooked through. Cooks jealously guard their recipes for boudin as there can be much variation in the ingredients, particularly in the seasonings. Petits pâtés salés make use of spiced chopped pork filet, which is seasoned, covered with classic French *pâté brisée* (short crust pastry), and then shaped into two-inch rounds before being baked. The majestic Christmas ham is characterized by its large size, 10–15 pounds on the bone, by its time-consuming preparation, and by its reddish sugar glaze, which was traditionally enhanced by the application of a clothes iron to the outside after the cooking.

One of the most important food-related festivals on the two islands is the long-standing annual Fête des Cuisinières (Festival of the Women's Cooking Association) on Guadeloupe. This event takes place in mid-August in honor of Saint-Pierre, the patron saint of the organization, and entails a parade in Point-à-Pitre, the capital, led by the 250 or so members of the Women's Cooking Association dressed in traditional skirts, scarves, and headdresses. The parade finishes with a celebratory lunch of local specialties for all participants.

There are also local agricultural or seafood festivals on both islands that celebrate and highlight specialties, such as the Fête du poisson et de la mer (Festival of Fishing and the Sea) on Guadeloupe in late April or early May, and the Semaine Gastronomique de Sainte-Marie (Week of Gastronomy in Saint Marie) on Martinique at the end of April, which provides culinary histories and recipes for traditional Caribbean foodstuffs such as yams, pineapple, coconut, and squashes.

Diet and Health

For French citizens residing in the overseas departments of Martinique, Guadeloupe, and French Guiana, life expectancy has continued to rise during the 2000s so that it now matches that of metropolitan France: 77 years for men and 84 years for women in 2005. This rise in life expectancy is almost entirely due to a decrease in infant mortality. In terms of health, high blood pressure, cancer, and cardiovascular disease are the most important threats to life expectancy on the islands, as they are in metropolitan France and in the West, generally. One enormous difference in the health of metropolitan and overseas French citizens is caused by endocrinal diseases, which kill at double the rate on Guadeloupe, Martinique, and French Guiana compared to the metropole. All of these pathologies are linked to diet, and endocrinal disease in particular is connected to type 2 or sugar diabetes, which can develop in those whose diets feature too much starchy and sweet food. Diabetes affects women in the overseas departments at a higher rate than men.

The rates and nature of alcohol-related problems also differ between the metropole and the islands. While alcoholic psychosis kills at a higher rate overseas, cirrhosis of the liver kills at a lower rate, with Guadeloupe being the island most affected by all alcoholic disorders. The reason for this discrepancy lies in the type of alcohol consumed: rum on the islands and wine in the metropole. These statistics notwithstanding, female alcoholism is lower on Martinique and French Guiana than in the metropole.

While health is assessed and medical care is provided on the islands in institutionally similar ways to metropolitan France, there exists nonetheless in the French Antilles an extensive body of folk remedies that rely on local plants for the production of botanical tonics (*rimèd razié*). Considered part of the legacy of slaves' knowledge of healing, this body of knowledge is currently experiencing a renewal of interest. On Guadeloupe, for example, the Association pour la promotion et le développement des plantes médicinales et aromatiques de Guadeloupe (Association for the Promotion and Development of Medicinal and Aromatic Plants of Guadeloupe) has inventoried 625 varieties of medicinal plants that can be used to create remedies. While some of these remedies are familiar to all localities where the particular plant grows—for instance, using cloves to soothe toothaches—there are many specific to the islands. Examples include a flower called *atoumo* in Creole ("against all evils"), whose petals in combination with rum and honey are considered to bring down fevers; the bark of the red gum tree (*gommier rouge*) macerated with allspice berries in rum, which is thought to soothe rheumatism; and a bath containing the leaves of the sugar apple (*pomme cannelle*), which is reported to lift fatigue.

Bertie Mandelblatt

Further Reading

Antilles Resto. http://www.antillesresto.com/.

Bourne, M. J., S. A. Seddon, and G. W. Lennox. *Fruits and Vegetables of the Caribbean.* Oxford: Macmillan Education, 1988.

Burton, David. *French Colonial Cookery: A Cook's Tour of the French-Speaking World.* London: Faber and Faber, 2000.

De Rozières, Babette. *Creole: Recipes from the Culinary Heritage of the Caribbean, Blending Asian, African, Indian, and European Traditions.* London: Phaidon, 2007.

Harris, Jessica B. *Iron Pots and Wooden Spoons: Africa's Gift to New World Cooking.* New York: Atheneum, 1989.

Ovide, Stéphanie. *French Caribbean Cuisine.* New York: Hippocrene Books, 2002.

Parkinson, Rosemary, Clem Johnson, and Ruprecht Stempell. *Culinaria the Caribbean: A Culinary Discovery.* Cologne, Germany: Könemann, 1999.

Wolfe, Linda. *The Cooking of the Caribbean Islands,* Alexandria, VA: Time-Life Books, 1970.

Mexico

Overview

The Republic of Mexico forms part of the North American continent; nonetheless, culturally and linguistically, it has greater affinity with Latin America. Some consider it part of Central America, which includes Guatemala, Belize, Honduras, Nicaragua, and Panama. Mountains form the backbone of the country and divide it into three geographic precincts: a central highland located in south-central Mexico, a southern highland in southern Mexico, and a southeastern highland in the southeastern part of the country. Economically and politically, the most important of these precincts throughout history has always been the central highland, where Mexico City is located at 7,000 feet above sea level. Throughout history the country has always been controlled from some seat of power in the central highland.

The population of Mexico is over 100 million, divided into 30 states. Catholicism is the predominant religion, making up 87 percent of the population, while Protestant evangelical groups form 7 percent of the population, with other religions making up the remainder. Geography plays an important role in determining the diet of Mexicans. The country occupies an area of 2,000 miles from north to south, with diverse plant and animal life, which is reflected in the food traditions of the various regions. Gastronomically, the country can be divided into six regional areas, based on local food traditions: northern Mexico, the Pacific Coast, western Mexico, central Mexico, the isthmus of Tehuantepec, and the Maya area.

The Mexican diet has a common substratum throughout the country, based on corn, beans, and chili peppers. There are many ways of preparing corn, different varieties and methods of preparing beans, and a great diversity of chili peppers and sauces that are popular in each region. Mexico produces a plenitude of fresh fruits and vegetables, whose preparation is also regional.

🍽 Food Culture Snapshot

Felipe and Aurora Urrutia live in an apartment in a middle-class neighborhood of Mexico City, known as La Irrigacion. Felipe is an engineer from Celaya, Guanajuato, and works at Teléfonos de Mexico. Aurora is from Guadalajara, Jalisco, and works in the accounting department of a local department store, El Palacio de Hierro. Their combined incomes allow them to live a comfortable life, without luxuries, but after the bills are paid, there is little money to save toward the purchase of their own home or for starting a family.

Their diet is simple Mexican and international-style food. They seldom eat out at good restaurants, because of the extra expense. Like most immigrants to Mexico City, they rely on friends, rather than family, for their social contacts. To save time, Aurora purchases nearly all of their food products at a nearby supermarket.

A typical day's food consumption for the Urrutias is as follows: Their day begins at about 6 in the morning with a cup of strong, black coffee to wake them up. This may be followed by a sweet roll, *pan dulce*, if there is time. Around 10 A.M., during their morning coffee break, they consume an *almuerzo,* or small breakfast, which Felipe buys from a street vendor and Aurora purchases at her place of work. This small meal may consist of juice or fresh fruit, along with any of the following: eggs, meat, beans, *chilaquiles* (a tortilla-based dish), tortillas, chili sauce, and coffee. Mexican sweet rolls are a favorite for this time of day.

The most important meal of the day is served in midafternoon, anytime between 2 and 4 P.M. Felipe and Aurora generally do not have enough time to go home on their lunch hours, so Aurora usually takes a hard-roll sandwich, called a *torta,* and a salad or leftovers from the previous night's dinner, which she can warm up in the microwave oven in her office. Pizzas are a popular take-out food for lunch. Felipe generally eats in a *fonda,* an inexpensive restaurant with a fixed menu that caters to office workers, or he may choose to resort to street vendors to sell him tacos or other fast food from a mobile street cart.

Felipe and Aurora eat a more substantial dinner than do middle-class people who have a heavy meal at midday. Their evening meal, served around 9 P.M., may consist of meat and a salad, tacos and beans, enchiladas, or tortilla-based dishes, such as *sopes, tlacloyos,* or *panuchos* (these are snacks but quite filling). Those who have a heavy meal at midday may prefer a light meal, or *merienda,* at night. This may consist of any of the following: soup, fruit, sweet bread, or tamales. A more ample dinner, or *cena,* may be shared with friends or family on more formal occasions.

During the past 50 years, supermarkets have become a favorite shopping center for housewives, who previously had to shop at several small specialty stores or buy at open-air markets. Today's supermarkets sell freshly baked breads, newly made tortillas, fruits and vegetables, and all products needed for cooking a complete meal. Large fruit and vegetable markets are still frequented by many housewives who have the time to shop there. Shopping at supermarkets saves valuable time.

Major Foodstuffs

The most important food product in Mexico is corn. Many Mexicans eat corn or maize products at every meal in a variety of ways and as snacks between meals as well. It makes up over 50 percent of the caloric intake of middle-class Mexicans and up to 80 percent of the indigenous diet. There are many ways of preparing corn. It can be boiled, toasted, roasted, ground into a fine corn flour, or used as whole kernels and added to a variety of stews. The most common use of corn in present-day Mexico is in the form of tortillas and tamales.

Fresh corn can be purchased year-round; it dries well and can be ground into cornmeal for making tortillas, tamales, and *atoles* (corn-based drinks). Mexican housewives can buy cornmeal to make their own tortillas or purchase ready-made tortillas at the supermarket or the *tortillería* (tortilla shop). Tortillas must be made every day, since they do not keep well overnight. Women in urban Mexico City are not willing to spend the necessary hours grinding corn to make handmade tortillas, although some purchase ready-prepared masa and make tortillas for special occasions. The corn gruel atole can be purchased in the supermarket as a semiprepared product. Corn tortillas are preferred in central and southern Mexico, while wheat-flour tortillas are popular in northern Mexico.

Beans have been an important ingredient in the Mexican diet throughout history. They are a good complement to corn in the diet and contain the amino acids lacking in corn. When consumed together, corn and beans provide the necessary protein requirements for a healthy diet. There are more than

Authentic Mexican dish of tamales with red peppers and pinto beans. (Shutterstock)

20 varieties of beans on the Mexican market; these are commonly known to the public by the color of their seeds, their shapes, or the region where they are grown. Beans are sold in a variety of colors, such as black, pink, white, and beige (*bayo*). Spotted (*pinto*) and mottled (*moteado*) beans are also distinguished, as are particular shapes, such as goat's-eye beans and peanut-shaped beans. Quick-cooking beans called *instantaneos* have become popular in recent decades. They are easily and quickly prepared by adding a small amount of water to the ground beans and frying them as refried beans. Beans are consumed daily by a majority of the Mexican population at any or all of the three meals.

Vitamins and minerals are provided by a variety of fruits and vegetables, some native to the country and others of European origin. Tomatoes, squash, onions, chili peppers, and tomatillos are the most consumed vegetables in the diet. A pear-shaped member of the squash family, called a chayote, is popular, as are cactus paddles, known as *nopales*. Avocados and jicamas, a tuber with white flesh and a radishlike texture, often eaten as a snack or in salads, are other vegetables native to Mexico that have been part of the Mexican diet since pre-Hispanic times. When the Spaniards arrived in the 16th century, they introduced vegetables from the Mediterranean area such as carrots, lettuce, cabbages, onions, garlic, cauliflower, broccoli, eggplant, radishes, okra, spinach, and many other vegetables that have become part of the Mexican diet over the years.

Citrus fruits play an important role in the Mexican food tradition. Sweet and sour oranges, grapefruit, tangerines, sweet and sour lemons, and limes arrived in Mexico soon after the Spanish conquest and adapted easily to the Mexican soil and climate. Many other fruits were brought to Mexico from other parts of the world. Apples, pears, cherries, mangoes, grapes, strawberries, plums, peaches, bananas, melons, and watermelons all arrived in the 16th or 17th century. Mangoes were brought from the Philippines by merchants on the Manila Galleon, which traded between Manila in the Philippines and Acapulco for 250 years. In Mexico, the finest mangoes are known as "manila mangoes." Mexico contributed many tropical fruits to the international diet, such as the papaya, as well as fruits from the *Anona* family like the custard apple, called cherimoya, and the *guanábana*. The *zapote* family includes the mamey, sapodilla (*chicozapote*), and several varieties of zapote distinguished by the color of their pulp, which are popular Mexican fruits, as are guavas. Fruits from the cactus plant include the prickly-pear fruit called *tuna* and the *pitahaya*. Their use in the Mexican diet dates from ancient times.

Special meat shops called *carnicerías* are popular for purchases of all kinds of meat products, as are meat stands in markets or in supermarkets. In Mexico beef is known as *carne de res* and is considered the highest-status meat available and the most expensive as well, making it out of reach for many Mexicans. Pork is a popular meat product and is used in many traditional Mexican dishes. Mutton is appreciated for roasting in a barbecue pit, and roast kid is a popular dish in northern Mexico. Chickens are inexpensive and probably the most popular meat on the market. Eggs are consumed widely and are a good source of protein. Fish is plentiful but more expensive than meat, making it a less popular choice for economy-minded housewives. It can be purchased at special fish shops called *pescaderías,* in markets, or in supermarkets.

Rice is a popular carbohydrate in the Mexican diet and is consumed on a daily basis as an accompaniment for the main dish. It can also be served as a "dry soup" with fried plantains on top or as an ingredient in liquid soups. *Arroz a la mexicana* is red rice, prepared with pureed tomatoes. In addition to white rice, green rice made with fresh cilantro, parsley, and roasted poblano-type peppers that have been pureed and added with the liquid to the cooking rice is a festive method of preparing rice. Black rice is prepared with black bean broth from the bean pot, known as *frijoles de olla.* White rice is also used for making rice pudding, *arroz con leche,* a typical and popular Mexican dessert of Spanish origin.

Sugar found new uses when it was introduced into Mexico in the 16th century. The sugar industry was established early in Mexico on land belonging to Hernán Cortés, at his great hacienda in the state of Morelos. It became a popular ingredient for making Mexican sweets and candy in the convents and nunneries and was also employed in the manufacture of rustic rum, called *chinguirito,* with a high alcohol content. The most important use of sugar today is in the manufacture of soft drinks, making Mexico the highest consumer of sugar in the world. Soft drinks are also manufactured with a fructose base. Mexican desserts are very sweet, but they are eaten only on special occasions, not on a daily basis. The candy industry is well developed in Mexico, often as an artisan product. Several regions of the country are known for the particular type of candy they produce.

Mexican cooking is well known for its spicy flavor, which mainly comes from the use of hot chili peppers; nonetheless, many other spices are also used for flavoring food. Black pepper, cinnamon, cumin seeds, sesame seeds, aniseed, oregano, cloves, and nutmeg are only a few of the spices on the market that are regularly used in cooking. Mexicans are especially fond of cinnamon, which is used in desserts, coffee (*café de olla*), hot chocolate, and cinnamon tea, as well as in breads and cookies. Mexico is the principal consumer of cinnamon in the world. Local spices include annatto (achiote) seeds, used almost exclusively in Yucatecan cooking. Green or white pumpkin seeds (*pepitas de calabaza*) are popular for cooking or eating as snacks. Chili peppers, garlic, onions, and tomatoes make up a seasoning often referred to as *a la mexicana.*

Cooking

Throughout Mexican history, the preparation of food has always been considered women's work. Men sometimes took part in outdoor cooking, such as barbecuing meat on a framework of sticks over an open fire or preparing the underground ovens called *pibs* in the Maya area, used for cooking large animals, massive tamales, or large fowl. Men may also have participated as cooks for feasts, banquets, and funerary rites; however, the principal role in everyday cooking was assigned to women.

Many cooking utensils found in present-day Mexican kitchens are cultural remnants of pre-Hispanic implements. Some are still being manufactured and used today. A typical example of this would be the griddle, or *comal,* used to heat tortillas. They are now manufactured from metal, rather than clay, but they serve the same purpose. *Metates* for grinding corn and spices can still be found in more traditional kitchens, as well as *molcajetes,* better described as a stone mortar and pestle, for grinding seeds, tomatoes, and chili peppers for salsas. Clay pots have a long tradition in food preparation in Mexico and can be found in many kitchens as storage vessels for water or grains. Small braziers, called *anafres,* are now made of tin rather than clay, but they are still being manufactured and used in Mexico.

Traditional Mexican cooking is labor-intensive and time-consuming. The cooking is generally done on gas stoves as electricity is expensive. Kitchens are fairly well equipped except in the poorer neighborhoods of Mexico City, where one can find only basic implements such as blenders for soups and salsas, pots and skillets, and sometimes a small refrigerator or icebox to avoid a daily trip to the marketplace.

Kitchens in middle- and upper-class homes in Mexico City are as well equipped as many American kitchens and include dishwashers, microwave ovens, blenders, hand beaters, garbage disposals, gas or electric ovens, toasters, electric coffeepots, and any other equipment they may find useful. Upper-class women are not known for their interest in the kitchen and hire household help for daily meals

Mixture of ingredients on a metate ready to grind into a Mexican paste-sauce called mole. (Leon Rafael | Dreamstime.com)

and use caterers when they invite guests to their homes.

Sautéing and deep-frying are the most common cooking techniques and are carried out in cast iron skillets. Boiling and soup making are done in deep pots; beans are cooked in pressure cookers, and electric blenders are necessary for preparing soups and salsas. Tortillas and spices are heated on cast iron griddles, or comales. Ovens are not a required item in Mexican kitchens, as they consume a lot of gas and cooks prefer stovetop cooking, when possible. Most middle- and upper-class kitchens do have ovens, but they are not used on a daily basis.

Typical Meals

The definition of a typical Mexican meal depends on the cultural group, setting (rural or urban), age group, social and economic level, and geographic region. One can, however, speak in general terms about Mexican food traditions. Corn is combined with beans, squash, chili peppers, tomatoes, and tomatillos to form the basic diet of the country. Secondary foods, which are eaten less frequently but are consumed throughout the country, are represented by native vegetables such as cactus paddles, avocados, vegetable pears, jicamas, and greens, known as *quintoniles, verdolagas,* or *quelites.* Peripheral foods may include seasonal crops such as insects, mushrooms, chokecherries, the fruits of the prickly pear, and small cactus fruits known as *biznagas.* These foods are produced during the rainy season and are generally collected by the rural population.

Tortillas and hot chili sauces accompany meals throughout Mexico at all social levels. These two elements can be considered a common food denominator among social classes. Small plates of salt and cut limes are common table accessories. Meals are eaten two, three, or more times a day, depending on the occupation and resources of the family and how one defines a meal. Rural Indian groups are at considerable nutritional risk, especially those who live in the southern states of Guerrero, Oaxaca, and Chiapas. The daily diet of some of the elderly members of these groups consists of tortillas, chili sauce, and little more.

Food and meal schedules in rural Mexico vary considerably according to local activities, resources, and customs. Breakfast may be eaten any time between 5 and 7 A.M. Farmers usually rise very early and have a light breakfast of atole or tortillas and chili. They take their midday meal, which may consist of corn prepared as *pozol,* made of fresh or fermented corn and water, into the cornfield. After they return home in the afternoon, a meal that includes hot tortillas, beans, chili sauce, and coffee or atole is eaten between 4 and 6 P.M. These are the general guidelines of an Indian diet.

In urban Mexico City, many Mexicans start the day with a cup of coffee, herbal tea, or hot chocolate. These beverages may be accompanied by a sweet roll. The beverage is followed later by a heavier meal called an almuerzo. This may be eaten around 10 A.M., depending on the work schedule and whether it is taken at home, on the street, or in a restaurant. A variety of dishes can be served at this meal. Juice and fresh fruit are popular dishes to begin the meal. Eggs, meat, beans, stew, salsa, and tortillas are the general elements of the almuerzo.

The most important meal of the day is served in midafternoon, sometime between 2 and 4 P.M. In provincial Mexico, families try to take the main meal of the day together; however, in large urban areas, it is generally no longer possible for the family to gather at home to eat because of work schedules and heavy traffic at this time of day. The meal may begin with an *antojito* (appetizers), such as a quesadilla, or directly with a bowl of hot soup. The custom of serving both a liquid broth or creamy soup, and also a dry soup, such as rice or pasta, has become less popular in recent years due to the extra calories two soups represent. The main course may be meat, fish, or chicken, served with a salad or vegetables. The most popular carbohydrate for accompanying meat dishes is rice. Beans may be served with the main course or as a separate dish following the principal dish. Desserts include fresh fruit, ice cream, rice pudding, or a custard called flan. The most common after-dinner beverage is coffee. Plain water or fruit-flavored water are common beverages for a meal. The younger crowd prefers soft drinks at any time of day.

After eating a substantial meal in midafternoon, most people do not feel like a heavy meal at night. A light meal, or merienda, may be served around 9 P.M., when light snacks, antojitos, tamales, soups, sweet rolls, or fruit may be eaten. A more formal dinner, cena, may be shared with family and friends on special occasions. This gastronomic scheme is by no means standard throughout the country. The majority of the population does not have sufficient resources to eat on such an elaborate scale. Life in provincial Mexico is less hectic than in Mexico City, and people enjoy their meals at a more leisurely pace.

A typical evening dish for the merienda are *sincronizadas,* or tortilla ham and cheese sandwiches. Sincronizadas may be considered fast food, but they can be very good, depending on the cheese used.

Sincronizadas

1 tbsp oil

12 small corn tortillas

6 slices Port Salut cheese

6 slices ham

6 tsp chili salsa

Heat a frying pan over medium heat, and add the oil. Top 6 of the tortillas with a slice of cheese and a slice of ham. Spread 1 teaspoon of salsa over the ham. Cover with a second tortilla and place in the hot skillet. The tortilla edges may be held together with a toothpick, so that they do not separate. Toast over medium heat until the cheese begins to melt and the tortilla begins to brown. Flip over and toast the other side. Transfer to a plate and keep warm. Serve guacamole sauce on the side.

Provincial Mexico

The typical Yucatecan dietary pattern is somewhat different than that in other parts of the country. In Mérida a businessman or white-collar office worker may begin his day with a cup of coffee or juice before rushing off to the office; then, around 10 A.M. he may order an almuerzo or *tentempie* (literally, a little something to keep him on his feet until lunch). This may consist of a torta with a *cochinita*

pibil (a pork-based dish) filling or some other meat filling. The food can be purchased at a market stand near his place of work. This is an important time to share experiences with fellow employees, although some comment that it is not healthy because of the high fat content in food eaten during this early morning recess.

If it is Monday, his midday meal will probably be a dish of beans with pork (*frijol con puerco*), as this is the typical Monday menu in middle- and upper-class homes and restaurants in Mérida. The dish may be accompanied by a vegetable soup, rice and tortillas or bread, and fruit-based water or a soft drink. The evening meal, taken at home or at a nearby restaurant, may consist of a Yucatecan antojito such as panuchos (small bean-stuffed tortillas, fried and topped with shredded chicken, pork, or turkey and pickled red onions), served with Yucatecan hot sauce. A dark Yucatecan beer usually accompanies this dish.

In northern Mexico a cattle rancher may begin his day with a hearty plateful of *machaca con huevos,* which is dried and shredded beef fried with tomatoes, onions, and green chili peppers and cooked with scrambled eggs. The dish may be served with pinto beans (*frijoles charros*), flour tortillas, and a mug of strong, black coffee. If he is in Monterrey for lunch, he may be served a cheese soup (*caldo de queso*), pickled shrimp (*camarones en escabeche*), and broiled kid (*cabrito al pastor*) with guacamole, onion, tomato, cilantro, and chili peppers and served with pot beans (frijoles de olla) sprinkled with cheese and *pico de gallo* sauce. A good selection to accompany this meal would be a cold Bohemia beer.

The evening meal would no doubt include a broiled strip of beef (*carne a la tampiqueña*) served with red enchiladas, beans, and guacamole, to be washed down with another cold Monterrey beer. Northern Mexican men are noted beef eaters and beer drinkers.

Frijoles con Tequila (Beans with Tequila)

Traditionally, *frijoles borrachos* (drunken beans) are made with beer and pieces of pork and bacon. In this recipe, tequila replaces the beer and is added twice—during the last stage of cooking and again just before serving.

1 lb pinto beans

10 c water

3 tbsp lard

1 tbsp salt

1 medium onion, chopped

1½ c tomatoes, seeded and chopped

4 serrano chilies

½ c tequila

2 tbsp chopped cilantro

Simmer the beans covered with water with 1 tablespoon of lard for about 2 hours or until soft (or cook them in a pressure cooker). Add 1 tablespoon salt after the first hour. Drain the water from the beans, reserving 1 cup of the broth.

Heat the remaining 2 tablespoons of lard in a large pot over high heat until it starts to smoke. Add the onion, tomatoes, chilies, and a little salt. Cook until the fat rises to the surface and the vegetables are soft, about 10 minutes. Add the beans and cook for 5 minutes, stirring constantly. Add the reserved broth and half the tequila. Continue cooking until almost all of the liquid has evaporated. Just before serving, add the remaining tequila and sprinkle cilantro leaves over the top.

Oaxaca is a gourmet's paradise. It is famous for serving seven different types of mole, and all are exceptionally good. One of the best places to try traditional Oaxacan food is in the main market, which begins serving meals very early in the morning. Clients sit at long, rustic wooden tables, covered with plastic tablecloths, with other clientele. There is nothing exclusive about eating in the Oaxaca market. A breakfast menu usually begins with fresh orange juice, followed by roasted cheese in green sauce (*quesillo oaxaqueño*); black turtle beans seasoned with avocado leaves, which gives them a distinctive flavor; large, hot corn tortillas called *tlayudas;* and coffee with brown sugar and cinnamon or hot chocolate. Oaxaca produces a variety of sweet rolls,

which are also favorite breakfast items. Lunch at the same market may include a cactus paddle and shrimp soup (*caldillo de nopales y camarón*) or an appetizer of tacos, made of corn tortillas filled with Oaxaca cheese and a sauce. Fried-grasshopper tacos with guacamole are also a favorite first course. Pork in yellow mole sauce is also popular, simply called *amarillo* (yellow) due to the yellow chili, *chilcoztli,* used to prepare it. Black beans usually accompany this dish. The meal may end with ice cream, for which Oaxaca is famous, and black coffee. The evening meal in Oaxaca is often Oaxacan tamales wrapped in banana leaves and served with atole or hot chocolate.

Mexican food is hearty and not for those who are watching their weight. Much of the food is fried and has a high calorie content, and ample portions are served. This is reflected in the obesity problem, which may contribute to diabetes and has become a serious health problem in the country.

Eating Out

Good food and good cooking have become fashionable in Mexico in recent years. The number of eating places, from simple *taquerías* that offer unpretentious fare to elaborate, upscale restaurants, where clients gather both to eat fine food and to see and be seen, have increased 10-fold since the early 1980s. In the past few years Mexico City has become a gourmet's delight.

The number of food stalls, taquerías, *torterías,* fondas, *loncherías,* cafés, and elegant restaurants catering to different social and economic levels is truly prodigious. Until the economic crisis of 2008–2009, people were increasingly eating outside the home, because women's increasing involvement in the labor force gives them less time and energy to spend in the kitchen.

Street foods play an important role in providing food for a large percentage of the Mexican population. Mexico has a long tradition in selling street food, which is food and drink sold on public streets, ready for consumption, and offered by nonpermanent sellers. Long before the arrival of the Spanish conquistadores, Aztec vendors were setting up their stalls in the Tlatelolco Market to serve the public. They sold a variety of stews, sauces, insects, fish dishes, and tortillas, prepared daily for the buyers and sellers of the great market. This custom continued throughout colonial times and is now more prevalent than ever. It also reflects the unemployment and underemployment Mexico City is experiencing due to the economic crisis.

Street food offers a good option for those workers who cannot afford to eat in a restaurant or fonda, as they sell inexpensive food with fast service. Street foods are sold on city corners, in markets, outside bus or train stations, in public parks, near factories or office buildings, or wherever there are plenty of people looking for a good, quick lunch. The preferred type of food sold in the stands is typical Mexican food such as tacos that can be eaten with the fingers, so no cutlery is needed. Some offer a complete meal of soup, served in a cup, with a meat stew, Mexican red rice, beans, and tortillas, served on a plastic plate. A soft drink, to be drunk straight out of the bottle, and a hot chili sauce complete the meal. This type of food is nutritious, filling, and probably cheaper than a housewife could prepare at home.

Fondas are another option for eating away from home. They are small, inexpensive restaurants that cater to office workers and set up their establishments near office buildings or wherever large groups of potential customers congregate. Many offer fixed menus, posted at the entrance. These usually include a soup, pasta or rice, tacos, enchiladas, beef stew or stuffed vegetables, and a simple dessert. These small restaurants are quite economical if one considers the amount of food received.

Mexican markets sell almost all of life's necessities, including good food. Market food stands open early for breakfast but really get into full swing about 10:30, when the almuerzo crowd arrives. They offer good, simple, inexpensive food such as tostadas, tacos, hearty broths, meat, eggs, and fruits and

A fast food stall in Papantla, Mexico specializing in antojitos. (StockPhotoPro)

fruit juice. One gets good value for one's money at a market stand.

Tacos are Mexico's favorite fast food. They can be eaten at any time of day and are sold in all types of eateries or in taquerías that specialize in tacos and other corn-based *botanas* or antojitos. Tortas are the Mexican equivalent of sandwiches, made with a hard roll called a *telera,* sliced horizontally and stuffed with a variety of fillings. Special restaurants called torterías prepare and sell thousands of tortas every day to people who must eat outside their homes. Tortas are also sold in baskets on the street, at bus stations, or near subway stations. They are an easy-to-eat finger food.

In recent decades Mexico City has become a cosmopolitan city where restaurants that specialize in food from all parts of the world can be found. Asian, African, Mediterranean, Caribbean, South American, European, North American, Middle Eastern, and Mexican restaurants abound throughout the city. Japanese sushi bars have become very popular in the past decade. Japan is also represented by fine restaurants that charge according to their status. French-style bistros are also popular eating places. Peruvian food has been discovered by the Mexican public, and the city has several fine Peruvian restaurants. Many restaurants belong to consortiums, with several restaurants, which may be owned by the same group of investors, sharing publicity and other expenses. There are a few top-notch restaurants that specialize in serving fine Mexican food. These are no doubt the finest Mexican restaurants in the world.

Special Occasions

Mexicans love a good fiesta and readily admit to being a fun-loving people when they say, "Somos muy fiesteros" (We are a very festive people). They have many opportunities to celebrate throughout the year, as the Mexican calendar is full of official, unofficial, and religious holidays. Rite-of-passage fiestas such as baptisms, first communions, coming-out parties for 15-year-olds, weddings, and funerals, as well as birthdays, saint's days, graduation parties, and fiestas on many other occasions give one a good

panorama of Mexican social life. The fiesta cycle can be considered one of Mexico's most distinctive cultural traits. Some festive occasions have become customary throughout the country and are considered national fiestas. These may coincide with religious or civic fiestas.

Rite-of-passage celebrations are carried out on a personal or family level. These include the baptism ceremony, confirmation in the Catholic Church, first communion events, coming-out parties for young girls when they turn 15, weddings, and funerals.

Some religious fiestas involve the participation of the entire community. Rural harvest festivals are held in early autumn, when most agricultural produce is harvested or harvests are about to begin. The rural population may give thanks for a particularly good harvest or ask for the protection of their crops until they can be gathered. To these activities, one must add a list of civic fiestas such as the Day of the Constitution, celebrated on February 5; the Battle of Puebla on May 5 (i.e., Cinco de Mayo); Independence Day festivities on September 15 and 16; and the Day of the Revolution, on November 20.

Food and drink are important elements in the fiesta cycle. Specific dishes may be associated with certain celebrations and are traditionally served at those functions. Typical fiesta dishes include tamales in all shapes, sizes, and flavors; a variety of mole dishes served with turkey, chicken, or pork; a codfish stew called *bacalao*; poblano-type chili peppers stuffed with chopped meat and dried-fruit stuffing and topped with a nut sauce, called *chiles en nogada*; barbecued kid, lamb, and beef; a pork and hominy dish called *pozole*; and many, many others.

When food is prepared for a community fiesta, the responsibility is shared by several members of the community. Every family in the community has to pay their share of the fiesta; if they do not cooperate, they are ostracized by the rest of the community. Festive food may depend on the customs of the particular region of the country preparing the celebration. It also depends on the economic resources of the participants and the social level of those involved.

One of Mexico's most colorful fiestas marks the Day of the Dead (Día de los Muertos) on November

1 and 2. It is one of the most important rituals in the Mexican fiesta cycle. It can best be described as a festival to welcome the return of the souls of the dead and provide them with the pleasures they enjoyed during their lifetimes. The fiesta incorporates elements of pre-Hispanic religious beliefs and practices, which differentiates it from other more orthodox Catholic fiestas on All Saints' and All Souls' Day. In Mexico, it is celebrated like in no other Catholic country in the world.

A unique bread called *pan de muerto* (bread of the dead) is baked especially for this occasion. It is generally a round, domed loaf with extra dough filleted on top in the shape of a head and extremities to symbolize a skeleton. Breads are also produced in the shape of skeletons and ghosts.

The Day of the Dead is essentially a private or family affair, as the core of the celebration is carried out within the family and takes place in the family home or at the family plot in the cemetery. Each household prepares its offerings of food and drink for their dead, which traditionally consist of the deceased person's favorite dishes. A temporary altar is set up on a table where the food is served in clay dishes, along with vases of marigolds (*cempasúchil*), white candles, and photographs of the dead and of the saint to which they were devoted. Small dishes of salt, glasses of water, and a plate of incense sanctify the ceremony. Hollow skulls made of sugar paste display the name of the dead person across the forehead.

November 1 is the day to celebrate children, particularly those who died during the year. The ringing of church bells on October 31 at 8 P.M. announces the arrival of the "spirits of the children." By this time altars have been set up where the food

Offerings being sold as part of the celebration of the Day of the Dead or Dia de los Meurtos, Mexico City, Mexico. (Jesús Eloy Ramos Lara | Dreamstime.com)

Sugar skulls are seen in a store window in Mexico City as part of celebrations for its Days of the Dead beginning on October 31. (AFP | Getty Images)

is placed. This consists of Day of the Dead bread, sweet tamales, fruit, ears of corn, atole, milk, candied pumpkin, and fruit jam, accompanied by yellow marigolds and sugar skulls. Fast foods, such as potato chips, Doritos, Coca-Cola, candy, and cookies, as well as plastic toys, may also be placed on the children's altars, demonstrating the change in the diet of Mexican children.

The main ceremony is held on November 2, when the souls of the adults are celebrated and given the most splendid offering the family can afford. Tamales are always included, as is a loaf of Day of the Dead bread and chicken or turkey in a mole sauce. Other dishes may include enchiladas and *chalupas* (small boat-shaped tortillas filled with beans and hot sauce), or other favorite dishes. Beverages range from coffee, chocolate, and atole to whatever alcohol the deceased preferred. A bottle of beer or a shot glass of tequila or *mezcal* (a distilled liquor from Oaxaca) will form part of the offering. If the person was a smoker, a package of his favorite cigarettes will be included. There is an element of pride and status in providing an elaborate offering for relatives.

The deceased's souls are believed to be present as spirits who have returned from the other world. The spirits are not seen; however, their presence is sensed. They do not physically consume the food and drinks but rather absorb their essence. When the souls have had their fill, it will be the turn of the living members of the family to share the offering. Some of the food will be taken to the cemetery to be placed on the graves of the deceased and consumed by family members at the grave site. Sometimes a path of marigold petals is laid out to lead the souls to their proper destination in the cemetery. The sight of thousands of candles lighting up the night cemetery on November 2 is indeed impressive.

Federal and city governments and cultural organizations now promote the celebration of the Day of the Dead as a way for Mexicans to express their identity. Contests are organized by these groups to encourage the population to set up altars in town squares, markets, or public buildings, and a prize is often awarded the most well-made display. Banks, hotels, supermarkets, public buildings, businesses, and cultural organizations have begun to offer a display of the altar of the dead to stress their commitment to this most Mexican of all customs. This celebration is not disappearing; rather, it is becoming more and more important in Mexican cultural life.

Diet and Health

Mexico is a country of profound and often conflicting contrasts. At the same time as government and health officials attempt to cope with malnutrition and anemia in rural Mexico, one in every three adults in urban Mexico is overweight, making obesity the most serious health problem in the country today. Solving the problems of malnutrition and anemia is proving to be easier to resolve than obesity, which has risen to epidemic levels during the past decade.

Mexican food habits have changed substantially in the past few years. Nutritionists have observed an increase in the consumption of wheat products, replacing corn, in the form of breads, cereals, pastas, cookies, and pastries. This is in part caused by the transition from a rural to an urban diet due to the heavy migration from the countryside to urban areas during the past few decades. The general availability of refined, high-fat, and high-sugar products in urban areas makes fast-food products convenient purchases.

The new products available on the market, introduced by the North American Free Trade Agreement in 1994, often replace rather than complement Mexican ingredients in the diet. The increased participation of women in the labor force results in less time for women to prepare family meals and forces them to rely on ready-made foods, which may be higher in fats and simple carbohydrates than home-made meals. There is also a tendency to accept the new food imports because of their higher status compared to the traditional diet, especially for those at middle and high income levels. The external influence is less dramatic on rural diets; however, the migration of undocumented Mexican laborers to the United States has proved detrimental to the rural diet as well, when workers return with a preference for diets high in animal fats and sugars. The frequency of obesity, diabetes, and cardiovascular problems as a result of the change to a more refined diet high in fats and sugars can be observed in both urban as well as rural Mexico.

For several decades, the Mexican government has carried out various programs in an attempt to improve the diet and nutrition of the Mexican population. These have included changes in economic policies, control of food prices, subsidies for the production of food, retail sale of government-subsidized foods, and programs of food distribution. These include free primary-school breakfasts in rural schools and food boxes or baskets containing products that make up the basic diet.

One of the most noted deficiencies in the Mexican diet at all social levels is iron, which reflects an inadequate diet. This has been shown to cause anemia in both children and expectant mothers, as well as retarded growth patterns in children. School-age children who are affected by an iron deficiency show less interest in learning, a reduced attention span, and chronic fatigue. Anemia is more prevalent in rural Mexico than in urban communities.

Nutrients have been added to industrialized food products in the form of vitamins and minerals since 1987 in an effort to improve the Mexican diet. The addition of vitamins and minerals to both wheat and corn flour plays an important role in the Mexican diet, as many products are made from these basic ingredients.

Obesity represents the most serious health problem in Mexico today. One in every three urban adults in Mexico is overweight or obese, and the prediction is for these numbers to continue rising for both children and adults in coming years. The increase in excessive weight and obesity is associated with chronic diseases such as type 2 diabetes mellitus, hypertension, atherosclerosis, high cholesterol, certain types of cancer, cardiovascular diseases, and orthopedic, respiratory, and psychological problems. Coping with the health costs that result from obesity is a heavy burden for the Mexican health system to carry. Thirty percent of obesity is attributed to cultural factors, such as the high-fat diet popular in Mexico and a general lack of discipline in food habits. Soft drinks, such as Coca-Cola and Pepsi, contribute heavily to obesity, because Mexicans drink on average more than a 12-ounce can of soda every day. Forty-five percent of the cases of obesity are attributed to nontransmissible environmental factors. The consumption of processed foods with a high oil content and of simple and refined carbohydrates, with less fiber and complex carbohydrates, plays a role in the surge in obesity.

Recent statistics indicate that 10.75 percent of Mexicans between the ages of 20 and 69 are afflicted by some type of diabetes mellitus, which is equivalent to more than 5.5 million persons. Almost 23 percent of those affected with diabetes are unaware they have the illness. It is one of the principal causes of death in Mexico, along with cardiovascular problems and cancer. Obesity has become one of the major factors in the risk of acquiring the disease. A diet high in carbohydrates, lack of exercise, excess weight, chronic stress, and inheritance all play a role in the disease.

Anorexia is a growing problem in Mexico and has increased considerably in the past five years. It is more prevalent among young women than in young men and affects mostly young people between the ages of 11 and 25. Food deprivation is not a novelty in Mexico. It was common behavior in Catholic convents, where food was considered a spiritual element that converted eating into a ritual act. The convent dining room was a space of penitence and purification, where food was transformed into something sacred through which the nuns could expunge their sins and purify their spirits. Fasting and penitence were methods by which they attempted to attain purification of their bodies and souls. To leave a morsel of their favorite dish on their plate for the guardian angel was considered a manifestation of high spirituality.

Janet Long-Solís

Further Reading

Carmichael, E., and C. Sayer. *The Skeleton at the Feast: The Day of the Dead in Mexico.* Austin: University of Texas Press, 1992.

Coe, S. *America's First Cuisines.* Austin: University of Texas Press, 1994.

Long, J., ed. *Conquista y Comida: Consecuencias del encuentro de dos mundos.* Mexico City: Universidad Nacional Autónoma de México, 1996.

Long-Solís, Janet. *Food Culture in Mexico.* Westport, CT: Greenwood Press, 2005.

Ortiz de Montellano, B. *Aztec Medicine, Health and Nutrition.* New Brunswick, NJ: Rutgers University Press, 1990.

Pelto, G., and L. A. Vargas, eds. "Introduction to Dietary Change and Nutrition." *Ecology of Food and Nutrition* 27, No. 3–4 (1992): 159–61.

Pilcher, J. *¡Que vivan los tamales! Food and the Making of Mexican Identity.* Albuquerque: University of New Mexico Press, 1998.

Super, J. C. *Food, Conquest and Colonization in Sixteenth-Century Spanish America.* Albuquerque: University of New Mexico Press, 1988.

Vargas, L. A., and L. Casillas. "Diet and Foodways in Mexico City." *Ecology of Food and Nutrition* 27, No. 3–4 (1992): 135–48.

Native Americans

Overview

The term *Native American* encompasses an extremely broad spectrum of peoples spread across the various regions of the United States; it is therefore impossible to speak of Native Americans as one monolithic entity or cultural group. Among the thousands of extant tribes in America are the Iroquois (Six Nations) of upstate New York; the Narragansetts, Micmacs, Pequots, and Mohegans of the northeastern United States; the Plains tribes, including the Blackfoot, Lakota, Sioux, Comanche, Apache, Pawnee, Wichita, and Osage; the Navajo, Hopi, and Pueblo in the Southwest; the Coeur d'Alene and Nez Perce in the Pacific Northwest; the Paiutes in the West; the Cherokees, Seminoles, and Choctaws of the Southeast; the Caddo of Texas and Louisiana; and the Inuits and Tlingits in Alaska. Additionally, the term *Native American* can also apply to the First Nations people of Canada and the various peoples of Central and South America.

Therefore, when speaking of Native American foodways, it is necessary to take each tribe's regional ecosystem into account, as food procurement and preparation, agricultural methods, and hunting techniques vary widely depending on each tribe's geographic location. However, one could argue that traditional Native American foodways of any stripe should serve as the model for locavorism, as much of their food practices are tied inextricably to their natural surroundings.

🍽 Food Culture Snapshot

Lucinda Crow is a 48-year-old Ojibwe who lives in northern Minnesota. She was recently diagnosed with diabetes, and her doctor has stressed the importance of changing her diet in order to manage this disease. Like 70 percent of Native Americans, Lucinda is overweight, which likely contributed to her developing diabetes. As she faces her important and very necessary lifestyle change, Lucinda must reconsider every meal and snack of every day.

Rather than purchase a box of pricey sugary cereal for her breakfasts, Lucinda instead chooses a box of plain oatmeal. With its high fiber content and low glycemic index, the oatmeal will keep Lucinda satisfied longer and keep her blood sugar in check. She also purchases some bananas and skim milk to round out a nutritious and diabetes-friendly breakfast.

Lucinda is a schoolteacher on her reservation, so she needs to pack healthy, filling lunches to take with her to work. She used to take microwavable frozen dinners, which are full of fat, salt, and unhealthy fillers. These days, she chooses a loaf or two of multigrain bread, some lean turkey lunch meat, some low-fat cottage cheese, a head of lettuce, carrots for a crunchy alternative to potato chips, and some apples or other seasonal fruit for a sweet finish to her meal.

For dinner, Lucinda plans balanced meals featuring a lean protein, at least one green vegetable, and a grain. Where she once would have purchased frozen potpies and pizzas, Lucinda instead buys salmon and chicken breasts, broccoli, and brown rice. The days of white breads and pastas are behind her now, as are prepackaged, processed desserts like cupcakes and brownies. If Lucinda wants a sweet treat, she purchases a low-fat frozen yogurt to enjoy in moderation.

Many Native Americans find that they have limited access to fresh foods, their choices circumscribed because their reservations are somewhat isolated. Often, grocery shopping takes place at convenience stores, supplemented with government-subsidy foods like cheese and beans. However, with careful planning and scrupulous attention to details like portion control, Native Americans like Lucinda can eat healthfully for life.

Major Foodstuffs

After a long, complicated, and painful history including displacement onto reservations and forced integration into mainstream America, most Native American tribes eat the same diet as non-Natives, like soft drinks, pizza, and so on. However, many Native American tribes have a particular food item that is integral not only to their diet but also to their tribal identities, reaching back to precontact times; this section provides an overview of some of these significant food items.

It is widely understood that, regardless of region or tribal affiliation, the most important Native American foodstuff is corn (maize). Many tribal origin stories, particularly among the southeastern tribes, feature the Corn Woman, who is responsible for the continued presence of corn on the American landscape. The foodstuffs most commonly associated with Native American foodways are the Three Sisters: corn, beans, and squash. The primary agricultural technique for these crops is companion planting, in which the three crops are planted in clusters on mounds, with corn occupying the central spot in the mound. The stalks provide poles for the climbing beans, while the squash plants spread out along the bottom of the mound to help prevent weeds; the squash leaves also act as mulch for the companion mound. Expert farming tribes include the Hopi and the Navajo in the Southwest and the Cherokee in the Southeast.

A traditional set-up for growing the Three Sisters—corn, beans, and squash—is utilized in this Cherokee garden. (Marilyn Angel Wynn | Nativestock.com)

The Ojibwe of the Great Lakes region rely on fishing, growing squash and maize, and cultivating *manoomin* (wild rice, which is actually a grass rather than a grain). Manoomin is an important part of the Anishinaabe (the larger umbrella group of Native peoples to which the Ojibwe belong) migration stories, in addition to being a dietary staple, a commodity to be sold, and a vital component of sacred ceremonies. Manoomin is native to the Great Lakes region and is harvested by canoe. Ricers bend the stalks of the rice plants over the side of the canoe and knock the ripe grains loose. After it is harvested, the rice is dried, roasted, and then "danced" in a process reminiscent of grape stomping in order to remove the husks.

Winnebago Wild Rice

1 c wild rice

1½ tsp salt

2½ c water

4 strips bacon

6 eggs

¼ tsp pepper

⅓ c melted butter or bacon fat

Put rice, 1 teaspoon salt, and water in a saucepan. Bring to a boil and reduce heat to a simmer until all water is absorbed. Cook bacon until crisp, and break into small pieces. Beat eggs with ½ teaspoon salt and pepper until fluffy. Cook eggs in the same skillet where the bacon was cooked. Combine bacon, eggs, and butter or bacon fat with wild rice. Serve warm.

Chokecherries are another plant-based staple in Native American foodways, particularly for the Plains tribes; they were especially important to the Blackfoot and Cheyenne. The cherries were pounded out, seeds included, then dried in the sun.

The Iroquois (Six Nations), based primarily in upstate New York, are credited with discovering the edible properties of maple syrup as early as the 1600s. One tribal legend credits the discovery of the sap to Chief Woksis, who, in frustration at having failed to successfully hunt for his family's food, threw his tomahawk into a tree, which caused sap to flow into his water bucket. His wife mistook the sap for water and used it to cook deer meat, which lent it a sweet taste and made the chief realize what had actually been in his pail. In actuality, the Iroquois likely discovered maple syrup by eating frozen icicles hanging from the sugar maple trees on their lands. They would set up winter sugaring camps amid groves of sugar maple trees and devote the cold months to harvesting the sap. To procure the sap, they would cut V-shaped slashes into the trees and collect the sap in a vessel of some sort. They would boil down the sap into solid hunks of maple sugar, which they would then use to season grains or to sweeten water for a special drink; they would also use the sugar for gifts or to trade.

Many Native American tribes have diets comprising mainly hunted proteins like fish and game. For example, the Inuit of Alaska and the Northwest Territories of Canada eat a very protein- and fat-heavy diet comprising whales, walrus, caribou, and seals. In fact, the seal is a prized catch for the Inuit, in that its meat is a valuable source of fat, iron, and vitamins A and B_{12}; additionally, the pelt provides much-needed warmth in the bitterly cold winter months. While seal hunting is an extremely controversial topic in Western culture, the Inuits' practices are protected in governmental bans and proscriptions against commercial seal hunting. When an Inuit boy kills his first seal or caribou, a feast is held in his honor.

The Salish (or Coast Salish) peoples of Oregon, Washington, and western Canada relied primarily on fishing but also maintained inland grasslands, which provided a variety of small game animals, as well as vegetables, roots, berries, and ferns such as bracken. Salmon and a freshwater fish called *kakanee* were staples, as well as shellfish like clams and cockles. The Salish hunted in the sea, air, and land for whale, fowl, and game.

The Tlingit of southern Alaska and the Yukon have a saying, "When the tide goes out, the table is set," which illustrates this people's heavy reliance on the sea for their primary diet. Among the foods available for harvest on the beach are razor clams, mussels, seaweed, oysters, and crabs. However, to eat "beach food" exclusively is to earn the contempt of tribesmen and is considered a sign of poverty. Salmon is the central foodstuff of the Tlingit, with seal and game closely following. To provide their bodies with essential vitamins and minerals alongside the protein found in the fish and game, the Tlingit eat every part of the animal; bones used in soup stock supply calcium as well as vitamin D and iron. Stomachs and intestines provide vitamin E and the vitamins in the B complex. Vitamin C can be found in plant matter. The Tlingit are also very fond of packaged and processed food like Spam and ice cream.

Bison was the primary game for the nomadic tribes among the Plains Indians; their weapon of

Buffalo meat dries at an Arapaho camp near Fort Dodge, Kansas in 1870. Once an agricultural people, the Arapaho migrated from Minnesota to the Great Plains in the late 1700s, when they began to hunt buffalo. (National Archives)

choice in hunting bison was the bow and arrow. Bison were a major source of several usable goods for tribes like the Blackfoot and the Sioux. In addition to being a primary source of food, the animals provided warmth, clothing, and shoes from their pelts; the makings of knives, arrowheads, and tools from their bones; and material for cups, rattles, ornaments, and switches from the horns, hooves, and tails. The edible parts of the bison such as the meat, bone marrow, tongue, liver, blood, and intestines were either cooked into a stew, using the stomach as a cooking vessel, and eaten right away, or preserved and made into jerky. Unfortunately, the U.S.

government began hunting bison, which numbered around 60 million, and encouraged commercial hunters to do the same in the 19th century (approximately 1872–1874) as a means of starving the Natives into extinction. Thousands of bison carcasses, stripped of their pelts, were left rotting on the plains, rendered worthless to the Natives who relied on them so heavily for food, trade, and culture. Only a few hundred bison remained in North America by the late 19th century; thanks to the efforts of a few private ranchers in the West and northern Plains states, the American bison was brought back from the brink of extinction. In fact, bison meat has become very popular, praised for its low fat content and nutritional qualities.

Buffalo Stew (Lakota)

Ingredients

Buffalo stew meat, cut into bite-sized chunks

Tsinpsila (prairie turnips)

Onions, sliced

Get a large pot and put in the meat, tsinpsila, and onions. Cover with water and boil until done.

Pemmican was another important foodstuff for Native American tribes, especially as the winter months or long hunts approached. The primary ingredient was lean meat from large game animals like elk, bison, or deer. The meat was cut into thin slices and dried until brittle. It was then pounded into a powder and mixed with melted fat; some recipes included dried and powdered cranberries, while blueberries, cherries, and/or chokeberries were used exclusively in ceremonial pemmican. The mixture was stored in rawhide pouches; if stored correctly, pemmican could last for very long periods.

The Caddo Indians of Texas and Louisiana were farmers who cultivated the Three Sisters crops. Additionally, the women would gather wild plant matter like blackberries, persimmons, and acorns while the men would hunt small game like deer, turkey, and rabbits in their local area. The men would also gather periodic hunting parties to hunt buffalo in the west.

Perhaps the most legible edible reminder of the troubled relationship between the Native peoples and the settlers is the Navajo fry bread. Many tribes have their own recipes for fry bread, but the Navajos are credited with inventing this beloved treat with a sad history. In the summer of 1863, the U.S. Army failed to elicit surrender from the Navajos, who had been raiding army forts that had infiltrated their lands in eastern Arizona and western New Mexico. The army then scorched the areas surrounding Navajo lands in order to starve the Natives and force them to surrender; the tactic worked, and thousands of Navajos surrendered. In January 1864, the army began a series of long walks from Navajo territory to the Bosque Redondo camp near Fort Sumner in southeastern New Mexico. Hundreds of Navajos died on these long walks. While they were interred in Bosque Redondo, the government supplied the Navajos with commodity foods like flour, lard, powdered milk, salt, sugar, and baking powder; the Navajo made fry bread out of these ingredients. It was adopted and adapted by many southwestern tribes and is now a common foodstuff found at powwows and restaurants across the Southwest, in addition to being a potent symbol of Indian solidarity and perseverance. Native author Sherman Alexie has said, "Frybread is the story of our survival."

Fry bread is the foundation of the Navajo or Indian taco, which contains a combination of beans or ground beef, chopped lettuce, tomatoes, and cheese, with green chili as an optional topping. After the fillings are added, diners roll up the plate-sized fry bread and eat the taco with their hands.

Fry Bread

4 c flour

2 tbsp baking powder

1 tbsp powdered milk

1 tsp salt

1 tsp cinnamon (optional)

½ c shortening

1 c warm water

Mix flour, baking powder, powdered milk, salt, and cinnamon. Add in the shortening and water gradually, until the dough sticks together. Knead dough until smooth, and make into large balls. Roll or pat them out into circles about the size of a small plate. Fry in hot cooking oil until brown on both sides. Drain on paper towels or blot to remove excess grease.

First Nations people know fry bread as bannock, and it does not carry the same political and cultural weight as it does for peoples like the Navajo.

Cooking

Native American women, regardless of tribe or geographic location, were tasked with the job of preparing food, in addition to gathering berries, plants, and roots for their families. They were extremely innovative in the wide variety of dishes they concocted out of maize, including mixing it with meat, fish, nuts, maple syrup, and berries. They did this using a variety of different cooking vessels and tools.

Common cooking utensils and tools included tongs, stirring sticks and paddles, ladles, and scrapers, often made from the horns and antlers of hunted game. *Metates* are flat surfaces used to break down grains, and mortars and pestles (called *molcajetes* in Central and South America) are still used today to grind herbs and spices, as well as maize; they were even sometimes used on meats.

One central cooking vessel was the kettle, as boiling was a primary preparation technique. Boiling took place either over a direct fire or by placing extremely hot stones into a kettle along with the food to be cooked. Sometimes the kettle was edible; as previously mentioned, the stomach of the bison could be used as a cooking vessel and then consumed along with the stew that was cooked in it. Other types of cooking vessels included clay bowls in the Southwest and tightly woven baskets among the southwestern Apache and the northwestern tribes.

Cherokee Succotash

2 lb fresh or dry lima beans

3 qt water

3 c fresh corn cut from cob

2 pieces smoked ham hock

Salt to taste

Pepper to taste (optional)

4–6 onions (wild or pearl)

2 tbsp melted bacon fat

Soak beans, if using dry ones, for 3–4 hours. Bring the water to a boil, then add the beans. Cook at a moderate boil for 10 minutes, then add the corn, ham hocks, salt and pepper, and onions. Add the bacon fat. Reduce heat, and cook for 1 hour on low heat.

Hopi (Arizona) women used a special griddle called a *piki* stone to prepare their revered blue-corn *piki* bread. Women prepared the stone in individualized rituals involving smoothing it with gravel and moistening it with cottonseed oil; it was then placed on four legs over a fire. The stone was handed down through generations, just as many women pass on their cast iron skillets to their daughters and granddaughters. The piki was made in a special house that contained the stone. The women would combine the blue maize meal, hot water, and ash, knead this into a batter, and then smear the batter toward their bodies across the hot piki stone. After a short time, the bread was ready, and it was peeled off the stone, rolled up like a crepe, then stacked and stored. A woman who was skilled in making piki was held in very high regard, much as a talented male hunter would be.

Because corn is still a central cultural and dietary staple for many Native American peoples, certain preparation rituals are still observed, such as roasting corn. At harvest time, Native Americans will dig a pit in the ground, which is then lined with rocks. They then burn wood on top of the rocks until it is reduced to embers and cover the embers with corn husks and stalks. They then place ears of corn on this heated bed, cover up the ears with more husks and stalks, pour water on the pit, bury it, and leave it for several hours. Southwestern Native Americans are credited with developing the process of making popcorn out of maize.

The Aztecs and Mayans of Mexico are credited with developing the process of nixtamalization, which is soaking corn in lime. This process breaks down the walls of the corn kernels and makes the protein inside more accessible. Once those thick walls have been broken down, the kernels can be ground into meal, which is then used in tortillas, tamales, cornbread, and so on.

Baking was another commonly employed cooking technique. The *horno* is an adobe oven used by Native peoples in the Southwest to bake breads, roast corn, and cook meats. It is shaped like a beehive and is heated by wood. To prepare the oven for use, the wood is burned until the horno has reached the appropriate cooking temperature. The embers are removed, and the bread is inserted. For preparing meats, the oven is brought to about 650 degrees Fahrenheit, the embers are moved to the back of the oven, and the meat is placed inside. Because the oven is made from adobe (dried mud), it is a naturally moist environment and results in tender, succulent, juicy meat.

Some Native peoples also steamed their food; in fact, the clambake is often attributed to certain tribes in Massachusetts who steamed their clams in large rock circles within which the mollusks were layered with rockweed (a type of seaweed) and heated until the clams broke open and steamed in their own juices.

Native Americans had to develop many methods of food preservation in anticipation of lean times and winter months. Drying food by laying it out in the sun or placing it close to a fire was the most common preservation method. Meat that wasn't consumed at the site of a successful hunt or fishing expedition was dried right away for later consumption. In the Pacific Northwest, women dried huckleberries for year-round use to sweeten various dishes and bitter plants. Smoking was also used to preserve meat, particularly salmon in the Pacific Northwest. In the Northeast, Native people preserved meats by sprinkling salt on fish or game and drying it near a fire. Other East Coast and Northern Plains tribes

A Pueblo woman in San Juan Pueblo, New Mexico, bakes bread in an adobe oven. (Marilyn Angel Wynn | Nativestock.com)

used the vinegar produced from fermented maple syrup to preserve venison.

Typical Meals

Due to the nearly complete assimilation of Native Americans into mainstream American culture, despite the geographic isolation of many reservations, the typical Native American meal looks identical to the average meal of a low-income family. (This is not to suggest that all Native Americans are of low socioeconomic status but to speak to the realities of life on the typical contemporary Native American reservation.) Portion sizes are typically very large, with fat intake between 30 and 40 percent of dietary calories. Typical foods are low in fiber and extremely heavy in refined carbohydrates and starchy vegetables like potatoes.

Breakfast begins much like any other American morning, with a bowl of cereal like Cheerios or Cocoa Puffs, or fried eggs with processed meats and coffee. Lunch might consist of a sandwich on white bread with Spam or lunch meat, cookies, chips, perhaps a can of fruit cocktail, and a sweetened soda to drink. For dinner, the menu might consist of a taco made with flour tortillas or fry bread, or macaroni with canned vegetables.

Where traditional Native American foodways once consisted of wild game, foraged wild greens, cultivated gourds, and other fruits, the reservation and government-subsidy systems have dramatically altered Native American lifestyles and effected a profound loss of culture, as reflected in their contemporary eating habits. The emphasis on processed foods devoid of proper nutrition, along with a shift away from a highly physically active to a largely sedentary lifestyle, has contributed to what might be described as an epidemic of obesity and obesity-related diseases among Native American and First Nations populations in the United States and Canada.

Eating Out

Most Native Americans who do not live in remote, rural areas practice the same dining-out habits as other Americans. They are just as likely to go to

McDonald's or any other restaurant as any other American. Most Native food is shared at home, but even then, more mainstream fare populates the plate. While Native American culture is not a restaurant culture per se, a number of restaurants across the country specialize in and focus on Native American foods, from dives in the Arizona desert to grilled seafood in the Pacific Northwest to fine dining in Santa Fe.

The Frybread House in downtown Phoenix is owned and operated by members of the Tohono O'odham tribe, and it specializes in various iterations of fry bread and Indian tacos. Diners can order fry bread loaded with refried beans, green or red chili beef, or chorizo, topped with lettuce, tomato, and cheese. Also on the menu is a variety of stews, including the ubiquitous southwestern specialty, green chili; hominy stew; and menudo. Dessert options include fry bread drizzled with honey or chocolate and butter. The average price for menu items is $6.

Also found in Phoenix is Kai, a fine-dining restaurant located in the upscale Sheraton Wild Horse Pass resort on the Gila River Indian Community reservation. Taking its name from the Pima word for "seed," Kai features Native ingredients, honoring the local Pima and Maricopa tribes and emphasizing sustainability via produce and other ingredients sourced from the Gila River Indian Community farms. The menu is presented in oral tradition and storytelling terms: Appetizers are labeled "The Birth," salads are named "The Beginning," and entrées, which range in price from $39 to $52, are "The Journey." The tasting menu, priced at $140, is called "Short Story."

Across the country at the National Museum of the American Indian, the Mitsitam ("let's eat" in the language of the Delaware and Picsatawney tribes) Native Foods Café showcases Native foods and ingredients from five discrete regions across the country. This includes buffalo burgers representing the Plains tribes, venison steak from the Pacific Northwest, and turtle chowder with pickled ramps from the Northern Woodlands.

In response to the relative dearth of Native chefs in American restaurants, the Native American Program at the Classic Cooking Academy in Phoenix, Arizona, recruits and trains Native American youth in its specialized culinary program. The six-month course focuses on classical French training, while a major component centers on Native American culinary history and the role of indigenous foods in contemporary diets.

Observant and informed diners may notice Native American foods and cooking practices reflected on the menus of their local restaurants. Salmon grilled on a cedar plank or fiddlehead fern salads are two such examples. Many Native dishes have been adapted into mainstream culinary culture. Dishes like chili, wild rice, gumbo, succotash, cornbread, fried green tomatoes, and even corn on the cob have their roots in early Native American food practices as well.

Special Occasions

At traditional weddings, rather than exchange rings, the bride and groom gifted one another with food. The groom would bring venison or other meats as a symbol of his commitment to provide for his family. The bride brought corn or bean bread to symbolize her commitment to nurturing her household. The wedding feast menu at a traditional Native American wedding includes fry bread, venison, squash, beans, corn, and fresh fruits like blueberries, raspberries, and strawberries, if available and in season. The food is placed on a blanket and served buffet style. After the food is blessed, the elders and officiant eat first, followed by the bride, groom, and guests. Any leftover food is given to the elders.

When a baby is born among the Pueblo of New Mexico, the baby's family rubs cornmeal on his or her body. The Hopi conduct naming ceremonies featuring maize rituals. When a girl comes of age among the Hopi, she must perform maize-grinding ceremonies (recall that the Hopi women are revered for their maize-handling skills at the piki stone). Later, when she wants to propose to a boy, she makes piki bread and, accompanied by her mother and an uncle, presents it to the boy's family; if they accept it, the betrothal is official, and the girl would next bring a basket of white cornmeal and blue piki bread.

One unusual (to contemporary minds) feast food was dog. The Oglala Sioux prepared and ritually consumed dog on three occasions: to honor prominent men, in healing ceremonies called *Yuwipi,* and at fraternal society rituals. The Chippewa boiled dog in bear grease in order to recognize the adoption of white captives or visitors. The Ojibwe annually stewed a dog in wild rice as part of a sacred feast.

Native American spirituality and religious beliefs are intimately connected to the land and to food and aim to ensure a continued supply. Even mundane activities like hunting and planting corn were considered sacred and holy. Therefore, many, if not the majority, of Native celebrations prominently feature food and its consumption or abstention from it. Every tribe has a number of ceremonial feasts with sacred foods attached to them. Here are just a few examples, many of which are feasts of first food, honoring the new seasons of corn, fish, and a variety of local agricultural products.

In the Pacific Northwest, many tribes practiced First Salmon rituals in the spring. In these rituals, the shaman would place the first catch of the season, which had been caught by a specially selected fisherman, on an altar, where it would be welcomed as an honored guest and then cooked over a newly built fire. The head of the fish would be placed upriver so that it could find its way home. After all in attendance had tasted of the fish, its head and bones would be returned to the river so that it could be reborn and continue its way upstream. This ritual marked the commencement of fishing season, and the people were careful to treat the salmon with respect to ensure its continued return to the river.

The interior of a traditional Nez Perce longhouse during the feast of roots, bulbs, salmon, and venison. This canvas and pole longhouse was built specifically for use in celebrating the First Fruits and First Salmon Rites ceremony by the Looking Glass Band of Nez Perce in Kamiah Idaho. (Marilyn Angel Wynn | Nativestock.com)

In June, the Iroquois held a Green Bean Ceremony, honoring the first crops of one of the Three Sisters. The Oneida held Strawberry Ceremonies in June as well, feasting on a wide variety of dishes featuring the summer fruit, including drinks, fry bread, and strawberry-flavored corn soups.

In the southeastern United States, the Creek and Seminoles observe Posketv, a Green Corn festival that emphasizes fasting in anticipation of celebrating the new year, marked by the midsummer growth of new corn. The Cherokees also celebrate Green Corn days; their festivities include feasting on roasted corn. Indeed, many tribes across North America hold Green Corn festivals, which are the most important harvest festivals of the year and feature fasting, dancing, games, sacred fire building, and feasts that ended the fasts.

The Miwoks of northern California held an acorn festival in late September, as the tree nut was a staple of their diet. The gathering was called the Big Time, and tribal members would come from their villages and harvest the nuts, feast, exchange news and supplies, and perform ceremonial dances. Acorns are traditionally pulverized on a grinding rock, then leached in water to remove the bitter tannins.

Acorn Griddle Cakes

Makes 12–15 cakes

$^2/_3$ c unbleached flour

$^1/_3$ c finely ground leached acorn meal

1 tsp baking powder

$^1/_3$ tsp salt

1 tbsp honey

1 egg, beaten

¾ c milk

3 tbsp melted butter

Combine dry ingredients. Mix together honey, egg, and milk, and add dry ingredients, forming a smooth batter. Add butter. Drop batter onto a hot greased griddle, and cook until browned and slightly puffy.

Diet and Health

Many of the most common causes of death among Native Americans are directly related to diet. Many medical and nutrition experts agree that the radical changes in Native diets due to displacement to reservations have had a direct effect on the physical health of this population. Heart disease is the leading cause of death among Native Americans, and diet-related obesity, high blood pressure, high cholesterol, and diabetes are all risk factors associated with heart disease. Experts indicate that, on average, 30 percent of Native adults are obese. In some areas, like Arizona, nearly 95 percent of Native diabetics are also overweight.

Fry bread is often scapegoated as a primary cause for obesity and diabetes in Native populations. Because it is fried bread drenched in grease, it has nearly no nutritional value and is ultimately a delivery mechanism for 25 grams of excess fat and 700 empty calories (U.S. Department of Agriculture). Fry bread, along with other government-supplied commodity foods like potted meats, lard, and processed cheese, is often blamed for the widespread obesity and diabetes "epidemic" among Native populations. Many Native activists feel that these problems are a direct result of government programs of relocating tribes to reservations, thereby cutting them off from their traditional lifestyles, which lent the Native American diet a natural form of regulated caloric intake, an optimal balance of nutrients, and survival-inspired dietary adaptations.

In addition to having extremely high-fat diets and sedentary lifestyles, malnutrition is also a problem among Native American peoples; studies show that a mere 21 percent eat the recommended amount of fruit on any given day, while 34 percent eat the recommended amount of vegetables. The extreme poverty of reservation life also leads to prevalent hunger: Native Americans are also four times more likely to report not having enough to eat than other U.S. households. Proper nutrition education would help to mitigate this problem.

Other, more obscure threats to Native diets present themselves in genetically modified organisms

(GMOs). While naturally growing wild rice crops in Wisconsin and Minnesota have dwindled to half in the past century, agricultural firms and food corporations have developed a way to grow cultivated or paddy "wild" rice, which poses a threat to the Ojibwe, who rely on proper wild rice for income and preservation of their culture and traditions. There is fear among the Ojibwe that genetically modified rice may come to contaminate the naturally occurring wild rice they depend on; residents of the White Earth reservation in Minnesota have launched the Save Wild Rice campaign to prevent this from happening.

Melanie Haupt

Further Reading

Berzok, Linda Murray. *American Indian Food.* Westport, CT: Greenwood Press, 2005.

Divina, Fernando. *Foods of the Americas: Native Recipes and Traditions.* Berkeley, CA: Ten Speed Press, 2004.

Fiple, Kenneth F., and Krimhil Coneè Ornelas, eds. *The Cambridge World History of Food.* Vols. 1 and 2. Cambridge: Cambridge University Press, 2000.

"Food System Preservation Program." The Native American Women's Health Education Resource Center. http://www.nativeshop.org/news/93-information/659-food-system-preservation-program.html.

Frank, Lois Ellen. *Native American Cooking: Foods of the Southwest Indian Nations.* New York: C. N. Potter, 1991.

"Fry Bread and Indian Tacos." BlackRedRoots.org. http://www.blackredroots.org/content/view/52/76/.2

Fussell, Betty. *The Story of Corn.* New York: Knopf, 1992.

Jennings, Jesse D., ed. *Ancient Native Americans.* San Francisco: W. H. Freeman, 1978.

Kavasch, E. Barrie. *Enduring Harvests: Native American Foods and Festivals for Every Season.* Old Saybrook, CT: Globe Pequot Press, 1995.

Kavasch, E. Barrie. *Native Harvests: Recipes and Botanicals of the American Indian.* New York: Vintage Books, 1977.

Mihesuah, Devon A. *Recovering Our Ancestors' Gardens: Indigenous Recipes and Guide to Diet and Fitness.* Lincoln: University of Nebraska Press, 2005.

Native American Cuisine. http://nativerecipes.com/1.html.

"Native Americans, Diet of." Nutrition and Well Being A–Z. http://www.faqs.org/nutrition/Met-Obe/Native-Americans-Diet-of.html.

Native Harvest Wild Rice Campaign. http://nativeharvest.com/node/6.

Native Web. http://nativeweb.org/.

Penner, Lucille Recht. *A Native American Feast.* New York: Macmillan, 1994.

Save Wild Rice. http://savewildrice.org/.

Sturtevant, William C. *Handbook of North American Indians.* Washington, DC: Smithsonian Institution, 1978–2001.

Nicaragua

Overview

With 46,430 square miles of area, Nicaragua is the largest country in Central America. The name of the country comes in part from the Nahuat-speaking Nicarao people, who inhabited the shores of Lago de Nicaragua at the time of the conquest, and in part from the Spanish word for water, *agua.* The country occupies the eastern portion of the Central American subcontinent and is comprised of three distinct geographic regions. A range of volcanic mountains defines an upland portion that divides the Pacific coastal plains from the Atlantic lowlands, an extensive underdeveloped and sparsely populated area known as La Mosquitia consisting of inland savanna with swamps and mangrove forest. The Corn Islands (Islas del Maíz) skirt the east coast of the country out in the Caribbean Sea. Nicaragua is bordered on the north by the Gulf of Fonseca and Honduras and on the south by Costa Rica.

Present-day Nicaragua includes over five million people, most of whom are considered mestizo, or of mixed ethnic ancestry. There are smaller populations of Europeans, Asians, and Afro-Antilleans as well as indigenous groups such as the Miskitu and Sumu, who inhabit La Mosquitia and neighboring areas. Nicaraguans often refer to themselves as *Nicas* but also as *pinoleros* in reference to the popular toasted maize and cacao beverage, *pinolillo* (see the following), which is an emblem of national identity. Almost half of all Nicaraguans live in rural areas and work in agricultural activities for their livelihood. The rural sector has an especially high incidence of poverty and malnutrition.

The abundant land and water resources and a relatively low population density have in Nicaragua accommodated an extensive, export-oriented agricultural sector since the time of the conquest. Production is differentiated across the country: Bananas, peanuts and soybeans, sesame seeds, sugarcane, sorghum, and livestock are produced in the Pacific region, whereas almost all the coffee, beans, and rice are produced in the Central region. In the Atlantic region, some rice, beans, and sugarcane are also grown. Agricultural holdings are unevenly distributed into a small number of commercially oriented, extensive private estates and a large number of very small subsistence-oriented family plots, creating two tiers in the farming sector. Most rural Nicaraguans are either landless agricultural laborers or small holders with plots (*milpas*) of 3.7 acres (1.5 hectares) or less. Farmers and farmworkers alike grow maize, beans, rice, and sorghum primarily for local use. Cacao, yucca, plantains, and other fruits and vegetables are also produced for household consumption and for sale in the local markets. In good years, it is possible to plant and harvest two crops; the first, or *siembra de primera,* is planted in June and harvested in August, providing food and income for the household. The second crop, *la postrera,* is planted in August and harvested in October. This latter crop provides seed for the next year's plantings, and any excess is sold to purchase chemical inputs, supplies, and equipment.

🍽 Food Culture Snapshot

Throughout the Northern Autonomous Region of the Atlantic (RAAN) on the Caribbean coast of

Nicaragua are towns such as Waspam overlooking the Rio Coco. Here, Miskitu Indians have made their living raising crops in small gardens, hunting in the forest, fishing in the river, and turtling in the nearby Miskito Keys since precontact times. Ernesto and Sylvia Kaisni share an elevated, two-room wooden frame house with their three children. Like many Miskitu men from Waspam, Ernesto works as a commercial lobster diver and is away from home for long periods of time. In a manner favored by Miskitu custom, Sylvia looks after the house and children and coordinates food purchasing, preparation, and parenting chores with her sisters and mother, who live nearby.

Miskitu custom also includes very clear ideas about food; some foods are taboo, and others are thought to have curative properties. Ideally, proper Miskitu meals must include two complementary elements, *tama* and *upan*. Tama includes all the starchy foods: cassava, cocoyam, sweet potatoes, maize, rice, and plantains. Tama must be complemented by upan, the protein component that provides a contrasting taste, texture, and nutrients not found in the tama. The most common form of upan in the Miskitu region is turtle meat. Fish and other wild game animals as well as beef and chicken are readily accepted by the Miskitu and are consumed with relative frequency. Fish, turtle, and other animals are butchered occasionally, but as there is no refrigeration, all meat foods must be consumed immediately. By custom, Miskitu give away meat foods to close relatives and friends and sell them to others. The demand is always greater than the supply, and much of the conversation and daily activity about food centers on locating the ephemeral upan foods. When upan foods are not included, the meal is said to be "sad," and such meals are often the cause of discord and unhappiness.

When at home, Ernesto will start his day around 6 A.M. and go to the plantation (milpa) to tend to the food plants or go to the river to fish with a seine net. He does not eat breakfast at home but may carry along fruit or partake of the ripe fruit found in the plantation. Miskitu do not regard fruit as a real food; rather, they snack on it opportunistically throughout the day. Those remaining in the house will have a breakfast of sweetened coffee and bread with an occasional egg. All cooking is done in a stand-alone kitchen house, on a wood-burning, horseshoe-shaped, baked clay stove known as a *kubus*. After the breakfast is prepared and served, the children leave for school and Sylvia begins her housework. Twice a month she travels to the central marketplace to buy rice, beans, flour, coffee, sugar, and lard. With a blend of store-bought and locally accessed provisions, she prepares the main meal, which ideally includes some form of upan—a fried fish or turtle meat. Boiled plantains or cassava serve as the tama for the meal along with an accompaniment of rice and beans or homemade bread, prepared with coconut milk. Ernesto and other adult men eat first and in silence. Conversation is reserved for other settings. Children and others eat in the second seating, and the women who have prepared the meal eat separately, often during the course of their housework. In the evening, leftover food from the main meal is served along with coffee. Afterward, people visit with family and friends and converse for a time before going to bed.

Major Foodstuffs

Many of the important Nicaraguan foods are produced locally. White maize, for instance, is well adapted to the climate and soil conditions and is a highly nutritious plant; it features prominently in the diets of all Nicaraguans. Typically, maize is harvested, dried, processed into masa flour, and consumed fresh, or processed into the forms of tortillas, tamales, or maize-based beverages such as pinolillo, which are enjoyed by people in all social groups.

Pinolillo

Ingredients

3 ears fresh maize on the cob

½ c cocoa powder

½ tsp cinnamon

½ tsp salt

2 tsp ancho chili powder

Sugar to taste

1. Remove husks and silk from maize, and boil ears of maize for approximately 12 minutes or microwave at high heat for 6 minutes (long enough to allow the kernels to be removed from the cob easily). Remove kernels from cobs and spread on a baking sheet; sprinkle lightly with salt and place in a 325°F oven for approximately 10 minutes, or until the kernels appear lightly toasted. Monitor closely to guard against burning.

2. Place all ingredients into a blender or food processor, and blend on low speed for about a minute or until the corn kernels are pulverized.

3. Pour mixture over ice or add to ½ glass of cold milk, and sweeten to taste.

Beans and rice are important foods in the field and on the table. Rice is grown in a wide range of climates, soils, and moisture conditions, with about a third of the crop grown in irrigated paddies. The greater part of the rice crop is grown under rain-fed conditions in upland areas, where it is planted either as monocrop or in mixed fields alongside other food crops including beans, which provide dietary fiber, calcium, iron, and vitamins and serve as a cheap source of protein when meat is unattainable.

Meat consumption conveys social status in Nicaragua. It was once customary for a middle-or upper-class family to have beef at least once a day, and beef was and remains a luxury for the poor. As consumers, Nicaraguans are thrifty, using organ meats, skin, hooves, and blood in various dishes. Nicaraguans also eat turtle eggs, lizards, armadillos, and other game animals, but poultry remains the most popular form of animal food.

While less significant in terms of overall consumption, Nicaraguans do eat fruits, including pineapples, bananas, plantains, mangoes, guavas, breadfruit, and coconuts. The consumption of root vegetables such as cassava provides an important source of calories, and other vegetables such as avocados, tomatoes, peppers, squash, cabbage, and carrots provide vitamins, minerals, and trace elements in the Nicaraguan diet. Cabbage is commonly consumed and is featured in the preparation of a staple

Nicaraguan side dish or condiment known as *curtido de repollo.*

Curtido de Repollo

Ingredients

1 cabbage head (shredded)

1 c water

1¼ c white distilled vinegar

1 tbsp salt (if using a giant cabbage head or a fairly large one, use 2 tbsp)

½ tsp sugar

2 serrano chili peppers or other green chili peppers

2 medium tomatoes, diced

1 medium or small onion, minced

2 spicy serrano chili peppers or other green spicy chili pepper, minced finely

1 medium lime, sliced

Place shredded cabbage in a large bowl. Combine water, vinegar, salt, sugar, and 2 chili peppers in a blender or food processor. Blend until peppers are liquefied, and pour over shredded cabbage and toss well together. Cover and refrigerate for 2 hours or more. Toss occasionally to pickle evenly. Drain all the excess liquid. Moments before serving, add the fresh ingredients: tomato, onion, and the remaining chilies. Dress liberally with lime juice y *¡buen provecho!*

Cooking

The processes and techniques used to prepare Nicaraguan dishes arise from various cultures and places. Some methods and materials are indistinguishable from those used in North America; others originate in South America and Mesoamerica, mirroring the ancestry of the Nicaraguan people. Some cooking equipment followed in the wake of European contact, while other methods and implements are likely blends of two or more ideas from varied origins. The most common form of food preparation in pre-Hispanic Nicaragua was likely cooking over an open fire. Contemporary grill cooking—*a la parrilla* or *asada*—is a direct descendant of this method, favored especially for cooking beef or poultry. Grilled *elotes* (ears of corn on the cob) are widely available as street food, served on a stick and seasoned with a smear of butter or mayonnaise, and then a topping of salt, lime juice, or chili powder. As there were few sources of animal fats in pre-Hispanic Nicaragua, frying was an unknown cooking technique but one readily adopted and favored by contemporary Nicaraguan cooks. Deep-frying in oil is the preferred method for preparing many foods ranging from plantains to yucca. Rice, too, is often fried in oil, often with finely diced red chilies or onions.

Typical Meals

As in other parts of Central America the daily meals in Nicaragua are designated *desayuno, comida,* and *cena.* The desayuno is eaten early in the morning and usually consists of eggs, cheese, rice and beans, and plantains, served with bread or tortillas. Fresh juice or coffee accompanies most Nicaraguan breakfasts. The main meal of the day is a late lunch known as the comida; many try to take this meal at home with their family. A characteristic comida might feature *indio viejo*—a stewed dish of shredded beef, onions, tomatoes, and peppers fried with shredded stale tortillas, then thinned with orange juice and broth and flavored with mint. The meal is often accompanied by deep-fried plantains, rice and beans, and curtido (see the preceding). There is great variety in the execution of the final meal of the day, the cena. In some cases the term is used to describe a formal meal shared with friends or family on special occasions; in other uses the cena is simply the family meal eaten very late in the evening. In the rural areas, this would be based on the staples of tortillas and *frijoles* (beans) and may include a stew of vegetables seasoned with garlic, onions, tomatoes, and chilies.

Eating Out

In Nicaragua the demand for eating out is proportional to the size and complexity of the settlement.

In small villages, "eating out" may mean eating at a friend or family member's house, whereas in the large towns or cities a range of establishments provide food for sale to the public. When Nicaraguans eat out in the city it typically means visiting street-food vendors or similar very casual dining establishments. Take-out foods available from itinerant vendors on the street include *quesillos* (a white corn tortilla topped with creamed cheese, salt, chopped pickled onions, and sour cream), roasted elotes, and *vigoron* (boiled yucca topped with *chicharrones*—crunchy pork rinds—and curtido) served up on a banana leaf. Eating out in the bigger cities does offer more variation, including restaurants that serve Nicaraguan cuisine along with other Latin American, European, and Asian cuisines. An influx of fast-food restaurants in recent years has affected the landscape of urban Nicaraguan food culture as well.

Beef and stewed yucca with banana tree leaves and vegetables available for sale in a street market in Leon, Nicaragua. (Shutterstock)

Special Occasions

Many Nicaraguan fiestas are focused on the Roman Catholic liturgical calendar. Christmas, Easter, Lent, and the saints' days are widely celebrated holidays. The Christmas cycle begins on December 7, with a celebration of the Immaculate Conception known as La Purísima. The festivities include la Noche de Gritería (the Night of the Screaming) as children and young adults roam the streets and sing for the Virgin Mary. They stop at each house, where treats are offered, including *rosquillas* (donuts similar to biscotti), oranges, lemons, and chopped *caña* (sugarcane). The height of the Christmas celebration comes on Nochebuena (Christmas Eve). Family and guests gather for the holiday and are served *gallina rellena navideña*—a chicken stuffed with papaya, chayote squash, capers, olives, raisins, and tomatoes.

The Easter holidays begin with Carnival, the celebration of excess preceding the austere Lenten period. Carnival (*carne vale*) is thought to derive from an expression meaning "farewell to meat." Per the fasting tradition, meatless dishes abound in Nicaragua during the 40 days of Lent. During the colonial period the Catholic Church declared the iguana a type of fish and therefore acceptable for consumption on meatless days. Throughout Lent and Holy Week, Nicaraguans cook dishes made from the meat and eggs of the iguana. Its popularity has placed the species under threat of extinction, and measures have been put in place to protect the lizard whose unfortunate nickname is "the chicken of the tree."

Diet and Health

Poverty is the main social determinant of the quality of diet and overall health status in Nicaragua, and the traditional diet has undergone a transition, fueled by globalization and urbanization. Major changes in trade and exchange among nation-states have meant for people on the ground an increased use of processed foods including sugar, refined flour, hydrogenated fats, and animal products coupled with a decline in the intake of whole grains, fruit, and vegetables of local provenance. Despite the availability of many healthful foods, the average Nicaraguan's diet is unbalanced. Various data concur that more than a fifth of the overall population is malnourished, and approximately one in four children in Nicaragua is stunted due to malnutrition. Paradoxically, Nicaragua has witnessed a growing incidence of obesity, diabetes, and cardiovascular disease in the same era. A health problem related to diet is the lack of access to sanitation and safe drinking water. Most rural dwellers in Nicaragua rely on contaminated water sources, and a significant proportion of the overall population does not have access to basic sanitation. Both factors amplify various health problems originating in poor diet.

Good health in Nicaragua is challenged by a wide array of health problems including a high prevalence of malaria and other parasitic diseases, various respiratory ailments, diarrheal diseases, anemia, periodic natural disasters, malnutrition, and high rates of maternal and infant mortality. The Sandinista regime substantially increased spending on health care, broadening and equalizing access to services. There was a substantial drop in infant mortality and the transmission of communicable diseases. However, the system was increasingly strained by shortages of funds. The current health care system aligned against these challenges mirrors the stratified nature of Nicaraguan society. Members of the upper classes rely on private physicians and hospitals, and often travel abroad for specialized care. The Nicaraguan Social Security Institute provides health care to the small segment of society employed in government and industry. The vast majority of the population is served at public facilities, and some 40 percent of Nicaraguans have no access to any health care services due to the uneven provision of services and the locations of health care facilities.

Various governmental and nongovernmental programs have taken aim at overall health status by improving people's food security and nutritional health. For instance, a program of free school meals for all primary-school children provides daily meals of rice, beans, corn, oil, and cereal, which are prepared by parents in rotation as part of a school-supervised food-aid program. Likewise, the government has distributed food-production packages including live-stock, seeds, and agricultural inputs to families in rural areas of Nicaragua to boost food production and stabilize rural communities.

Michael R. McDonald

Further Reading

Behnke, Alison, Griselda Aracely Chacon, and Kristina Anderson. *Cooking the Central American Way: Culturally Authentic Foods, Including Low-Fat and Vegetarian Recipes.* Minneapolis, MN: Lerner, 2005.

"Central American Recipes." http://www.food.com/recipes/central-american.

Dennis, P. A. *The Miskitu People of Awastara.* Austin: University of Texas Press, 2004.

McDonald, Michael R. *Food Culture in Central America.* Westport, CT: Greenwood Press, 2009.

Ortiz, Elizabeth Lambert. *The Book of Latin American Cooking.* New York: Alfred A. Knopf, 1979.

"Recipes from Nicaragua." Nicaragua.com. http://www.nicaragua.com/recipes/.

Tapia Barquero, Humberto. *Nicaragua, maiz y folklore.* Managua: Papelera Industrial de Nicaragua, División de Artes Gráficas, 1981.

White, Stephen F., and Esthela Calderon. *Culture and Customs of Nicaragua.* Westport, CT: Greenwood Press, 2008.

Panama

Overview

Panama is a nation-state located in Central America. It borders on Costa Rica on the west and Colombia on the southeast. Panama is considered one of the "crossroads of the world." During colonial times, Panama was a strategic place for the Spanish Empire, as a barrier between the Caribbean and the Pacific Ocean. In the 19th and 20th centuries, it became a commercial point of connection in the Americas. In 1821, Panama was incorporated into Gran Colombia after its independence from Spain; it became a republic when it declared its independence from Colombia in 1903. Panama has been the location of large and significant infrastructural projects, including the Panamanian Railroad (1850–1855), the French efforts to build a canal (1880–1889), and the U.S. construction of the Panama Canal (1904–1914).

Throughout its history as a nation-state, Panama has emphasized its Spanish roots. In fact, as a result of its geopolitical location, Panama's peoples represent a great diversity of cultures and ethnicities, including eight indigenous groups (Ngöbe, Buglé, Naso, Bokotá, Kuna, Emberá, Wounan, and Bri-Bri), five different waves of migration of peoples of African descent (connected to slavery in the 16th century and to voluntary migration from the British, Spanish, and French West Indies in the 19th and 20th centuries), and sizable numbers of immigrants from China, Greece, Spain, and India, among others. This ethnic diversity has produced a multiplicity of foodways as well as some dishes that are generally viewed as characteristic of the "national cuisine," such as *sancocho* (soup), arroz con pollo (rice with chicken), and *arroz con frijoles* (rice and beans).

Arroz con pollo, a Panamanian dish made with rice and chicken. (StockPhotoPro)

🍽 Food Culture Snapshot

Beatriz is an Afro-Antillean woman who lives with her youngest son in Bocas Town, Colón Island (Archipelago of Bocas del Toro). She is the mother of five children; her four daughters are married and have children of their own. All but one also live in the archipelago or the province of Bocas del Toro. Beatriz works as a cook and administrator of a bed and breakfast owned by a permanent resident expatriate. She cooks every day for herself and her family, in addition to working at the bed and breakfast. She also runs a small informal food business, preparing spicy sauce and other food items based on her own recipes. She sells these items at her home and in the few stores that cater specifically to tourists and resident expatriates.

A common meal that Beatriz cooks for her son and herself is a hearty meat-and-tubers soup. As is common among Afro-Antilleans, Beatriz prizes deep-fried food and uses large quantities of vegetable or coconut oil to fry her food. Some of the common dishes Beatriz cooks include rice and beans with coconut milk, *rondón* (fish soup with coconut milk and tubers), *michilá* (boiled ripe plantain with coconut milk), *chicheme* (boiled hominy with coconut milk, condensed milk, and spices), *bragadá* (fried codfish cake made with flour), ackee (the fruit of a tree brought to Bocas del Toro from Jamaica) with codfish, ackee with eggs, pig's tail, *sauce* or *souse* (pig's feet cooked with cucumber and vinegar), *patí* (a turnover of spicy meat), and *janny cake* (flour bread made with coconut and baked), also known as *journey cake*.

Beatriz is extremely proud of her cooking abilities and the opportunities her extensive knowledge of Afro-Antillean cuisine has brought her. She is praised by all the tourists who stay at the bed and breakfast where she works. Beatriz is particularly generous in sharing her knowledge and secrets with friends, particularly resident expatriates. This is not common in Bocas, as women who keep their cooking secrets may acquire status within the community through them. Accordingly, most women prefer to guard their cooking secrets, handed down from their grandmothers or neighbors, for themselves. These secrets become their personal intellectual and cultural wealth, as they guarantee their prestige in the community and further opportunities to be hired as cooks.

Major Foodstuffs

City- and town-dwelling Panamanians consume three main meals daily. A hearty breakfast with fish or other types of meat, *hojaldras* (deep-fried dough), *patacones* (fried plantains [*Musa paradisiaca*]), and fried rice is common. People eat lunch (either at home or out) between noon and 2 P.M. Lunch is generally composed of either soup or rice with meat (beef, pork, or chicken) and beans or lentils; tubers such as yucca, *ñampi* (a small gnarled yam [*Dioscorea* sp.]), *ñame* (yam), *otoe* (*Xanthosoma* sp., similar to taro), and dasheen (taro [*Colocasia* sp.]); and an occasional salad. Fried fish is also a common option for lunch, dinner, or a snack. Dinner is lighter and might include fried snacks. It is customary to eat a *bolsita* (literally, "small bag") in the afternoon, as an appetizer or in lieu of dinner. A bolsita consists of a piece of fried chicken with approximately three pieces of patacones, three pieces of fried yucca, or a few French fries. Bolsitas are sold in small restaurants or on the streets in a small paper bag (hence the name) for one to two dollars.

Processed snacks (colloquially known as *burundanga*) and Panamanian snacks are eaten very commonly. They include maize empanadas (fried corn-flour cakes filled with meat or cheese), *carimañolas* (fried yucca rolls filled with ground beef or chopped eggs), and tortillas (fried maize patties that are much thicker than the Mexican tortillas). These snacks are available on street corners and small restaurants, or they can be bought frozen in supermarkets to be fried at home.

Rural Panamanians and indigenous groups often do not follow a regular three-meals-a-day regimen, but the foodstuffs they consume on a daily basis do not vary much from those already listed, except that processed snacks are uncommon. Also, meat is consumed less frequently, not for lack of desire but for lack of availability.

As already noted, Panamanians have a cuisine understood to be the "typical" or "national" cuisine, along with regional cuisines, including indigenous, Afro-Antillean, Indian, Chinese, Greek, Spanish, and Italian, among others, represented by the larger minorities in the country. A recipe for one of those typical or national dishes, the soup *sancocho de gallina,* follows. Depending on the region of the country, the same dish will include fewer (if cooked among indigenous peoples) or more (if cooked among Afro-Antilleans) ingredients, transforming the consistency and flavor of the soup.

Sancocho de Gallina (A Recipe from Panama's National Cuisine)

Ingredients

1 chicken (3 lb), cut in pieces

1 medium-size onion

4 cilantro leaves (often called "Chinese parsley" in the United States)

2 sweet chilies

1 tsp oregano

½ c annatto seed water

Salt

2 lb ñame

Cook the chicken in pieces with the onion, cilantro, chilies, and oregano. Add annatto seed water. (To make the annatto seed water, boil the water and add 1 teaspoon of annatto seeds. Wait 20 minutes, then strain out the seeds.) When the chicken is tender, add salt and ñame in pieces, and wait until the ñame becomes tender.

Eating Out

It is common for city- and town-dwelling Panamanians of all social classes to eat out often. Whereas members of the middle and upper classes in Panama City visit upscale restaurants that offer international cuisine (Korean, Japanese, Chinese, Indian, French, Greek, Italian, Spanish, North American, Australian, Peruvian, Chilean, Argentinean, Brazilian, and Colombian food, just to name a few), members of the lower classes have access to inexpensive restaurants offering Chinese food, North American fast food, and Panamanian snacks.

Special Occasions

Panamanians celebrate special occasions by preparing and consuming dishes that are regarded as traditional and part of the national cuisine. Secular and religious festivities as well as life-transition events are marked by the consumption of these dishes; old-time favorites are sancocho and stewed, roasted, or fried chicken with rice and fried bananas. Among Afro-Antilleans in the provinces of Bocas del Toro and Colón, special occasions call for a hearty soup (including the Afro-Antillean version of sancocho) or rice and beans prepared with coconut milk and accompanied by chicken, fish, or turtle (in Bocas del Toro). Because of the overexploitation of marine resources—partly as a result of the growth of tourism—dishes that were considered daily meals, or *comida corriente,* are now considered delicacies, or *comida de fiesta,* and thus can be consumed only on special occasions. This is particularly true of lobster, octopus, and snails, among others. These resources are also scarce throughout the country and, thus, have become more commonly consumed for special events.

Diet and Health

Studies conducted in connection to the dietary practices of Panamanians indicate that excess consumption of oil and salt among most ethnic groups has produced frequent cases of hypertension and obesity, in both urban and rural areas. Exceptions include the diets considered traditional for rural populations and indigenous peoples, such as the Kuna, whose diet has been studied from nutritional and cultural perspectives recently. The Kuna who have moved to urban areas and away from their *comarcas* (administrative regions with substantial indigenous populations) have tended to adapt to the less healthy dietary norms of mainstream Panama. A similar situation occurs with the largest indigenous group in Panama, the Ngöbe. Among the Ngöbe, greater involvement in the cash economy and greater availability of cash, due to government subsidies and more people working for wages, have produced a substantial shift away from the traditional diet, which was nutritionally balanced overall. The Ngöbe diet now includes large quantities of purchased polished white rice and white sugar and less of the traditional healthy foods. Consequently, rates of undernutrition and malnutrition have risen substantially.

Carla Guerrón Montero

Further Reading

La Comisión Económica para América Latina (CEPAL), Social Development Division. *Poverty, Hunger and Food Security in Central America and Panama.* Santiago de Chile: United Nations, 2005.

McDonald, Michael R. *Food Culture in Central America.* Santa Barbara, CA: Greenwood Press/ABC-Clio, 2009.

Williams, Chuck, ed. *Essentials of Latin Cooking.* Birmingham, AL: Oxmoor House, 2010.

Paraguay and Uruguay

Overview

Paraguay and Uruguay are located in the Southern Cone of South America and are two of the smallest countries on the continent. Paraguay is a landlocked country of 5.2 million inhabitants, bordered by Argentina, Brazil, and Bolivia. The country is divided by the Paraguay River into two unequal and distinct portions. To the west is the Chaco prairie, an inhospitable and sparsely populated region that makes up over half of Paraguay's land area. Less than 3 percent of the population lives in the Chaco. The capital city of Asunción is located east of the Paraguay River, where most Paraguayans live. The country has suffered from isolation, civil war, dictatorships, and periods of extreme political and economic instability.

An important factor in Paraguay's food culture is the influence of the native Guaraní Indians, who likely lived in the region for thousands of years before the arrival of the Spanish conquerors in the 16th century. Today, over 90 percent of Paraguayans are considered mestizos, descendants of the native Guaranís and the Spanish colonists. Paraguay is unique in South America in that both Spanish and Guaraní are official languages, and the country's indigenous language is more widely spoken than its European one. Ninety percent of Paraguayans speak Guaraní, which they usually learn before Spanish. Today, Paraguayan gastronomy is a hybrid of European and Guaraní ingredients, cooking methods, and customs.

Uruguay is a Spanish-speaking country of 3.5 million people. Uruguay's only land border is with Brazil, to the north. The Río de la Plata and Uruguay River form the border with Argentina to the west, and to the southeast is the South Atlantic Ocean. Almost a third of the population lives in metropolitan Montevideo, the capital and largest city. Due to its advanced education system including a high literacy rate, large urban middle class, and relatively even income distribution, Uruguay is often said to have one of the highest standards of living in Latin America.

Uruguay was a Spanish colony until independence in 1828. It is a country of immigrants, mainly of European and chiefly of Spanish and Italian descent. Uruguayan food culture is therefore primarily European with minimal indigenous influence. Beef is the most fundamental element of Uruguayan cuisine. The country is one of the world's top per-capita consumers of red meat, often grappling with neighboring Argentina for the top spot.

Most Uruguayans are nominally Roman Catholic although most do not actively practice a religion. Church and state are officially separated, making it one of the most secular countries in Latin America. Religion therefore does not play a major role in the daily diet of Uruguayans. However, many European food traditions are practiced on major Christian holidays such as Easter and Christmas.

🍽 Food Culture Snapshot

Pedro Luis and Lucía Spagnolo live in a suburb of Montevideo. Their lifestyle is similar to that of a well-off Paraguayan family living in the capital city of Asunción. The Spagnolos have two children, Jimena and

Martín, who both live at home. Martín is in high school, and Jimena is in her mid-twenties (unmarried women tend to live at home). Family is important to the Spagnolos, and even some longtime friends are considered a part of the extended family. The Spagnolo household is always bustling, with friends and family frequently coming over for afternoon tea and snacks or a late dinner.

Lucía stays at home and is responsible for the bulk of the food shopping and preparation. She makes a trip to the supermarket a couple times a week to stock up on coffee, tea, pastas, potatoes, milk, eggs, cheeses, soft drinks, and dry goods. Most days she visits a local produce market to pick up fresh lettuce and tomatoes for salads and fruits for dessert, and she stops at the butcher down the street for fresh cuts of beef or chicken for making breaded cutlets, panfried steaks, or stews. Lucía tries to make a homemade lunch every day during the week, as it is important to her that the family eat together for this biggest meal of the day. However, sometimes Pedro Luis cannot make it home from work for lunch, instead eating a fixed-price meal at a favorite restaurant near his workplace, and Martín often picks up a quick sausage or steak sandwich at a café with friends. After lunch, Lucía visits a local bakery where she purchases breads or pastries with sweet or savory fillings to accompany the afternoon tea. For dinner, Lucía uses leftovers from lunch to make a soup or stew, orders take-out pizza and empanadas (savory turnovers) from a nearby pizzeria, or serves pasta with a sauce purchased at the supermarket.

While Lucía performs the daily shopping duties, Pedro Luis is in charge of visiting the local butcher on weekends to procure the meat for the Sunday *asado*, or barbecue. Because he is the man of the family, the asado is his domain. Pedro Luis has purchased meat from the same trusted butcher for many years. The asado is the most important and anticipated meal of the week, and Pedro Luis takes great pains to ensure its success.

Major Foodstuffs

The major foodstuffs of Uruguay are primarily of European, rather than indigenous, origin. The greatest European culinary influences come primarily from the countries of Italy, Spain, and France, but the cuisines of Germany, England, and other countries also play a role. These influences are due to the great waves of European immigration into Uruguay beginning in the mid-19th century. The largely European population solidified a food culture based on Old World culinary habits. Today, the foodstuffs that appear most on the tables of Uruguayans are beef, dairy, wheat, sugary pastries, and wine. The two other important foodstuffs in Uruguay, potatoes and yerba maté, are indigenous to the continent.

Paraguayan cuisine, or *tembi'u paraguái* as it is known in the Guaraní language, is a result of the combination of European culinary techniques and ingredients with those native to the region. The names of Paraguayan specialties often use both Spanish and Guaraní terms. Spanish colonists adapted European foodstuffs to use ingredients they found in the New World, such as substituting corn and yucca flours for wheat flour to make breads, and adding peppers and other native vegetables to stews. The major foodstuffs of Paraguay are beef, yucca, corn, dairy products, and yerba maté, plus squash, peppers, and beans.

When European colonists arrived in Uruguay, they found a land with a temperate climate, grasslands, and fertile coastal lowlands. The domesticated breeding animals they brought in the 17th century,

A traditional corn soup made in Paraguay. (Shutterstock)

such as cattle, pigs, sheep, and goats, thrived on the Pampas grasslands. Today, the Pampas are still important cattle-raising land and are home to large estancias and cattle ranches. Beef is the largest export and a main driver of the Uruguayan economy. Beef is also the central element of the Uruguayan diet and a marker of national identity as it is tied to the culture of the gauchos, Uruguayan cowboys. Indigenous wildlife plays a much smaller role in the diet of Uruguayans, but the native, flightless *ñandú* (rhea) is today raised on Pampas farms and has become an export item. The majority of land is devoting to raising livestock, but the fertile soil also supports food crops. Today, the main food crops in Uruguay are wheat and rice, followed by corn, potatoes, barley, sugarcane, and soybeans. Due to the small size of the Uruguayan population, a large percentage of meats and crops are exported.

Agriculture is also economically significant in Paraguay, especially cattle ranching and the industries with which it is associated. The traditional meat-based diet is reminiscent of a time when beef was cheap and abundant. While chicken, pork, and to a lesser extent lamb are eaten in Paraguay, beef is undoubtedly the most popular meat used for typical Paraguayan meals. Beef exports are substantial for such a small country, and Paraguay also produces cotton and soybeans for export. Due to increasing prices, many Paraguayans cannot afford to eat as much beef as is traditional.

The staples of the Paraguayan diet are two native ingredients: yucca and corn. Yucca (known as *mandioca* in Paraguay but variously called manioc or cassava) is a starchy tuber that is highly poisonous and must be properly processed before consumption. It was cultivated and processed by the Guaraní centuries before the arrival of the colonists and continues to be grown throughout the country. Yucca processing yields three distinct edible derivatives that are all used in Paraguayan cuisine: *fariña* (flour), *typyraty* (a dry, fibrous residue), and *almidón* (starch). Corn (maize) is similarly used in many forms and at different stages of maturation: *choclo* or *maíz tierno* (young, fresh corn), *choclero* or *maíz cau* (semimature corn), and *maíz* (dried corn). Many of the traditional foods of Paraguay are prepared from these

staple grains. Yucca appears boiled as a common side dish, in dough for empanadas (turnovers), in fried fritters called *bolitas de mandioca,* and in many other preparations. Corn also takes various forms, from toasted dried corn eaten as a snack, to a hominy-based stew called *locro,* to various forms of polenta (*mbaipy* in Guaraní). A uniquely Paraguayan polenta preparation is *kivevé,* a sweet pumpkin polenta served with grilled meats or as a dessert. Another classic is *mazamorra* (dried corn stew), one of the oldest and simplest indigenous dishes.

Chipás are Paraguayan breads that accompany most meals. There are over 80 different types of chipá, which range from crisp flatbreads to corn custards and use a range of ingredients such as peanuts or anise seeds. They are most frequently shaped like bagels or rolls and are made from yucca starch, cornmeal, fresh cheese, eggs, lard or butter, and/or milk. Common variants include *sopa paraguaya* (Paraguayan cornbread), made with cornmeal and fresh cheese; *chipá guazú* (big chipá), a creamy corn custard flavored with onion; *mbejú* or *mbeyú,* an unleavened fried pancake made from a crumbly dough of fresh cheese and yucca starch; and *chipá caburé,* which is cooked around a stick. Sometimes chipá are filled with ground meats or vegetables, like *chipá so'ó.*

Dairy plays a large role in Uruguayan and Paraguayan food culture. Milk, eggs, yogurt, cheese, and *dulce de leche* (caramelized sweetened condensed milk) are consumed daily. The Uruguayan cheese industry produces local versions of famous European cheeses such as mozzarella, Gouda, provolone, Brie, Camembert, and Parmesan. Cheese-making techniques were brought to Uruguay by immigrants chiefly from Italy, France, and Switzerland. The cheese most used in Paraguay is a salty cow-milk farmer cheese called *quesú paraguái* (Paraguayan cheese). It is used in a number of traditional dishes including breads and soups and is often the only variety of cheese available in the countryside.

For a country surrounded by water on three sides, seafood plays a surprisingly small role in the repertoire of traditional Uruguayan dishes, although along the Atlantic coast the Spanish culinary influence can be seen in the preparation of dishes that feature cockles, mussels, and shrimp. Beef remains paramount, however, especially in the interior. Although Paraguay is landlocked, the country's extensive river and lake system provides freshwater fish such as the dorado (a firm-fleshed white fish), the coveted *surubí,* and the popular *bagre* (catfish). Fish in Paraguay is grilled, fried, or stewed in soups and most often eaten in areas around the rivers and lakes.

The large number of Italian immigrants to Uruguay in the 19th and 20th centuries accounts for the popularity of fresh and dried pastas. Pasta is served with a variety of sauces including the popular *tuco* (meat sauce) and the Uruguayan Caruso sauce made from cream, beef stock, onions, ham, and mushrooms. Ravioli, lasagna, gnocchi, and baked cannelloni are also popular, and polenta and mashed potatoes are often topped with meatballs or braised meats. Italian-style pizza is also widely eaten in Uruguay, as well as *lehmeyun,* an Armenian pizza topped with ground meat and vegetables. Pies and turnovers abound, such as empanadas in a huge range of sizes and fillings and *pascualina* (spinach or Swiss chard pie).

The most popular vegetables and fruits in Uruguay and Paraguay are a combination of European and indigenous products. In Uruguay, the most-eaten vegetables are Swiss chard, red bell peppers, onions, spinach, lettuce, tomatoes, carrots, and squash. The most popular fruits are citrus, apples, and bananas. The Paraguayan diet incorporates indigenous foodstuffs such as squash, pumpkins, beans, and peanuts, all foods that were cultivated by the Guaraní before colonization. Onions, garlic, and various herbs and spices of European origin are also important to the Paraguayan diet. A wide variety of tropical fruits are also found and eaten in Paraguay.

The Spanish colonists introduced techniques for harvesting and processing sugarcane to the New World. Before the conquest, sweetness was provided by honey and fruits. Today, Uruguayans have a sweet tooth, and their desserts are rich and often very sweet. French pastries are especially popular in Uruguay, such as those incorporating meringues, mousses, soufflés, and cream. A typical Uruguayan dessert is *chajá,* a layered sponge cake with cream, jam, peaches, and meringue.

Postre Chajá

1 thin sheet of purchased sponge cake

2–3 tbsp orange liqueur

2 c heavy whipping cream, whipped to soft peaks

2–3 large peaches, peeled and sliced

1 lb purchased dry meringues, lightly crushed

Using a large round cookie cutter, cut circles from the sponge cake and brush each circle with liqueur to moisten the cakes. Top half of the rounds with a dollop of whipped cream and a few peach slices. Place the remaining rounds on top of the peaches and cover the cakes with whipped cream. Top each cake with pieces of meringue and the remaining peaches. Refrigerate for a few hours before serving.

Dulce de leche (caramelized sweetened condensed milk) is a national obsession in both Uruguay and Paraguay and is used to fill cookies, cakes, pastries, crepes, and *alfajores* (shortbread cookies), or as a topping for flan, a rich custard dessert originating in Spain. Sweet fruit pastes called *dulces* are popular in both countries and are used as fillings for empanadas, pastries, or cakes. A sweet quince paste called *dulce de membrillo* is especially popular in Uruguay and fills mini-shortbread cakes called *pasta frola.* A typical treat for breakfast, dessert, or a snack is *Martín Fierro,* named after an epic gaucho poem. It consists simply of a slice of cheese and a slice of dulce de membrillo.

Uruguay has produced its own beer and wine since the late 19th century. The country's wine industry is indebted to French and Italian immigrants and is the fourth largest in South America. Most Uruguayan wine is produced in the southern coastal departments. A red wine called Tannat is produced exclusively in Uruguay and southern France. In Uruguay, as in neighboring Argentina and coastal Chile, there exists a vast wine culture that is not found on the rest of the continent. Wines are consumed not only solo but also mixed in the form of *medio y medio,* a mixture of white wine and sparkling wine, or *clericó,* a mixture of fruits, fruit juice, and white wine. Often considered the Uruguayan national spirit, *grappamiel* claims Italian roots and is a potent spirit made with alcohol and honey. Gin Fizz is popular, especially in Montevideo, as is *limoncello,* an Italian lemon liqueur. In Paraguay, beer and a locally produced dark sugarcane spirit called *caña* are the most widely consumed alcoholic beverages.

A drink universally enjoyed in both Paraguay and Uruguay, regardless of geographic location or socioeconomic situation, is a bitter tea called maté. The drink is native to Paraguay and is made from the dried leaves of the *Ilex paraguariensis* shrub, which grows wild along the upper reaches of the Paraguay River. In pre-Columbian times, yerba maté was harvested by the Guaraní Indians. The Spanish subsequently adopted the beverage, and Jesuit missionaries in Paraguay and northeastern Argentina were the first to cultivate the shrub. Today, maté is consumed in vast quantities in Paraguay, Uruguay, and Argentina in a communal ritual that attests to the social nature of the culture of these countries.

Cooking

Cooking habits can differ greatly between urban and rural areas, although women are usually in charge of daily culinary tasks. Uruguayan and Paraguayan kitchens, especially those in cities, make good use of modern appliances like microwaves and blenders to ease the culinary workload. In Uruguay, most dishes involve techniques that originated in Europe, such as rolling fresh pastas and doughs, baking cakes and pies, making vinaigrettes, and pickling vegetables, meats, or seafood. The French culinary influence can be seen in the frequent use of *salsa blanca* (béchamel) and puff pastry. Today, many of these foodstuffs are available ready-made in supermarkets.

Traditional Guaraní cooking techniques and names are still reflected in the Paraguayan kitchen. Today, urban Paraguayans use a gas or electric stove, but a brick-and-clay oven called a *tatakua* ("fire hole" in the Guaraní language) was traditionally a fundamental part of Paraguayan food preparation. It is still widely used, especially in rural areas and for special occasions, for baking the breads called chipá or roasting meats. Many traditional dishes are available ready-made or partially made, canned, frozen, or packaged in supermarkets in urban areas. In rural areas, many families cannot afford the luxury of convenient ready-made products, so dishes are made from scratch.

Soups, stews, and braises are especially popular in Paraguay and Uruguay and combine European and native techniques and ingredients. They often begin with a *sofrito* of tomatoes, bell peppers, onions, garlic, and other aromatics. Various vegetables and beans are then added, as well as meats, depending on the economic means of the family. Soups and stews are traditionally prepared in cast iron or earthenware pots, but some modern kitchens use pressure cookers to speed cooking time.

Typical Uruguayan soups and stews include *buseca,* a winter tripe soup, and stews called *locros* or *pucheros,* made with meat, beans, lentils, and vegetables. The native ñandú (rhea) is used in stews, in either fresh or dried form. *Carbonada criolla* is a typical Uruguayan beef or veal stew with vegetables and fruit and is usually served in the shell of a winter squash.

In Paraguay, soups and stews are often finished with a handful of rice, milk, beaten eggs, or fresh cheese to stretch the dish. The popular *borí borí* is a meat soup with cornmeal and cheese dumplings. To make the much-loved traditional *so'o yosopy* (beef and rice soup), popularly called *soyo,* ground beef and rice are traditionally mashed together in a mortar to form a paste. This paste forms the base of the soup and is cooked with onions, peppers, tomatoes, and other aromatics in an iron pot with beef or pork fat. Today, many simplify the process by grinding the meat and rice in a blender and have made it healthier by using vegetable oils instead of animal fats.

So'o Yosopy (Beef and Rice Soup)

1 lb ground beef

2 tbsp white rice

2 medium onions, chopped

1 tomato, chopped

1 green bell pepper, chopped

3 tbsp lard or oil

1 tbsp flour

1½ qt cold water

1½ tbsp parsley, chopped

Salt

Pound meat and rice in a mortar or grind in a food processor until a paste forms. Remove, and then grind the onion, tomato, and pepper until smooth.

Heat the oil in a large, heavy-bottomed pot. Cook the vegetables until they begin to brown. Add the flour and stir for a minute. Then add the meat paste and water. Stir until the soup comes to a boil, and then cook for a few more minutes, just until the meat is cooked. Add parsley and salt to taste.

Typical Meals

The Uruguayan meal structure is similar to that in southern Europe, with three meals, an afternoon teatime, and snacks. Uruguayans eat a simple breakfast at home or in a café, most often consisting of coffee with milk or maté tea and simple pastries or croissants. Lunch is the main meal of the day and is traditionally homemade and eaten at home with the family, even on weekdays. A typical lunch involves three courses: an appetizer; a main dish of meat (usually beef) accompanied by potatoes, bread, and a simple green salad; and a simple dessert. Appetizers might be cold marinated beef tongue or *matambre,* a cold beef or veal roulade stuffed with vegetables, served with Russian salad (potatoes, peas, and carrots bound together with mayonnaise). The main-course meat dish is often steak, *milanesas* (fried breaded cutlets), stews, meat pies, *estofados* (braised meats), hamburgers, or pastas. Dessert might be fresh or canned fruit, or ice cream. Since lunch is the heaviest meal of the day, Uruguayans often take a siesta (nap), then return to work until 7 or 8 in the evening. At night they will have a light dinner, usually around 10 or 11. Dinner is usually low-fuss, with families eating take-out pizza, empanadas, or *bocatas* (sandwiches of cold cuts on a baguette) or repurposing leftovers from lunch into stews, soups, or casseroles. Milanesas or other simple beef dishes can also be eaten for dinner. Soft drinks, beer, and wine are commonly served at lunch and dinner, and juices and *licuados* (juices mixed with milk or water) are also popular in Uruguay.

Between lunch and dinner is the *merienda* (teatime) when people drink maté, a very important custom in both Uruguay and Paraguay. Maté is a tea that is sipped from a gourd using a metal straw in an elaborate ritual shared among family and friends. It is enjoyed everywhere—at work, at school, at home, or in the street. In Uruguay, maté is accompanied by snacks called *bizcochos,* which are buttery, flaky pastries of European origin with many sweet and savory variations. Paraguayans often drink a cold infusion of yerba maté leaves called *tereré.* Tereré is excellent for mitigating the intense heat of the Paraguayan summer.

In Paraguay, typical meals and mealtimes vary between the countryside and urban areas. Urbanites are likely to follow a European meal structure similar to that in Uruguay: a simple breakfast, a large lunch followed by a siesta, an afternoon teatime, and a light dinner. Rural Paraguayans are more likely to eat two meals a day, including a more substantial breakfast and a large lunch. The typical meal structure involves meat-based dishes such as milanesas or *bife koyguá* (steak topped with onions and fried eggs) accompanied by yucca, chipá, and simple salads.

Uruguayans and Paraguayans get together most weekends with family and friends to enjoy an asado, an event similar to the American barbecue that traces its roots to the culture of the gaucho. The asado is considered the national dish of Uruguay. The centerpiece of the asado is simply seasoned grilled beef, variety meats, and sausages, all cooked slowly over wood embers at a low temperature until well done. A generous one pound of meat per person is usually allotted, and the meat is handled almost exclusively by men. In Uruguay, the asado is accompanied by simple salads, sauces, bread, and fresh fruit or fruit salads for dessert. Yucca and chipá are also present at the Paraguayan asado. Wine, beer, and maté are always on hand, and music, dancing, and card games are enjoyed throughout the day.

Eating Out

While eating out is popular in the cities, country towns have limited options. Both Paraguay and Uruguay have their fair share of local fast food and street food that easily rivals competition from global multinational chains. Hamburgers and hot dogs (called *panchos*) are popular, but beef sandwiches called *chivitos* in Uruguay and *lomitos* in Paraguay, along with *milanesa al pan* (fried cutlet sandwiches) and *choripán* (sausage sandwiches), can be found on the streets, in bus or train stations, and, in Uruguay, in cafélike establishments called *confiterías*.

Other popular urban snacks sold on street corners or at stalls in Uruguay include *garrapiñada,* a mixture of peanuts, cocoa, vanilla, and sugar, and *tortas fritas,* fried cakes that are often topped with sugar, dulce de leche, or marmalade. The European influence on eating out in Uruguay can be seen in the popularity of cafés and pizzerias. Apart from pizzas cooked in wood-fired ovens, Uruguayan pizzerias typically offer a variety of empanadas and a specialty called *fainá* (chickpea-flour bread).

In Paraguay, chipás are sold as inexpensive roadside snacks, on buses, or by vendors called *chiperas* who ride bicycles around town or walk door-to-door selling their fresh breads in the late afternoon. *Asadito* stands are found in the streets offering roasted meat on a stick served with yucca. Paraguayan markets sell traditional ingredients and foods that are not available at the major supermarkets, such as fresh artisanal cheeses and game meat like ñandú (rhea) or deer. Vendors in these markets also sell many prepared traditional dishes, such as soyo with *tortillitas* (beef soup with fried cakes).

Uruguayans are mainly traditional in their eating habits, and most restaurants offer some combination of pastas, pizzas, salads, meat platters, and local beers and wines. The most expensive and exclusive eateries in Montevideo tend to offer French cuisine. It has been said there is a lack of ethnic eateries even in cosmopolitan Montevideo, and vegetarians often feel left out of the local cuisine. This is especially true at the ubiquitous *parrilla,* the most popular type of restaurant in the country. It is here that the asado is served in a public setting. Another specialty restaurant is the gaucho club, which specializes in typical gaucho dishes such as *asado con cuero* (beef cooked in its skin) and *mazamorra* (dried-corn stew). In Uruguayan cities and resorts along the Atlantic coast, restaurants offer freshly caught seafood.

Traditionally, meals have been eaten in the home with family, and this continues to hold high value in Paraguay, even though many living in big cities are forced to eat out at least once a day as urban sprawl and work schedules prevent a trip home. Restaurants continue to remain out of the budgetary reach of many Paraguayans, especially in rural areas where diners are conservative in their tastes and prefer traditional dishes and ingredients. Urban Paraguayans have a more adventurous palate, and Asunción has its fair share of eateries offering foreign food. The contribution of Paraguay's immigrant groups is seen in restaurants offering Italian, French, Chinese, Japanese, Korean, German, and Arab fare, as well as foods from neighboring Brazil and Argentina. Parrillas are a popular place to eat grilled meats as well as traditional Paraguayan dishes like chipá guazú, sopa paraguaya, and breaded and fried surubí. Until recently, typical Paraguayan foods were enjoyed almost exclusively in the home, but recently specialized restaurants and shops in urban areas have begun selling uniquely Paraguayan dishes in a "local" atmosphere.

Special Occasions

Because of the social nature of Uruguayan and Paraguayan culture, holidays and special occasions make great excuses for friends and families to gather and enjoy a special meal. In general, traditional special-occasion dishes are prepared by women, with the exception of the asado. Families in both countries hold asados to celebrate private events like birthdays, weddings, or the christening of a newborn. In Paraguay, chipá is considered a festive food and can be found at every popular religious celebration. Sopa paraguaya is the traditional dish served at weddings, for holidays, and on special occasions.

In Uruguay, the two major holidays are Christmas and Easter. Christmas falls at the height of summer in southern South America, so meals are light, with cold meats, salads, and seafood playing a central role. The most traditional Christmas dishes are *pan dulce* (sweet bread) and English pudding with dried fruits and nuts. Uruguayan Easter festivities begin in February with Carnival, a monthlong, countrywide celebration involving street parties, musical theater, masquerades, parades, music, dancing, singing, drinking, and eating.

For Christmas in Paraguay, the main celebratory meal occurs after midnight mass on Christmas Eve, and most Paraguayans prepare a mixture of traditional Paraguayan specialties along with more modern fare like a turkey or rice and meat dishes. Clericó, a mixture of fruit, wine, and sugar, is drunk throughout the day, and the arrival of Christmas is celebrated with a champagne toast. Holy Week calls for major celebration and features traditional Paraguayan dishes, especially various chipás, which are made more "special" by shaping them like animals and baking them in the traditional tatakua oven. During the days leading up to Easter, meatless preparations of traditional dishes are consumed, such as the corn-based *locro de Cuaresma* (Lent stew) or *locro blanco* (white stew). *Kyrype,* a fried tortilla of starch, cheese, egg, and onion, is also typically eaten during this time, as well as meatless *empanadas de Vigilia* (abstinence turnovers), which are typically filled with a tuna stuffing. After mass on Easter Sunday, families gather to celebrate and eat a festive meal centered on meat.

Another major Paraguayan holiday is the Feast of Saint John. It is enthusiastically celebrated all over the country on June 24, during Paraguay's winter. The day begins with mass, and many typical winter specialties such as polenta, *chipá asador* (chipá wrapped around a wooden dowel or broomstick and roasted over coals), or *payaguá mascada* (Indian fried fritters stuffed with ground beef, also known as *lampreado*) accompany the festivities. Pagan rituals and contests are enjoyed throughout the day, especially in the countryside, and include

pelota tata (kicking around a ball of fire), fire walking, climbing up greased posts, and the burning of Judas Iscariot in effigy.

Diet and Health

Uruguay has one of the best health systems in South America, and life expectancy is high for the region. The country has one of the lowest poverty levels on the continent, and energy and protein malnutrition are not serious threats. Most of Uruguay's health problems are those associated with excess. Obesity is quite prevalent and is caused by a high consumption of beef and dairy products, which lead to a diet rich in saturated fats. The Uruguayan diet also includes high consumption of sugars and carbohydrates in the form of potatoes, pastas, breads, sodas, alcoholic beverages, and sugary desserts. The major causes of death in Uruguay are diet related and include heart disease, cancer, and digestive disorders. Uruguay has the highest percentage of diabetics in South America. Studies suggest that Uruguayans' knowledge, attitudes, and practices concerning food and nutrition are inadequate, and measures are being taken to influence dietary choices to include more fruits, vegetables, fish, and fiber.

In Paraguay, access to proper health care and fresh drinking water varies greatly from city to countryside. Paraguay also has among the lowest rates of undernourishment and malnutrition in Latin America, yet deficiency disorders do occur, especially among the lowest-income population and in rural areas. The typical Paraguayan diet includes a high amount of carbohydrates and saturated fats. Yucca is the main source of carbohydrates, but corn products, sodas, fruit juices, sugar, and beer also contribute. Saturated fats come in the form of meat, especially beef, and animal fats used in cooking. Due to changing dietary trends and increasing knowledge among some sections of the population, some Paraguayans are changing traditional recipes by substituting vegetable oils for animal fats such as suet or lard. Cardiovascular diseases are among the leading causes of death for Paraguayan adults.

The botanical-medicinal heritage of the indigenous groups of Paraguay has been preserved to some extent, particularly in rural areas. Paraguayans frequently add herbs to the water used to brew tereré to heal minor ailments such as headaches or stomachaches. Certain traditional dishes are also believed to provide specific health and nutritional benefits. An example is *itacurú cué* (tripe soup), believed to restore health to the ill, provide strength to the frail, and increase milk production for women who are nursing.

Cari Sánchez

Further Reading

Kijac, Maria Baez. *The South American Table.* Boston: Harvard Common Press, 2003.

Livieres de Artecona, Doña Raquel. *La Cocinera Paraguaya.* Asunción, Paraguay: Editorial La Colmena SA, 1931. Available online at http://www.cocina-guarani.com.ar/.

Lovera, José Rafael. *Food Culture in South America.* Westport, CT: Greenwood Press, 2005.

"Paraguayan Gastronomy." Paraguay.com. http://www.paraguay.com/arts_and_culture/paraguayan_gastronomy.php.

Velilla de Aquino, Josefina. *Tembi'u Paraguái: Comida paraguaya.* 13th ed. Asunción, Paraguay: RP Ediciones, 2002.

Peru

Overview

Peru stretches from the Pacific coast of South America east to the Brazilian jungle. Ecuador and Colombia border Peru to the north, Chile to the south. Bolivia, formerly known as Upper Peru, lies southeast of Peru. Bolivia separated from Peru to become its own country in 1825. The capital of Peru, Lima, is located in the arid coastal section of the country and has its own world-renowned cuisine, sometimes called *cocina criolla.* The cuisines of the Andes Mountains, both the traditional indigenous cuisine and the more modern *cocina novoandina,* are also popular. The *selva* (jungle) region around the Amazon River is less developed but provides the country with beverages made from its exotic tropical fruits.

The Andes Mountains run north to south through Peru in at least three chains, with valleys and plateaus at different altitudes between them. The resulting vertical landscape, made up of diverse microclimates, has been under cultivation for centuries. Fertilization, natural pest-control techniques, cross-breeding, and crop development are practiced simultaneously in different climatic zones, perpetuating an agro-organic system that is better adapted to this geography than a monocrop plantation system, though there are large sugar and cotton plantations in the coastal area.

The Inca Empire, an empire made up of various indigenous tribes, existed for roughly 100 years before the Spanish conquest in 1532. After the conquest, indigenous foodways intersected with Spanish culinary traditions to form the basis of Peruvian cuisine. Labor shortages during the colonial period were addressed by the importation of slaves from Africa. Afro-Peruvians working in coastal agriculture, livestock production, and food preparation impacted Peruvian cuisine significantly, especially as it developed in the colonial period. In fact, the burst of creative culinary experimentation that eventually produced Peruvian cuisine was a result of the coming together of these three ethnicities—indigenous Peruvians, Spanish, and Africans. The introduction of new ingredients as a result of the Columbian Exchange and the growth of Lima, the capital and trade center of South America for much of the 16th, 17th, and 18th centuries, also impacted the development of Peruvian cuisine.

In the 19th century, immigrant groups like the Chinese, Japanese, and Italians inserted their food traditions into the Peruvian culture and influenced the cuisine. In Peru, new culinary ideas are embraced with a spirit of innovation. Peruvian Chinese food and Peruvian Japanese food are subgroups of Peruvian cuisine. Dishes from these traditions combine flavors from their ethnic roots with distinctly Peruvian tastes.

🍽 Food Culture Snapshot

Felipe and Giannina Quevedo live in a spacious apartment in the Surco district of Lima. Felipe is an industrial engineer, and Giannina is a professor of hospitality administration at St. Ignacio de Loyola University. They have two young children.

Felipe and Giannina have a simple breakfast of rolls and coffee each morning before going to work. If possible, they will both return home for the midday meal, which consists of typical Peruvian dishes, such as *arroz con pato* (rice with duck), *ají de gallina* (shredded chicken in a spicy sauce), or *carne asada* (grilled beef). A British-style afternoon tea is served around 5 P.M. It usually consists of tea, small sandwiches, and/or sweets. The family has a light supper later in the evening, which may include a soup or *tortilla de patata* (potato omelet).

Giannina buys most of their food and household supplies at a supermarket. She also shops at local specialty stores for items such as bread, milk, and meat. On Sundays, the family goes to Giannina's mother's home for a large meal with her brothers and sisters and their children. For this meal, they may purchase fish directly from the fishermen at the port of Callao, or they may visit the open-air market in Lima where they can purchase fresh produce or prepared specialty foods.

Major Foodstuffs

The potato and its distant relative the sweet potato are native to Peru and were unknown to the Old World before the Spanish conquest in 1532. The number of potato varieties grown in Peru may be as high as 4,000, not including the 2,000 varieties of sweet potatoes. Of all the varieties, the buttery, soft, and starchy yellow potato (*papa amarilla*) is one of the most popular. Before mills for grinding flour and baking ovens were widespread in Peru, Spanish nobles served platters of different-colored potatoes at banquets in place of bread. Today, many dishes, such as ceviche (raw fish marinated in lime), are typically served with a piece of boiled potato or sweet potato as a garnish. *Escribano,* a dish from Arequipa, is a type of potato salad soaked in *chicha de jora* (corn beer). *Causa* is a cold "torte" made out of layers of colorful vegetable or seafood salads and pureed potato. *Huanacayna* sauce, a creamy egg-based sauce, is always served over potatoes, as is *ocopa,* a sauce made with *huacatay* (Peruvian black mint).

A variety of potatoes being sold at a Peruvian market. (Dreamstime)

Huancayna Sauce

Sauce for 6 servings of papas a la huancayna
1 tbsp *ají amarillo* paste
½ lb *queso fresco*
½ lb ricotta
1 oz fresh breadcrumbs (no crusts), soaked in milk
1 egg, hard-boiled
1 c oil
3 lemons, juiced
2 saltine crackers
Salt and white pepper to taste

In a food processor, mix the ají paste, cheeses, soaked bread, and yolk from the hard-boiled egg. Add the oil and lemon juice to the cheese mixture slowly while food processor is on. Add the remaining milk from the soaked bread and saltine crackers. Thin the sauce with milk or thicken with saltines as needed; it should have the consistency of a light sauce to coat the potatoes. Season with salt and pepper.

Pour over cold potatoes and decorate with bibb lettuce, Peruvian olives, and hard-boiled eggs.

Corn (maize) was cultivated in Peru perhaps as early as 3000 B.C. There are 35 varieties of maize found today in Peru. *Choclo* is the Peruvian name for the large-kernel maize that is used in Peruvian cuisine. Like potatoes, choclo is often used as a garnish for traditional Peruvian dishes, such as ceviche. *Humitas* are soft maize pastes folded into leaves and cooked in steam, similar to Mexican tamales. Purple maize is boiled to provide a richly colored juice base for the dessert *mazamorra morada* and for the refreshing purple drink *chicha morada* (now sold in the United States as "natural Peruvian purple corn-based drink"). The juice of the purple maize is known to be high in antioxidants.

Quinoa, which is native to Peru, is a pseudograin containing all eight essential amino acids. Its high protein content made it a valued grain in the starch-based pre-Columbian diet of the Incas. Its recent popularity in the United States has led to an increase in production for export. Taking advantage of its newly acquired popularity, *novoandina* chefs use quinoa in haute cuisine preparations, creating such dishes as wild mushroom quinoa pilaf, "quinotto" (quinoa risotto) with truffle oil and *pallares* (giant lima beans), and quinoa-crusted flounder with grilled vegetables.

Quinoa contains saponins, toxins that leave a bitter taste on the grain. To remove the taste and the effects of the toxin, quinoa must be pre-rinsed or quick-boiled before cooking. Agricultural engineers have produced genetically modified strains of quinoa without saponins; however, this quinoa attracts pests and birds. Peruvian farmers prefer to sell the quinoa with its natural toxin rather than introduce pesticides into their agricultural practices.

Peruvian chili peppers are called *ají*. Their flavor is more subtle than the biting hot chili peppers found elsewhere in Latin America. Most Peruvian dishes contain ají in some form, though the cuisine, on the whole, is not overly spicy.

The Peruvian guinea pig, *cuy,* is a traditional meat item in Peru, especially in the Andean regions. Cuy are often kept in and around family homes, where they breed and require very little maintenance. They are slaughtered and prepared at home. The meat of the cuy is usually rubbed with an ají-spice mix, then roasted, stewed, or grilled. In Peru, cuy is considered a delicacy preferable to rabbit or suckling pig.

A large array of domesticated animals came into Peru's food supply as a result of the Columbian Exchange, including cows, pigs, goats, sheep, chickens, and rabbits. In the colonial period, the inability of cattle to reproduce at high altitudes, which persisted for some years after the conquest, as well as the indigenous Peruvians' fears of these large animals, kept the beef industry on the coast near the city of Lima, where it was also closer to the wealthier, beef-eating population of Europeans. From these early times, the beef industry was manned mainly by Africans. Cattle slaughterhouses were located in the San Lazaro district, the African section of the city, near the slave quarters and the slave market. Even today, the majority of the slaughterhouses are staffed by Afro-Peruvians. *Anticuchos,* Peruvian street food at its best, are made from beef hearts macerated in a spicy marinade, then threaded on skewers and grilled over a wood fire. Afro-Peruvians took advantage of their proximity to the slaughterhouses to create beef dishes like anticuchos that they could sell on the streets. Many bought their freedom with money earned from food-related side businesses. Dairy products were unknown in Peru before the Spanish conquest. Peruvian cuisine takes advantage of the textural qualities of cheese and evaporated milk but rarely exploits these ingredients for their flavor.

European plant foods that influenced Peruvian cuisine include wheat, grapes, olives, garlic, lemons, rice, and sugar. Peruvian *botija* olives were derived from a Spanish breed of black Alfonso olives. The name *botija* comes from the type of clay pot in which they were originally cured. Their purple color and creamy flavor come from a unique system that involves fermentation with live bacteria. Botija olives have become a specialty food export product. They are served in a type of olive mayonnaise with octopus in the Peruvian dish *pulpo al olivo.*

Peruvian lemons are similar to key limes. They are bright green and aromatic. Their flavor is smooth and sour, not quite as bitter as lemons. Peruvian lemons are important ingredients in ceviche and the cocktail *pisco sour.*

The closest Pacific port to the city of Lima is the Port of Callao. The particular way in which the Humboldt Current passes by this port draws in large quantities of plankton, making it a perfect feeding ground for a wide variety of fish. Before the conquest, indigenous *chasquis* (runners) had an established relay system whereby they delivered fresh fish, and other goods, from the Pacific coast to the Inca royalty in Cuzco at an altitude of 10,000 feet above sea level in less than 24 hours. The most famous Peruvian dish is ceviche, made from raw fish marinated in Peruvian lemon juice, similar to lime juice. Ceviche is usually served with a slice of sweet potato and a few kernels of choclo as a garnish.

Ceviche

Serves 6

2 lb wild striped bass or fresh grouper

25 limes or 50 key limes

Salt and pepper

Red onions, julienned and rinsed in cold water

Ají amarillo to taste, minced

Large-kernel corn, boiled

Sweet potato, boiled and cut in rounds

Cut fish into bite-size pieces. Place them in a glass or ceramic bowl. Add lime juice, salt, and pepper. (If using American limes, you may need to add a little orange juice concentrate if the acidity level is too high.) Add onions and ají. Garnish with sweet potato and corn. Keep cold in an ice bath. Serve refreshingly cool.

Peru's rivers also provide fish for dishes such as *chupe de camarones.* Large Peruvian freshwater crayfish are cooked whole to make this one-pot meal that includes breadcrumbs, garlic, onion, tomato, corn, peas, potatoes, rice, cheese, milk, stock, ají, and chicha de jora.

In the Andean highlands, the dry mountain air and dramatic temperature changes from day to night facilitated the development of techniques for producing freeze-dried and air-dried foods. Indigenous dried foods that are still present in Peruvian cuisine include *chuño* and *papas secas* (two types of dried potato), *charqui* (dried meat), dried, salted fish, and *cancha* (toasted, dry corn kernels). Papas secas are the main ingredient in the traditional dish *carapulcra,* a meat stew similar to chili.

Catholic European settlers, who used wine in the celebration of their religious liturgy and enjoyed it as a beverage as well, were eager to produce wine in the New World. However, it was not until 1560, when the fertile grape vineyards of the Ica region of Peru were fully developed, that the first vintage of New World wine was produced. Peru had a flourishing wine export industry until it was shut down in 1614 due to complaints from competing wine producers in Spain. The grape harvest was then used to produce *pisco* (Peruvian grape brandy), which became the main ingredient for the famous Peruvian cocktail, the pisco sour. Another pisco cocktail is *algarrobina,* made with pisco, condensed milk, and the sweet sap of the Peruvian *algarroba* tree.

Even when wine was abundant and cheap in Peru, the indigenous people preferred their own traditional drink, chicha de jora (maize beer). Euro-Peruvians from the colonial period also enjoyed chicha; the aristocratic Doña Josepha Escurrachea put a recipe for chicha de jora in her 1776 cookbook, listing it after a series of fruit drinks also called chichas. Contemporary Andean women continue to make chicha de jora at home. A red stick outside the door of one of their dwellings indicates that there is chicha for sale there. Modern chefs use chicha de jora for marinades and salad dressings.

Rice came to Peru from Spain via the Moors, who introduced it there in the Middle Ages, though strains of African rice breeds have been found among the Peruvian rice crops as well. In Peru, rice is often served with potatoes.

Olluquito con charqui is a traditional Peruvian dish that illustrates the blending of cultures in the cuisine. *Olluco* is a small tuber, native to Peru, with moist, juicy flesh. Olluco is popular with indigenous

Aymara, who liken it to "drops of rain." *Olluquito* is *olluco* with the Spanish diminutive *ito* attached. Charqui is dried meat. The word *charqui* is similar to the Quechua word for "dry," but it is also an Arabic word. In olluquito con charqui, the olluco and the charqui are cut in a fine julienne and cooked in an ají-garlic sauce. Ají is from Peru; garlic is from Europe. Olluqito con charqui is always served with rice, which indicates that the dish probably has Moorish or African roots, or both.

Three Peruvian tubers, olluco, *mashua,* and *oca,* are frost-resistant and grow together with potatoes in the highlands of Peru in an agro-organic system that controls pests and diseases. Although these tubers are part of the Andean diet, only the olluco is used in popular Peruvian cuisine. From the temperate highlands comes *lúcuma,* a tuberous fruit with a high starch content and flavor somewhat like coffee or maple. Lúcuma is the most popular ice cream flavor in Peru. Lúcuma is also used to flavor puddings and dessert beverages. Fresh lúcuma pulp can be frozen, making it useful for export along with other fruit purees.

Cooking

One-pot meals cooked in Spanish *ollas* (covered cooking pots) over wood fires are called *chupes* in Peru. *Ollas de barro* (clay pots) are traditional and are valued for the flavor they impart to food cooked on the wood fire. Wood-fired stoves are important for grilled dishes as well, such as anticuchos and *pollo a la brasa* (rotisserie chicken). Peruvians like to cook *chicharrón de cerdo,* pork fried to a crisp in its own fat, in large *sartenes* (pans) on open-air wood-fired stoves. Among the hardwoods that are used to fire these stoves, the wood of the Peruvian algarroba (a cousin of the mesquite) is valued. Since city dwellers rarely have wood-fired stoves in their homes or apartments, these dishes are usually enjoyed in restaurants or at vacation homes in the country.

Fried foods are popular in coastal cuisine. *Jalea* is a fried fish platter that includes fried plantains, fried yucca, and a corn salsa called *chalaca. Tacu tacu* is a fried "tortilla" made out of day-old rice and beans. It is used as a bed for meat, eggs, and/or

ripe plantains. *Lomo saltado* is a Peruvian stir-fry of beef tenderloin, onion, tomato, cilantro, soy sauce, garlic, and ají. It is served with rice and French fries. The stir-fry technique was introduced by Chinese immigrants in the 19th century. Lomo saltado is cooked in an extremely hot pan to produce a crisp, slightly charred flavor. Sometimes the pan is flamed with pisco as a finish to the dish.

For centuries in the high Andes, at the time of the potato harvest, indigenous families have met in the fields, where they cook humitas and new potatoes on heated stones buried in a pit. The festive meals cooked in these rustic outdoor cooking pits are called *pachamanca.* A large pachamanca, organized to celebrate the anniversary of a hacienda (ranch), may include meats, corn, potatoes, native tubers,

Lomo saltado, a Peruvian steak dish. (iStockPhoto)

and humitas. Coastal pachamancas use yucca and plantains. Harvest-time *huatias* are outdoor meals cooked in fires built under mounds of earth. Potatoes and fava beans cooked under these mounds are said to take on the deep, rich flavors of the minerals in the soil.

Potatoes and sweet potatoes are often served in their simplest form: boiled. Boiled potatoes of all colors are mashed or left whole to serve as the base for refreshing salads and spicy cold sauces. To prepare sauces, the *batan,* a large concave stone with a matching oval stone, used to grind grains, herbs, and ajís, is sometimes used. The batan is favored in Peru over the mortar and pestle for many culinary tasks.

Typical Meals

Typical breakfast fare in Peru is hard rolls, a cheese platter, butter and jam, and hot milk with coffee extract. *Almuerzo* is the main meal of the day. It usually falls between 1:30 and 2 P.M. and consists of two courses and a dessert. More recently, so as to adapt to the modern workday schedule, Peruvians have abandoned the traditional midday meal on weekdays. This means that the weekend almuerzo has become even more important. On workdays, people eat a small meal in the middle of the day and a heavier supper than usual in the evening.

For a weekend "family meal," the following are some popular first courses: *solterito* (a salad of fava beans, choclo, olives, and fresh cheese with a light vinaigrette), causa, papas a la huancayna, ceviche, anticuchos, or *papas rellenas* (meat-stuffed potato croquettes). In colder weather a soup, such as *parihuela* (Peruvian-style bouillabaisse) or chupe de camarones, may be served. The main course would be a heavier meat or fish dish, of which there are many in the classic repertoire of Peruvian cuisine. The cooking techniques, sauces, and accompaniments for most of these traditional main dishes are well known and well defined owing to the long food history of the country.

Desserts might include *suspiro a la Limeña,* which means "sighs of person from Lima" (a pudding of condensed milk, butter, and cream), *arroz con leche* (rice pudding), *milhojas* (layered pastry crisps with

manjar blanco—caramelized reduced milk like *dulce de leche*), or ice creams flavored with native Peruvian ingredients such as lúcuma, cherimoya, *guanábana,* purple maize, or algarrobina.

Merienda is the common Spanish and South American name for the snack taken around 5 P.M.; however, in Peru it is often referred to as *el té* and resembles British afternoon tea. Foods may be salty or sweet, formal or informal, depending on the day or the family traditions.

Supper is served sometimes as late as 9 P.M. It is a simple, one-course meal. Soups, *sangos* (porridges), or *locro* (a thick soup/stew made from Peruvian squashes and cheese) are popular. Sandwiches or cold cheese and meat platters may also be served.

Eating Out

Peruvians love to eat in public places, especially on weekends, surrounded by friends and relatives. Long-standing traditions of making, selling, and serving food outside of the home have created a varied, thriving restaurant and prepared-food industry. Perhaps the oldest type of Peruvian restaurant is the rustic *picantería,* typical of Arequipa. These family-run eateries are usually known for their spicy dishes and chichas.

Cocina criolla refers specifically to the traditional cuisine of Peruvian-born Europeans, but it can also refer to the cuisine of Lima. There are many restaurants in Lima, expensive and less expensive ones, where traditional cocina criolla is served. First courses almost always include ceviche, anticuchos, papas a la huancayna, and causa. Main entrées could be ají de gallina, *olluquito con carne,* carapulcra, jalea, *chicharrón,* or lomo saltado.

The most famous haute cuisine restaurant in Peru is superchef Gaston Acurio's Astrid y Gaston in Lima. Acurio is a French-trained chef who is determined to put Peruvian cuisine on the map. The restaurant is one of the first of several restaurants in Peru that have developed high-end standards and modern presentation styles for cocina criolla. These restaurants have also embraced the novoandina style of cooking, which showcases native Peruvian highland crops and indigenous cooking traditions in a haute cuisine setting. A high-end novoandina restaurant may serve the low-brow Afro-Peruvian staple tacu tacu (fried beans and rice) with seared yellowfin tuna, orange-endive salsa criolla, and a gooseberry–ají amarillo sauce.

Family-run sandwich shops in Lima, called *chicharronerías,* sell classic Peruvian fried pork sandwiches. *Cevicherías* are usually quaint, fun, family-owned seaside restaurants. The decor is unpretentious. Often, the owner is the fisherman, and his wife is the cook. Cevicherías compete with Japanese sushi bars, which serve sushi, sashimi, and Peruvian-style sushi called *tiraditos.* There are many inexpensive Chinese restaurants in Lima and other coastal cities. They have been an important presence in the country for over 100 years. Italian restaurants serving pasta dishes, like ravioli, are also familiar. The Miraflores district of Lima has a street dedicated almost entirely to pizzerias.

Street vendors have been a fixture in the plazas of Lima since the 16th century. Many of Peru's most beloved dishes, like anticuchos and chicha morada, were first sold as street food. Famous 19th-century street vendors include Erasmo, the "negro" sango vendor, and Ña Aguedita, who wrapped herself in woven scarves and dished out *fresceras, mazamorras,* and *champus* from three stone pots in Lima's open market. These colorful characters became iconic representatives of the multiethnic cuisine of Peru. In the more recent past, attitudes toward street vendors have been both positive and negative. With the increase in poverty and crime in the later 20th century, the streets and their vendors became less attractive than they once were. Nevertheless, recognizing the economic potential inherent in a quality street-food industry, the government has begun to make it easier for food businesses in the informal sector to legalize their enterprises and become more profitable.

Many of the famous Peruvian sweets were invented in convents, which competed with one another for the business of wealthy Peruvians, especially in the colonial period. Peruvian sweets often contain manjar blanco (Peruvian dulce de leche). Peruvian sweets are usually dense, very sweet rectangular confections that are cut into small squares and served in the afternoon or as a dessert after the main meal.

International fast-food chains such as McDonald's, Burger King, and Starbucks can be found in Peru only in the city of Lima. Tourist sites in the Andes and Amazonia tend to focus on ecotourists and those who desire an "authentic" Peruvian food experience. Local Peruvians prefer Peruvian food to all other foods. One of Gaston Acurio's goals is to market fast-food operations that will sell *pan con chicharrón* (Peruvian fried pork sandwiches) internationally as an alternative to the hamburger.

Peruvians have such a strong sentimental attachment to their cuisine that they welcome packaged and frozen foods that enable them to experience the flavors of Peru when they are elsewhere. Powdered versions of huancayna, ocopa, and other sauces are available. Ají can be purchased dried or canned. Frozen kits for making anticuchos can be found in Latin markets in the United States. One can even purchase a microwaveable vacuum-packed pachamanca, complete with choclo; yellow potatoes; Peruvian roots such as olluco, oca, mashua, *yacón,* and *maca;* along with humitas, as far away from Peru as Germany.

Special Occasions

Approximately 82 percent of Peruvians are Roman Catholic. While Catholic feasts, such as Christmas and Holy Week, are celebrated in Peru, days of fasting and abstinence are less common than in other countries because of *la bula,* a papal bull that gave privileges, including exemption from fasts, to Spain and her colonies. The bull was discontinued in the 1960s, but the spirit of feasting is still dominant in Peruvian culture.

El Señor de los Milagros is a specifically Peruvian feast celebrating a 17th-century mural painted by an Afro-Peruvian of a dark-skinned Christ on the cross. The mural stimulated popular piety but was not appreciated by local authorities, who made several unsuccessful attempts to have it removed from its prominent location. In 1655, when an earthquake reduced the entire section of the city in which the mural was located to rubble, the mural was found standing perfectly intact. The feast commemorating this event is celebrated on

October 18 after a number of days of penance in which people wear purple-colored penitential garments. On the actual feast day, copies of the mural are carried through the streets by crowds of people dressed in purple. These processions are followed by dinners that conclude with *turrone de Doña Pepa,* a pastry made of anise cookie logs bathed in a molasses-fruit glaze and covered with (purple!) sprinkles. Legend claims that Doña Pepa, a 17th-century Afro-Peruvian, made the first turrone to commemorate this feast after receiving the recipe in a dream from an angel.

The November feasts of All Saints' and All Souls' coincide with the returning rains of spring in Peru. During this time, guests visit family and friends to eat traditional dishes, particularly the favorite dishes of the deceased. Foods are also brought to cemeteries, where the dead are remembered with a joyful picnic. In Cuzco, the All Saints' Day feast traditionally includes a suckling pig and humitas (tamales).

Festivals of the saints and of the Blessed Virgin Mary are celebrated similarly throughout the country with processions, religious and folkloric ceremonies, traditional foods, and chicha. A feast that is popular among mixed-race Peruvians is that of the mulatto Peruvian saint Martin de Porres (1579–1639). Also called Fray Escoba (Friar Broom), St. Martin de Porres is known for his work feeding people and cleaning up after them. Many Peruvian homes have a small broom in the corner of their kitchen as a symbol of their devotion to this native Peruvian saint. He is known for having planted a famous olive grove in Lima, for preparing picnics and salads for the Dominican brothers in his convent, and for feeding the poor, especially the indigenous people, many of whom were homeless.

The Inca feast of Inti Rayni takes place in Cuzco at the winter solstice. It is a celebration in thanksgiving to the Sun God. The feast was banned in 1572 by the Catholic authorities, but it is celebrated today as a historical, folkloric, and religious festival. Among the festivities are many reenactments of Inca rituals, including a great feast consisting of meat, cornbread, chicha, and coca tea.

Christmas in Peru is a time to enjoy sweets. Sweet mango juice, bakery rolls, and *churros con chocolate* (fried donuts dipped in chocolate sauce) are popular. A common Christmas treat is imported Italian panettone and Peruvian-style chocolate milk made from evaporated milk, a chocolate bar, and cinnamon.

Carnival, the last day of feasting before the penitential season of Lent, generally does not include the kind of excessive eating and drinking often associated with this holiday in other countries. It is a day of "tricks" involving surprising people by bursting water balloons on them. In Cajamarca, guests are welcomed into family homes for papas a la huancayna, other traditional foods, and chicha de jora.

Holy Week is celebrated everywhere in Peru, but the most famous celebration is in the mountain city of Ayacucho. There, on the eve before Easter, it is customary to have a feast consisting of 12 typical Peruvian dishes. One of the dishes almost always included is *chiriuchu* (spicy roasted cuy). Chiriuchu is also served with beer, chicha, and cornbread on the vigil of the feast of Corpus Christi in June.

Diet and Health

Archaeological remains of preconquest indigenous Peruvians indicate that they were in good health. Protein sources included cuy (Peruvian guinea pig), game, fish, and quinoa. Dried foods and multiclimatic agricultural practices ensured food security. Moreover, recent analysis of the preconquest indigenous diet reveals that ingestion patterns increased nutrient absorption. The "appetizer" for the midday meal was *cancha* (dried maize). The rough texture of this foodstuff opened the alimentary passages, preparing them for increased nutrient absorption. Custom prevented the drinking of chicha de jora (maize beer) until the end of the meal, when enzymes in this fermented beverage could aid in the digestion of the complex carbohydrate–rich menu. This eliminated the danger of losing nutrients due to excess liquid or fiber pushing food through the digestive system too quickly.

Indigenous Peruvians have chewed the leaves of the coca plant, which are used to make the narcotic drug cocaine, for centuries. When the leaves are chewed alone, they produce a mild burst of energy. When they are chewed with an alkaline agent, usually in the form of vegetal ashes, the effect is heightened. The chewing of coca leaves does not have the extreme narcotic effect of the chemically pure alkaloid cocaine, nor does it seem to be addictive. It seems to help relieve the symptoms of altitude sickness.

Kelly O'Leary

Coca leaf vendors sell the leaves out of large bags in a Peruvian market. The cultivation and use of the coca leaf in Peruvian culture is a way of life. However, because the leaves are also the raw material used in the production of cocaine, the tradition has come under fire from the Peruvian and United States governments as Peru is one of the largest providers of coca leaves to Colombia, a country that provides cocaine to the rest of the world. (Corel)

Further Reading

Custer, Tony. *The Art of Peruvian Cuisine.* Lima, Peru: Fundación Custer, 2003.

Guardia, Sara Beatriz. *Una Fiesta del Sabor: El Peru y sus comidas.* (English translation in appendix). Lima, Peru: Ausonia, 2000.

Kijac, Maria Baez. *The South American Table.* Cambridge, MA: Harvard Common Press, 2003.

Lockhart, James. *Spanish Peru 1532–1560: A Social History.* 2nd ed. Madison: University of Wisconsin Press, 1994.

Lovera, José Rafael. *Food Culture in South America.* Westport, CT: Greenwood Press, 2005.

Super, John C. *Food, Conquest and Colonization in 16th Century Spanish America.* Albuquerque: University of New Mexico Press, 1988.

Puerto Rico

Overview

Puerto Rico is an archipelago located between the Caribbean Sea and the North Atlantic Ocean. It is composed of the main island of Puerto Rico, the smaller islands of Culebra and Vieques, and many uninhabited islands like Mona, Desecheo, and Caja de Muertos. Politically it is an unincorporated territory of the United States, or Estado Libre Asociado (Associated Free State). The food culture of Puerto Rico has been formed through centuries of adaptation, blending, and creation based on elements originating in Taino Arawak, Spanish, African, and U.S. cultures.

The precolonial indigenous inhabitants of Puerto Rico were Taino Arawaks, whose basic staple was yucca. They processed yucca by peeling and grating it, squeezing out the juice and its poisonous components, and drying it to form flour with which they made a flatbread called *casabe.* Yucca was supplemented with fish and shellfish, and with beans, maize, fruits, and vegetables that the Taino Arawaks cultivated in small plots of land called *conucos.*

The Spanish colonizers arrived in 1493, starting a colonial period that lasted four centuries. It redefined the ecosystem and the food culture of the archipelago. The Spanish learned local fishing and food-cultivation and -preparation techniques from the indigenous inhabitants, and they also introduced new foods and culinary techniques. Many of the foods considered essential by the Spanish were hard or impossible to produce in the Caribbean. Whereas pigs and cattle thrived on the islands, wheat flour, olive oil, *bacalao* (salt cod), and wine had to be constantly imported. These foods became an important part of Puerto Rican food culture even though they are not local foods. The Spanish successfully introduced many vegetables and fruits from Europe, Asia, and Africa, and today it is hard to believe that they did not originate in the Caribbean region. These include plantains, bananas, coffee, breadfruit, sugarcane, tamarinds, and mangoes. Dishes from different regions of Spain, including Moorish dishes, were slowly transformed as they were constantly adapted and reinvented using new ingredients and taste ideals. Contemporary Puerto Rican rice dishes like *asopao* (soupy rice) and arroz con pollo (chicken with rice) are based on *arroz caldoso* and Valencian paella, which have different versions all over Latin America and the Caribbean.

During the Spanish colonial period, Puerto Rico produced coffee and sugar for the Spanish market, and the food supply depended on subsistence agriculture and products imported from Spain. Thousands of slaves were imported from different regions of Africa. The Africans introduced vegetables like okra and *ñames* (true yams as opposed to sweet potatoes) as well as food-preparation techniques like the pounding and grating of plantains and other starchy vegetables to form savory cakes.

Contemporary specialties like *mofongo* (pounded fried plantains) clearly show an African lineage. As cooks on the plantations and in affluent homes, Africans had a formative role in the shaping of Puerto Rican cuisine. They were in charge of assembling and creating a new cuisine with disparate ingredients, techniques, and taste memories from diverse regions of the world.

When the United States invaded Puerto Rico in 1898, a distinctive cuisine already existed in the archipelago, but the local food culture continued to develop under U.S. colonial rule and its project of modernization. Important staples like rice and beans were increasingly imported from the United States, and the diet of Puerto Rican peasants in the U.S.-dominated sugar economy became more and more limited. Food aid and home economics instruction in the public school system helped to speed up the incorporation of cheap processed foods like oatmeal, dried milk, canned Vienna sausages, Spam, and canned corned beef. These and other U.S. products have been localized and incorporated into the matrix of Puerto Rican cooking. *Arroz con salchichas* (rice with Vienna sausages) and Thanksgiving turkey stuffed with mofongo are very common dishes. A more recent dimension of the impact of the relationship with the United States is the effervescence of a restaurant culture fueled by tourism, diasporic Puerto Ricans with professional culinary training and work experience acquired abroad, and the ambition of transforming Puerto Rican cuisine into the "grand cuisine" of the Caribbean. Another important aspect of contemporary Puerto Rican food culture is its resilient Caribbean character, constantly reinforced by cultural nationalism and by vibrant Cuban and Dominican communities that keep the Caribbean fusion constantly evolving.

🍽 Food Culture Snapshot

Middle-class Puerto Ricans do most of their food shopping at supermarkets. Many families supplement supermarket purchases with produce from the *plaza del mercado* (traditional food markets) and with a few items grown at home or received from relatives and friends who cultivate small plots. In rural areas many people keep chickens and pigs, and in coastal areas noncommercial fishing is common.

The Rivera family—Yesenia, David, and their three kids—go to the supermarket together. In the produce area they choose from a variety of imported fruits and vegetables like apples, peaches, and plums, as well as local and imported tropical fruits like coconuts, mangoes, papayas, and different varieties of bananas.

From the fresh vegetable area they get onions, garlic, tomatoes, potatoes, yucca, and *yautías* (the underground stem of a *Xanthosoma* plant), but they do not buy plantains and traditional flavoring ingredients like *ajíes dulces* (sweet chilies) and *recao* (long-leaf cilantro) because David grows them in their suburban backyard. From the refrigerated section they buy milk, eggs, sliced processed cheese, and several cartons of juice drinks including orange, passion fruit, and guava. From the dry foods aisles they pick up coffee, many bags of rice, canned and dried beans, canned tomato sauce, pasta, boxed cereals, and sandwich bread.

When looking at the meat section, the kids ask for hamburgers, but Yesenia shuns premade patties in favor of fresh low-fat ground meat, which she will season with an onion and garlic *adobo* (seasoning rub) to make her own burgers. She also selects packaged pork chops and chicken parts. At the frozen aisle they buy ice cream, fish sticks, and ready-made turnover wrappers to make savory *pastelillos*. Finally, in the bakery section they buy a loaf of *pan criollo* (Puerto Rican bread), which they will enjoy at breakfast the next day, and a lemon meringue pie, which the kids requested.

Sometimes Yesenia prefers to shop at her local plaza del mercado. She thinks that it is good for her children to experience the small-town atmosphere of the old-fashioned market, and she also likes the fresh local fruits and vegetables sold there. She buys three different varieties of yautía, one breadfruit, and a bunch of *guineos manzanos* (a short and fat variety of banana), which are rarely available at the supermarket. Before leaving they stop at the prepared-food stands where they eat *bacalaítos* (codfish fritters) and drink fresh fruit *batidas* (shakes).

Major Foodstuffs

Rice and beans are the main staples of the Puerto Rican diet even though the diet has become more diversified in recent decades. Coffee is a necessity for breakfast, and it is also enjoyed throughout the day and after meals. Rice could be of the short- or long-grain variety, but together with beans it is the center of most meals. Many people consider that they have not eaten a full meal if they have not eaten rice and beans, so it is not unusual to see pasta dishes like lasagna served with rice and beans on the side. A popular expression for making a living is *ganarse las habichuelas,* or "earning the beans." Red kidney beans and pink beans are the most common, together with chickpeas and *gandules* (pigeon peas).

Pork, chicken, and beef are the favorite meats. Many Puerto Ricans enjoy specialty dishes made with offal, like *mondongo* (tripe) and *mollejas* (gizzards), but there are many who dislike them. Canned meat products are very popular because their low price makes eating meat every day possible. Seafood is also appreciated, although at home it is not consumed as frequently as meat. Fresh fish is not widely available so people buy imported frozen fillets. Bacalao remains an important component of Puerto Rican cuisine, but nowadays imitation crabmeat is taking its place in many traditional dishes. Conch and octopus are well liked, and they can be found in many stores.

Viandas is a category of starchy foods that includes yucca, different varieties of yautía, ñames, *batatas* (white sweet potatoes), breadfruit, plantains, and green bananas. Viandas can be simply boiled and served as a side dish dressed with olive oil, or they are transformed into dishes like mofongo, *alcapurrias* (grated viandas stuffed with meat and fried), and *pasteles* (grated viandas stuffed with

A sign for a restaurant featuring mondongo, a Puerto Rican tripe dish. (iStockPhoto)

meat, wrapped in plantain leaves, and boiled). Simple lettuce and tomato salads, or salted avocado slices, are ways in which other vegetables are consumed. Fruits like oranges and bananas also have staple status, whether eaten for breakfast, dessert, or a snack.

Another important category of foods includes the items necessary to make *sofrito,* a seasoning made with ground ingredients, used in beans, rice, stews, and meat dishes. A basic sofrito contains onions, garlic, ajíes dulces, and recao. However, each cook adds one or more additional ingredients, making the sofrito unique. Possible additional ingredients include *cubanelle* or bell peppers, roasted red bell peppers, cilantro, oregano, pimento-stuffed olives, capers, ham, or olive oil. Lightly frying the sofrito in olive oil or lard that has been colored and flavored with achiote (annatto seeds) is the first step in Puerto Rican cooking, and it gives dishes their distinctive taste and aroma.

Fruits like mangoes, bananas, guavas, and oranges are grown in many backyards, and they are frequently eaten as a snack. Coconuts are prized for their refreshing water and for their sweet flesh, which is used grated or in milk form to make innumerable desserts. Some less widely available but equally popular fruits include *parcha* (passion fruit), *guanábana* (soursop), pineapples, papayas, *acerolas* (West Indian cherries), and *quenepas* (a round green fruit with a thin brittle skin and a large pit covered by sweet pulp).

Cooking

Daily Puerto Rican cooking combines traditional techniques with the use of modern equipment. Grating and pounding are two fundamental food-preparation techniques that are best performed with traditional tools. A simple hand grater (*guayo*) is indispensable when grating green plantains to make dumplings (*bollitos de plátano*) or when grating all kinds of viandas for alcapurrias and pasteles. Grating in a blender or in a food processor does not release enough stickiness in the viandas, which is necessary for them to form a cohesive dough or batter. Although it is indeed possible to make the batter for pasteles and alcapurrias in a food processor, purists insist that this method produces inferior results. The *pilón* (wooden mortar and pestle) is another essential kitchen tool, particularly to make mofongo. Only the pilón makes plantains and other viandas come together with the right balance of softness and chunkiness, and it also gives mofongo its domed shape. In restaurants it has become commonplace to serve mofongo in the pilón, sometimes with a meat or seafood stuffing. Another important food-preparation tool is the *tostonera,* a wooden press used to flatten plantain slices between the first and second frying to make *tostones.* Newer tostonera designs shape the plantain slices into cups that can be filled with meat or seafood to make *tostones rellenos.*

Gandules con Bollitos de Plátano (Pigeon Peas with Green Plantain Dumplings)

Serves 4

Ingredients

For the Bollitos

1 green plantain

½ tbsp olive oil

½ tsp garlic, crushed

¼ tsp salt

¼ tsp ground black pepper

For the Gandules

1½ tbsp olive oil

1 small onion, chopped

1 clove garlic, crushed

2 oz smoked ham, cubed

2 tbsp sofrito (available in the Latin American foods aisle of most supermarkets)

¼ c tomato sauce

1 can pigeon peas, drained

2½ c water

1 bay leaf

Salt and pepper to taste

Procedure

Peel the plantain, and grate it using the smallest holes of a box grater. The result should be wet and sticky. Mix the grated plantains with the oil, garlic, salt, and pepper. Take teaspoonfuls of the mixture and shape into small balls. Cover until ready to use.

Heat the oil in a large pot, and sauté the onion, garlic, and ham until the onion is translucent. Add the sofrito, stir, and cook for 3 minutes. Add the tomato sauce, stir, and cook for 3 more minutes. Add the pigeon peas and stir well. Add the water, bay leaf, salt, and pepper, and simmer for 15 minutes. Drop in the dumplings one at a time, and stir carefully after 5 minutes. Simmer for 30 minutes, or until the broth has thickened and the dumplings are cooked through. Serve with white rice.

The blender has become an important tool in the Puerto Rican kitchen primarily to make sofrito. Making sofrito in a blender rather than in the pilón is less labor-intensive and also gives excellent results. Additionally, the blender can easily make enough sofrito for a few weeks, which significantly reduces cooking time. Blenders, mixers, and food processors are used to make the occasional cake or flan (caramel custard), and microwave ovens are used mostly for reheating leftovers or for quick cooking of rice and beans.

The most important cooking vessel is a *caldero,* a thick and heavy pot similar to a Dutch oven. Cooking rice in the caldero produces *pegao,* a layer of crispy rice that sticks to the bottom of the pot and is considered a treat. Electric rice cookers have not become popular in Puerto Rico because they do not produce pegao. The caldero is also the preferred vessel for deep-frying tostones, alcapurrias, and many other snacks and appetizers. Calderos or regular pots are used to cook beans, soups, and stews. Pressure cookers are favored among many for their ability to cook dried beans and chickpeas quickly, which allows them to have home-cooked instead of canned beans.

Another important cooking vessel is a saucepan for making coffee. Water is heated to just below boiling before adding at least one heaping tablespoon of espresso coffee grounds for each cup of coffee desired. The coffee is stirred constantly for one minute without letting it boil, and finally it is strained with a *colador* (cloth strainer). The coffee can be drunk black or returned to the saucepan after heating up some milk in it. This technique produces coffee that is strong but not bitter, and most people prefer it to drip or espresso machines.

Today, the food industries offer many alternatives for busy Puerto Rican home cooks. Peeled and cut viandas are available frozen. Tostones and other fritters are available frozen and ready to fry. Many households use canned beans, chickpeas, and gandules rather than fresh, dried, or frozen ones. Canned tomato sauce is ubiquitous, as well as bouillon cubes, seasoning packets, and ready-made adobos. Sofrito is sold in jars or in frozen plastic tubs, and even those cooks who do not like to depend on these products keep one around just in case they run out of their own.

Typical Meals

Puerto Ricans do not eat traditional meals every day. Many people have eclectic food habits and like to experiment with new flavors and cuisines that they have come to know about from the media, travel, and restaurants. However, certain patterns remain easy to identify. Breakfast consists of coffee with bread or pastries like bakery-bought *quesitos* and *tornillos* (puff pastry cylinders stuffed with cream cheese or pastry cream). Other breakfast options include eggs, pancakes, and French toast. Cereals can be of the boxed variety, but hot cereals like oatmeal, farina, and cornmeal and custards made with cornstarch are still popular. Lunch is often eaten outside of the home, and it can be either a fast version of dinner or just a sandwich or fast-food items like burgers, fried chicken, or pizza.

Dinner more often than not consists of rice, beans, and a meat dish. Rice can be white rice that is simply cooked with salt and oil or lard. Yellow rice is cooked with sofrito, achiote, and tomato sauce, and sometimes it includes beans and/or meat. Rice becomes a one-pot meal when cooked as asopao, a thick soup with plenty of meat or seafood. Asopao is considered the ideal meal to warm up on a rainy day or to fight a cold. Beans are stewed with sofrito and tomato sauce. Different versions can include cubes of pumpkin, potato, ham, or fresh pork hocks. The most common meat preparations are pork chops, boneless pork loin cubes, or chicken parts rubbed with adobo and fried. Beef cubes, Vienna sausages, Spam, and canned corned beef are stewed following the same procedure of adding sofrito, tomato sauce, bouillon cubes, and potatoes. Beefsteak is served as *bistec empanado* (breaded and fried) or as *bistec encebollado* (cooked in vinegar and onions).

The rice, beans, and meat dinner is sometimes complemented by side dishes and snacks, mostly made with viandas. Green plantains are served as tostones or *arañitas* (crispy clusters of shredded plantain) on the side or as bollitos de plátano in a gandules stew. Ripe plantains, sliced lengthwise and fried, are another common side dish. Ripe plantain slices are also used to make *pastelón,* a layered ripe-plantain casserole with a beef, chicken, or pork filling. Other viandas appear as side dishes simply boiled or as mofongo.

Arañitas (Shredded Green Plantain "Spiders")

Yields 6 to 8 pieces

1 green plantain

1 clove garlic, crushed

¼ tsp salt or adobo

Oil for frying

Peel the plantain, and grate it using the medium-sized holes of a box grater. Sprinkle the salt or adobo evenly over the thin, long plantain strands. Heat 2 inches of oil to approximately 350°F. Take a heaping tablespoonful of plantain strands and press lightly with your fingers until the strands stick together forming a cluster. They should look like spiders with plenty of "legs" sticking out. Fry until golden and crispy. Sprinkle with salt to taste, and serve with a dipping sauce.

Dessert is served often but not daily. Traditional dessert options might include fresh fruit and homemade or store-bought flan, bread pudding, *dulce de lechosa* (semiripe papaya slices in syrup), or guava paste with *queso del país* (fresh cheese). Ice cream, cakes, pies, and pastries are other possibilities.

Eating Out

Many coffee shops are open for breakfast. They offer coffee, batidas, and freshly squeezed orange juice. These drinks can be accompanied by toasted bread with butter or by pressed sandwiches made with ham, cheese, and/or fried egg. A special treat of some old Spanish cafeterias and bakeries is the *mallorca,* a brioche-like bun covered with powdered sugar. Mallorcas are usually split, spread with butter or margarine, and toasted in a sandwich press.

The most popular places to eat lunch are *fondas* (cafeterias) and fast-food outlets. Fondas serve traditional Puerto Rican food at low prices and with no-frills service that allows working people to enjoy a full meal during their lunch hour. Customers choose from food counters that contain the menu items of the day, which typically include white and yellow rice, stewed beans, and a few meat options. Side dishes might include pegao, tostones (fried, squashed, and refried plantain), mofongo, *amarillos* (fried ripe plantain slices), and French fries. Puerto Rican–style spaghetti and lasagna are other possible options, as well as dishes that are not generally made at home like mondongo and goat stew. Competing with fondas are fast-food outlets like McDonald's, Burger King, KFC, and Taco Bell, which can be found everywhere. Most fast-food restaurants have made concessions to the Puerto Rican palate and include items like rice, beans, tostones, and flan in their menus.

Festivals are occasions for eating out in Puerto Rico. Whether the theme is music, art, dance, agriculture, or a specific food item, all festivals offer plentiful amounts of traditional food and drink. Festival food vendors have created new versions of traditional snacks, many of which are supersized versions of their predecessors. Bacalaítos are made dinner-plate size, and arañitas have become *nidos,* large grated plantain nests stuffed with meat or seafood salad. Ironically, the names of the original dishes mean "little codfish" and "little spiders," making their supersized versions seem incongruent. Piña colada, with or without rum, is always present at festivals, sometimes served inside a hollowed-out pineapple. Another favorite food item sold at festivals are traditional sweet confections made with guava, sweet potato, coconut, bitter orange, papaya, sesame seeds, or caramelized milk. Thanks to festivals many traditional foods that were unknown to younger Puerto Ricans are now easy to sample. These include *guanimes con bacalao* (boiled cornmeal dumplings with salted codfish salad) and the sweet treat called *gofio* (toasted cornmeal mixed with sugar).

Other weekend and holiday eating-out options are *lechoneras* (roast pork restaurants) and seafood and fritter stands by the beach. Lechoneras are located all over the rural mountainous areas. They roast whole pigs and serve the meat with accompaniments that include rice, beans, viandas, pasteles, and alcapurrias. Even though most of the pigs are more likely to be roasted in gas ovens than over natural wood charcoal, lechoneras retain their reputation for serving old-style Puerto Rican food. The atmosphere is like a party, with plenty of music, dancing, and beer. In the coastal areas seafood outlets serve fried fish, as well as seafood salads made with *carrucho* (conch), octopus, bacalao, *jueyes* (land crabs), king crab, or imitation crabmeat. Beachside kiosks are also famous for their generously sized fritters, like *alcapurrias de jueyes* (land crab–stuffed yautía and green plantain fritters).

There is a wide variety of restaurants. Each town has at least a fonda, a *criollo* (Puerto Rican) restaurant, a pizzeria, and a Chinese restaurant. Criollo restaurants of all price levels abound all over, and seafood restaurants are the specialty of coastal towns but do not necessarily serve local seafood. The large metropolitan area, which includes San

A whole pig being grilled in a marketplace in Puerto Rico. (Dreamstime)

Juan and other municipalities, has a dynamic restaurant culture with a wide variety of international cuisines. The most popular restaurant categories are seafood, Puerto Rican, Italian, and Asian, followed by steakhouse, Caribbean, Iberian, and international. There are a few French restaurants and many upscale eclectic restaurants with renowned chefs like Wilo Benet of Pikayo and Peter Schintler of Marmalade. Upscale restaurants serve both international tourists and the growing local population of fine-restaurant enthusiasts. There is also a large number of fusion restaurants where chefs incorporate local flavors and ingredients into dishes from different parts of the world, with an emphasis on Asia. Fusion restaurants serve innovations like sushi rolls wrapped with ripe plantain strips and tandoori chicken with plantains and guava paste.

Restaurant culture in Puerto Rico is currently at a high point. In 2007 the first restaurant guide, called *Sal!* was published, and it has a companion Web site with editorial content, a calendar of food-related events, recipes, and customer-written reviews of restaurants in Puerto Rico and abroad. Many restaurants have been featured in U.S. gourmet magazines, and Puerto Rican chefs participate in U.S. cooking shows and competitions. Chef Roberto Treviño of Aguaviva participated in *Iron Chef America,* and Wilo Benet participated in *Top Chef Masters.* Many chefs working in Puerto Rico have lived, traveled, worked, or trained in the United States, Spain, France, and beyond, which gives their restaurants an international flavor, whether they serve criolla or international cuisine.

Special Occasions

Traditional Puerto Rican food is expected at Christmastime. Even families without the time or expertise to cook the required dishes look for small caterers who sell specific dishes or full meals. The ideal menu consists of *arroz con gandules* (rice with pigeon peas), *pernil* (roasted pork leg), and pasteles in both the plantain and yucca varieties. These main dishes can be complemented with fritters and with store-bought snacks like potato chips, tortillas, and salsa. Traditional sweets are also required, particularly those made with coconut. Coconut flan, *tembleque* (cornstarch-thickened coconut milk custard), and *arroz con dulce* (thick coconut-milk rice pudding) are some of the favorites, and it is not rare to serve all three. Coconut milk is also the main ingredient in the Christmas drink *coquito,* which is often described as a coconut eggnog. Other treats expected for the Christmas meal are almonds, walnuts, hazelnuts, and *turrones* (almond nougats) imported from Spain. The Christmas meal is generally a gathering of the extended family, and throughout the holiday season schools, offices, clubs, and groups of friends have their own Christmas parties with a similar menu. The Christmas menu serves as the model for other family celebrations like New Year's Eve, Mother's Day, and Father's Day.

Thanksgiving is a part of the Puerto Rican holiday calendar. Families gather together to enjoy either a traditional Puerto Rican holiday meal, a traditional U.S. Thanksgiving meal, or a combination of both. Rice and beans could be served with a roasted turkey that has been generously rubbed with a garlicky adobo to make it taste like pernil. Turkey prepared in this way is known as *pavochón,* a combination of the words for turkey (*pavo*) and pork (*lechón*). The turkey could also be stuffed with plantain, breadfruit, or yucca mofongo. Dessert options are likely to include a pumpkin flan and homemade or store-bought pies.

Roman Catholicism is the dominant religion in Puerto Rico, although large numbers consider

Arroz con gandules, rice with pigeon peas, is one of the traditional dishes served at Christmastime in Puerto Rico. (iStockPhoto)

themselves nonpracticing Catholics, and many others combine elements of Catholicism with Afro-Caribbean religions like Santeria. This openness and eclecticism is manifested during Lent, particularly during Holy Week. Few Puerto Ricans abstain from meat in any officially prescribed way, but during Holy Week it is still customary for many families to consume seafood at home or in restaurants. Traditional peasant dishes like *serenata con bacalao,* a combination of boiled viandas served with a salted codfish salad, appear during this period, sometimes with more nostalgic than religious connotations.

For weddings and *quinceañeros* (15th-birthday celebration, particularly for girls), hiring a food caterer has increasingly become the norm. The menu could be similar to the Christmas meal, but often it consists of standard catering dishes that have been Puerto Ricanized. Such dishes include chicken legs in guava sauce and yucca-stuffed chicken breasts.

Diet and Health

A history of a plantation economy followed by one dominated by industries and services means that Puerto Rico imports the bulk of its food. There is small-scale production of coffee, bananas, vegetables, poultry, and dairy products, but it is not enough to satisfy local demand, and many local producers find it hard to compete with cheaper food imports. In the 20th century the Puerto Rican diet shifted from one based on agricultural products and frequent scarcity to one based on agroindustrial processed foods and relative abundance. The results are well known in all industrialized countries: widespread obesity, including high rates of childhood obesity, and related diseases like diabetes, high blood pressure, and heart disease. In 2007 the government of Puerto Rico initiated a campaign to make exercise and nutrition instruction available in all municipalities.

Puerto Ricans are trying to improve the quality of their food in many different ways. Vegetarianism has become established as a viable diet alternative, and many stores and restaurants cater to this lifestyle. There are a few small organic farms, some of which offer community-supported agriculture programs. Most people have switched from lard to olive or vegetable oil, and many try to reduce their consumption of the fried and high-carbohydrate foods that are abundant in the Puerto Rican diet: rice, beans, viandas, fritters. Sedentary lifestyles, an abundance of heavily processed foods, and confusion and misinformation regarding diet and health guidelines are the norm.

Zilkia Janer

Further Reading

Aboy Valldejuli, Carmen. *Puerto Rican Cookery.* New Orleans, LA: Pelican, 1983.

Benet, Wilo. *Puerto Rico True Flavors.* Baltimore, MD: Read Street, 2007.

El Boricua. http://www.elboricua.com/recipes.html.

Cabanillas, Berta, and Carmen Ginorio. *Puerto Rican Dishes.* San Juan: University of Puerto Rico Press, 1974.

El Colmadito. http://www.elcolmado.com/USRecipes.asp.

Díaz de Villegas, José Luis. *Puerto Rico: Grand Cuisine of the Caribbean.* San Juan: University of Puerto Rico Press, 2004.

Duprey de Sterling, Emma. *Puerto Rican Artisanal Cookery.* San Juan: University of Puerto Rico Press, 2008.

"Food and Drinks." Welcome to Puerto Rico! http://welcome.topuertorico.org/culture/foodrink.shtml.

Houston, Lynn Marie. *Food Culture in the Caribbean.* Westport, CT: Greenwood Press, 2005.

Janer, Zilkia. "(In)Edible Nature: New World Food and Coloniality." *Cultural Studies* 21, No. 2–3 (2007): 385–405.

Ortiz Cuadra, Cruz Miguel. *Puerto Rico en la olla, ¿somos aún lo que comimos?* Madrid, Spain: Doce Calles, 2006.

Puerto Rican Cooking. http://prcooking.com.

Suriname

Overview

Suriname is the smallest independent country on the South American continent. The country is part of the greater Caribbean Basin and borders the Atlantic Ocean to the north, French Guiana to the east, Guyana to the west, and Brazil to the south. Suriname's official language is Dutch, but the Surinamese dialect Sranang Tongo is frequently spoken. In the 17th century the first Europeans settled in the area. Due to the colonization the native population of Amerindians was forced into the margins of a new society. From 1667 until 1975 Suriname was a Dutch colony and had a plantation economy. At the end of the 18th century, the majority of the population consisted of West African slaves. After the abolition of slavery, in 1863, immigrants from northern India, Indonesia (Java), and China started to constitute the workforce.

What Surinamese eat is strongly determined by ethnic background, geography, and religion. In this ethnically highly diverse country, no religion predominates. At present, around 27 percent of the Surinamese are Hindus, while various forms of Christianity are practiced by much of the rest of the population, which is comprised of around 20 percent Creoles (descendants of West African slaves and Europeans) and 15 percent Maroons (descendants of escaped slaves) and descendants of Europeans. The 15 percent who are Javanese are either Muslim or Christian. The remainder of the population consists of minorities such as Amerindians, Chinese, Jews, and Brazilians. The vast majority of Suriname's total population of around 470,000 people live in the capital Paramaribo. Following independence in 1975, a third of the population migrated to the Netherlands, where at present approximately 350,000 Surinamese are living.

🍽 Food Culture Snapshot

Mavis Hofwijk was born in Paramaribo in 1939, where her husband Lesley was born in 1941. They were both raised in Suriname; the couple moved to the Netherlands in 1970, but they continue to live in Suriname as well, spending part of the year in each place. Lesley retired from teaching at an elementary school. Together with her daughter Candice, Mavis runs Surinaams Buffet, a well-known catering company in Amsterdam Zuidoost, a suburb where in the 1970s many Surinamese settled. The lifestyle and foodways of Mavis and Lesley are representative for many middle-class Surinamese, whose diet includes typical Surinamese but also Dutch and European-style dishes.

In Suriname the couple breakfasts on slices of bread or *Surinaamse puntjes* (Surinamese bread rolls) with *bakkeljauw* (salted dried cod), peanut butter, cheese, or jam. Breakfast is accompanied by a cup of tea or coffee. Every second or third day Mavis goes to the bakery to buy bread.

The couple eats a hot meal once a day, for either lunch or supper. Many times the meal is prepared with whatever is at hand or available, and served for lunch at around 1 or for dinner at 6. The main dish mostly consists of vegetables sautéed together with meat. Cooking is done without recipes. The taste of the dish should be good in the pot, and spices, salt, and pepper are added while cooking. The meal is always accompanied by rice. Together with rice, a few times a week boiled roots and tubers are served. The meal is accompanied by *zuurgoed* (sweet and sour pickles) that are prepared with either *bilimbi* (a cucumber-like vegetable that grows on a tree; *Averrhoa bilimbi*) or cucumbers and onions in a mixture of vinegar, water, sugar, and spices such as allspice, peppercorns, garlic, and bay leaf. For dessert fresh fruits such as bananas, mangoes, and oranges are eaten. When in season, fruit is collected from the garden.

Like most Surinamese households, Mavis has a larder filled with food supplies. Her larder always contains *zoutvlees* (salted beef), bakkeljauw, dried shrimp, rice, legumes, spices, roots, and tubers. She buys her groceries either in one of the many local grocery stores or at the market; both are open seven days a week. From fresh meats to toilet paper, the mom-and-pop type of grocery stores sells all kinds of products. Ingredients are bought depending on the season and availability. Like most Surinamese, Mavis judges the quality of fruits, vegetables, meats, and other foodstuffs "with the eye" by touching, smelling, and looking at their appearance.

Major Foodstuffs

In the 1700s the arrival of the colonists caused a major change in the diet. New foods like wheat, olive oil, beef, pork, chicken, beer, and wine and new preparation techniques (e.g., smothering in butter and/or oil and cooking in an oven) were introduced. The colonists that migrated to Suriname were foremost of English, Dutch, and Sephardic Jewish origin, and they brought with them their own culinary habits and traditions. During colonization and in the centuries that followed, these habits contributed to the development of Suriname's cuisine.

For centuries Suriname was a plantation economy with a strong focus on growing cash crops such as sugar, coffee, and cacao, so little attention was paid to agriculture. Since the colonial period grains, legumes, potatoes, beets, carrots, salt, meat, fish, and many other foods have been imported from abroad (Europe and North America). During the colonial period these costly imports provided the population with food but also ensured that the colonists could replicate their traditional foodways.

Suriname is an area that has a rich biodiversity. Over 90 percent of the country is covered with forest. Most of the agriculture and fishing takes place on the coast but hardly contributes to the country's economy. Of the 40 million acres (16.2 million hectares) of land, around 3.7 million acres are considered to have agricultural potential. Only 15 percent of the labor force works in agriculture. Rice accounts for about half of all cultivated land, and rice and bananas are the major export products. The small fishing industry mostly exports shrimp.

Historically, the livelihoods of Amerindians, Maroons, Creoles, and other small communities depend on the produce of home gardens and fishing. Long before Suriname was discovered, the indigenous people already cultivated more than 50 plants. In addition to agriculture and fishing, hunting and gathering of wild plants provided food.

The traditional and largely self-supporting system for food provision is still practiced by inland communities such as the Maroons and Amerindians. These communities are foremost located in remote areas that are covered by dense tropical rain forest with an abundance of flora and fauna. In these communities women are responsible for the household and the kitchen garden. To provide carbohydrates, they cultivate roots and tubers such as cassava, taro (*Xanthosoma* spp.), and sweet potatoes. Other cultivated crops include pineapple, corn, plantains, melons, pumpkins, and peppers (*Capsicum annum*), as well as edible fruits from palm species, cashew nuts (*Anacardium occidentale*), calabashes (*Crescentia cujete*), mangoes, guavas, lemons, coconuts, tropical almonds (*Terminalia catappa*), star fruit, bitter melons (or gourds), tomatoes, and all kinds of Chinese cabbages, legumes, and beans.

Surinamese hardly consume fresh milk. The use of powdered and (sweetened) condensed milk is very common. Condensed milk is frequently used for the preparation of pastries, porridges, and desserts. Sliced Dutch cheeses such as Edam and Gouda are imported and are popular eaten on bread.

Many different types of fresh- and saltwater fish can be found in the waters of Suriname. The fishing sector foremost thrives on the cultivation, catching, and export of shrimp. In the Surinamese kitchen

A Surinamese woman tends to her backyard garden. (iStockPhoto)

the use of (dried) shrimp and (imported) cod is very common. Besides catfish, grouper, mullet, shark, snapper, perch, snook, and anchovies, many kinds of known and lesser-known tropical fish from the ocean and the rivers are consumed. Fishing is done either privately or by local fishermen who sell their catch on the market.

Popular herbs and spices include allspice, bay leaf, celery, (black) pepper, masala (curry powder), cumin, coriander, nutmeg, and (hot) peppers. Due to the generous use of different kinds of chili peppers, Surinamese cuisine tends to be hot and spicy. The beloved Madame Jeanette pepper is one of the world's hottest. Other seasonings are salted meat (beef), bakkeljauw (salt cod), and dried shrimp. Surinamese celery is the most popular kitchen herb and is used in many dishes. Another distinctive feature of Surinamese cuisine is the balance between sweet, sour, and salt. For the proper balance of a dish, sugar, vinegar, salt, Aromat (a popular dry seasoning mix of salt, onion, mushroom, turmeric, and other spices), and stock cubes are added according to taste.

Surinamese love color. Red, yellow, blue, and green liquid colorings are frequently used to decorate pastry. The popular *schaafijs* (crushed ice) is flavored with sugar syrups made from almonds, roses, and tropical fruits such as passion fruit, pineapple, and coconut. The yellow fatty substances of the seeds of *masoesa* (*Renealmia exaltata* —a plant that belongs to the ginger family) are solely used for

the flavoring and coloring of *moksi alesi* (literally, "mixed rice").

Cooking

Surinamese cuisine is a mixture of ingredients and cooking techniques from local Indians, the colonial powers, African slaves, and Asian immigrants. Reflecting a rich and dynamic multicultural society, the cuisine became a melting pot and a patchwork that is continuously developing. Food and the preparation of specific dishes play a very important role in the daily and social life of the Surinamese community.

Depending on ethnicity, income, and social class, the Surinamese kitchen, kitchen equipment, cooking, and cooking techniques can vary immensely. During the colonial period many houses had an outdoor kitchen. Nowadays, the standard kitchen equipment in general consists of various aluminum or stainless steel cooking pots, a rice cooker, a (cast iron) wok, and several frying pans. Barbecuing is done on either a wood or charcoal fire. The possession of a *tawa* (a flat iron griddle) is common among Hindus.

Typical Meals

Social, geographic, and ethnic differences make it hard to describe a typical Surinamese meal. On average Surinamese eat three meals a day. Two hot meals a day are not exceptional, and in between one or two snacks (which many times consist of fresh fruits) are eaten. For breakfast, white bread rolls (known as Surinaamse puntjes) or slices of bread with butter or margarine, topped with cheese, jam, peanut butter, and occasionally fruit, are eaten. The preferred drinks are coffee, tea, and sometimes fruit juice. Milk is not drunk, but it is used in coffee and for the preparation of desserts.

Overall and all year round, nourishing soups and stews as well as baked and rice-based dishes are served. Lunch or dinner many times consists of one main dish accompanied by several side dishes and condiments. In general Surinamese eat a lot of chicken and meats such as lamb, beef (with the exception of Hindus), and pork (with the exception of Jews and Muslims). Larger cuts of meat are barbecued or boiled in stews and soups.

Boiled white rice, roots and tubers, and white bread are popular side dishes. The most popular rice variety is *Surinaamse rijst* (Surinamese rice), which has a very long and thin grain. Rice is either boiled or used for *alesi*—a mixed rice dish of which most Surinamese women prepare several varieties. Roots and tubers are commonly boiled in water. With or without meat, most vegetables are smothered or sautéed in oil or butter, in a pot or wok. Zuurgoed (sweet and sour pickles) accompanies most meals. The leftovers from hot meals many times end up on a slice of bread or a roll and are even consumed for breakfast.

Among the most frequently used vegetables are *kousenband* (gartner L. *Vigna unguiculata* subsp. *sesquipedalis*), *tajerblad* (taro leaf), *sopropo* (bitter melon), *klaroen* (Chinese spinach), *dagoeblad* (water spinach), *antroewa* (African eggplant), and (African) okra. Brown beans, yellow split peas, and lentils are the most popular pulses, and to a lesser extent soybeans, cowpeas, black-eyed peas, and mung beans are also used. Coconut milk and shredded coconut are used in many desserts and cakes such as the popular *bojo,* a flourless cake with grated coconut and grated cassava. Originally prepared from tapioca (cassava starch), *gomakuku* (corn-flour cookies) are the most distinctive cookies. Popular cakes include *fiadu* (a yeast-dough cake that is filled with butter, cinnamon, sugar, almonds, pineapple, and raisins) and *Engris boroe* (English cake) and *keksi* (cake). To preserve cakes these are either sprinkled with liqueur or spread with clarified butter.

Next to tea and coffee, popular drinks are *gemberbier* (ginger beer), *kasiri* (an alcoholic beverage from cassava juice), Parbobier (local beer), fruit syrups and lemonades, and fruit and egg punches prepared with and without alcohol.

Together with the development of a national cuisine, most Surinamese ethnic groups have managed to keep their own distinctive dishes and eating habits. The country's cuisine is a mixture of dishes with multiple foreign origins. Well-known dishes consumed by all Surinamese are roti (of Indian origin and prepared with baking powder), (Creole) peanut soup, *bakabana* (fried plantains), *telo met bakkeljauw* (fried cassava with clipfish), (Chinese) *bami* (noodles), *bruine bonen met rijst* (brown beans with rice), *her'heri* (literally, "fruits of the earth"), *peprewatra* (literally, "pepperwater"; a watery soup with catfish), moksi alesi (mixed rice), *pepperpot* (a savory stew and/or soup), cassava bread, and the Jewish Creole baked dish *pom.*

Pom

Within the Surinamese community pom is the most popular and best-known festive dish. Within and outside of Suriname, the oven dish is prepared by both men and women, and each Surinamese ethnic group makes a slightly different version. Hindus add piccalilli relish, Javanese add soy sauce, Jews use oil instead of butter, and Chinese add ginger or lychees.

Ingredients

2.2 lb grated *pomtajer* (fresh or frozen malanga or *yautía*)

7 oz piccalilli relish

1 stalk celery, finely chopped

1 small onion, chopped

2 chopped tomatoes

1 stick butter

7 tbsp sunflower oil

½ lb chicken pieces

1 onion, chopped

1 small can tomato paste

1 stalk celery, finely chopped

¾ c cold water

½ stock cube (chicken or beef)

5 tbsp sugar

½ tsp black pepper

Nutmeg to taste

Preheat the oven to 375°F.

Pomtajer preparation

Put the package of pomtajer in a bowl, put it in the refrigerator, and let it defrost overnight. Put the tajer in a bowl, add the piccalilli, celery, onions and tomatoes, and mix the pomtajer with a spoon or fork.

Preparation of the stewed chicken

Melt half the butter and oil in a large casserole over low heat. Add the chicken pieces, and sauté the chicken over high heat for about 4 minutes. Reduce the heat, add the onions, and fry, stirring occasionally, until tender, about 5 minutes. First, add the tomato paste, then the celery; stir once or twice, and simmer the chicken for 2 to 3 minutes on low heat.

Assembly

Mix the chicken thoroughly with the pomtajer. Add the water, crumble the stock cube into the pan, add the sugar, and stir well. Add salt, pepper, and nutmeg to taste. Put the pom on a greased baking tray. Put pieces of the remaining butter on top, and bake the pom in the oven for about 60 minutes. The pom is done when the inside is yellow and the crust is golden brown.

Surinamese cuisine is not regional but ethnically specific. Until the middle of the 19th century, Surinamese cuisine was foremost influenced by Amerindians, Europeans, and West Africans. Cassava bread, *cassareep,* and pepperpot are dishes of Amerindian origin. Pepperpot (or pepper pot) is a well-known savory stew and/or soup. In the region there are numerous pepperpot variations. The ingredients and thickness of the dish vary, but most recipes make use of hot (chili) peppers and cassareep: the thick boiled juice (syrup) of poisonous cassava that Amerindians used either as a preservative or as a cooking liquid. Depending on the season and availability, various meats and vegetables were added and boiled in the cooking pot, and, with addition of more meats and vegetables, it was frequently reheated.

During the colonial period, the European plantation owners considered food, like clothing, a sign of wealth. Especially in the 18th century this meant a rich dinner table. With soup as a starter and pineapple, oranges, and other fresh fruits for dessert, the main course often consisted of various meats, fish, and poultry. Stuffed pigs, ham, pork chops, lamb chops, game, pigeons, chicken, and pies were served together with fresh garden vegetables such as radishes, lettuce, endive, beans, celery, and parsley. Pickles and European wines, brandy, and liqueurs were imported.

The food on the table of Suriname's small but influential Jewish community was determined by the Jewish dietary laws. Eating pork and the consumption of milk and meat together are not allowed. Also, drinking of alcohol (wine and liquor) was not a habit. The Jews ate plenty of chicken and other poultry, fish, vegetables, fruits, and sweets. In the Jewish kitchen oil and spices, especially pepper, were used. For the Jewish holidays and Sabbath, special baked dishes, breads (challah), and matzos (for Passover) were prepared. The Jewish culinary influence includes the oven dishes pom and *popido* (prepared with rice with chicken).

Even as late as 1928, the diet of the former West African slaves still consisted of hard-to-digest starchy fruits and roots such as bananas (*Musa* spp.), *tajers* (both *Xanthosoma* and *Colocasia*), yams

Within the Surinamese community pom is the most popular and best known festive dish. (Dreamstime)

(*Dioscorea cayennensis Lam.*), *napi* (*Dioscorea trifida*), cassava, sweet potatoes, and rice. Vegetables and fruit were cultivated on so-called *kostgrondjes*—small plots of land or home gardens. The culinary influence of West Africa is reflected in the consumption of roots, tubers, plantains, okra, and dishes such as peanut soup, *tomtom* (balls of boiled plantain or roots and tubers), and her'heri.

Her'heri

This is plantains, sweet potatoes, Chinese taro (*Colocasia esculenta*), pomtajer (*Xanthosoma* spp.), and napi (*Dioscorea trifida,* a kind of sweet potato) with sautéed salt cod.

1 green plantain

1 yellow plantain

1 tsp salt (per quart of water)

½ lb peeled Chinese taro, in pieces

½ lb peeled pomtajer, in pieces

14 oz frozen cassava, in pieces

14 oz peeled napi, in pieces

14 oz peeled sweet potatoes, in pieces

14 oz bakkeljauw (salt cod)

Put a large pot of water on the stove, and bring to a boil. Meanwhile, peel the plantains. Add salt to the water, and put the plantains in the pot. Bring to a boil. Add the pieces of Chinese taro, pomtajer, frozen cassava, napi, and sweet potatoes. With a slotted spoon, remove the plantains after 30 minutes. Boil the rest of the tubers about 30 more minutes, and until tender.

Meanwhile, rinse the salt cod under cold running water. Cook it for 10 minutes in 2 quarts of boiling water. With a slotted spoon, remove the fish from the pot, and set aside.

Divide the fish into pieces. Use a slotted spoon to remove the tuber pieces from the pot. Serve the plantains and tubers with the fish and a little bit of its cooking liquid.

After the abolition of slavery in 1863, contract workers from Asia were hired. Between 1853 and 1913 approximately 50,000 new immigrants from the former Dutch East Indies (Java), British India (which part of India), and China arrived in Suriname, bringing along all kinds of ingredients and dishes from their own culinary traditions: rice, roti, soy sauce, chutney, piccalilli, noodles, ginger, Chinese cabbages, and lychee.

The ties with the motherland were always very close, and before and after Suriname's independence in 1975, many Surinamese settled in the Netherlands, where at present around 350,000 Surinamese are living. Upon arrival in the Netherlands, traditional food patterns were replicated. In order to be able to prepare Surinamese cuisine, ingredients such as cassava (manioc), taro, sweet potatoes, and bitter gourds (or melons) were either imported or replaced with locally available produce such as potatoes, endive, and spinach. Lacking familiar foods, many Surinamese suffered from homesickness. Two popular songs reflect the homesickness and the role of food within the Surinamese community abroad. At the same time, these songs, "Bruine bonen met rijst" (Brown beans with rice) and "Oh Nederland geef mij rijst met kousenband" (Please, Netherlands, give me rice with yard-long beans), familiarized the Dutch with Surinamese food. Due to the ongoing globalization, nowadays most Surinamese foodstuffs are available in the Netherlands.

Eating Out

Traditionally, cooking and entertaining are done at home. Street vending to make a livelihood is quite a common phenomenon in Suriname; in particular, many Surinamese women make a living selling all kinds of foods on the street. Surinamese are used to buying take-out foods and snacking in public. Street-food vendors sell all kinds of cakes, fruits, snacks, ice, drinks, sandwiches, and sausages. Due to globalization, and since Suriname is becoming a more popular vacation destination, the number of eateries and restaurants that serve a variety of foods is on the rise. In Paramaribo, eateries and restaurants that serve Javanese and Chinese cuisine are popular. Furthermore, a growing number of eateries and restaurants, ranging from outdoor food courts serving Javanese specialties to roti shops, sell a larger variety of seafood, pancakes, and curries.

Special Occasions

Surinamese are very hospitable, and no matter the occasion guests are usually expected to partake in a meal. Regardless of ethnicity, Surinamese serve huge amounts of food at special occasions and festivities such as weddings, birthdays, and especially at a *Bigi Yari,* the celebration of a jubilee year. The most popular Surinamese festive dish that is served on all special occasions is pom. The Surinamese expression "without pom there is no birthday" specifies one of the occasions for which pom is prepared.

In Javanese religious life, during the *sadjén* and *slametan* (rituals commemorating events such as birth, circumcision, marriage, and death), special dishes with rice, chicken, boiled eggs, various fruits, and seasoned vegetables, as well as drinks such as water with blossoms, tea, and coffee, are served.

During funerals of Hernhutters (a small Christian community) everything is either black or white. After the burial *Anitri beri* (literally, "Hernhutter burial") is served. The two ingredients—rice and boiled salted beef—are eaten together with taro leaf smothered in butter.

Diet and Health

Despite a wealth of natural resources and a small population of around 500,000, a large number of people in Suriname suffer from malnutrition and a poor health. According to a World Bank Report on Suriname, approximately 47 percent of the population lives in poverty and is deprived of sufficient and healthy nutrition. Although the government is responsible for the promotion, protection, and improvement of public health, Suriname's government lacks funding.

In Suriname, diet and health are intertwined. Hindus, Muslims, Jews, Creoles, and indigenous communities all follow their own medical system, and traditional healers are often consulted. The cuisines of the Chinese Surinamese and Javanese Surinamese communities are considerably healthier than those of the Creole Surinamese and Hindu Surinamese. The Hindu and Creole diets tend to be too fatty and monotonous. Many Creoles follow Winti, a traditional African practice, and largely a secret religion, with its own myths, rites, offerings, spirits, and taboos. In Suriname Winti is influenced by both Christianity and Judaism. In Winti taboos are often related to food and called *treefs* (from the Hebrew *tarefa,* for forbidden food). Similar to in Judaism, for followers of Winti certain types of animal food are prohibited such as turtle and deer but also plants like plantain. Also, *kaseri* (from the Hebrew word *kosher*) plays a role in forbidding, for instance, menstruating women preparing or touching food.

Karin Vaneker

Further Reading

"Recipes from the Surinam Cuisine." Tropilab Inc. http://www.tropilab.com/surinamkitchen.html.

Starke, A. A., and M. Samsin-Hewitt. *Groot Surinaams Kookboek.* Paramaribo, Suriname: Stichting Kakantrie, 1976.

Vaneker, Karin. *Mavis Kookt: De Surinaamse keuken volgens Mavis Hofwijk* [Mavis cooks: Surinamese cuisine according to Mavis Hofwijk]. 'sGravenland, the Netherlands: Fontaine, 2008.

Trinidad and Tobago

Overview

Trinidad and Tobago are the southernmost islands in the southern Caribbean island chain. Trinidad is a mere seven miles off the coast of Venezuela and was, geologically speaking, once part of the South American landmass, separated from the mainland by tectonic shifts. As such, the island features flora and fauna otherwise seen only in South America. Tobago, a true volcanic island formation, has a slightly different geology and lies 19 miles northwest of Trinidad. Trinidad is 1,864 square miles, roughly the size of Delaware, and Tobago is 116 square miles, roughly the size of Martha's Vineyard.

In addition to the indigenous plant and animal species, Trinidad and Tobago feature a wide variety of fruits and vegetables originally brought by colonial settlers of Spanish, Dutch, French, and, lastly, English descent. Some notable additions are the now-ubiquitous breadfruit, pineapple, and *otaheite* (Malay) apple brought to the Caribbean by Captain Bligh of the infamous *HMS Bounty*.

The first European to set foot on Trinidad was Christopher Columbus, who came to the island in the summer of 1498 on his third voyage across the Atlantic. It was he who named Trinidad (trinity) for the three mountain ranges that cross the island at its south, center, and north. Columbus met native Amerindians of the Carib and Arawak tribes upon his arrival on Trinidad and Tobago. While legend has it the Arawaks were more peaceful than the warlike Caribs, both tribes were equally subject to slaughter at the hands of Spanish settlers and were highly susceptible to European diseases. Those who were not decimated were absorbed into the fabric of the colony, which would come to include French Catholics, invited by the Spanish king, and finally the English, all of whom brought African slaves to the island. When slavery was abolished throughout the English Caribbean, Trinidad, a British colony since 1802, employed a system of indentureship that brought first Chinese, then East Indian laborers to work the islands' lucrative cane and cacao fields from emancipation in 1838 to 1917.

Today, Trinidadian foods are categorized in the local mind as either Indian or Creole; the latter refers to foods of either African or mixed European and African descent. The myriad peoples who came together through ambition and hardship on the islands of Trinidad and Tobago have evolved into a population of 1.3 million that is a montage of language, culture, and food unique to the Caribbean.

🍽 Food Culture Snapshot

Damian and Joy Luk Pat are young urban Trinidadians living in Port of Spain. Damian is of Chinese and Spanish-Venezuelan descent and works as an independent sales and marketing manager. He is president of the T&T Business Network, while his wife, Joy, is a senior marketing officer.

The couple define themselves as foodies. Damian is the family cook, often experimenting with foreign dishes or fusions of Trinidadian and foreign dishes. One of his favorite pastimes is ferreting out traditional and new eateries around the island and posting photos and reviews on Facebook.

Like most Trinidadians, the Luk Pats do their grocery shopping in a variety of venues, from traditional farmers'

Men spreading out cocoa beans in cocoa drying sheds around the turn of the century, Trinidad. (StockPhotoPro)

markets to Western-style supermarkets. Because of their relative affluence they can afford delicacies from gourmet markets from time to time as well as a fair amount of dining out, including at American specialty eateries and ice cream parlors such as Cold Stone Creamery. Many are newly opened in Trinidad but feature American prices that are cost prohibitive to most Trinidadians, as the exchange rate is roughly TT$6 to US$1.

Breakfast in the Luk Pat home is usually eggs and whole wheat toast or low-fat yogurt rather than the more traditional salted codfish, smoked herring, and fried *bake* (a kind of fried biscuit). Lunch and dinner fare is similar, featuring a mix of Trinidadian dishes in either the Creole, Chinese, or Indian style. Rice is a staple the couple enjoys, as well as potatoes and pasta. Salad is usually eaten, too. They most commonly eat beef, pork, chicken, and fish. While stewed beef often graces their table, steak is less common. Along with shrimp, the Luk Pats consider it a special-occasion item.

As Trinidad has become more global, a variety of new food styles have come to the island including Arabian,

Japanese, and Mexican, mainly from international franchises. The couple are avid experimenters and particularly love sushi. It is quite common for Damian to research those dishes and recreate them at home on weekends or special occasions, sharing with family and friends. His parents, in particular, are always willing to try new dishes in his company though they are a far departure from what they are accustomed to eating. The family also enjoys partaking of the rich variety of traditional street foods available in their island home.

Health has become an increasing consideration for the Luk Pats, and they are trying to eat more vegetables that are steamed rather than fried or stewed. They are staying away from fried, high-sugar, and high-sodium foods as hypertension and diabetes are increasingly common in Trinidad and Tobago.

The Luk Pats' favorite foods are varied and include traditional dishes such as stewed chicken; callaloo; curried beef, chicken, or goat with roti (flatbread); and modern items like sushi and steaks. Damian lists some typical Trinidadian foods among his least favorite items, including dasheen (taro), avocados, and *caraili* (bitter squash). Outside of his experimental cooking extravaganzas, when cooking at home during the workweek, Damian cooks items that are simple and fast to prepare including stewed chicken, mixed rice dishes, mashed potatoes, or items that make use of minced beef.

Major Foodstuffs

Like the rest of the colonized Caribbean, Trinidad and Tobago's value to their European rulers was their vast agricultural resources, particularly sugarcane, which was processed in the North American colonies not only into sugar but also into molasses, used in rum production. Sugarcane was also part of the triangular slave trade in which slave-produced sugarcane was shipped to America, processed into sugar, and sent to Europe. Europe in turn shipped it along with other goods to Africa to trade for more slaves to go to the Caribbean and work on sugarcane plantations. Although 80 percent of the sugarcane produced in Trinidad is used for export, the amount of sugar produced on the island has declined dramatically following the closure of the country's largest sugarcane estate, Caroni Ltd., in 1975.

By the late 1860s the cacao industry in Trinidad and Tobago became another major cash crop, produced on estates where indentured laborers worked. A crossbreed of Central American native *criollo* and *forestero* cacaos planted by the Spaniards, the resulting *trinitario* was considered superior in taste and hardiness, perfect for use in the then–newly discovered process of removing cocoa butter from the bean, which is necessary for the production of chocolate bars. While trinitario beans still fetch a high price on the world market, local production has steadily declined since 1920, and Central and South American trinitario beans, particularly from Colombia, have entered the market.

By the early 20th century petroleum production began in Trinidad and continued to grow, outpacing agriculture as the mainstay of the national economy. Today, agricultures comprises less than 1 percent of Trinidad and Tobago's gross domestic product while oil and natural gas comprise 40 percent.

Other major foodstuffs produced and eaten in Trinidad are directly related to the islands' heyday of sugar and cacao production, as a variety of fruits and vegetables were imported into Trinidad and Tobago from Africa, India, and the South Pacific as sustenance for farm laborers. Rice, brought by Indian laborers and produced on the island, has become a major starch in the Trinidadian diet and is eaten with Indian and Creole foods alike. It may be served as a side dish to curries or stewed meats and vegetables, or within a pilaf.

Pelau

Serves 6

Pelau is one of those dishes that really exemplifies Trinidadian cuisine because it is an admixture of various cooking styles. Pelau, or rice layered with meats and vegetables, is a variation of East Indian *pilau,* which originated in Persia where it is called *polow.* The Anglicized version of the dish is called *pilaf.* The process of browning meat in sugar for pelau is an African tradition, and ketchup is a New World addition. It likely has its basis in tomato chutneys available in British India and brought to Trinidad by the English.

Chicken is the most common meat in pelau, but tender cuts of stew beef or lamb work just as well. In Tobago, pelau is often made with crab. Green seasoning is an herb paste made of chives, cilantro, thyme, oregano, parsley, garlic, and water that can be bought in West Indian groceries or made fresh at home.

1 c dry or 1 (12-oz) can pigeon peas, pinto beans, or black-eyed peas

3 tbsp canola oil

¾ c sugar (white or brown)

1 (3-lb) chicken, cut into 8 pieces, skin removed

1 small onion, chopped

1 clove garlic, minced

1 c coconut milk

1 bay leaf

2 tsp green seasoning

½ c chopped parsley

1 sprig thyme

2 carrots, peeled and chopped

5 scallions, chopped (white and green parts)

2 c long-grain rice

2 c cubed fresh calabaza or butternut squash

1 small Scotch bonnet pepper, whole

½ c ketchup

1 tbsp butter

1. If using dried peas, soak them overnight in 3 cups of water. Drain. Bring 3 cups of fresh water to a boil in a saucepan, and add the peas. Simmer for 15 minutes, or until cooked almost completely through. Drain and set aside. If using canned beans, drain, rinse with cold water, drain again, and set aside.

2. Heat the oil in a Dutch oven or other heavy, deep pot. Add the sugar and swirl in the pot; allow it to caramelize to a light brown color. Add the chicken and stir well to coat.

3. Lower the heat to medium, and add the onion and garlic. Cook for 1 to 2 minutes, stirring constantly.

4. Add 2 cups of water, the coconut milk, bay leaf, green seasoning, parsley, thyme, carrots, and scallions to the chicken. Cover and simmer over medium-low heat for 10 minutes.

5. Wash the rice by placing in a bowl and running cold water over it to just cover. Swirl the rice around with your hand until the water becomes cloudy, then carefully pour off the water. Repeat the process four or five times until the water runs clear. Drain well, and stir the rice into the chicken mixture.

6. Add the squash, peas, hot pepper, ketchup, and butter to the chicken. Reduce the heat to low, cover, and cook for 20 minutes, or until the peas and vegetables are tender.

7. Remove the lid and fluff the rice. The rice should be moist but not sticky.

A variety of tubers and starchy vegetables, or *ground provisions* as they are collectively called, including yucca, Caribbean sweet potato (*boniato*), and pumpkin, are incorporated into a variety of dishes as a vegetable component, are used in desserts, or are simply boiled, fried, or roasted for use as a side dish with meats. Ground provisions also include breadfruit and plantains, though both are tree fruits.

Legumes are used by all Trinidadians, including dal (yellow split peas), *channa* (chickpeas), pigeon peas, black-eyed peas, and kidney beans. They are used in everything from breads to rice dishes to soups and stews to side dishes and desserts.

Breads and baked goods, both in the form of traditional Indian griddle breads and European-style breads and sweets, are heavily consumed in Trinidad and Tobago. Roti, a soft, round griddle bread cooked on a *tawa* (flat, round cast iron skillet), was brought from India by indentured laborers and includes variations like *dal puri*, a version of roti stuffed with ground, spiced lentils, and *buss up shut*, a version of roti that is torn up into pieces to resemble a "burst-up shirt." The latter is a late 20th-century addition to the Trinidadian bread repertoire. Bake, a savory beignet, is widely eaten for breakfast or as a sandwich roll.

Fish and fowl comprise most of the meat eaten in Trinidad and Tobago. The former is thanks to the abundant waters that both surround the island and form the rivers and streams inland. Kingfish, redfish, shark, salted codfish, smoked herring, shrimp, and crab are popular, but two—*Cascadura cascadoo,* a highly scaled fish in the catfish family that lives in muddy fresh waters, and flying fish, an ocean fish living in the waters between Tobago and Barbados—are the most prized. According to local legend, anyone who partakes of *Cascadura* is destined to return to Trinidad. Flying fish is so beloved that when the dredging of a deeper harbor in Barbados's capital disturbed the fish's habitat enough to cause a biomass migration to Tobago, it sparked an international argument.

The limited land for livestock rearing in Trinidad and Tobago, coupled with the limited palate for beef among Indian Hindus and pork among African and Indian Muslims, has made chicken the favored choice in the islands. Traditionally, every home, even in relatively crowded urban areas, kept "yard fowl" for both meat and eggs. However, increasingly, fowl are purchased from the local market or supermarket, supplied by large-scale poultry farms, as the society has moved away from its agrarian roots. Goat was and still is widely eaten on both islands because goats' small size means that even those who do not have large land tracts, which correlates to most of the country, can keep them with relative ease. Goat is most often eaten curried.

As a society Trinidadians eat a large quantity of vegetables, due in great part to cultural influence. Vegetarian Hindu Indians brought caraili, a bitter squash; *bodi,* long Indian string beans; eggplant; and more. Greens, such as spinach and callaloo (Indian dasheen), hearken from both the Indian and African traditions. Crops are varied and include corn,

Platter of typical local Trinidad food including bodi, salt-fish cod, fried accra, bread fritters, and vegetables with jonnycake bread. (Robert Lerich | Dreamstime.com)

tomatoes, zucchini, and other temperate-weather foodstuffs that have been adopted in the islands.

The diversity of fruits available on Trinidad and Tobago is far more varied than that in even some of the other Caribbean islands, as they include South American items in addition to those items native to Central America and the Caribbean. Coconuts are available year-round, and numerous varieties of mangoes, another popular fruit, are available for 10 months of the year. Although too many to mention, some more commonly used fruits include avocados, guavas, passion fruit, *pomme cythere* (June apple), *pommerac* (otaheite apple), pineapple, soursops, *barbadine* (a large greenish fruit with cream-colored flesh), and sapodilla. Watermelon, which arrived on the islands in the 1980s, is incredibly popular as well.

In terms of beverages Trinidad and Tobago are noted throughout the Caribbean for the production of Carib and Stag, two local beers, and for Angostura bitters, used in many cocktails, which has been made following a secret recipe on Trinidad since 1824. Local rums of varying grades are also produced, including increasingly aged sipping rums, such as 1919 and 1824, also from the House of Angostura.

Nonalcoholic beverages, such as green coconut water, ginger beer, *mauby* (a punch made from the bark of the carob tree and having a flavor similar to root beer), and sorrel (a sweet-tart ade made from dried hibiscus flowers) are widely drunk. Commercially produced local soft drinks, such as Solo and Chubby sodas, reflect the extreme sweet tooth of people in this sugar-producing country. Interestingly, the British soft drinks Pear Drax and, to some extent, Apple Drax are highly favored—particularly around Christmas—in Trinidad and Tobago, creating a market for the drinks that no longer exist in their native England.

Cooking

Historically, cooking in Trinidad and Tobago was most often done over a small fire on which an iron pot was directly set or hung, or on baking stones placed in the fire that a tawa could be settled upon. This method was based in the plantation era when slaves and laborers had only rudimentary wooden barracks. Outdoor cookhouses did exist in the plantation houses, but for poor, average folk a simple fire served the purpose and also kept the heat and danger of live fire away from the home.

This cooking method was used well into the mid-20th century throughout many parts of the island and is still extant in the popular "river lime" or "beach lime," in which a hot food picnic is cooked over an open fire. The hallmark of those events is that the food might be prepared in any kitchen and closely mimic those that were historically produced on an open flame including pelau, a rice dish incorporating stewed meat, beans, spices, and vegetables; stewed chicken, in which chicken pieces are first browned in caramelized sugar; dumplings; and boiled ground root vegetables.

Mud ovens, specifically for baking, and similar to what was used in Mesoamerica, were also used in Trinidad and Tobago well into the modern era and can still be found in rural communities on both islands. In communities with a high percentage of people with Amerindian and *Cocoa Panyol* (Venezuelan Spanish) roots, "buccaneer" cooking is still done; this is a method of smoking using native hardwoods, such as tonka or *samaan,* and wet banana leaves to smoke highly seasoned and marinated foods, particularly bush meats such as iguana, *manicou* (in the muskrat family), and *gouti* (hare). The method harkens back to the original cooking methods of island natives and is similar to the process of jerking in Jamaica, where wild boar and now domesticated pig are the preferred meats and allspice wood is used for smoking. Later, the form evolved to what became known as barbecue (from the word *barbacoa*).

Pickling provided a way to reduce the gaminess of bush meats or goat, or preserve out-of-season fruits. Indian hot pickles, such as lime or mango *achar,* or *kuchela,* made from shredded, peppered, and pickled green mango, are typical condiments. Non–Indian-style hot pickles are collectively called *chow chow* and are similar to the American versions. They mostly make use of vinegar or saltwater and plenty of hot pepper. Some common chows are mixed vegetables including cauliflower and caraili, the Indian bitter melon. Other chows include pineapple, pomme cythere, and mango, but any variety of green fruits or hard vegetables can be used in chow. Pepper sauces are an absolute must-have on the Trinidadian table and, generally, are still homemade, though national brands like Chiefs and Matouk's provide various kinds for those who cannot make it themselves.

Cookery in Trinidad and Tobago was based largely on what could be achieved using the preceding cooking methods—stews and soups, roasted meats, griddle breads, and boiled vegetables—but those cooking styles remain the hallmark of the modern Trinidadian kitchen. It is not uncommon for foreign ingredients or methods to be adapted to this type of cooking or to local ingredients. Home cooking in Trinidad remains the standard, and most people eat breakfast at home, often carry their lunch to work or school, and eat a home-cooked hot meal for dinner. Given the heat of the country, lunch was, at one time, the heaviest meal of the day, with a lighter supper following at nightfall.

Teatime was a beloved ritual in Trinidadian life, taking place in the mid- to late afternoon, as in the United Kingdom, continuing even after independence. As time has passed, tea has fallen away or might comprise only a cup of tea, sweetened with condensed milk as is the local custom, and a digestive biscuit or small roll. The afternoon snack taken by schoolchildren when they return home from their day is still collectively called "tea," regardless of what it might comprise, and this has more to do with the hour than the foods eaten.

With the advent of modern conveniences like air-conditioning coupled with Trinidad and Tobago's rapid rush toward being a First World, industrialized nation, daily schedules have moved closer to those of people in Europe and America, with an eight-hour workday, including a lunch break and a busy commute home. Additionally, it is fairly usual for both husband and wife to work outside of the home, so there is no one present to cook a hot meal to which the family can return after a busy day. The end result is that a variety of adaptations, including the use of packaged and frozen foods, or eating out, have rapidly become solutions for the evening meal. Within some affluent houses a cook, or lady who comes in to cook, may still be employed, similar to what was the norm even in middle-class families in colonial times, though the lady of the house would have been present. Today, this is fairly rare except among the most privileged.

Typical Meals

Breakfast in Trinidad and Tobago is a mix of European and ethnic cooking and food styles. Eggs scrambled, fried, or in an omelet and served with toast are equally popular to *egg chokha,* or eggs fried with tomatoes, onions, and spices. Salted codfish, or salt fish, is popular at breakfast when served as *buljol,* a dish in which it is fried with onion, tomato, and spices and served with fried bake (a fried biscuit or fritter). Smoked herring, cooked in a similar manner but served with dumplings, is another breakfast that makes use of a typically English ingredient cooked in the local style.

Guava jam or jelly is a must-have on the breakfast table as is tea, though coffee is increasingly served. Coffee beans are grown and processed right on the island. Hong Wing is the most established and popular brand. Rituals, a Starbucks imitator, has popped up all over the islands and serves as a pit stop for many breakfast-goers, though, for the most part, the American price levels (US$3.50 for a latte) puts those drinks mostly in the "treat" category.

For those who choose to eat their breakfast out, *doubles,* or spiced chickpeas layered between two pieces of fried yeast-based dough, is a beloved breakfast standard. Doubles vendors can be seen throughout the island every morning and in the wee hours of weekend nights to service partying club-goers.

Once based in heavy dishes, such as rice and beef stew, curried chicken, fried fish, and other extensive meals, lunch has morphed to include sandwiches and take-out foods, particularly from the many Western chains popping up around the island, such as Kentucky Fried Chicken or pizza. Still, the island's vibrant street-food culture does provide lunch for office workers, just as it did for laborers a century before. The most popular offerings include roti and curry, barbecue, corn soup, roast corn, *phoulourie* (fried balls of split pea–flour dough), shark and bake, cow-heel soup, callaloo soup (the "national" dish of Trinidad), and more. Soft drinks are commonly consumed with lunch.

Curried shrimp, a very popular dish in restaurants in Trinidad and Tobago. (StockPhotoPro)

Curried Shrimp

This is a popular curry in roti shops and is often paired with dal puri or *paratha roti* (a flat bread; see the following).

1 lb large shrimp, shelled and deveined

3 scallions, white and green parts, minced

1 small onion, chopped

½ tsp turmeric

½ tsp cumin

1 tbsp West Indian curry powder (such as Chief's Brand)

¼ Scotch bonnet pepper, minced

4 leaves *shado beni,* chopped, or 2 tbsp chopped cilantro

1 tbsp canola oil

2 Roma tomatoes, chopped

Salt and pepper to taste

1. Mix shrimp, scallions, onion, turmeric, cumin, curry powder, Scotch bonnet pepper, and shado beni together in a large bowl. Cover with plastic wrap and refrigerate for 2 hours.

2. Heat the oil in a large, deep frying pan, and add the tomatoes. Cook 1 minute, and add the shrimp mixture. Season with salt and pepper, and mix well.

3. Add 1 cup water and simmer until shrimp turns pink. Remove from heat and serve with dal puri or paratha roti.

_____

Paratha Roti

Makes 4

Roti

2 c all-purpose flour

2 tbsp baking powder, preferably Lion Brand

¼ tsp salt

Warm water as needed

Paste (Loya)

3 tbsp cold ghee

2 tbsp canola oil

Flour as needed

1. Whisk together flour, baking powder, and salt in a bowl and gradually add water, using your fingers to mix the flour and water together. Do not knead; simply gently combine the flour and water.

2. Continue adding the water until you achieve a soft, sticky dough that just comes together into a ball. Cover and set aside to rest for 15 minutes.

3. Make the paste by combining the ghee and oil. Set aside.

4. Flour a work surface and turn out the roti dough. Cut the dough into 4 large pieces and gently form into a ball. Flour your hands as needed to be able to handle the dough, and do not overknead.

5. Roll out each ball of dough into a circle ¼ inch thick, and brush with the Loya paste. Sprinkle the surface lightly with flour. Make a cut halfway through the middle of the circle and roll the dough away from you into a cone shape. Roll the cylinder into a ball by pushing the narrow end of the cone in towards the wider end, and pinching the edges closed. Repeat with the remaining pieces of dough and let the balls rest for 15 to 20 minutes on a floured surface.

6. Roll the rested dough into ⅛-inch-thick circles and place on a hot tawa or cast iron griddle. Brush with oil, immediately turn over, and brush with oil again. Continue to flip the dough until it is puffy. Remove from heat, and place in a clean dishtowel. Fold dishtowel to cover the rotis so they stay warm.

_____

What was once typical lunch fare has become the repertoire of dinners at home for those who have time to cook. Rice, curry, stewed meat and vegetable dishes, fried fish, Creole-style food, and the like are equally cooked regardless whether a home is primarily of Indian, African, or Creole descent. Takeout such as Chinese or pizza is often eaten as well.

In its most traditional form, dinner will include a green salad, and often a soup, followed by the main dish, which comprises a balance of protein, vegetable, and a larger portion of starch, whether that be rice, provisions (tubers), or bread. Bread is less often eaten at dinner except perhaps as roti and curry, though that is increasingly becoming lunchtime fare. Trinidadians tend to eat dinner fairly late by American standards, more aligned with those of Europe. It is not unlikely to find dinner taken at 8 or 8:30 P.M. in the average home. Water is the beverage most likely consumed at dinner, though wine is beginning to reach a larger audience. Drinks like beer are more often consumed separately, in the manner of a cocktail rather than accompanying food.

Trinidadians are champion snackers, enabled by the well-established and myriad street-food scene: _sahina_ (a fritter of split pea flour), dasheen (callaloo), phoulourie, oyster shooters, spiced fried channa (chickpeas), boiled _peewah_ (a fruit/nut in the palm tree family), and much more. A number of packaged snack food companies on the island provide Trinidadians with popular nosh—everything from potato chips to candy bars and English digestive biscuits, sold in packs of two.

Sugary snacks are ubiquitous and well consumed in the islands, most likely because of the abundance of sugar that has always been available. Indian sweets (collectively called _mithai_) are eaten by all and have a high sugar content. They include items like _kulma_ (a fried dough stick dusted with sugar), _golab jamun_ (syrup-soaked fritters), _jalebi_ (deep-fried batter like funnel cakes soaked in syrup), and various types of *barfi* (a kind of milk fudge). Other European preparations, such as fudge made from chocolate or coconut, cookies, cakes, and tarts, are supplemented by a wide variety of ice creams using local fruits. In 2009, Cold Stone Creamery opened in the capital city of Port of Spain.

Eating Out

The dining-out option that has existed for the longest time in Trinidad and Tobago is street foods. Initially simple food stalls that served estate laborers in the 19th century, as the years passed street-food vendors have become more elaborate in their setup. Stalls are supplemented with food trucks, and some vendors even provide makeshift outdoor seating. Today, the government board of health licenses street-food vendors, and patrons are discouraged from purchasing foods from unlicensed stalls.

The best-known street-food collective in Trinidad was, perhaps, The Breakfast Shed, started in 1920 to provide a hot breakfast option to local schoolchildren. Situated in a galvanized-roof warehouse in Port of Spain's harbor district, inside were various vendors of Creole-style food, set-up stalls, and some seating from which patrons could choose. The original building was torn down to make room for a waterfront revival and promenade. The New Breakfast Shed, housed in a modern building, has retained some of the former vendors but is, in the estimation of locals, a shadow of its former self.

Since 1990, a robust fast-food and fast-casual restaurant culture has sprung up on Trinidad and Tobago. While the beef-heavy McDonald's doesn't have

A Kentucky Fried Chicken in downtown Trinidad. (AFP | Getty Images)

a major presence, Kentucky Fried Chicken, Popeye's, and the local chain Royal Crown are well patronized. Papa John's and Pizza Hut compete with the local chains Pizza Boys and Mario's, which serve a pizza featuring the far sweeter (sugar-enhanced) tomato sauce that appeals to local tastes. Subway and Burger King are here as well. Most of the fast-food chains are concentrated around the capital and the large cities of Chaguanas, in the central part of Trinidad, and San Fernando, in the south. Chinese takeouts that serve "Trini-Chinee" food are numerous throughout the country and offer a number of specialties specific to Trinidad and Tobago, including dasheen pork and fried wontons.

American fast-casual chains such as TGI Fridays and Ruby Tuesday's enjoy a status above what they do in the United States, as they charge American prices (the exchange rate is about TT$6 to US$1). They are considered stylish and unique in their offerings of "typical" American fare.

In the past decade, a crop of fine-dining restaurants that are the bailiwick of chefs classically trained in the French culinary style in Europe or America have opened, particularly in the capital city. The most creative of those chefs mix their formal training with local ingredients, adapting traditional dishes to more formal presentation or preparations to good result. Mélange restaurant is one good example of the nouvelle Trinidadian cuisine, as is Battimamzelle.

Special Occasions

Celebrations are central to Trinidad and Tobago's culture, and the country is perhaps most known for holding one of the biggest parties on earth in its yearly pre-Lenten Carnival activities. The nation's population burgeons during the festivities, which feature reveling in the form of costumed street parades, steel drum music, and copious consumption of alcohol. Unlike other special occasions in Trinidad, Carnival is not particularly marked by certain foods. Instead, religious-based holidays and feast days are where food takes center stage.

Trinidad and Tobago's population is primarily Christian (75%) with a small percentage of groups that mix traditional West African religion with Christianity such as Shouter Baptists and practitioners of Orisha. Hindus comprise nearly 23 percent of the population, and Muslims nearly 6 percent. Some quick addition indicates that these numbers total well over 100 percent, which neatly tells the tale of religion in Trinidad: Like its people it is a mélange of practices that exist and intermingle, usually with no sense of dilution or lack of authenticity on the part of their practitioners.

Regardless of their self-proclaimed religious heritage, Trinidadians often celebrate holidays across religions. The Hindu festival of Diwali is a national holiday in Trinidad and Tobago and is most notable for Indian vegetarian foods such as vegetable and fruit curries and mithai, the traditional Indian sweets already mentioned.

Ramadan, the Muslim fast month, is shared with non-Muslim friends during Eftar, the breaking of the fast that starts with the consumption of a date and some water. Other foods are traditional Trinidadian foods that do not make use of pork. During Eid al-Fitr, the end of Ramadan, feasts are celebrated throughout the country and again feature Indian sweets, as the Trinidad Muslim tradition is largely Indian based though there is an increasing number of African Muslim converts. The small Trinidad Lebanese population tends to be Christian. *Sawine,* a vermicelli pudding, is a must-have during the feast.

Regardless of religion, nearly every Trinidadian celebrates Christmas in one fashion or another, and this is the occasion when food is most important. Much of the Trinidadian Christmas foods have their heritage in the Cocoa Panyol or Spanish community of the islands. Specialties like *pastelle,* a meat-filled corn turnover similar to a tamale, and *paymee,* a sweetened version of the same dish, without meat are also typical Christmas foods. Black cake, a descendant of Irish Christmas cake that was brought to Trinidad by the small population of Irish indentured laborers in the 19th century, is an absolute must-have for Christmas.

Popular holiday beverages include sorrel, ginger beer, and *ponche crème,* eggnog featuring condensed milk and Angostura bitters. Roasted turkey, imported from the United States, has become a major dish for Christmas dinner, and it is usually stuffed with a local stuffing made from *chataigne,* a starchy tree fruit in the breadfruit family.

Weddings across cultures are another major feasting occasion. In Indian families, particularly, hundreds of guests may attend a wedding celebration, often for days at a time. Cooks who are well versed in cooking for traditional Indian weddings are employed during this time, making three-foot-long rotis on four-foot-wide tawas and huge pots of food. Dal puri is most often served at these events because it is complex to make and requires a delicate hand.

Diet and Health

Trinidadian foods have come to be considered by nutritionists as overly carbohydrate- and fat-rich, based heavily in starches, once used to provide calories to field laborers along with limited protein and poorer, fattier cuts of meat unwanted by plantation masters. Oil, particularly coconut oil, was well used in African, Indian, and Chinese cooking and continues to be so today, even when vegetable or seed oils are substituted. In recent years, the government health department has undertaken health campaigns to promote more judicious use of fats and oils for heart health, as heart disease is the leading cause of disease-related death in Trinidad and Tobago.

According to the United Nations' Food and Agriculture Organization (FAO), obesity is not yet a problem in Trinidad and Tobago among children and young people, much like the United States, though the number of overweight individuals has increased as the country has moved away from an agrarian to an industrial society. The FAO reported in 1999 that nearly 17 percent of people over 20 are overweight, and within that group 31 percent are obese.

Childhood nutrition, particularly regarding the consumption of adequate calcium, is also a concern into which health officials are putting efforts. Hypertension and alcoholism are two other common diet-based health issues. Although no recent data have been gathered about food access, in 1995, 22 percent of the population was listed as living below the poverty level, half of which were considered "extremely poor" and therefore having limited access to food and proper nutrition. Most at risk for malnutrition in those households, according to the FAO, are children, the elderly, and pregnant and lactating women. While Trinidadians do eat a wide variety of fruits and vegetables on a daily basis, they also consume a great deal of sugar as alcohol, and diabetes is on the uptick.

Ramin Ganeshram

Further Reading

Ganeshram, Ramin. *Sweet Hands: Island Cooking from Trinidad and Tobago.* New York: Hippocrene Books, 2006.

Lai, Walton Look. *Indentured Labor, Caribbean Sugar: Chinese and Indian Migrants to the British West Indies, 1838–1918.* Baltimore, MD: Johns Hopkins University Press, 2004.

Mahabir, Noor Kumar. *Caribbean East Indian Recipes.* San Juan, Trinidad: Chakra, 1992.

Moodie-Kublalsingh, Sylvia. *The Cocoa Panyols of Trinidad, an Oral Record.* New York: St. Martin's Press, 1994.

Williams, Eric. *History of the People of Trinidad and Tobago.* London: A. Deutsch, 1964.

United States: The Mid-Atlantic

Overview

The mid-Atlantic states of the United States are here defined as the heavily urbanized and industrial region stretching from north of Virginia to the south of New England including New York, New Jersey, Pennsylvania, Delaware, and Maryland as well as the interior of these states. While this region shares many features with states to the north and south, it is unique in its remarkable ethnic and religious diversity as well as the food cultures associated with vibrant immigrant communities, which have been arriving in successive torrents since the 17th century. New York City, for example, hosts perhaps the most eclectic range of cuisines on earth; its food culture is in a sense a convergence of practically every tradition covered in this encyclopedia, adapted to local conditions and often having evolved into foods eaten today around the globe. Its role as a financial and commercial hub of world trade has also given this region an astoundingly cosmopolitan character, always ready to integrate new ingredients, recipes, and ways of eating. Thus one finds as common everyday fare dishes descended from English roasts to Irish stews, Italian pizza to Jewish bagels, Chinese lo mein to Polish kielbasa, as well as soul food introduced by African Americans who migrated from the South, and more recent introductions from virtually every corner of the earth. Here one can dine in some of the most acclaimed French-inspired restaurants in the world as well as find Indian, Russian, Salvadoran, or Korean cuisine—the list is endless. This region also produces many of the industrial foods most commonly eaten across the United States, whether it be Campbell's Soup from Camden, New

Jersey; Nabisco crackers, originally from New York; or Tyson chickens raised in Maryland. The majority of artificial flavors used in the United States are also developed in New Jersey. Thus one can rightly say that this region hosts the best and worst of American cuisine and every possible variety in between.

The original inhabitants of this region were the Lenape Indians. They survived by hunting and fishing as well as extensive agriculture based on native plants such as corn, beans, and squash. Although they suffered a devastating demographic catastrophe with the introduction of European diseases as well as more overt forms of aggression, the foods they consumed still form a solid backbone of mid-Atlantic food culture. New Jersey is still renowned for superior corn and tomatoes. Although many other New World plants were actually reintroduced to this region later, zucchini and peppers, for example, or potatoes introduced from South America—made into chips said to have been invented in Saratoga, New York—the legacy of the Native Americans remains in many favorite dishes: Maryland crabs, oysters all along the coast, native blueberries in the pine barrens of New Jersey, or native grape species made into wine in the Finger Lakes. Sunflowers, vitally important for their oil, seeds, and edible roots (Jerusalem artichokes), are native to eastern North America.

The first European settlers in this region were the Dutch, whose claim was staked with the explorer Henry Hudson in 1609. Within a few years a settlement named New Amsterdam was established on the island of Manhattan. The outpost of Albany up the Hudson River was established in 1614, and between these two points large Dutch landholders maintained patroonships that, virtually feudal in organization and structure, encompassed small farmers working the fields of large "patrons." The fortified port of New Amsterdam welcomed virtually anyone regardless of origin or religion to settle and engage in commerce, so from the start there was a mixed population of Dutch and other Europeans, Jews, and Africans. Dutch cuisine, although relatively simple, survives in this region in dishes such as waffles and pancakes as well as in the concept and word *cookie*. In a series of wars the English sought to oust the Dutch from the mid-Atlantic, and this was accomplished permanently in 1674, when the city and region kept the name New York.

To the immediate south there were Swedish settlements in what is now New Jersey and Delaware, though ultimately the most important group to settle along the Delaware River were religious exiles known as Quakers. William Penn founded the colony of Pennsylvania and its capitol, Philadelphia, which by the 18th century became the second-largest English-speaking city in the world. English culinary traditions were introduced, but equally important were those derived from German settlers, Mennonites, and Amish Anabaptists also seeking religious freedom. Pretzels are one of the most recognizably American foods introduced by Germans, but hot dogs, sauerkraut, and mustard, not to mention beer, are considered quintessentially American. To the south the colony of Maryland was formed as a haven for Catholics by Lord Baltimore, and in many respects it is here that a uniquely English cuisine survives, especially in the fishing culture of the Chesapeake.

In the early 19th century the population began to move westward and inland. This was aided by a series of canals to facilitate trade and later railroads. Eventually, major industrial cities like Pittsburgh and Buffalo sprang up, as well as farms in rural districts. But the most important event of the 19th century was the massive influx of immigrants hailing primarily from eastern and southern Europe. Southern Italians introduced pizza, spaghetti, and other dishes that are culinary staples—not to mention the Philly cheese steak sandwich. Jews fleeing religious persecution brought with them deli culture: corned beef and pastrami sandwiches, rye bread, and sour

dill pickles as well as bagels and lox. Irish immigrants escaping the potato famine as well as Poles and other eastern Europeans made their own contributions. In the wake of the Civil War there was a massive influx of former slaves to the North, bringing what is essentially Southern food; some of the best anywhere can be found in places such as Harlem.

Prominent immigrant groups adding to this incredibly eclectic culinary mix include Chinese, mostly from Canton, whose dishes are familiar and commonly eaten in Chinese restaurants by everyone. An enormous Hispanic community made up first of Puerto Ricans after the Spanish American War, followed by other Caribbean and Central American peoples as well as Mexicans, means that Latino cuisine is equally familiar to anyone living in this region. Although Americans in the mid-Atlantic states might not regularly cook dishes from more far-flung parts of the world, a thriving restaurant culture means that few people live far from an Indian or Thai restaurant, a Greek diner, a Japanese sushi bar, Spanish tapas bar, or any number of ethnic restaurants that have now become integral to the way everyone eats.

🍽 Food Culture Snapshot

Nina and Will Lok-Segal live in Prospect Heights, a middle-class neighborhood in Brooklyn. She is a senior researcher for a nonprofit foundation. He is an editor for a large publishing firm. Their lifestyle and eating habits are typical of professionals living in a cosmopolitan city where food has become a major preoccupation, and trying new foods only requires a hop on the subway. They are also influenced by their backgrounds: Nina was born in Hong Kong, and Will's mother grew up in Paris.

Nina and Will usually eat breakfast at home because neither of them needs to be at work until 10 A.M., thereby avoiding the worst of rush hour into Manhattan. While Nina often prepares oatmeal from scratch or fixes a bowl of cold cereal with sliced fruit and soy milk, Will sticks to black coffee and dry multigrain toast. On weekends they take turns preparing more elaborate meals: Nina makes frittatas with vegetables or herbs, while Will has a sweet tooth and a light touch with pancakes or French toast. Like many New Yorkers, the Lok-Segals either pack lunch (often leftovers) to eat at their desks or buy something at the many quick-service lunch places in midtown Manhattan. While Nina's favorite is a Korean buffet, Will is partial to the meatball sandwiches sold at a small Italian takeout shop. Very common are soup-and-salad chains and food trucks where people line up for ethnic specialties like halal chicken over rice, Indian *dosas,* and Belgian waffles. Will's office has a coffee bar stocked with cookies, chips, and other snack foods where employees graze whenever they are hungry or bored. Nina keeps a bag of pistachios and chocolate bars in her desk drawer, nibbling them along with the green tea she drinks throughout the day.

Dinner is eaten at 8:30 P.M. Either Nina or Will prepares something simple: a green salad, sautéed pork chops or a rotisserie chicken picked up on the way home, and rice. They have wine with dinner. On the weekends, especially if they are entertaining friends, dinner is more elaborate, an occasion to try out new recipes and fresh produce bought in Chinatown or at the Grand Army Plaza Greenmarket. On occasion they will also purchase cheese at Murray's or Dean & Deluca, or perhaps seafood at Citarella, which are among the most revered gourmet shops in the country. Dessert is either store-bought sorbet or fruit.

Major Foodstuffs

Three major influences on New York City's food habits are its geographic location, its role as a port city, and its long history of immigration. The Dutch and other early settlers of New Amsterdam cultivated potatoes, cabbages, onions, and apples on land that is now Upper Manhattan and the Bronx. As they moved up the Hudson Valley, apples were an important crop: sliced, dried, and used for pies all winter long, and pressed for cider. Cows were raised for milk and as a source of meat. Chickens, ducks, and geese provided eggs and the occasional roast. Pigs provided fresh meat and bacon, as well as sausages and headcheese. Farms north, west, and east of New York, including Long Island's East End, provided fresh vegetables and fruits, and its shores were a source of oysters, cod, lobsters, and other fish

and seafood. The borough of Queens was once the city's milk shed, ensuring a fresh and constant supply of milk.

Throughout its history, New York City has consumed the fruits of global trade. As a major port city, foods would pass through New York. Every technological innovation including refrigeration and steam engines brought new foods to the city. In the 1920s, a mere 12 percent of the produce consumed in the city was grown in New York State. After World War II, the number of farms within 200 miles of the city declined dramatically, as suburbs sprouted in the place of fields. In the 1950s, nearly 20 percent of the United States' food supply passed through New York State. Foods from every state in the nation and more than 30 countries were consumed on a regular basis.

Immigration has shaped and continues to shape New York City's food culture. Iconic foods include bagels (with a *schmear* of cream cheese) and pizza (thin crust). Knishes have been replaced with taco trucks, and sushi joints have become ubiquitous. Western European food practices continue to dominate; wheat products like bread, pasta, and cereals are consumed in large quantities. Corn is more likely to be consumed in processed foods than as tortillas, cornbread, or grits. Vegetables and fruits, particularly potatoes, onions, and apples, available at the city's farmers' markets, reflect both geographic constraints and people's tastes.

A drive toward more sustainable food practices is inspiring a resurgence of small-scale food processing and do-it-yourself classes being offered in butchering and sausage making. People are raising chickens and rabbits in backyards. Rooftop gardens are thriving as private as well as commercial enterprises. Though Mayor Bloomberg's otherwise-inspiring 2030 Plan for a sustainable future did not include food (nor did Robert Moses's and Jane Jacobs's competing visions), city agencies, nonprofits, and community organizations are responding with new policies, programs, and proposals for more local food production. East New York Farms and Value Added involve volunteers and schoolchildren in urban agriculture; Flatbush Food Coop is among several cooperatively owned and managed grocery stores; Cornell Cooperative Extension trains aspiring farmers, many of whom are recent immigrants, and helps them find land to lease as well as markets where they sell their produce.

Water, sodas, and fruit juices are commonly served with meals. Children drink milk (or soy milk) in school, and at meals eaten at home as well. Energy drinks, vitamin waters, smoothies, and other fortified beverages are consumed on the go. Coffee, light and sweet, is bought from coffee carts, and Starbucks has its lines of devotees. Throughout upscale residential neighborhoods, cafés roast their own fair-trade beans. Beer is part of the city's heritage. When Germans and Czechs immigrated to New York in the mid-19th century, they brought with them a taste for lager-style beers. Breweries were established throughout Brooklyn; a combination of mass production, mass marketing, and labor strikes caused their decline in the 1950s. Brooklyn Brewery and Six Points Brewery are marking a comeback of local beer. Wine is an important part of New York's thriving restaurant culture. It is also served at home in households with European roots. Among the many residents with roots in South and Central America, beer and/ or distilled liqueurs are more commonly consumed alcohols. Quality wines are produced in the Finger Lakes region in upstate New York, and on the North and South Forks of Long Island.

Cooking

Cooking in New York and the mid-Atlantic region varies broadly, and it is difficult to generalize. In some households cooking is an ordinary part of the daily routine with many family members pitching in. Especially in less affluent homes, cooking may be a necessity to feed the family affordably, especially with the prevalence of fast food. In busy homes, cooking is still usually done by the mother of the family, though constraints of time and the general hectic pace of life, when both parents work and children have after-school commitments, can seriously curtail the frequency of home-cooked meals eaten together as a family.

During the early decades of the 20th century, immigrants lived in crowded tenements. Many depended on foods cooked outside the home. Today, many New Yorkers continue to depend on take-out foods. While some pick up an entire meal (Chinese food, pizza, fast food, or other convenience options), others combine prepared foods with something cooked at home. Microwaves and rice cookers are as commonly used to prepare foods as are more traditionally European techniques like sautéing or roasting. Grilling is popular, whether in city parks, on apartment balconies, or in backyards across Queens, or Staten Island. In the vast suburban sprawl of the megalopolis, the barbecue grill is an absolute necessity for every backyard, wealthy or more modest. It is here, and often only here, that men take charge, wielding spatula and fork, flipping burgers or steaks, ribs, wings, or perhaps something more adventuresome like fish.

Otherwise, the standard kitchen is much like elsewhere in the United States, although with perhaps more attention to style and detail and less to utility. An average family will own a full four- or six-burner range and oven, a capacious refrigerator that allows shopping once a week for groceries, and sometimes a large separate freezer as well. Especially in suburban households, the fridge can be the center of the entire home. There will be cavernous cabinets to hold an array of canned goods, boxed cereals, and snack foods. There will invariably be a dishwasher, and perhaps a stand mixer, food processor, coffeemaker, toaster, and a range of other gadgets large and small. The irony, of course, is that much of the food consumed is frozen or requires little preparation—perhaps only a few minutes in the microwave.

There is, however, a growing percentage of the population, men and women, that treats cooking as a leisure activity. Perhaps inspired by cooking magazines or cooking shows on television, they socialize with friends by cooking a meal at home, showing off their latest culinary experiments and sharing good wine. Such people are open to new cuisines, trying new ingredients and following the latest trends avidly. They may try their hand at a pad Thai one night, a ceviche the next, without any qualms about mixing and matching flavors in a kind of homemade fusion cuisine.

Typical Meals

A typical breakfast consists of cold cereal with milk and fruit, toast with jam, or instant oatmeal, accompanied by coffee or tea and orange juice. People grab egg-and-cheese sandwiches at delis or McDonald's. Kids are sent to school with breakfast bars, toaster waffles, or other "grab-and-go" foods. On weekends, breakfast turns into brunch, and anything goes, from bagels and lox to diner-style platters of eggs, bacon, pancakes, and hashed browns. Waffles are served with whipped cream and fresh berries. Dim sum parlors attract large groups of all ethnicities. Whether savory or sweet, weekend breakfasts are occasions to indulge.

Lunch is usually a quick meal. For people working in offices, it means stepping out for half an hour, buying something in the vicinity, and eating in a nearby park, at a desk, or in an employee lunchroom. Sandwiches, whether "deli-style" piled high with cold cuts, lettuce, and mayo or European-style panini, are typical choices. Chains offering customized salads and soups are popular. Trucks and carts line the streets of business districts, offering a dizzying array of ethnic foods at good prices, attracting everyone from mail clerks to executives. Some people pack their lunch—sandwiches and a piece of fruit, or leftovers to be warmed up in the office microwave. The power lunch continues to exist for those with expense accounts—although the multi-course three-martini meal has been replaced with "express" options of single-course meals, often salads that include sliced steak or grilled shrimp, and lemonade or sparkling water.

At home, lunch is also a casual, quick affair consisting of sandwiches or leftovers. In addition to cold cuts, typical sandwiches include tuna and chicken salads, and the childhood classic, peanut butter and jelly. Chips or pretzels are often served as accompaniments, and a simple dessert like a cookie or piece of fruit completes the meal. Some cultural groups like Italian and African American families continue the tradition of a Sunday lunch as the main meal of the day.

Dinner is the main meal due to the organization of the working and school day. Whether eaten at home or in a restaurant, for many, dinner is the one hot meal of the day regardless of cultural or ethnic/national background. A typical dinner includes a portion of animal protein, whether meat or fish; a starch like potatoes or rice; and a vegetable. Stews and braises can be prepared ahead of time, with meat supplemented with root vegetables. These filling dishes are popular in the colder months. Summer means cold salads and grilled foods like burgers and sausages, corn on the cob, and watermelon. Pasta is a popular choice because it can be prepared cheaply and easily. Take-out foods ranging from pizza and fast food to entrées ordered at fine-dining establishments are a mainstay.

Eating Out

Restaurant culture thrives in the cities dotting the mid-Atlantic coast. These range from a simple aluminum pushcart with Sabrett hot dogs for those who like to dine *al fresco* to Michelin-starred restaurants owned by celebrity chefs. In fact, the presence of the Food Network Studios in New York City means that many food television stars have restaurants here—Bobby Flay and Mario Batali, for example. Everything in between amounts to literally thousands of restaurants. In some neighborhoods you will find half a dozen on every block, with an expensive formal white-tablecloth establishment jockeying for space with a Greek diner, an Italian pizzeria, a small Chinese take-out place, a Korean convenience store, an upscale bistro, and a Salvadoran *pupuseria*. For a quick pick-me-up, there are also native establishments like Papaya King for a hot dog or juice, as well as fast-food chains like McDonald's, Burger King, and KFC. New Yorkers probably dine out more than any other people on earth, and it is said that you could eat out in a different spot every single day of your life. It is often joked that wealthy New Yorkers have trophy kitchens decked out with high-tech ovens and appliances that they never use. It is true that some people don't even have a working kitchen, as there is always food to be bought within a few steps. In small apartments, dishwashers are used as dry storage; shoes are shelved in cabinets.

A shop on the corner in Chinatown, New York. (Shutterstock)

Urbanites in all major cities of the mid-Atlantic, including Washington, D.C., and Philadelphia, are extremely sophisticated and particular about their restaurant choices. With so many options, they can afford to be choosy, and it is true that unless a restaurant is well rated (the ubiquitous democratic *Zagat Guide* is one measure), it is bound to fold. Restaurants, not surprisingly, turn over remarkably quickly, and only the best withstand the test of time, and even then not always, if one thinks of the legendary Lutece or Le Pavillon.

In New York one can find not only fine, expensive restaurants but also many that set culinary trends globally, whether it be in fusion cuisine, the latest science-inspired "molecular gastronomy" establishment, or merely the newest as yet undiscovered corner of the world. If it exists anywhere, it will be found in New York; in fact, some culinary

traditions survive only here in exile, with the people themselves.

Special Occasions

Foods consumed on special occasions often erase regional distinctions in favor of national traditions. For example, Thanksgiving is observed with foods that are now considered traditional throughout the United States: turkey, sweet potatoes, pumpkin pie, and cranberry relish. The stuffing reveals the region's British influence, incorporating chestnuts and celery. The many immigrants living in New York City adopt Thanksgiving, making it their own by adding Bengali spices to cranberry sauce or rubbing a turkey with jerk seasoning. Summer is all about ball games; hot dogs are consumed with lager-style beer. In Prospect Park, as well as the greenways lining the

Hudson River, informal soccer, softball, and volleyball games attract food vendors. When the New York Philharmonic plays its annual concerts in Central Park, thousands gather with friends to dine on blankets under the stars. On Super Bowl Sunday, everyone suspends their diets to nosh on chicken wings and nachos piled high with cheese, sour cream, and pickled jalapeños. St. Patrick's Day means corned beef and cabbage, and green bagels, in a town where everyone claims Irish, Jewish, and Italian heritage as part of their civic identity.

Like elsewhere, Christmas is celebrated by practically everyone, sometimes even non-Christians, as an excuse to exchange gifts and decorate a Christmas tree. Not surprisingly, a large Jewish population celebrates Passover with unleavened bread and fasts on Yom Kippur, as well as enjoying many other food-centered holidays. African Americans celebrate Kwanzaa, and devout Muslims fast during Ramadan. Uniquely, it is perhaps only in this region that one will find all these holidays side by side, sometimes within the same household when there are parents of mixed heritage. Schools will often be shut for a range of holidays for children of various faiths. Memorial Day, the Fourth of July, and Labor Day are three-day weekends marking the start, middle, and end of summer. They are celebrated with picnics and barbecues.

Diet and Health

New York City faces the same challenges as the rest of the United States: Obesity/overweight and diabetes are threatening the well-being of large percentages of the population. Obesity, diabetes, and other diet-related diseases are strongly correlated with class, race/ethnicity, and neighborhood. While middle- and upper-income people like Will and Nina live in neighborhoods with many food choices including large grocery stores, specialty stores, restaurants ranging from fast food to full-service, and two farmers' markets within walking distance of their home, too many New Yorkers live in neighborhoods described as "food deserts." Access to fresh, healthy foods is a challenge in these food deserts, and residents are consigned to paying high prices for low-

quality foods. Often, they are dependent on bodegas and other small stores with limited selections. Not all vendors accept EBT (food stamps/electronic benefits), WIC coupons, and other forms of social supports, further limiting where people can shop. Compounded with long working hours (many low-income individuals work more than one job), and long routes to and from work, these factors mean shopping is difficult. Kitchens in public housing—let alone shelters and other temporary housing—are often in disrepair. Fast food offers quick satisfaction at a reasonable price—and long-term negative impacts on overall health. A number of recent government initiatives have been established to correct this situation, including federal funds that will help chain groceries build new stores in areas of the Bronx and Brooklyn that have low food access (a program piloted successfully in Philadelphia). GreenCarts is a Department of Health program that issues licenses to pushcart vendors who agree to sell produce in food deserts. Chain restaurants are required to post calorie counts in an effort to help consumers make more informed choices. Trans fats were banned several years ago, causing major food processors to adjust their recipes. The city sent advisors out to bakeries, restaurants, and local manufacturers to help them change their practices. Salt is the new target in an effort to lower rates of hypertension, especially prevalent among lower-income residents. While critics complain that Mayor Bloomberg is operating a "nanny state," diet-related diseases cost the city millions in health care and lost productivity every year. Without laws that force food processors to institute changes, it is very difficult to address these issues. A large city like New York has the market muscle to make this happen.

New York's Greenmarket program started in 1976 when a farmers' market opened at Union Square to provide farmers within a 200-mile radius of the city with a profitable outlet for their produce, and city residents with fresh fruits and vegetables. Today, Greenmarket operates nearly 50 markets, found in every borough of the city. There are more requests for markets than there are farmers to supply them. To encourage residents of lower-income neighborhoods to patronize the markets, many vendors have terminals that accept EBT. Most markets are seasonal and are open only one day a week, but they provide an important source of local foods, and an opportunity for people to mingle and socialize in ways that supermarkets don't encourage. Seasons are marked with food. Strawberries, asparagus, and peas announce the end of a long winter. In July, people chat while shucking corn. Tomatoes invite careful prodding. As New Yorkers have developed more sophisticated palates, and as Greenmarkets have ranged into more diverse neighborhoods, basil and cucumbers are now side by side with Asian greens, wasabi sprouts, cilantro and culantro, and freshly jarred kimchi. Growing concerns about factory-farmed meat have created a market for lamb, chicken, beef, and pork. Customers can talk to producers, learning why some grow organically while others bypass certification and depend on their customers' trust.

Supermarkets vary greatly by neighborhood. Whole Foods, with its full range of grass-fed beef, organic chicken, line-caught fish, and beautifully displayed produce, cheeses, and coffees, locates in well-to-do neighborhoods with high foot traffic like Columbus Circle, Union Square, and Chelsea. Shopping at Whole Foods duplicates the experience of wandering a market, while offering prices on basic goods that are comparable to those in less-luxurious grocery stores. Trader Joe's has wide appeal for their relatively low-cost prepared foods and snacks. They, too, are found only in well-to-do neighborhoods. Fairway's original store is on the Upper West Side. They have since opened stores in Harlem and in Red Hook, Brooklyn. Here, shopping is a contact sport, with great prices on produce combined with gourmet goods and a full-service butcher and fishmonger. In these "better" neighborhoods, even the national chains like Pathmark are nicely appointed and offer a wide selection of products.

In low- and moderate-income neighborhoods, supermarkets are run-down, selling tired-looking produce and limited selections of meat and poultry. Shelves lined with processed foods reinforce the health and diet problems facing residents. It's no problem finding 20 kinds of sugary cereal and juiceless fruit punch, but it is highly unlikely that these stores will carry natural peanut butter or bulk grains.

The tired argument is that healthy foods won't sell in lower-income neighborhoods, but studies find over and over that residents are well aware of the dangers of unhealthy choices for their community's health. Mobility is relative; in gentrifying neighborhoods, among the signs of change are people getting off the subways carrying bags of groceries from other, more affluent parts of the city. In Washington Heights, for example, the new professional classes shop at Fairway and West Side Market; long-time residents make do with the Associated with its shabby awning, rusty carts, and constant funk of spoiled meat. The prices are higher for most goods, except for Central American and Caribbean staples like plantains.

While New York City has not joined the mayor of Rome in declaring that access to healthy food is a civil right, many changes have been made to the school lunch, and breakfast, programs. Efforts have been made to reduce the total fats, salts, and sugars in school food and to increase total nutrients and fiber. Changes are incremental. Obstacles include lack of infrastructure (schools where cafeterias are designed to reheat, not cook, food), funding, and kids' tastes. Introducing a healthy option is pointless if it ends up in the trash. Nonetheless, the Department of Education is committed to introducing more cultural variety and more locally sourced foods. All apples purchased by the school system are now grown in New York State; local carrots will soon follow. Milk is now skim, not whole or chocolate, and soy milk is available for the many children of African and Asian descent who are lactose intolerant. For many lower-income children, the meals eaten at school (free or nearly free) are the only full meals they eat. Summer programs were introduced to fill in the gaps between school terms. Ensuring that these meals are nutritionally balanced and otherwise fulfilling is critical to long-term public health and to advancing justice through access to food.

Babette Audant and Ken Albala

Further Reading

Grimes, William. *Appetite City: A Culinary History of New York*. New York: North Point Press, 2009.

Hauck-Lawson, Annie, and Jonathan Deutsch, eds. *Gastropolis: Food and New York City*. New York: Columbia University Press, 2009.

Kurlansky, Mark. *The Big Oyster*. New York: Random House, 2006.

Rose, Peter. *The Sensible Cook: Dutch Foodways in the Old and New World.* Syracuse, NY: Syracuse University Press, 1989.

Weaver, William Woys. *Sauerkraut Yankees: Pennsylvania Dutch Food and Foodways*. Mechanicsburg, PA: Stackpole Books, 2002.

United States: The Midwest

Overview

The American Midwest comprises 12 states: Ohio, Michigan, Indiana, Illinois, Wisconsin, Minnesota, Iowa, Missouri, Kansas, Nebraska, South Dakota, and North Dakota. These states span the midcontinent from the western edge of the Allegheny Mountains on the east all the way to the high plains that abut the Rocky Mountains in the west. The Midwest is cut in two by the Mississippi, a river that drains all the waters from two-thirds of the continent, while the Great Lakes and the 49th parallel define the northern border and the Ohio River the southern boundary. The whole region encompasses 820,000 square miles and is occupied by 66 million inhabitants. Today, roughly 50 million people live in metropolitan areas and large towns, unlike the 1890s, when the farming population was much larger and farmers' food came directly from the land on which they lived.

Much of the Midwest is relatively flat prairie land but not entirely. It has been further subdivided into broad areas: the Great Lakes and Old Northwest, Ohio River and Trans-Mississippi River, and the Great Plains. Each subregion represents different landforms, natural resources, histories, ethnic origins, and dialects. This fact counters the common perception that the Midwest is nothing but a flat and endless plain with food to match. Many of the Midwestern states have more than one of these divisions within them, and that is important in considering local foodways.

Although home to major cities, such as Chicago, and heavy industrial production, agriculture lies behind the idea of the Midwest as America's food-producing heartland. Some of the most important agricultural-production technologies were invented in the Midwest, including the John Deere plow and the McCormick reaper. From the 1890s on, the region has been seen as filled with small towns and broad farmlands, occupied by people who are slow to adopt new cultural trends. For these reasons the Midwest is usually thought of as center of "normal" American culture. Food is an integral part of this image: The Midwest said to be the land of plain cooking, of casseroles and "white food," meaning mashed potatoes and cream sauces. In fact, Midwestern foodways represent a global food system with dishes and foods imported from the far corners of the world.

🍽 Food Culture Snapshot

Steve and Brenda Wilson live in Saint Louis, Missouri, with their young son and daughter. They are interested in locally produced food and, on Saturday, go to the weekly farmers' market in Tower Grove, one of the 1,500 farmers' markets in the Midwest. They cannot fulfill all their week's food needs at the open-air market because it does not sell breakfast cereals, milk, cheap commonly eaten meats, flour, sugar, salt and pepper, canned soups and sauces, cooking oils, butter and margarine, juices, frozen products, snack foods, and imported fruits and vegetables, such as bananas. These will be purchased later, while pushing a large food cart, from the food aisles and cases in a local supermarket. The children have a lot to say about what cereals and snacks the family buys. At the farmers' market the Wilsons can buy in-season, fresh sweet corn, lettuce and greens (such as kale and chard), green beans and fresh peas, tomatoes (including some old heirloom breeds), varieties of green and red peppers, different kinds of eggplants, potatoes, onions, garlic, carrots, rhubarb, melons, grapes, berries, pears, apples, peaches, and fresh herbs. Basil, tarragon, oregano, thyme, mint, rosemary, parsley, and cilantro (fresh coriander leaves) are popular and used in a number of dishes. All of these are sold directly by the farmers who grow them. In this market there are also animal farmers. Sustainably raised lamb, beef, pork, rabbit, sausages, chicken, and eggs straight from the farm, as well as cheeses, are all available for sale, and the Wilsons stock up on some of these, though the meats and produce are somewhat more expensive than supermarket food. This market also encourages freshly baked goods. Young women from a local Mennonite community, dressed in plain, long skirts and wearing small white kerchiefs, sell their homemade cakes, nut cakes and cookies, yeast breads, and quick breads. Other bakers have crusty Italian, French, and whole-grain breads.

From these ingredients the Wilsons will prepare daily breakfasts, lunches or dinners, and suppers. On Sunday they usually make a roast beef or chicken served with mashed potatoes, green beans, fresh bread and butter, and a freshly made fruit pie for dinner. On this day, they are buying ingredients to prepare a dish for a potluck

Corn chowder, a dish that mixes traditions from New England and the South, in Midwestern corn country. (Robyn Mackenzie | Dreamstime.com)

dinner at a nearby history museum. Steve grew up in a town on the Illinois/Indiana border where corn chowder has been made for generations. It is a dish that mixes traditions from New England and the South in Midwestern corn country.

Corn Chowder

Serves 6–8

¼ lb bacon, chopped

8 tbsp butter

2 large potatoes, diced (about ¾ lb)

1 large carrot, sliced into rounds

1 small onion, chopped

4 ears fresh sweet corn, shucked and kernels cut from cob

Water to cover

4 tbsp flour

2 c milk

1 tsp salt, or to taste

Ground black pepper to taste

Place bacon in a deep pan over medium heat. Cook bacon until the fat melts but the bacon is not crispy. Add 4 tablespoons butter, and melt. Add potatoes, carrot, and onion, and sauté in butter and bacon until the vegetables are coated and onion begins to wilt. Add just enough water to cover, and bring to a boil. Reduce heat to a simmer, cover pan, and cook until potatoes are tender, 15–20 minutes. Meanwhile, melt 4 tablespoons butter in a separate saucepan. Whisk the flour into the butter until completely blended. Stir the milk into the butter-flour mixture until smooth. When the vegetables are done stir them with a whisk or fork until the potatoes break up into small lumps. Stir in the milk mixture, stirring well. When thickened and heated through, add salt and pepper to taste and stir well. Serve with corn muffins or cornbread.

Major Foodstuffs

What people eat everyday is the result of environments, history, and technology. Although the Midwest states are agricultural powerhouses, much of what they produce is not grown for local consumption. Iowa, for instance, is the number one grower of soybeans, Illinois number two, and Minnesota number three, but tofu is not a regular part of the Midwestern diet. Iowa and Illinois are the top producers of feed grains for farm animals, and Iowa is the nation's premier hog farmer. Most of this massive output is processed by large food manufacturers and sold in national and international markets. Before World War II (1945), farmers and people living in small towns were able to produce enough food in gardens and from truck farms to feed their own families during the year: Only some supplies such as flour and sugar needed to be purchased from stores. But today, with some local exceptions, food eaten every day by Midwesterners is bought in food stores and supermarkets, a lot of it coming from as far as 1,500–3,000 miles away.

Midwesterners consume between 1,500 and 1,900 pounds of food annually. Of this, about 35–40 percent comes from animal products, including both meats and dairy, and more beef (about 75 pounds per year) is eaten than in other parts of the country. Thirty percent of the diet is vegetables, but 30 percent of that is potatoes. Grains compose 13–14 percent of the average diet, most of them processed. Wheat is the most popular, made in the form of breads, sweet baked goods, and breakfast cereals. Corn is also widely used, but much of it is used in processed foods, including animal feeds, cornstarches, and corn syrups. Fats, oils, sugars, and sweeteners compose most of the remaining daily calories. Dried legumes such as navy, pinto, and black beans are a small (about 8 pounds per year) but growing food segment, in part due to a rising Hispanic population. The average per-person caloric intake is about the national average of 2,600–3,000, though Midwestern states are generally at the middle to lower end of the national overweight and obesity scale.

Meat is the center of almost all Midwestern meals, whether home cooked or in restaurants. Beef, poultry, pork, and some fish are common. Ground beef is the most widely used form, often as patties (hamburgers) or loose for chili and similar dishes, including a famous sandwich style in Iowa. Poultry zoomed in popularity in the last quarter of the 20th century because it costs less and is thought to be lower in fat. Chicken is used year-round, with breast meat the favored cut. Turkey is also widely available and a necessity at holidays such as Thanksgiving and Christmas. A great deal of the poultry consumed comes from Midwestern states, especially Indiana and Ohio. Pork has declined in competition with poultry, but bacon and ham are staples of people's tables, often at breakfast and for lunches. Iowa remains a major producer. Though the region is surrounded by great lakes and big rivers, freshwater fish is less widely eaten than imported seafood, especially shrimp, salmon, and canned tuna. Of freshwater fish types, catfish is popular in southern parts of the Midwest and among African Americans, while along Lakes Michigan and Superior, local whitefish is used in fish fries and fish boils (in northern Wisconsin).

Other meats include game animals such as duck, goose, turkey, venison, squirrel, and rabbit, which appear during hunting seasons, especially in rural areas of the Midwest. With almost a million deer taken during the fall hunting season, venison is more widespread than might be supposed.

Animal-based proteins also come from dairy products. Like other Americans, people in the Midwest love milk in liquid state, as cheeses, and in ice cream. The amount of milk drunk per person has declined by 30 percent since 1970, but cheese use has increased by 100 percent over the same period (10 pounds of milk make 1 pound of cheese). Wisconsin, the Dairy State, produces more cheese than any other state, and its citizens are above-average cheese eaters (hence the common insult for Wisconsinites, "Cheeseheads"). A considerable amount of cheese is not eaten out of hand but instead used in pizza and pasta dishes. Ice cream is a highly favored dessert, and states such as Indiana, Illinois, and Minnesota are major ice cream makers. Not a basic component of Midwestern diets, yogurt has nonetheless increased in usage to as much as 4 pounds per person per year, as compared to 15 pounds for ice cream.

In days when more Midwesterners lived on farms, most vegetables and fruits were grown locally. Green beans, cabbages, carrots, peas, bell peppers, tomatoes, lettuces, spinach, cucumbers, potatoes, onions, parsnips, turnips, rutabagas, zucchini, squash, and pumpkins (Illinois is the number one pumpkin grower) were raised in gardens and fields and eaten regularly. What was not eaten fresh was canned at home for use over the winter. Potatoes, however, were the most popular tuber and remain so. Today, many more fresh vegetables are available in supermarkets, though few are grown nearby, except for those sold in local farmers' markets. Most of the same vegetables are consumed today as in the past with the addition of broccoli and cauliflower because of their high vitamin content and antioxidant qualities. Also, salad greens have become very popular, making for higher lettuce consumption than ever before. Instead of being home canned, a good portion of the vegetables eaten now are frozen, actually the best way to preserve their nutritional contents.

The Midwest enjoys abundant fruit production. Michigan is the sixth-largest fruit producer in the United States and the leading grower of sour cherries, which are used in pie fillings. Wisconsin is number one in cranberries, and until early in the 20th century southern Illinois led the nation in peach exports. Surprisingly, citrus fruits from Florida and California are the most popular fruits, most of them made into juices. Melons, peaches, pears, sweet cherries, and berries are frequently purchased, but more popular are bananas (imported) and apples. A good deal of apple consumption in the Midwest is in the form of processed juices, 33 percent higher than the rest of the country. Altogether fresh fruits and fruit juices make up only about 18 percent of the average diet.

Living in the midst of the nation's greatest producers of wheat and corn, Midwesterners ought to be great whole-grain eaters, but they are not. Most wheat and barley is milled and baked into breads, pastas, cakes, and other pastries. Wheats, including the red durums from the Great Plains, are processed, stripped of their main nutrients, and turned white, into the flour sold for home use. Where whole grains mainly appear is in breakfast cereals. Oats and cracked wheats are staple cooked hot cereals, while corn, wheat, barley, and flax are used in cold cereals. That is appropriate for the Midwest because the breakfast cereal industry was pioneered in Michigan, Ohio, and Illinois. Rice plays a smaller but important

role in Midwestern cuisine, none of it grown in the region and almost all of it milled to make it white, thus removing its natural vitamins and fiber.

Some historical local foods are still used even in the modern industrial food system, many of them gathered from the wild. American persimmons, mostly used for preserves and pies, are collected from trees in southern Ohio and especially southern Indiana and Illinois. Pawpaws, also called custard apples, or Hoosier bananas in Indiana, are found across the Midwest. Their creamy pulp is also used in sweet desserts and drinks. Both fruits are the focus of local late-summer festivals. Mushroom gathering is a popular pastime. Morels and chanterelles found in Midwestern forests are highly prized and widely consumed in season. Wild rice, Minnesota's state grain, in its true natural state is harvested by canoe from small lakes and streams, often by Native Americans. Although now farmed for national distribution, the wild version is very local. Fish, such as bass, perch, buffalo, and bluegills, is caught locally and widely consumed. Turtles and frogs (the legs) are in the same category, though eaten by relatively few Midwesterners in recent years.

Cooking

What people cook and how they cook it depends on income levels, availability of ingredients, and the cook's interest in good cooking. In times when the more people lived in rural areas and worked on farms, cooking was almost entirely in the hands of women. Farmwives and their daughters rose early in the morning to stoke fires in their wood- or coal-burning ovens and started cooking. These stoves usually had two ovens, one hot for baking, the other called a warming oven to keep cooked food hot. The stovetop had anywhere from two to four hot plates on which the cook could set pans and kettles. Because coffee was an essential beverage, kettles and coffeepots were kept on the stove the whole day through. Skillets were essential because Midwesterners, like all Americans, love fried food. Deeper pans were used for soups and stews and for cooking vegetables.

Inventories of kitchens from around 1900 show that many had dozens of cooking devices, ranging from knives to cooking spoons and spatulas, different-sized strainers, mortars and pestles, whisks, mixing bowls, baking pans of various sizes, apple corers, cherry pitters, hand meat grinders, sausage stuffers, and many others. Since few foods were pre-prepared, as now, cooking was labor-intensive. For the midday farm meal, meat had be cut to size and roasted or baked; and when the meat was done, gravy was made from the drippings. Potatoes were peeled and boiled, and vegetables like green beans picked, trimmed, and also boiled. Fresh bread had been made beginning with early morning preparations. Desserts were usually pies, the crusts made with lard that had been rendered at home, the fruit fillings prepared by hand. Most recipes were not elaborate, except for cakes, and many of the dishes prepared in country kitchens remain as staples of Midwestern cooking.

For more than 100 years American cooking has trended toward easier preparation and faster cooking. Inventions such as the gas and electric stove, refrigerator, home freezer, food mixers, food processor, and, more recently, the microwave oven have saved a lot of time in the kitchen. To accommodate these new implements food companies created food products that were easy to use and also fit American tastes. Many of these companies are Midwestern, and the people who created the foods grew up with Midwestern foodways. For instance, a favorite dish, Kraft boxed macaroni and cheese dinner, was invented in

A baked casserole with potato, sausage, onion, and cheese. (Teresa Kasprzycka | Dreamstime.com)

Chicago in 1937 using powdered American cheese and pasta, butter, and milk. It is really a casserole that is a characteristically Midwestern dish.

Modern-day cooking varies from person to person. For those who are keen on new food trends and fine dining, kitchens are equipped with the best stoves and many electric food-preparation devices. They also have the best ingredients including varieties of fresh herbs and spices. Some of these cooks make efforts to use locally sourced food products or at least foods that are organically grown, if not local. Although these innovative cooks are a significant part of the culinary scene, most kitchens and cooks are rather different, employing foods processed by industrial production techniques.

Modern stoves have the same functions as the old wood-burning ones: ovens for baking and roasting and cooktops for frying, sautéing, boiling, and steaming. Modern utensils are often made of heat-resistant plastics but serve the same functions as the old ones. Home cooking includes baked, roasted, or fried meats, but the rest of the meal might be prepared by heating pre-prepared dishes in a conventional or microwave oven. Casseroles, for instance, are often made with packaged or canned soup. Frozen foods are eaten in an average household six times each week, many of these heated by microwaves (the best way to preserve vitamin contents). These might be vegetables or the ever-popular pizza. Salads to accompany the meal often come from pre-cut and washed salad mixes and dressings from bottled preparations. Desserts are one kind of dish that remains traditional. Fruit pies are a Midwestern specialty, and many are made at home. However, a good many might be made from store-bought pie crusts and canned fruit fillings. Cakes, too, are commonly made from cake mixes, mixed with an electric blender and baked in the oven. Or whole meals can be purchased premade from food stores. Roughly 50 percent of all Thanksgiving dinners are served from this source.

Though the basic foodstuffs of Midwestern cuisine seem homogeneous, there is diversity in its peoples and their foodways. Immigration and local environments make for distinctive regional and local foodways.

Typical Meals

Native American peoples of what is now the Midwest used corn and gathered the same wild plants that people do now, wild rice and mushrooms, for example, but most modern foods came with later immigrants. The main English-speaking settlers followed two routes, the Ohio River in the south and northern trails. The southern areas of the Midwest tend to be hilly all the way from the Allegheny Mountains to the Missouri Ozarks. Settlers here came mainly from the American South and brought Southern, Appalachian foodways with them. Abraham Lincoln was one of them. In southern Indiana, Illinois, and Missouri, pioneer women cooked with corn more than other grains. Cornbread, johnnycakes, and hoecakes, all made from cornmeal, were cooked in skillets set over open fires, and later on in ovens. Wheat flour, usually mixed with butter or soured milk, was used to make biscuits. Meats were mainly pork, all raised, slaughtered, and processed by each family. All the family members participated in what was a major late-autumn or winter event in the farm year. Baked ham fried in home-rendered lard was a commonplace meal served with red-eye gravy (made from the pan drippings) and corn grits. Hunting, usually by the men in the family, also brought protein to the table. One of the most famous dishes is still burgoo, a stew made with squirrel and whatever other meats might have been available, all cooked up with vegetables in a big pot. Wild greens often accompanied meals. Desserts were usually fruit pies, the crusts made with lard, and sometimes the pies were fried in deep fat.

Modern food production has affected these old foodways. Lard, for example, has been largely replaced by vegetable shortening and margarine. But many of the same meal ingredients remain common in the southern, Ohio River, and Ozark regions. Grits and biscuits are still on breakfast tables, pork is more widely used than in other parts of the Midwest, and frying is king at home and in restaurants. Home cooks still make pies at home, and they are popular in restaurants throughout the Midwest. One specialty homemade treat is sugar pie, Indiana's official state pie, made of a simple pie crust, sugar, and cream.

English speakers, including Irish immigrants moving to the central and northern parts of the Midwest, came mainly from New York and New England. Their foods were based on beef, with some pork, and wheat, rather than the pork and corn common in the South. Roasted beef, stews, and fried steaks in various forms were the center of most meals along with potatoes, a cooked green vegetable, and gravy. Desserts were usually baked—pies, cakes, and lots of puddings. The main variation was chicken for Sunday dinner and, especially for Catholic families, fish on Fridays. Today, chicken is far more common on everyday dinner tables, but beef in various versions is still the dominant meat. Coleslaw, from a Dutch word for cabbage salad, was also a popular dish at home and in public settings, such as potluck meals and church socials. It is still made at home but is now mostly purchased from food stores. In the rural Midwest dinner was the main meal of the day, taken in the middle of the workday, at about noon. Supper was lighter, usually the dinner leftovers, served about 6 P.M. This word usage is still used in many parts of the Midwest, less so in cities, and early evening meals are still the rule.

A distinctive British food tradition came with miners from Cornwall from the middle of the 19th century. Working the tin, lead, copper, and iron mines in the hilly country of western Wisconsin and Michigan's Upper Peninsula was hard work and needed hearty food. The women of mining families made pasties for the men to take to work. Pasties are turnovers made with meat and vegetables such as potatoes. Cornish pasties were then taken up by Finnish migrants, and these homemade savories remain as an identifier of regional food culture.

In the 1850s Germans began to arrive in the Midwest in large numbers and settled on farms and in cities. Although their own religions and dialects varied, their foods were similar. Sausages and beer are important elements of German food culture. Noodles and various potato preparations, along with vinegar-laced preparations such as sauerkraut and sauerbraten, are all part of German cuisine. So are several types of cakes and cookies. It was not unusual for wealthier people in cities and farm households to employ young German women as cooks, and in this way, German foodways became part of Midwestern cuisine. Cities with large German populations—Milwaukee, Saint Louis, Chicago, and Detroit, among others—became famous for beer manufacturing. A light variety called pilsner became so popular that it is now what we think of as American beer. Beer is an important item in everyday American foodways. It is the most ubiquitous mildly alcoholic beverage, and few sporting events are held without it being served.

German food culture centers on sausages. Several of the many German types are now embedded in the Midwest. Bratwurst is a signature dish of Wisconsin: There is not a fair or ball game, picnic, or festival that does not feature bratwurst. These are often lightly boiled in beer, then grilled on an open fire, and finally served on a bun with German-based mustard and onions. The same holds for frankfurters (supposedly from Frankfurt in Germany) and wieners (Vienna sausages from Austria), which became hot dogs in the United States. Hot dogs are served in restaurants, at stands, and by street vendors. Chicago has distinctive hot dog styles as do Detroit and Cincinnati. Perhaps the most famous hot dogs of all come from a German-founded company in Chicago and Wisconsin, Oscar Mayer. Since the 1950s Oscar Mayer wieners have been eaten at home by children, an easily heated convenience food and an important part of Midwestern and American foodways.

One group of German speakers came to the Midwest in the decades around 1900 from Russia, where large numbers of them lived along a section of the Volga River. Settling in the Great Plains including Kansas and Nebraska, many lived on family farms, planting and harvesting the hard red wheat that they introduced to the Midwest. One dish they brought is called a *bierock* or *runza* and is virtually the state food of Nebraska. These are savory pastries, stuffed with cabbage and sometimes meat, that are traditionally baked at home as everyday food—eaten by the farm men in the fields—and for holidays. So popular are they that a chain of runza restaurants has spread across Nebraska.

Scandinavians from Norway, Denmark, Finland, and Sweden immigrated in the 19th and early 20th centuries in large numbers. Minnesota, Wisconsin, parts of Michigan, and cities such as Chicago and Minneapolis acquired the food habits of these new settlers. Most of the food preparations were like those in the rest of the Midwest, heavy on meats and potatoes (potato sausage with white sauce is a classic homemade dish), with creamy sauces laced with lots of dill common. Several dishes remain as indicators of local culture and are still features of home cooking, especially on holidays. *Lefse,* a kind of thick bread, made with potatoes and cooked on a flat griddle, is one, and *limpa,* a rye bread made with cardamom, anise, citron peel, and some sugar, is another. Lutefisk is dried whitefish that has been soaked in water mixed with lye and then cooked. Almost no one except Norwegian Americans likes fish prepared this way, but that is what makes it culturally important. One dish that has translated to general Midwestern food culture is the Swedish pancake. Beginning about 100 years ago, this sweet pancake topped with berries and whipped cream was served in restaurants, and it has remained a popular breakfast dish, often after church services, ever since.

Eastern European foods and cooking have played a large role in Midwestern food culture. Czechs, Poles, Russians, and other Slavic-speaking people arrived with Ashkenazi (eastern European) Jews beginning in the last years of the 19th century. On farms across the Midwest and especially in the newly industrialized cities, American began to learn about Polish pierogi (Polish filled dumplings) and *paczki* (jam-filled doughnuts), Czech *kolache* (small pastries made with butter and filled with fruit), Jewish blintzes (thin pancakes rolled up with fruit or cheese fillings, served with sour cream), bagels, *biyalis* (a small, flat roll similar to a bagel but without a hole and topped with onion and poppy seeds), latkes (potato pancakes), and sausages of all kinds, including the (Jewish) all-beef hot dog. All of these can be found in Midwestern supermarkets, especially in cities where people of eastern European descent live. Pastries such as paczki and kolache are holiday treats often made in homes by several generations of women in the family: grandmothers, mothers, and daughters. They are a few of the foods that serve as family binders.

Italian immigrants have had the greatest impact on Midwestern foodways—and those in the United

States as a whole. Beginning around 1900, most came from the southern parts of Italy and Sicily, bringing a whole range of pastas, breads, vegetables dishes, and tomato-based sauces. Though most were poor laboring families, before too long they entered the food business. Small Italian restaurants and green grocers sprang up in Chicago and other main cities, and some dishes became part of Midwestern cuisine. Eggplant, zucchini, greater use of garlic than elsewhere, lettuce, tomato sauce, lasagna, spaghetti, and casseroles are everyday cooking in homes everywhere in the Midwest. Spaghetti and meatballs is an Italian American dish, unknown in the mother country but suited to hearty Midwestern home cooking. Surveys show that pasta of some kind, not counting macaroni and cheese, is served at home once or twice a week, and pizza appears more often than that. Pizza is another Italian dish that became Americanized. The Chicago version, a very heavy, cheese-loaded version called deep dish, has been served in restaurants since the late 1940s. It is one of the characteristic dishes of that city. The largest chain of pizza restaurants, Pizza Hut, was founded in Wichita, Kansas, in 1958. One very local traditional Italian food called *cudighi* is characteristic of Michigan's Upper Peninsula. Invented for miners who worked in the Iron Mountain range in the 1930s by restaurateurs who came from northern Italy, this heavy, spiced pork patty sandwich can be made at home, but it is a common fast food for Yoopers, as the people there are known.

Two other important influences on Midwestern foods are African Americans and Latin Americans. In the early years of the 20th century and again just after World War II (post-1945), African Americans migrated from the Southern states to Midwestern cities in large numbers. In cities such as Chicago and Detroit some characteristic dishes came to be called soul food by restaurateurs in the 1960s. Southern fried chicken and fish, grits, greens, pork, biscuits, and certain cakes and pies are now staples in Midwestern cities, and ingredients are widely available in food markets. One important Southern food has crossed into general usage: barbecue. Around World War I, African Americans employed in the Kansas City, Missouri, region set up barbecue restaurants.

A backyard barbecue grill with pork meat on the slats and a bowl of homemade sauce on the side. (Eti Swinford | Dreamstime.com)

Today, Kansas City has dozens upon dozens of barbecue places and is world famous. Often made with a sweet, tomato or ketchup base, Midwestern barbecue has distinctive styles. It is made not only in restaurants but also at home, usually by men, as a type of backyard cooking or grilling. Weekends and holidays are the great days for such preparations, and often home-style barbecue cooks bring their creations to the many barbecue competitions held across the country.

People from various regions of Mexico entered the Midwest in the 1910s and settled to work in industrial towns and cities in small numbers. From the 1960s immigration increased exponentially not only in cities but also in the countryside, where more recent migrants work in agriculture. Many Mexican dishes have become Midwestern, eaten out or in the home. Tamale pies and taco casseroles are common home-cooked meals. Tacos and enchiladas eaten out of hand, loaded with Wisconsin cheddar cheese and not too spicy-hot tomato salsas, are regular fast-food dishes and are made at home. Often these come in ready-to-eat forms made by large food manufacturers. And there is hardly a sporting event that does not serve tortilla chips covered in a melted cheese-food product. From fine dining to small local restaurants run by newly immigrated families, Mexican food is now an important part of the region's foodways.

In many ways, Midwestern foodways are generically modern American with an increasingly global taste. But there are ongoing traditions of plain, hearty home cooking and regional dishes that set the Midwest apart from other parts of the United States.

Eating Out

Eating out in the Midwest varies by locations, incomes, and taste. Public dining places range from expensive fine-dining restaurants run by celebrated chefs (Chicago is a world leader in these kinds of eating houses) to middle-income facilities, both locally owned and corporate places, such as Applebee's and Olive Garden, and fast-casual establishments, of which McDonald's, Big Boy, Culver's, and Pot Belly are some Midwest-based examples. In between are many ethnic restaurants, local diners, and quick fast-food places. Of the latter, quick food, the Midwest has types that are closely identified with their communities. Chicago hot dogs loaded with condiments, Detroit coney dogs covered in meat sauces, Iowa loose meat sandwiches (Maid-Rite is the best known), and Cincinnati chili are examples. Few people eat family dinners at these places, but all are very popular for lunchtime dining and midday snacking.

Ethnic restaurants are mainly found in urban areas. Once, this kind of dining was confined mainly to Italian, Greek, German, eastern European, and Chinese restaurants. Today, diners in almost any city can choose from a much wider variety of international places, from Mexican to African, varieties of Indian, and Southeast Asian, among the most common. Thai and Vietnamese restaurants are widespread, and in northern cities such as Minneapolis, Hmong cuisine is popular. Green, red, and *massaman* curries, *sate* (grilled meat on a skewer), spicy soups, papaya salads, *pho* (beef soup), and many noodle dishes are regularly consumed by Midwesterners. One savory noodle dish, pad Thai, is so popular that it has become Thai American.

In former days, before the national interstate highway system was fully established, many towns had their own local restaurants. Often, the food was sourced from the nearby countryside, especially during the growing and harvest seasons. Fried chicken, pot roasts, and meat loaf, with baked or mashed potatoes and some overcooked vegetable, followed by homemade fruit pies with cream, were favorites. Today, most of these kinds of eating places have been replaced by corporate chain outlets, whether burger or family sit-down eateries.

Two kinds of restaurants with local roots remain, both of ethnic origin. Many cities and towns in the Midwest have Greek-owned diners, often called "family restaurants." Diners such as these serve meals all through the day, with dishes ranging from pancakes, bacon, and eggs for breakfasts, to soups and sandwiches at lunchtime, to full-scale meals for dinner. A common joke is that "Grecian chicken" is the standard dish. These kinds of restaurants fill an important dining niche that was once occupied by several kinds of places, such as coffee shops, cafeterias, and locally owned small eateries.

A broad swath of the Midwest has been called "the chop suey belt." Chinese American restaurants number in the tens of thousands in the United States and make more money than the major hamburger chains. Hardly a small town in the Midwest is without one, and hardly a Midwesterner has never eaten chop suey and chow mein, sweet and sour pork or chicken, fried egg rolls and wontons, sweet and sour soup, and egg foo yong. In many respects, Chinese American dishes are as Midwestern as beef and potatoes.

Special Occasions

Like all Americans, Midwesterners have plenty of holidays and festivals, all of them celebrated with the consumption of food in large quantities. Some celebrations are private, family affairs with meals, such as Thanksgiving, Christmas, and Passover. Others are both private and public, with family dinners and food served in public, examples being Eid al-Fitr (the end of the Muslim month of fasting), Asian New Year, and Easter. Other festivals are regular calendric events, such as the Fourth of July; state, county, and town fairs; and specific public food events, often called "Taste of ____." In most of them, Islamic fests excepted, alcoholic beverages are commonly served along with featured foods.

Thanksgiving is a uniquely American holiday and nowhere more revered than in the heartland from which so much of America's food comes. It is also an autumn harvest season fest. Roasted turkey is the centerpiece, usually stuffed with an herbed wheat or cornbread mixture, and accompanied by thick, fatty gravy made from the pan drippings. Served family style, meaning put in large bowls that are passed around the table, are mashed white or sweet potatoes, a green vegetable (particularly lightly boiled green beans), baked squash, cranberry sauce, bread rolls, and plenty of butter. There are also plenty of beverages. Desserts will usually be fruit pies, possibly mince pie, or a fruit cobbler, all served with ice cream. One variation of the standard table is the addition of macaroni in tomato sauce, or lasagna. Introduced by Italian immigrants around 1900, these dishes migrated to the African American and other communities to the point where Thanksgiving lasagna is not uncommon.

Virtually all of the foods at this table are the same as those on a Midwestern farm table a century ago. Potatoes, squash, green beans, cranberries, dairy products, fruits, and the turkey are all Midwestern products that can still be obtained fairly locally. If any single meal holds a Midwestern food identity, it is Thanksgiving.

Public fairs, the first held in Ohio in 1850, and food festivals are also occasions for plenty of eating in hearty Midwestern fashion. Fairs are often served by vendors who offer foods that can be found at similar events around the country: fried funnel cakes, doughnuts, hot dogs, hamburgers, and cotton candy, among many others. There are some special dishes that are either unique to one fair or another or characteristic of Midwestern food. Fried

A garish hot dog stand at a county fair in Ohio. (Dreamstime)

cheese curds, often breaded, remind us of Wisconsin, where they are a common snack dish; Indian tacos (fried bread filled with mildly spiced tomato sauce, ground hamburger, and shredded cheese) are Nebraska's and the Dakota's contributions to America's cuisine; and pork chops on a stick and roasted corn are examples from Iowa. Corn dogs (hot dogs coated in a cornmeal batter and deep-fried) are a specialty of the Illinois State Fair and are called Cozy Dogs named after a local restaurant that supposedly invented them (it did not). In Wisconsin, bratwurst is king, boiled in beer, then grilled on open charcoal fires, and served on a bun with grilled or fresh onions and German mustard. Apart from such sausages, ice creams, and candy, almost everything to be eaten at a Midwestern fair is deep-fried.

There are also many specialized festivals centered on regional foods. Mitchell, Indiana, and Taylorville, Illinois, among others, hold persimmon festivals in the fall of each year. This native American fruit is not commonly eaten today, but persimmon puddings and pies were staple dishes in early American cooking. Lake Snowden near Albany, Ohio is the scene of a pawpaw fest. A once-popular fruit, the pawpaw can be eaten fresh only for a short time and thus does not appear in supermarket produce aisles. Some food festivals are very large and cover varieties of foods. The world's largest is the Taste of Chicago, which draws more than 3.5 million visitors over a 10-day period in July. Foods, served mainly by the city's many ethnic restaurants, range from kebabs to sate, pizza, hummus, hot dogs, Italian beef, and, most famously, barbecues. So popular is this event that Midwestern cities such as Madison, Wisconsin; Cincinnati, Ohio; and many smaller towns and cities hold similar festivals with varieties of food that represent their own communities.

Diet and Health

Ideas about diet and health among Midwesterners do not spring from religious tenets, with several small exceptions, but from modern science and common sense. This has not always been the case, since in the 19th and early 20th centuries folk medicine and folktales were often invoked to cure illness and promote physical health. One collection of folklore from the 1930s shows that some rural people believed that goiters (a painful swelling of the thyroid gland, usually from a lack of iodine in the diet) could be cured by hanging a warty frog around the victim's neck or by boiling a frog alive and rubbing the fat on the goiter. At the same time, many herbal medicines were concocted and used locally. Sassafras tea, for instance, was widely used as a healthful tonic after a long winter when "the blood thickened" and people wanted to cleanse their systems by purging themselves. Nonetheless, in the absence of scientific research, patent medicines were also widely used, most of them sold by "quack" (phony) medical practitioners who laced their potions with lots of high-percentage alcohol.

Diet has always played an important role in people's ideas about good health. Rural people looked forward to the first wild greens of the spring and ate them as "sallets." When the first cultivated lettuces appeared, they, too, were consumed as health foods. Similar ideas about the obvious connections between diet and health drove the earliest health reformers, the most famous being Sylvester Graham in the early 19th century. He believed that chemical additives to foods were harmful and so promoted eating wholegrain flours. His graham cracker was widely known, though nothing like the biscuit of the same name today. His ideas were taken up by the Kellogg brothers, whose sanitarium (literally, "healthy place") in Battle Creek, Michigan, became hugely popular. People who came to restore their health ate a special diet consisting of many vegetables and high-fiber foods. One of these was corn flakes, which the Kelloggs invented and one of the brothers marketed nationally. Thus began the breakfast cereal industry, many of whose products are still marketed as important to a healthy diet. Several of the major cereal producers remain as Midwest-based companies.

If eating a good breakfast is important to health, so are other dietary procedures and products. In the present day, people in the Midwest are as concerned about diet and health as they are in other parts of the country. Overweight to the point of obesity, high blood pressure, blood serum cholesterol as a danger to the heart, and cancers are among the chief worries. As a result, and despite the notion of Midwestern food being filled with saturated fats, sugars, and high amounts of gluten, people have changed their diets in the last several decades. Fat and salt consumption has decreased, and leaner meats and fruits and vegetables are eaten in greater amounts than ever. Obesity levels and other health statistics in the Midwest are about in the middle range for American states—about 26 percent of the population. Life expectancy is also at the national average. This compares favorably with statistics from 1940 when the surgeon general of Illinois issued a report stating that the average life expectancy of an average male in the state was 60 years old, without hope of it ever getting better.

The single dietary factor leading to ill health in the Midwest is poverty. The urban poor's inability to find and pay for healthy foods (high-carbohydrate, high-fat, and high-salt foods are cheaper) is matched by the lack of money for similar foods among the rural poor. Obesity rates for such people in the Midwest are among the highest in the United States, ranging up to 36 percent. Obesity leads to many other health issues, from heart attacks to respiratory problems. Individuals know this, but their circumstances do not allow for healthier diets. As such, this is a major public health problem in America's agricultural heartland.

Bruce Kraig

Further Reading

Cayton, Andrew R. L., and Susan E. Gray, eds. *The American Midwest: Essays on Regional History.* Bloomington: University of Indiana Press, 2001.

Clark, Grace Grosvenor. *The Best in Cookery in the Middle West.* New York: Doubleday, 1955.

Long, Lucy M. *Regional American Food Culture.* Westport, CT: Greenwood Press, 2009.

Shortridge, Barbara, and James Shortridge. *The Taste of American Place: A Reader on Regional and Ethnic Foods.* New York: Rowman and Littlefield, 1998.

Shortridge, James R. *The Middle West: Its Meaning in American Culture.* Lawrence: University of Kansas Press, 1989.

Sisson, Richard, Christian Zacher, and Andrew R. L. Cayton. *The American Midwest: An Interpretive Encyclopedia.* Bloomington: University of Indiana Press, 2007.

United States: New England

Overview

New England comprises six states in the northeastern corner of the United States: Maine, Vermont, New Hampshire, Massachusetts, Rhode Island, and Connecticut. The most densely populated New England state is Massachusetts, where more than 6 million of New England's 14.3 million residents live—about 810 per square mile. The most sparsely populated states are Maine, with a total population of 1.3 million (41 per square mile), and Vermont, where there are about 620,000 residents (67 per square mile). Because Massachusetts played a central historical role in the move for independence from Great Britain, has a large, dense population, and is home to New England's largest city, Boston, the state is often viewed as the focal point of New England and as emblematic of the Yankee personality: resourceful, independent, ingenious, and innovative.

The ancestral roots of New England frame its historic food traditions. From north to south the emphasis differs somewhat: Vermont, New Hampshire, and Maine's roots are predominantly French Canadian, English, Irish, and German; Massachusetts's ancestors are Irish, Italian, French or French Canadian, and English; Rhode Island's are the same as Massachusetts but include Hispanic and Portuguese ancestry; and Connecticut has more Italian ancestry than its northern neighbors, followed by Irish, English, German, and French or French Canadian ancestry.

Although New England remains largely Caucasian, its historical food culture is overlaid by and enriched with food cultures introduced by modern immigrants. Blacks/African Americans, Hispanics/ Latinos, and Asians are growing populations in all the New England states. Massachusetts is home to many Central and South Americans as well, particularly Brazilians; Rhode Island has Liberian, Nigerian, and Ghanaian citizens; South Americans, Portuguese, and immigrants from former Soviet countries live in Connecticut. Supermarkets, grocery stores, and restaurants reflect this ethnic diversity.

New England has projected an energetic presence into American food culture and technology from its early days to modern times. The first cookbook authored by an American, *American Cookery,* was written by Amelia Simmons in 1796 and originally published in Hartford, Connecticut. In the 1960s, Massachusetts resident Julia Child brought French cooking into American homes with her book *Mastering the Art of French Cooking* and her public television cooking show, *The French Chef.* Many culinary tools were created in New England that embody the concept of Yankee ingenuity. For example, the first can opener was patented in 1858 by Ezra J. Warner of Waterbury, Connecticut. David Goodell of Antrim, New Hampshire, built a business on an improved apple parer that he invented in 1864. Turner Williams of Providence, Rhode Island, improved on the hand-operated egg beater by adding a second, interlocking beater in 1870, and his appliance became known as the Dover egg beater. Potato breeders in Vermont and Maine created hundreds of new potato varieties in the late 19th century. In the 1940s, following World War II, the home microwave oven was developed in Massachusetts as weapons manufacturer Raytheon looked to diversify its product portfolio. The Cuisinart food processor was invented in 1973 by Greenwich, Connecticut, native Carl G. Sontheimer.

The development of speedy global trade in all kinds of foodstuffs has flattened the distinctiveness and seasonality of everyday New England cookery in a broad sense by making a wide range of foods available year-round—similar to what any American can purchase in any local supermarket. Traditional New England foods that were once consumed on a daily basis due to the limitations of the seasons and of supply, such as baked beans, boiled puddings, salt pork and salted fish, breads and puddings made of cornmeal and rye flour, molasses, and seasonal fruits and vegetables, are now foods that are eaten by choice rather than necessity and that form the region's culinary identity. Many native foodstuffs, dishes, and foodways distinguish New England from other regions in the United States. Festivals, tourism, holidays, and family traditions acknowledge, support, and celebrate regional, traditional, and seasonal foods such as blueberries, strawberries, cranberries, and apples; corn, squash, and beans; lobsters, clams, oysters, mussels, and cod; maple syrup; and cheddar cheese. The Thanksgiving feast is a keystone of American identity that is based on the colonial-period New England harvest festival.

🍽 Food Culture Snapshot

In the 21st century, New Englanders spend more than half their food dollars, or about 10 percent of their net income, on meals prepared at home. They spend about 40 percent of their food dollars, or about 5 percent of their net income, on meals away from home.

Among foods purchased for home preparation, meats predominate, particularly poultry and beef. Following meats are fresh fruits and vegetables; cereals and bakery products; frozen prepared meals and other foods; canned and packaged soups; potato chips, nuts, and other snacks; condiments and seasonings, such as olives, pickles, relishes, sauces, and gravies; baking needs; other canned and packaged prepared foods, such as salads and desserts; and dairy products such as milk, cream, cheeses, sour cream, and buttermilk. Because of the time constraints imposed on families in which both parents are working, and even in single-person households where the priority is to spend less time in the kitchen and more time pursuing leisure activities, prepared meals are convenient, popular, and responsive to current trends and fashions in nutrition.

Like most Americans, New Englanders tend to do their shopping at supermarkets, and in urban areas they can shop online and have groceries delivered to their homes. Until the 1990s, independent grocers played a strong role alongside growing supermarket chains. But with the consolidation of supermarkets, independents and smaller grocers have a decreasing presence except in rural areas. In rural areas, independent grocers are more common.

As supermarkets penetrate a greater share of the market, at the same time New Englanders place increasing value on locally grown foods. Natural-foods supermarkets highlight organically grown, native, seasonal foods, as well as heirloom varieties of produce and breeds of poultry and livestock. Many shoppers seek organic produce, meat, poultry, baked goods, and dairy products at indoor and outdoor farmers' markets that operate year-round, fueled by a strong regional organization of organic farmers and gardeners. Supermarkets that recognize the growing consumer interest in local and organic foods also carry items from such producers. Smaller boutique markets emphasize locally grown or manufactured foods, from fruits and vegetables to breads and other baked goods, meats, poultry, cheeses, wines, beers, and soft drinks.

New Englanders have grown more health conscious in the 21st century and less physically active than their forebears. Dietary choices reflect the trend in the consumption of smaller quantities of meat and fats and greater quantities of fruits, vegetables, and grains than the preceding generations consumed. A typical breakfast might be fruit with dry cereal and milk or yogurt, or eggs and toast. A commuter might pick up a bagel with cream cheese or—on the heavier side—a breakfast sandwich with egg, ham or sausage, and cheese on the way to work. Coffee, tea, or citrus juice is commonly consumed with breakfast.

Lunches are light, perhaps prepared at home and brought to work or sent with children to school: a sandwich or soup, perhaps with a salad, accompanied by a soft drink, juice, or water. Dinners typically include a roast or broiled meat, a starch, vegetables or a salad, and sometimes a dessert. Casseroles, pastas, and other one-dish meals are also common, often accompanied by a salad or vegetable. Prepared meals bought at a supermarket, either fresh or frozen, are also common fare. New Englanders tend to drink wine at home more than any other alcoholic beverage, and they enjoy tea and fruit juice as their primary nonalcoholic drinks.

Major Foodstuffs

The geography of New England provides a rich landscape for growing and harvesting foodstuffs. With more than 6,000 miles of tidal shoreline and U.S. fishing rights that extend 200 miles from shore, its waters yield abundant fish and shellfish. The inland countryside offers an environment that supports both large- and small-scale farming as well as having the climate and soils necessary to produce the forage needed for dairy farming. Although the growing season is short, the income per farmed acre for all six New England states is among the top five regions in the country.

Colonial and Revolutionary New England was largely rural, and its economy was rooted in agriculture as a source of capital to support its developing economy. Growing urban populations in Boston and Salem, Massachusetts; Newport, Rhode Island; and Portsmouth, New Hampshire, provided markets for farm goods. The fish and shellfish industries played

Lobsters and clams steam over hot rocks at an annual clambake in Cape Cod, Massachusetts. (National Geographic | Getty Images)

a large role in New England's economy as well as on its dining tables. The codfish was so abundant in colonial times that it became a symbol of economic prosperity in New England. A gilded cod carved of wood has graced the State House in Boston since 1784, and the cape of Massachusetts is known as Cape Cod.

Contemporary New England agriculture and fishing are minor players on the national level, but the significant crops, fish, and shellfish of the region form a large part of the New England cultural and culinary identity. Its major crops—those for which its states are among the top 10 in acres harvested nationally—include wild blueberries, cranberries, raspberries, strawberries, apples, pears, pumpkins and other squashes, and potatoes. It has the largest number of maple trees tapped for syrup in the United States and also maintains a large inventory of milk goats and milk cows. Maine is known for American lobster and is the location of the majority of American lobster landings in the United States. Oysters, soft-shell and hard-shell clams, mussels, shrimp, scallops, and crab come from New England waters, as well as cod, haddock, bass, flounder, tuna, halibut, and many other fishes. Local and seasonal delicacies such as New England eggs and poultry, smelts, Maine shrimp, fiddlehead ferns, and wild or farmed mushrooms tend to stay in the region.

Maple sap is processed into maple syrup in the spring and is strongly identified with Vermont. Cow, goat, and sheep milks are made into butter, cheese, ice cream, and other dairy products by dozens of local and regional dairy processors. Berries are sold fresh in their summer season locally, as well as canned, frozen, baked into pies and muffins, and processed into jams and jellies. The apple harvest begins in early fall, when young, fresh apples are at their peak of flavor. As fall progresses, apples become cider and hard cider, jelly, and pies. Pumpkins are sold fresh and also processed, canned, and made into pies. From May to October, many varieties of potatoes are sold fresh or processed into frozen French fries and other potato products; beans are baked with molasses and pork and canned or sold dried for home cooking. Most fish and shellfish are exported, but regional demand and local festivals that celebrate fishing and shellfishing, such as the annual lobster festivals in Maine and New Hampshire, are helping to keep more of the catch local.

Cooking

Classic New England cookery is known for being simple, spare, seasonally based, and not highly spiced. Everyday modern New England cooking is much the same. Modern refrigeration and preservation have reduced the need for emphasis on seasonality, but certain iconic New England dishes that are distinguished by their style of cookery remain ritual around the seasons. More ethnic influences are evident in some of the variations on classic New England dishes, particularly in southern New England.

New England kitchens typically differ from urban to suburban/rural in the amount of space available—urban kitchens tend to be smaller—but major appliances are the same for the most part. In some of the more rural kitchens, a wood-burning cookstove/oven may serve the triple purpose of cooking, heating the room, and heating water, in addition to an electric or gas stovetop and oven used solely for cooking. Suburban and rural kitchens, given the luxury of space, serve as a center of the household, where socializing and family activities other than cooking take place. Like most modern American kitchens, any New England kitchen will have a gas or electric stovetop and oven, a refrigerator, a sink, a dishwasher, and sometimes a garbage-disposal system in the sink. Microwave ovens, mixers, toasters and toaster ovens, food processors, slow cookers, and other small appliances are common.

Eating in modern homes can take place in both formal and informal rooms. Informal eating usually happens in the kitchen. When entertaining or having a special meal, a dining room that is separate from the kitchen is used. In smaller, urban apartments, often there is only one multipurpose dining area.

Cooking outdoors is very popular in New England in the summertime. Summer is the backdrop for the classic clambake or lobster bake that takes place on rocky shores, sandy beaches, or backyard grills. New Englanders were slow to adopt the clambake tradition from Native Americans, rejecting shellfish as "savage" food, but once they accepted the tradition, many variations cropped up. The basic menu comprises hard-shell or soft-shell clams, potatoes, onions, and corn, and it may include lobster and fish. Other additions reflect ethnic influences, such as *Saugys* in Rhode Island, which are veal-based wieners that are known for the "snap" of their natural casings; Italian sausage; linguica (Portuguese sausage); and, sometimes, tripe. Clambakes are most often community gatherings or celebrations—a favorite for Independence Day.

There are many ways to assemble a clambake. One method popular along the Maine coast, where the focus is more on lobsters but soft-shell clams are almost always included, is to build a fire on a rocky shore, in a U-shaped hollow in the rocks that is open on one end, and over which a thick metal sheet can be laid. When the metal is heated, rockweed is piled on top. Also known as bladder wrack, rockweed is an intertidal seaweed that holds a great deal of moisture and imparts a unique flavor to the bake. Live lobsters are laid down in the first layer, followed by a layer of rockweed, then soft-shell clams that have been placed in mesh bags, then another layer of rockweed, followed by corn on the cob. All is topped off with a final layer of rockweed and a sheet of wet canvas; then seawater is poured over the whole. A bakemaster watches over the bake, stokes the fire, and determines when the shellfish and corn are done. Eaten outdoors at tables covered with newspaper, the bake is often accompanied by hot rolls or bread and potatoes. Bowls of melted butter are set out for diners to dip lobster and clams into, and everyone eats with their hands, tossing the shells into common shell bowls. Blueberry pie, made with the tiny, sweet, wild blueberries that are native to Maine and served with vanilla ice cream, and strawberry shortcake, made with a biscuit-style shortcake and sugared native strawberries topped with whipped cream, are perennial favorites for dessert.

Fall and winter cookery features hearty one-pot meals, stews, and chowders, from the traditional Yankee pot roast or New England boiled dinner to fish or clam chowder or oyster stew. Scallops and tiny sweet Maine shrimp appear in the markets from December to February. A popular way to eat Maine shrimp is to bake them whole in a hot oven until just done, separate the head and tail, and suck the shrimp meat from the tail. Another winter delicacy is smelt: small, silver fish with sweet white flesh. Fished through holes bored in the ice at the mouths of tidal rivers from December until March, often by local fishermen in small fishing shacks set up on the ice, the smelts are cleaned, coated in a mixture of flour, cornmeal, salt, and pepper, and skillet-fried. Smelts can be finger food or eaten with utensils, either plain or with a squeeze of lemon or dip of tartar sauce.

In the springtime, fiddlehead ferns appear in local markets, along with dandelion greens, rhubarb, and morel mushrooms. Fiddleheads, which are the young coiled heads of the ostrich fern, are blanched or steamed and then tossed with butter. A particularly delicious spring treat is to sauté the fiddleheads with the morels of the season or other mushrooms.

Typical Meals

New England meal patterns follow the same sequence through the day as meals across the United States: breakfast, which is typically a light morning meal; lunch at midday, which again tends to be on the lighter side; and dinner, the main meal of the day and also the heaviest. People who do physically demanding work are likely to consume heavier breakfasts and lunches than people who work in a more sedentary environment.

Meat, potatoes, and a vegetable or vegetables have long characterized the typical New England main meal. Usually the three elements are cooked separately, as in the New England boiled dinner of corned beef, potatoes, carrots, and turnips. Sometimes they are cooked together, as in a Yankee pot roast.

Yankee Pot Roast

Season a 4-pound top sirloin roast generously with salt and pepper. Heat some oil, bacon drippings, or other fat in a large, heavy-bottomed saucepan, and brown the roast on all sides. Pour a quart of boiling water over it and cover closely. Simmer as gently as possible for 2 hours, or until the roast is tender. Add peeled onions, carrots, turnips, and potatoes, cut into large pieces. Cook till the vegetables are tender; then remove the meat and vegetables from the pan and thicken the cooking liquid with 2 tablespoons of flour mixed smoothly with a little cold water. If necessary add more water while the roast is cooking so that there will be enough sauce to cover the vegetables.

It is useful to look at a typical day's meals in the early 19th century to note both the departures in modern eating as well as some of the traces of meals and foodways from the past that are carried into the present. Compared to the meals of preindustrial New England, contemporary meals are smaller and simpler. For example, an early 19th-century farmer's breakfast during the working week might include meats, such as sausages, ham, souse (pickled pig's ears, snouts, cheeks, and feet), or fried pork, and eggs, or pork and apples with a milk gravy, served with boiled potatoes. Salt mackerel and shad might be soaked overnight and then boiled. Baked goods served could include johnnycake (cornmeal and water) or "rye and Indian" bread made from rye flour and cornmeal, and possibly pie.

In the 21st century, a weekend breakfast or brunch—a combination of breakfast and lunch—might be on the heavier side: a breakfast meat, eggs, toasted bread, biscuits or pancakes, and fish cakes. Brunch is more a meal to be enjoyed at leisure and for the pleasure of eating than a practical meal, and it recalls the abundance of a farm breakfast. A typical weekday breakfast would be lighter, more expedient, and pragmatic, as already described: fruit with dry cereal and milk or yogurt, or eggs and toast. A commuter might pick up a bagel with cream cheese or—on the heavier side—a breakfast sandwich with egg, ham or sausage, and cheese on the way to work.

The 19th-century midday meal was known as dinner, and it was usually the big meal of the day and on Sundays could be a time for guests to visit and join in. The meal usually consisted of a roast, which was turned on a spit in front of the fire and could be tended by a child if necessary. Pies were frequent fare—baked in quantity in wintertime and frozen in a cold room, then thawed as needed for dinner.

Weekday dinners might consist of boiled corned beef and pork with a savory pudding and seasonal vegetables as well as cellared vegetables such as turnips, cabbage, pumpkins, and squashes.

Lunch is the modern New England midday meal. Like breakfast, it can be a bigger, more lavish affair on weekends as a brunch. During the workweek, it is normally a lighter meal consisting of a sandwich, a soup, or a salad, possibly composed of leftovers from the previous evening's meal, and perhaps a piece of fruit or other sweet for dessert.

Supper was the 19th-century evening meal, comprising the leftovers from dinner, along with such dishes as hasty pudding (made of cornmeal and water) with milk or molasses, brown bread and milk with stewed pumpkin, baked apples, berries when in season, pie, gingerbreads, and custards. Often, a pot of baked beans would be started on Saturday to eat the next day on the Sabbath.

Dinner is the modern evening meal and is the main meal of the day: a meat, a starch, and vegetables or a salad. Sunday dinner is usually the most elaborate of the week—a special roast meat or fowl—and for many the leftovers from Sunday become Monday's dinner. Dessert is not as common a coda to the evening meal as it once was and is often served only on special occasions. Baked beans, often called Boston baked beans because of their close identification with Boston, are still widely eaten today.

Boston Baked Beans

The first published recipe for baked beans appeared in 1829 in *The Frugal Housewife,* by Lydia Maria Child, and called simply for a pound of pork to a quart of beans with a sprinkling of pepper and nothing more. The following is a more flavorful recipe for Boston baked beans.

Rinse and pick over 1 pound of great northern or white navy beans. Soak in cold water overnight, then place the beans and soaking liquid in a large cooking pot. Simmer the beans until the skins burst when you blow on them—15 minutes or longer. Then place the beans in an earthenware baked bean pot, leaving the liquid simmering on the stovetop. Press a whole, peeled onion into the beans. Score deeply a ¼-pound piece of salt pork, and press it into the beans over the onion. Mix together ½ cup molasses, 1 teaspoon dry mustard, and ½ teaspoon each of salt and ground black pepper. Pour over the beans, then pour in the simmering water, adding more if necessary to cover. Put the lid on the pot, and bake in a preheated 250°F oven for 5 hours or until the beans are tender and cooked through. Baked beans are traditionally served with brown bread.

Baked Beans in a classic Boston Bean Pot. Beans are slow cooked in an oven with a variety of seasonings, some including onion, molasses, and sugar. (iStockPhoto)

Eating Out

There is a long history of eating out in New England. The ordinaries, taverns, and public houses of the 17th–19th centuries are the earliest examples of Americans eating away from home in a setting other than that of friends or family. Taverns were located on the owner's property, often next to the town's meetinghouse. In their earliest days they were meant to serve residents primarily, and then travelers. A typical tavern would provide food, drink, lodging, and space for horses, carts, and often livestock. The tavern or public house was a place of entertainment, social interaction, and business transactions for local residents, and a welcome stopping point for those bringing produce or livestock to market and for people traveling by stagecoach.

Early tavern fare was not known to be particularly good or abundant, but as the relationship of the tavern became more intertwined with the food trade, which was becoming more entwined with the alcohol trade, the food improved. Travelers could stop for a meal or a drink, or stay for lodging as well. Meals were served at communal tables and at appointed times. Dining rooms were separate from the taprooms where alcohol was served, and the better taverns served a breakfast that often included steaks, fish, eggs, cakes, and tea or coffee. Smaller taverns or country taverns might include pies, puddings, and cider at breakfast. Dinner was served in the afternoon and was a similar menu to breakfast. Supper was the evening meal, again with the table laid similarly to breakfast, but including cold fowl, ham, and other meats. Cider, ale, and distilled spirits, particularly rum, were served. As the urban landscape developed, taverns became hotels with a greater emphasis on finer dining and decor.

The American diner had its start in Providence, Rhode Island, in the early 1870s as a horse-drawn, mobile freight wagon that provided take-out sandwiches, pies, hot meals, and coffee outside the offices of the *Providence Journal* after restaurants had closed for the night. An entrepreneur in Worcester, Massachusetts, improved on the freight wagons by creating wagons with indoor seating and, later, indoor cooking that catered to late-night workers and public events. The improved diners added items such as baked beans, hamburgers, and clam chowder to their menus. By the early 20th century, public health and safety concerns necessitated that the mobile wagons become set in permanent locations, and by 1940 the classic stainless steel diner had been

developed. Diners might serve New England fare, or, if situated in an ethnic neighborhood, the menu would reflect the local tastes. Many diners survive from their heyday, and they continue to be popular casual eating-out destinations today.

In modern New England, a large diversity of options exist for eating out, from diners, carryouts, and clam shacks to upscale restaurants serving traditional New England fare, restaurants serving modern interpretations of traditional dishes, and a large diversity of ethnic eateries, from the very informal to very upscale.

Though dining-out options are myriad, residents of the Northeast comprise the smallest market share of Americans who do eat out, and when they do, it is most likely to be for dinner at a full-service restaurant. Tourism fuels a healthy restaurant economy, and when visitors come to New England, they look for traditional New England fare, particularly seafood.

Informal clam shacks and lobster shacks abound along the coastal areas, where diners can enjoy a shore dinner of lobster, steamed soft-shell clams, and corn on the cob; deep-fried seafood of all kinds including scallops, shrimp, oysters, and particularly clams; stuffed clams or *stuffies,* which are large hard-shell clams (quahogs) that are chopped, mixed with breadcrumbs and herbs, and stuffed back into the shells and baked—a Rhode Island specialty that can also be embellished with chorizo for a Portuguese touch; or lobster rolls and crab rolls, in which the lobster or crabmeat is mixed with a little mayonnaise and served on a toasted New England–style hot dog bun. Chowders can be "clear" clam chowder, a Rhode Island specialty that is not enriched with cream, or creamy chowder, which is common from Massachusetts north. Chowders can also be tomato-based, seen most often south of the "chowder line" in Connecticut, where clear or creamy New England clam chowder becomes tomatoey Manhattan clam chowder. Shacks usually offer hard ice cream, soft-serve ice cream, and various kinds of ice cream drinks that are known variously as milk shakes (Connecticut), frappés (Maine, Massachusetts), or cabinets (Rhode Island). Frozen lemonade—a slushy lemon drink of Italian origin—and coffee milk—milk with sweet coffee syrup—are popular treats in Rhode Island.

Stuffies

Scrub 12 live quahogs and rinse in cold water to remove grit. Bring a couple of inches of water to boil in a large pot, add the quahogs, and simmer covered for about 5 minutes, or until the clams open. Set clams aside to cool. Reserve the steaming liquid.

Finely mince a quarter of an onion, a stalk of celery, 2 cloves of garlic, and half a bell pepper. Sauté in olive oil with a big pinch of dried thyme until tender. Stir in 1½ to 2 cups of dried breadcrumbs and transfer to a large bowl.

Remove the quahog meat from the shells, and reserve the shells. Check for grit and dip into reserved steaming liquid to rinse if necessary. Chop roughly and add to vegetable and breadcrumb mixture, along with a handful of finely chopped parsley, the juice of half a lemon, a dash of Worcestershire sauce, and salt and pepper to taste. Mix thoroughly, adding 1 beaten egg and clam juice or strained steaming liquid as needed to moisten the mixture.

Heat oven to 425°F. Spoon the stuffing mixture into the shells and press it flat. Arrange the stuffed shells on a baking sheet, and bake for about 15 minutes until browned. Serve with lemon wedges.

Diner food often includes deep-fried fish and shellfish, but diners round out their offerings with other traditional New England foods such as pickled tripe, roast turkey with cranberry sauce and mashed potatoes, Yankee pot roast, and New England boiled dinner. Oyster stew, lobster stew and lobster bisque, and clam, fish, or corn chowder are also diner staples. Desserts run the traditional gamut, especially including pies of all kinds, which feature New England fruits and vegetables in season such as strawberries, rhubarb, blueberries, apples, raspberries, and pumpkin. Indian pudding, a dessert made of milk, cornmeal, and molasses that dates back to colonial times, is another popular item.

New England dishes are showcased in upscale settings as well. Locke-Ober restaurant in Boston, which has been in operation since the 1870s, offers such classics as lobster stew, lobster bisque, and clams casino. Clams casino—an elegant version of the stuffie composed of tiny cherrystone clamshells stuffed with a mixture of clam meat, breadcrumbs, bacon, onions, and bell peppers—was supposed to have been created in the early 20th century by the Little Casino in Narragansett, Rhode Island. Locke-Ober and many other restaurants throughout the six New England states use native New England ingredients and traditional recipes in innovative ways as well, sometimes putting a new spin on an older recipe or creating a recipe that folds a native ingredient, such as lobster, into a nonnative form, such as an Asian spring roll.

New England's native foodstuffs have often had a regional identity appended to them on menus or in markets that reflects a pride of place and skill in growing or manufacturing foods and food products. As the European concept of *terroir*—the influence of local growing conditions on the flavor of produce—has spread and combined with New England's pride in its products, native foodstuffs are increasingly and more specifically identified with their place of origin. Fish and shellfish are described in terms of where they are harvested, so diners or shoppers will often see "Point Judith" (Rhode Island) describing their calamari or "Duxbury" or "Wellfleet" (Massachusetts) or "Damariscotta River" (Maine) and dozens of other place-names describing their oysters. Produce of all kinds is often described by the name of the area where it was grown—for example, Roxbury Russet, Newton Pippin, and Rhode Island Greening apples. Cheeses are not simply varieties such as cheddar or chèvre, they are from specific dairies or creameries, often by one of the scores of licensed artisanal cheese makers in New England, particularly Vermont.

Besides traditional New England fare, there are many ethnic restaurants in New England, particularly in the southern states and more urban areas where immigrants are more concentrated. Italian, Portuguese, Caribbean, Brazilian, Mexican, Asian, African, and other ethnic eateries abound.

Special Occasions

The iconic American holidays of Independence Day and Thanksgiving spring from New England history.

Many of the foods and rituals surrounding the celebration of these holidays are still in practice today.

A secular, patriotic, and publicly celebrated holiday, Independence Day, or the Fourth of July, does not have a set feast menu associated with it, though drinking alcoholic beverages has always been associated with the Fourth. Toward the beginning of the 19th century, some towns began to hold public dinners featuring seasonal foods following the public speeches, parades, music, and other events of the day, and before the fireworks that capped the celebration. Picnics became very popular in the mid-19th century, either at home and eaten outdoors or packed up to take to a pretty spot. Cold meats, pickles, cheese, olives, bread, and pies were popular packable fare for a Fourth of July picnic, much as they are today. Later in the 19th century, whole poached salmon served with peas and new potatoes, or lamb with peas, appeared on celebratory menus, as did roast pig, clambakes, and chowders. Salmon, peas, and potatoes are the most iconic of New England Independence Day feasts.

The modern Thanksgiving celebration is based, at least in spirit, on a "harvest home" feast that was held on the occasion of bringing the last of the harvest home. The popular belief is that the first Thanksgiving occurred at Plymouth in 1621. The association is thanks to the efforts of Sarah Josepha Hale, who was the editor of *Godey's Ladies' Book.* Hale campaigned for many years to have Thanksgiving declared a national holiday and finally succeeded in 1863 when she persuaded President Abraham Lincoln to proclaim

the last Thursday of November as a day of thanks. In 1865 she wrote and published an editorial in *Godey's* that connected the events at Plymouth in 1621 with the first Thanksgiving holiday, and with it she captured the popular imagination.

The basic Thanksgiving menu that Americans cook up in their homes each November is composed of foods that are considered native to America, and are also native to New England. Roast turkey is the main course, and it is such a strong symbol that vegetarian substitutes made of tofu or wheat gluten are shaped to look like a turkey. Stuffing, often with oysters or chestnuts; cranberry sauce or relish; potatoes, usually mashed and served with gravy; and pumpkin, apple, or mincemeat pie for dessert are the classic elements of a modern Thanksgiving feast.

In the springtime, Vermont, Maine, and New Hampshire have sugaring-off parties to celebrate the end of maple syrup season. The centerpiece of the party is sugar on snow, maple syrup that is boiled to 230 degrees and poured in thin ribbons over bowls of snow, where it firms to a caramel-like consistency. The intensely sweet maple candy is served with sour pickles, which can be eaten alternately with the candy to cut through its sweetness. Raised doughnuts are traditionally served alongside.

In southern New England, saint's day feasts are held from June to October and feature Italian American food that is associated with immigrants from various regions of Italy. One feast of note is the Fisherman's Feast in Boston, established in the early 20th century. Sicilian fishermen pay respect to Madonna del Soccoroso (Our Lady of Help) and bless the fishing waters. The streets are filled with people, music, and vendors selling Italian goods and souvenirs as well as Italian sausages, calamari, pizza, pasta, and other Italian and Italian American treats.

Diet and Health

Research has established that a lack of physical activity coupled with unhealthy eating patterns contributes to obesity and a number of chronic diseases, including some cancers, cardiovascular disease, and diabetes. Compared with people who consume a diet with only small amounts of fruits and vegetables, those who eat more generous amounts as part

Thanksgiving dinner placed on table. (Corel)

of a healthful diet are likely to have reduced risk of chronic diseases.

Americans in general have been growing heavier over the last several decades, which can be viewed in part as a trend related to living in an affluent and well-nourished society. Changes in technology have allowed a more sedentary lifestyle; in most families, both parents usually work, and the proliferation of fast food and other convenience foods, which tend to be high in fat and simple carbohydrates, has also contributed to the increasing size of the American waistline.

Compared with other Americans, New England residents are among the least obese; relatively few have a body mass index, or BMI, of greater than 30. Obesity trends upward from south to north. New Englanders struggle more with overweight—a body mass index of 25–29.9. Here, the trend is reversed from north to south, with more overweight people in southern New England. The total population who are either overweight or obese is about 60 percent. Finally, about 40 percent of New Englanders are neither underweight nor overweight.

The optimal diet for maintaining good health, as established by governmental and independent studies, includes at least five servings of vegetables and fruits per day. While only about 30 percent of Americans report consuming the recommended amount, the New England states are in the top 20 of those who do so. Exercise is also a key component of good health. About 20 percent of New Englanders are considered to be at risk for health problems due to a lack of physical activity.

In recent years, medical practice in the United States is placing a greater emphasis on treating disease by prescribing lifestyle changes in diet and exercise as an adjunct to medication and other therapies. Complementary and alternative medicines are becoming more integrated into traditional medical practice. Such medicines and therapies include homeopathy and herbal medicines, mind-body balancing practices (such as yoga, meditation, or tai chi classes), acupuncture, massage and relaxation techniques, and energy healing therapies. The National Institute of Health created the National Center for Complementary and Alternative Medicine in 1999 to advance research on such therapies and make authoritative information available to the public.

Meg Ragland

Further Reading

Bureau of Labor Statistics. *Consumer Expenditure Survey: Current Expenditure Tables, Region of Residence, 2008.* http://www.bls.gov/cex/tables. htm.

Carlisle, Nancy, and Melinda Talbot, with Jennifer Pustz. *America's Kitchens.* Boston: Historic New England, 2008.

Center for Disease Control, National Center for Chronic Disease Prevention and Health Promotion. "Behavioral Risk Factor Surveillance System." http://www.cdc.gov/brfss/index.htm.

Feintuch, Burt, and David H. Watters, eds. *The Encyclopedia of New England.* Princeton, NJ: Yale University Press, 2005.

Gabaccia, Donna R. *We Are What We Eat: Ethnic Food and the Making of Americans.* Cambridge, MA: Harvard University Press, 1998.

Gutman, Richard J. S. *American Diner: Then and Now.* Baltimore, MD: Johns Hopkins University Press, 2000.

Long, Lucy M. *Regional American Food Culture.* Westport, CT: Greenwood Press, 2009.

Lukas, Paul. "The Big Flavors of Little Rhode Island." *New York Times,* November 13, 2002.

Maine Folklife Center. "Foodways." http://umaine. edu/folklife/research/foodways-research-a-taste-of-maine/.

Maine Organic Farmers and Gardeners Association. http://www.mofga.org/.

McWilliams, James. *A Revolution in Eating: How the Quest for Food Shaped America.* New York: Columbia University Press, 2005.

Mitchell, Edwin Valentine. *It's an Old New England Custom.* New York: Vanguard Press, 1946.

Morse, Alice Earle. *Stage Coach and Tavern Days.* New York: Macmillan, 1900.

National Marine Fisheries Service, Northeast Fisheries Science Center. "Brief History of the Groundfishing Industry of New England." http://www.nefsc.noaa.gov/history/stories/groundfish/grndfsh1.html.

Neustadt, Kathy. *Clambake: A History and Celebration of an American Tradition.* Amherst: University of Massachusetts Press, 1992.

Oliver, Sandra L. *Saltwater Foodways: New Englanders and Their Food, at Sea and Ashore, in the Nineteenth Century.* Mystic, CT: Mystic Seaport Museum, 1995.

Smith, Andrew. *Eating History: 30 Turning Points in the Making of American Cuisine.* New York: Columbia University Press, 2009.

Stavely, Keith, and Kathleen Fitzgerald. *America's Founding Food: The Story of New England Cooking.* Chapel Hill: University of North Carolina Press, 2004.

Thorne, John, with Matt Lewis Thorne. *Serious Pig: An American Cook in Search of His Roots.* New York: North Point Press, 1998.

United States: The Pacific Northwest

Overview

The Pacific Northwest is the North American geographic region along the northeastern edge of the Pacific Ocean. It is predominantly limited to the states of Washington and Oregon in the United States and the province of British Columbia in Canada, though it often includes Idaho, western Montana, southeastern Alaska, and northern California. This region's major metropolitan areas consist of Vancouver, British Columbia; Seattle, Washington; and Portland, Oregon, and the region's total population is approximately 16 million people. Many people from the region refer to it as "Cascadia"; in fact, talk of secession has been taking place in the region for nearly as long as Washington and Oregon have been part of the United States. Today, the region is still strongly identified with political liberalism and radicalism, though this is primarily concentrated in urban areas; most of the rural areas in the region are politically conservative.

Located along the Pacific Ocean, the Pacific Northwest is highly representative of America's so-called melting pot of cultures, and this is highly evident in the variety of ethnic cuisines commonly available throughout the region. Though the majority of the regional population is comprised of Caucasians of European descent, Latinos and Asians (immigrant and naturalized) are the second and third most populous. Of the provinces of Canada, British Columbia has the highest proportion of visible minorities, comprising 24.8 percent of the total population. Vancouver, British Columbia, has the second-largest Chinatown district in North America (after San Francisco, California), and 45 percent of all Japanese living in Canada live in British Columbia—more than in any other Canadian province. People of Asian origin also dominate foreign immigration to Washington. Commensurate with the situation in other regions of the United States, Latinos comprise the majority of immigrants to Oregon and the second-highest proportion of immigrants in Washington, representing the majority of the agricultural workforce in the Pacific Northwest.

Indigenous peoples (the aboriginal peoples of Canada, American Indians, and Alaska Natives) also make up a central part of the Pacific Northwest's cultural identity, though their populations in the region are only slightly higher than national averages. Alaska purports to have the region's highest proportion of indigenous people, with approximately 20 percent of Alaskans identifying themselves as American Indian or Alaska Native. Many Pacific Northwest indigenous people strongly advocate upholding their ancestral hunting and fishing rights in order to observe tradition as well as for subsistence.

Food Culture Snapshot

Matt and Sarah Roberts are a married couple in their early thirties. They're originally from the Midwestern United States but moved to Portland, Oregon, after graduate school to find work and live in a region that was more representative of their active, environmentally conscious lifestyle. Matt works at a large software company, and Sarah works for an environmental engineering firm. Their lifestyle and diets are typical of so-called DINK (dual-income, no kids) couples. They live in an older house in a neighborhood approximately

337

10 to 15 minutes from downtown and have a small backyard where they grow a few vegetables and have an old apple tree that was probably planted sometime in the 1920s. Rosemary grows well in the Mediterranean climate of the Pacific Northwest, and like many homes in the area, the Roberts have a large shrub of it in their front yard.

Instead of making large shopping trips to stock up on groceries, they usually make daily or near-daily shopping trips to their neighborhood grocery store, health-food store, or farmers' market, if the weather is nice. These trips are often made on the way home from work, to pick up ingredients to prepare that night's dinner.

The Roberts try to shop sustainably whenever possible—for them, this means buying primarily locally produced, organically grown meats and produce. Conversely, they make occasional visits to one of the Asian supermarkets that are common in their neighborhood. Imported Asian produce and packaged products are readily available in Pacific Northwest urban centers, thanks to the large number of immigrants from all over Asia. Many of these Asian products, such as tofu, miso, and a variety of Asian vegetables, are produced locally.

Sarah, like many young North American women, watches her caloric intake and leans toward a low-fat diet. She sometimes skips breakfast but tries to at least have a piece of wheat toast with peanut butter and a cup of green tea before she runs out the door to catch a bus to work. She usually brings lunch from home (often last night's leftovers) so she can have something healthy and save money. Matt usually opts to buy breakfast from some coffee shop near his workplace—usually a bagel or English muffin sandwich with scrambled egg and ham for breakfast (with a latte), and he will usually buy a burrito, a slice of pizza, or maybe some Vietnamese beef noodle soup for lunch. Dinner, at around 8 P.M., is often eaten in front of the television. Tonight's dinner will be wild-caught Alaska salmon fillets with rosemary-roasted baby potatoes and a green salad with some sliced apples on top. Sarah enjoys a glass or two of wine with dinner, and Matt usually has a microbrewed beer (in warmer weather he might opt for a domestic brew such as Pabst Blue Ribbon).

Major Foodstuffs

Seafood

Fisheries are a major economy in the Pacific Northwest, and this is reflected in the abundance of locally available seafood including wild-caught Pacific cod, albacore tuna, sole, Alaskan halibut, Dungeness and Alaskan king crab, pink shrimp and spot prawns, and more than 25 varieties of oysters raised in commercial beds in the chilly bays and sounds of Washington and British Columbia. But no other fish is more central to the cultural and regional identity of the Pacific Northwest than the salmon (*Oncorhynchus* spp.): Chinook, coho, and sockeye salmon and steelhead trout (a close relative of salmon) are the region's most important fish species, being generally available to commercial and/or recreational anglers during most of the year. Due to a variety of factors, populations of wild salmon have been on the decline for years, warranting the protection of some species under the U.S. Endangered Species Act. This decline has recently led to restrictions on commercial fishing in the Pacific Northwest.

Agriculture

Agriculture and viticulture are also important Pacific Northwest economies. The majority of North America's pomes and stone fruits (specifically sweet cherries) are produced in the Pacific Northwest,

Fresh grilled sockeye salmon steak dinner with asparagus and lemon wedges. (Sally Scott | Dreamstime.com)

particularly in Washington's Yakima Valley. The region's volcanic soils and mild, maritime climate are also ideal for growing berries and grapes. Berries in the *Vaccinium* genus such as huckleberries, cranberries, and blueberries thrive considerably in the deep, acidic soils of the region, though raspberries, blackberries, currants, gooseberries, and kiwi berries (a small, hairless variety of kiwi) are all commercially grown in the Northwest as well.

Hazelnuts (colloquially called *filberts*) are another regionally specific agricultural product. Only Turkey produces more hazelnuts than the Pacific Northwest, though Oregon produces vastly more than Washington or British Columbia (approximately 23,000 tons per year, compared to 100 tons in Washington and 360 tons in British Columbia).

Potent Potables

Oregon's Willamette Valley and Washington's Yakima Valley are second only to Germany in world production of hops, and this is reflected in the production and consumption of microbrewed beers in the Northwest. Since the 1980s, more than 360 microbreweries (breweries that produce fewer than 20,000 barrels per year) and brewpubs have become established in Oregon, Washington, and British Columbia.

Viticulture is a somewhat recent agricultural development in the region, taking off in the 1990s; however, the Okanagan Valley in British Columbia, Yakima and Walla Walla counties in Washington, and Yamhill County in Oregon are now considered to be comparable to grape-growing regions of France and Italy for their *terroir*. Enology and viticulture are highly commercially viable in the region because of economies of scale, with the region's wineries being typically small and family owned, compared to other major wine-producing regions such as California's Napa Valley.

More recently, connoisseurs of hard alcohol have followed suit, and artisanal distilleries have begun to comprise a niche market in the Pacific Northwest—of the approximately 100 distilleries in the United States, 20 are microdistilleries located in Oregon, producing fragrant gins, vodkas, and eaux-de-vie (literally, "water of life"; fruit brandy), all from locally produced ingredients. One Oregon microdistillery even produces an *eau-de-vie poire* with a small pear grown inside the bottle.

Dairies and Creameries

The Willamette Valley in northwestern Oregon is known as the "grass seed capital of the world." While most grass seeds are neither fit nor intended for human consumption, this achievement does point to the fact that the Pacific Northwest is good at growing grass, which is a preferred food of dairy-producing livestock (cows, sheep, and goats). As a result, the region is home to more than 80 artisanal creameries as well as several large-scale commercial dairies. Many independent cheese makers in the region rival the highest-quality European creameries.

Wild Foods

In addition to fishing, hunting is a popular pastime in the Pacific Northwest, and the region supports large populations of big game such as deer and elk (also antelope, moose, and bear, though these are hunted less frequently); upland birds such as turkey, grouse, quail, pheasant, partridge, and ptarmigan; and waterfowl including several species of ducks and geese. Though some hunters in the region participate for sport and keep trophies of their game, the majority are subsistence hunters and eat what they kill (trophy hunters are generally tourists to the region and are treated with disdain by locals). Many hunters utilize the numerous small-scale meat processors located throughout the region to butcher large game and convert meat scraps into sausage.

Gathering wild foods, particularly mushrooms and berries, is another hobby that has been growing in popularity over the past several years. The Pacific Northwest provides excellent habitat for expansive thickets of several species of wild huckleberries and an abundance of choice edible mushrooms such as chanterelles, boletes (known in Italy as porcini or in France as cèpe), oyster mushrooms, chicken-of-the-woods (a variety of *maitake*), cauliflower mushroom, white "Oregon" truffles, and matsutake. Recreational and commercial mushroom hunters tend to return to favorite spots year after year, the locations of which are often closely guarded (sometimes with firearms). Stories of mushroom hunters shooting their own family members during disputes over prime picking territories are common, but national forests and private properties closer to residential areas tend to be relatively safe for casual pickers.

Cooking

Like in most regions of North America, home cooking in the Pacific Northwest is typically performed by women, though men still comprise the majority of cooks and chefs in commercial kitchens. Most Pacific Northwesterners learn to cook from their mothers or other elder women in the family. Nearly all households come equipped with a standard four-burner electric or gas range, electric oven, and refrigerator/freezer. The majority of households also have an electric toaster and a microwave oven, though many health-conscious people in the region avoid using microwaves due to concerns that microwaves destroy the nutritional content of foods (these concerns have yet to be substantiated by scientific evidence).

Many households also equip themselves with electric slow cookers. These appliances allow busy people to safely and conveniently cook time-consuming foods like tougher cuts of meat and stews on a countertop without supervision (e.g., while away at work). Other small electric appliances such as toaster ovens, electric blenders, and food processors are also fairly common.

Sautéing in vegetable or olive oil and baking/roasting are two of the most commonly employed cooking techniques, likely due to their ease and relatively low health impacts. Vegetable fats tend to be preferred over animal fats for general cooking purposes.

Most households in the Pacific Northwest also have a means of outdoor cooking, such as a propane or charcoal grill. When weather permits, many people in this region prefer to cook outdoors and frequently have social gatherings centered around the cooking and consumption of foods. These gatherings are often erroneously called barbecues. Unlike the more regionally significant true barbecue of the southern United States, wherein proteins (generally large cuts of pork or beef) are slow-cooked for several hours (or even days) over indirect heat at low temperatures, Pacific Northwest "barbecues" consist of grilled foods that are generally prepared fairly quickly over direct heat and may include more vegetarian-friendly options such as hot dogs and burgers made from soy protein, fish fillets, and skewered vegetables.

One technique that is intrinsic to the Pacific Northwest is cooking fish, typically salmon, on a plank of cedar or alder wood over a direct heat source such as a flame or coals. This cookery method was adopted from indigenous people of the region, and wood planks specifically made for grilling salmon are readily available in the region. Smoking fish and meat for flavor and as a means of food preservation is still a fairly common practice in the Pacific Northwest, especially among recreational anglers. This has been particularly true since the advent of small electric, gas, and charcoal smokers and smoker-grills intended for home use.

Many younger people in the Northwest draw culinary inspiration from foreign cultures and are somewhat more adventurous with flavor than their parents were, preferring to prepare their foods with fresh rather than canned or frozen ingredients, and they tend to use more fresh herbs, garlic, chilies, and flavored oils and vinegars. It is also common to see younger home cooks prepare vegetarian or vegan versions of foods typically associated with a high amount of animal fats and proteins, such as making Southern-style biscuits and gravy using soy sausage and almond milk instead of pork sausage and cow milk for the gravy, or a Reuben sandwich with tempeh (a fermented soybean cake) instead of corned beef.

Typical Meals

Families tend to eat meals together, sometimes at the dinner table in the kitchen or dining room, but often in the living room or family room, seated in front of the television. Breakfast and dinner are usually eaten at home, but lunch is almost always eaten away from home (at school or at the workplace), at least on weekdays.

As in much of the United States and Canada, most people in the Pacific Northwest tend to eat fast breakfasts before school or work, such as cold breakfast cereals with milk; store-bought frozen waffles reheated in the toaster and served with a sweet topping such as maple syrup, nut butter, or a fruit spread; oatmeal with a bit of nuts or dried fruit; or a cup of yogurt that contains fruit. Toast and eggs are another common quick breakfast.

Among working people, weekdays in the Pacific Northwest often start with a cup of coffee and a bagel or pastry from a neighborhood coffee shop (though many people skip eating breakfast and opt only for coffee). The Pacific Northwest is the birthplace of Starbucks, and espresso and coffee drinks have been building in popularity in the region since the 1990s. Now, nearly every town in the Northwest has at least one place that serves espresso drinks—even rural gas stations have instant latte machines.

Preferred lunchtime fare in the Pacific Northwest is not particularly distinct from lunch foods across the United States and Canada. Women are more likely than men to bring lunch from home, often leftover dinner from the previous night. Many large companies in the region are sited on campuses that include employee cafeterias where restaurant-style foods are prepared by experienced cooks.

Most children eat a lunch that was prepared by one of their parents and brought from home, though many children instead eat lunch foods that were purchased in their school cafeterias. Children from low-income households may qualify for free lunches that are provided by their schools; these are the same lunches that are served to the rest of the student body, but they are offered at no cost to the child's family. Some public school districts also offer free breakfast to children from low-income families.

Dinners usually consist of a protein (meat or fish), a starch (pasta, rice, or potato), and a vegetable. This can be as simple as roasted chicken with mashed potatoes and green beans or as elaborate as coffee-rubbed venison tenderloin with polenta and wild mushrooms, depending on the cook's interest and skill in cooking. Sometimes these components are combined into a hearty soup or stew and served with a bread product such as a biscuit (a chemically leavened quick bread) or a dinner roll (a yeast-leavened bread). Soups, stews, and chowders are considered comfort food in the Northwest and are favored during the cooler, rainy months between October and April.

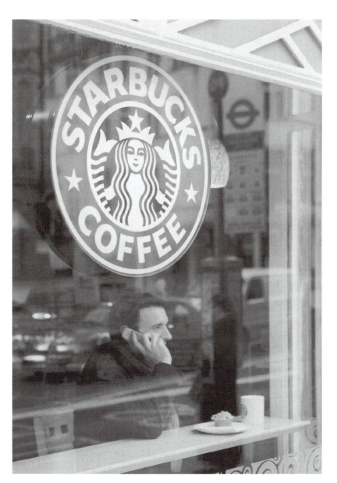

A busy Starbucks store in Seattle, Washington. (StockPhotoPro)

Thai-Spiced Salmon Chowder

This chowder combines the best of the Pacific Northwest: local salmon and Southeast Asian spices. Corn's sweetness pairs wonderfully with salmon.

Serves 4–6

Ingredients

2 tbsp butter

1 tsp olive oil

2 oz salt pork (or 2 slices bacon)

I celery rib, diced

½ jalapeño, seeded and minced

½ c red onion, diced

¾–I lb waxy potatoes (such as Yukon gold), diced

I c frozen corn

I can creamed corn

I c coconut milk

3½ c fish stock (or chicken stock)

2 bay leaves

½ tsp grated fresh galangal (or ginger)

3 star anise pods

2 tbsp basil chiffonade

8 oz coho salmon fillet, skinned and deboned

Salt and pepper to taste

Garnish: arugula chiffonade or chopped cilantro

In a large, heavy-bottomed pot, melt the butter over medium-high heat. Add the olive oil to prevent the butter from browning, and add the salt pork. Let the pork render for a minute, then add the celery, jalapeño, and onion (mirepoix). Toss in a pinch of salt so the mirepoix sweats (avoid browning the mirepoix).

Add the potatoes and frozen corn, and stir to coat with the buttery pork fat. Add the creamed corn, coconut milk and stock, the bay leaves, the galangal, and the star anise. Simmer over medium low until the potatoes are tender, approximately 20 minutes.

When the potatoes are nice and tender, turn off the heat and remove the bay leaves and star anise. Slice the salmon into bite-sized pieces and add to the soup with the basil. The latent heat from the soup will cook the salmon.

Pairs well with a peppery, slightly acidic Pacific Northwest Pinot Gris.

Eating Out

Breakfast and brunch establishments are highly popular in the Pacific Northwest. These are typically in-expensive neighborhood restaurants that also serve lunch and dinner, but they include some higher-end prix fixe restaurants that serve sophisticated weekend brunch items. Waits for a table at popular breakfast spots may exceed an hour on Saturday or Sunday. Typical brunch offerings consist of a scramble (eggs scrambled with vegetables and/or meat), home fries (fried or roasted cubed potatoes), and a piece of toast. This will typically be served with locally roasted coffee. Many people in the region also enjoy a breakfast cocktail during weekend brunch, such a screwdriver (orange juice with vodka), a Bloody Mary (tomato juice with vodka and a dash of horseradish and Worcestershire sauce, garnished with a rib of celery or pickled vegetables), or a mimosa (orange juice with champagne or Prosecco).

Recently Portland, Oregon, has received some notoriety for its populations of food carts. Food carts are a popular alternative to indoor dining establishments, and they tend to be clustered in parking lots in neighborhoods or streets that receive ample foot traffic. Food carts usually specialize in one type of cuisine, including Kazakh, Czech, Lebanese, Indian, Japanese, Vietnamese, Thai, and Mexican, though some are more generalist (e.g., "Mediterranean"). Some carts specialize in one type of food, such as barbecue, hot dogs, crepes, handheld pies, waffles, or Belgian-style *frites* (thin French fries). Neighborhood carts are often open very late to cater to crowds spilling out of closing bars, whereas the majority of the food carts located in the downtown area are frequented by lunch crowds and close after lunch.

Asian restaurants are widely available and usually provide diners with a substantial meal for little money—Japanese, Korean, Chinese, Vietnamese, Thai, and Indian restaurants are all common in the Pacific Northwest. In Vancouver, British Columbia, alone, there are more than 130 Japanese *sushi-ya* (sushi restaurants) and *izakaya* (restaurants serving small plates of grilled foods like *yakitori* and *robata*) that are tucked into every nook and cranny, providing diners with an experience reminiscent of wandering the streets of Tokyo. Vietnamese beef noodle soup (*pho*) houses are abundant in the Pacific Northwest, serving fragrant bowls of star anise–

spiked beef broth with thinly sliced beef and rice noodles. Adventurous eaters can usually order more traditional ingredients such as beef tendon or tripe. Authentic Hong Kong–style Chinese restaurants are also widespread, offering freshly roasted duck or pork, fried *yi mein* (thin wheat noodles, colored yellow with lye water), and seafood hotpots, in addition to traditional Cantonese dim sum.

The Pacific Northwest is also well known for its fine-dining establishments, though not all of them are necessarily expensive. These restaurants tend to be staffed with young, often heavily tattooed chefs who have their own style of cooking, though many rely on the implementation of European techniques with local, seasonal ingredients. An appetizer such as French-style pork pâté (made with local pork) served with house-pickled baby heirloom vegetables is an example of this marriage between technique and product and is commonly featured on menus. Most fine-dining and higher-quality casual establishments, even if not inherently French, also feature a salad of roasted beets with (local or French) bleu cheese, the ever-popular steak frites as an entrée, and a *pot de crème* (a chilled custard) or seasonal fruit dessert. Fresh seafood, if featured on the menu, tends to be obtained from local waters, and restaurants specializing in seafood dishes are fairly common.

A tattooed chef puts the finishing touches on a dish in a Portland restaurant, Oregon. (Richard Ross | Getty Images)

Special Occasions

Major holidays and events such Thanksgiving, Christmas, New Year's Eve, birthdays, and weddings are celebrated in the Pacific Northwest much in the way they are celebrated elsewhere in the United States and Canada. Meals on holidays and other special occasions are typically casual gatherings of family and friends.

Canadian Thanksgiving is celebrated on the second Monday in October, whereas American Thanksgiving is observed on the third Thursday of November. There are not really any components of the Thanksgiving feast that are specific to the Pacific Northwest; the meal typically focuses on roasted turkey served with cranberry sauce and a variety of side dishes that traditionally consist of mashed potatoes with gravy, stuffing (cubed bread cooked with onions, celery, and poultry broth, with variations in ingredients occurring among households, such as the use of oysters, cornbread, dried fruits, or nuts), green bean casserole (green beans baked with cream of mushroom soup or a béchamel sauce and topped with fried onions), and candied yams (technically a sweet potato, baked with butter and brown sugar, and often topped with marshmallows). Vegetarian households may prepare a product called tofurkey, which is a soy-based, savory loaf that bears little resemblance to turkey. Dessert traditionally consists of pumpkin pie, and an additional fruit pie might be served as well.

The Pacific Northwest does not have any particular meal or foods associated with New Year's Eve. Like elsewhere in the United States and Canada, the event is often celebrated with champagne or another sparkling white wine (or apple cider), with a toast to the new year being traditionally conducted at the stroke of midnight.

Canada Day (Canada) and Independence Day (United States) are national holidays observed on July 1 and July 4, respectively. Being summertime holidays, these are typically celebrated with outdoor parties—backyard cookouts and camping excursions are both common. Foods typically consumed during these holidays include grilled chicken (with or without barbecue sauce), hamburgers, hot dogs or sausages, corn on the cob, potato or macaroni salad (usually with a mayonnaise-based dressing), baked beans, and watermelon. Cold beer is often consumed in copious amounts during these holidays. The foods typically eaten during these holidays are similar to those eaten at American parties that celebrate sporting events.

Birthdays and weddings are typically associated with cake. A birthday cake may be homemade or purchased at a bakery or grocery store and is usually one or two layers of cake with frosting. If the cake is for a child, a dusting of colorful sugar sprinkles, toy figures, or other accoutrements may decorate the cake. One candle representing each year the honoree has been alive is another traditional topping; the birthday boy or girl then attempts to blow out the candles, and tradition speaks of a wish being granted if all candles are extinguished with one breath.

Wedding cakes tend to be much more elaborate, consisting of multiple tiers of (usually white) cake with buttercream icing or fondant and decorated according to the bride and groom's preferences and the season during which the wedding is being held (floral themes are common, though an autumn wedding may include colorful leaves as part of the decor). In the Pacific Northwest, this tradition is typically observed in the same way as in other parts of the United States and Canada, though whimsical alternatives to a cake may include a cupcake "tree" (a selection of cupcakes arranged on a tiered platter) or doughnuts arranged in a pyramid. One Portland, Oregon, doughnut shop caters weddings and allows wedding ceremonies to be conducted in their bakery. In addition to the traditional wedding cake, many weddings include a groom's cake. The groom's cake is usually a smaller, informal cake that is decorated in a way that represents the groom's interests or personality. Groom's cakes are usually a flavor other than vanilla.

Though Christmas is a Christian holiday, it is widely celebrated by non-Christians in the Pacific Northwest. At Christmastime, homemade cookies and candies are typically prepared and exchanged among friends and family members. Christmas dinners are granted a little more creative license than Thanksgiving, with no specific protein being symbolic of the holiday. Some households prepare another roasted turkey, while others serve a pork roast or roast beef. Side dishes vary as well. Coconut cream pie and desserts with a peppermint and chocolate component are fairly representative of American and Canadian Christmas celebrations.

Hanukkah, like most Jewish holidays, has symbolic foods that are traditionally eaten in observance of the holiday; Hanukkah's food is latkes. Latkes are fried potato pancakes that are often served with sour cream and/or applesauce. Children may be given *gelt,* which are thin chocolate wafers wrapped in gold foil to resemble coins. Dinner will often focus on a beef brisket. A traditional Hanukkah dessert, particularly among Sephardic Jews, is *sufganiot* (a raised donut dusted with powdered sugar).

Easter dinner is traditionally a ham, though lamb may be served instead (the lamb is viewed in Christianity as a symbol of Christ). Eggs are also symbolic of Easter, though this predates Christianity as a pagan fertility symbol. Hard-boiled eggs are colored with food-grade dyes and then hidden by adults for children to hunt for and place in a basket lined with plastic grass. These eggs can then be eaten as a snack or breakfast following Easter. Egg-shaped candies are also traditional gifts to children during the Easter celebration, along with chocolate bunnies (another remnant of pagan fertility celebrations).

The Passover seder is a ritual feast that has six symbolic components: The *maror* and *chazeret* are bitter herbs, symbolizing the bitterness and harshness of the slavery that the Jews endured in ancient Egypt. The maror is usually grated horseradish, and chazeret is usually a lettuce leaf. *Charoset* represents the mortar used by the Jewish slaves to build the storehouses of Egypt and is usually comprised of a blend of chopped nuts, apples, and sweet spices. *Karpas* is another vegetable (usually parsley, though celery or potato is sometimes used) that is dipped in saltwater or vinegar to symbolize the tears shed during slavery. *Beitzah,* a roasted egg, is a traditional symbol of the festival sacrifice (or may be interpreted as a symbol of mourning the loss of the Temple of Jerusalem). *Z'roa* is a roasted lamb shank bone that acts as an additional symbol of the Passover sacrifice.

Traditional seder dinners usually include gefilte fish (cakes of chopped whitefish), matzo ball soup, and brisket or veal, though modern households often prepare different versions of these dishes.

Diet and Health

The Pacific Northwestern diet is comparable to that in the rest of the United States and Canada, though it leans toward slightly healthier choices. The Pacific Northwest has a high proportion of vegetarians and vegans compared with elsewhere in the United States and Canada. Its major urban centers (Portland, Seattle, and Vancouver) are considered to be the top three vegetarian-friendly cities in North America according to surveys by the nonprofit organization People for the Ethical Treatment of Animals (PETA). Vegetarians and vegans in the Pacific Northwest tend to simply eat meatless versions of the same foods that omnivores eat or meat substitutes that are usually made of soy or textured vegetable protein (TVP). They also tend to rely more heavily on Asian cuisines, deriving much of their protein intake from tofu (soybean curd originally from China but now widespread across Asia), tempeh (fermented soy or grain cakes from Indonesia), and seitan (solid wheat gluten from China, Japan, and Vietnam). Many vegetarians add nutritional supplements to their foods as seasonings—Bragg Liquid Aminos (a salty-tasting source of 16 amino acids that resembles tamari or soy sauce) and nutritional yeast flakes (a source of B-complex vitamins that is often used for flavoring cheese substitutes) are in nearly every vegetarian kitchen in the Pacific Northwest.

Ecologically conscientious or so-called green lifestyles are common in the Pacific Northwest, and this is reflected in the dietary choices that are made

People shopping for farm-fresh produce, including peaches and plums, sold by a local farmer in Eugene, Oregon. (Lee Snider | Dreamstime.com)

by many of its residents. Organically grown produce and free-range, organic meats are readily available at most mainstream grocery stores, and specialty stores that provide a wide selection of locally grown meats and produce are relatively common, even in smaller cities. Many heirloom varieties of vegetables and fruits are grown and sold in the region, and these are more available and affordable than in other parts of the United States or Canada. Many of the region's restaurants have received accolades for taking advantage of the Pacific Northwest's bounty by showcasing local flora and fauna on their menus. Some restaurants even have their own farms.

Farmers' markets are another successful means of closing the gap between farm and table, in that the people who grow or raise the foods can sell directly to the consumer. Most neighborhoods or districts in each urban center have a farmers' market (usually open one day per week), and even smaller urban areas (especially college towns like Eugene, Oregon, and Olympia, Washington) tend to have at least one farmers' market. Community-supported agriculture, or CSAs, enable individuals or families to purchase a yearly share of a local farm's seasonal produce (sometimes delivered directly to their homes), while simultaneously providing income to small, organic farmers.

Heather Arndt-Anderson

Further Reading

Aquilar, George W., Sr. *When the River Ran Wild! Indian Traditions on the Mid-Columbia and the Warm Springs Reservation.* Portland: Oregon Historical Society/University of Washington Press, 2005.

Burmeister, Brett, and Lizzie Caston. *A Guide to Food Carts in Portland.* http://foodcartsportland.com.

Cook, Langdon. *Fat of the Land: Adventures of a 21st Century Forager.* Seattle, WA: Skipstone Press/Mountaineer Books, 2009.

Long, Lucy M. *Regional American Food Culture.* Westport, CT: Greenwood Press, 2009.

Manning, Ivy. *The Farm to Table Cookbook: The Art of Eating Locally.* Seattle, WA: Sasquatch Books, 2008

Parr, Tami. *Artisan Cheese of the Pacific Northwest: A Discovery Guide.* Woodstock, VT: Countryman Press, 2009.

Williamson, Jacqueline B. *The Way We Ate: Pacific Northwest Cooking, 1843–1900.* Pullman: Washington State University, 1996.

United States: The South

Overview

The American South, a cultural and political region of the United States, is loosely defined as the 11 states of the former Confederacy. They are historically linked by the devastating shared experience of defeat in the American Civil War in which they defended chattel slavery, followed by decades of poverty. The South, larger geographically than Germany and France combined, and home to a population of roughly 100 million Americans, is considered as having one of the most vibrant of American cuisines.

Five states border the Atlantic Ocean: Virginia, North Carolina, South Carolina, Georgia, and Florida; four others stretch westward from Florida, on the Gulf of Mexico: Alabama, Mississippi, Louisiana, and Texas. Two other states, Tennessee and Arkansas, connect on opposite sides of the Mississippi River and stretch westward from Virginia to Texas. The region also includes the southern parts of the border states to the north that still allowed slavery when the Civil War began, stretching westward from Delaware across Maryland, West Virginia, Kentucky, and Missouri. (These border states remained in the Union, with West Virginia—a mountainous area with few slaves—separating from Virginia over the issue of secession and becoming a new state in 1863.)

The mass migration of several million African Americans (the black diaspora) during and after the post–Civil War period of Reconstruction created large pockets of Southern cultural infusion, including the blues, jazz, and food, in Chicago, Cleveland, Detroit, Los Angeles, New York City, Washington, D.C., and elsewhere. The migration accelerated after World War II and the early years of the civil rights movement.

Many nationalities converged over time into the American South already inhabited by Native Americans: Spaniards and French arrived beginning in the 16th century, later moving into Louisiana, where they became known as Creoles, a designation ultimately including Caribbean free persons of color. In the 17th century, the English settled in Virginia and South Carolina, followed by Scots, Scots-Irish, Irish, and Welsh. French Huguenots took advantage of John Locke's declaration of religious freedom to settle in Charleston, joining sons of Barbadian planters, capitalist-minded Quakers, Jews, and German Lutherans.

African slaves of many tribal groups and nations were shipped across the Atlantic, especially from Senegal. French Acadians settled in Louisiana after great tribulation. Diverse groups of Germans settled in concentrated areas, as did smaller numbers of Italians and Greeks. Small groups of Chinese were brought over to work building the canals of Augusta, Georgia, and as laborers in the Mississippi delta.

The latest influx of primarily white inhabitants began with the advent of air-conditioning. The civil rights movement was the catalyst for the South's full reunion with the rest of America—sometimes referred to as the Second Reconstruction, with both white and black in-migration; much of the latter returning natives were lured by family ties and the opening of new job opportunities. Late 20th-century additions include Latinos, primarily from Mexico and Central America, Puerto Ricans, and Cubans. Each of these nationalities brought with them their cultural and food heritage, melding primarily African and European cuisines shared by blacks and whites.

The South is frequently referred to as the Bible Belt of the United States, as religion has always had a strong influence. Overwhelmingly Protestant, ranging from High Episcopalians to the dominant Baptists, Methodists, and a host of fundamentalist groups, it includes expanding Catholic and Jewish populations as well as Amish and even Baha'i. Little religious prejudice still exists, in part due to numbers of interfaith marriages. (Greeks and Jews were accepted by whites on the basis of skin color.) In more recent years the Muslim (including Nation of Islam) population has slowly expanded, with its incumbent dietary restrictions and often little-noticed morgues in larger cities.

African Americans tend to be concentrated among African Methodist Episcopal (AME), American Baptist, and other historically black congregations. Although many white and black congregations are technically integrated, it is often said that Sunday is the most segregated day of the week. Religious institutions frequently provide extensive social activity and child care, as well as providing a meal after the service. African American communities are known for their church food, with such delicacies as fried chicken and sweet fruit pies, providing a refuge from de facto segregation, but in both white and black congregations volunteer and home cooking is being replaced by church kitchen staffs.

The region's late 20th-century in-migration has muted the level of religiosity of the South, but religion continues to play a more significant role than elsewhere in America in shaping political and social attitudes.

🍽 Food Culture Snapshot

Betty Sue and Ryan Bradley live in Atlanta, Georgia, part of the middle class returning from the suburbs to live in central cities after their children are grown. Betty Sue is a pharmacist, and Ryan is an attorney. The Bradleys' lifestyle and foodways are typical of college-educated Southerners. Their food interests are broad, including foods of many nationalities. The only meals where they eat together are evenings and weekends. The average Southerner eats three meals a day and several snacks.

The Bradleys rise at 6:30 each weekday, with Ryan going for a two-mile run. Betty Sue prepares a breakfast tray holding Diet Coca-Cola; cereal with raisins, pecans, and bananas; and commercial fresh Florida orange juice, returning to bed to eat. Ryan makes a weekly refrigerator batch of low-fat yogurt, canned pineapple, raisins, pecans, wheat germ, and oatmeal, eating a bowl of it each day along with a sliced banana, a glass of orange juice, and coffee brewed from freshly ground beans. He eats while briefly watching the news before work.

Midmorning, at work, Betty Sue sips a caffeinated Diet Coke and eats a snack of peanut butter crackers; Ryan drinks his third cup of coffee, accompanied by an oatmeal cookie or a doughnut. For lunch, Betty Sue eats in a small restaurant, ordering a Caesar salad topped with ham followed by a dessert of fried beignets sprinkled with powdered sugar. (For her grandparents this was the major meal of the day and was called dinner.) Ryan meets a client for a lunch of curried chicken with sautéed turnip greens, rice, and a wedge of caramel cake for dessert. This traditional cake is light and has a caramelized icing. Both Betty Sue's and Ryan's desserts are typical Southern indulgences that busy people rarely fix at home.

Midafternoon, each will eat a sweet or a piece of fruit. After work they have a glass of wine and a snack of cheese straws (baked from cheese, flour, and butter) or celery filled with pimento cheese (a mixture of pureed pimento peppers, mayonnaise, garlic, and onions.)

At 7 P.M., the Bradleys cook dinner (formerly called supper) together. Betty Sue tosses a salad of fresh arugula, basil, thyme, lemon balm, or mint from their garden with dried cherries, a slice or two of Parmigiano Reggiano cheese, and a sliced pear, covered in a vinaigrette dressing of sherry vinegar and olive oil. Ryan grills a fresh-caught Carolina red snapper. Betty Sue cooks rice, which she grew up eating daily, and steams a green vegetable. This main meal of their day is cooked and eaten within 45 minutes, before they each turn to their computers for work and relaxation.

Their children are college students studying away from home at Southern colleges. One is eating fried chicken while drinking a highly caffeinated, sugared soda. The other is eating fried local farm-raised catfish, hush puppies (fried balls of a cornmeal mixture), and coleslaw. Even with their eclectic, international diet chosen from the broad array of foodstuffs of the world, historically Southern food still resonates with the Bradleys and their children.

Although the Bradleys' day is sprinkled with reminiscences of Southern meals, it is very different from what either Betty Sue or Ryan ate while growing up. Both their mothers cooked a substantial breakfast each morning of biscuits, eggs, sautéed ham with red-eye gravy, and grits (cornmeal mush). Lunch, consisting of an apple or banana and a peanut butter sandwich taken to school in a lunch box or paper bag, was washed down with sweetened iced tea, called sweet tea to differentiate it from unsweetened tea, or chocolate milk from a carton. Dinner was eaten with the entire family sitting down at the table in the formal dining room. It might have consisted of rice, macaroni (traditionally spaghetti is called macaroni), or potatoes; a green vegetable; pork chops; and canned fruit on top of iceberg lettuce topped by commercial mayonnaise, followed by pudding for dessert.

The Bradleys are in marked contrast to the many that remain mired in extreme poverty in the South. This includes both blacks and whites, with the blacks proportionally more disadvantaged than whites. Poverty affects their dietary habits considerably, with more reliance on heavily salted, fat-laden processed foods due to their need to work one or more jobs, leaving less time for grocery shopping and cooking.

Major Foodstuffs

The American South's major foodstuffs vary according to the geography, weather, soil content, and primary origin of its immigrants. The early English colonists brought cattle, chickens, and pigs; curries and spices; and wheat, oats, and other grains, along with root vegetables and beans. Africans, through ship captains and others, brought peas, okra, melons, eggplants, *benne* (sesame) seeds, and rice. Indigenous foods included beans, squash (including pumpkins),

poke "salat" or pokeweed (supplemented by English and African greens), muscadine and other wild grapes, plums, wild game, and seafood. Tomatoes from Central and South America were early arrivals.

Growing seasons vary from two or three in the lower South to one in mountainous areas. Until World War II, the South was predominantly agrarian. Many homes had a milk cow and chickens. This was due in part to the lack of refrigeration, which made food highly perishable, and was a way for the family to save money. Milk was left overnight to thicken and sour (*clabber*) before being churned into butter. Buttermilk, the residual liquid, was used as a tenderizer for soaking chicken, in cooking (the combination of buttermilk and baking powder caused a higher rise in baked goods), and as a beverage.

The primary breads are cornbread and biscuits. The rise of commercial baking powder in the mid- to late 19th century enabled Southerners to cook quick breads such as biscuits and cornbread, which require less time in a hot kitchen than yeast breads, which were reserved for special occasions. By the end of the 19th century, low-gluten soft-wheat flour was milled from winter wheat, producing delicate, airy cakes, pies, and cheese straws, with baking (originally adapted from English cookbooks) considered an art. Coconuts brought in as ballast for incoming ships gave rise to coconut cake as well as the coconut industry. Pastries include pecan, lemon, lime, and fruit pies.

Food Processor Biscuits

2½ c self-rising flour

½ c shortening or lard, frozen

¾–1 c milk or buttermilk

¼–⅓ c melted butter

¼ c all-purpose flour for shaping

Preheat the oven to 500°F. Add 2 cups of the flour to a food processor using the steel or pastry blade. Cut one half of the shortening into ¼-inch cubes; cut the second half into ½-inch cubes and refrigerate. Add the cold ¼-inch cubes to the food processor. Pulse one or two times until it is like cornmeal;

add the remainder of the shortening and process until pea sized. Add the ¾ cup of milk. Pulse 2 or 3 times until the shortening is cut in and the milk is incorporated, looking a bit like cottage cheese. The mixture should loosely cling to a finger. Add more flour or milk as needed. Lightly flour a work surface. Pat dough to ¼ inch thick. Fold in half. Pat out again. Fold again. Repeat two more times. Pat out ¼ inch thick. Brush half the dough with the melted butter. Fold the dough over to make it 4 inches thick. Dip a 2-inch round metal cutter into the flour. Cut out rounds in the dough, starting at the outside, avoiding the fold. Move biscuits to a greased sided cookie sheet or iron skillet next to each other. Bake for 10–12 minutes on the second rack of the oven.

Ham Biscuits

5 dozen baked biscuits, each the size of a 50-cent piece (see previous recipe)

¾ c butter, softened

1 small onion, finely chopped

2 tbsp poppy seeds

2–3 tsp Dijon mustard

1 lb shaved ham

Split the baked biscuits. Mix together the butter, onion, poppy seeds, and mustard. Spread the bottom halves of the biscuits with the mixture. Top with the shaved ham. Replace the top halves of the biscuits. Arrange the biscuits in a basket or on a platter and serve immediately, or store the finished biscuits, tightly covered in foil, in the refrigerator for up to 2 days. To freeze, wrap the biscuits in foil, then place in a freezer bag. To reheat, defrost in the refrigerator overnight. Reheat biscuits from the refrigerator in the tightly wrapped foil until heated through.

Rice, prevalent in the lower coastal South, had a symbiotic relationship with slavery. Slaves from rice-growing areas of Africa had the skill, knowledge, and ability to grow rice. Hurricanes and other disasters did away with rice as a primary crop in the Carolinas by the beginning of the 19th century, although it continued to be eaten there. The primary Southern rice-growing states into the 21st century were Arkansas, Louisiana, Mississippi, Missouri, and Texas.

Corn was of extraordinary value in the South. Whether as cornbread dunked in clabber (soured milk), freshly boiled and buttered off the cob, scraped to be "creamed" in a frying pan, or fried as fritters, corn, coupled with pork, provided sustenance all year. Grits, cornmeal, and corn flour are integral by-products of ground corn. Grits are increasingly served as a dinner starch rather than at breakfast. Whole-kernel corn hominy, primarily sold canned, is rarely eaten anymore.

Louisiana developed two unique cuisines, distinct from other Southern food. The Cajun cuisine, a form of country cooking created by French Acadians, is broad and flavorful. The "holy trinity" (onions, celery, and bell pepper) and "the pope" (garlic) are its base. Its bursts of spiciness derive from the need to use what was available, from crawfish to sassafras. Creole cuisine is New Orleans city food, a sophisticated, rich mélange of Spanish, French, Italian, and African foods. The major Louisianan thickeners are roux, primarily made from slowly browning flour with vegetable oil; filé powder (ground sassafras); and okra. Hot pepper sauces, both homemade and commercial, provide an important condiment all over the South. The semi-isolated Gullahs (also known as Geechees) of Georgia and South Carolina barrier islands also have a specific cuisine, which includes many soul food dishes.

African foodstuffs brought to the South, most likely by ship captains, are beloved among the broad expanse of Southerners, without regard to color and income. The South is unlike cultures where the elite reject peasant food such as peas and beans. The legacy of poverty suffered by both races after the Civil War combined with the presence of black cooks (first as slaves, then as servants) in white middle-class homes until the late 1960s melded both cooking styles and methods of cooking with available local ingredients. Cooks had "toting" privileges, allowing them to bring excess food home, reinforcing the shared cuisine. Each race brought something to the table, one teaching baking, the other rendering lard or frying.

Race-based superior social status for whites, who could not be mistaken for black, allowed both cultures to eat the same comforting and filling foods, which have been called soul food for the last quarter century. *Chitlins* (pork intestines) were used by both blacks and whites in rural regions but have fallen in disfavor, due to the need for arduous cleaning and cooking. There are still festivals celebrating them (boiled or fried) as well as grits, peanut, oyster, shrimp, and other food festivals.

Numerous varieties of peas, descended primarily from the wild African cowpea, *Vigna unguiculata* and other species, were imported, including pigeon peas, field peas, black-eyed peas, butter peas, Crowder, zipper, leather britches, and lady peas. This was due in large part to President Thomas Jefferson's interest in them. After their original importance in feeding African slaves familiar food, they have been embraced throughout Southern food culture, with greater variety than is seen elsewhere in the United States. They are an inexpensive, important source of nutrition often combined with seasoning meat, rice, and/or hot cornbread.

The peanut (which grows under the soil and is not a nut at all) has become a significant Southern financial and nutritional asset, with worldwide dietary influence. Southerners are as likely as other Americans to eat peanut butter sandwiches and salted peanuts. Only in the South, however, do people savor freshly harvested peanuts boiled in the shell. Soybeans are a cash crop, rotated with crops such as rice and cotton, as they supplement the soil. Pole beans, a long, wide bean with a thick string, were the dominant bean until the late 20th century when smaller runner and half runner beans came into use. Other green vegetables include butter beans, broccoli (a favorite of President George Washington), brussels sprouts, cabbage, celery, asparagus, and fennel.

Turnip and collard greens remain an important source of nutrients, especially among low-income residents. The heat of the kitchen and traditional African one-pot cooking encouraged cooking tough greens and pole beans slowly on the back of the stove with a slice of smoked pork and a hot pepper. Young greens are now sautéed, braised, or even used in salads, but there is still a great affection at all income levels for the older style, eaten with cornbread, particularly when there is a nip in the air. The broth (called *pot likker*) adds nutritional value and warmth.

Root vegetables, such as turnips, carrots, Jerusalem artichokes (sunchokes), sweet potatoes, and Irish potatoes, are boiled, sautéed, baked, mashed, or grilled. Vidalia, Georgia, and Texas have developed *terroir* providing for specialty onions, sweet enough to eat out of hand. Pecans are plentiful, grown commercially primarily in Georgia, South Carolina, and Texas. Peaches are the principal stone fruit, with abundant apples, blueberries, figs, strawberries, cantaloupes and watermelons, and various plums, as well as Florida's Valencia oranges, limes, lemons, tomatoes, mangoes, other tropical fruits, and avocados. Kitchen gardens of tomatoes, beans, squash, root vegetables, and herbs have never gone out of favor.

Blue crabs, eaten from the shell or as soft shells, range from Maryland down the Atlantic coast to the Gulf of Mexico. The three varieties of shrimp change with temperature, depth, and latitude. Their flavor varies with the marshes, bayous, and waterways where they feed. Oysters, farm-raised mussels, and clams from many coves add to the available shellfish, as does the Florida snow crab. A wide array of round and flat fish include sea bass, sea trout, grouper, flounder, and varieties of snapper. Sturgeon is nearly extinct after once being plentiful. Inland lakes, ponds, and streams provide the indigenous catfish,

Platter of fried fish, cole slaw, hush puppies, and french fries. (Danny Hooks | Dreamstime)

wild and farmed. Freshwater trout, stocked by state agencies, may be found along with indigenous bass and crappie. Catfish and crawfish are both wild and farmed.

Chicken, pork, and beef remain the prevalent meats. Each part of the region has developed its own process for preserving pork, usually smoked and salted, with Virginia's the most renowned. Country ham is served thin, like an Italian prosciutto, cut into half-inch to one-inch slices for sautéing, or soaked, boiled, and then glazed in the oven.

Historically, the use of meat depended on class and income, with agrarian and less fortunate families using meat primarily as a condiment during the week and eating chicken or roasts only on Sundays. Cheaper cuts of pork, such as fat back, belly fat, hog jowls, neck, and so on, called "seasoning meats," were utilized to season vegetables and provide protein. Game is a hobby food, with quails and pigeons commercially farm-raised.

Sugarcane and sorghum developed the Southern sweet tooth—a proclivity toward sugary desserts. Sorghum "molasses" syrup was prominent from the Civil War through World War II, when less expensive refined sugars became available. Cold, carbonated, caffeinated beverages, including Coca-Cola and Dr. Pepper, found wide acceptance in the South long before becoming international. The home cook might make custards, peanut brittle, pralines, benne seed wafers, or toffee as a treat. Sweetened condensed milk was used for fudge and caramelized for a sauce, caramel being a relished flavor, as in caramel cake.

Bourbon, a whiskey that started illegally as corn moonshine, has long been an accepted part of the Southern table, whether for marinating meat, making bourbon balls for dessert, or being served with "branch water" (fresh stream water), Coca-Cola, or muddled mint, ice, and sugar in a silver mint julep cup. Kentucky whiskey is now made from a sour-mash distilled product of corn, rye, barley, and fresh limestone spring water.

In Texas, only the eastern part of the state remains oriented toward Southern food; western Texas is oriented toward Southwestern and Mexican food. Tortillas, guacamole, and salsas had become part of the Southern diet by the late 1980s, with Mexican and Hispanic food gaining in the following decades. Florida maintains a Southern cuisine in the areas close to Georgia; below that is a more Hispanic style, frequently called "Miami cuisine."

Cooking

Home cooking constantly evolves as more women have begun working. Outside cooks have disappeared in the middle-class home. Cooking duties fall primarily to women, but men are increasingly helpful. The average family shops for food once a week, with perhaps a stop for fresh milk, fruit, or a specialty item.

Grocery shopping in the South has altered significantly. A half century ago, home deliveries were made by grocery stores, and dairies, bakeries, and local neighborhood markets were found within walking distance. Today's urban large chain grocery stores and supermarkets are not easily accessible for the poor, requiring transportation. These stores sell a vast array of easily heated frozen and prepared foods; frozen and fresh fruits and vegetables; mixes for cakes, pies, biscuits, and breads; one-pot dinners; and other convenience foods. Many poultry or meat products are premarinated and sold in easily cooked, boneless cuts.

Distribution of locally grown products has expanded through local farmers' markets and acceptance by some grocery stores. Typical homes have a stovetop with four burners, an oven, a microwave, and a refrigerator with a freezer and ice maker, as well as a hot/cold-water sink. A dishwasher is found in most middle-class homes. The disadvantaged utilize electric hot plates, portable ovens, a sink with inadequate hot water, and a secondhand refrigerator.

Braising, boiling, steaming, roasting, and sautéing are the prevalent methods of cooking. Virtually no deep-frying occurs in the middle-class home. The iron skillet is associated with Southern cooking even if not used to the same degree as nonstick pans. Baking pans, saucepans, and frying pans, along with a variety of knives, measuring cups, teaspoons, tablespoons, and wooden spoons, remain. Measures are taken with measuring cups (in ounces) and measuring spoons (the largest, a tablespoon, is equal to three teaspoons). Nearly every home has a grill, whether outside or built into the stove, grill pans, or small electric grills. Men typically do the outdoor grilling.

Typical home evening meals include fresh or frozen vegetables, a starch, and a meat, with an occasional meatless pasta or rice meal. Everything is served at one time rather than in courses. Soups, both commercially prepared and fresh, are frequently served as an entrée rather than a starting dish, perhaps with a salad and crackers, biscuits, cornbread, or yeast rolls, for lunch or dinner.

Typical Meals

Three meals a day is the norm, with morning and afternoon snacks and, after dinner, chips, cookies, and/or ice cream while watching television before bedtime. Cereals for breakfast, skim milk, sandwiches, and low-calorie salad dressings are daily norms, with few elaborate breakfasts at home. The occasional Sunday breakfast with fried eggs, featherlight biscuits or hotcakes, and country ham sautéed in a frying pan with its pan (red-eye) gravy poured over hot grits is a treat.

The goal of most home cooks is to prepare and serve the dinner meal in 45 minutes, preferably less. Families try to eat together, but middle-class children have many activities, making shared mealtimes difficult. Chicken breasts are a favorite meat because of the ease of preparation. Boneless or marinated legs and thighs are a distant alternative. Other quick-cooking favorites are pork tenderloins and scaloppini, shrimp pilaf, crawfish, ground beef, steaks, and an occasional stir-fry. The amount of deep-frying has decreased considerably in the last 40 years. Coastal areas eat much more seafood, and mountain and inland people have eaten more freshwater or frozen fish until the last 25 years, as transportation has improved.

Meals are eaten with knife, fork, and spoon, and paper or cloth napkins are used. Food is served either from the stove or family style in serving bowls where individuals serve themselves. Homemade desserts are rare during the week, with the exception of cake or brownies from a mix. Many families batch-cook on weekends, preparing stews, roasts, gumbos, chicken and dumplings (made from biscuit dough

A typical country breakfast made up of grits and biscuits. (iStockPhoto)

or pasta) or other soup meals, meat loaves and other items made from ground beef, macaroni and cheese, or roasted chicken or chicken parts that will provide several meals. "Scratch" baking is usually done on the weekends.

During the week commercial loaf bread, cornbread, or freezer-to-oven biscuits are eaten with meals. Once every week or two, pizza, a Chinese meal, barbecue, or fried chicken might be purchased (or delivered) to eat at home. Cooked rotisserie chickens from the grocery store are used as they are, or the cooked meat is incorporated into other dishes such as soups, stews, and salads.

Eating Out

The Civil Rights Act of 1964, which outlawed racial discrimination at restaurants and interstate accommodations, was pivotal in changing the South's social structure. Prior to this time, by state law or custom, white-only restaurants predominated, whether lunch counters at the Woolworth's dime store serving tuna salad sandwiches or Continental restaurants with escargot. Clubs were segregated.

African Americans had separate facilities and clubs. After integration, previously black-only barbecues and soul food restaurants reached a new national appeal, with black Southern music forms such as jazz and the blues paving the way for increasing social interaction. The opening up of social accommodations not only broke social barriers, especially among young adults, but also created stronger recognition of the biracial heritage of Southern food. The act also outlawed employment discrimination. With blacks and whites beginning to work together as equals in the workplace they not only sat together at restaurants but also engaged in lively conversation and recognized the commonality of their food.

Money earned by blacks employed in previously white-only jobs resulted in a larger market for goods and services, and African Americans supplied an experienced workforce for a growing economy in the 20th century's final 30 years, helping to fuel eating out for blacks and whites in the new fast-food restaurants. The enhanced economic growth, together with black withdrawal from domestic work, led to more whites eating out. This opened the way for development of a new and lighter Southern cuisine, using local products and classic European cooking techniques.

Every sizable Southern city historically had at least one popular Greek restaurant. Chain and other diners, such as Waffle Houses at interstate highway exits, are highly patronized, most serving grits all day long as a breakfast or side dish. Bistro and fine-dining restaurants have multiplied, stressing fresh local ingredients and fresh-caught seafood as well as making their own charcuteries. "Family" restaurants provide inexpensive choices, allowing each member of a family to order his or her preferred meal. Southern ingredients are cooked in new as well as traditional ways. Fried seafood restaurants, even in coastal areas, frequently import seafood and sell it cheaply. Buffet restaurants are primarily Southern and economical.

Barbecue is one of the most beloved foods. Barbecue restaurants, whether primarily carryout or sit down, are known for their specialty ingredients. On the East Coast, shredded pork barbecue is the norm; moving westward toward Tennessee, ribs become more popular. Further west, barbecues are most often beef.

Special Occasions

Barbecues are prominent on the Fourth of July, Independence Day. Ideally, a whole pig is cooked in a pit, called a "six-pack pit" as it takes two men one six-pack of beer to dig the pit. The butterflied pig, wired to a rack, cooks slowly all night over an open fire, swabbed with local versions of sauce. After much of the meat and crispy skin have been removed and chopped, eaters vie for any leftover meat clinging to the bones. It is served with coleslaw, potato salad, Brunswick stew, and white bread. Homemade cakes are set out on a large table, along with peach ice cream ready to go on top.

Wedding receptions historically serve cheese straws; crustless cucumber, chicken salad, or pimento cheese sandwiches; and tiny ham biscuits. The low country adds hot shrimp and grits. When a death occurs, neighbors, friends, and family bring covered dishes as they would to a church picnic, and the food is left accessible for whoever drops by, with a preponderance of hams, fried chicken, and cakes. After the funeral food is frequently served at the place of worship.

Coastal families may grill or bake whole snapper or other ocean fish for Thanksgiving, or serve an oyster stuffing in roast turkey, while other areas add ham to the table. A wide range of vegetables is available in bowls on the table. At Christmas, Latino communities serve *lechón de Navidad,* a pit-roasted pig stuffed with sour oranges, garlic, lemons, and rosemary. Coastal communities serve oyster stew on Christmas Eve, with other communities serving sliced ham or turkey. Cured hams make their appearance during Christmas and New Year's Eve, with less-salty processed hams taking more of a modern role.

Black-eyed peas are eaten on New Year's Eve, usually combined with rice and called *hoppin' John,* as a sign of good luck, in part because, when the Union soldiers foraged Southern gardens and foodstuffs during the Civil War, they spurned the peas that helped keep Southerners alive, both black and white. Traditionally, cooked turnips or collard greens foretell "green backs" (dollars) all year long.

Mardi Gras is elaborately celebrated in Louisiana. Kings cake, which has a tiny baby (once a piece of jewelry) inserted as a surprise, is a ritual. The main Easter meal is served midafternoon, a throwback to when dinner was served at three o'clock or later in the afternoon in high society such as in Charleston. Ham (rather than fresh lamb), asparagus, fresh local lettuces for salads, and a daffodil or other cake are served.

Diet and Health

The American South has the highest rate of obesity in the United States. Despite much talk about curtailing sugar, salt, and fat, the South's middle class complicates this by dietary inconsistency, spurning low-fat seasoning meat such as smoked neck in vegetables and instead cooking bacon with brown sugar or adding sugar-laden products to a barbecue sauce. Hidden calories in condiments such as tomato sauce and prepared foods are frequently ignored, as are visible calories in starchy vegetables such as baked potatoes with sour cream.

Although the rising obesity among the poor is attributed to unhealthy home cooking—frying a pork chop, for instance, or seasoning meat in the vegetables—snacking and frequent eating in fast-food restaurants with more calories in less-filling foods are more likely the culprit. Fresh fruits and vegetables, as well as meat lower in fat, are expensive out of season. Small neighborhood grocery stores accommodating the poor tend to be more expensive or have been supplanted by stores attached to gasoline stations, which offer high-carbohydrate snacks and canned products high in salt. Food stamps have the possibility for improved nutrition and can now be used where fresh products are available, such as farmers' markets. Fad diets abound. Yet those with access to fresh food find that eating all things in moderation not only is pleasing but also, in the long run, is healthier and reduces obesity.

Nathalie Dupree

Further Reading

Dabney, Joseph E. *Smokehouse Ham, Spoon Bread and Scuppernong Wine.* Nashville, TN: Cumberland House, 2008.

Dupree, Nathalie. *New Southern Cooking.* New York: Alfred A. Knopf, 1986.

Egerton, John. *Southern Food.* New York: Alfred A. Knopf, 1987.

Folse, John D. *The Encyclopedia of Cajun and Creole Cuisine.* Gonzales, LA: Chef John Folse, 2004.

Fowler, Damon Lee. *Classical Southern Cooking.* Salt Lake City, UT: Gibbs-Smith, 2008.

Hess, Karen. *The Carolina Rice Kitchen: The American Connection.* New York: Columbia University Press, 1981.

Long, Lucy M. *Regional American Food Culture.* Westport, CT: Greenwood Press, 2009.

Southern Foodways. http://www.southernfoodways.com/.

Taylor, John Martin. *Hoppin' John's Lowcountry Cooking.* New York: Bantam Books, 1992.

United States: The Southwest

Overview

The U.S. Southwest comprises the states of Arizona, Colorado, New Mexico, and Utah, including some parts of Texas. This region mainly comprises the Colorado Plateau, ranging between 5,000 and 8,000 feet in elevation, separated by deep canyons. In southern Arizona, the terrain drops from 2,000 feet down to the arid Arizona-Sonora Desert. As well, in northwestern Utah, the plateaus drop down into the Great Basin Desert. In short, this region is marked by both some of the hottest areas in the United States and some of the coldest.

Prehistorically, the Southwest was settled by different groups of ancestral Native Americans. The Puebloan peoples primarily concentrated in the Four Corners region and along New Mexico's Rio Grande River, supported through the practice of small-scale agriculture. Puebloan peoples subsisted on a combination of three basic foods: corn, beans, and squash. Other groups, such as the more nomadic Navajo (the Diné), Apache, and Utes, maintained a hunting and gathering lifeway, exploiting the animal and plant resources available in both the mountain and desert regions of Arizona, Utah, and New Mexico. In 1598, the first Spanish and Mexican settlers traveled from Mexico City to establish the Spanish towns of Albuquerque and Santa Fe, settling in northern New Mexico. The Spaniards brought with them European fruits, vegetables, and grains, including wheat, orchard fruits, grapes, and other Old World grains. As well, they introduced domesticated animals, including cattle, horses, sheep, goats, and pigs. Early Spanish and Mexican expansion into Texas gave rise to the Tejano culture and ancestral traditions that characterize South Texas. As a result, South Texas shares common foods and food traditions with the Mexican ranching families of New Mexico and southern Arizona.

By the early 1800s, Anglo traders and explorers established contacts in the Southwest, and following the Mexican-American War in 1846, Mexico ceded all lands between Texas and the Pacific Ocean to the United States. Anglo settlers and ranchers brought with them the tradition of cattle ranching and small-scale dryland farming. Incorporating regional food traditions, Anglo settlers also introduced new foods and cooking methods that came to characterize a recognized "cowboy" cuisine. While cowboy cuisine may characterize what is more commonly recognized as a Western cuisine, these peoples and their foodways comprise both historical and modern components of the food culture of the Southwest. West Texas shares the ranching tradition that marks the regions of eastern New Mexico and Arizona, a lifeway that gave rise to cowboy cuisine.

During the early 20th century, many Mexicans temporarily immigrated to the Southwest under the Bracero Program, and since the end of this program, Mexican immigrants have continued to settle in the U.S. Southwest, bringing with them new cultural practices, regional variations in Spanish language, and different foodways. This influence is expressed more in the foodways of southern Arizona and New Mexico.

Many Americans associate Southwestern cuisine with Mexican food, grouping together a set of intraregional foodways that mark cultural and ethnic differences within the Southwest. The food cultures of the Southwest more accurately reflect the history of the region, bringing together Native Americans, Spanish and Mexican settlers, Anglo ranchers, and, more recently, Mexican national immigrants. In general, Southwestern food cuisine reflects a fusion of different cultural groups and their respective foodways. It is characterized by extensive use of beef and pork, chili, pinto beans, rice, and corn.

Yet, within the region, important differences persist. While the rest of the United States may group these different intraregional cuisines together, no discussion sparks more fervor than those surrounding the use of certain spices, chilies, and/or beans. Southwestern cuisine in Arizona is influenced by indigenous foodways, Anglo ranching cuisine, and Sonoran food traditions. New Mexican cuisine is much simpler than Mexican cuisine, grounded in the combination of beef, green chili, potatoes, and/or corn. In contrast with Tejanos, New Mexicans cook with a basic combination of onion, garlic, and small amounts of oregano, not using cumin or jalapeño chilies to the degree that their eastern neighbors do. Tex-Mex is consumed in the areas of western and southern Texas, reflecting the culinary adaptations of Mexican American immigrants. Tex-Mex cuisine is marked by extensive use of beef, pinto beans, cheese, red chili, and cumin in the red chili sauces. Tex-Mex cooks may opt for the shortcut chili gravy, that is, canned red chili or enchilada sauce, to season their dishes. In the Southwest, how one prepares "Southwestern" cuisine represents an important marker of ethnic identity, both reinforcing solidarity within a group and marking distinctive boundaries between others.

Green Chili Sauce

Ingredients

½ c vegetable oil

2 cloves garlic, minced

1 c onion, minced

1 tbsp flour

2 c chicken broth

2 c diced green chili (hot, preferably)

Salt to taste

Sauté garlic and onion in oil in saucepan. Blend in flour. Add broth and green chili. Bring to a boil and simmer, stirring frequently, for 5–8 minutes.

Green Chili Enchiladas

Serves 2

Ingredients

6 corn tortillas

2 tbsp vegetable oil

1 clove garlic

2 c green chili sauce (previous recipe)

1 tbsp flour

2 c grated cheddar or Monterey Jack cheese

¼ c minced onion

Heat the tortillas on a griddle, and keep warm under a kitchen towel. Heat the garlic in the oil, then discard garlic. Blend flour into the oil. Stir in green chili sauce, and heat thoroughly. If mixture is too thick, add water or chicken broth. Add salt to taste. Layer tortillas with sauce, minced onion, and cheese on ovenproof plates. Sprinkle cheese on top. Place in oven to allow cheese to melt. For an authentic New Mexican touch, place a fried egg on top.

🍽️ Food Culture Snapshot

In her village in northern New Mexico, Doña Manuela Luján rises early on the morning of Christmas Eve, noticing that the snow has continued to fall all night and now covers the neighboring mountains. Despite the cold and continuing snowfall, she hurriedly carries dry wood outside to her adobe oven, her *horno,* located in the patio behind her home. She checks on the red chili tamales she prepared yesterday, carefully stacked on the back porch where they froze overnight.

Once she starts the fire in the outdoor oven, she returns to her kitchen to make the bread from the dough she left rising the night before. She divides the dough into two parts, one part for the bread and one part for the traditional sweet rolls, the *molletes.* She shapes the bread dough into loaves, leaving them to rise in the pans. Turning to the sweet rolls, she separately beats eggs, sugar, aniseed, and lard to create a mixture added to the bread dough. Kneading the sweet dough, she carefully shapes the rolls, cutting a cross in the center of each roll. From the sacks of dried corn, she scoops lime-treated hominy into a boiling pot of water, leaving it to cook.

While the bread and sweet rolls bake outside in the horno, Doña Manuela turns her attention to the *bizcochitos,* anise-flavored sugar cookies traditionally made for Christmas. Starting with sugar, Doña Manuela beats fresh pig lard into the sugar, whipping the mixture to incorporate air until it approaches the consistency of whipped cream. Adding a pinch of aniseed, she then adds a mixture of whole wheat flour, salt, and baking powder. After shaping the bizcochitos by hand, she places them in the gas stove to bake, now turning to make the empanadas, which are meat pastries. She mixes the filling from cooked meat, cooked dried apples, cinnamon, ground cloves, ginger, molasses, and raisins. Leaving the mixture to cook on the stove, Doña Manuela rolls out the pastry dough, cutting the rounds for the empanadas.

As the sun disappears below the horizon, she hears children singing as they process through the village. Stopping at her door, they sing a hymn, recreating the tradition of the *posadas,* in which Joseph and Mary searched for lodging in Bethlehem. She invites the children in to share in the molletes, bizcochitos, and sweet rolls, all representing traditional symbols of Christmas gifts.

After the children leave, Doña Manuela goes to her storeroom to take dried red chili pods from the strands that hang in storage. She removes the stems and seeds, washing the pods; she then adds the chili, oregano, salt, garlic, and onion to the *posole* stew. Bringing the frozen tamales in from the back porch, Doña Manuela stacks them carefully in the tamale cooker, leaving them to steam. Bundling her coat and scarf around her to protect against the winter cold, she hurries to the church for Christmas Eve midnight mass. Gathering around the bonfires outside the church, friends and family greet each other, wishing each other happiness for the season. Later, following mass, the family and extended kin return for an early Christmas breakfast of empanaditas, posole, and tamales.

Major Foodstuffs

For many Americans, Southwestern cuisine is characterized by some combination of corn, beans, chili, and/or meat. Within this complex of foods, the intraregional variation in cuisines is constructed by different combinations of similar ingredients. For the Southwesterner, these apparently subtle differences in types of beans, or the method of preparing chili, for example, represent important markers that distinguish intraregional cuisines. These seemingly slight differences in ingredients are neither minor nor trivial. As some Mexican cooks in southern New Mexico will say, "Ahora es cuando el chile verde le ha de dar el sabor al caldo" (Now is when the green chili gives the flavor to the soup).

Corn historically represented the most important food throughout the Southwest. For Native Americans, corn has comprised the dietary staple and provided the central ingredient in many regional dishes.

Some typical sauces from the Southwest, including green chile, guacamole, and mole. (Dreamstime)

The domestication of maize occurred in the highland regions of Mexico and Guatemala in prehistoric times, and indigenous farmers first brought domesticated maize varieties into the Rio Grande Valley in about 700 A.D. Corn's important role in Native American agriculture and foodways thus led to its incorporation into important religious rituals, creation narratives, and ancestral legends. For Native Americans in the Southwest, corn came to be sacred, a symbolic representation of their ancestral mother and the essence of culture itself. Prayers are offered to the corn, in order to ensure the plant's maturity and productivity. Once harvested, corn is used in different forms in traditional ceremonies, including the plant, the seed, and the corn pollen.

Across the Southwest, five different varieties of corn predominate: blue, white, red, yellow, and speckled. Blue, red, and speckled corn are more commonly associated with the foodways of the Puebloan peoples, including both the Rio Grande Pueblos and the Western Pueblos, including Hopi and Zuni. Blue corn is traditionally used in baking, stews, and traditional breads, such as the Hopi *piki*. Red corn is used stews and parched corn, while speckled corn is used in a range of baked goods.

When the Spaniards arrived in New Mexico, they brought European foods with them, but they also incorporated corn into their diet, reflecting both the influences from Mexico and shared foodways with indigenous peoples. Corn was incorporated into some of the most traditional Hispanic dishes of the region, including the hominy used in posole and *chicos,* which are small dried kernels of corn, used in stews in northern New Mexico. Unlike Mexican cooks to the south, neither Spanish settlers in New Mexico nor Mexican settlers in Arizona or Texas used corn in tortillas, preferring flour tortillas to accompany meals.

Beans were first domesticated in Mesoamerica, and indigenous farmers spread the common pinto bean throughout the Southwest in prehistoric times. Pinto beans are commonly used throughout different regional cuisines of the Southwest, readily adopted by Spanish and Anglo settlers. Among different Native American groups, a wide variety of beans, including white, blue, red, yellow, and multicolored ones, were used through the prehistoric and historic periods, although their use has declined in modern times. In the Arizona desert, the Tohono O'odham used the tepary bean, known for its drought tolerance. In more recent times, Arizona chefs and food activists have incorporated tepary beans into regional dishes in an effort to revive consumption of indigenous beans. As well, in prehistoric and historic times, the Tohono O'odham of the Arizona desert, the Mescalero Apache of New Mexico, and different Native American groups in Texas gathered wild mesquite beans for consumption. In Hopi and Rio Grande Pueblo dishes, beans are often combined with corn or squashes in the same dish to construct simple vegetable stews.

In their migrations from the Mexican interior, Spanish and Mexican settlers brought with them the acquired taste for pinto beans. In northern New Mexican cuisine, both the pinto bean and the *bolita,* a round, light brown bean, are used interchangeably in preparing beans, while the pinto bean is more commonly used throughout Arizona and Texas. Across Mexican and Mexican American cuisines in the Southwest, pinto beans are usually prepared separately; that is, they accompany the main dish. Thus, the chili with beans first prepared by the historic chili queens on the downtown plaza of San Antonio represented a historic creation, a culinary strategy to stretch a meat-based dish. In addition, Spanish and Mexican settlers in the Southwest brought with them the beans and pulses of the Old World, in particular, garbanzo beans and lentils. In the cuisines, these foods are now more often associated with dishes consumed during the Lenten period, when devout Catholics abstain from eating meat.

Chili peppers of the *Capsicum* genus are widely used throughout the Southwest, although the different varieties characterize regional diversity. In southern Arizona and northern Sonora, chiltepins, small wild chili peppers, are found in the protected transition zone between the desert and mountain ranges. These extremely hot, small red chilies were used by indigenous populations to add flavor and spice to vegetable dishes. In addition to using chilies as a food spice, Native American women put the hot chili pepper powder on their nipples to initiate weaning in their toddlers. In modern times, chiltepins may be dried, crushed, and then sprinkled judiciously over soups and stews. Reflecting a history of Mexican migration from Sonora, Arizonan cuisine more often includes the use of milder Mexican chilies, such the Mexican poblano and dried ancho.

In New Mexico, the Anaheim chili is used, a long, varied, narrow chili, used both as a fresh green chili and, once ripened, as a dry red chili. Green chilies are traditionally roasted, to peel off the outer skin and leave the meaty flesh. Green chili sauces are simple, comprised primarily of green chili. In contrast, red chili sauces may be made from either fresh chili, dried red chili, or dried chili that has been ground to a powder. In either case, the cook will often add thickeners, such as flour, and other spices, including ground cumin and/or oregano, to the final sauce. In Texas, jalapeño chilies are more often used in dishes and stews, reflecting culinary influences from Mexican immigrants.

Of the domesticated vegetables, squash represented the most important food in the Native American diet. Along the Rio Grande and in northern Arizona, Native American farmers grew primarily winter squash, such as varieties of pumpkins, acorn, cushaw, and gourd squashes. These squashes were grown for their edible seeds and fruits, as well as to be used as tools and containers. When the Spaniards arrived, they brought with them the summer squashes, also known as *calabacitas,* which were commonly used in the stews and sautéed dishes of Mexican cuisine. As well, Spaniards introduced new vegetables and fruits, such as tomatoes, melons, and cantaloupes, which were quickly incorporated into Native American foodways.

In addition to domesticated plants, wild-gathered plants also contributed important foods to the Native American diet. In the Arizona desert, the Tohono O'odham harvested juice from the saguaro cactus and gathered fruits from the prickly pear and cholla cactus. In cooler climates at higher altitudes, Native Americans of northern Arizona and northern New Mexico seasonally gathered wild greens, such as lamb's-quarter, mustard, wild mint, purslane, and wild onions. When the Spaniards arrived, they often incorporated these greens, known also as *verdolagas* or *quelites,* into stews and vegetable dishes.

During the prehistoric period, Native Americans acquired meat through hunting, incorporating small amounts of wild game and small animals into their diet. Grounded in indigenous beliefs in animal spirits, Native American hunters ceremonially sought the permission of animal spirits before killing animals. The meat of large game, such as elk or bison, was usually dried into a jerky, while smaller animals, such as jackrabbits or cottontails rabbits, were normally used in stews or grilled. Wild birds and fish also represented an occasional protein source in indigenous diets.

With the arrival of the Spaniards and Anglos, European food plants and animals also became part of the Southwestern foodways. Old World domesticated animals were integrated into Southwestern foodways, including, in particular, sheep, cattle, goats, and pigs. As the Diné adopted a subsistence pattern of herding sheep, lamb, or mutton, became a more common meat item in their stews and other dishes.

In dishes that include meat, beef is most common across the Southwest in general, but preparation methods vary significantly by region. In the Arizona desert, the Tohono O'odham traditionally dried meat in the sun, producing a dried meat flesh that required no refrigeration. Adopted by American soldiers and trappers, this product became beef jerky; for the Mexicans, the dried beef became *carne seca,* or dried beef.

Cooking

Throughout the Southwest, the most common cooking methods include sautéing, deep-frying, and stewing, that is, stovetop methods that reflect ancestral traditions of cooking over an open fire. Sautéing normally begins by gently frying some combination of onion, garlic, chili, and/or herbs in oil, to which vegetables or meat are then added for longer, gentler cooking. Different flavors in the sauces are thus created by different combinations of standard food ingredients.

As a cooking method, deep-frying was introduced in historic times and is more commonly used in the preparation of snack foods, such as fry bread or sopaipillas, or Mexican foods more commonly recognized as snack foods in Mexico, such as *taquitos,* more commonly known as rolled tacos throughout the Southwest, or chiles rellenos.

Stewing is a cooking method that draws on the tradition of Mexican *caldillos,* combining red or green chili with meat and, often, some combination of vegetables. Prepared through long hours of stovetop simmering, these dishes served to both stretch meat among many family members and use vegetables seasonally available from household gardens. In the Southwest, stews are traditionally seasoned simply, usually based on an initial sauté of onion, garlic, and chili.

In general, baking is not a preferred method of preparing most food dishes. Baking is specifically limited to the preparation of breads, cookies, or empanadas, foods that are often associated with special occasions or feast days. The Spaniards first introduced the earthen oven, the horno, to the Pueblo Indians during the colonial period. The horno is located outside the residence, and Puebloan peoples will often place one to four hornos together, so that bakers may work together in preparing bread for community feasts. In Hispanic households, baking empanadas or cookies, in particular, bizcochitos, often marked the beginning of the Christmas season.

Typical Meals

Historically in the region, most farming and ranching households would consume three to five meals a day, with the main meal at midday. In modern times, most people eat three meals a day, with dinner in the evening being the main meal of the day. The following are examples of typical meals in middle-class families in seven different regions of the Southwest.

In the Arizona-Sonoran household, a traditional dinner might center on *machaca,* a meat stew made of reconstituted dried beef jerky, stewed with mild chilies and tomatoes until the meat is soft and shreds easily. The meat's smoky flavor is enhanced by marinating it in garlic and citrus juices, followed by hours of sun-drying. Accompanying this stew would be huge white flour tortillas found only in Sonora and Arizona, often measuring up to 16 inches across. More recently, Arizonans have become accustomed to the infamous chimichanga, a burrito comprised of a flour tortilla wrapped around machaca and then deep-fried. Various restaurants in border towns, including Tucson and Nogales, all claim to have invented the chimi, as it is affectionately known in Arizona.

In a traditional Tohono O'odham household, the dinner meal of vegetable stew would include tepary beans, similar to pinto beans, and a particular O'odham squash, both adapted to desert climates. Accompanied by a juice or fruit ade made of prickly pear cactus, these foods are characteristically low glycemic, thus metabolizing slowly in the body and controlling blood sugar levels.

Southern New Mexican regional cuisine has been more heavily influenced by Mexico. Thus, a typical dinner meal would include red chili enchiladas, usually including chunks of beef or pork, often topped with grated cheese. These enchiladas would be prepared in a casserole-style baking dish and then baked in the oven. As a main dish, enchiladas would be accompanied by refried pinto beans and Mexican-style rice. The rice is prepared by first sautéing it in vegetable oil before it is cooked in chicken broth combined with a blend of tomatoes, garlic, and onion. The sautéing gives the prepared rice a bite that distinguishes the rice from the soupier Tex-Mex rice.

In northern New Mexico, Hispanic families might partake of green chili stew for dinner, a thick stew comprised of chopped, roasted green chili, cubed meat (either beef or pork), and small chunks of potatoes. In more rural and traditional households, this stew might contain chicos, small dried corn kernels, harvested from a traditional, small-kerneled corn still grown throughout northern New Mexico. Accompanying the green chili stew would be white flour tortillas, warmed on the griddle and served folded beneath the bowl. For dessert, under special circumstances, families might have sopaipillas, a small square of fried bread, hot and puffy, with honey drizzled over it.

Among the Rio Grande Pueblos of northern New Mexico, including also the more western Pueblos, such as Zuni or Hopi, dinner might include a meat-based stew of either beef or mutton, which would

Texas-style chili con carne, now recognized as the official dish of Texas. (Dreamstime)

contain vegetables such as corn and squash. In general, vegetable and meat stews in Native American communities are milder, not including the spices and chili that characterize stews in Mexican or Mexican American households.

In West Texas, a rural family might sit down to a beef stew, also known as chuckwagon stew, or chili con carne, made with ground beef, tomatoes, red chili powder, and beans, accompanied by sourdough biscuits. In South Texas, dinner might consist of Texas-style chili con carne, now recognized as the official dish of Texas. In this region of the Southwest, chili is a stew of small pieces of beef, cooked in a broth of red chili. The red chili pods are boiled, peeled, chopped, and then liquefied in a broth. Lazy cooks may prepare the red broth with chili powder, but true chili aficionados can recognize the difference readily. Historically, in San Antonio, pinto beans were added to the chili as a means of stretching the stew. In the

late 1800s, Mexican American women, known as the "chili queens," traditionally prepared chili stew in San Antonio's downtown plaza in the evenings. Patrons would gather to sup on red chili stew and large flour tortillas, entertained as well by strolling mariachi musicians. In 1937, the San Antonio health department imposed new sanitary regulations on the chili stalls, effectively shutting them down permanently.

Eating Out

Historically, dining out was never common throughout the Southwest. During the 1800s, for travelers and traders throughout the West, small establishments offered lodging and sustenance for nonlocals. Some of the earliest restaurants in Arizona, New Mexico, and Texas were originally established as stage stops along major routes from the East to California. In modern times, restaurants are evaluated by a discerning clientele, critiqued for the freshness of their tortillas, the heat of the chili, and the flavor of the salsas. Loyalties to different establishments are deep-seated and earnest, reflecting a discernment of taste developed through many years of savoring homemade and locally prepared food. While fast-food "Mexican" establishments abound, locals continue to patronize traditional, locally owned restaurants. However, across the board, local Southwestern restaurants are characterized by reasonably priced food.

For many Southwesterners, Santa Fe, New Mexico, represents a foreign world, populated by movie stars, artists, visiting dignitaries, and wealthy tourists. Although Santa Fe is recognized as one of culinary capitals of the world, most regional residents find little connection between the foodways of their ancestral heritage and Santa Fe's nouvelle cuisine. Grounded in the creative combination of traditional Southwestern ingredients and standards from other cuisines, Santa Fe dinners are both a delight for the eye and an experience in unique and unusual flavor combinations. While taking relatives visiting from outside the Southwest to Santa Fe, a visiting Southwesterner might partake of foie gras flavored with figs and chili and honey-grilled giant shrimp, followed by a main dish of peppered elk tenderloin.

Snack foods have been commonly consumed in the Southwest since prehistoric times. Among Native Americans, grains and seeds provided the basis of foods that could be carried over long distances. In historic times, foods such as pumpkin seeds, roasted piñon (pine) nuts, parched corn, and dried desert fruits have become more commonly recognized as snack foods.

Among Mexican and Mexican American populations in southern Arizona, southern New Mexico, and South Texas, snack foods draw on the rich heritage of Mexican cuisine. Tortilla-based food items, such as gorditas, taquitos, and chimichangas, among others, are widely available at evening food stands, at take-out establishments, and, as fresh processed items, in every grocery store. Most famous is the traditional burrito, a large flour tortilla wrapped around ingredients including either chopped meat flavored with red chili or mashed refried pinto beans accompanied by grated cheese. Popular folk legend attributes the burrito's creation to taco vendors during the Mexican Revolution in Ciudad Juárez, Chihuahua, located across the U.S.-Mexican border from El Paso, Texas, who offered "wrapped" snacks to urban patrons. Along this border region, including southern New Mexico and West Texas, burritos may comprise a wide range of different kinds of meat, including shredded beef (*deshebrada*), pork with mole, beef stomach, tripe, and/or tongue.

Special Occasions

In this region, special foods are served both for community or family feast celebrations and for public consumption, reflecting the long tradition of tourism in the Southwest. Within the Native American community, during feast days, the meals are served in common dishes, with guests and family coming and going, eating and visiting, as they arrive. Some Native American communities allow tourists to come and watch their traditional celebrations; other communities may ban outsiders. In cases where outsiders are allowed, feast foods, such as stews, snack foods, or special breads, may be available for purchase; in other cases, residents may invite visitors into their homes, serving them foods in compliance with their ancestral traditions. Some of the most important feast breads include piki bread and fry bread.

Piki is a tissue-thin corn wafer that is unique to the northern Pueblos. Traditionally made throughout the northern Pueblos, it is more common among the Hopi, although piki is undergoing a renaissance in specific Pueblos, in particular, Tesuque and San Ildefono. Piki may be made from blue, red, or yellow corn, depending on personal preference and the specific ceremony. Piki batter is comprised of a mixture of water, finely ground cornmeal, and small amounts of chamisa ash. The ash imparts the traditional grayish-blue color that distinguishes traditional piki. Pueblo women cook piki on traditional

A man at a traditional Native American fry bread food stall at the Gourd Show in Arizona. (StockPhotoPro)

piki stones, which are large, smooth, flat stones that have been passed down from mother to daughter for generations. The stone is heated by a prepared fire underneath. Once it reaches sizzling, the woman quickly spreads a paper-thin layer of piki batter, moving her hand quickly over the batter to smooth out lumps while at the same time avoiding burning her hand. The batter is laid on in overlapping strips, resulting in a thin paperlike wafer. The first piki is fed to the fire, as an offering, and subsequent piki sheets are either rolled or gently folded before they harden. Piki is traditionally offered to friends and family during the summer Katchina dances.

Fry bread is often served at public feast days both in the New Mexico Pueblos and on the Navajo reservation. It is a flat dough made of wheat flour, leavened with yeast or baking powder, and then deep-fried in oil, shortening, or lard. Fry bread was created during the 1880s by Native Americans from the rations (lard, flour, salt, baking powder, and powdered milk) distributed by the U.S. government. Once symbolically a starvation food product, it has since come to be a "traditional" food. Fry bread is now associated with Native American powwows, feast days, and public events. Traditionally, fry bread is served with honey or powdered sugar as a sweet. In other instances, the fry bread may be slit open and then pinto beans, ground beef, grated cheese, and/ or shredded lettuce are inserted, thus transforming it into what is known as an Indian or Navajo taco. In more recent years, fry bread has come to represent a controversial symbol of the impact of processed, high-fat foods on Native American diets, and some nutritionists allege fry bread plays a role in Native American obesity and high incidence of type 2 diabetes.

Fry Bread

Makes 6–8 large fry breads

Ingredients

3 c all-purpose flour

1 tbsp baking powder

1 tsp salt

1¼ c warm water

Extra flour for processing

Vegetable oil for frying, or lard (traditional)

Blend the flour with the baking powder and salt in a mixing bowl. Make a well in the center of the flour mixture, and pour in the warm water. Mix the flour and water with a wooden spoon. Take the dough from the bowl, and mix gently with hands on a board until dough is thoroughly mixed. Excessive kneading will make a heavy fry bread. Form into a ball. Cover dough with a kitchen towel, and let rest for 10 minutes. Place dough on a cutting board, and cut dough into 6–8 pieces. Shape and pat each piece into a disk 5–7 inches in diameter.

Place vegetable oil or lard in deep, heavy pan. Oil should be a minimum of 1 inch deep. Heat oil to about 350°F. Place formed dough gently in oil, and press down on dough as it fries so the top is submerged in the hot oil. Don't overcrowd pan. Fry until some browning occurs, approximately 2–3 minutes, then flip and fry other side. Bread is done when surface is dry to the touch and smooth.

Among Southwestern Hispanics, ceremonial foods are most often associated with important Catholic feast days throughout the liturgical calendar, including Christmas, Lent, Easter, and All Saints' Day, more recently recognized as the Día de los Muertos. These feast foods are traditionally served to extended family and friends, although they may also be available for visiting tourists.

For Christmas, both posole and tamales are traditional feast foods. Posole is a thick stew made with pork, red chili, onions, garlic, and hominy corn. In some areas of northern New Mexico, particularly among the Pueblos, a "green" or "white" posole may be more common, containing the same stew ingredients already listed except the red chili.

Tamales are made from a thick masa, that is, cornmeal dough, blended with rich pork lard to the consistency of whipped cream. Throughout most of the Southwest, tamales contain meat, usually pork, and red chili. Pre-Christmas festivities often begin with the *tamalada,* the tamale-making party, in which family and friends join as a group to make the tamales. Tamale making is labor-intensive, requiring hours of careful hand labor to construct and roll the tamales. In addition to red pork chili tamales, sweet tamales, made with a filling of brown sugar, walnuts, raisins, and spices, such as nutmeg, cinnamon, and/or ginger, may be prepared for Christmas. As well, for many Mexican immigrant and Mexican American households, tamales with dark chocolate mole are traditionally served on Christmas Eve, accompanied by hot chocolate.

Diet and Health

For many Americans, Southwestern foodways are more commonly conceptualized as a cuisine marked by the heavy use of chili, fat, and meat. In modern times, health experts have watched with alarm the increased rates of obesity and type 2 diabetes among minority populations, including both Native Americans and Latinos, in the U.S. Southwest. Pointing to the traditional foodways as a culprit, public health specialists and dieticians have proposed radical changes in traditional diets, in an attempt to head off a future health disaster. Other experts call for a more judicious analysis of the foodways of the Southwest, often citing the healthier aspects of an earlier, more traditional diet based on vegetables, complex carbohydrates, little animal fat, and no processed foods. For these food activists, drawing on the ancestral heritage of Native American, Hispanic, and Anglo frontier foodways represents an opportunity to improve diets while at the same time allowing ancestral foods to play important roles in conserving cultural heritage.

Lois Stanford

Further Reading

Abarca, Meredith. *Voices in the Kitchen: Views of Food and the World from Working-Class Mexican and Mexican American Women.* College Station: Texas A&M Press, 2006.

Arnold, Sam'l P. *Eating Up the Santa Fe Trail.* Boulder: University Press of Colorado, 1990.

Cabeza de Baca, Fabiola. *Good Life: New Mexico Traditions and Food.* 3rd ed. Santa Fe: Museum of New Mexico Press, 2005.

Cabeza de Baca, Fabiola. *We Fed Them Cactus.* 2nd ed. Albuquerque: University of New Mexico Press, 1994.

Counihan, Carole. *A Tortilla Is Like Life: Food and Culture in the San Luis Valley of Colorado.* Austin: University of Texas Press, 2009.

Dent, Huntley. *Feast of Santa Fe: Cooking of the American Southwest.* New York: Simon & Schuster, 1993.

DeWitt, Dave. *Cuisines of the Southwest: An Illustrated Food History with More Than 160 Regional Recipes.* Phoenix, AZ: Golden West, 2008.

Dunmire, William W., and Gail D. Tierney. *Wild Plants of the Pueblo Province: Exploring Ancient and Enduring Uses.* Santa Fe: Museum of New Mexico Press, 1995.

Foster, Nelson, and Linda S. Cordell, eds. *Chiles to Chocolate: Foods the Americas Gave the World.* Tucson: University of Arizona Press, 1992.

Frank, Lois Ellen. *Foods of the Southwest: Indian Nations.* Berkeley, CA: Ten Speed Press, 2002.

Jamison, Cheryl Alters. *The Border Cookbook: Authentic Home Cooking of the American Southwest and Northern Mexico.* Cambridge, MA: Harvard Common Press, 1995.

Janer, Zilkia. *Latino Food Culture.* Westport, CT: Greenwood Press, 2008.

Kavena, Juanita Tiger. *Hopi Cookery.* Tucson: University of Arizona Press, 1980.

Long, Lucy M. *Regional American Food Culture.* Westport, CT: Greenwood Press, 2009.

Miller, Mark. *The Great Chile Book.* Berkeley, CA: Ten Speed Press, 1991.

Muller, Frederick R. *La Comida: The Foods, Cooking, and Traditions of the Upper Rio Grande.* Boulder, CO: Pruett, 1995.

Nabhan, Gary Paul. *Renewing America's Food Traditions: Saving and Savoring the Continent's*

Most Endangered Foods. White River Junction, VT: Chelsea Green, 2008.

Romero, Regina. 1998. *Flora's Kitchen: Recipes from a New Mexico Family.* Tucson, AZ: Treasure Chest Books.

Sewell Linck, Ernestine, and Joyce Gibson Roach. *Eats: A Folk History of Texas Foods.*

Fort Worth: Texas Christian University Press, 1989.

Tausend, Marilyn. *Cocina de la Familia: More Than 200 Authentic Recipes from Mexican-American Home Kitchens.* Whitby, ON: Fireside, 1999.

Walsh, Robb. *The Tex-Mex Cookbook: A History in Recipes and Photos.* New York: Broadway, 2004.

Venezuela

Overview

The continent of South America hosts four major landscape types, from the Andean heights to the Amazonian basin, from vast central grasslands to coastal regions bordering three different oceans. Venezuela, occupying the continent's northeastern perch with 1,740 miles of Caribbean coastline, includes all four of them. And just as these landscapes differ geographically, each contributes its own particular elements to the cultural stew that is modern-day Venezuelan cuisine, including native plants, local economies, and regional traditions.

The Andean range, traveling up the continent's west coast, makes a gentle turn to the east in Colombia, then spills into the sea along Venezuela's north coast. With it comes some of the most sophisticated of pre-Columbian traditions such as terraced farming, drying as a technique of food preservation, and that all-important Andean vegetable, the potato. At the southern tip of the southernmost state, 70,000 square miles of Amazonian river basin lap across the Brazilian border into the least populated region in the country. Here, small Indian tribes hunt, fish, and farm cassava as their primary foodstuff just as their ancestors did.

The Orinoco, the second-largest river on the continent, with the third-largest water volume in the world, fertilizes vast grasslands, or *llanos,* as it travels across the country from east to west. Here, *llaneros* herd the cattle descended from those brought by the Spaniards, turning beef into an essential element of the Venezuelan diet. Finally, coastal cultures are often closer in lifestyle and food traditions to those of the Caribbean islands than to those in the country's inland areas.

Today, corn and beans remain all important, and cassava, or yucca as it is called here, is still a major ingredient. Venezuelan food culture and cuisine blend these with a hint of Africa and a powerful dose of Spain to produce its *cocina criolla.*

Food Culture Snapshot

Maria Reyes, who lives in Caracas, is thinking of the evening meal as she studies the empty pantry shelf where the bag of *masarepa* used to sit. She had better take immediate action, or there will be no arepas for dinner. The Venezuelan equivalent of tortillas, these pillow-like rounds are an absolute necessity. A trip to the market is in order. While she is out, she might as well pick up a week's worth of supplies.

In busy Caracas, the nearby supermarket is the best place to fill up on bulk products, but Maria is a good bargainer and can get better prices on meat and produce at the traditional market down the street. Here she can compare quality, and, in a worldly city like Caracas, the riotous displays of food connect her to the countryside far more than the grocery stores or fancy food shops.

Before she proceeds to the produce stalls, she stops to replenish her all-important supply of black beans, so important in Venezuelan cuisine that they are popularly known as *criollo caviar.* She loads up on onions, garlic, tomatoes, and bell peppers to make a week's worth of *sofrito,* a sauté, soup, or stew base. A package of presoaked cassava goes into her basket along with a bunch of plantains and a couple of pounds of potatoes. She grabs several bunches of cilantro, then thoughtfully selects the freshest vegetables she can find. The spinach, green beans, and eggplant all look good.

Maria visits the meat vendors to pick out both pork and beef. Pork is the family's favorite, but beef stays good and cheap thanks to local production in the llanos. She moves to a cheese stall to pick out some soft native cheese for breakfast arepas. Nearby are the fruit stalls piled high with mangoes, papayas, cherimoyas, soursops, and guavas. She selects a few of each, adds some avocados for *guasacaca,* the Venezuelan equivalent of guacamole, and, with a basket filled to bursting, heads toward home, a week's menu already worked out in her head.

Major Foodstuffs

Strong as the influence of Spain has been on the way Venezuelans eat, it is more visible in the cities than the countryside, among the wealthy than the poor, and during holidays and special events than every day. Imported ingredients such as olives, capers, wine, and spices signal the Spanish influence and are found mostly in the cities and at holiday times. Wheat, also a Spanish gift, plays a similar role since its flour is more expensive than corn products, though wheat breads are very popular.

Corn and beans still form the backbone of the rural diet and remain central to urban foodways as well. Arepas, made from processed corn flour, still accompany almost every meal, and fresh corn kernels along with local cheese are often mixed into wheat flour to make *cachapas,* a favorite pancake. Whole corncob chunks are incorporated into hearty stews, or *sancochos.*

Except in the llanos, country dwellers eat less meat than city dwellers do, and, because pigs are easy to raise at home, the meat is more likely to be pork than beef. Llaneros, like the gauchos of Argentina, herd their cattle freely over the grasslands and continue the tradition of slaughtering an entire cow to roast over a fire. Meanwhile, the diet of the Amazon remains relatively unchanged from pre-Hispanic times.

Cachapas, which are corn dough patties filled with cheese. This is a popular food item in Columbia and Venezuela. (iStockPhoto)

Cooking

At the time of the Spanish conquest in the early 16th century, most of Venezuela's population was organized into disparate farming communities subsisting on corn, yucca, beans, and vegetables. Meals were eaten twice a day. Cooking was done by roasting, grilling, or boiling. There were no fats, and, except for the occasional treat of honey, sweets were unheard of. The rivers and oceans supplied fish, while hunters supplemented the diet with game.

While the diet may have been simple, its preparation was not. Sophisticated technology allowed cooks to keep their communities alive and healthy. They soaked, cooked, and fermented yucca to eliminate its bitter toxins. They softened corn by soaking it in wood-ash-suffused water, then ground it to make flour. In the process, they liberated otherwise-unavailable nutrients from corn, which, when combined with beans, provided their people with an adequate supply of protein.

The Spaniards not only introduced new ingredients and improved cooking implements but also brought an entirely new technology. Frying in olive oil had been an important cooking method in Spain, but olive trees did not grow well in the New World. Instead, they turned to lard. They brought a means of enhancing flavor by sautéing onions, garlic, and leeks until soft to make a sofrito before adding other ingredients to the pot. In a perfect example of the Columbian Exchange, the New World added tomatoes and peppers to the sofrito, which today flavors Venezuela's favorite dishes.

Typical Meals

Meals are usually taken twice a day in the countryside and three times in the cities. Though an increase in the pace of life has driven the urban lunch from the home to the workplace, breakfast and dinner remain relatively unchanged. Breakfast is based on bread, which can be made with wheat or, more commonly, corn flour. Arepas are a favorite, often pulled open and filled with a runny cheese somewhat like crème fraiche.

Dinner is the biggest meal of the day, a time when families gather together to enjoy several courses. Soups are usually part of the menu, and, though beans may dominate in rural meals, they are rarely absent on the tables of the wealthy. Rice is extremely popular as well. But Venezuelans love meat, poultry, and seafood, so those who can afford it usually include it in the evening meal.

Arepas

The classic bread of Venezuela is made with precooked white corn flour called masarepa, *harina precocida,* or *masa al instante.* It is not masa harina or tortilla flour. Look for it in Latin American stores under the brand name Harina P.A.N.

2 c masarepa

1 tsp salt

2 c water (approximate)

Preheat oven to 350°F.

Whisk together arepa flour with salt in a large bowl. Stir in water to make a relatively stiff dough. If mixture doesn't blend properly, add water in small increments. Let dough stand for 5 minutes, then form into balls and flatten into cakes 3 inches across and a half-inch thick.

Cook on a lightly greased griddle over moderate heat for 5 minutes to a side. Place on baking sheets, and bake for 20 to 30 minutes, turning occasionally. Fully cooked arepas sound hollow when tapped gently.

Pabellon Criollo con Caraotas Negras (Beef with Black Beans and Plantains)

Considered Venezuela's national dish, *pabellon* is truly a Creole concoction. It is always served with black beans. White rice, cooked with a simple sofrito of onions and garlic, is also essential.

Serves 6

For the Beef

1½ lb flank or skirt steak, cut to fit in a large saucepan

3 onions, one cut into large chunks, two chopped

Beef broth to cover

A woman preparing arepas, typical corn fritters of Venezuela. (StockPhotoPro)

3 tbsp olive oil

3 cloves garlic, minced

I red bell pepper, seeded and chopped

I lb fresh or canned tomatoes, peeled, seeded, and chopped

I tsp salt

Black pepper to taste

For the Beans

2 c black beans

3 tbsp olive oil

I onion, chopped

I red bell pepper, seeded and chopped

4 cloves garlic, smashed and chopped

I tsp cumin

I tsp ground sugar

Salt, pepper, and sugar to taste

For the Plantain

I ripe plantain or 2 underripe bananas

2 tbsp olive oil

Place the meat and onion chunks into a large sauce-pan and cover with beef broth. Bring to a boil over medium heat and simmer, covered, until the meat is tender, 1½ to 2 hours. Allow to cool, remove cooled meat from stock, and shred finely. Strain stock and set aside.

Heat 3 tablespoons of oil over medium heat, add shredded meat, and brown, stirring lightly. Reduce heat to medium and stir in onions, garlic, bell pepper, tomatoes, salt, and pepper. Cook, uncovered, about 20 minutes, moistening with stock if necessary to create a dense sauce. Adjust salt and pepper.

Wash and pick over the beans. Cover with cold water and soak from 4 hours to overnight. Add enough water to cover the beans by 1 inch, bring to a boil, and simmer, covered, checking periodically, until they are tender, about 2 hours. Stir more frequently toward the end to keep beans from sticking to the pot.

In a skillet, heat 3 tablespoons oil and sauté onion and bell pepper until soft. Add garlic, cumin, and

sugar, and sauté partly covered over low heat for 30 minutes. Add to the beans, cook briefly to blend flavors, and then add salt, pepper, and sugar to taste.

Just before serving, peel plantain or bananas, cut into 3 pieces, and slice each lengthways. Fry in the 2 tablespoons remaining oil over low heat, 3 minutes to a side. Arrange the beef, beans, and rice on a large platter garnished with plantain.

Eating Out

While urban workers are likely to bring lunch from home, fast food is available to anyone looking for an inexpensive meal. This doesn't just mean Mc-Donald's, though the U.S. chains are well-enough entrenched. Venezuelans today boast their own fast-food joint, the *arepera*. The country's ancient bread is split open and the doughy inner portion torn out. Then it is stuffed with all manner of beans, meats, cheeses, or stews to make *arepas rellenas*. Vendors produce them in huge quantities, wrap them in napkins, and sell them on paper plates.

Restaurants began to appear in Venezuela in the 19th century and are now well established, from unpretentious *luncherías* to fine-dining places. Many are owned by descendants of foreigners, particularly Italians, but just about any cuisine can be found in the cities, from Chinese to Indian to French.

Special Occasions

Most dining out in Venezuela is reserved for special occasions. Birthdays, engagements, anniversaries, and weddings may be celebrated at restaurants, but important holidays, community achievements, and saint's days are recognized at home. None of these is more important than Christmas and Easter.

Christmas, in addition to churchgoing, is a time for gathering and feasting with the family, usually at the home of the senior member. The pièce de résistance may be a stuffed turkey or glazed ham that looks as if it came straight off an American table, but the plate of *hallacas* beside it is all Venezuelan. Similar to Mexican tamales, these cornmeal dumplings are stuffed with sautéed meat, wrapped in banana leaves rather than corn husks, and boiled rather

Hallacas, cornmeal dumplings stuffed with sautéed meat, wrapped in banana leaves, and boiled are traditional Christmas food in Venezuela. (iStockPhoto)

than steamed. They are essential to any Christmas meal.

While many take Holy Week, or Semana Santa, as an opportunity for a vacation, others observe it quite seriously. Residents of South America add to the repertoire of accepted Lenten dishes to include amphibians, reptiles, and water-dwelling mammals. Venezuelans particularly relish the meat of the semi-aquatic capybara, the world's largest rodent, to the point where poaching is common and there is some fear that the population may be threatened.

Diet and Health

Early Spanish commentators noted the glowing good health of South America's indigenous peoples, including those of Venezuela. They talked of strong, healthy stature, shining hair, and gleaming teeth, properties soon to disappear with the deadly onslaught of foreign germs, slavery, and, as even 16th-century commentators suggested, the Spanish diet. Like all conquerors, the Spanish imported as much of their own diet as possible. In addition to new vegetables, herbs, and wheat, they brought farm animals, fat, sugar, and the expectation of three meals a day. They taught the local population to fry their foods in lard.

In terms of flavors and technology, the Spanish contribution merged with indigenous ingredients and techniques and gave birth to cocina criolla, something greater than the sum of its parts. But today the cuisines of Venezuela and other Latin American countries are much higher in fat and sugar than those of the pre-Hispanic period. Frying is widely used. Sugary sodas are as popular as fruit juices. Those with enough money now confront the evils of the Western diet. At the same time, class distinctions leave some people with too little money to buy meats, fats, and sweets in any large quantity and others with too little to eat at all. Only in the last decade have Venezuelans connected the dots between overconsumption of animal fats and ill health. Within recent years, the use of lard has declined while vegetable oils have rallied, hopefully a first step in a healthier direction.

Nancy G. Freeman

Further Reading

Cordova, Regina, and Emma Carrasco. *Celebración: Recipes and Traditions Celebrating Latino Family Life.* New York: Main Street Books, 1996.

Dineen, Mark. *Culture and Customs of Venezuela.* Westport CT: Greenwood Press, 2001.

Kijac, Maria Baez. *The South American Table: The Flavor and Soul of Authentic Home Cooking from Patagonia to Rio de Janeiro with 450 Recipes.* Boston: Harvard Common Press, 2003.

Lovera, José Rafael. *Food Culture in South America.* Westport CT: Greenwood Press, 2005.

Ortiz, Elizabeth Lambert. *The Book of Latin American Cooking.* Hopewell, NJ: Ecco Press, 1994.

Raichlen, Steven. *Healthy Latin Cooking: 200 Sizzling Recipes from Mexico, Cuba, Caribbean, Brazil and Beyond.* New York: St. Martin's Press, 1996.

Rojas-Lombardi, Felipe. *The Art of South American Cooking.* New York: Harper Collins, 1991.

"Venezuela." Recipes 4 Us. http://www.recipes4us.co.uk/Venezuelan%20Recipes.htm.

"Venezuelan Recipes." Food.com. http://www.food.com/recipes/venezuelan.

"Venezuelan Recipes." Mikel Rodriguez's Web site. http://www.cs.ucf.edu/~mikel/Recipes/Venezuelan_Recipes.htm.

About the Editor and Contributors

Ken Albala, Editor, is professor of history at the University of the Pacific in Stockton, California. He also teaches in the gastronomy program at Boston University. Albala is the author of many books, including *Eating Right in the Renaissance* (University of California Press, 2002), *Food in Early Modern Europe* (Greenwood Press, 2003), *Cooking in Europe 1250–1650* (Greenwood Press, 2005), *The Banquet: Dining in the Great Courts of Late Renaissance Europe* (University of Illinois Press, 2007), *Beans: A History* (Berg Publishers, 2007; winner of the 2008 International Association of Culinary Professionals Jane Grigson Award), and *Pancake* (Reaktion Press, 2008). He has co-edited two works, *The Business of Food* and *Human Cuisine.* He is also editor of three food series with 29 volumes in print, including the Food Cultures Around the World series for Greenwood Press. Albala is also co-editor of the journal *Food Culture and Society.* He is currently researching a history of theological controversies surrounding fasting in the Reformation Era and is editing two collected volumes of essays, one on the Renaissance and the other entitled *The Lord's Supper.* He has also coauthored a cookbook for Penguin/Perigee entitled *The Lost Art of Real Cooking,* which was released in July 2010.

Julia Abramson has visited France on a regular basis for more than 25 years to study, research, travel, and eat. She has published essays on aspects of food culture from vegetable carving to gastronomic writing and is the author of the book *Food Culture in France.* Abramson teaches French literature and culture and food studies at the University of Oklahoma, Norman.

M. Shahrim Al-Karim is a senior lecturer of food service and hospitality management at the Universiti Putra Malaysia. His research interests include food and culture, culinary tourism, food habits, and consumer behavior. He received a BS in hotel and restaurant management from New York University; an MBA from Universiti Teknologi MARA, Malaysia; and a PhD in hospitality and tourism from Oklahoma State University, United States.

E. N. Anderson is professor emeritus of the Department of Anthropology, University of California, Riverside.

Laura P. Appell-Warren holds a doctorate in psychological anthropology from Harvard University. Her primary focus of research has been the study of personhood; however, she has also studied the effects of social change on children's play. She has done research among the Bulusu' of East Kalimantan, Indonesia, and among the Rungus Momogon, a Dusunic-speaking peoples, of Sabah, Malyasia. In addition, she has traveled widely throughout Arctic Canada. She is the editor of *The Iban Diaries of Monica Freeman 1949–1951: Including Ethnographic Drawings, Sketches, Paintings, Photographs and Letters* and is author of the forthcoming volume entitled *Personhood: An Examination of the History and Use of an Anthropological Concept.* In addition to her current research on cradleboard use among Native North Americans, she is a teacher of anthropology at St. Mark's School in Southborough, Massachusetts.

Heather Arndt-Anderson is a Portland, Oregon, native who draws culinary inspiration from many world cuisines but prefers cooking from her own backyard. She is a part-time natural resources consultant and a full-time radical homemaker; in her (rare) spare time she writes the food blog *Voodoo & Sauce.*

Michael Ashkenazi is a scholar, writer, and consultant who has been researching and writing about Japanese food since 1990. In addition to books and articles on Japanese society, including its food culture, he has written numerous scholarly and professional articles and papers on various subjects including theoretical and methodological issues in anthropology, organized violence, space exploration, migration, religion and ritual, resettling ex-combatants, and small arms. He has taught at higher-education institutions in Japan, Canada, Israel, and the United Kingdom, directing graduate and undergraduate students. He is currently senior researcher and project leader at the Bonn International Center for Conversion in Germany, with responsibility for the areas of small arms and reintegration of ex-combatants. He has conducted field research in East and Southeast Asia, East and West Africa, the Middle East, and Latin America.

Babette Audant went to Prague after college, where she quickly gave up teaching English in order to cook at a classical French restaurant. After graduating from the Culinary Institute of America, she worked as a chef in New York City for eight years, working at Rainbow Room, Beacon Bar & Grill, and other top-rated restaurants. She is a lecturer at City University of New York Kingsborough's Department of Tourism and Hospitality, and a doctoral candidate in geography at the City University of New York Graduate Center. Her research focuses on public markets and food policy in New York City.

Gabriela Villagran Backman, MA (English and Hispanic literature), was born in Sweden and raised in Mexico and the United States; she currently lives in Stockholm, Sweden. She is an independent researcher, interested in food studies, cultural heritage, writing cookbooks, red wine, and the Internet.

Carolyn Bánfalvi is a writer based in Budapest. She is the author of *Food Wine Budapest* (Little Bookroom) and *The Food and Wine Lover's Guide to Hungary: With Budapest Restaurants and Trips to the Wine Country* (Park Kiado). She contributes to numerous international food and travel publications and leads food and wine tours through Taste Hungary, her culinary tour company.

Peter Barrett is a painter who writes a food blog and is also the Food & Drink writer for *Chronogram Magazine* in New York's Hudson Valley.

Cynthia D. Bertelsen is an independent culinary scholar, nutritionist, freelance food writer, and food columnist. She lived in Haiti for three years and worked on a food-consumption study for a farming-systems project in Jacmel, Haiti. She writes a food history blog, *Gherkins & Tomatoes,* found at http://gherkinstoma toes.com.

Megan K. Blake is a senior lecturer in geography at the University of Sheffield. She has published research that examines the intersections between place and social practices. While her previous work focused on entrepreneurship and innovation, her recent work has examined food practices and family life.

Janet Boileau is a culinary historian who holds a master of arts degree in gastronomy from Le Cordon Bleu Paris and a doctorate in history from the University of Adelaide.

Andrea Broomfield is associate professor of English at Johnson County Community College in Overland Park, Kansas, and author of *Food and Cooking in Victorian England: A History.*

Cynthia Clampitt is a culinary historian, world traveler, and award-winning author. In 2010, she was elected to the Society of Women Geographers.

Neil L. Coletta is assistant director of food, wine, and the arts and lecturer in the MLA in gastronomy program at Boston University. His current research includes food and aesthetics and experimental pedagogy in the field of food studies.

Paul Crask is a travel writer and the author of two travel guides: *Dominica* (2008) and *Grenada, Carriacou and Petite Martinique* (2009).

Christine Crawford-Oppenheimer is the information services librarian and archivist at the Culinary Institute of America. She grew up in Ras Tanura, Saudi Arabia.

Anita Verna Crofts is on the faculty at the University of Washington's Department of Communication, where she serves as an associate director of the master of communication in digital media program. In addition, she holds an appointment at the University of Washington's Department of Global Health, where she collaborates with partner institutions in Sudan, Namibia, and India on trainings that address leadership, management, and policy development, with her contributions targeted at the concept of storytelling as a leadership and evidence tool. Anita is an intrepid chowhound and publishes on gastroethnographic topics related to the intersection of food and identity. She hosts the blog *Sneeze!* at her Web site www.pepperforthebeast.com.

Liza Debevec is a research fellow at the Scientific Research Centre of the Slovene Academy of sciences and arts in Ljubljana, Slovenia. She has a PhD in social anthropology from the University of St. Andrews, United Kingdom. Her research interests are West Africa and Burkina Faso, food studies, Islam, gender, identity, and practice of everyday life.

Jonathan Deutsch is associate professor of culinary arts at Kingsborough Community College, City University of New York, and Public Health, City University of New York Graduate Center. He is the author or editor of five books including, with Sarah Billingsley, *Culinary Improvisation* (Pearson, 2010) and, with Annie Hauck-Lawson, *Gastropolis: Food and New York City* (Columbia University Press, 2009).

Deborah Duchon is a nutritional anthropologist in Atlanta, Georgia.

Nathalie Dupree is the author of 10 cookbooks, many of which are about the American South, for which she has won two James Beard Awards. She has hosted over 300 television shows on the Public Broadcasting Service, The Food Network, and TLC. She lives with her husband, Jack Bass, who has authored 9 books about the American South and helped with her contribution to *Food Cultures of the World*.

Pamela Elder has worked in food public relations and online culinary education and is a freelance writer in the San Francisco Bay area.

Rachel Finn is a freelance writer whose work has appeared in various print and online publications. She is the founder and director of Roots Cuisine, a non-profit organization dedicated to promoting the foodways of the African diaspora around the globe.

Richard Foss has been a food writer and culinary historian since 1986, when he started as a restaurant critic for the *Los Angeles Reader*. His book on the history of rum is slated for publication in 2011, to be followed by a book on the history of beachside dining in Los Angeles. He is also a science fiction and fantasy author, an instructor in culinary history and Elizabethan theater at the University of California, Los Angeles, Extension, and is on the board of the Culinary Historians of Southern California.

Nancy G. Freeman is a food writer and art historian living in Berkeley, California, with a passion for food history. She has written about cuisines ranging from Ethiopia to the Philippines to the American South.

Ramin Ganeshram is a veteran journalist and professional chef trained at the Institute of Culinary Education in New York City, where she has also worked as a recreational chef instructor. Ganeshram also holds a master's degree in journalism from Columbia University. For eight years she worked as a feature writer/ stringer for the *New York Times* regional sections, and she spent another eight years as a food columnist and feature writer for *Newsday*. She is the author of *Sweet Hands: Island Cooking from Trinidad and Tobago* (Hippocrene NY, 2006; 2nd expanded edition, 2010) and *Stir It Up* (Scholastic, 2011). In addition to contributing to a variety of food publications including *Saveur, Gourmet, Bon Appetit,* and epicurious.com, Ganeshram has written articles on food, culture, and travel for *Islands* (as contributing editor), *National Geographic Traveler,*

Forbes Traveler, Forbes Four Seasons, and many others. Currently, Ganeshram teaches food writing for New York University's School of Continuing Professional Studies.

Hanna Garth is a doctoral candidate in the Department of Anthropology at the University of California, Los Angeles. She is currently working on a dissertation on household food practices in Santiago de Cuba. Previously, she has conducted research on food culture, health, and nutrition in Cuba, Chile, and the Philippines.

Mary Gee is a medical sociology doctoral student at the University of California, San Francisco. Her current research interests include herbalism and Asian and Asian American foodways, especially with regards to multigenerational differences. Since 1995, she has actively worked with local and national eating disorders research and policy and advocacy organizations as well as for a program evaluation research consulting firm.

Che Ann Abdul Ghani holds a bachelor's degree in English and a master's degree in linguistics. She has a keen interest in studying language and language use in gastronomy. She is currently attached to the English Department at Universiti Putra Malaysia. Her research interests range from the use of language in context (pragmatics) to language use in multidisciplinary areas, namely, disciplines related to the social sciences. She also carries out work in translation and editing.

Maja Godina-Golija is research adviser at the Institute of Slovenian Ethnology, Scientific Research Centre of Slovenian Academy of Science and Arts, Ljubljana, Slovenia.

Annie Goldberg is a graduate student studying gastronomy at Boston University.

Darra Goldstein is Frances Christopher Oakley Third Century Professor of Russian at Williams College and the founding editor-in-chief of *Gastronomica: The Journal of Food and Culture.*

Keiko Goto, PhD, is associate professor at the Department of Nutrition and Food Sciences, California State University, Chico. Dr. Goto has more than 15 years of work experience in the field of nutrition and has worked as a practitioner and researcher in various developing countries. Dr. Goto's current research areas include food and culture, child and adolescent nutrition, sustainable food systems, and international nutrition.

Carla Guerrón Montero is a cultural and applied anthropologist trained in Latin America and the United States. She is currently associate professor of anthropology in the Department of Anthropology at the University of Delaware. Dr. Guerrón Montero's areas of expertise include gender, ethnicity, and identity; processes of globalization/nationalism, and particularly tourism; and social justice and human rights.

Mary Gunderson calls her practice paleocuisineology, where food and cooking bring cultures alive. Through many media, including the sites HistoryCooks.com and MaryGunderson.com, she writes and speaks about South and North American food history and contemporary creative living and wellness. She wrote and published the award-winning book *The Food Journal of Lewis and Clark: Recipes for an Expedition* (History Cooks, 2003) and has authored six food-history books for kids.

Liora Gvion is a senior lecturer at the Kibbutzim College of Education and also teaches at the Faculty of Agriculture, Food and Environment at the Institute of Biochemistry, Food Science and Nutrition Hebrew University of Jerusalem.

Cherie Y. Hamilton is a cookbook author and specialist on the food cultures and cuisines of the Portuguese-speaking countries in Europe, South America, Africa, and Asia.

Jessica B. Harris teaches English at Queens College/City University of New York and is director of the Institute for the Study of Culinary Cultures at Dillard University.

Melanie Haupt is a doctoral candidate in English at the University of Texas at Austin. Her dissertation, "Starting from Scratch: Reading Women's Cooking Communities," explores women's use of cookbooks and recipes in the formation and reification of real and virtual communities.

Ursula Heinzelmann is an independent scholar and culinary historian, twice awarded the prestigious Sophie Coe Prize. A trained chef, sommelier, and ex-restaurateur, she now works as a freelance wine and food writer and journalist based in Berlin, Germany.

Jennifer Hostetter is an independent food consultant specializing in writing, research, and editing. She has degrees in history and culinary arts and holds a master's degree in food culture and communications from the University of Gastronomic Sciences in Italy. She also served as editorial assistant for this encyclopedia.

Kelila Jaffe is a doctoral candidate in the Food Studies Program at New York University. Originally from Sonoma, California, and the daughter of a professional chef, she has pursued anthropological and archaeological foodways research since her entry into academia. She received a BA with distinction in anthropology from the University of Pennsylvania, before attending the University of Auckland, where she earned an MA with honors in anthropology, concentrating in archaeology. Her research interests include past foodways, domestication, and zooarchaeology, and she has conducted fieldwork in Fiji, New Zealand, and Hawaii.

Zilkia Janer is associate professor of global studies at Hofstra University in New York. She is the author of *Puerto Rican Nation-Building Literature: Impossible Romance* (2005) and *Latino Food Culture* (2008).

Brelyn Johnson is a graduate of the master's program in food studies at New York University.

Kate Johnston is currently based in Italy, where she is an independent cultural food researcher and writer and a daily ethnographer of people's food habits. She has a degree in anthropology from Macquarie University in Sydney, Australia, and a recent master's degree in food culture and communication from the University of Gastronomic Sciences, Italy. She was also editorial assistant for this encyclopedia.

Desiree Koh was born and raised in Singapore. A writer focusing on travel, hospitality, sports, fitness, business, and, of course, food, Koh's explorations across the globe always begin at the market, as she believes that the sight, scent, and savoring of native produce and cuisine are the key to the city's heart. The first and only female in Major League Eating's Asia debut, Koh retired from competition to better focus on each nibble and sip of fine, hopefully slow food.

Bruce Kraig is emeritus professor of history at Roosevelt University in Chicago and adjunct faculty at the Culinary School of Kendall College, Chicago. He has published and edited widely in the field of American and world food history. Kraig is also the founding president of the Culinary Historians of Chicago and the Greater Midwest Foodways Alliance.

R. J. Krajewski is the research services librarian at Simmons College, where among other things he facilitates discovery of food-culture research, especially through the lens of race, class, and gender. His own engagement with food is seasonally and locally rooted, starting in his own small, urban homestead, much like his Polish and German ancestors.

Erin Laverty is a freelance food writer and researcher based in Brooklyn, New York. She holds a master's degree in food studies from New York University.

Robert A. Leonard has a PhD in theoretical linguistics from Columbia. He studies the way people create and communicate meaning, including through food. He was born in Brooklyn and trained as a cook and *panaderia-reposteria* manager in the Caribbean; his doctoral studies led him to eight years of fieldwork in language, culture, and food in Africa and Southeast Asia. In the arts, as an undergraduate he cofounded and led the rock group Sha Na Na and with them opened for their friend Jimi Hendrix at the Woodstock Festival. Leonard is probably one of a very few people who have worked with both the Grateful Dead and the Federal Bureau of Investigation, which in recent years recruited him to teach the emerging science of forensic linguistics at Quantico.

Jane Levi is an independent consultant and writer based in London, England. She is currently working on her PhD at the London Consortium, examining food in utopias, funded by her work on post-trade financial policy in the City of London.

Yrsa Lindqvist is a European ethnologist working as the leading archivist at the Folk Culture Archive in Helsinki. Her research about food and eating habits in the late 1990s, combined with earlier collections at the archive, resulted in 2009 in the publication *Mat, Måltid, Minne. Hundraår av finlandssvensk matkulur.* The book analyzes the changes in housekeeping and attitudes toward food. She has also contributed to other publications focusing on identity questions and has worked as a junior researcher at the Academy of Finland.

William G. Lockwood is professor emeritus of cultural anthropology at the University of Michigan. His central interest is ethnicity and interethnic relations. He has conducted long-term field research in Bosnia-Herzegovina and the Croatian community in Austria and also among Roma and with a variety of ethnic groups in America, including Arabs, Finns, and Bosnians. He has long held a special interest in how food functions in ethnic group maintenance and in reflecting intra- and intergroup relations.

Yvonne R. Lockwood is curator emeritus of folklife at the Michigan State University Museum. Her formal training is in folklore, history, and Slavic languages and literatures. Research in Bosnia, Austria, and the United States, especially the Great Lakes region, has resulted in numerous publications, exhibitions, festival presentations, and workshops focused on her primary interests of foodways and ethnic traditions.

Janet Long-Solís, an anthropologist and archaeologist, is a research associate at the Institute of Historical Research at the National University of Mexico. She has published several books and articles on the chili pepper, the history of Mexican food, and the exchange of food products between Europe and the Americas in the 16th century.

Kristina Lupp has a background in professional cooking and has worked in Toronto and Florence. She is currently pursuing a master of arts in gastronomy at the University of Adelaide.

Máirtín Mac Con Iomaire is a lecturer in culinary arts in the Dublin Institute of Technology. Máirtín is well known as a chef, culinary historian, food writer, broadcaster, and ballad singer. He lives in Dublin with his wife and two daughters. He was the first Irish chef to be awarded a PhD, for his oral history of Dublin restaurants.

Glenn R. Mack is a food historian with extensive culinary training in Uzbekistan, Russia, Italy, and the United States. He cofounded the Culinary Academy of Austin and the Historic Foodways Group of Austin and currently serves as president of Le Cordon Bleu College of Culinary Arts Atlanta.

Andrea MacRae is a lecturer in the Le Cordon Bleu Graduate Program in Gastronomy at the University of Adelaide, Australia.

Giorgos Maltezakis earned his PhD in anthropology with research in cooperation with the Institute Studiorium Humanitatis of the Ljubljana Graduate School of the Humanities. His dissertation was on consumerism, the global market, and food, which was an ethnographic approach to the perception of food in Greece and Slovenia.

Bertie Mandelblatt is assistant professor at the University of Toronto, cross-appointed to the departments of Historical Studies and Geography. Her research concerns the early-modern French Atlantic, with a focus on commodity exchanges at the local and global scales: Her two current projects are the history of food provisioning in the Franco-Caribbean and the transatlantic circulation of French rum and molasses, both in the 17th and 18th centuries.

Marty Martindale is a freelance writer living in Largo, Florida.

Laura Mason is a writer and food historian with a special interest in local, regional, and traditional foods in the United Kingdom and elsewhere. Her career has explored many dimensions of food and food production, including cooking for a living, unraveling the history of sugar confectionery, and trying to work out how many traditional and typically British foods relate to culture and landscape. Her publications include *Taste of Britain* (with Catherine Brown; HarperCollins, 2006), *The Food Culture of Great Britain* (Greenwood, 2004), and *The National Trust Farmhouse Cookbook* (National Trust, 2009).

Anton Masterovoy is a PhD candidate at the Graduate Center, City University of New York. He is working on his dissertation, titled "Eating Soviet: Food and Culture in USSR, 1917–1991."

Anne Engammare McBride, a Swiss native, food writer, and editor, is the director of the Experimental Cuisine Collective and a food studies PhD candidate at New York University. Her most recent book is *Culinary Careers: How to Get Your Dream Job in Food,* coauthored with Rick Smilow.

Michael R. McDonald is associate professor of anthropology at Florida Gulf Coast University. He is the author of *Food Culture in Central America.*

Naomi M. McPherson is associate professor of cultural anthropology and graduate program coordinator at the University of British Columbia, Okanagan Campus. Since 1981, she has accumulated over three years of field research with the Bariai of West New Britain, Papua New Guinea.

Katrina Meynink is an Australia-based freelance food writer and researcher. She has a master's degree in gastronomy through Le Cordon Bleu and the University of Adelaide under a scholarship from the James Beard Foundation. She is currently completing her first cookbook.

Barbara J. Michael is a sociocultural anthropologist whose research focuses on social organization, economics, decision making, and gender. Her geographic focus is on the Middle East and East Africa, where she has done research with the pastoral nomadic Hawazma Baggara and on traditional medicine in Yemen and is working on a video about men's cafes as a social institution. She teaches anthropology at the University of North Carolina Wilmington and has also worked as a consultant for several United Nations agencies.

Diana Mincyte is a fellow at the Rachel Carson Center at the Ludwig Maximilian University-Munich and visiting assistant professor in the Department of Advertising at the University of Illinois, Urbana-Champaign. Mincyte examines topics at the interface of food, the environment, risk society, and global inequalities. Her book investigates raw-milk politics in the European Union to consider the production risk society and its institutions in post-Socialist states.

Rebecca Moore is a doctoral student studying the history of biotechnology at the University of Toronto in Ontario, Canada.

Nawal Nasrallah, a native of Iraq, was a professor of English and comparative literature at the universities of Baghdad and Mosul until 1990. As an independent scholar, she wrote the award-winning *Delights from the Garden of Eden: A Cookbook and a History of the Iraqi Cuisine* and *Annals of the Caliphs' Kitchens* (an English translation of Ibn Sayyar al-Warraq's 10th-century Baghdadi cookbook).

Henry Notaker graduated from the University of Oslo with a degree in literature and worked for many years as a foreign correspondent and host of arts and letters shows on Norwegian national television. He has written several books about food history, and with *Food Culture in Scandinavia* he won the Gourmand World Cookbook Award for best culinary history in 2009. His last book is a bibliography of early-modern culinary literature, *Printed Cookbooks in Europe 1470–1700.* He is a member of the editorial board of the journal *Food and History.*

Kelly O'Leary is a graduate student at Boston University in gastronomy and food studies and executive chef at the Bayridge University Residence and Cultural Center.

Fabio Parasecoli is associate professor and coordinator of food studies at the New School in New York City. He is author of *Food Culture in Italy* (2004) and *Bite Me: Food and Popular Culture* (2008).

Susan Ji-Young Park is the program director and head of curriculum development at École de Cuisine Pasadena (www.ecolecuisine.com); project leader for Green Algeria, a national environmental initiative; and a writer for LAWEEKLY'S Squid Ink. She has written curriculum for cooking classes at Los Angeles Unified School District, Sur La Table, Whole Foods Market, Central Market, and Le Cordon Bleu North America. She and her husband, Chef Farid Zadi, have co-written recipes for *Gourmet Magazine* and the *Los Angeles Times.* The couple are currently writing several cookbooks on North African, French, and Korean cuisines.

Rosemary Parkinson is author of *Culinaria: The Caribbean, Nyam Jamaica,* and *Barbados Bu'n-Bu'n,* and she contributes culinary travel stories to Caribbean magazines.

Charles Perry majored in Middle East languages at Princeton University, the University of California, Berkeley, and the Middle East Centre for Arab Studies, Shimlan, Lebanon. From 1968 to 1976 he was a copy editor and staff writer at *Rolling Stone* magazine in San Francisco, before leaving to work as a freelance writer specializing in food. From 1990 to 2008, he was a staff writer in the food section of the *Los Angeles Times.* He has published widely on the history of Middle Eastern food and was a major contributor to the *Oxford Companion to Food* (1999).

Irina Petrosian is a native of Armenia and a professional journalist who has written for Russian, Armenian, and U.S.-based newspapers. She is the coauthor of

Armenian Food: Fact, Fiction, and Folklore and holds degrees in journalism from Moscow State University and Indiana University.

Suzanne Piscopo is a nutrition, family, and consumer studies lecturer at the University of Malta in Malta. She is mainly involved in the training of home economics and primary-level teachers, as well as in nutrition and consumer-education projects in different settings. Suzanne is a registered public health nutritionist, and her research interests focus on socioecological determinants of food intake, nutrition interventions, and health promotion. She has also written a series of short stories for children about food. Suzanne enjoys teaching and learning about the history and culture of food and is known to creatively experiment with the ingredients at hand when cooking the evening meal together with her husband, Michael.

Theresa Preston-Werner is an advanced graduate student in anthropology at Northwestern University.

Meg Ragland is a culinary history researcher and librarian. She lives in Boston, Massachusetts.

Carol Selva Rajah is an award-winning chef and food writer currently based in Sydney, Australia. She has written 10 cookbooks on Malaysian and Southeast Asian cuisine. Her book *The Food of India* won the gold award for the Best Hardcover Recipe Book at the prestigious Jacob's Creek World Food Media Awards.

Birgit Ricquier is pursuing a PhD in linguistics at the Université Libre de Bruxelles and the Royal Museum for Central Africa, Tervuren, Belgium, with a fellowship from the Fonds de la Recherche Scientifique (FNRS). The topic of her PhD project is "A Comparative Linguistic Approach to the History of Culinary Practice in Bantu-Speaking Africa." She has spent several months in central Africa, including one month in the Democratic Republic of the Congo as a member of the Boyekoli Ebale Congo 2010 Expedition and two months of research focused on food cultures in Congo.

Amy Riolo is an award-winning author, lecturer, cooking instructor, and consultant. She is the author of *Arabian Delights: Recipes and Princely Entertaining Ideas from the Arabian Peninsula, Nile Style: Egyptian Cuisine and Culture,* and *The Mediterranean Diabetes Cookbook.* Amy has lived, worked, and traveled extensively through Egypt and enjoys fusing cuisine, culture, and history into all aspects of her work. Please see www.amyriolo.com, www.baltimoreegypt.org, and diningwithdiplomats.blogspot.com for more information and further reading.

Owen Roberts is a journalist, communications instructor, and director of research communications for the University of Guelph in Guelph, Ontario, Canada. He holds a doctorate of education from Texas Tech University and Texas A&M University.

Fiona Ross is a gastrodetective whose headquarters is the Bodleian Library in Oxford, United Kingdom. She spends her time there investigating the eating foibles of the famous and infamous. Her cookery book *Dining with Destiny* is the result: When you want to know what Lenin lunched on or what JFK ate by the poolside, *Dining with Destiny* has the answer.

Signe Rousseau (née Hansen) is Danish by birth but a long-term resident of southern Africa and is a researcher and part-time lecturer at the University of Cape Town. Following an MA in the Department of English and a PhD (on food media and celebrity chefs) in the Centre for Film and Media Studies, she now teaches critical literacy and professional communication in the School of Management Studies (Faculty of Commerce).

Kathleen Ryan is a consulting scholar in the African Section of the University of Pennsylvania Museum of Archaeology and Anthropology, Philadelphia. She has carried out research in Kenya since 1990, when she began a study of Maasai cattle herders in Kajiado District.

Helen Saberi was Alan Davidson's principal assistant in the completion of the *Oxford Companion to Food.* She is the author of *Noshe Djan: Afghan Food and Cookery;* coauthor of *Trifle* with Alan Davidson; and coauthor of *The Road to Vindaloo* with David Burnett; her latest book is *Tea: A Global History.*

Cari Sánchez holds a master of arts in gastronomy from the University of Adelaide/Le Cordon Bleu in South Australia. Her dissertation explores the global spread of the Argentine *asado.* She currently lives in Jacksonville, Florida, where she writes the food and travel blog *viCARIous* and is the marketing manager for a craft brewery.

Peter Scholliers teaches history at the Vrije Universiteit Brussel and is currently head of the research group "Social and Cultural Food Studies" (FOST). He studies the history of food in Europe in the 19th and 20th centuries. He co-edits the journal *Food and History* and is involved in various ways in the Institut Européen d'Histoire et des Cultures de l'Alimentation (Tours, France). Recently, he published *Food Culture in Belgium* (Greenwood, 2008). More information can be found at http://www.vub.ac.be/FOST/fost_in_english/.

Colleen Taylor Sen is the author of *Food Culture in India; Curry: A Global History; Pakoras, Paneer, Pappadums: A Guide to Indian Restaurant Menus,* and many articles on the food of the Indian Subcontinent. She is a regular participant in the Oxford Food Symposium.

Roger Serunyigo was born and lives in Kampala, Uganda. He graduated from Makerere University with a degree in urban and regional planning, has worked in telecommunications, and is now a professional basketball player for the Uganda National Team. He also coaches a women's basketball team (The Magic Stormers).

Dorette Snover is a chef and author. Influenced by French heritage and the food traditions of the Pennsylvania Dutch country, Chef Snover teaches exploration of the world via a culinary map at her school, C'est si Bon! in Chapel Hill. While the stock simmers, she is writing a novel about a French bread apprentice.

Celia Sorhaindo is a freelance photographer and writer. She was the editor of the 2008 and 2009 *Dominica Food and Drink Guide* magazine and content manager for the Dominica section of the magazine *Caribbean Homes & Lifestyle*.

Lyra Spang is a PhD candidate in the Department of Anthropology and the Food Studies Program at Indiana University. She has written about food, sex, and symbolism; the role of place in defining organic; and the importance of social relationships in small-scale food business in Belize. She grew up on a farm in southern Belize and is a proud promoter of that country's unique and diverse culinary heritage.

Lois Stanford is an agricultural anthropologist in the Department of Anthropology at New Mexico State University. In her research, she has examined the globalization of food systems both in Mexico and in the U.S. Southwest. Her current research focuses on the critical role of food heritage and plant conservation in constructing and maintaining traditional foodways and cultural identity in New Mexico. In collaboration with local food groups, she is currently developing a community food assessment project in the Mesilla Valley in southern New Mexico.

Aliza Stark is a senior faculty member at the Agriculture, Food, and Environment Institute of Biochemistry, Food Science, and Nutrition at the Hebrew University of Jerusalem.

Maria "Ging" Gutierrez Steinberg is a marketing manager for a New York City–based specialty food company and a food writer. She has a master's degree in food studies from New York University and is a graduate of Le Cordon Bleu. Her articles have appeared in various publications in Asia and the United States.

Anita Stewart is a cookbook author and Canadian culinary activist from Elora, Ontario, Canada.

Emily Stone has written about Guatemalan cuisine in the *Radcliffe Culinary Times,* and she is at work on a nonfiction book about chocolate in Central America. She currently teaches journalism and creative writing at Sun Yat-sen University in Guangzhou, China.

Asele Surina is a Russian native and former journalist who now works as a translator and interpreter. Since 1999 she has worked at the Institute of Classical Archaeology at the University of Texas on joint projects with an archaeological museum in Crimea, Ukraine.

Aylin Öney Tan is an architect by training and studied conservation of historic structures in Turkey, Italy, and the United Kingdom. Eventually, her passion for food and travel led her to write on food. Since 2003, she has had a weekly food column in *Cumhuriyet,* a prestigious national daily, and contributes to various food magazines. She was a jury member of the Slow Food Award 2000–2003, with her nominees receiving awards. She contributes to the Terra Madre and Presidia projects as the leader of the Ankara Convivium. She won the Sophie Coe Award on food history in 2008 for her article "Poppy: Potent yet Frail," presented previously at the Oxford Symposium on Food and Cookery where she's become a regular presenter. Currently, she is the curator of the Culinary Culture Section of Princess Islands' City Museum. She is happy to unite her expertise in archaeology and art history from her previous career with her unbounded interest in food culture.

Nicole Tarulevicz teaches at the School of Asian Languages and Studies at the University of Tasmania.

Karen Lau Taylor is a freelance food writer and consultant whose food curriculum vitae includes a master's degree in food studies from New York University, an advanced certificate from the Wine and Spirits Education Trust, and a gig as pastry cook at a five-star hotel after completing L'Academie de Cuisine's pastry arts program. She is working toward a master's degree in public health while she continues to write, teach, test recipes, eat, and drink from her home in Alexandria, Virginia.

Thy Tran is trained as a professional chef. She established Wandering Spoon to provide cooking classes, culinary consultation, and educational programming for culinary academies and nonprofit organizations throughout Northern California. Currently, she is a chef instructor at the International Culinary Schools at the Art Institute of California–San Francisco and Tante Marie's. She is also the founder and director of the Asian Culinary Forum. She co-authored The Essentials of Asian Cooking, Taste of the World, and the award-winning guide, *Kitchen Companion*.

Leena Trivedi-Grenier is a Bay-area food writer, cooking teacher, and social media consultant. Her writings have appeared in *The Business of Food: Encyclopedia of the Food and Drink Industry, Culinary Trends* magazine, and the *Cultural Arts Resources for Teachers and Students* newsletter and will be featured in several upcoming titles by Greenwood Press. She also runs a food/travel/gastronomy blog called *Leena Eats This Blog* (www.leenaeats.com).

Karin Vaneker graduated from the AKI Academy of Visual Arts in Enschede, the Netherlands. She later attended Sint-Lukas Hoger Instituut voor Schone Kunsten in Brussels, Belgium. She has written for numerous Dutch newspapers and magazines, specializing in trends and the cultural and other histories of ingredients and cuisines, and has published several books. Furthermore, Vaneker has worked for museums and curated an exhibition about New World taro (L. *Xanthosoma* spp.). At present she is researching its potential in domestic cuisines and gastronomy.

Penny Van Esterik is professor of anthropology at York University, Toronto, where she teaches nutritional anthropology, advocacy anthropology, and feminist theory. She does fieldwork in Southeast Asia and has developed materials on breast-feeding and women's work and infant and young child feeding.

Richard Wilk is professor of anthropology and gender studies at Indiana University, where he directs the Food Studies Program. With a PhD in anthropology from the University of Arizona, he has taught at the University of California,

Berkeley; University of California, Santa Cruz; New Mexico State University; and University College London and has held fellowships at Gothenburg University and the University of London. His publications include more than 125 papers and book chapters, a textbook in economic anthropology, and several edited volumes. His most recent books are *Home Cooking in the Global Village* (Berg Publishers), *Off the Edge: Experiments in Cultural Analysis* (with Orvar Lofgren; Museum Tusculanum Press), *Fast Food/Slow Food* (Altamira Press), and *Time, Consumption, and Everyday Life* (with Elizabeth Shove and Frank Trentmann; Berg Publishers).

Chelsie Yount is a PhD student of anthropology at Northwestern University in Evanston, Illinois. She lived in Senegal in 2005 and again in 2008, when performing ethnographic research for her master's thesis at the École des Hautes Études en Sciences Sociales in Paris, on the topic of Senegalese food and eating habits.

Marcia Zoladz is a cook, food writer, and food-history researcher with her own Web site, Cozinha da Marcia (Marcia's Kitchen; www.cozinhadamarcia.com.br). She is a regular participant and contributor at the Oxford Symposium on Food and History and has published three books in Brazil, Germany, and Holland— *Cozinha Portuguesa* (Portuguese cooking), *Muito Prazer* (Easy recipes), and *Brigadeiros e Bolinhas* (Sweet and savory Brazilian finger foods).

Index

Boldface numbers refer to volume numbers. A key appears on all verso pages.

Aboriginal Australians, **3**:1–8; cooking, **3**:3–4; Damper Bread, **3**:4; diet and health, **3**:6–8; eating out, **3**:5; food culture snapshot, **3**:1–2; major foodstuffs, **3**:2–3; meals, typical, **3**:4–5; overview of, **3**:1; Quandong Crumble, **3**:2; special occasions, **3**:5–6

Accras de morue, **2**:210–11

Achaar (tomato pickle), **3**:188–89

Acorn Griddle Cakes, **2**:240

Adzhapsandali, **4**:124–25

Afghanistan, **3**:9–20; ashak, **3**:13; aush, **3**:10; Burani Bonjon, **3**:14–15; cooking, **3**:12–14; diet and health, **3**:20; eating out, **3**:15–16; food culture snapshot, **3**:9–11; major foodstuffs, **3**:11–12; mantu, **3**:10, **3**:14, **3**:16; meals, typical, **3**:14, **3**:15; overview of, **3**:9; Qabili Pilau, **3**:18–19; rice pilaeu, **3**:19; shola-e-zard, **3**:17; special occasions, **3**:16–18, **3**:19

Africa, **1**:1–214; Algeria, **1**:3–10; Angola, **1**:11–18; Benin, **1**:19–22; Burkina Faso, **1**:23–30; Central Africa, **1**:31–41; Côte d'Ivoire, **1**:43–47; Egypt, **1**:49–58; Ethiopia and Eritrea, **1**:59–70; Ghana, **1**:71–74; Guinea, **1**:75–79; Kenya, **1**:81–89; Liberia, **1**:91–96; Maasai, **1**:97–103; Madagascar, **1**:105–13; Mauritania, **1**:115–18; Morocco, **1**:119–24; Mozambique, **1**:125–35; Namibia, **1**:135–39; Nigeria, **1**:141–49; Senegal, **1**:151–59; Sierra Leone, **1**:161–65; Somalia, **1**:167–71; South Africa, **1**:173–81; Sudan, **1**:183–87; Swahili City-States, **1**:189–95; Swaziland, **1**:197–201; Uganda, **1**:203–8; Zimbabwe, **1**:209–14

Akoho sy Voanio, **1**:112

Aleluja, **4**:345–46

Algeria, **1**:3–10; cooking, **1**:5–7; diet and health, **1**:9–10; eating out, **1**:8; food culture snapshot, **1**:3–4; harira (soup), **1**:8, **1**:9; Harsha (Quick Semolina Bread for Ramadan), **1**:9; major foodstuffs, **1**:4–5; meals, typical, **1**:7–8; overview of, **1**:3; special occasions, **1**:9; tagine (stew), **1**:5, **1**:6, **1**:7

Aliciotti con l'indivia (fresh anchovies with escarole), **4**:210

Aloko (Deep-Fried Plantains), **1**:44

Americas, **2**:1–373; Argentina, **2**:1–5; Aruba and Bonaire, **2**:7–13; Barbados, **2**:15–30; Belize, **2**:31–35; Bolivia, **2**:37–45; Brazil, **2**:47–54; Canada, **2**:55–64; Chile, **2**:65–74; Colombia, **2**:75–83; Costa Rica, **2**:85–90; Cuba, **2**:91–99; Curaçao and Sint Maarten, **2**:101–7; Dominica, **2**:109–17; Dominican Republic, **2**:119–27; Ecuador, **2**:129–34; El Salvador, **2**:135–39; French Guiana, **2**:141–45; Grenada, **2**:147–52; Guatemala, **2**:153–58; Guyana, **2**:159–63; Haiti, **2**:165–73; Hawaii, **2**:175–82; Honduras, **2**:183–90; Inuit, **2**:191–98; Jamaica, **2**:199–206; Martinique and Guadeloupe, **2**:207–16; Mexico, **2**:217–29; Native Americans, **2**:231–41; Nicaragua, **2**:243–48; Panama, **2**:249–52; Paraguay and Uruguay, **2**:253–61; Peru, **2**:263–71; Puerto Rico, **2**:273–81; Suriname, **2**:283–89; Trinidad and Tobago, **2**:291–301; United States, **2**:303–67; Venezuela, **2**:369–73

Angola, **1**:11–18; Caldeirado de Cabrito (Goat-Meat Stew), **1**:16, **1**:18; cooking, **1**:14–15; diet and health, **1**:18; eating out, **1**:17; food culture snapshot, **1**:12–13; funji (Manioc Puree), **1**:16; major foodstuffs, **1**:13–14; meals, typical, **1**:16–17; muamba de galinha (Angolan-style chicken),

Vol 1:	**Africa, Middle East**
Vol 2:	**Americas**
Vol 3:	**Asia and Oceania**
Vol 4:	**Europe**

1:15–16; overview of, 1:11–12; special occasions, 1:17–18

Antarctica, 3:285–90; cooking, 3:287–88; diet and health, 3:289–90; eating out, 3:289; major foodstuffs, 3:285–87; meals, typical, 3:288–89; overview of, 3:285; special occasions, 3:289

Aoatol, 3:211

Arabian Peninsula, 1:217–29; cooking, 1:221–22; diet and health, 1:229; eating out, 1:225; food culture snapshot, 1:219–20; machbous, 1:224; major foodstuffs, 1:220–21; meals, typical, 1:222–24; overview of, 1:217–19; special occasions, 1:225–28; Stuffed Camel, 1:228

Arañitas (shredded green plantain "spiders"), 2:277–78

Arepa, 2:75–76, 2:87, 2:371

Arepas, 2:75, 2:81, 2:371

Argentina, 2:1–5; chimichurri, 2:3; cooking, 2:3; diet and health, 2:5; eating out, 2:3–4; empanadas, 2:1, 2:4; food culture snapshot, 2:1–2; major foodstuffs, 2:2–3; meals, typical, 2:3; overview of, 2:1; special occasions, 2:4–5

Armenia, 4:1–10; Chuchkhel, 4:2; cooking, 4:4–5; diet and health, 4:9–10; eating out, 4:7; food culture snapshot, 4:1–2; gata, 4:6, 4:8–9; major foodstuffs, 4:2–4; meals, typical, 4:5–6; overview of, 4:1; spas (yogurt soup), 4:6–7; special occasions, 4:7–8

Arroz con pollo, 2:2, 2:249, 2:273

Ärtsoppa (yellow pea soup), 4:363

Aruba and Bonaire, 2:7–13; cooking, 2:8–9, 2:10; diet and health, 2:12; eating out, 2:11; food culture snapshot, 2:7–8; funchi, 2:11; keshi yena, 2:9–10; major foodstuffs, 2:8; meals, typical, 2:10–11; overview of, 2:7; special occasions, 2:11

Ashak, 3:13

Asia and Oceania, 3:1–281; Aboriginal Australians, 3:1–8; Afghanistan, 3:9–20; Australia, 3:21–29; Bangladesh, 3:31–36; Brunei, 3:37–41; Cambodia, 3:43–47; Central Asia, 3:49–59; China, 3:61–72; Hmong, 3:73–81; Hong Kong, 3:83–92; India, 3:93–101; Indonesia, 3:103–11; Japan, 3:113–25; Kazakhstan, 3:127–34; Korea, 3:135–45; Lao People's Democratic Republic (Lao PDR), 3:147–52; Macau, 3:153–58; Malaysia, 3:159–68; Mongolia, 3:175–84; Māori, 3:169–73; Nepal, 3:185–91; Pakistan, 3:193–202; Papua New Guinea Foodways, 3:203–13; Philippines, 3:215–23; Portuguese in Asia, 3:225–34; Singapore, 3:235–45; Sri Lanka, 3:247–52; Thailand, 3:253–61; Tibet, 3:263–73; Vietnam, 3:275–81

Aush, 3:10

Australia, 3:21–29; Carpetbag Steak, 3:24; cooking, 3:23–25; diet and health, 3:28; eating out, 3:27; food culture snapshot, 3:21–22; major foodstuffs, 3:22–23; meals, typical, 3:26–27; meat pie, 3:27; overview of, 3:21; special occasions, 3:27–28

Austria, 4:11–19; cooking, 4:14–15; diet and health, 4:19; eating out, 4:18; food culture snapshot, 4:12–14; Gulyás (goulash), 4:16; major foodstuffs, 4:14; meals, typical, 4:15–17; overview of, 4:11–12; special occasions, 4:18–19; Wiener schnitzel, 4:12, 4:16

Babka, 4:34, 4:37

Bacalao a La Criolla (Codfish a La Dominicana), 2:123

Bacalhau, 3:154, 3:155, 3:227

Bairam Palovi (Uzbek Wedding Pilaf), 3:55

Baked Sweet Plantains with Cheese, 2:185

Bammy, 2:201, 2:203

Bananas, 1:82

Bandeja paisa, 2:81

Bangladesh, 3:31–36; Bengali sweets, 3:34; cooking, 3:33; diet and health, 3:35–36; eating out, 3:34–35; food culture snapshot, 3:32; major foodstuffs, 3:32–33; malpoa, 3:35; meals, typical, 3:33–34; overview of, 3:31; rezala (white lamb curry), 3:31–32; special occasions, 3:35

Barbados, 2:15–30; breakfast or tea, 2:25–26; cooking, 2:23–25; Coucou, 2:22–23; diet and health, 2:30; dinner or supper, 2:27; eating out, 2:27–28; food culture snapshot, 2:16–18; lunch or breakfast, 2:26–27; major foodstuffs, 2:18–22; meals, typical, 2:25–27; midmorning snacks, 2:26; overview of, 2:15; special occasions, 2:28–29; Steamed Flying Fish, 2:23; tea, 2:27

Barbados Coucou and Flying Fish, 2:22–23

Barboucha, 1:232

Bariai. *See* Papua New Guinea Foodways

Barszcz (beet soup), 4:275

Basque territory, **4**:21–29; cooking, **4**:25–27; diet and health, **4**:28–29; eating out, **4**:27–28; food culture snapshot, **4**:21–22; major foodstuffs, **4**:22–25; marmitako, **4**:26; meals, typical, **4**:25–27; overview of, **4**:21; special occasions, **4**:28

Beef Laap, **3**:150

Beef Rendang, **3**:163–64

Beignets (deep-fried donuts), **1**:6, **1**:8, **1**:32, **1**:37

Bejgli, **4**:188

Belarus, **4**:31–38; cooking, **4**:33–34; diet and health, **4**:37–38; dranniki (potato fritters), **4**:34, **4**:35; eating out, **4**:35–36; food culture snapshot, **4**:31–32; kalduny (dumplings), **4**:33, **4**:34–35; major foodstuffs, **4**:32–33; meals, typical, **4**:34–35; overview of, **4**:31; special occasions, **4**:36–37

Belgium, **4**:39–49; Blinde Vinken or Oiseaux Sans Tête (Blind Finches), **4**:43–44; cooking, **4**:41–42; diet and health, **4**:48; eating out, **4**:44–45, **4**:46; food culture snapshot, **4**:39–40; Konijn met Pruimen or Lapin Aux Prunes (Rabbit with Plums), **4**:40–41; major foodstuffs, **4**:40, **4**:41; meals, typical, **4**:42–43, **4**:44; overview of, **4**:39; smoutebollen or beignets (doughnut balls), **4**:47; special occasions, **4**:46–48; Stoemp met Spruitjes or Stoemp Aux Choux de Bruxelles (Mashed Potatoes with Brussels Sprouts), **4**:46

Belize, **2**:31–35; diet and health, **2**:35; eating out, **2**:34–35; food culture snapshot, **2**:32; major foodstuffs, **2**:32–33, **2**:34; meals, typical, **2**:34; overview of, **2**:31–32; Rice and Beans, **2**:33–34; special occasions, **2**:35

Benin, **1**:19–22; cooking, **1**:20; diet and health, **1**:22; eating out, **1**:21–22; food culture snapshot, **1**:19; major foodstuffs, **1**:20; meals, typical, **1**:21; Moyau (Chicken Stew), **1**:20; overview of, **1**:19; special occasions, **1**:22

Berbere, **1**:64–65

Berbers and Tuaregs, **1**:231–38; barboucha, **1**:232; cooking, **1**:234; diet and health, **1**:237–38; eating out, **1**:236; food culture snapshot, **1**:232; major foodstuffs, **1**:232–33; meals, typical, **1**:234–36; overview of, **1**:231; special occasions, **1**:236–37

Berlinerkranser (Norwegian Berlin Wreath Cookies), **4**:265

Beshbarmek, **3**:133

Beurre manié, **4**:371

Bibimbap, **3**:143

Bigilla, **4**:233

Bigos (Hunter's Stew), **4**:275

Bint al-sahn, **1**:320

Black-Eyed Peas with Chard, **4**:84

Blaff de poisson blancs (fish blaff), **2**:211–12

Blinde Vinken or Oiseaux Sans Tête (Blind Finches), **4**:43–44

Blómör, **4**:195

Boil-Up, **3**:172–73

Bolivia, **2**:37–45; chuno (preserved potatoes), **2**:39, **2**:40, **2**:41; cooking, **2**:39–40; diet and health, **2**:44–45; eating out, **2**:42–43; empanadas, **2**:41; food culture snapshot, **2**:38; major foodstuffs, **2**:38–39; meals, typical, **2**:40–42; overview of, **2**:37–38; picante de pollo (chicken in spicy sauce), **2**:40; special occasions, **2**:43–44

Bonaire. *See* Aruba and Bonaire

Borsch soup, **4**:378

Borscht, **4**:303

Bosnia and Herzegovina, **4**:51–60; cooking, **4**:54–55; diet and health, **4**:59–60; eating out, **4**:57; food culture snapshot, **4**:52; major foodstuffs, **4**:52–54; meals, typical, **4**:55–57; overview of, **4**:51–52; special occasions, **4**:57–59; urmašice (Bosnian dates), **4**:58

Boston Baked Beans, **2**:330

Bouillon d'awara, **2**:143–44

Bourekia, **4**:85

Braai (act of barbecuing), **1**:136, **1**:138, **1**:176, **1**:177, **1**:178

Brændende kærlighed, **4**:99

Brazil, **2**:47–54; caipirinha, **2**:52; diet and health, **2**:53–54; eating out, **2**:51–52; feijoada, **2**:51; food culture snapshot, **2**:48; grouper moqueca, **2**:50–51; major foodstuffs, **2**:48–50; meals, typical, **2**:50, **2**:51; overview of, **2**:47–48; special occasions, **2**:52–53

Breskvice, **4**:78

Brinjal (eggplant) sambal, **3**:250

Brunei, **3**:37–41; cooking, **3**:39; diet and health, **3**:40–41; eating out, **3**:40; food culture snapshot, **3**:37–38; major foodstuffs, **3**:38–39; meals, typical, **3**:39–40; Nasi lemak, **3**:38; overview of, **3**:37; Prawn Sambal, **3**:40; special occasions, **3**:40

Bryndzové halušky (dumplings), **4**:336

Buffalo Stew (Lakota), **2**:235

Bulgaria, **4**:61–70; cooking, **4**:66; diet and health, **4**:70; eating out, **4**:69; food culture snapshot, **4**:62; kavarma, **4**:67; major foodstuffs, **4**:62–66; meals, typical, **4**:66–69; moussaka, **4**:62; overview of, **4**:61–62; special occasions, **4**:69–70

Burani Bonjon, **3**:14–15

Vol 1:	**Africa, Middle East**
Vol 2:	**Americas**
Vol 3:	**Asia and Oceania**
Vol 4:	**Europe**

Burek, **4**:51–52

Bur katuunboow, **1**:170

Burkina Faso, **1**:23–30; cooking, **1**:25–26; diet and health, **1**:29–30; eating out, **1**:26–28; food culture snapshot, **1**:23–24; major foodstuffs, **1**:24–25; meals, typical, **1**:26; overview of, **1**:23; Riz Gras, **1**:28–29; special occasions, **1**:28, **1**:29

Cachapas, **2**:106, **2**:370

Caipirinha, **2**:52

Caldeirado de Cabrito (Goat-Meat Stew), **1**:16, **1**:18

Caldo verde (kale and potato soup), **4**:283, **4**:285

Camarones Guisados (Shrimp Stew), **2**:123–24

Cambodia, **3**:43–47; Cambodian Pork and Eggplant Stir-Fry, **3**:44–45; Caramelized Fish, **3**:46; cooking, **3**:44; diet and health, **3**:47; eating out, **3**:46; food culture snapshot, **3**:43–44; major foodstuffs, **3**:44; meals, typical, **3**:45–46; overview of, **3**:43; special occasions, **3**:46

Cambodian Pork and Eggplant Stir-Fry, **3**:44–45

Canada, **2**:55–64; Atlantic provinces, **2**:59; British Columbia, **2**:58; Canadian north, **2**:59–60; cooking, **2**:60–61; diet and health, **2**:63; eating out, **2**:61–62; Elora Road Butternut Squash and Buttermilk Soup, **2**:56; food culture snapshot, **2**:55–57; major foodstuffs, **2**:57–60; meals, typical, **2**:61; Ontario and Quebec, **2**:58–59; overview of, **2**:55; prairie region, **2**:58; special occasions, **2**:63

Canh chua Ca Loc (sour broth), **3**:279

Canjeero, **1**:169

Caramelized Fish, **3**:46

Caril de galinha à Moçambicana (Curried Chicken, Mozambican Style), **1**:133

Carne asada, **2**:184–85

Carpetbag Steak, **3**:24

Cassareep, **2**:161–62

Cazuela, **2**:68, **2**:69, **2**:71

Ceebu jën, **1**:155

Central Africa, **1**:31–41; beignets (deep-fried donuts), **1**:32, **1**:37; Chikangue, **1**:33; chikwangue, **1**:32, **1**:35, **1**:36–37; cooking, **1**:35–37; diet and health, **1**:40; eating out, **1**:39–40; food culture snapshot, **1**:32–33; fufu, **1**:36; major foodstuffs, **1**:33–35; meals, typical, **1**:37–39; overview of, **1**:31–32; poulet à la moambe (Chicken with Palm Butter), **1**:37; special occasions, **1**:40

Central Asia, **3**:49–59; Bairam Palovi (Uzbek Wedding Pilaf), **3**:55; cooking, **3**:53–54; diet and health, **3**:58–59; eating out, **3**:55–57; food culture snapshot, **3**:50–51; koq chuchvara (Uzbek green dumplings), **3**:57; major foodstuffs, **3**:51–53; meals, typical, **3**:54–55; overview of, **3**:49–50; samsa, **3**:51–52, **3**:54; special occasions, **3**:57, **3**:58

Cepelinai (Zeppelins/Potato Dumplings), **4**:226–27

Cesnekova polevka (garlic soup), **4**:90

Cevapcici (sausage), **4**:328, **4**:329–30

Ceviche, **2**:266

Chamuças (Chicken Turnovers), **1**:130–31

Cheese Bread, **4**:313

Cheese Fondue, **4**:374–75

Cheese-stuffed pupusas, **2**:137

Chelo, **1**:241–42

Cherokee Succotash, **2**:236

Chicken adobo, **3**:218, **3**:219–20

Chicken piri-piri, **4**:286

Chicken Rice, **3**:241–42

Chikangue, **1**:33

Chikwangue, **1**:32, **1**:35, **1**:36–37

Chile, **2**:65–74; cazuela, **2**:68, **2**:69, **2**:71; cooking, **2**:68; curanto, **2**:70; diet and health, **2**:72–74; eating out, **2**:71; empanadas, **2**:72; food culture snapshot, **2**:66; major foodstuffs, **2**:66–68; meals, typical, **2**:69, **2**:70–71; overview of, **2**:65; pastel de choclo, **2**:69–70; special occasions, **2**:71–72; wines, **2**:67–68

Chimichurri, **2**:3

China, **3**:61–72; cooking, **3**:64–65; diet and health, **3**:69–72; dim sum, **3**:65, **3**:164; eating out, **3**:68–69; food culture snapshot, **3**:61–62; major foodstuffs, **3**:62–64; meals, typical, **3**:65–67; overview of, **3**:61; Red-Cooked Pork, **3**:68; special occasions, **3**:69; Stir-Fried Greens, **3**:67; Sweet and Sour Fish, **3**:67–68

Chubbagin, **1**:117

Chuchkhel, **4**:2

Chuno (preserved potatoes), **2**:39, **2**:40, **2**:41, **2**:266

Chupe de pescado (Fish Soup), **2**:132

Colcannon, **4**:204

Colombia, **2**:75–83; arepa, **2**:75–76; bandeja paisa, **2**:81; cooking, **2**:78–79; diet and health, **2**:83; eating out, **2**:82; empanadas, **2**:80; food culture snapshot, **2**:76–77; major foodstuffs, **2**:77–78; meals, typical,

2:79–80, 2:81–82; overview of, 2:75–76; Sobrebarriga Bogotá (flank steak), 2:80–81; Sopa de Frijoles Canarios (Canary Bean Soup), 2:79; special occasions, 2:82–83

Corn chowder, 2:314

Costa Rica, 2:85–90; cooking, 2:87; diet and health, 2:89–90; eating out, 2:89; food culture snapshot, 2:85; gallo pinto (beans and rice), 2:86; major foodstuffs, 2:86–87; meals, typical, 2:87–89; overview of, 2:85; special occasions, 2:89

Côte d'Ivoire, 1:43–47; aloko (Deep-Fried Plantains), 1:44; cooking, 1:44–45; diet and health, 1:46–47; eating out, 1:46; food culture snapshot, 1:43; foufou (Boiled Cassava), 1:45; Kédjenou de Poulet, 1:46; major foodstuffs, 1:44; meals, typical, 1:45–46; overview of, 1:43; special occasions, 1:46

Crab Backs, 2:112

Cranachan, 4:323–24

Croatia, 4:71–79; breskvice, 4:78; cooking, 4:73–74; diet and health, 4:78–79; eating out, 4:77–78; food culture snapshot, 4:71–73; Gulyás (goulash), 4:72, 4:76; major foodstuffs, 4:73; meals, typical, 4:74, 4:75–77; overview of, 4:71; Palascintas, 4:76; Rab cake, 4:75; sarma (stuffed cabbage), 4:74–75; special occasions, 4:78

Cuba, 2:91–99; cooking, 2:95; diet and health, 2:98–99; eating out, 2:97–98; food culture snapshot, 2:92–93; major foodstuffs, 2:93–95; meals, typical, 2:95–96; Moros y Cristianos (Cuban Black Beans and Rice), 2:93; overview of, 2:91; picadillo,

2:96–97; special occasions, 2:98

Curaçao and Sint Maarten, 2:101–7; cooking, 2:103–5; diet and health, 2:107; eating out, 2:106; food culture snapshot, 2:102; Iguana Stew, 2:104; major foodstuffs, 2:102–3; meals, typical, 2:105–6; overview of, 2:101–2; special occasions, 2:106

Curanto, 2:70

Curried shrimp, 2:297–98

Curtido, 2:137

Curtido de repollo, 2:245

Cyprus, 4:81–85; Black-Eyed Peas with Chard, 4:84; bourekia, 4:85; cooking, 4:82–83; diet and health, 4:85; eating out, 4:84; food culture snapshot, 4:81–82; halloumi cheese, 4:82; major foodstuffs, 4:82; meals, typical, 4:83–84; overview of, 4:81; Souvlakia Me Pitta (Kebabs in Pita Bread), 4:83; special occasions, 4:84–85

Czech Republic, 4:87–92; cesnekova polevka (garlic soup), 4:90; diet and health, 4:92; eating out, 4:91; food culture snapshot, 4:88; major foodstuffs, 4:89–90; meals, typical, 4:90–91; overview of, 4:87–88; special occasions, 4:91; Vepřo-Knedlo-Zelo (Pork Dumplings and Vegetables), 4:88–89

Dal makhani, 3:96–97

Damper Bread, 3:4

Denmark, 4:93–101; Brændende kærlighed, 4:99; cooking, 4:97–98; diet and health, 4:100–101; eating out, 4:99–100; food culture snapshot, 4:94–95; major foodstuffs, 4:95–97; meals, typical, 4:98–99; overview of, 4:93–94; special occasions, 4:100

Dikons, 3:90

Dim sum, 3:65, 3:89, 3:164

Dominica, 2:109–17; cooking, 2:112–13, 2:114; Crab Backs, 2:112; diet and health, 2:116–17; eating out, 2:115–16; food culture snapshot, 2:109–10; major foodstuffs, 2:110–12; Manicou or Agouti (Dominican Game), 2:114; meals, typical, 2:114–15; overview of, 2:109; special occasions, 2:116

Dominican Republic, 2:119–27; Bacalao a La Criolla (Codfish a La Dominicana), 2:123; Camarones Guisados (Shrimp Stew), 2:123–24; cooking, 2:121–22; diet and health, 2:126; eating out, 2:125; empanadas, 2:125; food culture snapshot, 2:120; Habichuelas con Dulce (popular Easter dish), 2:126; LaBandera Dominica, 2:123; major foodstuffs, 2:120–21; mangu, 2:122; meals, typical, 2:122–23, 2:124; overview of, 2:119–20; pasteles en hoja (Banana-Leaf Bundles), 2:126; Pudín o Bizocho (Special Dominican Holiday Cake), 2:126; Puerco Asado (Pork Roast), 2:124; sancocho (holiday stew), 2:126; special occasions, 2:125–26

Doro Wat, or Zegeni (Chicken in Red Pepper Paste), 1:65

Dovi (Peanut Butter Stew), 1:211–12

Dranniki (potato fritters), 4:34, 4:35

Dublin Coddle, 4:200

Dumplings, 2:149–50

Easter Spice Bun, 2:204

Ecuador, 2:129–34; chupe de pescado (Fish Soup), 2:132; cooking, 2:132; diet and health, 2:134; eating out,

Vol 1:	**Africa, Middle East**
Vol 2:	**Americas**
Vol 3:	**Asia and Oceania**
Vol 4:	**Europe**

2:133; food culture snapshot, 2:129–30; major foodstuffs, 2:130–32; meals, typical, 2:132–33; overview of, 2:129; special occasions, 2:133–34

Egg hoppers, 3:250

Egypt, 1:49–58; beans, 1:52; coffee, 1:54; cooking, 1:54; diet and health, 1:57; eating out, 1:56; fats, 1:53; food culture snapshot, 1:50–51; fowl, 1:53; fruits, 1:52; grains, 1:51–52; herbs, 1:54; legumes, 1:52; major foodstuffs, 1:51–54; meals, typical, 1:56; meat, 1:53; nuts, 1:54; overview of, 1:49; poultry, 1:53; seafood, 1:53; Shorbat Maloukhiya (Jew's Mallow Soup), 1:55–56; special occasions, 1:56; spices, 1:54; t'amaya (Egyptian Fava Falafel), 1:54–55; tea, 1:54; vegetables, 1:52–53

Elora Road Butternut Squash and Buttermilk Soup, 2:56

El Salvador, 2:135–39; cheese-stuffed pupusas, 2:137; cooking, 2:137–38; curtido, 2:137; diet and health, 2:139; eating out, 2:138–39; food culture snapshot, 2:135; major foodstuffs, 2:135–37; meals, typical, 2:138; overview of, 2:135; special occasions, 2:139

Empanadas, 2:1, 2:4, 2:41, 2:72, 2:80, 2:125, 2:362

Eritrea. *See* Ethiopia and Eritrea

Ethiopia and Eritrea, 1:59–70; berbere, 1:64–65; cooking, 1:63, 1:64, 1:65–67; diet and health, 1:69–70; Doro Wat, or Zegeni (Chicken in Red Pepper Paste), 1:65; eating out, 1:68–69; food culture snapshot, 1:60; injera, 1:63–64; major foodstuffs, 1:60–63; meals, typical, 1:67–68; niter kibbeh (Spiced Butter), 1:65; overview of, 1:59–60; special occasions, 1:69

Europe, 4:1–384; Armenia, 4:1–10; Austria, 4:11–19; Basque territory, 4:21–29; Belarus, 4:31–38; Belgium, 4:39–49; Bosnia and Herzegovina, 4:51–60; Bulgaria, 4:61–70; Croatia, 4:71–79; Cyprus, 4:81–85; Czech Republic, 4:87–92; Denmark, 4:93–101; Finland, 4:103–10; France, 4:111–22; Georgia, 4:123–31; Germany, 4:133–45; Great Britain, 4:147–59; Greece, 4:161–70; Gypsies, 4:171–79; Hungary, 4:181–89; Iceland, 4:191–96; Ireland, 4:197–205; Italy, 4:207–18; Latvia, 4:219–23; Lithuania, 4:225–30; Malta, 4:231–38; Moldova, 4:239–44; Netherlands, 4:245–57; Norway, 4:259–69; Poland, 4:271–79; Portugal, 4:281–88; Romania, 4:289–97; Russia, 4:299–310; Saami, 4:311–16; Scotland, 4:317–25; Serbia, 4:327–31; Slovakia, 4:333–37; Slovenia, 4:339–46; Spain, 4:347–57; Sweden, 4:359–66; Switzerland, 4:367–75; Ukraine, 4:377–84

Fårikål (mutton-in-cabbage), 4:263

Fattoush, 1:281, 1:291

Fatush (Flatbread Salad), 1:271–72

Feijoada, 2:51

Fenugreek, 1:295, 1:296, 1:319, 1:321

Féroce D'avocat, 2:212–13

Finland, 4:103–10; cooking, 4:104; diet and health, 4:109–10; eating out, 4:106–7; food culture snapshot, 4:103–4; Joulu-torttu, 4:109; meals, typical, 4:104–6; overview of, 4:103; Poronkäristys, 4:105; special occasions, 4:107–9

Fish-ball soup with noodles, 3:239–40

Flatbrau, 4:195

Foie gras, 4:121

Food Processor Biscuits, 2:349–50

Foufou (Boiled Cassava), 1:45

France, 4:111–22; cooking, 4:115–16; diet and health, 4:121–22; eating out, 4:118–19; foie gras, 4:121; food culture snapshot, 4:113–14; major foodstuffs, 4:114–15; meals, typical, 4:116–17, 4:118; overview of, 4:111–13; Poulet Aux Poireaux (Chicken with Leeks and Tarragon), 4:117–18; Ratatouille (Summer Vegetable Stew), 4:117; special occasions, 4:119–20

French Guiana, 2:141–45; bouillon d'awara, 2:143–44; cooking, 2:143; diet and health, 2:144–45; eating out, 2:144; food culture snapshot, 2:142; major foodstuffs, 2:142–43; meals, typical, 2:143, 2:144; overview of, 2:141–42; special occasions, 2:144

Frijoles con Tequila (Beans with Tequila), 2:222–23

Fry Bread, 2:235, 2:365

Fufu, 1:36

Funchi, 2:11

Funji (Manioc Puree), 1:16

Fuul Sudani (Sudanese Fava Bean Stew), 1:185–86

Gado-gado, 3:106

Gai yang (Lao-Style Barbecue Chicken), 3:149, 3:150

Gallo pinto (beans and rice), 2:86

Gandules con Bollitos de Plátano (Pigeon Peas with Green Plantain Dumplings), 2:276

Gata, **4**:6, **4**:8–9

Gaza, Palestine Territories, **1**:292–93

Gemini Mashed Potatoes, **3**:293

Gemista (stuffed vegetables), **4**:166

Georgia, **4**:123–31; adzhapsandali, **4**:124–25; cooking, **4**:126–27; diet and health, **4**:130–31; eating out, **4**:129–30; food culture snapshot, **4**:124; Georgian wine, **4**:128–29; khachapuri, **4**:124, **4**:129–30; major foodstuffs, **4**:125–26; meals, typical, **4**:127–29; overview of, **4**:123–24

Germany, **4**:133–45; cooking, **4**:139–40; diet and health, **4**:144; eating out, **4**:141–42; food culture snapshot, **4**:133–34; Kartoffelsuppe (Potato Soup), **4**:134; Kohlrouladen (Cabbage Rolls), **4**:136–37; major foodstuffs, **4**:134, **4**:135–36, **4**:137–39; meals, typical, **4**:140–41; overview of, **4**:133; special occasions, **4**:142–43

Ghana, **1**:71–74; cooking, **1**:72–73; diet and health, **1**:74; eating out, **1**:73–74; food culture snapshot, **1**:71; Groundnut Stew, **1**:73; major foodstuffs, **1**:71–72; meals, typical, **1**:73; overview of, **1**:71; special occasions, **1**:74

Gibanica, **4**:342

Glaze, **2**:205

Goan vindalho, **3**:228–29

Goi Ga, **3**:279–80

Golabki (cabbage rolls), **4**:276

Grape leaves, **1**:239, **1**:271, **1**:278, **1**:280, **1**:297

Great Britain, **4**:147–59; cooking, **4**:152–54; diet and health, **4**:158–59; eating out, **4**:155–57; food culture snapshot, **4**:148; major foodstuffs, **4**:148–52; meals, typical, **4**:154–55; overview of, **4**:147;

Rich Fruitcake, **4**:157; Roast Beef and Yorkshire Pudding, **4**:155; special occasions, **4**:157–58

Grechnevye Bliny (Russian Buckwheat Pancakes/Crepes), **4**:308

Greece, **4**:161–70; cooking, **4**:164–65; diet and health, **4**:169–70; eating out, **4**:167–68; food culture snapshot, **4**:161–63; gemista (stuffed vegetables), **4**:166; major foodstuffs, **4**:163–64; meals, typical, **4**:165–66, **4**:167; overview of, **4**:161; sfougato (omelet), **4**:166–67; special occasions, **4**:168–69

Green Chili Enchiladas, **2**:358

Green Chili Sauce, **2**:358

Grenada, **2**:147–52; cooking, **2**:150–51; diet and health, **2**:152; Dumplings, **2**:149–50; eating out, **2**:151–52; food culture snapshot, **2**:148; Grenadian Oil-Down, **2**:149, **2**:150, **2**:151; major foodstuffs, **2**:148–49, **2**:150; meals, typical, **2**:151; overview of, **2**:147–48; special occasions, **2**:152

Grenadian Oil-Down, **2**:149, **2**:150, **2**:151

Griyo (glazed pork), **2**:167

Groats, **1**:298

Groundnut Stew, **1**:73, **1**:144

Grouper moqueca, **2**:50–51

Guadeloupe. *See* Martinique and Guadeloupe

Guatemala, **2**:153–58; cooking, **2**:155–56; diet and health, **2**:157–58; eating out, **2**:157; food culture snapshot, **2**:153–54; major foodstuffs, **2**:154–55; meals, typical, **2**:156, **2**:157; overview of, **2**:153; Pepián, **2**:156–57; special occasions, **2**:157

Guinea, **1**:75–79; cooking, **1**:77; diet and health, **1**:79; eating

out, **1**:78; food culture snapshot, **1**:75; maffe hacco (Cassava-Leaf Sauce), **1**:76–77; major foodstuffs, **1**:76, **1**:77; meals, typical, **1**:77–78; overview of, **1**:75

Gulyás (goulash), **4**:16, **4**:72, **4**:76, **4**:184–85

Guriltai Shol (Mutton Soup with Noodles), **3**:177–78

Guyana, **2**:159–63; cassareep, **2**:161–62; cooking, **2**:160–61; diet and health, **2**:163; eating out, **2**:162; food culture snapshot, **2**:160; major foodstuffs, **2**:160; meals, typical, **2**:161, **2**:162; overview of, **2**:159–60; pepperpot, **2**:161; special occasions, **2**:162–63

Gypsies, **4**:171–79; cooking, **4**:175–76; diet and health, **4**:177–78; eating out, **4**:176; food culture snapshot, **4**:173–74; major foodstuffs, **4**:174–75; meals, typical, **4**:176; overview of, **4**:171–73; sarmi, **4**:177; special occasions, **4**:176–77; trgance, **4**:174

Habichuelas con Dulce (popular Easter dish), **2**:126

Haiti, **2**:165–73; cooking, **2**:168–69; diet and health, **2**:172–73; eating out, **2**:170; food culture snapshot, **2**:165–66; griyo (glazed pork), **2**:167; major foodstuffs, **2**:166–68; meals, typical, **2**:169–70; overview of, **2**:165; Sos Pwa Rouj (Red Beans in Sauce), **2**:169; special occasions, **2**:170–72

Hákarl, **4**:195

Hallacas, **2**:372–73

Halloumi cheese, **4**:82

Halushky (dumplings), **4**:336, **4**:380

Ham biscuits, **2**:350

Hangikjöt, **4**:195

Harira (soup), **1**:8, **1**:9, **1**:124

Vol 1:	**Africa, Middle East**
Vol 2:	**Americas**
Vol 3:	**Asia and Oceania**
Vol 4:	**Europe**

Harsha (Quick Semolina Bread for Ramadan), **1**:9

Hawaii, **2**:175–82; cooking, **2**:177–78; diet and health, **2**:181–82; eating out, **2**:179–80; food culture snapshot, **2**:175–76; Hawaiian-Style Kalbi, **2**:180; major foodstuffs, **2**:176–77; meals, typical, **2**:178–79; overview of, **2**:175; poi, **2**:177; Salmon Poke, **2**:176; special occasions, **2**:180–81

Hawaiian-Style Kalbi, **2**:180

Her'heri, **2**:288

Herzegovina. *See* Bosnia and Herzegovina

Hmong, **3**:73–81; cooking, **3**:75–76; diet and health, **3**:79–81; dikons, **3**:90; eating out, **3**:77; food culture snapshot, **3**:74–75; major foodstuffs, **3**:75; meals, typical, **3**:76; overview of, **3**:73–74; Sour Soup, **3**:76; special occasions, **3**:77–79; Zeub Nfsuab (Boiled Pork and Mustard Greens), **3**:76

Honduras, **2**:183–90; Baked Sweet Plantains with Cheese, **2**:185; carne asada, **2**:184–85; cooking, **2**:186; diet and health, **2**:189–90; eating out, **2**:188; food culture snapshot, **2**:183–84; major foodstuffs, **2**:184, **2**:185–86; meals, typical, **2**:186–88; overview of, **2**:183; special occasions, **2**:188–89

Hong Kong, **3**:83–92; cooking, **3**:86–87; diet and health, **3**:91–92; dim sum, **3**:89; eating out, **3**:88–90; food culture snapshot, **3**:83–84; major foodstuffs, **3**:84–86; meals, typical, **3**:87–88; Mock Shark's-Fin Soup, **3**:90; overview of, **3**:83; special occasions, **3**:90–91

Hrútspungar, **4**:195

Huancayna sauce, **2**:264–65

Hungary, **4**:181–89; Bejgli, **4**:188; cooking, **4**:183–84; diet and health, **4**:188–89; eating out, **4**:187; food culture snapshot, **4**:181–82; Gulyás (goulash), **4**:184–85; major foodstuffs, **4**:182–83; meals, typical, **4**:184, **4**:185–86; overview of, **4**:181; Paprikás Csirke (Paprika Chicken), **4**:186–87; special occasions, **4**:187–88

Huushuur (Mongolian fried meat-filled pastries), **3**:180–81

Iceland, **4**:191–96; Blómör, **4**:195; cooking, **4**:193; diet and health, **4**:195–96; eating out, **4**:194; Flatbrau, **4**:195; food culture snapshot, **4**:191–92; Hákarl, **4**:195; Hangikjöt, **4**:195; Hrútspungar, **4**:195; Lifrarpylsa, **4**:195; major foodstuffs, **4**:192–93; meals, typical, **4**:193–94; overview of, **4**:191; Rúgbrau, **4**:195; special occasions, **4**:194–95; Svid, **4**:195

Iguana Stew, **2**:104

Imam bayaldi, **1**:306

Impala (African Antelope), **1**:200–201

India, **3**:93–101; cooking, **3**:95–96; Dal makhani, **3**:96–97; diet and health, **3**:100–101; eating out, **3**:98–99; food culture snapshot, **3**:93–94; laddoos, **3**:99; major foodstuffs, **3**:94–95; meals, typical, **3**:96, **3**:97–98; overview of, **3**:93; special occasions, **3**:99–100

Indonesia, **3**:103–11; animal proteins, **3**:105; beverages, **3**:107; cooking, **3**:107–8; diet and health, **3**:110–11; eating out, **3**:108–9; food culture snapshot, **3**:103–4; gado-gado, **3**:106; lontong opor, **3**:107; major foodstuffs, **3**:104–7; meals, typical, **3**:108; nasi tumpeng, **3**:109–10; overview of, **3**:103; plant sources, **3**:105–7; rice, **3**:103; special occasions, **3**:109–10; starches, **3**:104–5

Injera, **1**:63–64

Inuit, **2**:191–98; cooking, **2**:195; diet and health, **2**:197–98; eating out, **2**:196; food culture snapshot, **2**:192; major foodstuffs, **2**:192–95; meals, typical, **2**:196; overview of, **2**:191–92; special occasions, **2**:196–97

Iran, **1**:239–47; chelo, **1**:241–42; cooking, **1**:241, 243–44; diet and health, **1**:246; eating out, **1**:244–45; food culture snapshot, **1**:239–40; koreshte geymeh, **1**:242–43; lamb biryani, **1**:241; major foodstuffs, **1**:240–41; meals, typical, **1**:244; overview of, **1**:239; special occasions, **1**:245–46

Iraq, **1**:249–57; cooking, **1**:251–52; diet and health, **1**:256–57; eating out, **1**:253–54; food culture snapshot, **1**:249–50; Kleichat Tamur (Date-Filled Cookies), **1**:255, **1**:256; major foodstuffs, **1**:250–51; Margat Bamya (Okra Stew), **1**:253; meals, typical, **1**:252–53; mutton briyani, **1**:250; overview of, **1**:249; special occasions, **1**:254–56

Ireland, **4**:197–205; colcannon, **4**:204; cooking, **4**:201; diet and health, **4**:204; Dublin Coddle, **4**:200; eating out, **4**:202–3; food culture snapshot, **4**:197–98; major foodstuffs, **4**:198–201; meals, typical, **4**:201–2; milk and dairy, **4**:200; overview of, **4**:197; pork, **4**:200; potatoes, **4**:199–200; Shepherd's pie, **4**:198; soda bread, **4**:201; special occasions, **4**:203–4; tea, breads, and cakes, **4**:201

Israel, **1**:259–66; cooking, **1**:261–62; diet and health, **1**:265; eating out, **1**:263; food culture snapshot, **1**:259–60; Israeli Salad, **1**:263; latkes, **1**:264; major foodstuffs, **1**:260–61; meals, typical, **1**:262–63; overview of, **1**:259; shakshuka (Eggs with Tomatoes), **1**:264; special occasions, **1**:264

Israeli Salad, **1**:263

Italy, **4**:207–18; Aliciotti con l'indivia (fresh anchovies with escarole), **4**:210; cooking, **4**:210–11; diet and health, **4**:216–17; eating out, **4**:212–14; food culture snapshot, **4**:207; major foodstuffs, **4**:207–10; meals, typical, **4**:211–12; overview of, **4**:207; Pappa al Pomodoro (Tuscan Tomato and Bread Soup), **4**:208; saffron risotto, **4**:208; special occasions, **4**:214–16

Jamaica, **2**:199–206; animal protein, **2**:201; bammy, **2**:201, **2**:203; breakfast, **2**:203; coffee, **2**:202; cooking, **2**:203; diet and health, **2**:205–6; dinner, **2**:204; Easter Spice Bun, **2**:204; eating out, **2**:204; fish and shellfish, **2**:201; food culture snapshot, **2**:200–201; Glaze, **2**:205; lunch, **2**:203–4; major foodstuffs, **2**:201–3; meals, typical, **2**:203–4; overview of, **2**:199–200; pepper shrimp, **2**:201; plant sources, **2**:201–2; rum, **2**:202–3; special occasions, **2**:204; spices, **2**:202; starches, **2**:201

Jamun (Bengali sweet), **3**:34

Japan, **3**:113–25; cooking, **3**:116–17; diet and health, **3**:123–24; eating out, **3**:118–21; food culture snapshot, **3**:113–14; Kamo/Niku Namban Soba (Duck or Beef and Noodle Soup), **3**:118; major foodstuffs, **3**:114–16; meals, typical, **3**:117–18; overview of, **3**:113; ozoñi, **3**:122; Red and White Salad, **3**:123; special occasions, **3**:121–23

Jerk chicken, **2**:113, **2**:201

Jollof rice, **1**:144

Jordan, **1**:267–75; cooking, **1**:270–71; diet and health, **1**:274–75; eating out, **1**:272–73; fatush (Flatbread Salad), **1**:271–72; food culture snapshot, **1**:268–69; major foodstuffs, **1**:269–70; mansaf, **1**:273–74; meals, typical, **1**:271; overview of, **1**:267–68; special occasions, **1**:273–74; za'atar, **1**:270, **1**:272

Joulutorttu, **4**:109

Kadayif, **1**:311

Kaiserschmarrn, **4**:17, **4**:18, **4**:340

Kalduny (dumplings), **4**:33, **4**:34–35

Kamo/Niku Namban Soba (Duck or Beef and Noodle Soup), **3**:118

Kanafeh, **1**:311

Kapusnica, **4**:337

Kartoffelsuppe (Potato Soup), **4**:134

Kavarma, **4**:67

Kaya, **3**:238–39

Kazakhstan, **3**:127–34; Beshbarmek, **3**:133; cooking, **3**:131–32; diet and health, **3**:134; eating out, **3**:132; food culture snapshot, **3**:127–28; major foodstuffs, **3**:128–30, **3**:131; meals, typical, **3**:132; overview of, **3**:127; plov,

3:131; samsa, **3**:130; special occasions, **3**:132–34

Kédjenou de Poulet, **1**:46

Kenya, **1**:81–89; bananas, **1**:82; beverages, **1**:85; cooking, **1**:85–86; diet and health, **1**:88; eating out, **1**:87–88; food culture snapshot, **1**:82–83; major foodstuffs, **1**:83–85; meals, typical, **1**:86, **1**:87; overview of, **1**:81–82; special occasions, **1**:88; sukuma wiki, **1**:86–87; ugali (cornmeal porridge), **1**:82, **1**:83, **1**:87

Keshi yena, **2**:9–10

Khachapuri, **4**:124, **4**:129–30

Kimchi, **3**:136–38, **3**:140, **3**:145

Kleichat Tamur (Date-Filled Cookies), **1**:255, **1**:256

Kohlrouladen (Cabbage Rolls), **4**:136–37

Konijn met Pruimen or Lapin Aux Prunes (Rabbit with Plums), **4**:40–41

Koq chuchvara (Uzbek green dumplings), **3**:57

Korea, **3**:135–45; bibimbap, **3**:143; cooking, **3**:139–40; diet and health, **3**:144–45; eating out, **3**:141–43; food culture snapshot, **3**:137; kimchi, **3**:136–38, **3**:140, **3**:145; major foodstuffs, **3**:137–39; meals, typical, **3**:140–41; overview of, **3**:135–37; special occasions, **3**:143–44

Koreshte geymeh, **1**:242–43

Korma (lamb stew with yogurt), **3**:196

Kulesh (millet, potato, and lard soup), **4**:379

LaBandera Dominica, **2**:123

Laddoos, **3**:99

Lamb biryani, **1**:241

Lao People's Democratic Republic (Lao PDR), **3**:147–52; Beef Laap, **3**:150; cooking, **3**:149; diet and health, **3**:151; eating

Vol 1:	**Africa, Middle East**
Vol 2:	**Americas**
Vol 3:	**Asia and Oceania**
Vol 4:	**Europe**

out, **3**:150–51; food culture snapshot, **3**:147; Gai yang (Lao-Style Barbecue Chicken), **3**:149, **3**:150; major foodstuffs, **3**:147–49; meals, typical, **3**:150; overview of, **3**:147; special occasions, **3**:151

Latkes, **1**:264

Latvia, **4**:219–23; cooking, **4**:221; diet and health, **4**:223; eating out, **4**:222; food culture snapshot, **4**:219; major foodstuffs, **4**:219–21; meals, typical, **4**:221–22; overview of, **4**:219; Rīga sprats, **4**:221; skaba putra (sour barley porridge), **4**:222; special occasions, **4**:222–23

Lebanon, **1**:277–83; cooking, **1**:279–80; diet and health, **1**:282; eating out, **1**:281; fattoush, **1**:281; food culture snapshot, **1**:277–78; major foodstuffs, **1**:278; meals, typical, **1**:280–81; Mjaddara (Pockmarked Rice and Lentils), **1**:280; overview of, **1**:277; Samak bi-Tahini (Fish in Tahini Sauce), **1**:279; special occasions, **1**:281–82

Liberia, **1**:91–96; cooking, **1**:94; diet and health, **1**:95; eating out, **1**:95; food culture snapshot, **1**:91–92; major foodstuffs, **1**:92–94; meals, typical, **1**:94, **1**:95; overview of, **1**:91; Palm Butter Soup, **1**:95; special occasions, **1**:95

Lifrarpylsa, **4**:195

Lithuania, **4**:225–30; Cepelinai (Zeppelins/Potato Dumplings), **4**:226–27; cooking,

4:228; diet and health, **4**:230; eating out, **4**:229; major foodstuffs, **4**:227–28; meals, typical, **4**:228–29; overview of, **4**:225–26, **4**:227; Šaltibarščciai (Cold Beet Soup), **4**:228; special occasions, **4**:229–30

Lomo saltado, **2**:71, **2**:267

Lontong opor, **3**:107

Luwombo, **1**:206

Maasai, **1**:97–103; blood and, **1**:102; clans of, **1**:97–98; cooking, **1**:99–100; diet and health, **1**:102–3; eating out, **1**:101; fats and, **1**:102; food culture snapshot, **1**:98; major foodstuffs, **1**:98–99; meals, typical, **1**:100–101; meat feast, **1**:101–2; overview of, **1**:97–98; sections of, **1**:97; special occasions, **1**:101–2

Macau, **3**:153–58; bacalhau, **3**:154, **3**:155; cooking, **3**:155–56; diet and health, **3**:157–58; eating out, **3**:156–57; food culture snapshot, **3**:153–54; major foodstuffs, **3**:155; meals, typical, **3**:156; minchi, **3**:154–55; overview of, **3**:153; special occasions, **3**:157

Machbous, **1**:224

Madagascar, **1**:105–13; akoho sy voanio, **1**:112; cooking, **1**:108–9; diet and health, **1**:112–13; eating out, **1**:110–11; food culture snapshot, **1**:106; major foodstuffs, **1**:106–7, **1**:108; meals, typical, **1**:109, **1**:110; overview of, **1**:105–6; romazava, **1**:108, **1**:109–10; special occasions, **1**:111–12; varenga, **1**:107–8

Maffe hacco (Cassava-Leaf Sauce), **1**:76–77

Malaysia, **3**:159–68; Beef Rendang, **3**:163–64; cooking, **3**:161–63; diet and health, **3**:167; eating out, **3**:164; food culture

snapshot, **3**:159–60; major foodstuffs, **3**:160–61; meals, typical, **3**:163, **3**:164; Nasi lemak, **3**:159, **3**:160; overview of, **3**:159; special occasions, **3**:165–67

Malpoa, **3**:35

Malta, **4**:231–38; bigilla, **4**:233; cooking, **4**:234; diet and health, **4**:237; eating out, **4**:235–36; food culture snapshot, **4**:231–32; major foodstuffs, **4**:232–34; meals, typical, **4**:234–35; overview of, **4**:231; special occasions, **4**:236–37

Mamaliga (polenta), **4**:242

Mangu, **2**:122

Manicou or Agouti (Dominican Game), **2**:114

Mansaf, **1**:273–74

Mantecados, **4**:356

Mantu, **3**:10, **3**:14, **3**:16

Margat Bamya (Okra Stew), **1**:253

Marmitako, **4**:25, **4**:26

Martinique and Guadeloupe, **2**:207–16; accras de morue, **2**:210–11; blaff de poisson blancs (fish blaff), **2**:211–12; cooking, **2**:210–11; diet and health, **2**:215–16; eating out, **2**:213–14; Féroce D'avocat, **2**:212–13; food culture snapshot, **2**:207–8; major foodstuffs, **2**:208–10; meals, typical, **2**:211, **2**:212; overview of, **2**:207; special occasions, **2**:214–15

Matooke, **1**:204–5

Mauritania, **1**:115–18; chubbagin, **1**:117; cooking, **1**:116; diet and health, **1**:118; eating out, **1**:118; food culture snapshot, **1**:115; major foodstuffs, **1**:115–16; meals, typical, **1**:116–18; overview of, **1**:115; special occasions, **1**:118

Mawa (Bengali sweet), **3**:34

Meat pie, **3**:27

Mexico, **2**:217–29; cooking, **2**:220–21; diet and health, **2**:227–29; eating out, **2**:223–25; food culture snapshot, **2**:217–18; Frijoles con Tequila (Beans with Tequila), **2**:222–23; major foodstuffs, **2**:218–20; meals, typical, **2**:221–22, **2**:223; mole sauce, **2**:220, **2**:223, **2**:227; overview of, **2**:217; sincronizadas, **2**:222; special occasions, **2**:225–27

Mhammara, **1**:300–301

Mid-Atlantic (United States), **2**:303–11; cooking, **2**:306; diet and health, **2**:309–10; eating out, **2**:307–8; food culture snapshot, **2**:304–5; major foodstuffs, **2**:305–6; meals, typical, **2**:307; overview of, **2**:303–4; special occasions, **2**:308–9

Middle East, **1**:215–322; Arabian Peninsula, **1**:217–29; Berbers and Tuaregs, **1**:231–38; Iran, **1**:239–47; Iraq, **1**:249–57; Israel, **1**:259–66; Jordan, **1**:267–75; Lebanon, **1**:277–83; Palestine Territories, **1**:285–96; Syria, **1**:297–303; Turkey, **1**:305–16; Yemen and Oman, **1**:317–22

Midwest (United States), **2**:313–24; cooking, **2**:316–17; corn chowder, **2**:314; diet and health, **2**:323–24; eating out, **2**:321; food culture snapshot, **2**:313–14; major foodstuffs, **2**:314–16; meals, typical, **2**:318–21; overview of, **2**:313; special occasions, **2**:321–23

Minchi, **3**:154–55

Minchi (Macanese Ground Meat), **3**:232–33

Mititei (grilled sausage rolls), **4**:241, **4**:242, **4**:293, **4**:295

Mjaddara (Pockmarked Rice and Lentils), **1**:280

Mnazzlit Ahmar wa-Aswad, **1**:301–2

Mock Shark's-Fin Soup, **3**:90

Moldova, **4**:239–44; cooking, **4**:241–42; diet and health, **4**:243; eating out, **4**:242–43; food culture snapshot, **4**:239; major foodstuffs, **4**:239–41; mamaliga (polenta), **4**:242; meals, typical, **4**:242; moussaka, **4**:240; overview of, **4**:239; special occasions, **4**:243; zama (chicken and noodle soup), **4**:241–42

Mole sauce, **2**:220, **2**:223, **2**:227

Momo, **3**:189, **3**:190, **3**:268

Mongolia, **3**:175–84; cooking, **3**:179–80; diet and health, **3**:183–84; eating out, **3**:181–82; food culture snapshot, **3**:176–77; Guriltai Shol (Mutton Soup with Noodles), **3**:177–78; huushuur (Mongolian fried meat-filled pastries), **3**:180–81; major foodstuffs, **3**:178–79; meals, typical, **3**:181; overview of, **3**:175–76; special occasions, **3**:182–83

Māori, **3**:169–73; Boil-Up, **3**:172–73; cooking, **3**:172; diet and health, **3**:173; eating out, **3**:173; food culture snapshot, **3**:169–70; major foodstuffs, **3**:170–72; meals, typical, **3**:172; overview of, **3**:169; Roroi Kūmara, **3**:172; special occasions, **3**:173

Morocco, **1**:119–24; cooking, **1**:121; diet and health, **1**:124; eating out, **1**:123; food culture snapshot, **1**:119; major foodstuffs, **1**:119–21; meals, typical, **1**:121–22; overview of, **1**:119; qotban (Brochettes), **1**:123; Soupe aux Carottes (Carrot Soup), **1**:122–23; special occasions, **1**:124

Moros y Cristianos (Cuban Black Beans and Rice), **2**:93, **2**:94, **2**:187

Moussaka, **4**:62, **4**:240

Moyau (Chicken Stew), **1**:20

Mozambique, **1**:125–35; caril de galinha à Moçambicana (Curried Chicken, Mozambican Style), **1**:133; chamuças (Chicken Turnovers), **1**:130–31; cooking, **1**:129–30; diet and health, **1**:134; eating out, **1**:131–32; food culture snapshot, **1**:128; major foodstuffs, **1**:128–29; meals, typical, **1**:131; overview of, **1**:125–28; special occasions, **1**:132–33

Muamba de galinha (Angolan-Style Chicken), **1**:15–16

Mutton briyani, **1**:250

Namibia, **1**:135–39; braai (act of barbecuing), **1**:136, **1**:138; cooking, **1**:137; diet and health, **1**:138–39; eating out, **1**:138; food culture snapshot, **1**:136; grains and starches, **1**:136; major foodstuffs, **1**:136, **1**:137; meals, typical, **1**:138; oshifima, **1**:136–37; overview of, **1**:135; special occasions, **1**:138

Nasi lemak, **3**:38, **3**:159, **3**:160, **3**:239

Nasi tumpeng, **3**:109–10

Native Americans, **2**:231–41; Acorn Griddle Cakes, **2**:240; Buffalo Stew (Lakota), **2**:235; Cherokee Succotash, **2**:236; cooking, **2**:236–37; diet and health, **2**:240–41; eating out, **2**:237–38; food culture snapshot, **2**:231–32; Fry Bread, **2**:235; major foodstuffs, **2**:232, **2**:233–35; meals, typical, **2**:237; overview of, **2**:231; special occasions, **2**:238–40; Three Sisters, **2**:232, **2**:235; Winnebago Wild Rice, **2**:233

Nepal, **3**:185–91; achaar (tomato pickle), **3**:188–89; cooking,

Vol 1: **Africa, Middle East**
Vol 2: **Americas**
Vol 3: **Asia and Oceania**
Vol 4: **Europe**

3:187; diet and health, 3:191; eating out, 3:190; food culture snapshot, 3:186; major foodstuffs, 3:186, 3:187; meals, typical, 3:187–88, 3:189, 3:190; momos, 3:190; overview of, 3:185–86; special occasions, 3:190; Tama ko Tarkari (Bamboo-Shoot Curry), 3:186–87

Netherlands, 4:245–57; birthdays, 4:256; Carnival, 4:255; Christmas, 4:256; condiments, 4:248; cooking, 4:249; dairy, 4:246–47; diet and health, 4:256–57; Easter, 4:255; eating out, 4:253–54; Fairs, 4:255; fish, 4:248; food culture snapshot, 4:246; food preservation, 4:248–49; fruit, 4:247–48; major foodstuffs, 4:246–49; meals, typical, 4:249–53; meat, poultry, and game, 4:248; New Year's, 4:254; oliebollen (doughnut balls), 4:254–55; overview of, 4:245–46; potatoes and vegetables, 4:247; Queen's Day, 4:255; Sint Maarten and Sinterklaas, 4:255–56; special occasions, 4:254–56; spices, 4:248; stamppot boerenkool (kale with sausage and potato), 4:251; vegetable hotchpotch, 4:251

New England (United States), 2:325–35; Boston Baked Beans, 2:330; cooking, 2:328–29; diet and health, 2:333–34; eating out, 2:330–32; food culture snapshot, 2:326–27; major foodstuffs, 2:327–28; meals, typical, 2:329–30; overview of, 2:325–26; special occasions, 2:332–33; Stuffies, 2:332; Yankee Pot Roast, 2:329

Nicaragua, 2:243–48; cooking, 2:245–46; curtido de repollo, 2:245; diet and health, 2:247–48; eating out, 2:246; food culture snapshot, 2:243–44; major foodstuffs, 2:244, 2:245; meals, typical, 2:246; overview of, 2:243; pinolillo, 2:244–45; special occasions, 2:247

Nigeria, 1:141–49; cooking, 1:145; diet and health, 1:148–49; eating out, 1:146–47; food culture snapshot, 1:142–43; Groundnut Stew, 1:144; jollof rice, 1:144; major foodstuffs, 1:143–45; meals, typical, 1:145–46; overview of, 1:141–42; special occasions, 1:147–48

Nihari (beef stew with ginger), 3:199–200

Niter kibbeh (Spiced Butter), 1:65

Norway, 4:259–69; Berlinerkranser (Norwegian Berlin Wreath Cookies), 4:265; cooking, 4:261, 4:262; diet and health, 4:267–68; eating out, 4:263–65; fårikål (mutton-in-cabbage), 4:263; food culture snapshot, 4:259; major foodstuffs, 4:259–61; meals, typical, 4:262–63; overview of, 4:259; Palesuppe (Bergen Young Saithe Soup), 4:261–62; special occasions, 4:265–66

Oatmeal Biscuits, 4:319

Oliebollen (doughnut balls), 4:254–55

Oman. *See* Yemen and Oman

Oshifima, 1:136–37

Ozoñi, 3:122

Pabellon Criollo con Caraotas Negras (beef with black beans and plantains), 2:371–72

Pacific Northwest (United States), 2:337–46; agriculture, 2:338–39; cooking, 2:340; dairies and creameries, 2:339; diet and health, 2:345–46; eating out, 2:342–43; food culture snapshot, 2:337–38; major foodstuffs, 2:338–40; meals, typical, 2:340–41; overview of, 2:337; potent potables, 2:339; seafood, 2:338; sockeye salmon, 2:338; special occasions, 2:343–45; Thai-Spiced Salmon Chowder, 2:341–42; wild foods, 2:339–40

Pad Thai (Thai fried noodles), 3:257–58

Pakistan, 3:193–202; breads, 3:197–98; cooking, 3:195; diet and health, 3:201–2; eating out, 3:200; food culture snapshot, 3:194; kebabs, 3:197; korma (lamb stew with yogurt), 3:196; major foodstuffs, 3:194; meals, typical, 3:195–200; meat and grain dishes, 3:196–97; meat and gravy dishes, 3:195–96; nihari (beef stew with ginger), 3:199–200; overview of, 3:193–94; roghan josh, 3:195–96; sewian, 3:197; special occasions, 3:200; sweet dishes, 3:197

Palascintas, 4:76

Palestine Territories, 1:285–96; cooking, 1:290–91; diet and health, 1:296; eating out, 1:293–94; food culture snapshot, 1:286; Gaza and, 1:292–93; major foodstuffs, 1:286–90; meals, typical, 1:291–92; overview of, 1:285; qatayef pancakes, 1:295; shakshuka, 1:286; special occasions, **1**:294–95; the Triangle in, **1**:292; West Bank region of, **1**:293

Palesuppe (Bergen Young Saithe Soup), **4**:261–62

Palm Butter Soup, **1**:95

Panama, **2**:249–52; arroz con pollo, **2**:249; diet and health, **2**:251–52; eating out, **2**:251; food culture snapshot, **2**:249–50; major foodstuffs, **2**:250; overview of, **2**:249; Sancocho de Gallina (recipe from Panama's national cuisine), **2**:251; special occasions, **2**:251

Pannkakstårta (birthday pancake cake), **4**:361–62

Pappa al Pomodoro (Tuscan Tomato and Bread Soup), **4**:208

Paprikás Csirke (Paprika Chicken), **4**:186–87

Papua New Guinea Foodways, **3**:203–13; aoatol, **3**:211; diet and health, **3**:211–13; eating out, **3**:206; major foodstuffs, **3**:203–4; meals, typical, **3**:204–6; overview of, **3**:203; Sago processing, **3**:210; special occasions, **3**:206–11; tapiok, **3**:208; Taro, origin of, **3**:207

Paraguay and Uruguay, **2**:253–61; cooking, **2**:257; diet and health, **2**:260–61; eating out, **2**:259; food culture snapshot, **2**:253–54; major foodstuffs, **2**:254–57; meals, typical, **2**:258–59; overview of, **2**:253; Postre Chajá, **2**:256; so'o yosopy (beef and rice soup), **2**:257–58; special occasions, **2**:259–60

Pastel de choclo, **2**:69–70

Pasteles en hoja (Banana-Leaf Bundles), **2**:126

Pelau, **2**:28–29, **2**:113, **2**:293–94

Pelmeni, **4**:300

Pepián, **2**:156–57

Pepperpot, **2**:26, **2**:161, **2**:162, **2**:287

Pepper shrimp, **2**:201

Peru, **2**:263–71; Ceviche, **2**:266; cooking, **2**:267–68; diet and health, **2**:270–71; eating out, **2**:268–69; food culture snapshot, **2**:263–64; huancayna sauce, **2**:264–65; lomo saltado, **2**:267; major foodstuffs, **2**:264, **2**:265–67; meals, typical, **2**:268; overview of, **2**:263; special occasions, **2**:269–70

Philippines, **3**:215–23; Chicken adobo, **3**:218, **3**:219–20; cooking, **3**:217–19; diet and health, **3**:223; eating out, **3**:220–22; food culture snapshot, **3**:215–16; major foodstuffs, **3**:216–17; meals, typical, **3**:219, **3**:220; overview of, **3**:215; special occasions, **3**:222–23

Pho, **3**:65, **3**:278

Picadillo, **2**:89, **2**:96–97, **2**:187

Picante de pollo (chicken in spicy sauce), **2**:40, **2**:41

Pierogi, **4**:274

Pinolillo, **2**:244–45

Pintxo, **4**:27

Plasas, **1**:163

Plov, **3**:131

Poi, **2**:177

Poland, **4**:271–79; barszcz (beet soup), **4**:275; bigos (Hunter's Stew), **4**:275; cooking, **4**:273; diet and health, **4**:278–79; eating out, **4**:277; food culture snapshot, **4**:271–72; golabki (cabbage rolls), **4**:276; major foodstuffs, **4**:272–73; meals, typical, **4**:274–75, **4**:276–77; overview of, **4**:271; pierogi, **4**:274; special occasions, **4**:277–78

Pom, **2**:286–87

Poronkäristys, **4**:105

Portugal, **4**:281–88; bolo rei, **4**:287; caldo verde (kale and potato soup), **4**:283, **4**:285; chicken piri-piri, **4**:286; cooking, **4**:285; diet and health, **4**:287–88; eating out, **4**:286; food culture snapshot, **4**:282; major foodstuffs, **4**:283–84; meals, typical, **4**:286; overview of, **4**:281–82; special occasions, **4**:286–87

Portuguese in Asia, **3**:225–34; cooking, **3**:228, **3**:229–30; diet and health, **3**:233–34; eating out, **3**:231; food culture snapshot, **3**:225–26; Goan vindalho, **3**:228–29; major foodstuffs, **3**:226–28; meals, typical, **3**:230–31; minchi (Macanese ground meat), **3**:232–33; overview of, **3**:225; sarapatel, **3**:227, **3**:232; special occasions, **3**:231–32, **3**:233

Postre Chajá, **2**:256

Potato and Mushroom Pirozhki, **4**:306–7

Potica, **4**:345

Poulet à la moambe (Chicken with Palm Butter), **1**:37

Poulet Aux Poireaux (Chicken with Leeks and Tarragon), **4**:117–18

Prawn Sambal, **3**:40

Pudín o Bizocho (Special Dominican Holiday Cake), **2**:126

Puerco Asado (Pork Roast), **2**:124

Puerto Rico, **2**:273–81; arañitas (shredded green plantain "spiders"), **2**:277–78; cooking, **2**:275–77; diet and health, **2**:280; eating out, **2**:278–79; food culture snapshot, **2**:274; Gandules con Bollitos de Plátano (Pigeon Peas with Green Plantain Dumplings), **2**:276, **2**:280; major foodstuffs, **2**:274–75; meals, typical, **2**:277, **2**:278; overview of, **2**:273–74; special occasions, **2**:279–80

Qabili Pilau, **3**:18–19

Qatayef pancakes, **1**:295

Qotban (Brochettes), **1**:123

Quandong Crumble, **3**:2

Vol 1:	**Africa, Middle East**
Vol 2:	**Americas**
Vol 3:	**Asia and Oceania**
Vol 4:	**Europe**

Rab cake, **4**:75

Ratatouille (Summer Vegetable Stew), **4**:117

Recipes: achaar (tomato pickle), **3**:188–89; Acorn Griddle Cakes, **2**:240; adzhapsandali, **4**:124–25; akoho sy voanio, **1**:112; aleluja, **4**:345–46; Aliciotti con l'indivia (fresh anchovies with escarole), **4**:210; aloko (Deep-Fried Plantains), **1**:44; arañitas (shredded green plantain "spiders"), **2**:277–78; ärtsoppa (yellow pea soup), **4**:363; aush, **3**:10; Bacalao a La Criolla (Codfish a La Dominicana), **2**:123; Bairam Palovi (Uzbek Wedding Pilaf), **3**:55; Baked Sweet Plantains with Cheese, **2**:185; Barbados Coucou and Flying Fish, **2**:22–23; barszcz (beet soup), **4**:275; Beef Laap, **3**:150; Beef Rendang, **3**:163–64; berbere, **1**:64–65; Berlinerkranser (Norwegian Berlin Wreath Cookies), **4**:265; Beshbarmek, **3**:133; beurre manié, **4**:371; bigilla, **4**:233; bigos (Hunter's Stew), **4**:275; bint al-sahn, **1**:320; Black-Eyed Peas with Chard, **4**:84; blaff de poisson blancs (fish blaff), **2**:211–12; Blinde Vinken or Oiseaux Sans Tête (Blind Finches), **4**:43–44; Boil-Up, **3**:172–73; Boston Baked Beans, **2**:330; bouillon d'awara, **2**:143–44; brinjal (eggplant) sambal, **3**:250; bryndzové halušky (dumplings), **4**:336;

Buffalo Stew (Lakota), **2**:235; Burani Bonjon, **3**:14–15; Bur katuunboow, **1**:170; caipirinha, **2**:52; Caldeirado de Cabrito (Goat-Meat Stew), **1**:18; caldo verde (kale and potato soup), **4**:285; Camarones Guisados (Shrimp Stew), **2**:123–24; Cambodian Pork and Eggplant Stir-Fry, **3**:44–45; Canh chua Ca Loc (sour broth), **3**:279; canjeero, **1**:169; Caramelized Fish, **3**:46; caril de galinha à Moçambicana (Curried Chicken, Mozambican Style), **1**:133; carne asada, **2**:184–85; Carpetbag Steak, **3**:24; cassareep, **2**:161–62; Ceebu jën, **1**:155; Cepelinai (Zeppelins/Potato Dumplings), **4**:226–27; cesnekova polevka (garlic soup), **4**:90; cevapcici (sausage), **4**:329–30; Ceviche, **2**:266; chamuças (Chicken Turnovers), **1**:130–31; Cheese Bread, **4**:313; Cheese Fondue, **4**:374–75; cheese-stuffed pupusas, **2**:137; chelo, **1**:241–42; Cherokee Succotash, **2**:236; Chicken adobo, **3**:219–20; Chicken Rice, **3**:241–42; chimichurri, **2**:3; chubbagin, **1**:117; chupe de pescado (Fish Soup), **2**:132; corn chowder, **2**:314; Crab Backs, **2**:112; cranachan, **4**:323–24; Curried shrimp, **2**:297–98; curtido, **2**:137; curtido de repollo, **2**:245; Dal makhani, **3**:96–97; Damper Bread, **3**:4; Doro Wat, or Zegeni (Chicken in Red Pepper Paste), **1**:65; Dovi (Peanut Butter Stew), **1**:211–12; dranniki (potato fritters), **4**:35; Dublin Coddle, **4**:200; dumplings, **2**:149–50; Easter Spice Bun, **2**:204; Elora

Road Butternut Squash and Buttermilk Soup, **2**:56; fårikål (mutton-in-cabbage), **4**:263; fatush (Flatbread Salad), **1**:271–72; Féroce D'avocat, **2**:212–13; Food Processor Biscuits, **2**:349–50; foufou (Boiled Cassava), **1**:45; Frijoles con Tequila (Beans with Tequila), **2**:222–23; Fry Bread, **2**:235, **2**:365; fufu, **1**:36; funchi, **2**:11; funji (Manioc Puree), 16; Fuul Sudani (Sudanese Fava Bean Stew), **1**:185–86; gado-gado, **3**:106; Gai yang (Lao-Style Barbecue Chicken), **3**:150; gallo pinto (beans and rice), **2**:86; Gandules con Bollitos de Plátano (Pigeon Peas with Green Plantain Dumplings), **2**:276; gata, **4**:8–9; Gemini Mashed Potatoes, **3**:293; gemista (stuffed vegetables), **4**:166; Glaze, **2**:205; Goan vindalho, **3**:228–29; Goi Ga, **3**:279–80; golabki (cabbage rolls), **4**:276; Grechnevye Bliny (Russian Buckwheat Pancakes/Crepes), **4**:308; Green Chili Enchiladas, **2**:358; Green Chili Sauce, **2**:358; Grenadian Oil-Down, **2**:149; griyo (glazed pork), **2**:167; Groundnut Stew, **1**:73, **1**:144; grouper moqueca, **2**:50–51; Gulyás (goulash), **4**:184–85; Guriltai Shol (Mutton Soup with Noodles), **3**:177–78; Habichuelas con Dulce (popular Easter dish), **2**:126; halushky (dumplings), **4**:380; ham biscuits, **2**:350; Harsha (Quick Semolina Bread for Ramadan), **1**:9; Hawaiian-Style Kalbi, **2**:180; Her'heri, **2**:288; huancayna sauce, **2**:264–65; huushuur (Mongolian fried meat-filled pastries), **3**:180–81; Iguana Stew, **2**:104; Impala (African

Antelope), 1:200–201; injera, 1:63–64; Israeli Salad, 1:263; jollof rice, 1:144; kalduny (dumplings), 4:35; Kamo/Niku Namban Soba (Duck or Beef and Noodle Soup), 3:118; kapusnica, 4:337; Kartoffelsuppe (Potato Soup), 4:134; kaya, 3:238–39; Kédjenou de Poulet, 1:46; keshi yena, 2:9–10; khachapuri, 4:130; Kleichat Tamur (Date-Filled Cookies), 1:255, 1:256; Kohlrouladen (Cabbage Rolls), 4:136–37; Konijn met Pruimen or Lapin Aux Prunes (Rabbit with Plums), 4:40–41; koq chuchvara (Uzbek green dumplings), 3:57; koreshte geymeh, 1:242–43; korma (lamb stew with yogurt), 3:196; kulesh (millet, potato, and lard soup), 4:379; LaBandera Dominica, 2:123; laddoos, 3:99; luwombo, 1:206; machbous, 1:224; maffe hacco (Cassava-Leaf Sauce), 1:76–77; malpoa, 3:35; mamaliga (polenta), 4:242; mangu, 2:122; Manicou or Agouti (Dominican Game), 2:114; mansaf, 1:274; Margat Bamya (Okra Stew), 1:253; marmitako, 4:26; mhammara, 1:300–301; minchi, 3:154–55; minchi (Macanese ground meat), 3:232–33; mititei (grilled sausage rolls), 4:295; Mjaddara (Pockmarked Rice and Lentils), 1:280; Mnazzlit Ahmar wa-Aswad, 1:301–2; Mock Shark's-Fin Soup, 3:90; momo, 3:268; momos, 3:190; Moros y Cristianos (Cuban Black Beans and Rice), 2:93; Moyau (Chicken Stew), 1:20; muamba de galinha (Angolan-Style Chicken), 1:15–16; nihari (beef stew with ginger), 3:199–200; niter kibbeh (Spiced Butter), 1:65; Oatmeal Biscuits, 4:319; oliebollen (doughnut balls), 4:254–55; oshifima, 1:136–37; Pabellon Criollo con Caraotas Negras (beef with black beans and plantains), 2:371–72; pad Thai (Thai fried noodles), 3:257–58; Palascintas, 4:76; Palesuppe (Bergen Young Saithe Soup), 4:261–62; Palm Butter Soup, 1:95; pannkakstårta (birthday pancake cake), 4:361–62; Pappa al Pomodoro (Tuscan Tomato and Bread Soup), 4:208; Paprikás Csirke (Paprika Chicken), 4:186–87; pastel de choclo, 2:69–70; pasteles en hoja (Banana-Leaf Bundles), 2:126; pelau, 2:293–94; Pepián, 2:156–57; pepperpot, 2:161; picadillo, 2:96–97; picante de pollo (chicken in spicy sauce), 2:40; pinolillo, 2:244–45; plasas, 1:163; plov, 3:131; pom, 2:286–87; Postre Chajá, 2:256; Potato and Mushroom Pirozhki, 4:306–7; poulet à la moambe (Chicken with Palm Butter), 1:37; Poulet Aux Poireaux (Chicken with Leeks and Tarragon), 4:117–18; Prawn Sambal, 3:40; Pudin o Bizocho (Special Dominican Holiday Cake), 2:126; Puerco Asado (Pork Roast), 2:124; Qabili Pilau, 3:18–19; qotban (Brochettes), 1:123; Quandong Crumble, 3:2; Ratatouille (Summer Vegetable Stew), 4:117; Red and White Salad, 3:123; Red-Cooked Pork, 3:68; rezala (white lamb curry), 3:31–32; Rice and Beans, 2:33–34; Rich Fruitcake, 4:157; riz gras, 1:28–29; Roast Beef and Yorkshire Pudding, 4:155; romazava, 1:108, 1:109–10; Roroi Kūmara, 3:172; salata dugwah (Peanut-Paste Salad), 1:184–85; Salmon Poke, 2:176; Salmorejo Cordobes (Cold Pureed Salad), 4:351–52; Šaltibarščciai (Cold Beet Soup), 4:228; Samak bi-Tahini (Fish in Tahini Sauce), 1:279; samaki wa kupaka, 1:191–92; sancocho (holiday stew), 2:126; Sancocho de Gallina (recipe from Panama's national cuisine), 2:251; sarma (stuffed cabbage), 4:74–75; Sarmale cu varza (Stuffed Cabbage Leaves), 4:293–94; sarmi, 4:177; Sautéed Reindeer, 4:315; sewian, 3:197; sfougato (omelet), 4:166–67; shabril, 3:272; shakshuka (Eggs with Tomatoes), 1:264; shola-e-zard, 3:17; Shorbat Maloukhiya (Jew's Mallow Soup), 1:55–56; sincronizadas, 2:222; skaba putra (sour barley porridge), 4:222; smoutebollen or beignets (doughnut balls), 4:47; Sobrebarriga Bogotá (flank steak), 2:80–81; so'o yosopy (beef and rice soup), 2:257–58; Sopa de Frijoles Canarios (Canary Bean Soup), 2:79; Sos Pwa Rouj (Red Beans in Sauce), 2:169; Soupe aux Carottes (Carrot Soup), 1:122–23; Sour Soup, 3:76; Souvlakia Me Pitta (Kebabs in Pita Bread), 4:83; spas (yogurt soup), 4:6–7; stamppot boerenkool (kale with sausage and potato), 4:251; Stir-Fried Greens, 3:67; Stoemp met Spruitjes or Stoemp Aux Choux de Bruxelles (Mashed Potatoes with Brussels Sprouts), 4:46;

Vol 1:	**Africa, Middle East**
Vol 2:	**Americas**
Vol 3:	**Asia and Oceania**
Vol 4:	**Europe**

Stuffed Camel, **1**:228; Stuffies, **2**:332; sukuma wiki, **1**:86–87; Sweet and Sour Fish, **3**:67–68; Tama ko Tarkari (Bamboo-Shoot Curry), **3**:186–87; t'amaya (Egyptian Fava Falafel), **1**:54–55; Thai-Spiced Salmon Chowder, **2**:341–42; Tom Kha Gai (Coconut Chicken Soup), **3**:256–57; trgance, **4**:174; urmašice (Bosnian dates), **4**:58; varenga, **1**:107–8; Vepřo-Knedlo-Zelo (Pork Dumplings and Vegetables), **4**:88–89; Wiener schnitzel, **4**:16; Winnebago Wild Rice, **2**:233; Yankee Pot Roast, **2**:329; Yassa, **1**:155–56; Yogurt Sauce, **4**:330; zama (chicken and noodle soup), **4**:241–42; Zeub Nfsuab (Boiled Pork and Mustard Greens), **3**:76; zhug, **1**:319; Zürich Veal Stew, **4**:371

Red and White Salad, **3**:123

Red-Cooked Pork, **3**:68

Rezala (white lamb curry), **3**:31–32

Rice and Beans, **2**:33–34

Rice biryani, **1**:82, **1**:189, **1**:243, **1**:251

Rice pilau, **3**:19

Rich Fruitcake, **4**:157

Rīga sprats, **4**:221

Riz gras, **1**:28–29

Roast Beef and Yorkshire Pudding, **4**:155

Roghan josh, **3**:195–96

Romania, **4**:289–97; cooking, **4**:292–93; diet and health, **4**:296–97; eating out, **4**:295–96; food culture snapshot, **4**:290; major foodstuffs, **4**:290–92; meals, typical, **4**:294–95; mititei (grilled sausage rolls), **4**:295; overview of, **4**:289–90; Sarmale cu varza (Stuffed Cabbage Leaves), **4**:293–94; special occasions, **4**:296

Romazava, **1**:108, **1**:109–10

Roroi Kūmara, **3**:172

Rúgbrau, **4**:195

Russia, **4**:299–310; borscht, **4**:303; cooking, **4**:304–5; diet and health, **4**:309–10; eating out, **4**:307; food culture snapshot, **4**:299–301; Grechnevye Bliny (Russian Buckwheat Pancakes/Crepes), **4**:308; major foodstuffs, **4**:301–4; meals, typical, **4**:305–6; overview of, **4**:299; pelmeni, **4**:300; Potato and Mushroom Pirozhki, **4**:306–7; special occasions, **4**:307–9

Saami, **4**:311–16; Cheese Bread, **4**:313; cooking, **4**:313, **4**:314; diet and health, **4**:316; eating out, **4**:315; food culture snapshot, **4**:311–12; major foodstuffs, **4**:312–13; meals, typical, **4**:314–15; overview of, **4**:311; Sautéed Reindeer, **4**:315; special occasions, **4**:315–16

Saffron risotto, **4**:208

Sago processing, story of, **3**:210

Salata dugwah (Peanut-Paste Salad), **1**:184–85

Salmon Poke, **2**:176

Salmorejo Cordobes (Cold Pureed Salad), **4**:351–52

Šaltibarščciai (Cold Beet Soup), **4**:228

Samak bi-Tahini (Fish in Tahini Sauce), **1**:279

Samaki wa kupaka, **1**:191–92

Samsa, **3**:51–52, **3**:54, **3**:130

Sancocho (holiday stew), **2**:80, **2**:124, **2**:126, **2**:249

Sancocho de Gallina (recipe from Panama's national cuisine), **2**:251

Sarapatel, **3**:227, **3**:232

Sarma (stuffed cabbage), **4**:53, **4**:58, **4**:74–75

Sarmale cu varza (Stuffed Cabbage Leaves), **4**:293–94

Sarmi, **4**:67, **4**:177

Sautéed Reindeer, **4**:315

Scotland, **4**:317–25; cooking, **4**:320; cranachan, **4**:323–24; diet and health, **4**:324–25; eating out, **4**:322; food culture snapshot, **4**:317–18; major foodstuffs, **4**:318–20; meals, typical, **4**:321–22; Oatmeal Biscuits, **4**:319; overview of, **4**:317; special occasions, **4**:323, **4**:324; tatties and neeps, **4**:318, **4**:323

Senegal, **1**:151–59; Ceebu jën, **1**:154–55; cooking, **1**:153–54; diet and health, **1**:158–59; eating out, **1**:156–57; food culture snapshot, **1**:151–52; major foodstuffs, **1**:152–53; meals, typical, **1**:154, **1**:155, **1**:156; overview of, **1**:151; special occasions, **1**:157–58; Yassa, **1**:155–56

Serbia, **4**:327–31; cevapcici (sausage), **4**:328, **4**:329–30; cooking, **4**:328–29; diet and health, **4**:330–31; eating out, **4**:330; food culture snapshot, **4**:327–28; major foodstuffs, **4**:328; meals, typical, **4**:329; overview of, **4**:327; special occasions, **4**:330; Yogurt Sauce, **4**:330

Sewian, **3**:197

Sfougato (omelet), **4**:166–67

Shabril, **3**:272

Shakshuka (Eggs with Tomatoes), **1**:8, **1**:264, **1**:286

Shepherd's pie, **4**:198

Shola-e-zard, **3**:17

Shorbat Maloukhiya (Jew's Mallow Soup), **1**:55–56

Sierra Leone, **1**:161–65; cooking, **1**:164; diet and health, **1**:165; eating out, **1**:165; food culture snapshot, **1**:161–62; major foodstuffs, **1**:162–64; meals, typical, **1**:164–65; overview of, **1**:161; plasas, **1**:163; special occasions, **1**:165

Sincronizadas, **2**:222

Singapore, **3**:235–45; Chicken Rice, **3**:241–42; cooking, **3**:238; diet and health, **3**:245; eating out, **3**:242; fish-ball soup with noodles, **3**:239–40; food culture snapshot, **3**:236–37; Kaya, **3**:238–39; major foodstuffs, **3**:237–38; meals, typical, **3**:239–41; overview of, **3**:235–36; special occasions, **3**:243–45

Sint Maarten. *See* Curaçao and Sint Maarten

Skaba putra (sour barley porridge), **4**:222

Slovakia, **4**:333–37; bryndzové halušky (dumplings), **4**:336; cooking, **4**:335; eating out, **4**:336; food culture snapshot, **4**:334; kapusnica, **4**:337; major foodstuffs, **4**:334–35; meals, typical, **4**:335–36; overview of, **4**:333–34; special occasions, **4**:336–37

Slovenia, **4**:339–46; aleluja, **4**:345–46; cooking, **4**:342–43; diet and health, **4**:346; eating out, **4**:344; food culture snapshot, **4**:339–40; gibanica, **4**:342; major foodstuffs, **4**:340–42; meals, typical, **4**:343–44; overview of, **4**:339; Potica, **4**:345; special occasions, **4**:344–45

Smoutebollen or beignets (doughnut balls), **4**:47

Sobrebarriga Bogotá (flank steak), **2**:80–81

Sockeye salmon, **2**:338

Soda bread, Irish, **4**:201

Somalia, **1**:167–71; Bur katuunboow, **1**:170; canjeero, **1**:169; cooking, **1**:168–69; diet and health, **1**:171; eating out, **1**:170; food culture snapshot, **1**:167; major foodstuffs, **1**:167–68; meals, typical, **1**:169–70; overview of, **1**:167; special occasions, **1**:170

So'o yosopy (beef and rice soup), **2**:257–58

Sopa de Frijoles Canarios (Canary Bean Soup), **2**:79

Sos Pwa Rouj (Red Beans in Sauce), **2**:169

Soupe aux Carottes (Carrot Soup), **1**:122–23

Sour Soup, **3**:76

South (United States), **2**:347–55; cooking, **2**:352–53; diet and health, **2**:355; eating out, **2**:353–54; food culture snapshot, **2**:348–49; Food Processor Biscuits, **2**:349–50; Ham Biscuits, **2**:350; major foodstuffs, **2**:349, **2**:350–52; meals, typical, **2**:353; overview of, **2**:347–48; special occasions, **2**:354–55

South Africa, **1**:173–81; braai (act of barbecuing), **1**:176, **1**:177, **1**:178; cooking, **1**:177–78; diet and health, **1**:180–81; eating out, **1**:179–80; food culture snapshot, **1**:174–75; major foodstuffs, **1**:175–77; meals, typical, **1**:178–79; overview of, **1**:173–74; special occasions, **1**:180

Southwest (United States), **2**:357–67; cooking, **2**:361–62; diet and health, **2**:366; eating out, **2**:363–64; empanadas, **2**:362; food culture snapshot, **2**:358–59; Fry Bread, **2**:365; Green Chili Enchiladas, **2**:358; Green Chili Sauce, **2**:358; major foodstuffs, **2**:359–61; meals, typical, **2**:362–63;

overview of, **2**:357–58; special occasions, **2**:364–66

Souvlakia Me Pitta (Kebabs in Pita Bread), **4**:83

Space, **3**:291–94; cooking, **3**:291–93; diet and health, **3**:294; eating out, **3**:293–94; Gemini Mashed Potatoes, **3**:293; major foodstuffs, **3**:291; meals, typical, **3**:293; overview of, **3**:291; special occasions, **3**:294

Spain, **4**:347–57; cooking, **4**:354; diet and health, **4**:357; eating out, **4**:355–56; food culture snapshot, **4**:350; major foodstuffs, **4**:350–51, **4**:352–54; mantecados, **4**:356; meals, typical, **4**:354–55; overview of, **4**:347–49; polvorones, **4**:356; Salmorejo Cordobes (Cold Pureed Salad), **4**:351–52; Spanish seafood paella, **4**:351; special occasions, **4**:356–57

Spanish seafood paella, **4**:351

Spas (yogurt soup), **4**:6–7

Sri Lanka, **3**:247–52; brinjal (eggplant) sambal, **3**:250; cooking, **3**:248–49; diet and health, **3**:251–52; eating out, **3**:250; egg hoppers, **3**:250; food culture snapshot, **3**:247–48; major foodstuffs, **3**:248; meals, typical, **3**:249–50; overview of, **3**:247; special occasions, **3**:250–51

Stamppot boerenkool (kale with sausage and potato), **4**:251

Stir-Fried Greens, **3**:67

Stoemp met Spruitjes or Stoemp Aux Choux de Bruxelles (Mashed Potatoes with Brussels Sprouts), **4**:46

Stuffed Camel, **1**:228

Stuffies, **2**:332

Sudan, **1**:183–87; cooking, **1**:185; diet and health, **1**:187; eating out, **1**:186; food culture snapshot, **1**:183–84; Fuul Sudani

Vol 1:	**Africa, Middle East**
Vol 2:	**Americas**
Vol 3:	**Asia and Oceania**
Vol 4:	**Europe**

(Sudanese Fava Bean Stew), **1**:185–86; major foodstuffs, **1**:184, **1**:185; meals, typical, **1**:185, **1**:186; overview of, **1**:183; salata dugwah (Peanut-Paste Salad), **1**:184–85; special occasions, **1**:186–87

Sukuma wiki, **1**:86–87

Suriname, **2**:283–89; cooking, **2**:285; diet and health, **2**:289; eating out, **2**:288–89; food culture snapshot, **2**:283–84; Her'heri, **2**:288; major foodstuffs, **2**:284–85; meals, typical, **2**:285–86, **2**:287–88; overview of, **2**:283; pom, **2**:286–87; special occasions, **2**:289

Svid, **4**:195

Swahili City-States, **1**:189–95; diet and health, **1**:194; eating out, **1**:193–94; food culture snapshot, **1**:190–91; major foodstuffs, **1**:192–93; overview of, **1**:189–90; samaki wa kupaka, **1**:191–92; special occasions, **1**:194

Swaziland, **1**:197–201; cooking, **1**:199; diet and health, **1**:201; eating out, **1**:200; food culture snapshot, **1**:197; Impala (African Antelope), **1**:200–201; major foodstuffs, **1**:197–98; meals, typical, **1**:199–200; overview of, **1**:197; special occasions, **1**:200

Sweden, **4**:359–66; ärtsoppa (yellow pea soup), **4**:363; cooking, **4**:362–63; diet and health, **4**:365; eating out, **4**:363–64; food culture snapshot, **4**:359–60; major foodstuffs,

4:360–61, **4**:362; meals, typical, **4**:363; overview of, **4**:359; pannkakstårta (birthday pancake cake), **4**:361–62; special occasions, **4**:364–65

Sweet and Sour Fish, **3**:67–68

Switzerland, **4**:367–75; beurre manié, **4**:371; Cheese Fondue, **4**:374–75; cooking, **4**:370–72; diet and health, **4**:375; eating out, **4**:373; food culture snapshot, **4**:367–68; major foodstuffs, **4**:368–70; meals, typical, **4**:372–73; overview of, **4**:367; special occasions, **4**:373–74, **4**:375; Zürich Veal Stew, **4**:371

Syria, **1**:297–303; cooking, **1**:299; diet and health, **1**:303; eating out, **1**:302; food culture snapshot, **1**:297; groats, **1**:298; major foodstuffs, **1**:297–99; meals, typical, **1**:299–300, **1**:301, **1**:302; mhammara, **1**:300–301; Mnazzlit Ahmar wa-Aswad, **1**:301–2; overview of, **1**:297; special occasions, **1**:302–3

Tagine (stew), **1**:5, **1**:6, **1**:7

Tama ko Tarkari (Bamboo-Shoot Curry), **3**:186–87

T'amaya (Egyptian Fava Falafel), **1**:54–55

Tapiok, **3**:208

Taro, origin of, **3**:207

Tatties and neeps, **4**:318, **4**:323

Thailand, **3**:253–61; cooking, **3**:255–56; diet and health, **3**:259–60; eating out, **3**:257; food culture snapshot, **3**:253; major foodstuffs, **3**:254–55; meals, typical, **3**:256; overview of, **3**:253; pad Thai (Thai fried noodles), **3**:257–58; pho, **3**:65, **3**:278; special occasions, **3**:258–59; Tom Kha Gai (Coconut Chicken Soup), **3**:256–57

Thai-Spiced Salmon Chowder, **2**:341–42

Three Sisters, **2**:232, **2**:235

Tibet, **3**:263–73; cooking, **3**:269–70; diet and health, **3**:272–73; eating out, **3**:270–71; food culture snapshot, **3**:263–65; major foodstuffs, **3**:265–69; meals, typical, **3**:270; momo, **3**:268; overview of, **3**:263; shabril, **3**:272; special occasions, **3**:271–72

Tobago. *See* Trinidad and Tobago

Tom Kha Gai (Coconut Chicken Soup), **3**:256–57

Trgance, **4**:174

The Triangle, Palestine Territories, **1**:292

Trinidad and Tobago, **2**:291–301; cooking, **2**:295–97; Curried shrimp, **2**:297–98; diet and health, **2**:301; eating out, **2**:299–300; food culture snapshot, **2**:291–93; major foodstuffs, **2**:293, **2**:294–95; meals, typical, **2**:297, **2**:298–99; overview of, **2**:291; pelau, **2**:293–94; special occasions, **2**:300–301

Tuaregs. *See* Berbers and Tuaregs

Turkey, **1**:305–16; cooking, **1**:310–11; diet and health, **1**:315; eating out, **1**:312–13; food culture snapshot, **1**:305–7; imam bayaldi, **1**:306; kadayif, **1**:311; kanafeh, **1**:311; major foodstuffs, **1**:307–10; meals, typical, **1**:312; overview of, **1**:305; special occasions, **1**:314–15; zarf, **1**:315

Turkish delight (rahat lokum), **4**:56, **4**:58

Ugali (cornmeal porridge), **1**:82, **1**:83, **1**:87, **1**:101, **1**:190

Uganda, **1**:203–8; diet and health, **1**:207–8; eating out, **1**:207; food culture snapshot, **1**:203–4; luwombo, **1**:206;

major foodstuffs, **1**:204–7; matooke, **1**:204–5; meals, typical, **1**:207; overview of, **1**:203; special occasions, **1**:207

Ukraine, **4**:377–84; Borsch soup, **4**:378; cooking, **4**:379–81; diet and health, **4**:384; eating out, **4**:382–83; food culture snapshot, **4**:377–78; halushky (dumplings), **4**:380; kulesh (millet, potato, and lard soup), **4**:379; major foodstuffs, **4**:378–79; meals, typical, **4**:381–82; overview of, **4**:377; special occasions, **4**:383–84

United States, **2**:303–67; Mid-Atlantic, **2**:303–11; Midwest, **2**:313–24; New England, **2**:325–35; Pacific Northwest, **2**:337–46; South, **2**:347–55; Southwest, **2**:357–67

Urmašice (Bosnian dates), **4**:58

Uruguay. *See* Paraguay and Uruguay

Varenga, **1**:107–8

Vegetable hotchpotch, **4**:251

Venezuela, **2**:369–73; arepas, **2**:371; cachapas, **2**:370; cooking, **2**:370–71; diet and health, **2**:373; eating out, **2**:372; food culture snapshot, **2**:369–70; hallacas, **2**:372–73; major foodstuffs, **2**:370; meals, typical, **2**:371; overview of, **2**:369; Pabellon Criollo con Caraotas Negras (beef with black beans and plantains), **2**:371–72; special occasions, **2**:372–73

Vepřo-Knedlo-Zelo (Pork Dumplings and Vegetables), **4**:88–89

Vietnam, **3**:275–81; Canh chua Ca Loc (sour broth), **3**:279; diet and health, **3**:280–81; food culture snapshot, **3**:275–76; Goi Ga, **3**:279–80; major foodstuffs, **3**:276–79, **3**:280; overview of, **3**:275

West Bank region, **1**:293

West New Britain Province. *See* Papua New Guinea Foodways

Wiener schnitzel, **4**:12, **4**:16

Winnebago Wild Rice, **2**:233

Yankee Pot Roast, **2**:329

Yassa, **1**:155–56

Yemen and Oman, **1**:317–22; bint al-sahn, **1**:320; cooking, **1**:319–20; diet and health, **1**:322; eating out, **1**:321; fenugreek, **1**:319, **1**:321; food culture snapshot, **1**:318–19; major foodstuffs, **1**:319; meals, typical, **1**:320–21; overview of, **1**:317–18; special occasions, **1**:321–22; zhug, **1**:319

Yogurt Sauce, **4**:330

Za'atar, **1**:270, **1**:272, **1**:287–89

Zama (chicken and noodle soup), **4**:241–42

Zarf, **1**:315

Zeub Nfsuab (Boiled Pork and Mustard Greens), **3**:76

Zhug, **1**:319

Zimbabwe, **1**:209–14; cooking, **1**:212; diet and health, **1**:214; Dovi (Peanut Butter Stew), **1**:211–12; eating out, **1**:213; food culture snapshot, **1**:210–11; major foodstuffs, **1**:211, **1**:212; meals, typical, **1**:212–13; overview of, **1**:209–10; special occasions, **1**:213–14

Zürich Veal Stew, **4**:371